WOMEN, RELIGION, and SOCIAL CHANGE

WOMEN, RELIGION, and SOCIAL CHANGE

Edited by
Yvonne Yazbeck Haddad
and
Ellison Banks Findly

State University of New York Press

"The Future," from a triptych entitled "Towards Light." Oil on canvas, Turkman S. S. R. 1970. Painted by Chary Amangeldyev, Art Museum, Ashkabad. The editors would like to thank Mr. Edward Malayan, Soviet Embassy, Washington D.C., for assistance in procuring permission for the use of the cover.

Published by
State University of New York Press, Albany

Printed in the United States of America

For information, address State University of New York Press, State University Plaza, Albany, N.Y., 12246

Library of Congress Cataloging in Publication Data

Haddad, Yvonne Yazbeck 1935-
Women, religion, and social change.

Includes index.
1. Women and religion—Addresses, essays, lectures.
2. Social history—Addresses, essays, lectures. I. Findly, Ellison Banks. II. Title.
BL458.H33 1985 291.1'78344 85-4747
ISBN 0-88706-068-4
ISBN 0-88706-069-2 (pbk.)

CONTENTS

Acknowledgments

This book brings together studies which were solicited specifically for the symposium on "Women, Religion and Social Change," held at Hartford Seminary, Hartford, Connecticut, October 21–22, 1983. It was sponsored by Hartford Seminary, Trinity College and Saint Joseph College.

The project was supported by grants from the Connecticut Humanities Council, the National Endowment for the Humanities, Aetna Life and Casualty, The Jodik Foundation, Hartford Consortium for Higher Education, National Conference of Christians and Jews and the Intercultural Studies Program at Trinity College. The viewpoints and recommendations expressed are those of the authors and do not necessarily reflect those of the Connecticut Humanities Council, the National Endowment for the Humanities, or other sponsoring organizations.

The organizing committee wishes to thank the Woman's Board of Hartford Seminary and the World Affairs Center, Inc. for co-sponsoring the event; Ms. Ruth Billyou, Coordinator of the Hartford Consortium of Higher Education, Ms. Jane Christie Smith, Assistant Director, Connecticut Humanities Council, Mr. Robert Roggeveen, Law Manager, Corporate Public Involvement of Aetna Life and Casualty, Mr. Charles Sardeson, Executive Director of the National Conference of Christians and Jews, Mrs. Richard Gates, President of The Jodik Foundation, and Ms. Marjorie Anderson, Executive Director of the World Affairs Center for their sustaining encouragement and support; Ms. Marilyn Denny and Ms. Cindy Sanford of the Faculty Grants Office of Trinity College for their untiring efforts in securing funds for the symposium; and Mrs. Sylvana Stratton, Comptroller, Hartford Seminary, for managing the finances of the project.

We are especially grateful to Mr. Ronald Spencer, Associate Academic Dean, Trinity College and Mrs. Elizabeth A. D'Amico, Assistant to the Director, Duncan Black Macdonald Center, Hartford Seminary for their expert editing skills—their insights and efforts immensely lightened the task of compiling the materials herein—, to Ms. Elizabeth Schick, Trinity College, for her work on the index and to Ms. Gay Weidlich, Religion Department, Trinity College and Mrs. Sheryl Wiggins, Hartford Seminary for all their assistance in helping to prepare the manuscript.

Preface

This book grew out of an interest in expanding the scope of scholarly investigation about the role of women in religion to include a variety of traditions and to encompass a broad span of years. At a time when women in the contemporary world are experiencing both exhilaration at increased opportunities for political, social and economic power and frustration at continuing circumstances of male control of many of the structures of change, it is increasingly important to look afresh at some of the ways in which women in various times and places have succeeded in effecting change. Because such change has often come about through the manipulation and transformation of the very religious institutions and beliefs which had hitherto served to maintain the status quo, new attempts to examine the dynamics of the relationship between women and traditional religious systems in times of transition are needed.

Interest in women's roles and experiences has been heightened by the feminist revolution, which has resulted in the wide range of studies now available on women. Moreover, the study of religion by American and European scholars in the past several decades has broadened considerably, leading to a new recognition of the importance of understanding the experiences of participants in religious traditions outside of the western context. The symposium was the context for a group of scholars to address issues cutting across the two fields of women's studies and history of religions, with specific attention to the ways in which women from a number of religious traditions have been able to effect social change within their respective societies. We see this as part of a continuing attempt to consider such issues as (1) whether there is a shared human experience in the way religious institutions and beliefs have functioned to either facilitate or inhibit women's participation in social change, and (2) how women have used theological structures and their attendant religious institutions, in either a traditional or refashioned form, to protect against or to legitimate the existing social order during periods of upheaval.

One thesis would suggest that women take a more active part in public life, and in the establishment of new religious structures, during periods of social crisis when the normal functioning of society breaks down. Many of the papers presented during the symposium were designed specifically to challenge, modify or confirm the hypothesis that women become especially prominent during periods of social upheaval and that religion is often the tool and/or object of such change. The symposium's participants explored such questions as the following: In what ways and in what times are women the initiators of social change? If it is true that women become prominent in times of social crisis, is it because their traditional roles as maintainers and transmitters of values are threatened, or is it because traditional roles for both sexes have been abandoned altogether and, as a result, women no longer have to act like women at all? Are women more likely than men, especially in times of crisis, to seek a creative ordering of life, a cohesive worldview, and do they, therefore, perceive their function as providing community stability and integration? Or are women marginal actors outside the arena of power who assume leadership roles for a brief period, taking advantage of prevalent discord, only to fade into the background when new leadership is legitimized or a new consensus is formulated?

Central to the investigation is the commonly accepted distinction between social change, which refers primarily to actual human behavior, and cultural change, which refers to changes in the symbol system by which humans make order of and find meaning in their lives. In applying such a distinction to the materials at hand, one is able to examine the relationship between changes in religious behavior as determined by religious institutions (social change) and changes in the structures of religious belief, expressed not only in theology but in religious art, music and literature as well (cultural change). The issues become even more complex when religious institutions both influence and are influenced by changes in other, secular social structures, or when changes in religious beliefs affect or are affected by changes in other ideological systems.

In each of the major sessions of the symposium consideration was given to the role of women both as transmitters and maintainers of cultural norms and values, and as the potential instruments through which those norms and values are challenged and redefined. Results of the various investigations differed, and were sometimes even contradictory; women's appropriation of the vision of themselves as bearers of culture leads to an acceptance of traditional religious structures. This is in marked contrast to those who use these structures to change their environment or who, in the process, even change the structures themselves.

The last fifteen years have produced a growing number of studies on various aspects of women and religion. A substantial portion of this literature, however, emphasizes the manner in which theological formulations in the classical periods of various religious traditions were proposed by men in order to control women. Other literature tends to distinguish between male and female forms of religion, ascribing to men a cerebral function concerned mainly with rational theological formulations and to women an emotive function concerned mainly with such things as ritual. Moreover, it is becoming increasingly the case that the role and status of women are addressed within a specific religious tradition. While these studies have produced new insights, they have tended to assume that each specific religion has a static worldview that has fixed the definition of women's roles which are then related to a revelation ascribed to divine authority. It was our intent that this symposium, in contrast, through a close examination of periods of social change would be part of a continuing effort to analyze those perhaps exceptional moments when accepted norms appear to be openly violated and new formulations acquire sanction and legitimacy. Such examination can shed new light on the function of religion in sanctioning or impeding changes in the roles of women, on the role of women in formulating and perpetuating norms and values, on factors that appear to encourage or discourage women's participation in such an endeavor, and, more generally, on the role of religion in periods of social crisis.

The papers presented in this symposium thus aimed at breaking new ground by focusing on variables, which are primarily interdisciplinary in nature, by drawing upon materials from different areas of the world and addressing issues across a broad span of years, and by raising, with specific reference to women and religion, the question of social change. It is our hope that we have at least provided a model for examination and discussion that will challenge others interested in the study of women and religion in traditional and contemporary societies to continue such investigations.

Y.Y.H. and E.B.F.

Introduction

Nancy Falk

Western scholarship has finally begun to recognize the complex interplay between religion and social change. Social scientists and religionists have known for a long time that religion is among the foremost of institutions which conserve society, encoding stabilizing worldviews and values and transmitting these from generation to generation. Scholars are now beginning to acknowledge that religion has been equally significant as an agent of social transformation; for that which encodes can recode, framing prophetic new views of human possibility and releasing the enormous bursts of energy that are necessary to move peoples and polities in altered directions. In fact, as that which alone could alter the root-paradigms which framed the decisions and directions of entire cultures, religion was the most powerful transformative force in society during times prior to the modern era.

The editors and authors of the present volume have already performed a service to seekers of understanding just by documenting this intricate waltz of religion and social change within a variety of historical and contemporary contexts. But they enhance their offering by adding a seldom-asked question: What has been the role of women during this process? The question is important, for women are the great "sleepers" of history. Often as much ignored by the religious and political establishments of their own times as they have been by modern Western historians, women often provide the unpredicted balance of support that determines whether a new direction "takes."

As contributors to this volume demonstrate well, such support from women has been evident in the initial phases of most of the great world religions. Women were prominent both as converts and as opponents to the message of Muhammad while the prophet's turbulent career was in process, and women both joined the Buddha's renunciant community and provided its all-important requisites of food, clothing, and shelter (see, respectively, chapters by Jane I. Smith and Janice Willis). Nor was Buddhism the only new movement attractive to women during the period of the eighth through sixth centuries B.C.E. which saw the rise of India's great heterodoxies. Although we know nothing of her following, and indeed little of her philosophical stance outside of her role in a famous, but possibly legendary, debate, the memory of the great teacher Gārgī attests to the presence of women in these explorations.

When we speak of transformative movements that occurred so many years ago, it is often, however, far easier to demonstrate that women were significant in such movements than to explain precisely why they were prominent. Part of our difficulty lies in the all-too-frequent haziness of our knowledge of antecedent social history: we cannot tell whether the active role of women represents a change from previous practice or a continuation of earlier circumstances. Both Jane I. Smith's study of women in early Islam and Ellison Findly's analysis of Gārgī's debate nonetheless suggest an intriguing hypothesis. For early Islam and the Indian heterodoxies both seem to have developed at times of declining status for women—in other words, in times that would leave women receptive to proposals for constructing alternative social worlds.

The premise that women are drawn to worldviews that permit them to affirm themselves as humans and as women receives important confirmation from Nancy Schuster's identification of the texts most studied by early nuns in the Chinese Buddhist tradition. For in a tradition where women briefly flourished—for example, the Buddhism that was transplanted from India into China at roughly the beginning of the Common Era—women studied and were inspired most by the texts which incorporated the most positive views of women. Dr. Schuster, significantly, also suggests that lively and vibrant women turned to the newly-transplanted Buddhism because their options were being restricted by the indigenous Confucian ideology.

The case of rabbinical Judaism, with its rigid separation and subordination of women, seems at first to represent an anomalous departure from established patterns of women's participation in the formative stages of religious movements. But perhaps it is less of an anomaly than it seems. For the prescriptions of the rabbis were less an unfolding of a new vision than a retrenchment intended to save the viable vestiges of an old one following the disaster of two failed rebellions and the destruction of the temple at Jerusalem. Moreover, as Judith Baskin points out, the prescriptions seem less a reflection of contemporary social practice than a vision of an ideal community framed from the perspective of a group of pious males.

As an advanced phase in the development of a long-established tradition, the rabbinic teachings may well represent another trend in the evolution of religions. For just as women seem to be prominent during initial phases of religious development, so they often seem to find their roles diminished as a movement congeals and begins to draw its internal lines more tightly. Jane I. Smith has acknowledged this phenomenon in Islam and traced its sources to an early acceptance of exclusion and seclusion both among leaders of the Islamic community and among Muslim women. Nancy Schuster also points out that women moved to the periphery during the later history of the Buddhist community in China.

In fact, as religious movements evolve, women appear to be less and less the agents of change and more and more its victims. An accompanying phenomenon, frustrating to the researcher, is an increasing disappearance of women from the historical record. For records are forged by those in power, and they pay scant attention to the powerless. Articles by art historians Jane Dillenberger and Walter Denny point to one possible resource for reconstructing women's history during those periods of less dramatic change when women fade from visibility. But drawing conclusions from art about social history can be tricky. For art does not solely reflect a given tradition's everyday life and values—as have, that is, many of the manuscript illustrations cited by Walter Denny. Art also provides a model for living. Thus, for example, the image of the penitent Mary Magdalen is far less a valid memory of Jesus' principal female follower than it is a vision of an ideal possibility which has reflected the values of each succeeding age that shaped it.

Rituals and songs are other resources which can help us to identify women's concerns and experiences. For even in traditions which are strikingly dominated by males, women frequently carve out some ritual corner of their own—as, for example, women have appropriated the *vratas*, or domestic rites, of the Hindu tradition. Moreover, especially in complex traditions such as Hinduism, as Sandra Robinson and Donna Wulff both demonstrate, certain currents within the tradition may prove more "friendly" to women than others. The *bhakti* (devotional) tradition of Hinduism is one such example of an historically friendly current. Donna Wulff shows how women of Bengal have drawn out and adapted its central themes to assert their own power and significance as women. However, Sandra Robinson's analysis of the legend justifying the *Itu vrata* adds a cautionary note: the rites which women perform (or the songs which women sing) will not necessarily articulate a perspective on women's status and roles that differs significantly from the views framed by men of the same tradition. Given no exposure to an alternative vision, women may simply rearticulate the values that lead to their own bondage.

But to learn how rituals and songs are used—and, indeed, to flesh out whatever skimpy impression we may have of the ways in which women, religion, and change have been interwoven in the past, we must inevitably draw on understanding derived from contemporary observation. Rosalind Hackett, writing of women's religious roles in Nigeria, offers a fascinating contemporary portrayal of the sort of religious stew that often simmers during periods of intensive social change or breakdown; students of religion know that such co-existence of a variety of models is often a preface to the emergence of transformative new movements. The stew in the Nigerian town of Calabar includes remnants of indigenous religious societies, Christian missionary churches, and examples of the new, post-missionary African independent churches. Women have been prominent in many of these institutions. But Dr. Hackett also offers an important caution: religious activity in Calabar presently represents more of a steam valve for releasing social tension than a movement towards revolutionary transformation.

Moreover, since the rise of nation-states and secular ideologies, radical social change has far more often been accomplished by means that are political rather than religious. Yet it would be a mistake to presuppose that the great political cataclysms that we call revolutions are wholly different in character from prophetic religious movements. For both are commonly fired by dynamic visions of restructured human relationships and institutions. Moreover, both articulate their visions and mobilize participants by generating ideologies, manipulating symbols, and staging public demonstrations of commitment—that is, rituals. We have even seen, in recent years, the advent of revolutions that are explicitly religious in ideology—that is to say, the vision of a new order that inspires the revolution has its source in a religious revelation. The classic example is, of course, the Islamic revolution in Iran. As we might expect, women have been prominent in twentieth-century revolutions, just as they have supported transformative religious movements of the past. They find themselves caught between varying ideologies that seek to transform their lives in accordance with the demands of modern life and the heritage of values and traditions grounded in scriptures. Yvonne Haddad shows that Arab women are integrally involved in the revolutionary process, captured by its fervor and advocating its goals. Their vision of liberation tends to reflect the corporate will for the liberation of the whole society rather than a feminine rebellion against the statutes of the prevalent order. Contributor William Darrow sustains her argument by analyzing the status of women under the new Iranian constitution and ideology. He shows that the same revolution which has putatively extended "greater rights" and "value and nobility" to women has in effect simply engendered a new and more attractive rationale for ancient patterns of exclusion and seclusion.

The remaining essays of this volume's section on Women and Revolution demonstrate that even secular revolutions have had noteworthy ties to religion. Author Lou Ratté, for example, shows how India's national liberation movement made use of powerful female images from India's Hindu heritage. But she argues also that the male leadership of this movement was more comfortable with powerful female images than it was with the prospect of political power and authority for women.

Many commentators have noted that the Marxist ideology which fed both the Russian and the Chinese revolutions is religious in structure. For the paradigm of "class struggle" is little more than a secularized version of the ancient myth of the battle between good and evil; while the "classless" society is particularly reminiscent of the Christian Kingdom of Heaven which knows neither Jew nor Greek, slave nor free, male nor female. It is nonetheless surprising to find in addition an infusion of American Methodism in the early stages of the Chinese revolution. Contributor Michael Lestz has explored the influence of Methodism upon the Soong sisters, daughters of a convert and one-time missionary, who married revolutionary leaders Sun Yat-sen and Chiang Kai-shek.

Religion has played a far more immediate and widespread role, however, in a Marxist revolution of the past decade. For the Sandinista movement which overthrew the Somoza regime of Nicaragua drew on a populace which was recovering its sense of dignity and outrage at injustice via the Roman Catholic liberation theology movement and the work of the "base communities" which were established as part of this movement. Pauline Turner explains the conspicuous role of women in the Sandinista movement and shows how constructing their own political base has helped these women, thus far, to reverse a past pattern of severe oppression.

One benefit of travel, whether literal or via the pages of a book, is that it sharpens our ability to recognize the subtle dynamics of our own society when we finally return home. Editors Haddad and Findly have wisely chosen to end their journey through two-and-a-half millenia and a dozen cultures by coming home at last to North America. But the first chapter of their final section reminds us, like the essay on the Nicaraguan revolution that precedes it, that America does not consist only of the European-import culture which we all-too-frequently associate solely with this term. Annemarie Shimony's contribution is set apart from the remainder of both its section and its volume because it documents a rare instance—the Native American Iroquois tradition—in which a process of religious and social change has moved women into roles of increasing prestige and influence.

The remaining four essays carry us through a tumultuous era of United States history, from the first feminist stirrings of the nineteenth century through a struggle still in process to redefine women's roles in the Roman Catholic and Jewish traditions. Ann Braude assesses the Spiritualist movement of the mid- and late-nineteenth century and finds it to be one of the many means through which women of the time challenged the conventional subordination of women's roles. Possessing spirits motivated women to speak on behalf of the fundamental equality of men and women—a striking echo of the motif of supernatural impulsion that has fired other, more powerful movements of prophetic transformation. And yet in other ways Spiritualists simply recapitulated the style, fads, and values of the Victorian period. The Grimké sisters, described by Frank Kirkpatrick, represented another type of religious motivation: drawing on an impulse towards moral perfection fostered by experiences of evangelical conversion, the Grimkés became social activists, leaders of the abolitionist movement.

A volume which explores the relationship between women, religion, and social change could scarcely be complete without attending to the efforts by women to effect changes in religion that have occurred during recent decades of the twentieth century. Antoinette Iadarola offers an unusual perspective on Catholic feminists' efforts to reform the status of women within the church by locating these efforts within the history of the hierarchy's conservative responses to women's suffrage, the birth control movement, women's employment, and protective labor law. Finally, Ellen Umansky traces and evaluates the efforts of American Jewish women to claim their tradition for themselves.

What conclusions can we draw from this rich and sometimes bewildering array of studies? Let me tentatively offer at least the following:

First, the relationship between women, religion, and social change has taken a wide variety of forms. Women have worked within religious movements that were revolutionary in their implications. Women have worked within revolutionary movements that were (at least partially) religious in their inspiration. Women have been inspired individually by religion to take part in movements working for changes in society; women have been prompted by social changes to work for changes in religion. Religion has been an instrument of liberation for women. But religion has just as often become an instrument of women's social oppression.

Second, recurrent patterns do seem to appear in this relationship. Women have been prominent both in emerging religious movements and in the contemporary revolutionary movements which have supplanted these as a means of achieving radical social transformation.

But third, we must approach these patterns with utmost caution—especially when seeking to offer explanations. Our data is often too scanty to support grand theories. Moreover, no matter what common factors might strike us as significant, the movement of women both into and out of transformative movements also depends on many discrete nuances of each movement's previous social context and history.

Fourth, the relationship between women, religion, and social change seems well worthy of far more extensive investigation.

And fifth, the planners, sponsors, and participants of the Hartford Symposium on Women, Religion and Social Change deserve our warmest thanks for sharing with us this exploratory volume.

PART I

Women and the Formation of Religious Tradition

CHAPTER ONE

*The Separation of Women in Rabbinic Judaism**

JUDITH BASKIN

Women did not play an active part in the development of rabbinic Judaism, nor were they granted a significant role in that tradition's religious life.[1] By examining the way the rabbis divided the world between men and women, however, particularly in light of insights derived from anthropological and structuralist approaches to social life and religious traditions, the general separation of the sexes can be seen as part of a larger system of dichotomies and oppositions. In fact, rabbinic Judaism's definition of women shares many characteristics with that of other conservative societies. Here, as elsewhere, women do not emerge as beings inferior to men, but are instead a creation completely and necessarily different from the unblemished male who alone can serve God fully. In rabbinic Judaism, no woman is deemed capable of any direct experience of the divine.

*The following abbreviations are used in the notes: *M. (Mishnah), B. (Babylonian Talmud), P. (Palestinian Talmud), T. (Tosephta),* and *Gen.R. (Genesis Rabbah).*

RABBINIC JUDAISM

The *Mishnah,* rabbinic Judaism's earliest surviving definitive record of prescriptions, was the production of one particular group of Jews who lived in the land of Israel during the early third century C.E. These rabbis attempted to address and provide legal direction for all areas of human existence by compiling and arranging according to subject matter the judicial and homiletic dicta stemming from centuries of intensive study of the Hebrew Bible. Yet, at the time when much of the Mishnah was initially formulated there was a variety of Judaisms, each convinced of its own authority and the validity of its understanding of revealed literature.[2] Only after the unsuccessful rebellions against Roman rule in the first two centuries of the Common Era did rabbinic Judaism gradually emerge as the normative mode of Jewish observance and practice. The *Mishnah* was embroidered and enlarged with generations of voluminous commentary, called the *Gemara.* Ultimately, the *Mishnah* and *Gemara* became the *Talmud,* which with the Hebrew Bible served as the basis for Jewish practice from the sixth to the twentieth century.

While the authors of the Mishnah saw their work as an extension of Biblical revelation, it goes far beyond any Biblical imperative in its intent to define "the whole range and realm of reality."[3] But it is impossible to know which of its numerous laws and ordinances were actually in effect at the time they were recorded. As Jacob Neusner has written, "The social parameters of the system are defined by the people who made it up, not by the world in which they lived."[4] Thus, the ideal vision of the relation between the male and the female, as between the divine and the human, which was proposed but not necessarily lived by one particularly pious group of men, ultimately became the guidebook and practical pattern for ensuing forms of Jewish life.[5]

WOMEN IN THE SYSTEM OF RABBINIC JUDAISM

Rabbinic Judaism places women at a severe disadvantage. As Leonard Swidler has documented,[6] the woman's position is subordinate to the man's in every aspect of life—social, legal and religious. As Montefiore and Loewe commented some decades ago:

> The difference in the relations of men and women to each other makes a constant difference between the Rabbis and ourselves. It is always cropping up. . . . Women were, on the whole, regarded as inferior to men in mind, in function and in status.[7]

Rabbinic Judaism was produced within a patriarchal society by a group of sages who imagined a man's world, with men at its center.[8] Rabbinic legislation, perceived by its authors as divinely ordained, therefore considers woman only in her relationship to man and as she falls under his control and can contribute to his comfort.[9] Women are expected to "fulfill their numerous household and family obligations, provide a loving and supportive atmosphere within the home, and realize their spiritual potential through the merits of their fathers or husbands."[10] As long as they fulfill these expectations women are revered and honored;[11] rabbinic literature is not lacking in words of praise for the supportive, resourceful and self-sacrificing wife,[12] nor is there a lack of consideration for her physical and emotional needs and welfare.[13] All good for the woman, however, is predicated upon her remaining subordinate.[14]

Woman's dependent and separate status in rabbinic literature can be illustrated in a number of ways. In a court of law, for instance, women are unacceptable witnesses;[15] in this instance, as a number of others, women are consigned to the same category as slaves and children.[16] In terms of observance, women are exempt from most regular religious obligations, especially those bound to be performed communally at specified times;[17] these came to include study, which was itself seen as a form of prayer. As a consequence, women were excluded from religious activities which took place in the public sphere, and from those endeavors, particularly intellectual pursuits, which conferred social and religious status. It is often suggested that women were exempted from time-bound commandments because of family responsibilities and obligations which might prevent their regularly fulfilling them.[18] Certainly there may be something to this, but it will be suggested below that the exemption of women from these activities is a profound statement of rabbinic Judaism's view of woman's nature and perceived lack of religious capacities. Whatever the reason, however, "In essence, all the important ways in which Judaism defined what it meant to be a Jew were either partially or completely closed to women."[19]

Because rabbinic Judaism has endured as the basis of the religious practice of a significant number of Jews, its attitudes towards women have recently been assailed by those holding feminist and egalitarian views; partisans for change in the Jewish woman's role continue to come into conflict with those who maintain the sanctity and rightness of ancient traditions. As Judith Hauptmann writes, "as a result of the great changes in the technological age and woman's increasing sense of her own value and her potential contribution to society at large, a re-examination of the legal institutions and social structures dictated by rabbinic literature is urgently needed."[20] Neither polemic nor apologetic, however, can disguise the fact that rabbinic Judaism considers women to be different from men in a number of significant and immutable ways, some of which will always defy change within the system.

One of the most revelatory indications of rabbinic Judaism's male-centered system of reality is still a part of the liturgy of traditional Jewish practice. This is a three-fold prayer recited daily which reads:

> Blessed art thou, Lord our God, King of the Universe, who hast not made me a gentile. Blessed art thou, Lord our God, King of the Universe, who has not made me a slave. Blessed art thou, Lord our God, King of the Universe, who hast not made me a woman.[21]

Woman's otherness from men is stressed throughout rabbinic literature. While women are credited with more compassion and concern for the unfortunate than men, perhaps as a result of their maternal roles,[22] they are also linked with witchcraft and wantonness, licentiousness and sexual abandon.[23] The rabbis taught that women possess four traits: they are greedy, eavesdroppers, slothful and envious.[24] They are also prone to steal and be frivolous.[25] "Ten measures of speech descended to the world," says the Talmud, "and women took nine of them."[26] Despite Biblical examples of vigorous and resourceful women,[27] and in the face of influential and admirable women of their own times,[28] the rabbis generally diminish women's abilities and qualities in their Biblical exegeses, general comments, and personal anecdotes. Thus, Beruriah, the wife of the second-century sage, Rabbi Meir, is virtually the only woman whom the Talmud describes as learned in Jewish law, yet she is transformed in later traditions into an adulteress and a suicide.[29] Other women who display unusual sagacity meet early deaths.[30] The Biblical judge Deborah is likened to a wasp and the prophetess Huldah to a weasel;[31] other Biblical heroines are similarly disparaged. Wherever a woman does utter words of wisdom in a rabbinic story it is generally to deliver a rebuke to someone in need of chastisement. To be bested by a woman is punishment indeed.[32]

Similar instances of the diminishment of women can be found throughout rabbinic literature, but a litany of such passages is of limited use if it is not put in a context. One way these texts may be evaluated is by exploring what women are separated from and with whom they are linked. What stands out in many of the rabbis' statements is not just the unpleasant way women are dismissed, but the conviction that women are limited from calling upon the divine name and therefore must be connected with others who are also disqualified from full religious rights and privileges. In one of its rulings, the Mishnah says that "All are subject to the command to appear before the Lord [at the Temple] excepting a deaf-mute, an imbecile, a child, one of doubtful sex . . . women, slaves that have not been freed, a man that is lame, or blind, or sick or aged, and one that cannot go up to Jerusalem on his feet."[33] Here women are linked with males who are incomplete or damaged in some way: they are disdained, are separated, in effect, because they are not whole or wholesome. And because of what they are not, they are ineligible to appear before God. Similarly, women are also, as we have seen, frequently grouped with slaves and other property, again probably because all are less than complete who are subject to a master.[34] Women by nature belong to a separate category of being from the righteous man who can achieve sanctity.

In this respect, it is important to look at the three rabbinic precepts which apply specifically to women. These are the lighting of candles to signal the advent of the Sabbath; the breaking off and burning of a bit of dough used in forming the Sabbath loaf (*challah*); and the observance of the laws of *niddah* (legislation pertaining to the menstruating woman) which strictly limit a woman's contact with any man during and for a week following her menstrual period. It is a crucial fact that rabbinic tradition does not regard these ordinances as *mitzvot,* that is, as divine commandments whose observance enhances the religious life of the observer and assures divine favor. Rather these precepts are described as eternal punishments brought upon woman to remind her of Eve's responsibility in the death of Adam, and therefore in all human mortality:

> Concerning menstruation: The first man was the blood and life of the world . . . and Eve was the cause of his death; therefore has she been given the menstruation precept. The same is true concerning *Challah* (leaven); Adam was the pure *Challah* of the world . . . And Eve was the cause of his death; therefore has she been given the Challah precept. And concerning the lighting of the [Sabbath] lamp: Adam was the light of the world . . . And Eve was the cause of his death; therefore has she been given the precept about lighting the [Sabbath] lamp.[35]

According to the *Mishnah,* disregard of these commandments brings dire results: "For these transgressions do women die in childbirth: for heedlessness of the laws concerning their menstruation, the Dough offering, and the lighting of the Sabbath lamp."[36]

It is fascinating that all three of these commandments specifically directed at women have to do with separation. All three can symbolize the chasm between the sacred and the profane, the holy and the secular, the realm of men who obey commandments and that of women who suffer disabilities, and ultimately between the realms of life and death themselves.

ANTHROPOLOGICAL APPROACHES

By viewing rabbinic Judaism as a cultural system, and by examining the ways in which rabbinic strictures correspond to ordering patterns found in societies throughout the world, rabbinic separation can be seen in a sharper light. One particularly useful anthropological distinction is that between public and private domains. Michelle Zimbalist Rosaldo has attempted to explain why "cultures everywhere have given men, as a category opposed to woman, social value and moral worth."[37] She suggests that this dichotomy in every range of human experience can be understood by one "near universal fact of human existence: in most traditional societies, a good part of a woman's adult life is spent giving birth to and raising children."[38] This has led to a "differentiation of domestic and public spheres of activity" which Rosaldo suggests has shaped a number of aspects of human social structure and psychology.[39] Where a strong separation between public and private arenas of activity exists, and where women are isolated from each other and placed under a single man's authority in the home, they are valued least.[40] It is true that women may find ways of exerting power within the home, or of obtaining emotional and social satisfaction in groups made up of other women, but as Rosaldo makes clear, real power and societal prestige lie beyond the household.[41] Wherever women and the domestic are synonymous, men are predominant.

In the Talmud's ordering of life, the sexes are separated as much as they can be. As wives, women belong in the home nurturing children. Acceptable alternatives to wifehood do not exist. Accordingly, women are barred from the public domain not only by custom but by detailed legislation which discourages female participation in most of the society's communal and power-conferring activities. Since these endeavors, in rabbinic Judaism, have to do mostly with participation in religious service, learning, and the execution of judgments according to Jewish law, women are simultaneously isolated from sources of spiritual and intellectual sustenance. Because there is little ground on which the public and private can meet, women are seen as not having religious or intellectual function or need.

Saul Berman has pointed out that many of the social and legal disabilities women suffer in rabbinic Judaism are accidental by-products of the system's insistence on her confinement to the domestic sphere.[42] As he says,

> The exemption from communal presence seems to be a central element of women's status in Jewish law, necessary to ensure that no mandated or preferred act conflict with the selection of the protected role.[43]

But inequities, such as deprivation of opportunities for positive religious identification, a disadvantaged position in areas of marital law and civil procedure, and relegation to an enabling role, can, he argues, be counter-productive and ultimately work against the attainment of central social goals.[44] The more women are isolated and alienated from the system, the less they feel a part of it, and given attractive alternatives, defections are not unlikely. Recognizing some of these dangers, the rabbinic law-making process has historically sought to be flexible in easing difficulties which women encounter because of the system's inherent discriminations against them. Hauptmann points out how various authorities have tried to alleviate some female disabilities such as the inability to divorce a husband, or to contest a husband's wish to divorce. Similarly, the laws governing remarriage of a woman whose husband has disappeared but cannot be proved dead were construed as leniently as possible.[45]

The sages of the *Mishnah* and *Talmud*, however, were determined that women should not have significant roles in the public arena. Yet various literary and archaeological data suggest that during the centuries of rabbinic Judaism's formulation some Jewish women, even while married, exercised legal options independently through litigation, successfully managed complicated financial affairs, and even served in positions of religious leadership and patronage. The New Testament Gospels, for example, portray women as a prominent and independent group in society.[46] Neusner notes that the discovery in a Judean desert cave of legal documents belonging to a Jewish woman of the early second century gives a similar impression:

> The account of the affairs of this woman, Babata, leaves no doubt of her legal capacities. She received all the properties of her hus-

> band during his own lifetime and took possession of them when he died. She remarried and inherited another large property. She undertook and effected numerous important litigations and in general supervised what was hers. Any picture of the Israelite woman of the second century as chattel and a dumb animal hardly accords with the actualities revealed in the legal documents of Babata.[47]

Bernadette Brooten also presents evidence that women were active in the public sphere of Jewish society. On the basis of a number of inscriptions in Greek and Latin, dating from the first century B.C.E. to the sixth century C.E. and ranging in locale from Italy to Asia Minor, Egypt and Phoenicia, in which women bear such titles as "head of the synagogue," "leader," "elder," "mother of the synagogue" and "priestess," Brooten suggests that contrary to previous scholarly consensus, Jewish women did assume positions of leadership in the ancient synagogue.[48] Brooten is correct in pointing out that all that is known about women from rabbinic Judaism is what its male authors thought about them, and she predicts that "As we begin to evaluate all of the sources for Jewish women's history in the period in question, including inscriptions and papyri, a much more differentiated picture will emerge."[49] Thus we may conclude that in strictly confining woman to the sphere of the domestic the rabbis were not just sanctifying accepted traditions and norms of life. Theirs was a vision of an ideal society which they believed conformed to divine will; their legislation enabled them to reject, in God's name, a number of aspects of the wider Jewish and gentile worlds around them, including female autonomy. The sharp dichotomy between men and women in rabbinic literature is a deliberate political and religious statement.

A second anthropological distinction which is relevant here is that between culture and nature. Sherry Ortner has noted that wherever a society recognizes a difference between the operation of nature (biological needs and processes) and culture (human consciousness and its products), culture will be perceived as both separate from and superior to nature.[50] Women's "pancultural second-class status" could be accounted for by the fact that women are linked more closely with nature, while men identify themselves with cultural creativity.[51] Certainly this schism is strongly present in rabbinic Judaism which jealously preserves culture, that is learning and study, as a male prerogative. The first-century sage, Rabbi Eliezer, maintained that "If a man teaches his daughter Torah [Biblical teachings and their rabbinic interpretations] it is as though he taught her lechery."[52] Elsewhere, this same scholar is quoted as having said, "The wisdom of woman is only in her distaff. . . . May the words of Torah be burned rather than be given to women."[53] The *Talmud* clearly states that Torah study is not a female obligation when it asks, "And how do we know that she has no obligation? . . . Because it is written [Deut. 6:7]: 'And you [masculine singular] shall teach your sons . . .' but not 'your daughter.' "[54] Of this exclusion Montefiore writes,

> Very few women were students of the Law: it was not intended that they should be. Yet the highest and most adorable thing in the world was to study the Law. The greatest and purest joy in the world was to fulfil all the commandments and ordinances of the Pentateuch and Rabbinic codes. But women need not, and could not, observe them all.[55]

Similarly, Hauptmann notes that women who continue to live within rabbinically oriented societies are removed from Judaism's central religious experiences:

> Prayer, an ongoing quest for an I-Thou confrontation with God, and study, the intellectual encounter with God's revealed word, requires much time, effort and skill. Women, because their role in life does not permit them to make the effort or acquire the skills, do not pray with regularity, nor do they delve into the study of the Jewish tradition.[56]

Why did rabbinic Judaism exclude women from the realm of culture? As Ortner notes, in all societies women are seen as closer to nature because of the "natural procreative functions specific to women alone."[57] She stresses, however, that this perception is more a construct of culture than a fact of nature:

> Woman is not "in reality" any closer to (or further from) nature than man—both have consciousness, both are mortal . . . but various aspects of woman's situation (physical, social, psychological) contribute to her being seen as closer to nature, while the view of her as closer to nature is in turn embodied in institutional forms that reproduce her situation.[58]

Rosaldo has also pointed out that cultural notions of the female often center around natural or biological characteristics: fertility, maternity, sex and menstrual blood.[59] Women, she writes, are defined almost exclusively in terms of their sexual functions, and these are often frightening or threatening to men; therefore, "women will be seen as anomalous and defined as dangerous, dirty, polluting, as something to be set apart."[60] Rabbinic Judaism, too, is most anxious to circumscribe, defuse and control the sexual attributes of the female as both polluter and temptress.

The concept of womanly uncleanness, particularly as linked to menstrual and post-partum discharges, is fundamental to the rabbinic separation of women.[61] Put simply, the unclean woman is a potential source of danger to male holiness which can be polluted in a number of ways. The question of what constitutes clean and unclean in Jewish tradition, as Jean Soler has shown, can be understood in structural terms. For instance, in the Biblical dietary laws which became the basis of the system of permitted and forbidden foods in rabbinic Judaism:

> unclean animals are marked by a blemish; they show an anomaly in their relation to the element that has brought them forth . . . or to the organs characteristic of life in that element. If they do not fit into any class, or if they fit into two classes at once, they are unclean [and] they are unclean because they are unthinkable [in this cosmos]. . . . Man, God, the animals and the plants are strictly defined through their relationship with one another in a series of opposites. The Hebrews conceived of the order of the world as the order underlying the creation of the world. Uncleanness then, is *simply disorder,* wherever it may occur.[62]

Soler goes on to say that the sexual and dietary prohibitions of the Bible are coordinated, and that both are based on separating classes of being, for to abolish distinctions would be to subvert the order of the world.[63]

In *Purity and Danger,* Mary Douglas also discusses the dietary laws, particularly as they are formulated in Leviticus. She concludes that in this text holiness is exemplified by completeness, and that holiness demands that individuals conform to the class to which they belong.[64] She comments that holiness means keeping distinct the categories of creation and involves correct definitions, discriminations and order. It is by rules of avoidance that holiness achieves physical expression, at every encounter with the animal kingdom, at every meal,[65] and at every possibility of an improper contact with a woman.

That these insights are also relevant to the separation between male and female realms mandated by rabbinic Judaism seems obvious. In this context it is easier to understand the view that it is better to burn the words of Torah than give them to a woman, for to do so would be anomalous, a subversion of the divine intent; it would disastrously confuse the assigned purposes of two separate categories of creation. Women are by definition not a part of the covenant, the *B'rit*, that exists between man and God, and whose symbol is circumcision; divine revelation, in the rabbinic system, is given only to men.

Douglas's remarks also prompt us to ask if holiness is possible where uncleanness is periodically present. If man can maintain holiness by avoiding any possible contact with a menstruating woman—and a considerable section of an order of the *Mishnah* and its talmudic commentary is devoted to just how a man can do this—can the woman herself ever be holy? Although she can be purified after her periodic uncleanness to preserve her husband from profanation, it seems that for herself the answer in rabbinic terms is no. At best it may be said that this is not a question rabbinic Judaism is interested in answering.

Women are also dangerous to men through the stimulation of sexual desire. In his discussion of the dietary laws, Soler defines uncleanness as disorder and anomaly. The woman, whose biological makeup tends towards disorder—in herself, and others—is doubly anomalous in an ordered male world. Left unchecked, she will be a constant reminder of untamed nature in a society which aspires to the divine. If the menstruating woman, therefore, should not enter the synagogue at all, the non-menstruating woman must sit separately and out of sight so that men will not be distracted from their prayers by her enticing presence.[66] The rabbinic remark that woman is "a pitcher full of filth with its mouth full of blood, yet all run after her"[67] is in its own terms less an opinion than a statement of fact. In rabbinic Judaism, a woman incarnates her disturbing and anomalous differences from men.

In his study of the Mishnah's order (or division) of Women (*Nashim*), Jacob Neusner calls particular attention to the theme of woman as aberration: in the patriarchal world of rabbinic Judaism man is normal and woman is abnormal.[68] This order, which is concerned with the contracting and dissolving of marriages, is anxious to keep women subject to men and to establish rules that regulate the transfer of a woman from her father to a husband. As Neusner writes, "The regulation of the transfer of woman is *Mishnah*'s way of effecting the sanctification of what, for the moment, disturbs and disorders the orderly world which *Mishnah* deems desirable."[69] Thus, the goal and purpose of *Mishnah*'s order of Women is "to bring under control and force into stasis all the wild and unruly potentialities of sexuality."[70]

The anomaly of woman, therefore, is worked out by assigning her to man's domain.[71] That women were seen to accept the premises of the system is confirmed by the talmudic story which praises a "young girl who fervently prayed that no man would unwittingly be led astray by her and thus lose his place in Paradise."[72] Similarly, the parlous state of the unprotected widow, always an anomalous figure, is poignantly illustrated in another talmudic tale:

> Rava's wife found out that Huma, the widow of a prominent rabbi, had perhaps inadvertently enticed her husband, whereupon she chased Huma out of town, exclaiming that she would not let Huma kill another man.[73]

Needless to say, the heroine of this story, nameless as she is, is Rava's wife!

In the ideal rabbinic master plan for society, woman looms as a potential source of pollution and disorder whose life and impact on men must be regulated. Her nature and essence are different from man's; as a consequence she must be kept separate from centers of holiness and the holy books. She must be maintained in a specific realm of the ordinary where her fearful powers will be controlled.

The ways in which rabbinic Judaism separates women from men reflect the rabbis' methods of regulating and sanctifying society, illustrating their conviction that the world below should mirror what they take to be the heavenly reality above. Anthropological studies show that rabbinic Judaism's perceptions of women are by no means unique or even unusual. But it still must be said that such a system of separation, with its attendant distancing of women as "other," will always bring with it a profound and persistent diminution of the human spirit.

NOTES

1. Rabbinic Judaism is a religious tradition which has its origins in post-Biblical Judaism (approximately 450 B.C.E.–70 C.E.), and which emerged and developed in the rabbinic period (the first six centuries of the Common Era) to become the normative form of Jewish practice up to the modern era. Its founders, careful readers and interpreters of the Hebrew Bible, were known in the post-Biblical period as Scribes and later, Pharisees. During the rabbinic period, the movement's leaders were called rabbis (teachers). On the rabbis and the rabbinic period, see Judah Goldin, "The Period of the Talmud (135 B.C.E.–1035 C.E.)," in *The Jews: Their History*, Louis Finkelstein, ed. (New York: Schocken Books, 1970), pp. 119–224.

2. On the varieties of Judaism in this period, see Marcel Simon, *Jewish Sects at the Time of Jesus* (Philadelphia: Fortress, 1967), or Michael Stone,

Scriptures, Sects and Visions. A Profile of Judaism from Ezra to the Jewish Revolts (Philadelphia: Fortress, 1980).

3. Jacob Neusner, *Method and Meaning in Ancient Judaism*, Brown Judaic Studies, no. 10 (Missoula, Montana: Scholars Press, 1979), p. 80.

4. Ibid., p. 83, n. 3.

5. Ibid., p. 95. Here Neusner writes: "Only in later times would the Israelite world come to approximate, and even to conform to, *Mishnah's* vision of reality."

6. Leonard Swidler, *Women in Judaism: The Status of Women in Formative Judaism* (Metuchen, New Jersey: The Scarecrow Press, 1976), p. 82.

7. G. C. Montefiore and H. Loewe, *A Rabbinic Anthology* (1938; reprint ed., Philadelphia: Jewish Publication Society, 1960), pp. xviii–xix.

8. Neusner, *Method and Meaning*, p. 95.

9. Ibid., see also Judith Hauptmann, "Images of Women in the Talmud," in *Religion and Sexism: Images of Woman in the Jewish and Christian Traditions*, Rosemary Radford Ruether, ed. (New York: Simon and Schuster, 1974), pp. 184–212, who writes, "A woman's prime function in life is to concern herself with man's welfare and to provide for his physical comfort" (p. 197).

10. Ellen Umansky, "Women in Judaism: From the Reform Movement to Contemporary Jewish Religious Feminism," in *Women of Spirit: Female Leadership in the Jewish and Christian Traditions*, Rosemary Ruether and Eleanor McLaughlin, eds. (New York: Simon and Schuster, 1979), p. 335.

11. Ibid.

12. See Hauptmann, "Images of Women," pp. 197–208, and Montefiore and Loewe, *Rabbinic Anthology*, pp. 507–15, for praise of women as wives and mothers.

13. Hauptmann writes, "Furthermore, the rabbis provided for a woman's emotional, social and sexual satisfaction in marriage," and she provides a number of talmudic citations to this effect. "Images of Women," pp. 186, 186–88 respectively. Similarly, Montefiore and Loewe write that "it must readily be admitted that the Rabbis seem to have loved their wives, that they all apparently, had only one wife each, and that the position of the wife was one of much influence and importance." *Rabbinic Anthology*, p. 507. Neusner too notes that woman's status in rabbinic Judaism "is not utterly lacking a measure of autonomy, dignity, and control of her own affairs." *Method and Meaning*, p. 94. As he adds, however, "The measure, to be sure, is not overflowing."

14. Hauptmann writes, "Women were protected by the rabbis from exploitation and had their basic rights safeguarded; men still occupied the dominant position." "Images of Women," p. 186. See also Neusner, *Method and Meaning*, pp. 94–95.

15. *M. Shebuot* 4:1: "The law about an oath of testimony applies to men but not to women." See Swidler, *Women in Judaism*, pp. 115–16 for a detailed discussion of this matter.

16. Examples include, *M. Berakot* 3:3: "Women and slaves and minors are exempt from reciting the Shema and from wearing phylacteries," and *M.*

Sukkah 2:7, "Women, slaves and minors are exempt from [the law of] the Sukkah."

17. *M. Kiddushin* 1:7; *B. Ketubot* 29a.

18. Thus, Swidler summarizes a number of contemporary Jewish commentators. *Women in Judaism,* p. 84. He points out, however, that this rule is often contradicted "when rules which are not time-bound are said not to oblige women." Ibid., pp. 84–85. Hauptmann also notes that exceptions to the general principle abound, suggesting that "The rule is more like an observation based on a large number of cases rather than a prescription for all possible contingencies." "Images of Women," p. 191.

19. Aviva Cantor Zuckoff, "The Oppression of the Jewish Woman," *Response* 18 (1973): 49.

20. Hauptmann, "Images of Woman," p. 210; also see Ellen Umansky's article in this volume.

21. Philip Birnbaum, trans., *Ha-Siddur Ha-Shalem: Daily Prayer Book* (New York: Hebrew Publishing Company, 1949), pp. 15–17.

22. Hauptmann, "Images of Woman," pp. 200–201.

23. Women are linked with wantonness and licentiousness in *M. Sotah* 3:4, and *B. Ketubot* 65a. They are connected with witchcraft in *M. Aboth* 2:7, which reads "Many women, much witchcraft"; the saying "The most virtuous of women is a witch" is found in several rabbinic sources, including *P. Kiddushin* 4, 66b, and *Soferim* 41a.

24. *Gen.R.* 45:5.

25. *B. Shabbat* 33b.

26. *B. Kiddushin* 49b.

27. One might cite Miriam (Exod. 15, 21; Num. 12); Rahab (Josh. 2); Deborah (Judg. 4–5); Jael (Judg. 4:18); and Huldah (2 Kings 22:12–20) among many others.

28. Hauptmann cites numerous rabbinic anecdotes reflecting on female intelligence and women's influence on men. "Images of Women," pp. 197–208. Also see below note 46.

29. On Beruria, see Swidler, *Women in Judaism,* pp. 97–104.

30. Hauptmann cites the example of Rabbi Samuel's daughters who "not only quoted Jewish law but actually utilized it in a shrewd way in order to obtain permission to marry a *cohen* [priest] after having been returned from captivity" (*B. Ketubot* 23a); while the daughters did marry, they died untimely deaths (*P. Ketubot* 2:6). "Images of Women," p. 204.

31. Thus, *B. Megillah* 14b: "R. Nahman said: haughtiness does not befit women. There were two haughty women, and their names are hateful, one being called hornet [possible meaning for Deborah] and the other a weasel [possible meaning for Huldah]."

32. See Hauptmann, "Images of Women," pp. 197–208, for a number of examples.

33. *M. Hagigah* 1:1.

34. *M. Kiddushin* 1:1, 1:2, 1:8.

35. *P. Shabbat* 2, 5b, 34; *Gen.R.* 17:7.

36. This ruling is found in *M. Shabbat* 2:6; *T. Shabbat* 2:10; *B. Shabbat* 31b–32a; *P. Shabbat* 2, 5b, 34; and *Gen.R.* 17:8.
37. Michelle Zimbalist Rosaldo, "Woman, Culture, and Society: A Theoretical Overview," in *Women, Culture and Society,* Michelle Zimbalist Rosaldo and Louise Lamphere, eds. (Stanford, CA: Stanford University Press, 1974), p. 22.
38. Ibid., p. 23.
39. Ibid., p. 36.
40. Ibid.
41. Ibid., p. 42.
42. Saul Berman, "The Status of Women in Halakhic Judaism," in *The Jewish Woman: New Perspectives,* Elizabeth Koltun, ed. (New York: Schocken Books, 1976), p. 123.
43. Ibid.
44. Ibid., pp. 115–16.
45. Hauptmann, "Images of Women," pp. 189–90.
46. Neusner, *Method and Meaning,* p. 92.
47. Ibid., pp. 92–93.
48. Bernadette J. Brooten, *Women Leaders in the Ancient Synagogue,* Brown Judaic Studies no. 36 (Chico, CA: Scholars Press, 1982), p. 1.
49. Ibid., p. 150.
50. Sherry Ortner, "Is Female to Male as Nature is to Culture?" in Rosaldo and Lamphere, *Women, Culture and Society,* p. 73.
51. Ibid.
52. *M. Sotah* 3:4. There is some disagreement about whether on this question Rabbi Eliezer represents mainstream views (Swidler, *Women in Judaism,* p. 93), or a minority opinion (Hauptmann, "Images of Women," p. 203). All seem to agree, however, that the Jewishly educated woman was a rarity.
53. *B. Yoma* 66b; *M. Sotah* 3:4.
54. *B. Kiddushin* 29b.
55. Montefiore and Loewe, *A Rabbinic Anthology,* pp. xviii–xix.
56. Hauptmann, "Images of Women," p. 193.
57. Ortner, "Is Female to Male," pp. 73–74.
58. Ibid., p. 87.
59. Rosaldo, "Woman, Culture and Society," p. 31.
60. Ibid., p. 32.
61. As Swidler points out, rabbinic Judaism saw ritual purity as a religious ideal. To incur uncleanness is to "somehow separate oneself from God, to be displeasing to God." He notes that there were three main causes of impurity: "leprosy; dead bodies of certain animals, and particularly human corpses; and issue from sexual organs" (based mainly on Lev. 11–17). "Of the three, the last is the most important and frequent, and clearly it is the woman that is most involved." A woman, as a man, is unclean after sexual intercourse, for seven days after any menstruous discharge of blood, for thirty-three days after the birth of a male child, and for sixty-six days after the birth of a female child (based on Lev. 12:2–5). Anything the unclean

woman touches, or anyone, also becomes unclean for a day. *Women in Judaism*, pp. 130–33.

62. Jean Soler, "The Dietary Prohibitions of the Hebrews," *The New York Review of Books* 26 (14 June 1979): 29.

63. Ibid., 30.

64. Mary Douglas, *Purity and Danger: An Analysis of the Concepts of Pollution and Taboo* (London: Routledge & Kegan Paul, 1966), p. 53.

65. Ibid., p. 57.

66. The restriction forbidding the menstruous woman to enter the synagogue is post-Talmudic, appearing first in the composition of the tenth century, *Baraita de-Niddah*. Swidler discusses this work and the stringency of its measures, *Women in Judaism*, p. 138. Brooten considers the question of whether women were separated from men during worship in the ancient synagogue. While she believes such a separation was not typical during the first five or six centuries of the Common Era, there is no doubt that by the tenth century it had become a feature of rabbinic Judaism. *Women Leaders*, pp. 103–38.

67. *B. Shabbat* 152a.

68. Neusner, *Method and Meaning*, p. 97.

69. Ibid.

70. Ibid.

71. Ibid., p. 100.

72. *B. Sotah* 22a, quoted in Hauptmann, "Images of Women," p. 205.

73. *B. Ketubot* 65a, quoted in Hauptmann, "Images of Women," p. 198.

CHAPTER TWO

Women, Religion and Social Change in Early Islam

JANE I. SMITH

Although women often play vital and significant roles in times of profound religious change, change accompanied by some form of social upheaval, normally these roles are substantially diminished when the upheaval has ceased and social change is gradual rather than dramatic. This hypothesis has been advanced as an attempt to identify a common pattern in the relationship of women and social change across a wide variety of religio-cultural contexts. My task in this article is to try to test the hypothesis against the events at the time of the establishment of Islam in the sixth century C.E. in Arabia.

At first glance it might seem that the case is so obvious as to present little challenge. An overview of the very early history of Islam provides a general picture of increasing segregation, seclusion and degradation of women. While several of the wives of the Prophet and other women played strong roles in the period of Islam's naissance, women soon came to be considered—and in most cases therefore to be—passive and submissive and consequently more and more isolated. That there were individual exceptions of women playing significant roles in society after the death of the Prophet does not negate the overall truth of this circumstance. Or so it would seem.

It is not true that women in general were insignificant members of society in the days of pre-Islamic Arabia, suddenly became active participants in religious revolution in the time of the Prophet Muḥammad, and then again lost status as their rights and privileges began to disappear. While the Qur'ān apparently did improve the legal circumstances for women in many aspects of family relations over those of the period immediately before the revelations to the Prophet, women in pre-Islamic Arabia were not completely without power and authority. These women are known in many cases to have been proud and strong-willed participants in battle as well as holders of significant religious status as seers and soothsayers, judge-arbiters, and (although rarely) even prophetesses.

It also seems to be the case that for most of his life Muhammad himself respected and trusted women, was strongly influenced by a number of forceful females, and attempted to provide for equal participation of women in the religious life of the new community. Is one to conclude, then, that the status of women was high and the opportunity for them to play significant social roles readily available before the advent of Islam as well as in its immediate formative period, and that it was only after the death of Muḥammad and the beginnings of solidification of the new community that women ceased to be taken seriously as active participants in society? I think not, although the evidence initially might seem to point that way.

Let us look first at some of what is known about women in pre-Islamic Arabia. While significant research has been done by Nabia Abbott, Robertson Smith, Ilse Lichtenstadter and others, far too often the results of their work are ignored in the effort to highlight the advantages (or, in some cases, the disadvantages) for women of the Islamic system as compared to its pagan background. Much contemporary Muslim apologetic, for example, thrives on the fact that the Prophet through revelation banned female infanticide and that unlimited polygyny was replaced by the Islamic limitation of four wives to a husband.

Apart from fairly simplistic attempts to categorize the general situation for women in pre-Islamic Arabia as poor in order to stress the virtue of the Islamic improvements, it is not easy to generalize about women before the time of the Prophet. Are we talking about the many centuries from the time of the Sabaen Kingdoms of South Arabia or about that period immediately before the Prophet which Muslims call the *jāhilīya* or time of ignorance? Are the records adequate to provide anything like a clear picture of any period? Even if we could know all the facts, would our distance from them in terms of time, geography and cultural orientation not color our responses so as to make the attempt to understand the early Arabian situation in context next to futile?

While recognizing such problems—only several among many—we can nonetheless assume that we do know some things and try to make generalizations about what the facts may mean. That women in ancient Arabia were not always subservient to men is clear from the chronicles of pre-Islamic Arab queens. Nabia Abbott in her detailed study[1] indicates that there are records of some twenty-four such queens over sixteen centuries. Some of the queens are known also to have been priestesses of the local gods. After about the fourth century C.E. we have little record of female rulers as such, though we do know that poets recognized and paid tribute to many strong women of their day.[2]

Despite these very notable exceptions, it is also true that females overall figure relatively little in the available records about life in pre-Islamic Arabia. A number of possible reasons may be adduced for this: (1) women in general were never in positions of social prominence; (2) an earlier prominence, at least in the case of certain individuals, gave way to a loss of public prestige during the period of ignorance; (3) the records are simply so inaccurate, or incomplete, that we have a skewed picture; (4) compilations of reports by second- and third-century Muslim recorders were subject to the anti-female prejudices of those recorders and thus misrepresent the actual situation.

It does appear in general that women's power and prestige were lower in the days immediately preceding the time of the Prophet than they were earlier. Scholars for a while accepted Robertson Smith's work[3] as proving that in many ancient Arabian tribes matriarchy and polyandry were the rule. This thesis, however, has come to be disregarded as improbable for any significant numbers. It is the case that in pre-Islamic Arabia several types of marriage existed, from matrilineal and matrilocal to patrilineal and patrilocal. In the jāhilīya period the latter clearly came to predominate, with the result that women seem to have been increasingly regarded as the property of males who had the right to unlimited polygamy. (At the time of the Prophet acquiring wives by capture was still widespread. The woman who was captured automatically became a member of the captor's tribe.)

Despite the patriarchal orientation of most marriages, a woman's blood kinship with her own tribe was retained and, if necessary, she could seek protection with her own people if ill-treated by her husband. The woman, then, was not without resources, but in fact the alternatives always left her under the charge of a male—either her husband or her nearest male kinsman. Both men and women could repudiate a marriage, although it is hard to know from available records how often women experienced this right.

Attempts to assess the degree of freedom and influence enjoyed by women in the jāhilīya have, of course, varied. Without question, as is almost universally the case, their primary sphere was the home and their primary roles were those of wife and mother.[4] In that context they were highly valued, the occasional practice of burying alive a female child notwithstanding. Women were important in the social life of the tribe because feuds and even battles arose over them, and families eagerly negotiated for the freedom of captured women. None of this is to credit women with having played significant decision-making or leadership roles outside the family context, although they sometimes served as mediators. Perhaps more interesting for the modern observer is the fact that women did take an active role in warfare. They were not armsbearers, however, but served by taking care of the wounded on the battlefield and by joining together in coteries to urge the warriors on to victory.

Few observers have gone so far as did Reynold Nicholson when he affirmed that the position of women in pre-Islamic Arabia was high and their influence great.[5] Stressing that poets sang of women and warriors fought for them, he eloquently argued that this was proof of their nobility and high rank in society. Unfortunately for Nicholson, perhaps, a contemporary feminist would turn his argument upside down and point out that what he is illustrating is precisely the passive role that permitted women to be considered objects for possession rather than full participants in the social structure of the tribe.

In fact, however, passivity does not at all seem to characterize the lives of women in pre-Islamic Arabia. In one sense women were protected and apparently seen, to some degree, as a kind of property. On the other hand they were of necessity strong and resilient, prepared to lead the hard life of a primarily desert land whose dangers included the constant threat of war and plunder in which they might be the booty. This helps explain their evident courage and even enthusiasm for a good fight. It seems that they did take some part in the events of public life and did exercise a kind of influence that was more or less lost in the later developments of Islamic society.

One way in which individual women were able to exercise influence was as participants in leadership roles in the religious life. Even up to the time of the Prophet there are recorded instances of a woman as soothsayer, as priestess, and as prophetess. (There is, however, only one known prophetess and even the priestesses were quite rare.)[6] The term *rabbat al-bait* literally means mistress of the temple in this context. Abbott observes that before the advent of Islam, *rabba* and *rabb* were applied to female and male human beings, respectively, who played the roles of priestesses and priests. After Islam the term *rabb* was generally limited to the deity. *Rabba* was not.[7] It is beyond the scope of this essay to pursue the implications of this, but future scholars may wish to examine the relationship of the emergence of a monotheistic cult, in which the deity is apparently understood as masculine, to the general conviction that it is impossible for women to play roles of religious leadership equal to men.

It does seem to be the case that women did not have an active part in the political life of Mecca on the eve of Islam. Under the leadership of Quṣayy, head of the Quraish tribe at the time of the Prophet, government decisions were made by a Council of Elders on which no woman sat. A woman would on occasion give her opinion in public, but attempts to exert influence generally were limited to private persuasion of the men in her family and clan. This, it is obvious, is a timeless strategy which women employ in the face of otherwise limiting male power structures.

In comparing women in pre-Islamic Arabia to those after the advent of Islam two observations can be made. One is that the position of a woman and her place in society were not determined by codified law. This meant that the role a woman was able to play depended to a great extent on her own personality. Is it possible that the very codification of Islamic law was in itself part of the cause of the segregation of women and the apparent lessening of their opportunities to participate in public life? Second, despite the obvious fact that to some extent women were simply understood by males to be their property— valued, perhaps even esteemed, but still property—they enjoyed one clear advantage over their sisters to come: they did not suffer the devastating restriction of seclusion.

From this general background on women in pre-Islamic Arabia, let us turn to the situation that prevailed during the time of the Prophet Muhammad and the founding of the new religion of Islam. Several episodes recorded during and after the life of the Prophet point to certain women having potential, and in some cases real, power. These seem to reflect the authority accorded women by virtue of their participation in, or association with, religious or cultic practices that were holdovers from earlier days.

A number of accounts record that at the time that Mecca surrendered to the Muslims, the keys of the Kaʿba were in the hands of a woman named Hubba, daughter of Hulayl, the last priest-king of Mecca.[8] It seems that little can be made of this, however, as Hubba's role was clearly secondary to that of not only her father but also her husband and the men of her tribe. More interesting is the case of a group of women who have come to be known as the harlots of Hadramaut. This part of South Arabia had been strongly opposed to the increasing influence of Muhammad. When the Prophet died a group of women apparently were so overjoyed that they gathered together for singing, dancing and open celebration. A.F.L. Beeston[9] speculates that they were perhaps priestesses of the old pagan religion of South Arabia who hoped that Muhammad's death signalled the end of Islam and therefore the resurgence of their own power and influence.

Regardless of what is really to be made of the incident, three points are of interest for our consideration. First, in that part of Arabia there evidently were women who, along with male priests, played an active religious role before the coming of Islam. Second, these women felt secure enough in that function to make a public demonstration of their joy at the death of the founder of Islam. Third, and closely related to the above, the new caliph Abū Bakr feared these women to the point that he sanctioned severe punishment for them. It seems clear, then, that these women did have the capacity to exert influence on the course of events, a capacity enjoyed by virtue of their pre-Islamic status and not one occasioned by the religio-social revolution of the Prophet.

The power of the spoken word, particularly in poetic form, was formidable in early Arabia and helps explain the force of the verbalized revelations of the Qurʾān. At the time of the Prophet a select group of persons was recognized as possessing the gift of poetry, including some of the women in tribes bitterly opposed to Muḥammad. One ʿAsmāʾ bint Marwān, for example, was considered so dangerous that the Prophet was anxious to get rid of her once and for all. While apparently he did not give orders for her death, the records cite his enormous relief when one of his followers, sensing Muhammad's alarm, had her executed.[10] After the final victory Muhammad extended amnesty to most of those who had fought against Islam. The only ones it appears he could not forgive, very likely out of concern for their continuing influence, were those (especially women) who had ridiculed him in songs and poems. This constitutes interesting testimony of the power of their position, as well as of the recited word.

Just as women had participated in battle before the time of Muhammad, usually cheerleading rather than bearing weapons, so they continued to be very much in evidence fighting both for and against the Prophet. In some cases their participation took the form of nursing, particularly in the setting up of field hospitals in mosques to care for the wounded. Often their roles were most notable when they were seeking revenge, and we have reports of women physically attacking enemy warriors with swords and clubs. One popular story of the early Islamic period, for instance, describes Sumayya, wife of ʿAmmār b. Yāsir. Both Sumayya and ʿAmmār were early converts to Islam. When ʿAmmār was tortured and killed by the Quraish, Sumayya went out to attack in retaliation and was herself killed, becoming the first woman martyr in Islam.[11]

One of the most interesting and well-known personages at the time of the Prophet was the redoubtable Hind, a woman to swell the heart of any firm-minded feminist. Her husband Abū Sufyān was the leader of the Quraish army, and it is clear that Hind was a figure of consequence in her own right—intelligent, proud, and seemingly fearless. Her rage against the Muslims was fueled by the fact that she had lost her father, uncle and brother at the Battle of Badr. At the subsequent battle of Uhud, Hind seized the opportunity for retaliation. She and some fifteen other women led the charge, singing and dancing and playing the tambourine onto the battlefield with the men following. When her father's murderer, Hamza, was himself killed in the fight Hind reportedly took long-awaited revenge by ripping out and biting his liver, cutting off his ears and nose and performing other grisly acts. There is little doubt that such reports are greatly exaggerated, but there is even less doubt that she was a women of strong will and courage. When Abū Sufyān himself later converted to Islam she became even more outraged, publicly striking her husband and calling for his death. "Kill this old fool, for he has changed his religion," she is reported to have cried. When she realized that her attempts were in vain she turned on her idols, smashing them and lamenting that she had trusted in them.[12] Hind herself later converted to Islam and fought for the new religion as she once fought against it.

As one of the leading women of Mecca, Hind was part of a group of women giving formal allegiance to Islam after the conquest of the city. Having women take the oath of allegiance to Islam had been part of Muhammad's overall plan from shortly after the emigration to Medina when he had his friend, the future caliph ʿUmar, administer it in his name. After this it was not uncommon for women to come to the Prophet in groups to vow their allegiance. There is some controversy about whether Muḥammad actually clasped the hands of the women as he did those of the men,[13] but the details are considerably less important than the fact that he clearly regarded women as creatures with sufficient independence from their husbands and families to make their own commitment. An astute politician, he also doubtless realized that a community with the active support of its women would be greatly strengthened. (Muḥammad's bond with the women is recorded in S. 60:12.) The fact that many women were included among the earliest converts to Islam does seem to indicate that women were influential in the ultimate conversion of both Mecca and Medina.

The first person to take the message of the Prophet seriously, and in that sense the first convert, was his first and at that time only wife, Khadīja, then about fifty-five years old. Her economic and social position as an independent merchant is of interest not only as an indication that such an occupation was open to women at the time of the Prophet, but also because it may have influenced others to listen to her husband's preaching. While much of the evidence is unreliable, it appears that together with some of Muḥammad's female relatives there were women converts from both high social rank (those who were members of the Quraish tribe) and the lower ranges of society. Clearly some women converted because of pressure from their husbands or families, but the records certainly make plain that for many it was a decision over which they had personal control.

Various tales are related of strong women who defied their families and would not give up their new faith in Islam, such as Umm Sharīk who was tortured by her husband's relatives and then left exposed to the sun with no water for three days. The story has it that finally a bucket of water came down from heaven to revive her.[14] The point is that while such narratives are certainly of doubtful authenticity and had the clear purpose of glorifying Islam rather than of praising women, they do indicate that women were significant enough in the life of the young community at least to be cited and credited with this kind of strength of character.

What we see, then, is that because women in pre-Islamic Arabian society had a measure of freedom and some participation in public affairs (though with little real opportunity for leadership), they were prepared for the most part to be equally active in either helping to oppose or to establish the new faith. The question then becomes, how did women fare once the battles were won and Islam was a recognized religio-political community?

There seems little question that for most of his active life Muḥammad recognized women as having the right to full participation in his new Islamic society, and in fact that he probably was more progressive on that score than many of his co-religionists. Despite the Prophet's apparent insistence on equal responsibilities in the religious sphere, however, events toward the end of his lifetime did lead to a situation in which the freedom and participation of women that characterized the earlier days were very seriously curtailed. Much of the change hinged directly on the issue of sexuality and the perceived need to "protect" the woman in ways which became greatly inhibiting. Some would see it as a direct result of Muḥammad's having overextended himself in the accumulation of wives to the point where intrigues in his harem were rife and the situation was close to unmanageable.[15]

In the meantime revelations came to the Prophet from God which were seen as eternal and universal, and yet also as directed toward the solution of particular problems facing Muḥammad and his community. When his favorite wife ʿĀ'isha was accused of misconduct after having stayed behind on a trip to search for a lost necklace, it was finally divine revelation which assured Muḥammad of her innocence.[16] This is not the place to describe in detail legal stipulations for women which the Prophet incorporated into the governing structure of the new community on the basis of Qur'anic revelation. Equally important as what was revealed and then codified is the fact that the process did take place. Whether the regulations on marriage, divorce and protection are equitable between men and women is probably of less consequence for women than the fact that once they were recognized as divine, and thus immutable, the possibility of alternative structures or modes of action was foreclosed.

Aside from this, it seems to me that two very significant and interrelated factors in early Islam not only contributed to but were determinative of the rather rapid decline of women from the (limited) position they held before the time of the Prophet. One is exclusion and the other seclusion. By exclusion I mean the fact that despite the obvious intention of the Prophet that women be part of the religious life of Islam, they increasingly were deprived of the opportunity to share in the communal aspect of that life. In particular, from the beginning they were excluded from participation in Islam's most significant leadership roles. By seclusion I mean that process—beginning most specifically with the Prophet's relegation of his wives to a place apart from normal social intercourse with men—that led to the functional withdrawal of women from the normal rounds of what came to be essentially male society.

For the purposes of this discussion I would say that the really interesting point is not that these things did happen, but that they could happen despite the significant role played by women before and during the Islamic revolution and despite the fact that they seem clearly not to have been the intent of the Prophet, at least in his earlier days. Thus I would argue that while in one sense the establishment of the new religion resulted in a diminished role for women, this could not have come about had the prevailing attitude of males not permitted and even encouraged such a diminished role. The two realities which I have called exclusion and seclusion seem both to have resulted from and given encouragement to the already present—and probably always existing—assumption by the males in the community that women in general are somehow ontologically unsuited for full societial participation. First the matter of exclusion.

That the Qur'ān makes explicit the full religious responsibility of women is very clear. They are enjoined to participate in the expressed obligations and are assured, equally with men, a just judgment and eternal condition commensurate with the degree of their piety. Yet in practical effect, the question of whether women's responsibilities, particularly that of the daily communal prayer, could be carried out in full company with men is less clear. There are various narratives which insist that Muḥammad did allow women to pray in his company, and even encouraged it, while other reports suggest that in fact this permission was granted only if the husband was in full agreement. The fact is that the inevitable sifting and coloring process of the transmission of narrative reports makes it very difficult to know what was in the mind of the Prophet. In any case it does appear that even the Prophet suggested rules for women somewhat different than those for men. One finds, for instance, testimony from ʿĀ'isha that Muḥammad indicated that the only time women should assemble was for a funeral or at the mosque and that women at morning prayer should be so wrapped up as to be unrecognizable.[17]

There are several instances of traditions from Umm Salāma, another of the Prophet's wives, which indicate that the Prophet felt a woman is better off praying in her own home, although chains of transmission for that are weak. One famous narrative, repeated in a variety of forms, attributes to the Prophet the suggestion that the most appropriate place for a woman to pray is her own hut, followed, in descending order of preference, by her enclosure, her compound, her clan's mosques, and finally (and least desirable) the mosque of Muḥammad.[18] This apparently was said in response to the case of a single woman and might be explained as pertaining only to her circumstances. It has, of course, been used through the centuries to admonish women to stay at home.

Muḥammad did order women not to pray during menstruation, a decree for which there is ample documentation and which apparently also precluded their attendance at the mosque during those times. Again this has become one of the classical supports for the unsuitability of women to act as imams or leaders of the prayer; an argument, in fact, made to me by a Philippine Muslim not long ago. A commonly circulated tradition, sometimes attributed to the Prophet, holds that prayer can only be interrupted by a dog, an ass, or a woman, an association over which ʿĀʾisha was understandably furious.[19]

The question of whether women should attend the mosque engaged the attention of the early Muslim doctors. It is obvious that many (one may presume most) of these authorities did not wish to have them present, but were constrained by such traditions as that which says that women cannot be prevented from attendance, although they must not be perfumed. There are also narratives attributed to the Prophet which say women should not raise their heads before the imam raises his (nothing similar is stipulated for men), and that women should exit from the mosque before men. ʿĀʾisha herself is supposed to have said that if Muḥammad had seen what she saw of the women he would not have allowed them to go to the mosque, a statement made after the death of the Prophet under the strict rule of the second Caliph ʿUmar, who forbade women to attend public worship.[20] There is some slight evidence that from the beginning women were separated from men at worship, but that does not seem to have become an explicit requirement until later.

Circumstances for women became considerably more constrained under the rule of ʿUmar, only a few years after the death of the Prophet. ʿUmar tried to limit women to prayer at home, but even his own wife and son opposed him. He achieved virtually the same effect by appointing separate imams for men and for women. He also forbade Muḥammad's wives to go on the pilgrimage, a decree which he later (and seemingly without explanation) reversed. The reversal, however, did not signal a change of any significance in the obvious and accelerating trend toward the exclusion of women from the worship life—as from the other aspects of public life—of the young Muslim community.

Some would argue that if we can indeed identify an increasing exclusion of women, it is precisely because of the specific fact of seclusion, beginning most obviously with the Qur'anic injunction that the wives of the Prophet be secluded behind a curtain. "And when you ask anything of the Prophet's wives," says S. 33:53, "ask it of them from behind a curtain; this will be more pure for your hearts and for their hearts." It is idle to suggest that this injunction, or others in the Qur'ān indicating ways in which to protect the female believers from insult, represented a direct attempt to subjugate and isolate women. The intent obviously was to offer women, and in particular the honored group of Muḥammad's wives who were to be leading examples to others in the community, protection and a means of preserving family honor. (It is true that the huts of Muḥammad's wives were all in the courtyard of the great mosque of Medina in full view of a constant stream of visitors.) One of the immediate causes for concern over protecting the honor of the Prophet's wives seems to have been the famous incident of ʿĀ'isha and the lost necklace.

The particular institution of the *ḥijāb* or seclusion behind a curtain, sanctioned by its inclusion as divine revelation, does seem to have signalled a significant move toward a reduction in opportunities for women. Such freedoms as they had soon became virtually nonexistent, and regulations originally intended for the wives of the Prophet were quickly extended to apply to all of the women of the community. "Thus was laid the foundation stone," writes Nabia Abbott, "of what was to prove in time one of the most stubborn and retrogressive institutions in Islam—the segregation of the women behind curtains and veil."[21]

While the devastating effects of the institution of the hijāb can hardly be overestimated, it is nonetheless worth asking whether it really created conditions markedly different from those women had experienced earlier. The evidence, as we have seen, is mixed, and yet it seems that the fact of seclusion could not have been perceived by the Prophet's wives to be shocking in the way it appears shocking to a twentieth-century observer. We have no record that any of the wives took issue with the decree, not even Umm Salāma and ʿĀ'isha, who were not known for reticence. Does not this apparent acceptance suggest that women in fact really did not expect to participate in the life of the community? The same could be asked of the later acquiescence by the mothers of the faithful to ʿUmar's decision that they not be allowed to make the pilgrimage. In other words, one is led to believe that even in the tumultuous days of the establishment of the new religion, women never had any expectation that as a group they would have significant parts to play outside of the home and family.

Again it seems important to return to the question of women in leadership roles. Here exclusion, I would argue, was not a consequence of seclusion but a result of the prevailing mentality that understood women to be inherently unfit for such roles. The wives of the Prophet were perceived as female role models, but clearly were not considered to be leaders in the public life of the community. (An interesting possible exception is ʿĀ'isha, to whom we shall return shortly.) The general inability to function in this capacity seems to have characterized women from the jāhilīya right through the founding of the new religion. It was noted earlier that before the time of the Prophet some women were leaders in religious, though not political, spheres. Even this possibility was more or less lost under the governance of the Prophet. An essential inequality on this score seems to be built into the basic presuppositions of Islam. The distinguished German orientalist Ignaz Goldziher says that the Qur'anic insistence on equal religious responsibility for women and men proves that women were not prevented from achieving the same importance as men in inner religious life. He does note, however, that there were what he calls "some theological limitations of entirely theoretical nature," one of which he identifies as the inability of women to reach the grade of prophet. He implies that this is theoretical because in any case there can be no more prophets after Muḥammad.[22] It must surely be argued, however, that the fact that women by definition cannot play this, the ultimate leadership role, is not theoretical at all, but has obvious implications for the understanding of women's capacity to serve as leaders.

We have already noted the problems understood to be inherent in a woman's becoming an imam. Later Muslim legislation decreed that this is an impossibility, but the issue is somewhat less clear for the time of Muḥammad. Some sources, for example, say that Umm Waraqa did function as an imam to her household at the request of the Prophet.[23] If she served both men and women in this capacity, as seems to have been the case, she is the only woman recorded as having done so. There are other instances of women leading prayers for other women; most often mentioned is ʿĀ'isha. These references, not surprisingly, are to the period after women were secluded from the common worship life.

On the whole it seems apparent that at no time during or immediately after the time of the Prophet did women have strong positions of leadership in the religious sphere. A possible exception lies in the fact that a few women in the early community served as collectors and transmitters of traditions. The most important source of information about the habits and opinions of the Prophet came from the widows of Muḥammad, particularly ʿĀʾisha, who were privy to a great deal of personal material. They were, therefore, the original authorities for much of what was attributed to the Prophet as well as the mediums through which the information was transmitted. In this sense they were influential in helping determine the standard of behavior for the young community. It is clear that ʿĀʾisha memorized a great many of the sayings of Muḥammad, as did Umm Waraqa who even made her own collection. In such isolated cases, women in the early community to a limited extent did assist in the redaction of the Qurʾān. I think it can be argued, however, that even in these instances when women were clearly influential in the formulation of the emerging legal structures of Islam, it was strictly because of their privileged positions as the ones nearest to the Prophet rather than because of recognition of their inherent abilities to exercise direction and authority.

If there were occasional possibilities for female leadership in the area of religion during and after the time of the Prophet, the same does not seem to have been true with respect to public affairs. Nothing in the Qurʾān even suggests a woman's eligibility for public service. There is no record that any woman served as a counselor to the Prophet, other than Khadīja in the earliest days, or as a deputy representing the interests of Islam. Again ʿĀʾisha, the spirited favorite of the Prophet, seems to have been an exception. She did in fact take an active part in political affairs after Muḥammad's death, violating the principle of seclusion when she fought in the Battle of the Camel and later when she tried to influence the course of community leadership. By virtue of her position as the wife closest to Muḥammed she was always highly respected and her opinion was sought on a number of matters. When the Caliph ʿUmar appointed a council of six to determine his successor, at his request they were to meet either in a place close to ʿĀʾisha's house or in the house itself. Perhaps unfortunately for the future course of women in Islam, however, even ʿĀʾisha was not able to maintain a leadership role. Militarily she was defeated in the Battle of the Camel, and politically she never could attain any degree of real power. Despite ʿUmar's desire for her proximity, she herself was not elected a member of his six-man council, nor could she even participate in the selection of its members.

With the rapid expansion of Islam, persons from a variety of cultures came to be included in the community. The addition of large numbers of captive slave women under the Umayyads resulted in the creation of a kind of two-class system of free Arab women and slaves.

Reputed to have loose morals, the slave women came to be very popular. In a parallel movement, free Arab Muslim women were increasingly "protected" by seclusion from the areas of social intercourse and a general receding of their influence. Many have defended the Islamic system by insisting that social conditions more than religious or political factors led to the gradual but steady enforcement of veiling and seclusion. "In order to observe historical justice," says Goldziher, "it must be admitted that degradation of women in Islam is the result of social influences for which the principles of Islam are unjustly made responsible, but which were in fact the outcome of the social relations of the peoples converted to Islam."[24] It can scarcely be denied, however, that the groundwork for this development had been solidly and effectively laid by the injunctions of the Qur'ān, no matter how one might wish to justify the social significance of these injunctions.

As was true before and during the time of the Prophet, individual women in the first century of Islam still were able to exert influence in a variety of ways. One can point, for example, to such persons as Muḥammad's great-granddaughter Sukāyna, a renowned figure in the social circles of the Hijāz, who had sufficient aplomb to choose and reject her husbands at her own will.[25] It is also the case that a select group of women were recognized in the community for their piety and religious learning, such as the Prophet's great-great-great-granddaughter Sayyida Nafīsa and others of the women scholars who studied and taught the Islamic sciences.

It is clear, however, whether we are discussing the time before, during or after the Prophet, instances of strong women playing leadership roles in any capacity were far from the norm. It may be lighthearted to say that the exception proves the rule, but I have tried to make the case that whether one is talking about the queens of early Arabia, individuals such as Hind or 'Ā'isha, or the small class of women who were influential in the religious realm, they in one sense are significant precisely because they are exceptional. For whatever reasons—and they would surely include some of the issues discussed here—the prevailing and dominant understanding of women simply hardened so that fewer such exceptions were possible.

It would seem to me, then, that on the basis of these rather general observations about the circumstances of women at the time of the founding of Islam, several tentative conclusions might be offered:

1. Before, during and after the time of the Prophet it was highly exceptional for a woman to play a significant leadership role—and then primarily in the religious rather than the political realm. Therefore

there is no convincing evidence that the social revolution engendered by the founding of Islam afforded women opportunities for leadership hitherto unavailable to them.

2. The establishment of Islam as a religio-cultural system significantly diminished the number of opportunities for women to participate openly in society. Two factors directly affecting their increased exclusion from normal social intercourse seem to have been (1) the codification of law based on divine revelation and (2) the imposition of seclusion, also based on divine revelation.

3. The fact that exclusion and seclusion came to prevail quickly and in increasing measure seems to have resulted from: (1) the prevailing male attitude about the inherent unsuitability of women for roles of full public participation and leadership; and (2) an apparent willingness on the part of women to accept the restrictions imposed on them and to acquiesce in the limitations then understood to be part of divine ordination.

It is obvious that these conclusions are preliminary and that considerably more investigation needs to be done before a clearer picture of the situation of and for women at the time of the Prophet can emerge. However, one last observation might be made about the scope of the project beyond the mere uncovering of data. The suggestion was made earlier that further reflection is needed on the issue of how a dominant conception of the deity as masculine may have led to a lessening of opportunity for women to play leadership roles in the religious structure. I think that the study of women and religion has now progressed to the point where we recognize the need to give greater attention to the possible connection between monotheism as a theological orientation and the understanding of inherent female potential. The ramifications of such a consideration, it is clear, might be significant for the study not only of Islam but of all the great monotheistic traditions as well. I suspect that when attention is given to this issue we will be able to shed more light on the question of women's participation in religious revolution.

NOTES

1. Nabia Abbott, "Pre-Islamic Arab Queens," *The American Journal of Semitic Languages and Literatures* 58 (1941):1–22.

2. See especially Reynold Nicholson, *A Literary History of the Arabs* (Cambridge: The University Press, 1962).

3. W. Robertson Smith, *Kinship and Marriage in Early Arabia* (Cambridge: The University Press, 1885 and reprints).

4. Ilse Lichtenstadter, *Women in the Aiyam al-ʿArab* (London: Royal Asiatic Society, 1935), chap. 4.

5. Nicholson, *Literary History*, p. 87.

6. Nabia Abbott, "Women and the State on the Eve of Islam," *The American Journal of Semitic Languages and Literatures* 58 (1941):260–61.

7. Ibid., 261–62. There have been some exceptions to this; *rabba* has occasionally been used in popular Islam to refer to a female religious functionary.

8. See, e.g., Ibn Saʿd, *Kitāb al-ṭabaqāt al-kabir* (Leiden: E. J. Brill, 1905–1940), 1:39ff.

9. A.F.L. Beeston, "The So-Called Harlots of Ḥaḍramaut," *Oriens* 5 (1952): 16–22.

10. Ibn Hishām, *Sīrah, Das Leben Muhammeds*, ed. F. Wüstenfeld (Göttingen, 1859) p. 134.

11. Faiz S. Abu Jabar, "The Status of Women in Early Arabic History," *Islam and the Modern Age* 4 (1973):69.

12. Abbott, "Women and the State on the Eve of Islam," 275 from Wāqidī, *Kitāb al-Maghāzī*, ed. A. von Kremer (Calcutta, 1856),pp. 308ff.

13. Gertrude H. Stern, "Muḥammad's Bond with the Women," *Bulletin of the School of Oriental and African Studies* 10 (1940–42):196.

14. Gertrude H. Stern, "The First Women Converts in Early Islam," *Islamic Culture* 13 (1939):297–98.

15. See, e.g., Nabia Abbott, *Aishah, the Beloved of Muhammad* (Chicago: University of Chicago Press, 1942), pp. 41–61.

16. Qur'ān, S. 24:11–15.

17. See Stern, "The First Women Converts," *Islamic Culture* 13 (1939): 300–303 for a summary of narrative materials on the general subject of women and prayer.

18. Aḥmad b. Ḥanbal, *Musnad* (n.p.: al-Maṭbaʿah al-Maymanīyah, 1895), 6:301.

19. Ibid., 42.

20. Ibid., 69.

21. Nabia Abbott, "Women and the State in Early Islam," *Journal of Near Eastern Studies* 1 (1942):110.

11. Ignaz Goldziher, *Muslim Studies* (London: George Allen and Unwin, 1971), 2:274.

23. Ibn Saʿd, *Ṭabāqāt*, 8:335; Aḥmad b. Ḥanbal, *Musnad*, 6:504.

24. Goldziher, *Muslim Studies*, 2:271.

25. See, e.g., J. C. Vadet, "Une personalité féminine du Ḥiğāz au 1er/VIIe siècle: Sukayna, petite fille de ʿAlī," *Arabica* 4 (1957):261–87.

CHAPTER THREE

Gārgī at the King's Court: Women and Philosophic Innovation in Ancient India

ELLISON BANKS FINDLY

In a tradition fully aware of the struggle for social prominence of the Aryan over the Dasyu, and of the brahman over the kṣatriya, there is very little to reflect the uneven and probably painful process by which men and women settled into the highly specialized gender roles characteristic of traditional Indian society. Unlike the numerous tales of conflict we find between "civilized" invader and "barbarian" inhabitant, and between ritually oriented priest and secular warrior, reference to conflict between the sexes for social or religious place appears as only an occasional break in the smooth veneer of male/female role delineation. We do know that women appear in places of prominence throughout Indian history: as scholars, teachers and even priestesses of the Vedic[1] and early Buddhist age,[2] as queens in their own right in both north and south India, Kashmir and Orissa,[3] and as poetesses in the medieval devotional movement which grew up throughout the sub-continent.[4] But the traditional vision of women as the silent and invisible bearers of the culture is a vision perpetuated not only by the tradition itself but also by modern scholars. Sengupta, for instance, says that traditional customs, both secular and religious, "have been preserved because of women's persistence in ancient traits,"[5] and Altekar maintains that "the continuance of . . . . moral fervour and spiritual tradition is largely due to the zeal, sincerity and devotion of women."[6]

Rarely, however, have these same scholars investigated the possible cracks in the veneer of India's past, cracks that may show women not only as bearers of a preserved cultural tradition but also, perhaps, as precisely the opposite: vehicles for cultural innovation and, more interestingly, for heterodox ideas and practices.[7] One of these cracks in the veneer is the appearance of a woman philosopher, Gārgī Vācaknavī, at the philosophical tournament held at the court of King Janaka of Videha some time around the beginning of the Upaniṣadic era (c. 600 B.C.E.). Her performance there raises serious questions about the social intentions of the Upaniṣad in which the account appears, the Bṛhadāraṇyaka, about the inclinations (feminist or otherwise) of the subject of interrogation and eventual winner of the contest, and about the literary motivations of the composers who attribute to Gārgī not only the most spirited and prickly personality of all the characters present but also the most heterodox of philosophic styles.

Early Indian Society in Transition

Gārgī's appearance in this Upaniṣad occurs at a time when two important changes in Indian life were about to take place: a dramatic reversal of the hitherto relatively favorable fortunes of women, and the replacement of the traditional system of Vedic ritual by a variety of more satisfying religious structures, one of them being the religion of the Upaniṣads. Although the history of women in ancient India reflects an increasingly inflexible social structure that, over the centuries, came to undermine whatever status women may have had as independent participants in civic and intellectual affairs, the Vedic period (c. 1200–600 B.C.E.) in many ways represents an era of unsurpassed advantage and opportunity for women.

Opportunities for a woman in this early period were based upon an understanding of the adult female as *ardhāṅginī*, partner to her husband in religious rites (ŚB.5.2.1.10; Manu.9.45), an ideal so strong that no sacrifice could be performed without her.[8] The gods, in fact, would not accept a sacrifice offered by a bachelor, and a husband had to call his wife to accompany him in the symbolic ascent to heaven during the worship (ŚB.5.2.1.8, 10).[9] The conception of the woman as half the spiritual body of her husband gave rise, at least in the early centuries, to some practices which, by modern standards, would seem relatively liberal. Not only could women participate in the sacred rites in the domestic sanctuary, as we see in the Mahābhārata and Rāmāyaṇa, and in the solemn ritual with her husband, as we see in the Śatapathabrāhmaṇa, but she could also, at least early in the Vedic period, perform the sacrifice herself. The priestess Viśvavārā (RV.5.28.1) and the poetess Apālā (RV.8.91), both of the Atri family, are each connected by the Ṛgveda to some important aspect of the preparation of the sacred ritual. Moreover, in this early period a wife usually performed the musical chanting of the Sāman songs (ŚB.14.3.1.35), a task later entrusted to a special class of male priests called Udgātṛs. Co-participation with her husband in religious affairs, albeit fairly limited, was combined with the wife's responsibility to him as a philosophical guide. She was called a *sahadharmiṇī*, an intellectual companion to her husband in issues of the mind, who still exercised a good deal of independent judgment.

Such activity presupposed a substantial education for the wife, who could marry, some early sources say, only after concluding a specified period of study.[10] This may account for the coeducational nature of the early forest universities,[11] and most certainly meant that parents had the responsibility for educating their daughters[12] and beginning such an education with the traditional ritual of education, the *upanayana*.[13] The only difference between boys and girls during studenthood was that girls were not to grow matted hair, were not to wear deerskin or bark garments, were not to go out to beg their daily food but were to beg in their own homes instead, and were not to be taught by anyone except a near male relative.[14] Vedic education for girls appears to have been serious and rigorous, at least in the early period, for the Ṛgveda notes a number of female sages *(ṛṣis)*[15] and later literature honors three women scholars in the *ṛṣitarpaṇa*, a list of the sages to whose memory a daily tribute of respect must be paid.[16]

Out of this early emphasis upon education a widespread tradition of female scholarship developed. Women were allowed to study freely and could become ascetics *(brahmacariṇīs)* or live in single-sex hostels.[17] There were, in general, two classes of female students, both of whom learned Vedic hymns and prayers and studied the manuals by which the sacraments were to be performed: the *sadyovadhūs*, who studied until their marriage at the age of fifteen or sixteen, and the *brahmavādinīs*, who studied for a lifetime.[18] It was the *brahmavādinīs* who not only memorized liturgical materials but also carried on specialized studies in Pūrvamīmāṅsā, a dry and difficult science by which the diverse philosophical problems connected with the Vedic sacrifice were discussed.[19] The Pūrvamīmāṅsā was perhaps *the* intellectual challenge of the day,[20] and the literature suggests that these very same women students spoke out at the popular assembly *(vidatha)*,[21] and that their performance there more than equalled that of men.[22] Moreover, a broad class of female teachers *(upādhyāyānīs* and *āchāryās)*[23] was prevalent throughout society, and it is probable that teaching was the most common profession open to women. With teaching, a woman could become economically self-reliant and, with a wide range of subjects to offer (grammar, poetry and literature, in addition to theology and philosophy) she could attract a broad range of students, male as well as female.[24]

Gradually, however, the position of women declined and by the time of the Dharmaśāstras, in the early centuries B.C.E., women were looked upon as equal to men of the lowest caste as far as formal education was concerned. Reflecting this new attitude, one prominent legislator says, "even women of good family come to ruin by independence" (see Nārada.16.30).[25] The ceremony of marriage, for instance, came to be recognized by legislators as taking the place of the *upanayana* for women, for whom, according to Manu, "zeal in the service of their husbands. . . . [was to stand] instead of dwelling with a spiritual father; and the care of home instead of the maintenance of the sacred fire."[26] The role of the wife as *sahadharmiṇī* was supplanted by that of the wife as *pativratā*, whereby a woman lost herself in the personality of her husband and would, as asceticism became more prominent, retire to the forest with him[27] and even, in time, be expected to immolate herself on his cremation pyre. Throughout society the same class of people who had previously excelled in Vedic theology and participated in their own right in Vedic sacrifices, who had spoken out with such composure and success at public assemblies,[28] and who had appeared in great numbers so prominently as scholars and preachers under the rigorous discipline of the Buddhist Order of nuns,[29] now became disenfranchised from the mainstream of religious affairs.

Most scholars feel that there are two reasons for this general decline, and especially for the exclusion of women from institutional aspects of religion: first, the longer time that was needed to memorize a rapidly growing tradition and, second, the new fashion of child marriage. With lowered marriage age increasingly in vogue (now well before puberty), there was little time left for the study of an ever-more cumbersome tradition. Furthermore, with the growing emphasis on sacrifices to the ancestors which only males could perform, sons came to be increasingly preferred over daughters. Consequently young women more and more had to focus their attention on producing a sufficient number of male sacrificers. Male children were also more desirable economically and socially, for not only could they provide the life-long labor needed to support an extended family but they did not have to be equipped with lavish dowries. A young woman's real *dharma*, then, came to be that of mothering male children by one of her own caste.[30] To legitimize this new low status of women, Manu (9.18) finally declared that women were impotent *(nirindriya)* and equivalent to falsehood *(anṛta)* itself.

The second major change taking place at this time was the replacement of the traditional system of Vedic ritual by new religious structures. According to the old system, the cosmos was magically created through complex machinations on the ritual ground, and man was deemed virtuous only if he mastered the intricate techniques of the ritual. Seen as increasingly ineffective, however, this system was gradually supplanted by others, the most important of which for our purposes is that of the heir to the Vedas, the Upaniṣads.

Coming long after the end of Aryan nomadism and the rise of the agricultural lifestyle, the Bṛhadāraṇyaka, as the oldest of these secret doctrinal texts, reflects a society no longer concerned with the safety of its borders or the stability of its economic system, but rather one willing and able to support both leisure-time activities, such as philosophical tournaments, and leisure-time classes and institutions. The widespread (and not always orderly) retreat into the forest reflected in Upaniṣadic literature was followed by the appearance of numerous ascetic religious movements (*śramaṇa* groups), as well as institutional forms of new philosophic systems, for example, the Buddhists and the Jains.[31] Characteristic of these systems was a structural isolation from the general run of society coupled with a unique dependence upon it: *śramaṇa* groups drew material benefits from society at large and in return bestowed spiritual merit upon particular donors. Such reciprocity was possible, in part, because philosophic issues were taking on a new importance in the wake of the decline of Vedism.

Since this period—at least during its earlier centuries—acknowledged the intellectual prowess of women, it would follow that the Upaniṣadic movement should have been even more beneficial to them. As the family unit's hold over the traditional spiritual life of the individual broke down (due to the increasing neglect of the sacrifice and its attendant institutions), we would expect that droves of women would take advantage of an opportunity for participation in the intellectual life of the culture. As it is, women appear significantly in only the first Upaniṣad, the Bṛhadāraṇyaka. The conspicuous absence of women from the later Upaniṣads is due most likely to the contemporaneous effects of social Brahmanism, for the movement towards more serious philosophic inquiry could in no way check the tightening hold of priestly legalism over the patterns of social and religious life for women. When the Dharmaśāstras finally took account of these new developments, their compilers saw women as even more necessary to the maintenance of the family unit as men retreated into the forest.

THE TOURNAMENT AT JANAKA'S COURT

It is on the eve of this precipitous decline in the intellectual life of women[32] and of the shift in religious life from ritualism to contemplation, that the tournament at Videha occurs. King Janaka has offered a prize of one thousand cows plus ten thousand gold coins to whichever of the brahmans present can demonstrate knowledge of the supreme Brahman.[33] A teacher named Yājñavalkya immediately appropriates the cows by asking his student, Sāmaśravas, to drive them home. The other brahmans become angry, and one by one put questions to Yājñavalkya to find out if he is in fact the greatest of the brahmans. What follows (Bṛhadāraṇyakopaniṣad 3.1.3–9.28) is perhaps the most significant example of the dialectical mode of argumentation we have from the period, in which the contributions made by Yājñavalkya in response to the nine sets of questions posed to him[34] lift Vedic thought finally and irrevocably out of its mire of liturgical symbolism. In the interrogation which ensues, Gārgī speaks not once but twice (the only one to do so) and distinguishes herself as the most eminent of the philosophers present. It is because of her performance at the tournament that she has been consistently singled out as one of the most striking female minds in Indian literature.

The questioning is opened by Aśvala, one of Janaka's priests (BĀU.3.1.2–10) who is concerned with sacrificial analogies. Although Yājñavalkya shows that he is well-versed in the symbolic correspondences between parts of the sacrifice and nature, the Bṛhadāraṇyaka will lead from this point on to show that ritualism is outdated,[35] especially as a means of overcoming death. Ārtabhāga, son of Jaratkāru (BĀU.3.2.1–13), begins the second round of questioning with a series on the essence of the senses and, as he proceeds to his final question about what survives death, he is able to elicit from Yājñavalkya the doctrine of man's return to nature according to his "just desserts":

man's body, he suggests, will return to the elements according to the principle of sympathetic magic, that is, like will return to like. What survives, however, is "deed" *(karma)*, but this new doctrine (that one "becomes" good by a good deed, and evil by an evil one) is so innovative and/or controversial that it cannot be discussed in public, and Yājñavalkya leads Ārtabhāga from the room by the hand in order to finish the discussion in private.

The third set of questions is put forth by Bhujyu, son of Lāhya (BĀU.3.3.1–2), who is interested in psychic research and elicits from Yājñavalkya a description of the succession of divine worlds where the great men of old have gone. He is followed by Uṣasta, son of Cakra (BĀU.3.4.1–2) who, at last, begins the posing of serious philosophical problems. Uṣasta is concerned with the soul *(atman)* which is within everything, and Yājñavalkya's response points to a universal subject which is of necessity different from its object: "you cannot see the seer of sight," he says, nor "hear the hearer of sound." Uṣasta's questions are taken further by Kahoḍa, son of Kuṣītaka (BĀU.3.5.1.), who discovers from Yājñavalkya that the only personal response to knowledge of such an *atman* is "the guileless life of a child,"[36] that of the *muni*, the silent sage, who lives transcending opposites and is a spiritual achiever simply "by [being] what he is" *(yena syāt)*.

Gārgī is the sixth questioner (BĀU.3.6.1) and using the ancient ritual imagery of the warp and the woof (for example, the weaving of the Ṛgvedic sacrifice), she moves Yājñavalkya back towards a first principle in a series of infinitely regressive questions until he stops her abruptly. "You are questioning too much," he says "about a divinity we are not to ask too much about." With this rebuke, Gārgī remains silent, and Uddālaka, son of Aruṇa (BĀU.3.7.1–23), father of the famous Śvetaketu (Chan.6.1), takes up her imagery of the woven thread and elicits from Yājñavalkya the innovative doctrine of *antaryāmi*, the inner controller, the principle immanent in all objects in the universe and yet separate from it. Not put off by Yājñavalkya's rebuke, however, Gārgī (BĀU.3.8.1–12) again questions him about that on which the universe is strung and threaded. When Yājñavalkya tells her "ether," she diplomatically repeats her questions and, to keep clear of all logical inconsistencies, Yājñavalkya then describes the principle in question the only way he can, with a long series of negatives: not coarse, not fine, not short, not long, etc. Brahman is, as before, a universal subject not bound by objects, attributes or referents.

The ninth and last questioner is Vidagdha, son of Śākala (BĀU.3.9.1–26), an irritating and persistent brahman who takes Yājñavalkya detail by detail through the resting places of the various gods and spirits. Finally, using a method similar to Gārgī's regressive questioning, Vidagdha elicits from Yājñavalkya a more sophisticated version of the earlier series of negatives, the famous doctrine of *neti, neti,* "not this, not this." When asked himself, however, about the nature of this Upaniṣadic person known merely by *neti neti,* Vidagdha, a "most importunate and self-opinionated critic,"[37] cannot respond and the curse which has been so lightly bandied about among the participants in the tournament—"if you do not know, your head will fall off"—is finally cast upon him, and robbers carry off his bones.

Gārgī's Achievement

The tragic conclusion to the tournament does not, however, hide the achievements of the participants. To be sure, the most significant aspects of the events in Janaka's court are the philosophic structures elicited from Yājñavalkya. From his remarks here, the foundation for the development of Vedānta is laid and any further concern with the ideology of ritual is seriously undermined. In assessing the performance of the interrogators themselves, however, it is Gārgī whose contributions (and style) are judged the most important:

> the lady philosopher Gārgī was held by common consent to be more astute than others and was allowed a second chance to confront the redoubted philosopher. Yājñavalkya had already found her a tough disputant. Her array of questions on the origins of things in an infinite regressive series was so exasperating to Yājñavalkya that he had to curb her curiosity by portending death if she persisted.[38]

> The subtlest philosophical questions were initiated for discussion by the lady philosopher Gārgī, who had the honour to be the spokesman of the distinguished philosophers at the court. She launched her attack on Yājñavalkya, the newly arrived philosopher, with an admirable coolness and confidence. . . . The searching cross-examination of Yājñavalkya by Gārgī shows that she was a dialectician and philosopher of a high order.[39]

> It is against this glorious background [of the Ṛgveda] that the dignified Vācaknavī Gārgi [*sic*] of the Upaniṣadic fame can be well appreciated. It is no wonder, therefore, that she steered clear of the temptations of wealth known to be proverbially fickle and chose the stony way of knowledge. . . . we hear of this woman boldly and confidently asking a series of questions. . . .[40]

Gārgī has an "unquenchable thirst for philosophical knowledge,"[41] and "actively participate[s] . . . [in] the search for a foundational conciousness."[42] Showing that a learned woman can "cope successfully with men in display,"[43] Gārgī stands out "in bold relief due to . . . [her] intellectual acumen and spiritual strength . . . [having] boldly . . . [risen] on behalf of the humiliated assemblage"[44] to respond to Yājñavalkya. She is, then, "the lady philosopher who stands out as the most outstanding personality among the philosophical interlocutors opposing" the successful brahman.[45]

Any evaluation of the scholarly consensus that Gārgī is the wisest and most articulate of the interrogators, however, must take account of the other tradition as well, that in which the assessments of her are condescending and perhaps even derogatory. In spite of the fact that Edgerton claims "the text here gives no evidence that she was regarded as exceptionally presumptuous,"[46] several scholars interpret the text in precisely this way.[47] For some her performance was, in fact, decidedly feminine for she seemed "abashed at this great display of the intellectual skill of her adversary, and as would become her female modesty, characteristically desisted from further questionings."[48] This tradition of scholarship charges that, in "her impudence," she tormented Yājñavalkya "with question after question"[49] and that "she exhibited the inordinate curiosity of the female kind especially when given to philosophy, which leads necessarily to a regress ad infinitum."[50] Finally, one scholar implies that when she insisted on asking more questions, "having previously been warned [off] by Yājñavalkya,"[51] she exhibited traits typical of women, who cannot refrain from speaking over and over again.

This contradictory assessment of Gārgī suggests that there may be more to the Bṛhadāraṇyaka account of the tournament than a simple recounting of events. As evaluators, we are now presented with two choices. Either, we can take the text at face value, as most scholars do, and understand Gārgī as the wisest and most eloquent of the disputants, though with a spirited and courageous personality that gets her into trouble with her philosophic adversary. Or, we can understand the text as a literary narrative, designed not only for the transmission of knowledge, but for amusement and pleasure as well. If the intent of the text is the latter, that is aesthetic, then Gārgī may be a literary vehicle for introducing and sustaining certain essential narrative elements—suspense and levity, for example—or, more significantly, heterodox philosophic ideas that may be decidedly dangerous in any other context. Consonant with the derogatory assessments of Gārgī, we might ask, what better way to introduce slightly off-beat elements than through the character of a woman?

The composers of the Bṛhadāraṇyaka, then, would in the first instance have to be highly commended for their liberal and decidedly "feminist" stance. In addition to this extended account of Gārgī in chapter 3, we find an extraordinary dialogue between Yājñavalkya and one of his two wives, Maitreyī, in chapter 4 (BĀU.4.5.1–15), in which Maitreyī, a *brahmavādinī* (BĀU.4.5.1), renounces her share of Yājñavalkya's property and because of her searching questions is judged capable of receiving her husband's esoteric teachings. This passage, moreover, casts Yājñavalkya as an early champion of women's economic rights: against the background of an on-going debate about whether a sonless "widow" should inherit her husband's wealth,[52] he, about to undergo a "spiritual death," hopes to divide all his property between his two wives. Finally, consonant with this liberal outlook, the composers of this Upaniṣad prescribe a ritual (BĀU.6.4.17) for those householders who hope for the birth of a scholarly daughter.[53]

In the second instance, however, the authors may be suspect, for the other wife of Yājñavalkya, Kātyāyanī, is described as *strīprajñaiva,* "of an essentially feminine outlook" (BĀU.4.5.1.), glossed by Śaṅkara as "minding household needs,"[54] hardly a comment appropriate to the feminist vision. Moreover, Maitreyī, from the narrative point of view, may be nothing more than a foil for Yājñavalkya's questions, a partner in dialogue only in so far as Yājñavalkya's brilliance becomes even more obvious in comparison with her ignorance.

In order to best assess the treatment of Gārgī, we will consider first the possibility of a conscious literary characterization. That there may be specific literary, even dramatic, intent in the Bṛhadāraṇyaka, and especially in the tournament episode, seems quite likely. In the Upaniṣads, says one source,

> a dramatic element may sometimes be introduced . . . by eschewing the narrative or hortatory form and substituting for it the dialogue form. . . . Single sustained episodes with a prevailingly poetic story form . . . exhibit a growing artistic consciousness, the highwater mark being reached in the Yājñavalkyakāṇḍa of the Bṛhadāraṇyaka . . . there is great art displayed [here]: . . . the discussion starting with what might appear as puerile priestly questions . . . [and] the language alternately rising and falling in answer to surging inward emotion . . . .The entire effect is unutterably solemn.[55]

It is the dialogue form of the episode which suggests that the Bṛhadāraṇyaka may contain more than just a descriptive account of the tournament. Like other, earlier dialogues in the Brāhmaṇic tradition, particularly the *saṃvāda* or so-called *ākhyāna* "conversation" hymns of the

Ṛgveda, this Upaniṣad may embody a nascent dramatic tradition not fully evident until centuries later.[56] The dialogue structure, if used here consciously, would have the advantage not only of rendering the event vivid and immediate but of portraying the vices and virtues of a personality in action.

While we have no obvious precedent to the casting of Gārgī as merely an amusing character, her relationship with Yājñavalkya does fit, for instance, the standard pattern set for women in later Sanskrit drama. R. Dikshit has shown that in almost every Sanskrit play the one theme that dominates is the view of "woman as the companion of man," of the "heroine [as] completely depend[ent] upon her relations with the hero"[57] for character delineation—of the woman, that is, as *ardhāṅginī*, a necessary half without which the unit cannot be whole. The relationship between Gārgī and Yājñavalkya, though not one of marriage, is certainly one of intimate collegiality, and while Gārgī no doubt makes her mark only in relation to Yājñavalkya, he is just as dependent upon her and her pointed questioning for the verbalization of his doctrine. Gārgī is not only Yājñavalkya's most acerbic opponent and therefore his most useful dialectical ally, but also, surprisingly, his greatest admirer and enthusiast. She is the only one to legitimize the contest by calling it a *brahmodya*,[58] and the only one to recognize Yājñavalkya's clear intellectual preeminence and eventual victory. The *ardhāṅginī* model, then, seems most fitting here, with Gārgī cast as Yājñavalkya's somewhat Platonic *sahadharmiṇī* who, though she may thwart, contrast, disrupt and distract, uniquely enables Yājñavalkya to play off her to advance the discussion.

Unlike any of the other interrogators, with the exception perhaps of the fussy and digressive Vidagdha, Gārgī is given a strong personality by the composers of the Upaniṣad. She is depicted not only as a spirited and intellectually courageous woman, but one who in discussion can be at best prickly and at worst prone to violent bouts of temper: "As a chief's son. . . . would string his unstrung bow and take in his hand two arrows to smite his enemies and stand forth (to combat)—just so I stand forth against you with two questions. Answer me them!"[59] To her credit, however, she is not only diplomatic, recognizing the need for decorum and form when Yājñavalkya rebukes her (BĀU.3.6.1), but also mature: the bursts of aggression easily give way to praise when met with a new argument or a compelling personal manner. Moreover, she has an exquisite sense of humor. When Yājñavalkya answers her question about the principle immanent in the phenomena of experience with "ether," she pays him homage—obviously with tongue in cheek, for it is a terrible answer—

and repeats her question exactly,[60] this time getting a response of more substance.

Second, and perhaps more striking, in the treatment of Gārgī is the possibility of a conscious philosophic characterization. There is no doubt that she, like the others present, moves Yājñavalkya on to new ground. Her persistence in the question about the immanent principle allows him to lay at last the foundation for his famous negative theology. When she presses him about the support of the visible world, and especially about a description of what supports ether, he is, according to Śaṅkara, faced with a serious problem. If he does not explain the principle, he will lay himself open to the charge of what in logic is called "non-comprehension"; if he does try to explain it, however, he will be guilty of what is called a "contradiction," an attempt to explain what cannot be explained.[61] It appears as well, if again we believe Śaṅkara, that Gārgī herself thought the question unanswerable,[62] but she presses Yājñavalkya, nevertheless, to provide an image for the futility of language in this regard—which he does. Yājñavalkya's response, then, hopes to evade both charges: first by passing the answer off onto someone else—"this is what brahmans refer to as . . . "—and second by stating that Brahman is without attributes. Thus, on the one hand, he says nothing controversial and, on the other, shows that he has understood the question.

Yājñavalkya's response to Gārgī in BĀU.3.8. is significant in two ways. First, and clearly most important, is the doctrine of *via negativa* implicit in his long series of what Brahman is not (BĀU.3.8.8) and expressed more succinctly in his subsequent answer to Uddālaka as *neti neti* "not this, not this" (BĀU.3.9.26). This doctrine of negativism, which stands in contrast to Gārgī's (and Maitreyī's) persevering quest for a positivist doctrine,[63] is at the heart of Yājñavalkya's thought and it is to Gārgī's great credit that she was able to elicit it from Yājñavalkya for the first time. Second, and perhaps more moderate, is Yājñavalkya's doctrine of immanence, described as dynamic in response to Gārgī and as static in response to Uddālaka.[64] We know that there must be an imperishable Brahman, Yājñavalkya tells Gārgī, because of the order present in the world around us. Moreover, not only is this principle reflected in the order in its world, but we can infer a design there as well: Brahman being in control of the movements of the seasons and the rivers, for example (BĀU.3.8.9), the world is as he willed it.[65]

These achievements of Gārgī are found, for the most part, in the account of her second series of questions. What she is known for most, however, is the consequence of her first series of questions when, because of "her intellectual impudence," Yājñavalkya is forced to respond with "a philosophical rudeness unbecoming in anyone gifted with the art of chivalry."[66] Yājñavalkya's action in this instance may be seen as abrupt, perhaps even violent, but it is unlikely that it is unnecessary. The Yājñavalkya of the Bṛhadāraṇyaka is a feisty, even irascible,[67] man whose nature nevertheless is tempered by prudence and kindness.[68] He is also, however, an eminent philosopher whose instincts of the mind must be trusted, for this Upaniṣad, which elevates as supreme the thought of this man, is not likely to preserve accounts of his arguments which are irrational or arise out of temper.

What, then, does Gārgī do to provoke such treatment? Gārgī, like the other interrogators, is interested in the nature of the first principle. She pursues her quest, however, with a method whose questions ultimately cannot be answered. In the "regressive" method,[69] "every new question . . . [carries] us behind the answer to the previous question":[70] for example, On what is water strung? On wind. On what is wind strung? On ether [and so forth] (BĀU.3.6.1). According to Śaṅkara,

> The idea is to show how an aspirant . . . can realise his own self, which is immediate and direct, which is within all and beyond all relative attributes, by taking up each relatively external element and eliminating it. . . .
>
> [If] whatever is an effect . . . is respectively pervaded by that which is the cause . . . [then] each preceding element must be pervaded by the succeeding one, till we come to the self that is within all.[71]

If this kind of a sequence of questions could, as appears possible on the surface, lead to the self as the first principle, then Yājñavalkya's rebuke is uncalled for. This is not the case, however, for according to tradition Gārgī is disregarding the proper method of inquiry into the nature of the absolute, knowledge of which, we are told by Śaṅkara, must come about "only through personal instruction": "The nature of the deity is to be known from the scriptures alone."[72] Gārgī's transgression, then, is not that she does not understand the ineffable nature of an absolute which lies beyond the bounds of language, but that she attempts to get to this knowledge through unorthodox means. Instead of meditating upon the scriptures of ancient tradition or affirming the new tradition by consulting a forest teacher, Gārgī does the obvious thing: she asks a series of straightforward questions[73] using the relationships she observes in the world.

The issue of tradition is central. Of all the interrogators only Gārgī is not persuaded by the traditionally accepted teachings of the Veda (as are Aśvala and Bhujyu) or the new (and eventually traditional) teachings of Yājñavalkya (as are Ārtabhāga, Uṣasta, Kahoḍa and Uddālaka). Her silence following Yājñavalkya's rebuke is more of a courtesy than an acquiescence. To his credit, Vidagdha, one of Gārgī's successors, perseveres with the infinitely regressive questioning (BĀU.3.9.20–26), and is eventually faced with Yājñavalkya's *neti neti* formulation and his own tragic end—evidence again of Yājñavalkya's difficulty with this method. With Gārgī's initial questions, it seems, Yājñavalkya is being asked (perhaps for the first time) to rely not upon tradition or belief in any *a priori* philosophical principle, but upon something else. If taken to their extreme, then, Gārgī's questions would violate the sanctity of *guru*-knowledge as currently formulated by Upaniṣadic society—secret wisdom not personally discovered from one's own experience, but understood and accepted (with personal insight, to be sure) as given by the master. Gārgī transgresses not only the sacred givenness of the Vedic tradition—though notice how beautifully she uses the ancient image of weaving (the ritual)—but also, and much more significantly, the new social code of the forest enclave, *guru-śiṣya* (teacher-student) etiquette.

Moreover, Gārgī's method of inquiry is foreign to that of the Vedic tradition upon which the Upaniṣads rest. When the poets of the Ṛg- and Atharvavedas become real philosophers and begin to ask abstract questions about a first principle, the type of question raised is almost always journalistic—*Who* did such and such a cosmic deed? *What divine name* does a god have when such and such a condition is evident? *What* did the gods use to make the world? *How* was the division into specific phenomena made? and *Why* is man the way he is?—all questions which could be given a specific answer and do not, in and of themselves, lead to a new question. Likewise in the Brāhmaṇa period, all speculation about a first principle is specific in nature: *What reward* will I get if I do such and such in the ritual? *What* is the natural correlate of such and such liturgical element? In this way, philosophical questions prior to the Upaniṣadic period, first, are understood as answerable and, second, are in time answerable only with doctrine from within the system.

With the Upaniṣadic period, however, epistemology is taken more seriously. K. N. Jayatilleke speaks of three classes of thinkers: the Traditionalists, who derive their knowledge from a scriptural tradition and interpretation based upon it; the Rationalists, who formulate theories based upon reasoning or logical argument; and the Experientialists, who depend upon direct personal, that is, intuitional, knowledge and experience (including ESP) for the basis of their theories.[74] Gārgī's type of inquiry, though relied upon and altered by dialecticians somewhat more acceptable to Yājñavalkya (e.g. BĀU.3.9.20–24; 4.3.2–6), cannot be characterized as belonging specifically to any of these three types. Rather, the *regressus ad infinitum* conforms much more closely to the type of experientially-based reasoning found in early Buddhist *suttas*, a literary and philosophical form some two or three centuries younger than the account in the Bṛhadāraṇyaka. The Pāli texts show that the early Buddhists were concerned primarily with causality, a principle applicable to all states and conditions of existence, regardless of how "mental" a particular one may be:

> When this is present, that comes to be;
> from the arising of this, that arises.
> When this is absent, that does not come to be;
> on the cessation of this, that ceases.[75]

This general formula of causation—"When this exists, that exists"—rests upon an experientially-based epistemology: "knowledge of causation is obtained through experience, and knowledge of causal uniformity is obtained through inference based on experience."[76] The culmination of this concern is the doctrine of *paṭiccasamuppāda*, an infinitely regressive (or progressive) cycle that symbolizes experience as a web of causal relations with no foundational principle or first cause. Gārgī's form of questioning, then, is very close to that of the early Buddhists. Compare, for instance:

> *Gārgī & Yājñavalkya*: On what is water strung and threaded? On wind. On what is wind strung and threaded? On ether. On what is ether strung and threaded? [and so forth]. (BĀU.3.6.1.)

> *Sāriputta & Gotama*: Birth, on what is it based? Becoming. Becoming, on what is it based? Grasping. Grasping, on what is it based? Craving [and so forth].[77]

That Gārgī's style of questioning does not become the norm until the period of the early Buddhists[78] raises a significant question of heterodoxy and the possibility that Gārgī is rebuked at Janaka's court for what her colleagues perceive to be heresy. Says Sastri, "Yājñavalkya has no sympathy with . . . [her] argument or with . . . [her] method, since as an Absolutist he cannot recognize the validity of the causal series."[79] If hidden in his rebuke is, in fact, a confrontation between accepted modes of interrogation and a mode not conducive to the Upaniṣadic goal, between questions which give rise to meditationally obtained altered states of consciousness and those which provide rationalistic analyses of experience (leading to meditation, to be sure, but of an entirely different order), then Gārgī's posture at the tournament must be seen in a new light. Since it is unlikely that Gārgī is a heretic, herself self-consciously defying tradition (for certainly that kind of information would have survived in the literature), we must suppose that she is simply an anomaly here, a thinker somewhat "before her time" trying out a new method with the kind of cocky self-confidence any philosopher might have if he were in possession of an innovative style.

Furthermore, the rebuke itself is significant in setting new doctrine. Under the ever-present curse that one's head will fall off, Gārgī will literally put herself in grave physical danger if she continues questioning. Moreover, it is implied here that too much questioning is dangerous for the mind. From Yājñavalkya's later responses to Gārgī, and to Vidagdha, it becomes clear that the only significant spiritual response in recognition of metaphysical truth is silence. Any other reply would be superfluous, digressive and entirely misleading. When, in her persistent questioning, Gārgī is finally gagged, a new quietistic tradition is acknowledged which culminates in the eloquent silence of the Buddha:

> "Now, master Gotama, is there a self?"
> At these words the Exalted One was silent.
> "How, then, master Gotama, is there not a self?"
> For a second time the Exalted One was silent.
> Then Vacchagotta the Wanderer rose from his seat
> and went away.[80]

Such silence may reflect either a skepticism about the ability of human thought to grasp what lies beyond the world of phenomena or a pragmatism which, because of the urgency of bringing suffering to an end, describes any metaphysical speculation as a useless waste of time. In the case of the Buddha, it is probably the latter; in the case of Yājñavalkya, it is most certainly the former.

The Bṛhadāraṇyaka, then, foreshadows Buddhism with at least two important doctrines: the series of infinite regress, reflected in the Buddha's inferential theory of causality, and the inability of language to approach metaphysical truth, reflected in the Buddha's silence. Both are new, and both are associated with Gārgī. Certainly Janaka's tournament brings forth other new material—Ārtabhāga and *karma*, Kahoḍa and the *muni*, and Uddālaka and the *antaryāmi*—and certainly the development of Buddhism out of and in response to the Upaniṣads is a ubiquitous affair. But what remains significant is that in the earliest Upaniṣad, and in the one which most clearly lays the foundation of classical Vedānta, there is open hostility to a style of inquiry that later becomes not only acceptable but basic to Buddhist thought—hostility that could only be based on Yājñavalkya's fear that if he responds authentically to Gārgī's infinite regress of questions, his own elaborately fabricated system will crumble, as happens in time to Upaniṣadic thinkers when questioned by the Buddha.

Any assessment of Gārgī, then, must consider the literary and philosophic agenda of the text. First, there are definite feminist tendencies in the Bṛhadāraṇyaka[81] which render it unique among the Upaniṣads of its period and which establish the clear possibility that Gārgī is faithfully rendered as a remarkable "lady philosopher" at the leading edge of her field.[82] Such an assessment would stand in contrast to, but not necessarily exclude, a second view that she is characterized as a typical female: on the one hand, that (perhaps for dramatic interest) she introduces suspense and comic relief by thwarting, disrupting and even side-tracking the discussion or, on the other, that (consonant with the *ardhāṅginī* model) she is the necessary partner, the "other half," to Yājñavalkya's dialetical search for truth, without whom the truth could not be found. In either case, her character would be a literary tool in the hands of the composers designed to confirm traditional views about women in a decidedly untraditional format. Third, the Bṛhadāraṇyaka, and the whole Upaniṣadic movement, would have gained immensely from any dramatic renunciation of heterodoxy; if there was such a concern, Gārgī's character may have been used to illustrate the results of philosophical confusion, the foibles of persistent ("Buddhistic") questioning, and the desirability of acquiescence to a new tradition and to its central system of *guru-śiṣya* etiquette.[83] Since no text is totally devoid of literary and rhetorical concerns, all "uses" of Gārgī are certainly possible and, to some extent, even probable. Nevertheless, it would be hard to deny the overall significance of Gārgī as perceived by the Indian tradition: an affirmation of women as productive colleagues in the on-going search for truth.

Notes

1. E.g., Viśvavārā and Apālā of the Atri family, and Ghoṣā Kākṣīvatī. Note: the following editions and translations of the Bṛhadāraṇyakopaniṣad have been consulted for this article: Franklin Edgerton, *The Beginnings of Indian Phi-*

losophy (Cambridge: Harvard University Press, 1965), pp. 135–69; Robert Ernest Hume, trans. *The Thirteen Principal Upanishads*, 2nd ed. rev. (London: Oxford University Press, 1931), pp. 73–176; and S. Radhakrishnan, ed. and trans., *The Principal Upaniṣads* (London: George Allen & Unwin, 1953), pp. 147–333.

2. See I. B. Horner, *Women Under Primitive Buddhism: Laywomen and Almswomen* (New York: E. P. Dutton and Company, 1930), and the article in this volume by Janice D. Willis.

3. See Padmini Sengupta, *The Story of Women of India* (New Delhi: Indian Book Company, 1974), pp. 80–81, 128–30.

4. E.g., Andal, Avvai and Mira Bai.

5. Sengupta, *Women of India*, p. 20.

6. A. S. Altekar, *The Position of Women in Hindu Civilization*, 2nd ed. (Delhi: Motilal Banarsidass, 1956), p. 207.

7. In a culture where personal insult could go so far as it did in, of all places, the early Buddhist Order, where "a nun, though 100 years old, must stand in reverence before a monk, though he may have just been initiated in the Church" (Ibid., p. 208), we also find reference to a sweetheart who flatly declines to marry her lover because she suspects he is reluctant to reveal to her secret Vedic theologies (TB.2.3.10) (Ibid., p. 201). Cracks in the surface such as this are rare, however, and are probably due to the ubiquity and heavy-handedness of the Brāhmaṇic redactors and to the thoroughness by which the Brāhmaṇic social schema was implanted.

8. Shakambari Jayal, *The Status of Women in the Epics* (Delhi: Motilal Banarsidass, 1966), p. 297.

9. Altekar, *Women in Hindu Civilization*, p. 197.

10. See C. Kunhan Raja, *Some Aspects of Education in Ancient India* (Adyar, Madras: The Adyar Library, 1950), pp. 106–11.

11. Sengupta, *Women of India*, p. 45; see also Bhagwat Saran Upadhyaya, *Women in Ṛgveda* (New Delhi: S. Chand & Co., 1974), pp. 178–80.

12. Jayal, *Women in the Epics*, p. 21.

13. Pandurang Vaman Kane, *History of Dharmaśāstra*, 5 vols. (Poona: Bhandarkar Oriental Research Institute, 1930–62); 2 (1941): 294–95.

14. Altekar, *Women in Hindu Civilization*, p. 200. Draupadī confesses, for instance, that she had instruction from brahmans (appointed to teach her brother) while sitting on her father's lap (MBh.3.32.60ff.).

15. E.g., Lopāmudrā, who composed RV.1.179 jointly with her husband Agastya; Viśvavārā, composer of RV.5.28; Apālā, authoress of RV.8.91; and Ghoṣā, with two long hymns to her credit (RV.10.39, 40). Ghoṣā, foremost of the female *ṛṣis*, daughter of the *ṛṣi* King Kakṣīvat, was (like Apālā) afflicted with some skin disease, possibly leprosy, and so remained unmarried in her father's house until the Aśvins cured her of the disease and gave her a husband.

16. Gārgī Vācaknavī, Vaḍavā Prātitheyī and Sulabhā Maitreyī (Āś.G.S. 3.4.4.).

17. Sengupta, *Women of India*, p. 69.

18. Eventually, a debate occurred amongst the law-makers as to whether *brahmavādinīs* could marry, but the application of the title to both Draupadī (MBh.4.1.3; 13.2.83; 14.95; see Jayal, *Women in the Epics*, p. 21, n. 6) and Maitreyī (BĀU.4.5.1), two women famous precisely because of their marriage(s), indicates the broad appeal of scholastic life for women.

19. Altekar, *Women in Hindu Civilization*, pp. 10–11.

20. That a good number of women were attracted to the study of Mīmāṅsā is suggested by the coining of a term *kāśakṛtsnā*, which designates a female scholar of the Mīmāṅsā work called Kāśakṛtsnī composed by the theologian Kāśakṛtsana (Mahābhāṣya.4.1.14; 3.155). Ibid., p. 11.

21. Upadhyaya, *Women in Ṛgveda*, p. 188; Jayal, *Women in the Epics*, p. 232. N.B. RV.10.85.26, 27.

22. Jayal, *Women in the Epics*, pp. 258, 296, 298.

23. *Āchāryā*, the female teacher, is not to be confused with *āchārāṇyī*, the male teacher's wife.

24. Altekar, *Women in Hindu Civilization*, pp. 13–23, 179.

25. Kane, *History of Dharmaśāstra*, 3 (1946):536. See also Manu.5.147–49; 9.2–4.

26. Manu.2.67; see also 9.18. Clarisse Bader, *Women in Ancient India*, Chowkhamba Sanskrit Studies, vol. 44, trans. Mary E.R. Martin (Varanasi: Chowkhamba Sanskrit Series Office, 1964), p. 17. Raja notes, "it is the irony of the situation that although women were authors of some of the *Vedic* hymns, they were later denied the right to study the *Vedas*," *Education in Ancient India*, p. 108.

27. Jayal describes the practice of *vānaprastha* as an occasional option for women ascetics in the epics as well, *Women in the Epics*, pp. 188–89.

28. MS.4.7.4 explicitly informs us that women no longer go to public assemblies.

29. See especially Horner, *Women Under Primitive Buddhism*. Buddhist nunneries went out of vogue somewhat later, finally disappearing around the fourth century C.E.

30. Kane, *History of Dharmaśāstra*, 1 (1930): 235.

31. "When the Buddha . . . took to itinerant preaching, he was only perfecting what had already been a recognized mode of promulgating philosophy." S. K. Belvalkar and R. D. Ranade, *History of Indian Philosophy*, vol. 2: *The Creative Period* (Poona: Bilvakuñja Publishing House, 1927), pp. 460–61.

32. The period of the Sūtras is generally seen to be the time when the rigidity of castes sets in, with "its roots in a period at least as early as the rise of Jainism and Buddhism," E. J. Rapson, ed., *The Cambridge History of India*, 6 vols. (1922–63; 3rd. Ind. rpt., Delhi: S. Chand & Co., 1968), 1:197.

33. Belvalkar and Ranade describe such scenes as follows: "a royal court or a sacrificial session, crowded with throngs of men gathered together from different places and impelled by different motives high and low," *History of Indian Philosophy*, p. 139.

34. Belvalkar and Ranade suggest that although each Brāhmaṇa is given to a distinct opponent, it seems that Brāhmaṇas 3 and 7, 6 and 8, and 4 and 5

may be "different versions of the same episode[s]," *History of Indian Philosophy*, p. 114.

35. Śaṅkara's commentary on BĀU 3.8.10, in fact, and a response to Gārgī, says that rites alone may not release one from the round of rebirth into knowledge of the immutable. Swāmī Mādhavānanda, trans., *The Bṛhadāraṇyaka Upaniṣad with the Commentary of Śaṅkarācārya*, 4th ed. (Calcutta: Advaita Ashrama, 1965), p. 524.

36. Belvalkar and Ranade, *History of Indian Philosophy*, p. 197.

37. D. Venkataramiah, "Maitreyi's Choice" in *Prof. M. Hiriyanna Commemoration Volume*, N. Sivarama Sastry and G. Hanumantha Rao, eds. (Mysore: Prof. M. Hiriyanna Commemoration Volume Committee, 1952), p. 221.

38. Ibid., p. 221.

39. Altekar, *Women in Hindu Civilization*, p. 12.

40. M. D. Paradkar, "Contributions of Women to Ancient and Medieval Sanskrit Literature," *Bhāratīya Vidyā*, 26.1–4:30.

41. Kane, *History of Dharmaśāstra*, 2 (1941):366.

42. P. S. Sastri, "Two Women Thinkers of the Upanishadic Age," *Prabuddha Bharata*, March 1954, p. 171.

43. E. W. Hopkins as quoted by Jayal, *Women in the Epics*, p. 257.

44. Basana Devi, "Great Women of the Vedic Times," *Prabuddha Bharata*, March 1954, p. 164.

45. Mādhavānanda, *Commentary*, p. xviii.

46. Franklin Edgerton, *The Beginnings of Indian Philosophy* (Cambridge: Harvard University Press, 1965), p. 135.

47. As if RV.8.33.17—"Even Indra said 'the mind of woman cannot be controlled; moreover, her intellect is slight'"—were the controlling sentiment even in this Upaniṣad. Translation is a paraphrase of Kane, *History of Dharmaśāstra* 2 (1941):368.

48. Belvalkar and Ranade, *History of Indian Philosophy*, p. 200.

49. R. D. Ranade, *A Constructive Survey of Upanishadic Philosophy* (Poona: Oriental Book Agency, 1926), pp. 61, 19, respectively.

50. Ibid., p. 40.

51. Mādhavānanda, *Commentary*, p. 512.

52. For a discussion of the issues in the development of this debate, see K. M. Kapadia, *Hindu Kinship* (Bombay: The Popular Book Depot, 1947), pp. 184–203, xiv–xv.

53. "Śaṁkara, in whose day women were debarred from learning the Vedas, could not but explain the word 'paṇḍitā' [here] as referring to proficiency in domestic work"! Kane, *History of Dharmaśāstra*, 2 (1941):366. Altekar points out that although this ritual did not become as popular as the comparable one for a son, there is a tradition of desire for learned daughters. Some think "that a talented and well behaved daughter may be better than a son (*Sam. Nik.*, III 2, 6). In cultured circles such a daughter was regarded as the pride of the family" (*Kumārasambhava*, VI, 63), *Women in Hindu Civilization*, pp. 3–4.

54. Mādhavānanda, *Commentary*, p. 772.

55. Belvalkar and Ranade, *History of Indian Philosophy*, pp. 140–41.

56. There is considerable debate about the origin of Sanskrit drama, its Aryan or non-Aryan heritage and, in particular, its relation to the "*ākhyāna* hymns." On the origins of Sanskrit drama see the discussions in I. Shekhar, *Sanskrit Drama: Its Origin and Decline* (Leiden: E. J. Brill, 1960), pp. xiii–xxvii, 1–13, and R. Dikshit, *Women in Sanskrit Dramas* (Delhi: Mehar Chand Lachhman Das, 1964), pp. 1–24. For a recapitulation of the *ākhyāna* debate see L. Alsdorf, "The *Ākhyāna* Theory Reconsidered," *Journal of the Oriental Institute* (Baroda), 13 (1963/64):195–207.

57. Dikshit, *Women in Sanskrit Dramas*, p. 16.

58. A theological debate about Brahman, often accompanying a sacrifice (BĀU.3.8.1, 12).

59. Edgerton's translation, *Beginnings of Indian Philosophy*, p. 145.

60. Says Śaṅkara of this repetition: "All this has been explained. The question and the answer are repeated in this and the next paragraph in order to emphasise [*sic*] the truth already stated by Yājñavalkya. Nothing new is introduced." Mādhavānanda, *Commentary*, p. 516.

61. Ibid., pp. 516–17.

62. Ibid., p. 516.

63. Sastri, "Women Thinkers," *Prabuddha Bharata*, March 1954, p. 171.

64. Ranade, *Upanishadic Philosophy*, pp. 56, 61.

65. The cosmological argument suggested here is supported by the physico–theological proof: "The argument from design and the argument from order are merely the personal and impersonal aspects of the physico-theological argument," Ranade, *Upanishadic Philosophy*, p. 257.

66. Belvalkar and Ranade, *History of Indian Philosophy*, p. 197.

67. Ranade, *Upanishadic Philosophy*, p. 19.

68. Ibid., pp. 19–20.

69. For a detailed discussion of this and the other methods of inquiry used in the Upaniṣads, see Ibid., pp. 34–40.

70. Ibid., p. 40.

71. Mādhavānanda, *Commentary*, p. 494.

72. Ibid., p. 495.

73. Śaṅkara describes Gārgī's manner of inquiry as inferential (Ibid., pp. 494–95), a process of reasoning whereby one starts from one or more propositions accepted as true and passes to another proposition or propositions whose truth one believes to be involved in the truth of the former.

74. As described in David J. Kalupahana, *Buddhist Philosophy: A Historical Analysis* (Honolulu: University Press of Hawaii, 1976), pp. 8–18.

75. Ibid., pp. 28–29; David J. Kalupahana, *Causality: The Central Philosophy of Buddhism* (Honolulu: University Press of Hawaii, 1975), p. 90.

76. Kalupahana, *Causality*, p. 108. Kalupahana describes the Buddha's epistemological process as one of inductive inference: "after verifying a number of causal relations, such as between birth and decay and death, the Buddha made inductive inferences concerning the future" (Ibid., p. 107)—similar, according to Śaṅkara, to the process used by Gārgī. On this, see above note 73.

77. Extracted from Mrs. Rhys Davids, trans., *The Book of the Kindred Sayings*

(Saṁyutta-Nikāya), Pt. 2 (London: Oxford University Press, for the Pali Text Society, n.d.), p. 39.

78. Buddhism, though a *śramaṇa*-based group, is a contradiction in terms for it is a teacher-centered tradition that cuts through any salvific power the teacher may be said to have.

79. Sastri, "Women Thinkers," *Prabuddha Bharata*, March 1954, p. 173.

80. F. L. Woodward, trans., *The Book of the Kindred Sayings (Saṁyutta-Nikāya)*, Pt. 4 (London: Oxford University Press, for the Pali Text Society, n.d.), p. 281.

81. E.g., BĀU.3.6.1; 3.8.1–12; 4.5.1–15; 6.4.17.

82. That the Bṛhadāraṇyaka has *exaggerated* Gārgī's achievements because of any feminist tendencies it may have is highly unlikely given the generally conservative environment in which all such literature was composed, compiled and transmitted—notwithstanding, of course, the social and religious ferment of the time.

83. Why Gārgī is not cursed to die like Vidagdha, having committed "philosophic sins" of almost equal magnitude, is not altogether clear. Most certainly her eventual silence and perceived acquiescence are significant, but the Dharmaśāstric injunctions against the killing of women may have been influential as well (see Manu. 9.232; 11.88, 89), as might, of course, the chivalrous nature of Yājñavalkya.

CHAPTER FOUR

Nuns and Benefactresses: The Role of Women in the Development of Buddhism

JANICE D. WILLIS

Recently a number of studies have appeared which address the issue of the portrayal of women in Buddhist literature.[1] Such studies are valuable and timely to be sure, since they begin to provide us with an entree into the relatively neglected area of Buddhism's relationship to, and view of, women. They have sought to investigate the complex and changing status of women in relationship to Buddhist doctrine and practice and to paint a picture of women's place and standing within the Buddhist fold over time. To date, however, in order to present such a picture, all the studies have relied exclusively upon data supplied by the Buddhist scriptures themselves, viewed in isolation. Of course, such an approach ultimately proves to be too limiting. While the texts certainly inform us about the various orthodox Buddhist views regarding women, they cannot themselves be expected to tell us how such views were received or acted upon by the women—and men—who have throughout Buddhist history called themselves "Buddhists."[2]

It is now time, in my opinion, to attempt to go beyond reliance solely upon the sacred scriptures of Buddhism; to attempt to fill out, if possible, the contours of what may be called an actual social history of Buddhism, using the issue of women as a base. For such a social history, two pools of information have to be used together: (1) the Buddhist scriptures which address the issue of women, and (2) secular histories of the periods relevant to the composition and dissemination of those scriptures.

Granted, the attempt to fashion a social history of Buddhism as it relates to women is no easy task. The main source of difficulty is the very nature of the two primary pools of information related to this issue. On the one hand, we have the Buddhist texts themselves. These evidence a wide typology of diverging images and views regarding the female and the feminine, ranging from quite negative (even clearly misogynous) ones early on, to "acceptable" and more positive ones over time. Dating of the texts, moreover, often is problematic, making it difficult to correlate a particular composition with a specific historical period. The authors of the texts in all cases were men,[3] monk-scholars, often with various agendas of their own. Finally, in many cases it is difficult to gauge the size and make-up of the audience of a given text and consequently to assess its impact and influence on the larger community.

On the other hand, when we look to the purely historical studies (that is, secular histories as opposed to religious histories or scriptural examples) we come upon the perennial problem that history is indeed most often "*his*-story," and thus the depiction of the participation of women (as well as other "minority" groups) in affecting events and change is conspicuously absent. Still, we must do the best we can.

Having noted these drawbacks, what I wish to do here is focus upon women and the Buddhist tradition, upon both those women who served the cause as nuns and those who, as laywomen, served in the important capacity of benefactresses of the dharma. In short, I wish at least to begin the discussion of Buddhism's impact on women and their impact in turn on it. I do so, first, by tracing some of the images of women (and of the feminine) presented in a number of Buddhist texts, from the early Theravāda period through the crown-jewel representatives of the developed Mahāyāna tradition;[4] and second, by mentioning some of the known historical facts regarding how certain women, notably certain laywomen, were impacting upon Buddhism at the time some of those texts were enjoying a good deal of popularity. While this is only a preliminary study, I think it can be adequately demonstrated that women played a key role in supporting and literally "maintaining" Buddhism in India and beyond.

I.

During the last forty-five years of his life, Siddhārtha Gautama (563–483 B.C.), the "Buddha," the "path-shower" and founder of Buddhism instructed monks, nuns, laymen, and laywomen. Like so many other teachers of his time, however, his primary aim, at least initially, had been to establish a monastic organization—an order of celibate monks—for the propagation of his teachings. Women, therefore, played no pivotal role in the formation or formulation of the early Buddhist tradition. Or so it would seem.

Given the social and cultural context of sixth-century B.C. India and the importance of celibacy to the early Buddhist monastic organization, it is not surprising that women *qua* women would have been devalued in some of the early literature. In India, as in China, women were subservient to three masters: to their parents when young, to their husbands when mature, and to their children when old. They were helpmates at best and burdens at worst, but always they were viewed as being inferior, second-class citizens.

In spite of such cultural bias, however, some five years[5] after establishing his male *saṅgha*, or Order, the Buddha did something quite radical. Along with the Mahāvīra (founder of Jainism, and an older contemporary of Siddhārtha), the Buddha attacked the caste system of the Brahmans; he condemned the outmoded language of the *Vedas* together with the vedic practice of ritual animal sacrifice; *and* he allowed for the "going-forth" of women from home into the homeless life. He admitted women into the community of his enrobed religious practitioners.

The monk, Ānanda, perhaps the Buddha's favorite disciple, is shown in the scriptures to be a chief advocate for women;[6] and honor falls to him for having pushed for the admission of women into the Order. According to the early scriptures, the woman destined to become the first Buddhist nun was Mahāprajāpatī, the Buddha's aunt and the woman who had raised him since he was seven days old.[7] The *Cullavagga's*[8] account of Prajāpatī's admission into the Order begins as follows:

> At one time the Awakened One, the Lord, was staying among the Sakyans at Kapilavatthu in the Banyan monastery. Then the

Gotamid, Pajāpatī the Great, approached the Lord; having approached, having greeted the Lord, she stood at a respectful distance. As she was standing at a respectful distance, the Gotamid, Pajāpatī the Great, spoke thus to the Lord:

> "Lord, it were well that women should obtain the going forth from home into homelessness in this *dhamma* and discipline proclaimed by the Truth-finder." "Be careful, Gotami, of the going forth of women from home into homelessness in this *dhamma* and discipline proclaimed by the Truth-finder." And a second time. . . . And a third time did the Gotamid, Pajāpatī the Great speak thus to the Lord: "Lord, it were well . . . ." "Be careful, Gotami, of the going forth of women from home into homelessness in this *dhamma* and discipline proclaimed by the Truth-finder."

Then the Gotamid, Pajāpatī the Great, thinking: "The Lord does not allow women to go forth from home into homelessness in the *dhamma* and discipline proclaimed by the Truth-finder," afflicted, grieved, with a tearful face and crying, having greeted the Lord, departed keeping her right side towards him.

Later, speaking to the Buddha on Mahāprajāpatī's behalf, Ānanda queried, "Are women competent, Revered Sir . . . to attain the fruit of once-returning . . . of never returning, to attain Arhatship?"[9] The Buddha did not deny their competence but predicted that, as a result of the founding of a women's Order, his doctrine would not abide long in India.[10] Moreover, the Buddha declared "eight weighty regulations"[11] which had to be accepted by Mahāprajāpatī prior to her admission. These eight special regulations for women served to make clear the nun's separate and inferior status compared to the monks'. According to F. Wilson's[12] translation, the eight rules were as follows:

> (1) In the presence of monks, O Ānanda, women are expected to request ordination to go forth as nuns. I announce this as the first important rule for women to overcome the obstructions so that instruction can be maintained throughout life.
> (2) In the presence of monks, O Ānanda, a nun must seek the teaching and instructions every half month. I announce this as the second important rule . . . .
> (3) No nun may spend a rainy season, O Ānanda, in a place where no monks are resident. This, O Ānanda, is the third important rule . . . .
> (4) After the rainy season a nun must have both orders [monks

> and nuns] perform the "end of the rainy season" ceremony for her with reference to the seeing, hearing, or suspicion [of faults committed by her]. This is the fourth important rule. . . .
> (5) It is forbidden that a nun, Ānanda, accuse or warn a monk about transgression in morality, heretical views, conduct, or livelihood. It is not forbidden for a monk to accuse or warn a nun about morality, heretical views, conduct, or livelihood. This is the fifth important rule I announce . . . .
> (6) A nun, Ānanda, should not scold or be angry with or admonish a monk. I announce this as the sixth important rule for women . . . .
> (7) When a nun violates important rules, O Ānanda, penance must be performed every half month. This I declare as the seventh important rule . . . .
> (8) A nun of one hundred years of age shall perform the correct duties to a monk. She shall, with her hands folded in prayerful attitude, rise to greet him and then bow down to him. This will be done with appropriate words of salutation. I declare this as the eighth important rule . . . .
> "If, O Ānanda, Mahāprajāpatī Gautamī will observe these important rules as a religious duty, then she shall go forth from a home life, take ordination, and become a nun."

Mahāprajāpatī is said to have gladly accepted the "eight rules" and taking them as "a garland of lotus flowers,"[13] she placed them upon her head, swearing never to transgress them. Moreover, the "five-hundred Sākyan women"[14] accompanying her are said to have done likewise.

Once the door was opened to them, women flocked into the order of nuns.[15] To be sure, one can imagine that the addition of a women's order would have caused problems. Early on, there were no permanent structures—no monasteries, or *vihāras*—to house either the monks or nuns.[16] The religious life was physically hard and rugged. In the eyes of contemporary onlookers, no doubt, a dangerous situation prevailed with monks and nuns living in close proximity to each other; and undoubtedly the Buddha himself knew as well that many of his monk converts had but recently abandoned the worldly life with all its ties to womenfolk. Now these very women had entered the monastic confines.

Perhaps this new situation accounted for the prediction the Buddha reportedly voiced to Ānanda immediately after allowing Mahāprajāpatī to enter the order. Again, the *Cullavagga*[17] records:

> If, Ānanda, women had not obtained the going forth from home into homelessness in the *dhamma* and discipline proclaimed by the Truth-finder, the Brahma-faring, Ānanda, would have lasted long, true *dhamma* would have endured for a thousand years. But since, Ānanda, women have gone forth . . . in the *dhamma* and discipline proclaimed by the Truth-finder, now, Ānanda, the Brahma-faring will not last long, true *dhamma* will endure only for five hundred years.
>
> Even, Ānanda, as those households which have many women and few men easily fall a prey to robbers, to pot-thieves, even so, Ānanda in whatever dhamma and discipline women obtain the going forth from home into homelessness, that Brahma-faring will not last long.

But the Buddha did allow women to take the robes and, having been admitted, they lost no time in proving their capacity and ability to cope with the rigors and to scale the heights of the religious life. Many became widely renowned as teachers of the Buddha's Dharma,[18] and a number of nuns attained the ultimate fruit of Nirvāṇa itself. Their *aññas* or "songs of triumph" are recorded in the text known as the *Therīgāthā*, or *Psalms of the Sisters*.[19] (It should be added that while individual nuns are praised as great teachers, they are always depicted as imparting teachings only to other women; and that while some may have possessed an individualized style or unique delivery, their teachings did not depart from the standard message as articulated by the Buddha himself.)

Even though the scriptures show that there were problems associated with the women's Order,[20] it was not the nuns who presented the major problems. These women were at least confined and controlled under the "rules" of the Order. Instead those who posed the greatest threat to the early Buddhist enterprise were the non-robed, unconfined women: women in their "natural" state. As with all monastic organizations, a precarious tension prevailed. Having deliberately chosen the life apart and isolated from worldly domestic realms, the enrobed community yet remained dependent upon that domestic realm for its very existence and maintenance. The *saṅgha* depended upon gifts from the laity. Moreover, monks who had recently left mothers, wives, children, and sweethearts were forced daily to interact with them in order to collect their very food. An early scripture records the following exchange between Ānanda and the Buddha:[21]

> "Master," says Ānanda, "how shall we behave before women?"—"You should shun their gaze, Ānanda."—"But if we

see them, master, what then are we to do?"—"Not speak to them, Ānanda."—"But if we do speak to them, what then?"—"Then you must watch over yourselves, Ānanda."

That woman is the monk's most dreaded threat is attested to by many scriptures of the Theravāda. Representing everything that is the antithesis of his quest for ultimate salvation, she becomes a symbol for all that he wishes to escape from. Entangled in family life and reproduction, in some texts woman is made a veritable synonym for *saṃsāra*[22] itself. I cite a few examples of such negative imagery:
The *Anguttara-Nikāya* states:

> Monks, I know of no other single form, sound, scent, savour, and touch by which a woman's heart is so enslaved as it is by the form, sound, scent, savour and touch of a man. Monks, a woman's heart is obsessed by these things.[23]

(As Paul has pointed out, "the passage immediately prior to this citation discusses the equivalent obsession men have for women."[24]) Three other passages may also be cited from the *Anguttara* collection. Thus i, 11, I, 72 records:

> Monks, womenfolk end their life unsated and unreplete with two things. What two? Sexual intercourse and childbirth. These are the two things.[25]

At *Anguttara-Nikāya*, xxiii, 6, III, 190, the following is said:

> Monks, there are these five disadvantages to a monk who visits families and lives in their company too much. What five? He often sees womenfolk; from seeing them, companionship comes; from companionship, intimacy; from intimacy, amorousness; when the heart is inflamed, this may be expected: Either Joyless he will live the godly life, or he will commit some foul offense or he will give up the training and return to the lower life. Verily, monks, these are the five disadvantages . . . .[26]

And, again, at vi, 5, III, 56:

> Monks, a woman, even when going along, will stop to ensnare the heart of a man; whether standing, sitting or lying down, laughing, talking or singing, weeping, stricken, or dying, a woman will stop to ensnare the heart of a man. Monks, if ever one would rightly say: "It is wholly a snare of Māra, verily, speaking rightly, one may say of womanhood: It is wholly a snare of Māra."[27]

Another corpus of early texts, referred to collectively as the *Jātakas*, or "Previous-Birth stories of the Buddha," also contain numerous accounts "designed to point the moral of feminine iniquity."[28] Coomaraswamy summarizes the *Jātakas'* contents as follows:

> "Unfathomably deep, like a fish's course in the water," they say, "is the character of women, robbers with many artifices, with whom truth is hard to find, to whom a lie is like the truth and the truth is like a lie. . . . No heed should be paid either to their likes or to their dislikes."[29]

And the *Kuṇālajātaka* (verses 24–25) records:

> No man who is not possessed should trust women, for they are base, fickle, ungrateful, and deceitful. They are ungrateful and do not act as they ought to; they do not care for their parents or brother. They are mean and immoral and do only their own will.[30]

Clearly, the passages cited above—far from accurately describing the female's nature—betray the fear of women felt by some of the early writers. That sword of fear was double-edged. Coomaraswamy notes, "For of all the snares of the senses which Ignorance sets before the unwary, the most insidious, the most dangerous, the most attractive, is woman."[31] Such fear produced a thoroughly misogynist polemic even in a text which later found its way into an early Mahāyāna collection known as the *Mahāratnakūṭa* (or, *Collection of Jewels*).[32] I quote a number of verses translated by Paul from "The Tale of King Udayana of Vatsa."[33]

> Fools
> Lust for women
> Like dogs in heat
> They do not know abstinence.
>
> They are also like flies
> Who see vomited food.
> Like a herd of hogs,
> They greedily seek manure.
>
> Women can ruin
> The precepts of purity.
> They can also ignore
> Honor and virtue.
>
> Causing one to go to hell
> They prevent rebirth in heaven.

Why should the wise
Delight in them? . . .

If one listens
To what I have said
They can be reborn, separated
From women.

Then theirs will be
The majestically pure heaven
And they will attain
Supreme Enlightenment . . . .

Those who are not wise,
Act like animals,
Racing toward female forms
Like hogs toward mud.

Fools cannot see
The vice in desires
And ignorantly focus on them
Like blind men . . . .

Because of their ignorance
They are bewildered by women who,
Like profit seekers in the market place,
Deceive those who come near.

Foolish men close to desire
Enter a realm of demons.
Like maggots
They are addicted to filth . . . .

Ornaments on women
Show off their beauty.
But within them there is great evil
As in the body there is air.

With a piece of bright silk
One conceals a sharp knife.
The ornaments on a woman
Have a similar end.

So much for one (tormented!) man's view of women.

When we come to the scriptures proper of the Mahāyāna—with its more universal outlook and appeal, its emphasis upon compassion and "selflessness," its "more sympathetic [attitude] to the existential concerns of the laity"[34] and its recognition of its growing dependency upon the laity (resulting in the concomitant elevation of all members of the laity, both male and female)—we would expect to find less explicit disparagement of women. Happily, this is generally the case. However, the specific means to this end were not direct, but proceeded in stages. That is, while the Mahāyāna conceded that women might attain to ultimate enlightenment, some of its early texts required that women first change their sex.[35] For example, an early Mahāyāna text, the *Lotus Sūtra*,[36] recorded:

> If a woman, hearing this Chapter of the Former Affairs of the Bodhisattva Medicine King, can accept and keep it, she shall put an end to her female body, and shall never again receive one.[37]

In another famed passage of the *Lotus*, we find the following episode recounted:

> At that moment, the venerable Sāriputra spoke to the daughter of Sāgara, the Nāga king: "Good daughter, you have certainly not wavered in awakening to the thought of enlightenment, and have immeasurable wisdom. However, the state of Supreme, Perfect Enlightenment is difficult to realize. Good daughter, even a woman who does not falter in diligence for many hundreds of eras and performs meritorious acts for many thousands of eras, completely fulfilling the six perfections still does not realize Buddhahood. Why? Because a woman still does not realize five types of status. What are the five types? (1) The status of Brahma, (2) the status of Śakra (Indra), (3) the status of a great king, (4) the status of an emperor, and (5) the status of an irreversible Bodhisattva."[38]

It should be pointed out that in the scenario which immediately follows the one just cited above, the eight-year old Nāga princess, after offering her priceless Nāga-jewel to the Buddha, magically transforms her "sexual" self, changing first into a male Bodhisattva and then into a Buddha possessing the "thirty-two major marks."[39] She thereby demonstrates that her sexual transformation is performed out of compassion for the still-ignorant Prajñākūta and Śariputra, and in full accordance with *her* realization of the ultimate teachings of Śūnyatā (that is, voidness of inherent self-existence). Still, the bias against the female sex per se remained in a number of Mahāyāna works.

This bias is also evidenced in some non-canonical (that is, non-sūtra) Mahāyāna works. A key example is provided by the famed *Bo-*

dhisattvabhūmi, composed in the fourth century A.D. by the renowned philosopher, Asaṅga. In the "Chapter on Enlightenment" *(Bodhipaṭalam)*, Asaṅga writes:

> All Buddha-s are exactly the same (in respect to their spiritual attainments). However they may be distinguished according to four factors: with regard to 1) length of life *(ayur)*, 2) name *(nāma)*, 3) family *(kula)*, and 4) body *(kāya)*. . . .Completely perfected Buddha-s are not women. And why? Precisely because a bodhisattva [i.e., one on his way to complete enlightenment], from the time he has passed beyond the first incalculable age (of his career) has completely abandoned the woman's estate *(strībhāvam)*. Ascending (thereafter) to the most excellent throne of enlightenment, he is never again reborn as a woman. All women are by nature full of defilement and of weak intelligence. And not by one who is by nature full of defilement and of weak intelligence, is completely perfected Buddhahood attained.[40]

Fortunately, a number of Mahāyāna texts seek to put an end to such disparagement of the female sex. They do so by building on the all important philosophical theory of śūnyatā (that is, voidness), and by carrying this theory to its logical conclusion. Thus a number of the *Prajñāpāramitā sūtras*,[41] or "Perfection of Wisdom" texts, challenge head-on the ill-conceived idea that distinctions of sex or gender can have any bearing whatsoever on a being's attainment of ultimate enlightenment. Thus, in one *Prajñāpāramitā* text,[42] the Buddha is reported to have said:

> Those who by my form did see me,
> And those who followed me by voice
> Wrong the efforts they engaged in,
> Me those people will not see.
>
> From the Dharma should one see the Buddhas,
> From the Dharmabodies comes their guidance.
> Yet Dharma's true nature cannot be discerned,
> And no one can be conscious of it as an object.[43]

When the Buddha is made to say that those who saw him by his form (that is, by his body, bearing the "thirty-two major marks") did not see him in truth, the argument is made against the notion that maleness (or femaleness) has any bearing on enlightenment. Firmly based upon "voidness," it forcefully asserts that questions of sexuality are irrelevant to the spiritual quest.

But perhaps the two Mahāyāna sūtra-s which best exemplify the spirit of "voidness" as it pertains to the issue of women and Buddhist practice and attainment are the *Vimalakīrti-nirdeśa-sūtra*[44] and the *Śrīmālā-sūtra.*[45] Importantly, both of these sūtras are addressed to and focus upon the laity, as opposed to the monastic community, and both portray the former as possessing higher insight.

In the *Vimalakīrtinirdeśa-sūtra*, a goddess who lives in the house of the layman, Vimalakīrti, instructs Śāriputra (who here represents the old conservatism of the Theravāda monastic community) that a female form is no hindrance to comprehending the ultimate, void, nature of reality. The thrust of the passage is that reality transcends all distinctions, including those associated with a given sex. It reads:

> *Śāriputra*: Goddess, what prevents you from transforming yourself out of your female state?
>
> *Goddess*: Although I have sought my "female state" for these twelve years, I have not yet found it. Reverend Śāriputra, if a magician were to incarnate a woman by magic, would you ask her, "What prevents you from transforming yourself out of your female state?"
>
> *Śāriputra*: No! Such a woman would not really exist, so what would there be to transform?
>
> *Goddess*: Just so, reverend Śāriputra, all things do not really exist.[46]

Lastly, the *Śrīmālā-sūtra* must be cited. Its chief protagonist is the Queen Śrīmālā, who is characterized as having "roared the lion's roar" of the Buddha's Doctrine. The text was composed in the Andhra region of South India in the third century A.D. It enjoyed immediate popularity in India, and later became influential in China as well, particularly during the reign of the famed T'ang Empress, Wu Tse-t'ien. In the *Śrīmālā*, one sees the full flowering of female capability. I quote Paul's summary of this unique text:[47]

> The sutra of *Queen Śrīmālā Who Had the Lion's Roar* is an exceptional text in several distinctive ways. (1) The assembly of those who listen to Queen Śrīmālā consists entirely of laymen and laywomen who are the attendants and citizens in Queen Śrīmālā's court and kingdom. The religious community of monks and nuns are *[sic]* absent. (2) Queen Śrīmālā is the central figure, preempting even the Buddha, with regard to the length and content of the speeches. No other Bodhisattvas share the center stage

> with Śrīmālā, which was not the case in other texts depicting female Bodhisattvas. (3) The entire exposition is addressed to both the good sons and daughters who love and accept the true Dharma, teaching all other living beings to do likewise. These good sons and daughters are compared to a great rain cloud pouring forth countless benefits and rewards, reminiscent of the parable in the *Lotus Sutra*. They are also compared to the great earth which carries the weight of the sea, mountains, vegetation, and sentient life, bestowing compassion like a great Dharma mother of the world. At no time is there a hierarchical pattern of the division of labor in which good sons are the administrators and teachers while good daughters are the assistants. (4) After the discourse, the order of the conversion of the citizens in Queen Śrīmālā's kingdom is extraordinary. First, the women of the city seven years of age and older are converted; then Queen Śrīmālā's husband, and finally the men of the city who were seven years of age and older. The preeminence of women over men in the order of conversion may either suggest a concession for the sake of the narration since Queen Śrīmālā is the central figure, or it may suggest that there was either a prominent woman in the ruling class at that time or that women could ideally have such a societal and religious position in a Buddhist community.

There shall be occasion to speak of the *Śrīmālā-sūtra* again; but for now I must close off the discussion of images of women in Buddhist literature.[48]

II.

Let me now shift briefly to what may be called a more socio-historical account of Buddhism's relationship to women. As Buddhism developed, and especially as the Mahāyāna took shape (c. 100 B.C.–200 A.D.), ties to the laity of necessity had to be strengthened. Not only was there the question of dependency in terms of simple daily alms; now the laity's support was necessary to fund the construction of more permanent and ever-larger monastic complexes as the number of clerics increased, and to fund the construction of stūpas,[49] or reliquary structures for public worship, as the number of lay followers increased.

Responding to the needs of the increasing number of lay devotees, the Mahāyāna proclaimed that the bodhisattva's course was open to all—regardless of whether one was a cleric or not and, as we have seen, regardless of whether one was a man or a woman. In place of the great emphasis on *śīla* (discipline and restraint) advocated by the early Theravāda monastic community, the Mahāyāna gave primacy to *dāna*, or giving. Indeed, *dāna* was made first in the list of the Mahāyāna's so-called "six perfections" (or *pāramitās*) of practice, this formulation replacing the Theravāda's "three-fold training" *(tri-śikṣapāda)*—in monastic discipline, meditation, and insight. If one did not have the good karmic fruit of being able to practice the monastic life, one could still practice Buddhism, gain merit through giving, and mount the successive stages of the bodhisattva to finally reach enlightenment. Naturally, such a doctrine appealed to popular religious sentiments and aspirations.

During his own lifetime, owing to his birthright (he was the son of the Śākyan king, Śuddhodana), the Buddha moved freely in well-to-do circles.[50] He consorted with royalty, merchants, and other wealthy laypersons. Many of these people were converted to his religious cause. Others at least remained loyal supporters. Such support did not disappear following the Buddha's passing.

It is not accidental that Romila Thapar, in her *History of India*[51] (vol. 1, p. 109), discusses both Buddhism and Jainism in the chapter headed "The Rise of the Mercantile Community (c. 200 B.C.–A.D. 300)." Thapar notes:

> The occupation of north-western India by non-Indian peoples was advantageous to the merchant, since it led to trade with regions which had as yet been untapped. The Indo-Greek kings encouraged contact with western Asia and the Mediterranean world. The Shakas, Parthians, and Kushanas brought central Asia into the orbit of the Indian merchant and this in turn led to trade with China. The Roman demand for spices and similar luxuries took Indian traders to southeast Asia and brought Roman traders to southern and western India. Through all India the merchant community prospered, as is evident from inscriptions, from their donations to charities, and from the literature of the time. Not surprisingly, the religions supported by the merchants, Buddhism and Jainism, saw their heyday during these centuries.[52]

And Robinson,[53] speaking specifically of Buddhism, remarks:

> Throughout its history, Buddhism has appealed particularly to the merchant class, especially those engaged in the caravan trade and in large-scale finance. Mercantile ideas of accountability and

> responsibility underlie the doctrines of merit and karma. A world view in which fortune is rational, the regular result of specific acts, appeals to enterprising men who would rather shape their destiny than just let fate happen to them. And the doctrine of the conversation of virtue reassures them that even if they fail in business they can succeed in religion.[54]

But let us return to the issue of women. While the Buddha may have been reluctant to found the Order of nuns, early scriptural accounts attest to the fact that he did not disdain to accept gifts (often quite elaborate and expensive ones) from devout (and often quite wealthy) laywomen followers. It is, I suggest, in regard to female lay patronage that we may begin to formulate answers to the question of the role of women in the formation and development of Buddhism in India and other countries.[55]

It appears in fact that from his earliest days as a teacher, the Buddha was patronized[56] by a number of wealthy women—by women merchants, wealthy courtesans, and royal queens. Moreover, it may be argued that such material support from women not only embellished but actually sustained the continuance of Buddhism in India right up to its final "disappearance" from the sub-continent.

In one of the early scriptures, the woman Visākhā, "a rich citizen commoner of Śrāvastī," is described by the Buddha as his "chief Benefactress."[57] Further described as "the mother of many blooming children [she is reported to have had ten sons and ten daughters], and the grandmother of countless grandchildren [said to have numbered 8,400],"[58] she is portrayed as having lavished gifts upon the Buddhist Order and as having generously catered to its every need. Having tried surreptitiously to donate her jewels, valued at "ninety millions," she instead donated money to the *saṅgha* at three times their value. Visākhā made a gift of treasured property at Śrāvastī,[59] built a monastery upon the site, and single-handedly provided for the needs of the Order whenever its members resided there. Her story is long and cannot be recounted here in detail. Instead, I quote a passage from the text which summarizes her donations:

> For four months did Visākhā give alms in her monastery to The Buddha and to the congregation which followed him; and at the end of that time she presented the congregation of the priests with stuff for robes, and even that received by the novices was worth a thousand pieces of money. And of medicines, she gave the fill of every man's bowl. Ninety millions were spent in this donation. Thus ninety millions went for the site of the monas-

> tery, ninety for the construction of the monastery, and ninety for the festival at the opening of the monastery, making two hundred and seventy millions in all that were expended by her on the religion of The Buddha. No other woman in the world was as liberal as this one who lived in the house of a heretic.[60]

The last sentence of this passage is quite interesting, for history shows that it was often the case that the husbands of the Buddha's wealthy benefactresses were followers of some other religious tradition.[61]

The benefactresses of the Buddha's Order were not limited to the "respectable" classes. The wealthy courtesan, Ambapālī,[62] who later became a nun under the Buddha's charge, is lauded in the scriptures as having been, while still a lay follower, "one of the most loyal and generous supporters of the Order."[63] An account of her life is found in the *Therīgāthā*,[64] but Coomaraswamy has summarized the occasion of her chief offering to the Buddha—a *vihāra* on her mango grove in Vesālī—as follows:

> Then the Master proceeded to Vesālī. At this time, also, there was dwelling in the town of Vesālī a beautiful and wealthy courtesan whose name was Ambapālī, the Mango-girl. It was reported to her that the Blessed One had come to Vesālī and was halting at her Mango Grove. Immediately she ordered her carriages and set out for the grove, attended by all her train; and as soon as she reached the place where the Blessed One was, she went up toward him on foot, and stood respectfully aside; and the Blessed One instructed and gladdened her with religious discourse. And she, being thus instructed and gladdened, addressed the Blessed One and said: "May the Master do me the honour to take his meal with all the Brethren at my house tomorrow." And the Blessed One gave consent by silence. Ambapālī bowed down before him and went her way . . . .
>
> The next day Ambapālī served the Lord and all the Brethren with her own hands, and when they would eat no more she called for a low stool and sat down beside the Master and said: "Lord, I make a gift of this mansion to the Order of which thou art the chief." And the Blessed One accepted the gift; and after instructing and gladdening Ambapālī with religious discourse, he rose from his seat and went his way.[65]

The intricate and intimate connections between the medieval Indian courtesans and the royalty of that day make for a fascinating story. The *Therīgāthā*, for example, tells us that four famous courtesans became nuns under the Buddha. Ambapālī has just been mentioned. The three others were Vimalā, Addhakāsī, and the monk Abhaya's mother, Padumavatī. The latter had been known as "the town-belle of Ujjeni," and "her boy, Abhaya, was King Bimbisāra's son."[66] (It can also be noted here that one of the actual wives of Bimbisāra, Queen Kṣemā, was converted and became a prominent nun under the Buddha.[67])

While mention has been made of women from the merchant class and of wealthy courtesans, undoubtedly the most important women supporters of Buddhism were the queens of the various historical periods. This fact becomes ever more evident as one traces the later development of Buddhism, in India and in the countries to which it spread.

That Buddhism prospered in India under the beneficence of wealthy queens is well attested to by a close reading of historical studies. The phenomenon seems to have occurred in both the southern and northern centers of Buddhism and to have continued from the second and third centuries A.D. up through the twelfth century. In connection with a key example of this situation in southern India, I ask you to think once again about the *Śrīmālā-sūtra*. Recall that this sūtra was written in South India in the third century A.D. What was the historical situation? Following the fall of the south Indian Sātavāhana empire around 220 A.D., the region was partitioned into several kingdoms, the Andhra region coming to be ruled by the Ikshvākus. Nilakanta Sastri[68] describes this royal house as follows:

> The reign of [Siri Chāntamūla's] son Vīrapurisadāta formed a glorious epoch in the history of Buddhism and in diplomatic relations. He took a queen from the Śaka family of Ujjain and gave his daughter in marriage to a Chutu prince. Almost all the royal ladies were Buddhists: an aunt of Vīrapurisadāta built a big stupa at Nāgārjunikonda for the relics of the great teacher, besides apsidal temples, *vihāras*, and *mandapas*. Her example was followed by other women of the royal family and by women generally as we know from a reference to one Bodhisiri, a woman citizen.

The Waymans suggest that by "taking these facts into consideration, one may postulate that the *Śrī-Mālā* was composed partly to honor the eminent Buddhist ladies who were so responsible for this glorious period of South Indian Buddhism."[69]

Nor should we fail to mention that a few centuries later, in China, the *Śrīmālā-sūtra* enjoyed increased popularity and prestige when Empress Wu liberally patronized Buddhism there (in exchange, one might add, for the propaganda campaign carried out on her behalf by her Buddhist supporters!).[70]

To return to India, what was true in South India was true in the North as well. Historical records show that particularly for the important northwestern center of Buddhism, that is, the regions around Kashmir, the Tradition enjoyed the continuous support of the queens of the period. Buddhism having fallen on hard times following the fall of the Kushana empire,[71] its revival in the North is partly—if not wholly—attributable to certain notable queens. Thus, Nalinaksha Dutt[72] provides the following glimpses into the history of Mahāyāna's development in the North:

> Meghavāhana, a descendant of Yudhiṣṭhira I, was brought by the people from Gandhāra and placed on the throne. He had a soft corner for Buddhism, hailing, as he did, from Gandhāra, a predominantly Buddhistic country. His queen Amṛtaprabhā of Prāgjyotisa is said to have built for the use of Buddhist monks a lofty vihāra called Amṛtabhavana . . . .[73]
>
> During the reign of Raṇāditya, one of his queens called Amṛtaprabhā placed a fine statue of Buddha in the vihāra built by a queen of Meghavāhana. Raṇāditya was succeeded by his son Vikramāditya, who was a devotee of Śiva. His minister Galuna had a vihāra built in the name of his wife, Ratnāvalī. . . .[74]
>
> Bālāditya [mid-eighth century A.D.] was succeeded by his son-in-law, Durlabhavardhana, whose queen set up the Anaṅgabhavana-vihāra, referred to by Ou K'ong as Ānanda or Ānaṅga vihāra. The king himself as also his successors were mostly Viṣṇu-worshippers. . . .[75]
>
> Jayamatī, queen of Uccala, built two monasteries, one of which was in honor of her sister Sullā. This, it is said was completed by King Jayasiṃha, the illustrious ruler, who succeeded Uccala. King Jayasiṃha patronised literary men and there was once more a revival of learning in Kashmir. He looked after the Maṭhas and Vihāras, the first of which that attracted his attention was the one built by his queen Ratnādevī. His chief minister Rilhaṇa was also very pious. He showed his veneration to both Śiva and Buddha, and erected a monastery in memory of his deceased wife Sussalā. Sussalā must have been a great devotee of Buddha, as she erected [a vihāra] on the site of the famous Caṅkuna-Vihāra, which had

been destroyed. It had a magnificent establishment for the Buddhist monks. Cintā, wife of Jayasiṃha's commander Udaya, adorned the bank of the Vitastā by a monastery consisting of five buildings, and Dhanya, one of the ministers, commenced the construction of a vihāra in honour of his late wife. Evidently, therefore, the reigning period of Jayasiṃha [1128–49 A.D.] marked a revival of the Buddhist faith in Kashmir.[76]

Conclusion

When we attempt to arrive at an accurate picture of the role played by women in the formation and subsequent development of Buddhism, two main sources of material are available. One is the vast corpus of Buddhist literature itself. Such scriptures present a variety of images of women, of the female, and of the feminine, with such portrayals generally getting more positive as we advance from the early to later texts. It can be noted that women were elevated, presented more positively, and granted more esteem in the texts *at the same time* that such elevation and esteem were accorded to the laity in general. Still, if only the texts are relied upon, a one-sided picture emerges in which women as a whole are most often portrayed as being reacted to (or, against) rather than as being active participants in their own right.

The other major source is the information provided in secular (as distinct from religious) histories. A close reading of this material shows women as independent and active in the world, and as capable of affecting and, in some cases, even of shaping, the development of the Buddhist tradition. Contrary to the Buddha's prediction that his Doctrine would not long abide in India because he now admitted women to his Order, history shows that women's support at least in some cases may actually have been responsible for the Tradition's flourishing on the subcontinent for as long as it did.

Both pools of information must be used together. The women who became followers of the Buddha served him as nuns and as lay benefactresses. While neither group can be said to have actively influenced the early Teachings per se, both groups of women proved that by practicing them they could attain spiritual heights equal to those of their male counterparts. Moreover, though the Order of nuns did not remain a strong factor in Buddhism's historical development, laywomen supporters did play a significant role in nourishing and sustaining the growth and development of the Tradition.

NOTES

1. See, for example, Nancy Falk, "An Image of Woman in Old Buddhist Literature: the Daughters of Māra," in *Women and Religion*, Judith Plaskow and Joan Arnold, eds. (Chico, CA: AAR/Scholars Press, 1974), pp. 105–12; Diana Paul, *Women in Buddhism: Images of the Feminine in Mahāyāna Tradition* (Berkeley: Asian Humanities Press, 1979); Nancy Schuster, "Changing the Female Body: Wise Women and the *Bodhisattva* Career in Some *Mahāratnakūṭasūtras*," *Journal of the International Association of Buddhist Studies* [hereafter *JIABS*] 4, no. 1 (1981):24–69; André Bareau, "Un Personnage Bien Mysterieux: L'espouse du Buddha," in *Indological and Buddhist Studies; Volume in Honour of Professor J. W. de Jong* (Canberra: Faculty of Asian Studies, 1982), pp. 31–59; and Yuichi Kajiyama, "Women in Buddhism," *Eastern Buddhist* (new series) 15, no. 2 (Autumn 1982): 53–70.

2. Speaking to this problem in relationship to early Christianity and current New Testament scholarship, Wayne Meeks, in his *The First Urban Christians; the Social World of the Apostle Paul* (New Haven: Yale University Press, 1983), pp. 1–2, states:

> [an] air of unreality . . . pervades much of the recent scholarly literature about the New Testament and early Christianity. A clear symptom of the malaise is the isolation of New Testament study from other kinds of historical scholarship—not only from secular study of the Roman Empire, but even from church history. Some New Testament students have begun to retreat from critical history into theological positivism. Others no longer claim to do history at all, but favor a purely literary or literary-philosophical reading of the canonical texts . . . .If we ask, "What was it like to become and be an ordinary Christian in the first century?" we receive only vague and stammering replies.
>
> To be sure, ordinary Christians did not write our texts and rarely appear in them explicitly. Yet the texts were written in some sense for them, and were used in some ways by them. If we do not ever see their world, we cannot claim to understand early Christianity.

3. Even the *Therīgāthā*, a collection of hymns recording the "triumphant songs" (or *aññas*) said to have been composed by women *arhatīs* upon their attainment of deliverance, was compiled, written, edited, and extensively commented upon by a monk named Dhammapāla. All the texts comprising the orthodox Buddhist Canon (of whatever country) were authored exclusively by men.

4. "Theravāda" and "Mahāyāna" are terms denoting the two main divisions of Buddhist thought and practice: 1) the early and more conservative or "individualist" phase called here the Theravāda, and 2) the later, more progressive and "universalist" phase known as the Mahāyāna.

5. For references to the lapse of "five years" between the Buddha's establishing his male Order and his decision to found a female Order, see I. B.

Horner, *Women Under Primitive Buddhism* (1930; reprint ed., New Dehli: Motilal Banarsidass, 1975), pp. 98, 103, and 295.

6. Horner, *Primitive Buddhism*, devotes an entire section to Ānanda and Gautama Buddha's relationship to women (see pp. 295–312). Horner writes on p. 295: "Of all Gotama's disciples, Ānanda was the most popular among the almswomen. . . they would have felt that in him they had a friend—one who had a definitely feministic bias." What is so interesting about the overall character of Ānanda as described in the scriptures (and what reveals their humor—as well as posits the reason for Ānanda's strong connection to feminine causes) is that, prior to his conversion, Ānanda's chief (saṃsāric) bondage was his addiction to women. A number of humorous passages in the scriptures show the lengths to which the Buddha had to go in order to wean Ānanda from this addiction so that in the end he joined the *saṅgha.* In I. B. Horner, trans., *The Book of the Discipline (Vinaya-Piṭaka)*, vol. 20 of the *Sacred Books of the Buddhists* (1952; reprint ed., London: Pali Text Society, 1975), p. 353, she notes that at "*Vin.* ii 289 . . . Ānanda was charged at the Council of Rajagaha with having persuaded Gotama to admit women to the Order, thus causing its decay."

7. According to Mahāyāna accounts, Buddhas are "always said to be born parthenogenetically, that is, without the sexual intercourse of the parents." Additionally, all mothers of Buddhas are destined "to die seven days after giving birth in order to preclude any sexual intercourse after such a miraculous event," Paul, *Women in Buddhism*, p. 63. In this world age, Queen Mahāmāyā, Gautama Buddha's mother, died seven days after his birth. From that time on he was raised by his aunt, Mahāprajāpatī. Both Horner, *Primitive Buddhism*, p. 102, and Paul, *Women in Buddhism*, p. 81, suggest that the myth-making process may have intruded into the orthodox account of the founding of the women's order, for its history parallels in many ways that of the Jains. In Jaina accounts also, it is Mahāvīra's aunt, Canda, who instigates the establishment of a nun's order.

8. See Horner, trans., *Cullavagga* 10 (i.e., "Lesser Division," chap. 10). The chapter is found in part 5 of the *Vinaya-Piṭaka*, or *The Book of the Discipline* (vol. 20 of the *Sacred Books of the Buddhists*), p. 352.

9. Again *Cullavagga* 10; here my own translation. This passage is also cited, with slight differences in translation, by Horner, ibid., p. 354; Henry Clarke Warren, *Buddhism in Translations* (Cambridge: Harvard University Press, 1896; reprint ed., New York: Atheneum, 1968), p. 443; and Ananda K. Coomaraswamy, *Buddha and the Gospel of Buddhism* (London: George Harrap and Co., 1916; reprint ed., New York: Harper Torchbooks, 1964), p. 161.

10. In fact, the Buddha says that his Doctrine's presence in India would be cut in half. The explicit words of the Buddha's predictions are given in the text of this article, following.

11. This is Warren's translation for the Pāli, *garudhammā*. See his *Buddhism in Translations*, pp. 444–47. Otherwise, the eight are referred to generally as the "eight chief rules."

12. In Paul, *Women in Buddhism*, pp. 85–86. Other translations of this pas-

sage differ, giving stronger wording especially with regard to the chief rule listed here as eighth. For example, Warren, *Buddhism in Translations*, p. 444, writes: "A priestess of even a hundred year's standing shall salute, rise to meet, entreat humbly, and perform all respectful offices for a priest, *even if he be but that day ordained.*" Similar wording is found in Horner, *Primitive Buddhism*, p. 119, and in Horner's translation in Edward Conze, *Buddhist Texts Through the Ages* (Oxford: Bruno Cassirer, 1954; reprint ed., New York: Harper Torchbooks, 1964), p. 24. Clearly such a rule was intended to solidify for all time the subordinate place of women within the Buddhist Order. Moreover, in addition to an extra two-year probationary period for nuns, there were more rules set down for them than for monks. Further, it often happened that monks incurred a lesser penalty than did nuns for a similar kind of offense.

13. See Horner, *Cullavagga* 10, p. 355; Warren, *Buddhism in Translations*, p. 446; and Conze, *Buddhist Texts*, p. 25.

14. See Paul, *Women in Buddhism*, pp. 86–87; and Caroline A.F. Rhys-Davids, trans., *Psalms of the Sisters* (the *Therīgāthā*) (London: Pali Text Society, 1948), p. 7.

15. A similar phenomenon had happened earlier, when women were allowed to become Jaina nuns. Referring to Sinclair Stevenson's *Heart of Jainism*, Horner, *Primitive Buddhism*, p. 102, states that "more than twice as many women as men, thirty-six thousand women to fourteen thousand men, left the world and became nuns under the Śvetāmbara sect of the Jain Order." That Jaina nuns have continued until the present to outnumber Jaina monks is attested to by Padmanabh Jaini's recent study, *The Jaina Path of Purification* (Berkeley: University of California Press, 1979), pp. 246–47. Horner, *Primitive Buddhism*, reiterates what she notes on p. 115, namely that "women . . . flocked in large numbers to ask for admission."

16. For a history of the development of permanent monastic structures, see Sukumar Dutt, *Buddhist Monks and Monasteries of India* (London: George Allen and Unwin, 1962).

17. Horner, *Cullavagga* 10, p. 356.

18. According to such texts as the *Apadāna* and *Therīgāthā*, several nuns became famous as preachers of the Dharma: Paṭācārā, Sukkā, Mahāprajāpatī, Dhammadinnā, Thullanandā, Bhaddā Kāpīlanī, and Khemā. The *Apadāna* cites seven illustrious women, calling them the "Seven Sisters." They were Khemā, Uppalavannā, Paṭācārā, Bhaddā, Kisāgotamī, Dhammadinnā, and Visākhā (the last mentioned being a famed laywoman disciple). On numerous occasions throughout the *Therīgāthā*, women are said to have joined the Buddhist Order after listening to a discourse propounded by a "brilliant-talker" *(citta-kathī)* nun. For more on the specific epithets used of these teachers, see Horner, *Primitive Buddhism*, pp. 254–58.

19. See Caroline A.F. Rhys-Davids, *Psalms of the Sisters (Therīgāthā).*

20. See Horner, *Cullavagga* 10, pp. 357ff. It should also be noted that the *Bhikkuni-vibhaṅga*, "The Nun's Analysis," or rules for the nuns, found in I.B. Horner, trans., *Vinaya-Piṭaka*, part 6 (in vol. 2 of the *Sacred Books of the*

Buddhists) (London: Luzac and Co., 1966), pp. 80–122, is comprised of rules laid down by the Buddha in response to individual occasions of specific problems associated with the nun's Order.

21. Cf. Coomaraswamy, *Gospel of Buddhism*, p. 160.

22. The point is forcefully made by Falk, "An Image of Woman in Old Buddhist Literature," in Plaskow and Arnold, *Women in Religion*.

23. Cf. Paul, *Women in Buddhism*, p. 51.

24. Ibid.

25. Cf. Ibid.

26. Ibid., p. 52.

27. Ibid.

28. This is the assessment of the *Jātakas* in Coomaraswamy, *Gospel of Buddhism*, p. 159.

29. Ibid., p. 160.

30. Cf. Paul, *Women in Buddhism*, p. 51.

31. Coomaraswamy, *Gospel of Buddhism*, p. 160.

32. The *Mahāratnakūṭa* is an early Mahāyāna anthology of texts, comprised of forty-nine individual tales. The text was translated into Chinese by Bodhiruci between 706 and 713 A.D. The tales of the anthology are quite diverse and seem clearly not to have been composed either by a single author or in a single location.

33. See Paul, *Women in Buddhism*, pp. 31–41.

34. See Richard Robinson, *The Buddhist Religion; A Historical Introduction* (Belmont, CA: Dickenson Publishing Co., 1970). When describing the early precursor to the Mahāyāna, i.e., the Mahāsaṅghika, p. 37, Robinson notes: "The Mahāsaṅghikas admitted upāsakas and non-arhant monks to their meetings, and were sensitive to popular religious values and aspirations."

35. Regarding this interesting phenomenon in early Mahāyāna accounts, see Schuster, "Changing the Female Body," *JIABS* 4, no. 1 (1969):24–69, and Paul, *Women in Buddhism*. Paul devotes an entire chapter (pp. 166–216) to what she terms "The Bodhisattvas with Sexual Transformation."

36. The *Lotus Sūtra* (Skt. *Saddharmapuṇḍarīkasūtra*) is one of the earliest and most influential of the Mahāyāna scriptures. It was composed sometime between 100 B.C. and 100 A.D. Two popular English translations of the *Lotus* are H. Kern, trans. (from the Sanskrit), The *Saddharma-Puṇḍarīka or the Lotus of the True Law ("Sacred Books of the East,* vol. 21, 1884; Oxford: Clarendon Press, 1909), and Leon Hurvitz, trans. (from the Chinese of Kumārajīva), *Scripture of the Lotus Blossom of the Fine Dharma (The Lotus Sūtra)* (New York: Columbia University Press, 1976).

37. Hurvitz, *Scripture*, chap. 23, p. 300.

38. This translation is by Paul, *Women in Buddhism*, p. 189.

39. In some of the early Mahāyāna literature, the claim is put forward that a woman's physical characteristics bar her from becoming either a Buddha or a *cakravartin* (i.e., "world monarch"), this by virtue of the fact that both of these conform to a specific physical type, called the *Mahāpuruṣa* or "Great Man" having thirty-two major marks (Skt. *lakṣaṇa*) and eighty minor marks. Listed

tenth among the thirty-two marks is "having the male sex organ concealed within a sheath." A pre-Mahāyāna, Pāli scripture, the *Lakkhana-suttanta* discusses these thirty-two major marks in detail. See *Dīgha-nikāya*, 3, translated by T. W. Rhys-Davids as *Dialogues of the Buddha* in *Sacred Books of the Buddhists*, vol. 4 (Oxford: Oxford University Press, 1921; reprint ed., London: Pali Text Society, 1977), pp. 132–67.

40. My own translation, from the Sanskrit version of the *Bodhisattvabhūmi*, ed. Nalinaksha Dutt (Patna: Jayaswal Research Institute, 1978), chap. 7, p. 66. See also Har Dayal's summary of some of this literature in his *The Bodhisattva Doctrine in Buddhist Sanskrit Literature* (London: Routledge and Kegan Paul, 1932; reprint ed., New Delhi: Motilal Banarsidass, 1975), p. 224.

41. The "Perfection of Wisdom" literature was composed primarily in southern India and over a few centuries, beginning circa 100 B.C. and continuing well beyond the fifth century A.D. For a detailed review of this literature, see Edward Conze, *The Prajñāpāramitā Literature* (The Hague: Mouton and Co., 1960) and the Introduction to his *Selected Sayings from the Perfection of Wisdom* (Boulder: Prajna Press, 1978).

In *The Prajñāpāramitā Literature*, p. 10, Conze offers a very interesting suggestion regarding the southern Indian origins of the female deity known as "Prajñāpāramitā," the "Mother of all Buddhas." He notes that the "Perfection of Wisdom" Goddess first appeared in an area of southern India where "both Dravidian and Greek influences made themselves felt. . . . In view of the close analogies which exist between the Prajñāpāramitā and the Mediterranean literature on Sophia, this seems to me significant. Also the Andhras were a non-Aryan people . . . and the matriarchal traditions of the Dravidians may well have something to do with the introduction of the worship of the 'Mother of the Buddhas' into Buddhism."

42. The *Diamond-sūtra* (Skt. *Vajracchedikā-sūtra*), composed circa fourth century A.D.

43. See E. Conze's translation of the *Diamond-sūtra* in his *Buddhist Wisdom Books* (London: George Allen and Unwin, 1958; reprint ed., New York: Harper Torchbooks, 1972), p. 63.

44. The *Vimalakīrti-nirdeśa-sūtra* was composed circa first century A.D. It is one of the oldest and most popular works of the Mahāyāna. Two English translations are popular: Charles Luk's translation from the Chinese, *The Vimalakīrti Nirdeśa Sūtra* (Boulder: Shambhala, 1972), and Robert A. F. Thurman's translation of the sūtra from the Tibetan, *The Holy Teachings of Vimalakīrti; A Mahāyāna Scripture* (University Park: Pennsylvania State University Press, 1976).

45. The *Śrīmālā-sūtra* is thought to have been originally composed in the Andhra district of South India sometime during the third century A.D. Alex and Hideko Wayman have translated the sūtra. See their *The Lion's Roar of Queen Śrīmālā* (New York: Columbia University Press, 1974).

46. Thurman, *Teachings of Vimalakīrti*, p. 61.

47. Paul, *Women in Buddhism*, pp. 287–88.

48. One could go on to mention later examples of women who excelled in

Buddhist practice, especially in connection with the development of the Buddhist tantric systems—such as Niguma, the "sister" of Nāropa, who developed her own system known as the "Six Yoga-s of Niguma"; bDag-med-ma, Marpa's accomplished wife; and Ma-gcig-lab-sgron-ma, who founded the celebrated system of *gCod* practice—but there is no space to go into these here.

49. For more on the important connections between the development of *stūpas* and the rise of the Mahāyāna, see Akira Hirakawa, "The Rise of Mahāyāna Buddhism and its Relationship to the Worship of Stūpas," in *Memoirs of the Research Department of the Toyo Bunko*, no. 22 (Tokyo: Toyo Bunko, 1963).

50. The scriptures show that the Buddha consorted with important kings of his day—such as King Bimbisāra of Magadha (who donated the famed Bamboo Grove located six miles outside of Rājagṛha), his son and successor, Ajātasatthu, and Prasenajit of Kośala—as well as with powerful merchants. His first lay converts are reported to have been the wealthy merchant couple who were the father and mother of Yasa, the "noble youth" who became the Buddha's sixth monk-disciple. The powerful merchant, Anāthapiṇḍaka, donated the land for the famous Jetavana monastery at Śrāvastī. Thus, as Robinson notes in *The Buddhist Religion*, p. 34, "even during the Buddha's lifetime his saṅgha became a wealthy landowner."

51. Romila Thapar, *A History of India*, 2 vols. (Middlesex, England: Penguin Books, 1966; reprint ed., Baltimore: Penguin Books, 1969).

52. Ibid., 1:109.

53. Robinson, *The Buddhist Religion.*

54. Ibid., p. 32.

55. For whatever reasons, the Order of nuns did not remain a strong component of Buddhism's development. Though exceptional personalities were counted among the nuns described in such texts as the *Therīgāthā*, as Paul notes, *Women in Buddhism*, p. 82:

> the nun's life is not well marked in the Mahāyāna sūtra tradition or in the philosophical writing of that tradition. Participation in an intellectual life by the Mahāyāna Buddhist nun is not recorded. The nun seems not to have been a significant part of the student body of the great Buddhist universities which were the central gem in the crown of the monk's order, an order which was extensive, prosperous, and productive of extraordinary thought and art.

Women benefactresses, on the other hand, played as shall be seen, a powerful role in developing and sustaining the Tradition.

56. I am well aware of the problems associated with the use of such terms as "patron" and "patronize" in these contexts. Though the *American Heritage Dictionary* (p. 961) defines "patron" as "anyone who supports, protects, or champions; a benefactor," the term clearly derives from the Latin *pater* and, even earlier, the Sanskrit *pati*, both denoting a male and meaning "father" or "protector." The closest feminine counterpart, i.e., "matron," is clearly inadequate here.

57. The life of Visākhā, also known as the "mother of Migāra," is recounted

in the *Dhammapada* commentary, and references to her are found in the *Udāna* and in the *Anguttara-nikāya*. Warren gives a translation of her life in his *Buddhism in Translations*, pp. 451–81. Horner, *Primitive Buddhism*, pp. 345–61 and Coomaraswamy, *Gospel of Buddhism*, pp. 163–64 also mention her. Coomaraswamy quotes H. Oldenberg (*Buddha, his Life, his Doctrine, his Order*, trans. from the German by W. Hoey [London, 1882]) as saying:

> Pictures like this of Visākhā, benefactresses of the Church, with their inexhaustible religious zeal, and their not less inexhaustible resources of money, are certainly, if anything ever was, drawn from the life of India in those days: they cannot be left out of sight, if we desire to get an idea of the actors who made the oldest Buddhist community what it was.

58. Warren, *Buddhism in Translations*, p. 471. Visākhā is said to have "lived to be a hundred and twenty years old, but there was not a single gray hair on her head—always she appeared as if about sixteen."

59. Śrāvastī was an important city during the Buddha's day and a main seat for his Order. It figures as the setting of numerous sūtras.

60. Warren, *Buddhism in Translations*, pp. 477–78.

61. That is, they were usually Hindus and worshipped either Viṣṇu or Śiva.

62. Ambapālī is also known as "Amrapālī." Her name means "daughter of the mango-guardian" according to the *Therīgāthā* LXVI. Her life is found recorded in that text because she later became a Buddhist nun. She is said to have had a son (named Vimala-Kondañña) who became a monk under the Buddha's care. That son, it is said, taught Ambapālī the meaning of the Buddhist doctrine of impermanence by illustrating it in relationship to her own aging body. She was thus "converted."

63. Horner, *Primitive Buddhism*, p. 89.

64. See Caroline A.F. Rhys-Davids, *Psalms of the Sisters* (i.e., *Therīgāthā* LXVI), pp. 120–25.

65. Coomaraswamy, *Gospel of Buddhism*, pp. 74–75. A contingent of "Licchavi princes" are said to have become upset when the Buddha refused their invitation to dine with them in order to honor his former acceptance to do so with Ambapālī.

66. See Horner, *Primitive Buddhism*, p. 89, and Caroline A.F. Rhys-Davids, *Psalms of the Sisters* (i.e., *Therīgāthā* XXVI), p. 30. Padumavatī, too, it is said in the *Therīgāthā*, was converted to the Buddha's teaching after hearing her son preach the Dharma.

67. King Bimbisāra apparently had three wives: 1) Khema (Skt. Kṣema), called his "queen-consort," 2) a princess from Videha, sometimes called Kośala-devā, who was the sister of King (?) Prasenajit (and the mother of Ajātasatthu), and 3) Chellana. Queen Kṣema was said to have purposely tried to avoid meeting the Buddha since, addicted to her own beauty, she was afraid of his censure. When through a trick carried out by King Bimbisāra she and the Buddha did meet, having listened to the Buddha's discourse, she attained arhatship (one of the only persons said to have done so while not enrobed).

For more on this woman who became a famous nun teacher, see *Therīgāthā* LII, and Horner, *Primitive Buddhism*, pp. 36, 167–69, 180, 183, 191, etc.

68. Nilakanta Sastri, *A History of South India* (Madras, 1963), p. 96. Cf. Alex and Hideko Wayman, *The Lion's Roar of Queen Śrīmālā*, p. 2.

69. Alex and Hideko Wayman, *The Lion's Roar of Queen Śrīmālā*, p. 2.

70. The T'ang Empress Wu Tse-t'ien apparently invited Bodhiruci, the famous Indian translator, to China and for some twenty years she and her two sons and successors provided support for him. Schuster, "Changing the Female Body," *JIABS* 4, no. 1 (1981):26 claims that,

> In return, Bodhiruci lent his prestige to the Empress' claim to be legitimate ruler of China in her own right. . . . The Empress' Buddhist supporters, with at least the tacit approval of Bodhiruci, agreed further that the Empress' reign had been predicted by the Buddha himself in certain Mahāyāna sūtras (the *Ratnamegha, Pao-yü ching*, and the *Mahāmegha, Ta-yün ching*). One of the sūtras Bodhiruci retranslated for the Empress was the *Śrīmālā-sūtra*.

71. The Kushana empire (or Kuṣāṇa Dynasty) in Northwest India (with its famed king, Kaniṣka, assession date 78 A.D. [?]) lasted from the first century A.D. until the middle of the third century A.D. From that time onward, the Northwest region came under Iranian influence following the victorious invasion by the Sāsānian dynasty of Persia.

72. See Nalinaksha Dutt, *Mahāyāna Buddhism* (New Delhi: Motilal Banarsidass, 1977).

73. Ibid., pp. 56–57.

74. Ibid., p. 57.

75. Ibid., p. 58.

76. Ibid., pp. 61–62.

Chapter Five

Striking a Balance: Women and Images of Women in Early Chinese Buddhism

Nancy Schuster

I. Buddhism in China: First through Fifth Centuries C.E.

Buddhism was brought to China from India around the beginning of the Common Era. It was a case of transplanting very sophisticated ideas from one highly developed culture to an equally advanced culture which had already created religious and philosophical systems of its own. Although the early Buddhist missionaries made some converts, the new religion from the west was slow to catch the interest of most Chinese. The assimilation of Buddhist doctrines, attitudes and values was a long, slow process.

The Buddhist missionaries came from all parts of the Buddhist world to China: there were monks and lay teachers from India and Kashmir, from the borders of the Persian empire, and from the various Buddhist cities which had sprung up in the oases along the great Central Asian trading routes. They brought Buddhist scriptures with them and, if they were able, translated them into Chinese after they had established themselves in their new homes. Each missionary brought with him texts which he himself knew well and had specialized in studying and preaching in his homeland. The range of Buddhist literature was vast, even in those days, but only a small part of it was at first accessible to Chinese Buddhists.

By the second half of the third century, native Chinese Buddhists like Fa Hu[1] and Shi-xing[2] were trekking westwards across the Central Asian deserts to search for more Buddhist texts to study and translate: an appetite for Buddhist learning was rapidly developing. Until around 300 C.E. the Central Asian trade routes were wide open to travellers, since the Chinese Empire under the Jin Dynasty was for the moment secure and the Central Asian oases themselves were enjoying peace and prosperity. Thus Fa Hu was able to bring back huge loads of scriptures from the Buddhist centers he visited in the western regions, and after his return he remained in close contact with his co-religionists in Kashmir, Kučā, Khotan and elsewhere, who from time to time sent him still more texts to translate.[3]

Fa Hu and other third-century travellers were eclectic in their tastes; they brought to China an assortment of scriptures: some major ones which were destined to fire the imaginations of Chinese Buddhists and to remain popular and influential for centuries, and others which were translated but never became well known and soon faded into obscurity. By the time of Fa Hu's death early in the fourth century, the Chinese Buddhist communities were already acquainted with many of the basic Mahāyāna Buddhist[4] scriptures, in particular the *Prajñāpāramitā (Perfection of Wisdom) sūtras*, the *Sukhāvatīvyūha-sūtra (Pure Land of the Buddha Amitabha)*, the *Vimalakīrtinirdeśa (the Teachings of the Bodhisattva Vimalakīrti)*, the *Śūraṅgamasamādhi-sūtra* (the *Meditation on the Hero's Course*) and the great *Lotus* scripture (*Saddharmapuṇḍarīkasūtra*).

There was a new surge of translating activity in China from the late fourth to mid-fifth centuries. It was the fruit of a second era of feverish quests for scriptures along the Central Asian "silk roads" and in the Indian subcontinent. Indefatigable Chinese pilgrims like Fa-xian[5] travelled all the way to India and Śrī Lankā looking for texts on the monastic rules, which the Chinese monks and nuns sorely lacked. Others went west to study meditation at the feet of renowned masters of Buddhist yoga and stayed on in Kashmir, which at that time was the acknowledged center for meditation training in the Buddhist world. When these latter pilgrims returned they brought meditation texts with them, and sometimes Kashmiri meditation teachers as well. Western specialists in the *Vinaya* (monastic rules), in meditation, in the philosophy of the various Hīnayāna and Mahāyāna schools, or in the newly composed or expanded great Mahāyāna sūtras, flowed eastward in a steady stream to China.[6] The Chinese appetite for Buddhist learning had become insatiable; Chinese Buddhists wanted it *all*, and they joyously welcomed anyone who could bring the scriptures to them. During the fourth and especially the fifth centuries, thanks to the translating and exegetical success of gifted foreign missionaries such as Kumārajīva from Kuča in Central Asia, Buddhabhadra, Dharmakṣema and Guṇabhadra from India, and Saṅghadeva, Buddhayaśas, Dharmamitra and Guṇavarman from Kashmir, Chinese Buddhists were able at last to let their minds wander freely through a huge and varied library of Buddhist literature. Chinese Buddhists, in turn, were sifting and assimilating what they found in the Buddhist books. They were mastering Buddhist thought and beginning to use it creatively to form their own distinctive forms of Buddhism. Chinese Buddhists of the late fourth and the fifth centuries were becoming very sophisticated in their comprehension of Buddhist thought, and Buddhism was, in turn, becoming a significant force in Chinese society.

II. Women in Buddhist Scriptures

Among the many Buddhist texts introduced into China, there were some which had special words to speak about women. Some sūtras have women as the principal interlocutors in dialogues with the Buddha or his followers; most of these are short texts, and most have known but ephemeral popularity. Several such texts were translated by Fa Hu and others during the third century. Somewhere in the bulk of the larger and more famous Mahāyāna sūtras, such as the *Lotus*, the *Vimalakīrtinirdeśa*, the *Perfection of Wisdom in 8,000 Lines* and the *Śūraṅgamasamādhi-sūtra*, one also finds occasional passages about women. The women who appear in these sūtras are literary creations, not historical personalities. They are ideal images, sometimes even mythical figures—supremely wise and witty teachers of the Buddhist Dharma, miracle-workers, precociously clever little girls, queens and princesses and magical goddesses who are all devotees of the Buddha. The few texts about real women (mostly nuns who were the immediate disciples of the Buddha) which do exist in the Buddhist Canon have never been well known in China, and were in any case not translated into Chinese until the end of the fourth century or later.[7]

The texts known to Fa Hu and his contemporaries contained mostly positive images of women. The women in them are often *bodhisattvas*, that is, heroic beings who are completely committed to attaining the perfect enlightenment of the Buddhas so that they may lead other beings to liberation from all suffering. *Bodhisattvas* may be male or female, clerics or laypeople, and they may be of any age. The female *bodhisattvas* in texts such as the *Lotus*, the *Vimalakīrtinirdeśa*, the *Vimaladattā-paripṛcchā* and the *Sumati-sūtra*[8] are all wise and eloquent women who engage the most prestigious of the Buddha's disciples in subtle debate and vanquish them ignominiously. There is no question in these texts that these women, ideal types though they are, are infinitely superior in intellect and virtue to all the males present save for the Buddha himself.

Nonetheless, the central issue in these sūtras and many others is whether or not women can become Buddhas (fully enlightened beings). Since the time of Gautama the Buddha himself (c. 500 B.C.E.), it had always been recognized that women and men could equally attain *nirvāna*, or liberation from the persistent unhappiness experienced in the unremitting round of rebirths *(saṃsāra)*.[9] Resolute cultivation of the mental and moral discipline taught by the Buddha would invariably lead the persistent disciple to freedom from unhappiness and rebirth through the attainment of enlightened understanding of the true nature of existence in this world. This accomplishment was not sex-based. But in Mahāyāna Buddhism, and in the older Buddhist schools, the idea that beings other than Gautama himself might win Buddhahood began to be entertained, and a debate ensued as to whether a woman could reach that exalted degree of perfection. Her physical body, after all, was visibly different from the male body of the historical Buddha. A woman could certainly *aspire* to Buddhahood, it was asserted—and in Mahāyāna Buddhism that meant she could be a *bodhisattva* and tread the *bodhisattva*-path toward enlightenment—but somewhere along the way, in the course of her own rebirths, she would have to cease to be female and go on being born only as a male. Otherwise she could never be a Buddha.[10] Sūtras like the *Vimalakīrti*, the *Vimaladattā*, the *Lotus*, *Śūraṅgama* and others directly countered these charges by *playing* with the notion of the change of sex. The goddess in the *Vimalakīrti*, for example, uses her supernormal powers to change freely back and forth from female to male, in order to demonstrate to Śāriputra, her monk antagonist, that maleness and femaleness are not ultimately real at all but are empty like a show of magic.[11] The conclusion reached in these texts, then, is that, so far as living the spiritual life and attaining its highest goals are concerned, a distinction between male and female is made only by the unenlightened worldling, and not by a truly wise *bodhisattva*.

The *Vimalakīrtinirdeśa* was widely read by Chinese Buddhists in the third, fourth and fifth centuries, and has continued ever since to be one of the most beloved Buddhist sūtras in China. It, the *Lotus Sūtra* and the other texts which convey the same message about women, have been extremely influential in shaping attitudes among Chinese Buddhists.[12] On the whole, it seems that early Chinese Buddhists received from the scriptures they read and discussed views of women which were largely positive.[13]

The second great period of translation activity (late fourth/early fifth centuries) introduced to Chinese Buddhists a much greater variety of Buddhist scriptures, monastic rule books, philosophical treatises and meditation manuals. While the *Lotus, Vimalakīrti, Perfection of Wisdom-sūtras* and *Śūraṅgama* were not displaced, and in fact became increasingly influential, other important texts joined them at the center of Buddhist attention. Some of these newer texts powerfully reaffirmed the belief that there is no difference between men and women in the ability to live the spiritual life and to attain the highest religious goals. In the *Śrīmālādevīsūtra*, translated in 436 by the Indian monk Guṇabhadra, a woman, Queen Śrīmālā, explains the most profound doctrines and converts many to Buddhism. The question of whether it is appropriate for a woman to do this is never even raised. Śrīmālā seems very nearly to be a female Buddha.[14] Similarly the *Gaṇḍa-vyūha-sūtra* introduces a number of female teachers whose understanding has reached the highest level; among them is a nun, some laywomen, even a prostitute. The *Gaṇḍavyūha* was translated by the Chinese monk Sheng-jian between 388 and 407 (T294) and by Buddhabhadra, the illustrious meditation master from India and Kashmir, between 418 and 422 (T278).[15] There were other *sūtra*s and commentaries on sūtras, too, which portrayed women as the spiritual equals of men,[16] but there were also some texts newly offered to the Chinese public which worked to undermine that egalitarian attitude.

It was from Kashmir that many of the missionaries came to China during the fifty years between 380 and 430; at least ten of the major teacher-translators who reached China during this period were from Kashmir.[17] In addition, several other foreign and Chinese monks studied for a time in Kashmir, were strongly affected by the instruction they had received there and remained in touch with scholars in that land even after they themselves had returned to China. Kashmir was, in the fourth and fifth centuries, one of the major centers of Buddhist learning in all of Asia. It was chiefly Buddhist meditation which was studied there. And it is in a few meditation manuals, a literary genre characteristic of Kashmiri Buddhism,[18] that one finds clearly misogynist outbursts, perhaps for the first time in Chinese Buddhism.

Kumārajīva[19] translated a short text called *Carnal Desire Reproved by the Bodhisattva* (T615) which is meant to cure the meditator's lustfulness by teaching him to meditate on the pain caused by his lustful mental attitude. The text, however, quickly slides into a shrill denunciation of women, the objects of lustfulness:

> As to the characteristics of a woman, her words are like honey but her heart is like poison . . . she is like a treasure cave on a golden mountain with a lion dwelling inside. . . . A woman . . . ruins the clan and destroys the family . . . And she is like a fine-meshed net: all the fish jump into it, and then she rips out their entrails and serves up their flesh on a platter. . . .[20]

Similar passages and similar images are found in some other guides to meditation which were circulating in the fifth century.[21] Since meditation is the most fundamental and universal practice of Buddhists, texts like these may have influenced some people, but their impact was probably far less than that of the better known, more frequently studied and preached, *Lotus, Vimalakīrtinirdeśa* and *Perfection of Wisdom sūtras*.

III. Women in Chinese Buddhism

There is scarcely any information available about women Buddhists in China before the fourth century, and precious little after that. There are occasional references in Buddhist sources and even in the traditional Chinese histories to Buddhist laywomen and female patrons of the monks' and nuns' orders. In the biography of the Kashmiri monk Dharmayaśas, for example, we read of a woman lay-devotee in Canton around 400 who went to the master for instruction.[22] Because of their prominent social positions, one hears a little more about Buddhist empresses, princesses and other women of the highest classes who patronized Buddhism in Jiankang (modern Nanjing) in the fourth and fifth centuries. Empress He of the Eastern Jin Dynasty founded a nunnery in Jiankang in 354, the Yong-an-si. Empress Chu, also of Eastern Jin, had founded the Yan-xing-si for some favored nuns a few years earlier and the Qing-yuan monastery as well, both at Jiankang.[23] The empress, who was a potent political force at the Jin court for forty years (she died in 384), maintained close contact with several nuns. Empress Yuan of the succeeding Liu Song

Dynasty invited the Kashmiri monk Dharmamitra to the palace, soon after his arrival in Jiankang in 424, to celebrate Buddhist rituals for herself, the crown prince and the princesses.[24] The imperial concubine Pan greatly admired the nun Ye-shou and in 438 paid for the elaborate enlargement of her convent.[25] Another noble lady, Madame Fan, had founded the convent for Ye-shou in 426; she converted the ancestral temple of one of her clan's prominent forebears into a Buddhist foundation, making Ye-shou the abbess.[26] The nun Hui-qiong was the recipient of a gift of land from a great lady, Madame Wang, mother of a Song princeling. Hui-qiong was generously patronized by many wealthy donors, and with their gifts she was able to have a convent built on the site (441).[27] Especially after about 380 C.E., Buddhism steadily increased its political influence at the Jin and Song courts, and in this process Buddhist women, including empresses, court ladies and nuns, played a prominent role.[28]

Such bare facts are all that we know of the great Buddhist ladies; we know nothing about the many humble women who no doubt made up a significant proportion of the Buddhist communities in north and south China at the time. Fortunately this paucity of information about Buddhist laywomen is somewhat offset by the existence of a fascinating document, the *Bi-qiu-ni-chuan, Lives of Eminent Nuns*, which preserves more than sixty-five biographies of some notable Chinese nuns who were active between 317 and 516 C.E.[29] The Chinese order of nuns or *bhikṣuṇī (bi-qiu-ni)* was formally established in the mid-fourth century,[30] and continues to this very day in the People's Republic of China and in Taiwan in an unbroken tradition.

IV. Chinese Buddhist Nuns

The *Bi-qiu-ni-chuan* (BQNC) does not offer a portrait of the nuns' community as a whole. Its author, the monk Bao-chang, selected only those nuns he considered most remarkable for their learning and success as teachers, for their accomplishments in meditation, for their extreme asceticism or for their faith and steadfastness.[31] Most of those women Bao-chang has immortalized fall into the first two categories, and they were no doubt the elite of the nun's order. They were also the ones who appealed most to Bao-chang's own tastes. Furthermore, nearly all the nuns in the BQNC lived in the south, and in the immediate vicinity of Jiankang (Nanjing), the capital of the southern dynasties and the most splendid and cultured city in China at the time.

What is most striking about the nuns we meet in the BQNC is what influential people they were in the society of their day. From the time the first nuns arrived at Jiankang around 340, they were generously patronized by the most powerful ministers at court and by empresses and emperors. Several were welcomed as special friends by members of the innermost circles of power, and at court nuns served not merely as religious instructors to pious rulers, but were sometimes involved in political decision–making as well.[32] It was of course precisely because the nuns had become such a significant presence in Chinese society at the southern capital that Bao-chang wrote their biographies.[33]

Undoubtedly the most influential and political nun at the Jin court was Miao-yin, the abbess of the Jianjing-si in Jiankang.[34] In the 380s she was a close friend of Emperor Xiao-wu (reigned 373–397) and his most powerful ministers, and later of those around his successor Emperor An (reigned 397–419). She was a woman well-educated in the Chinese classics as well as in Buddhist scriptures, and she composed literary works herself (they have not survived). She was constantly being invited to court to discuss literature and trade compositions with Emperor Xiao-wu, the Great Preceptor Si-ma Dao-zi (the real power behind the throne) and court scholars. Because she was respected and renowned, Si-ma Dao-zi established the Jianjing convent for her in 385 and made her abbess. Thereupon her fame as a learned nun and as a political friend worth cultivating increased exponentially; she attracted over a hundred religious disciples, but far more lay hangers-on who jostled each other at the gates of her convent each morning, hoping for her help to advance their own causes. In 398, the ambitious Huan Xuan, a rising political force who had always been cool to Buddhism, felt obliged to go to her as the one person who could discreetly persuade the Emperor and the Preceptor to appoint *his* choice to a crucial office. She did so, thus enabling Huan Xuan to begin his ascent toward the ultimate usurpation of the imperial power (402–404). Ironically, it was Huan Xuan who later killed Miao-yin's first and most loyal patron, Si-ma Dao-zi, in 402, because the old minister stood between him and the throne. It is not known how Miao-yin reacted to this. She apparently ended her own days in peace, certainly in prosperity. The date of her death is not recorded.

The Song royal family were even more assiduous cultivators of friendships with nuns than the Jin had been, although no cases quite comparable to Miao-yin's engagement in political intrigue are recorded. The nuns Bao-xian and Fa-jing of Pu-xian convent were appointed in 466, by imperial decree, to be the Regulator of the Nuns' Order, and the Director of the Nuns' Daily Monastic Routines, respectively, at the capital.[35] Both nuns were known as persons of extraordinary intellect, who were persuasive teachers and effective at managing practical matters. Fa-jing, the Director, was apparently an attractive personality who drew people to her in droves. She got on especially well with other women. In the capital region, women of the imperial household as well as ordinary laywomen and a great many nuns were constantly seeking her company. Others, who lived further away, wrote volumes of letters to her (unfortunately not extant). Bao-xian, the Regulator of the Nuns' Order, was a "majestic" person, more inclined to intellectual pursuits and administrative activities, it seems, than to close friendships. She was abbess of the Puxian-si as well as Regulator of Nuns for the capital region. When reading her biography, one senses that most people were awed by her austere character and her incredible abilities. She performed her administrative duties with great efficiency and care and directed the nuns' community most successfully. Emperors Wen, Xiao-wu and Ming-di of the Song, who reigned in succession from 424 to 473, treated her with respect and courtesy, giving her gifts and appointing her to high position. Yet, while they may have been persuaded by her religious teaching, she never became their close friend.

Most of the convents were in cities, in contrast to the monasteries which were often located in picturesque mountain settings some distance from urban centers. Monks often lived insulated from secular influences because of where their monasteries were situated, but the nuns were always in the thick of things, especially in Jiankang. This afforded them the opportunity to influence their powerful disciples in court circles, but also left them vulnerable to the secular interests of those same prominent followers, who were too close at hand to be escaped. Because of the abundance of devoted patrons, the nuns' order flourished in the fourth, fifth and sixth centuries. But the nuns were rarely able to lead the secluded lives dedicated to spiritual development which some might have preferred.

Bao-chang's nuns were a very learned group; in this respect, Miao-yin, Bao-xian and Fa-jing were not alone. It is impossible to measure the general level of education of nuns from this elite group, but it is clear that the leaders of the nuns' communities in Jiankang and, earlier, in the northern city of Luoyang were not only thoroughly conversant with the Buddhist classics but with those of secular Chinese literature as well. The learned nuns had many disciples, and they spent much of their time preaching Buddhist scriptures to the general public. They were major contributors to the dissemination of Buddhist ideas in China.

Dao-xing of the Eastern Convent in Luoyang[36] applied herself zealously to learning the sūtras when she was a young novice. By the time of her ordination at the age of 20 she knew the *Lotus* and the *Vimalakīrtinirdeśa* by heart. Her favorite sūtra, however, was the *Perfection of Wisdom in 8,000 Lines.* She was exceptionally gifted at explaining things and moreover got along easily with other people, so she was a very effective teacher. She was, according to Bao-chang, the first of a series of nuns who were marvellous preachers of the sūtras, and she was considered by everyone the greatest teacher in the province.

Dao-yi[37] came from a distinguished family, was married to a rising young official but was widowed at the early age of twenty-two. She immediately became a nun; her famous nephews Hui-yuan and Hui-ji were ordained at about the same time. She was already well educated in secular and religious literature when she became a nun, and was soon known as an impressive expounder of the *Lotus, Vimalakīrti* and the *Perfection of Wisdom in 8,000 Lines.* In 397 she moved to the He-hou convent in Jiankang, for she had heard that new sūtras and discipline texts *(Vinaya)* were being translated there and Buddhism was flourishing. (This was a period of enthusiastic patronage of Buddhism by the court; Miao-yin was at the height of her prestige then.) Dao-yi became a specialist in the *Vinaya;* she died at the age of seventy-eight highly respected by both clergy and laity throughout the Jiankang region.

Both these nuns were masters of the same texts, the *Lotus, Vimalakīrti* and *Perfection of Wisdom in 8,000 Lines,* which are certainly three of the most important Mahāyāna scriptures ever written. Other texts were studied by the BQNC nuns, too—the *Śūraṅgama-sūtra, Perfection of Wisdom in 25,000 Lines* and the *Mahāparinirvāṇa-sūtra* are mentioned. All these, as I have pointed out, are significant for the attitudes they express about women. No text, however, was as favored as the *Lotus,* which was chanted, studied or preached by at least eleven of the sixty-five nuns whose lives are recorded.[38] Other important texts translated for the first time during the fifth century may not yet have been widely known. The *Śrīmālādevī,* for example, is not mentioned until we reach the biography of a nun who lived at the very end of the fifth century, under the Chi Dynasty; the *Avataṃsaka* not until the sixth century.[39]

There is no record of any meditation texts used by the fourth and fifth century nuns, although many of them were indeed famous meditators. Meditation begins to be frequently mentioned by Bao Chang only when he gets to the nuns of the Song Dynasty (420–479). From the *Gao Seng Chuan (Biographies of Eminent Monks)* we know that there was an influx of meditation masters, many from Kashmir, into south China at the end of the Jin and beginning of the Song. Nuns were among their students, and many of the nuns themselves became meditation masters. Fa-bian[40] (active ca. 420–463) studied with the foreign monk Kālayaśas of the Dao-lin monastery and awakened her mind. She also had a connection with the Upper Forest of Contemplation monastery founded near Jiankang by the Kashmiri meditation master Dharmamitra in 435. His teaching lineage was preserved there for some time after his death in 442. Both these foreign masters are known to have taught visionary forms of meditation; among their translations were sūtras on the techniques of visualizing various Buddhas and *bodhisattvas*.[41] Fa-bian in trance, however, is described as stiff like wood and rock, precisely the words used in the Daoist classics, the *Dao-de-jing* and the *Zhuang-zi*, to characterize the Daoist masters' deep trances. Other meditating nuns are also said to have practiced death-like, deep meditation; for example, there was Seng-guo of the Guang-ling convent in Jiankang (active 429–441) who could remain concentrated for a whole day at a time.[42] Exactly what methods these nuns used is not known. The descriptions of trance states may have been borrowed, as conventional literary language, from the Daoist classics; or Daoism, which was an energetically growing religion in the fifth century, may really have had some influence on Buddhist practices. But it is more probable that most nuns used the better-developed Indian and Kashmiri Buddhist techniques of mindfulness of bodily processes and the like, or of visualization of Buddhas and bodhisattvas. It is rather frequently reported that meditating nuns cultivated visions of Buddhas in their paradises.

Those who did excel at meditation might become quite renowned. Jing-cheng[43] of the Bamboo Forest convent and a nun companion practiced meditation in the mountains and were regarded as saints. They were invited by some northern tribespeople to come and live with them. The nuns, not liking the border regions, looked for an excuse to return south. They began to play the glutton and the fool, and the tribespeople were glad to let them go. This episode resembles the kind of tale found frequently in Daoist and later in Chan Buddhist literature of the enlightened master who deliberately behaves eccentrically in order to "cover his traces" so that he can be free to live the religious life without being bothered by worldly people. In this early, pre-Chan Buddhist tale, it is very interesting that two women are the central figures and, like a female Han Shan and Shi-de, they are accompanied by a mysterious tiger who guards their meditation.[44]

These early Buddhist nuns, no matter what their accomplishments, were appreciated for what they themselves had done, for their own worth. Unlike the "Confucian" ideal of feminine conduct, which was expected to be the norm for women of the upper classes at this time, the Buddhist nuns were respected precisely because they were individuals following a path they had chosen, and doing a very good job of it. They were not judged on the basis of their relationship to a father, a husband or a son. The nun An Ling-shou,[45] who lived in north China in the first half of the fourth century, was intelligent and learned, and she spent her days enjoying the study of Buddhist teachings. Her father complained that she should marry, and Shou countered, "I am committed to the religious life, my resolution will not be shaken. Why must I conform to the Three Obediences before I can be thought to behave properly?"[46] Shou and her father then talked with the foreign monk Fo-tu-deng about it, and he reconciled the father to the girl's wishes by assuring him it was her destiny to become a nun and that she would bring profit and honor to her family if she were allowed to do it. After she had been a nun for some years, and had drawn a throng of disciples to her through her brilliant teaching, the Hun ruler of north China was so moved by respect for her that he promoted her father to an important position at court. Thus Shou's biographer has it both ways: because she has lived as a good Buddhist, she proves also to be the most filial of daughters, for rewards pour down upon her family as the result of her own accomplishments. By being a Buddhist, she has neglected neither her family nor the society she lives in, but has really served them both. This is the *bodhisattva* ideal, but it is also the Confucian ideal, albeit realized in an unorthodox manner. If the Chinese were to learn to live with Buddhism, they had to believe that it was in essential harmony with their own most cherished ideals. But as one sees in this case, the Buddhist life really did offer an alternative to the conventional, dependent life of a Chinese woman. It gave women, and men too, a genuine chance to realize their full potential as individual human beings with social consciousness.

V. A Woman's Options in Early Medieval China

The Chinese Buddhist nuns of the BQNC were a highly literate, active, influential group of women. Undoubtedly their characters and their aspirations were molded by many factors, but I believe that one of the most significant influences on them was the image of the forceful female teacher which they found in Buddhist scriptures. Similar models could be discovered outside Buddhist circles, but they were not common.

In early medieval China, a woman's life was normally defined by her role in a family. She was not meant to lead an autonomous existence. Indeed, a woman of the upper classes could not claim an independent place for herself in society; she owed her status entirely to the position of her father, husband or son. During the Han Dynasty (206 B.C.E.–220 C.E.) Confucian scholars had gradually formulated rules to govern the conduct of women; it was the upper classes who showed most interest in the rules. A woman was to marry and her life was to be completely centered on the home where she was to attend to her husband and her in-laws, busy herself with all the household duties and serve the ancestral cult.[47] A girl of the upper classes was not supposed to be given the extensive education in literature, composition, history, mathematics, music and some sciences which was normally provided to boys; she was trained instead to be a support to the family.[48]

Other ideas about the place of women were also current in China at the time; Confucian values did not yet dominate Chinese social thinking so completely or so rigidly as they came to do after about the tenth century. In north China women had far more freedom and responsibility than they had in the south, which may be because of customs introduced by the various Hun, Turkish and Mongol peoples who had settled in the north after the fall of the Han Dynasty.[49] The fourth and fifth centuries were a period of wrenching social and political disorder, and the old Confucian value system had been partially undermined.

Bao Chang presents his nuns as women who were willing to uphold Confucian values, especially chastity and filial piety, while at the same time they were confounding the whole Confucian family structure by abandoning a woman's normal roles for a life of celibacy and study. Many of the nuns in the Jin and Song sections of the BQNC came from upper class families, where Confucian traditions were most pervasive; we know that eight out of forty-five nuns were definitely from the upper classes and probably several others were as well, perhaps half of the total of forty-five. More than half—about twenty-six—were certainly literate for they read sūtras and lectured on Buddhist doctrine, but of these only five are definitely said to have been educated in the Confucian classics. Sixteen of the nuns came from the north and may have been influenced by non-Chinese social ideas as well as by the Buddhist doctrines which they allowed to pattern their lives.

The literate nuns became public figures, prominent in the society of their time and famous for their teaching. Some were people of outstanding intellect. As nuns they could live actively outside the avenues usually open to women and they could devote themselves to study and to contemplation. To be sure, there were educated women in those days even inside some Confucian families, and some were important writers.[50] On the fringes of Confucian society there were also women alchemists who had mastered a special kind of science; many of them were Daoists.[51] There were also prostitutes who, although they may have been sold into the profession, were able to live lives of relative freedom and were often allowed to study poetry, composition and music. Some became famous poets.[52] Thus, life in a Buddhist convent was not the only choice open to an intelligent woman who wished to devote her energies to study, teaching and writing, but it was certainly one of the most attractive and secure alternatives. And for the woman who had a genuine religious vocation and a taste for public life besides, it was unquestionably the best option.[53]

VI. Nuns and Images of Women in Buddhist Literature

According to the BQNC, early Chinese Buddhist nuns read only a few sūtras. It must be remembered, however, that information about the nuns of this period is definitely not complete. I would like to believe that they did read some of the lovely short texts about wise women even if they did not lecture on them; unfortunately we shall probably never know. It is true, however, that Chinese Buddhists, when they finally had before them Chinese translations of the mountains of religious texts Indian Buddhists had produced, realized it would be impossible to deal with them all. After struggling for a while with the mind-boggling assortment of doctrines, interpretations and claims in the whole body of Buddhist scriptures, they turned up their noses at all but the most exciting, and left the rest to sink into quiet oblivion. This is certainly ironic, since they had once hungered so to have all Buddhist literature at their command. When they came around to creating their own, very Chinese, schools of Buddhism in the sixth, seventh and eighth centuries, they based them on just a few texts, the very ones Chinese Buddhists had first come to know and to venerate: the *Lotus*, the *Pure Land sūtra*s, the *Perfection of Wisdom*, the *Avataṃsaka*.

The sūtras which the nuns and other Buddhists definitely did read conveyed images of women which are, I think, positive and exhilarating. The women in the *Vimalakīrtinirdeśa* and other sūtras are wise and witty and in no sense inferior to men; they are articulate mistresses of Buddhist doctrine who are peerless in debate and in subtle argument; they are able and compassionate teachers. And they are so close to Buddhahood that they can *play* with words, with ideas, with prejudices and preconceptions, as though they were great magicians.

The nuns' biographies never tell us that a particular nun was especially inspired by an image of a woman or an idea about women which she encountered in a Buddhist scripture. But compare the nuns' actual accomplishments with the sūtras' tales about women: the nuns studied and taught and debated, they were leaders among clerics and laity, they were admired for their virtue and their dedication to religion, they compassionately helped those in need and they were themselves models for other women to emulate. The best of the nuns were themselves like incarnations of the wise women of the Buddhist *sūtra*s. The influence seems to me unmistakable.

In Buddhist sūtras the real ideal is, of course, the *bodhisattva* who is actually asexual, neither male nor female. In the best Buddhist sūtras, the question "could a woman do that?" is never raised, for the authors themselves were not thinking in a sexist way. They were thinking about the bodhisattva ideal, which embraces both genders.[54]

Whatever they read, and however they understood the texts, the nuns passed on their understanding to the Buddhist public, for they were their teachers. The personal self-confidence and dignity they obviously manifested won them the respect of great numbers of people. These qualities left a lasting impression on those who knew them. The nuns' strength of character and personal confidence, forged in the fires of hard practice and deep contemplation, were communicated to the people they taught. The veneration the people felt for the nuns was inspired by the lives these women led. Presumably it was buttressed, too, by the stories they heard from the nuns about wise women in the Buddhist scriptures.

The Buddhist lay public read and listened to some sūtras, but they were certainly not exposed to as many as the monks and nuns were. Many monks, Chinese and foreign, worked on the translation teams which produced the Chinese versions of all sorts of texts. Chinese monks were influenced by the egalitarian ideas of the great Mahāyāna scriptures, for a century or two later the founders and shapers of the Chinese *Tiantai* school proclaimed unequivocally that women could become Buddhas; and the masters of the *Chan* school saw no difference between male and female *bodhisattva*-teachers.[55]

Foreign monks were an important and influential group in Chinese society of the fourth and fifth centuries. The foreign monks who transmitted all the various Buddhist texts to the Chinese had already absorbed their attitudes. But they, unlike the impatient Chinese, had mastered many texts. They must have been pulled in opposing directions, for or against equality, depending on which Indian school's texts they were reading. Some of these missionaries, like Kumārajīva and Dharmamitra, Buddhabhadra and Dharmakṣema, transmitted some texts which were hostile to women, and also some which championed them. And when one reads their biographies, one finds them teaching and helping both men and women with great kindness and betraying none of the monkish misogyny which has too often been attributed to all clerics. Guṇavarman, who translated the *Bodhisattvabhūmi*, a text which argues that women are inherently weak in intellect and virtue, was instrumental in advising and preparing for ordination a group of Chinese nuns—and in the very same year he was working on the *Bodhisattvabhūmi*. These actions are not contradictory, of course, for a monk could easily be a teacher to a woman without believing her to be the full equal of a man. It is worth pointing out, however, that the foreign monks seem to have tried conscientiously to behave like *bodhisattva*s themselves, that is, like beings who do not discriminate between male and female.

VII. The Nuns' Legacy

For the nuns of the BQNC, the fourth and fifth centuries sound like a veritable golden age. They were women living independent lives which they had chosen, appreciated for what they had accomplished, respected and rewarded for their intellectual excellence and their service to society, influential, taken seriously. It was a very good time for them, without a doubt, and they did a great many things. After examining the surviving Buddhist records from the fourth/fifth centuries one would have to conclude, nonetheless, that the nuns were oddly absent when all the really important work was being done. The nuns appear not to have written much compared to the monks; so far as we know they did not work on the great translation projects which occupied so many Chinese and foreign monks; they never became real leaders of the whole Buddhist community of nuns, monks and laity.[56] The information we have about the nuns and about the Buddhist community as a whole is far from complete, however. Perhaps the nuns did more than we know. The BQNC does mention that some nuns were prolific writers; since no works ascribed to them are now known we must assume that their compositions have perished —or that some anonymous works of the period preserved in the Buddhist canon are actually theirs! And certainly we know that the nuns at Jiankang performed tasks which were of enormous and lasting importance. *They* were the great transmitters of the doctrine to large segments of southern Chinese society, and their interpretation of scripture has inevitably helped form Chinese comprehension of Buddhist ideas.

The records suggest also that the nuns did not aid in the birth of the indigenous Chinese schools of Buddhism in the sixth century, and this may be true since the nuns' influence then seems to have been restricted mostly to the Jiankang area. Jiankang was the southern capital, a splendid metropolis and an important Buddhist intellectual center, but the new Chinese Buddhist schools were conceived in places of solitude, far from the turmoil of the cities. In Jiankang the nuns were busy answering the demands of their powerful patrons, and perhaps they hadn't the opportunity the monks had to quietly ponder the Buddha's teachings. For it was the monks, secluded from interfering patrons in their mountain retreats, who shaped the direction Buddhism was to take in China: it was they who founded the new Chinese Buddhist schools.

Although the nuns were enthusiastically sought out and highly respected for a few generations, in a few special places, it was finally the monks who gained and held the loyalty of the majority of Buddhists. The *Vinaya* rules give the monks authority over nuns, and in China as elsewhere the monks kept the real power in their own hands. The flowering of the Buddhist nuns' order in the fourth and fifth centuries in China was brilliant but brief. After the sixth century, Buddhist women as a *group* were never of such consequence again. The nuns' order flourished while Buddhism was still in the process of finding its place in China. By the late sixth century, the monks had consolidated their power and were leading Buddhism in the direction they wished it to travel. The nuns' order has survived, to be sure, but its glory is in the past.

Notes

1. The family of Fa Hu (Sanskrit Dharmarakṣa) was one of Yue-zhi stock from Central Asia, but they had settled at Dunhuang, on the northwesternmost edge of Chinese territory, a few generations before Fa Hu's birth. Fa Hu himself was thoroughly sinicized, well educated in the Confucian classics as well as Buddhist scriptures, and fluent in Chinese and several other languages. See his biography in *Gao Seng Chuan* (GSC), T2059, pp. 326.c.2–327.a.12. (T = *Taishō Shinshu Daizōkyō* edition of Chinese Buddhist Canon.)

2. E. Zürcher, *The Buddhist Conquest of China* (Leiden: E.J. Brill, 1972), 1:61–63.

3. It is not known exactly which countries Fa Hu himself visited, but it is known that in the late third century there were direct contacts between the Jin court and the important Central Asian states of Khotan, Kučā, Shan-shan, Qarašāhr and Ferghana. It is probable that Fa Hu visited some or all of these countries. Possibly he even reached India itself during his extensive travels. See Zürcher, *Buddhist Conquest*, 1:57–70; GSC, T2059, pp. 326.c.2–327.a.12.

4. Mahāyāna Buddhism, the "Great Vehicle," is one of the three major branches of Buddhism, the others being Hīnayāna, the "Small Vehicle," and Vajrayāna, the "Diamond Vehicle." Each of the three great branches was subdivided into schools. The Hīnayāna schools were the oldest and the Mahāyāna was essentially a reformation movement against them, an effort to "get back to the basics" of what Gautama the Buddha *really* taught. The Mahāyāna movement emerged perhaps in the first century B.C.E. Although many Hīnayāna monks did go to China as missionaries, and took their schools' texts with them, it was primarily Mahāyāna literature and Mahāyāna thought which were embraced by the Chinese. China, and the Far Eastern countries which learned of Buddhism through China, have remained Mahāyāna Buddhist until the present day. Vajrayāna Buddhism, often called Tantric Buddhism, is a later development out of the Mahāyāna. It fully accepts Mahāyāna doctrines while using some distinctive meditation practices of its own. It has been influential in China and Japan, but less so than the Mahāyāna itself.

5. Fa-xian was not the first Chinese monk to travel to the west, but he is one of the most famous, for his account of his travels has survived and has been published in an English edition. See J. Legge, *A Record of Buddhistic Kingdoms* (Oxford: The Clarendon Press, 1886; reprint ed., New York: Paragon Book Reprint Corp. and Dover Publishing, 1965). Fa-xian left China for India in 399 and returned in 414. He was past sixty when he set out on his extraordinary adventure!

6. The Western Jin Dynasty, which had briefly brought all China together once again under a unified rule, collapsed in 317 and China remained fragmented in a myriad of short-lived kingdoms for almost 300 years thereafter. The north was ruled by a host of non-Chinese rulers, Huns (Xiung-nu), Tibetans and other tribes from the Mongolian plains. These "barbarian" rulers were eager to keep the doors open to the west, which included their own homelands. Many of these "barbarian" kings were Buddhists themselves, and looked with favor on the Buddhist travellers. Southern China was ruled by a succession of native Chinese dynasties, beginning with the Eastern Jin in 317 with its capital at Jiankang (Nanjing). Many of the Chinese intelligentsia fled south in the wake of the Hun invasions. Needless to say, the cultures of north and south China differed considerably from each other during these centuries of chaos, but after 385 and especially in the first decades of the fifth century, people who wished to could travel relatively freely between north and south. Buddhists especially seem to have taken advantage of this freedom of movement, and travelled from Buddhist center to Buddhist center, spreading ideas.

7. In the very early collections of sūtras called the *Nikāyas* (in Pāli) or the *Āgamas* (in Sanskrit and Chinese), there are a few sūtras which describe early nuns preaching, or having discussions with the Buddha or some other prominent person. There are also occasional portraits of the lives of anonymous laywomen. For the Pāli versions of some of these see: *Saṃyutta Nikāya*, vol. 4, ed. Leon Feer (1894; reprint ed., London: Luzac and Co., for the Pali Text Society, 1960), 374–80; *Majjhima Nikāya*, vol. 1, ed. V. Trenckner (1888; reprint ed., London: Luzac and Co., for the Pali Text Society, 1964), 299–305; *Anguttara Nikāya*, vol. 3, ed. E. Hardy (1897; reprint ed., London: Luzac and Co., for the Pali Text Society, 1958), 36–37. The only female contemporary of the Buddha who *was* well known to the Chinese as early as c. 300 C.E. was Mahāprajāpatī, the aunt and step-mother of Gautama the Buddha who became the first Buddhist nun. One sūtra about her, T144, was translated before 307 C.E.; another, T1478, was translated between 397–439. Whether or not Mahāprajāpatī actually was a historical figure cannot be discussed here. But see A. Bareau, "La Jeunesse du Buddha dans les *Sūtrapiṭaka* et les *Vinayapiṭaka* anciens," *Bulletin de l'École Française d'Extrême-Orient* 61 (1974):199–274; and, "Un personnage bien mysterieux: l'epouse du Buddha," in *Indological and Buddhist Studies, Volume in Honor of Professor J.E.W. de Jong on his 60th Birthday*, ed. L. Hercus et al (Canberra: Faculty of Asian Studies, 1982), pp. 31–59. The *Āgamas* were translated into Chinese in their entirety between 384 and 443: T26, *Madhyamāgama* and T125, *Ekottarāgama*, begun by Dharmanandin in 384 and reworked or retranslated by Samghadeva in 397–98 (see P. Demiéville, "La *Yogācārabhūmi* de Saṅgharakṣa," *Bulletin de l'École Française d'Extrême-Orient* 44 (1947–50):373–74 and note 1; T1, *Dīrghāgama*, translated by Buddhayaśas and Zhu Fo-nian in 413; T99. *Saṃyuktāgama* translated by Gunabhadra between 435–443.

8. All four of these texts were translated by Fa Hu between 286 and 308. His translation of the *Lotus*, T265, was the first made in China and was widely read, but it was Zhi Qian's translation of the *Vimalakīrtinirdeśa* which was used. It had been completed between 223 and 228 C.E. in Jiankang: T474. *Vimaladattāparipṛcchā* and *Sumati-sūtra* are two of the less well known sūtras with women as protagonists, mentioned above. Unlike the *Lotus* and *Vimalakīrti*, the sole content of each of these sūtras is the debate between the heroine and male spokesmen for certain Buddhist views. Fa Hu's translations are T338 and T334, respectively.

9. In a very early text in the Pāli *Saṃyutta Nikāya*, for example, one reads:

> Whoever has such a carriage, whether a woman or a man,
> Shall indeed, by means of that carriage,
> Come to *Nirvāṇa*.
> (*Saṃyutta Nikaya*, 1:33)

10. The arguments about whether a woman could become a Buddha, and why, and how, are fairly complicated and cannot be detailed here. The reader is referred to the following: N. Schuster, "Changing the Female Body: Wise Women and the *Bodhisattva* Career in Some *Mahāratnakūṭasūtras*," *Journal of*

the International Association of Buddhist Studies (hereafter *JIABS*) 4 (1981):24–69; Y. Kajiyama, "Women in Buddhism," *The Eastern Buddhist* (new series) 15 (1982):53–70; D. Paul, *Women in Buddhism, Images of the Feminine in Mahāyāna Tradition* (Berkeley: Asian Humanities Press, 1979), pp. 166ff.

11. The *Vimalakīrtinirdeśa* teaches the doctrine of emptiness *(śūnyatā)* originally expounded in the *Perfection of Wisdom* scriptures: what is real is beyond definition, for everything exists dependent on everything else. Thus nothing can be defined by itself, for nothing has a unique essence which distinguishes it from everything else. Translations are available of the delightful *Vimalakīrtinirdeśa*, which is one of the literary and philosophical masterpieces of Buddhist literature: R. A. F. Thurman, *The Holy Teaching of Vimalakīrti* (University Park, PA: Pennsylvania State University Press, 1976); E. Lamotte, trans., *L'Enseignement de Vimalakīrti (Vimalakīrtinirdeśa)*, Université de Louvain, Institut Orientaliste, Bibliothèque de *Muséon*, vol. 51 (Louvain: Publications Universitaires, 1962). The change of sex episode is in "The Goddess" chapter.

12. The *Lotus'* version of the change of sex motif was perhaps the first to appear in Buddhist literature, and it lacks the finesse and clarity of the *Vimalakīrtinirdeśa* incident. In the *Lotus* a young girl changes in a moment from an unenlightened female to a perfected male Buddha, and does it by magic. Modern Chinese Buddhist nuns are quite familiar with the *Lotus*, and a group of them in Taiwan recently told an American researcher that the essential point of the transformation passage is that the difference between Buddhahood and delusion is merely a single moment of right thought and the apparent sex of the enlightened one is irrelevant! See M. Levering, "The Dragon Girl and the Abbess of Mo-shan: Gender and Status in the Chan Buddhist Tradition," *JIABS* 5 (1982):22–24. For an English translation of Kumārajīva's fifth-century version of the *Lotus Sūtra*, see L. Hurvitz, *Scripture of the Lotus Blossom of the Fine Dharma* (New York: Columbia University Press, 1976). The sex-change incident is on pp. 201 and 379.

13. This must remain a tentative conclusion for now since I have not been able to examine *all* early translations of texts which have something to say about women. There are many. However, frankly misogynist statements do seem to be rare in texts circulated in China before the fifth century. For another opinion, see Paul, *Women in Buddhism*, Part I, "Traditional Views of Women."

14. T353. On the *Śrīmālā*, see Paul, *Women in Buddhism*, pp. 281ff. The sūtra has been translated into English: D. Paul, *The Buddhist Feminine Ideal* (Missoula: Scholars Press, 1980); A. and H. Wayman, *The Lion's Roar of Queen Śrīmālā* (New York: Columbia University Press, 1974).

15. The *Gaṇḍavyūha* is a section of the huge *Avataṃsaka Sūtra (Flower Garland Scripture)*. The entire *Avataṃsaka* was translated by Buddhabhadra, only the *Gaṇḍavyūha* section by Sheng-jian. By the sixth century, the *Avataṃsaka* had taken its place beside the *Lotus, Perfection of Wisdom, Vimalakīrti*, and the *Sukhāvatī (Pure Land) Sūtra* as one of the best known and most influential sūtras in Chinese Buddhism, and it remains so even at the present day. On the

women of the *Gaṇḍavyūha*, see Paul, *Women in Buddhism*, pp. 94–105 and 134–65. On the *Gaṇḍavyūha* in China, see Jan Fontein, *The Pilgrimage of Sudhana* (The Hague: Mouton, 1968).

16. Two interesting texts, which again play with the motif of changing sex, are both commonly known as *Strīvivartavyākaraṇā-sūtra (Scripture of the Prediction of Buddhahood of the Woman Who Changes)*. T564 was translated by the Kashmiri meditation master Dharmamitra between 424 and 441, T566 by another Kashmiri, Dharmayaśas, in 415. T564 is one of the few Buddhist sūtras I know which speaks with genuine sympathy of the pains and injustices endured by real women in their ordinary lives:

> During the nine months that a child is carried within the body, one's sufferings are many. And at the time of giving birth, the body endures great pain and anguish and life itself is threatened . . . Because of other's commands . . . she must . . . pound herbs and hull rice, cook and grind . . . card and spin . . . and do all sorts of unpleasant work without measure . . . A woman must suffer with this body . . . (T564, p. 919.b.5–21)

On T564, see N. Schuster, "Yoga Master Dharmamitra and Clerical Misogyny in Fifth Century Buddhism," forthcoming in *The Tibet Journal* 9 (1984). A few other works translated about this time should be cited for their somewhat more positive than negative attitudes toward women: *Suvarṇabhāsa-sūtra* (T663) and *Mahāmegha-sūtra* (T387), both translated by the Indian Mahāyāna teacher Dharmakṣema between 414 and 426; *Mahāparinirvāṇa-sūtra*, translated also by Dharmakṣema, 414 to 421 (T374) and again by the Chinese pilgrim Faxian with the help of Buddhabhadra in either 410–11 or 417–18. In addition, the *Da-zhi-du-lun*, T1509, Kumārajīva's stupendous translation of the encyclopedic commentary on the *Perfection of Wisdom in 25,000 Lines*, clearly tries to mute the anti-feminine attitude often found in Buddhist scholastic literature of this kind. Kumārajīva worked on his translation from 402 to 406. On the other hand, Kumārajīva's other great translation of a Buddhist commentary, the *Shi-zhu-pi-po-sha-lun*, T1521, commentary on the *Daśabhūmika-sūtra*, is a mixed offering, containing both pro- and anti-feminine passages. It was completed sometime between 402 and 412. The *Daśabhūmika-sūtra* itself had been translated by Fa Hu in 297 (T285) and was translated again by Kumārajīva between 402–409 (T286). The sūtra describes in detail the ten stages in a *bodhisattva*'s career and says that a *bodhisattva* cannot remain a woman after the seventh stage. This text had some influence in monastic communities at least.

17. Saṃghabhadra and Saṃghadeva arrived just after 380, Puṇyatara, Vimalakṣas, Buddhayaśas and Dharmayaśas before 410, Buddhajīva, Guṇavarman and Dharmamitra in the 420s. Buddhabhadra, although a native of India, lived and studied for several years in Kashmir and brought Kashmiri-style Buddhism with him to China when he arrived in 406. Kumārajīva, who was born in Kuča and arrived in China in 402, studied for a time in Kashmir and later worked with Kashmiri masters in China. The Chinese monks Zhi-

yan and Bao-yun also studied in Kashmir as did the Chinese lay-devotee Ju-qu Jing-sheng. For biographies of all of these, see GSC, T2059, *juan* 2 and 3.

18. Demiéville, "La *Yogācārabhūmi* de Saṅgharakṣa," *Bulletin* 44 (1947–50):339–436, especially 362, note 1.

19. Biography in GSC, pp. 330.a.11–333.a.12. For an English summary of his life, see K. Ch'en, *Buddhism in China, A Historical Survey* (Princeton: Princeton University Press, 1964), pp. 81–83. On the meditation manuals translated by Kumārajīva, see *Chu-san-zang-ji-ji*, T2145, pp. 11.a, 14.c, 75.b, 101.b.27; and *Kai-yuan-shi-jiao-lu*, T2154, pp. 513,a., 664.c.

20. T615, p. 286.a.29-b.17.

21. Demiéville, "La *Yogācārabhūmi* de Saṅgharakṣa ," *Bulletin* 44 (1947–50): 361 and note 1, and Schuster, "Yoga Master Dharmamitra . . ." forthcoming in *Tibet Journal* 9 (1984). Perhaps more influential, at least in some Chinese monastic communities, was the *Bodhisattvabhūmi* written by the Indian *Yogācāra* master Asaṅga which says that every woman is by nature a person of many impurities and poor understanding, and therefore a *bodhisattva* must, at a certain point early in his career, cease to be reborn as a female. This is a fourth century repetition of the much older notion referred to earlier in this essay, and it certainly reflects a conservative attitude not shared by all Buddhists. For the reference see *Bodhisattvabhūmi*, ed. N. Dutt (Patna: Jayaswal Research Institute, 1966), p. 66. The *Bodhisattvabhūmi* was translated into Chinese by Dharmakṣema from India, between 414–426 (T1581) and by Guṇavarman of Kashmir in 431 (T1582). Similarly influential in some monastic communities in China were *Vinaya* texts, books of monastic rules which also contain stories about the foundation of the orders of monks and nuns. At least one of the *Vinaya*s, that of the Mahīśāsaka school which was translated into Chinese in 423 by Buddhajīva of Kashmir, contains the old charge that a woman cannot become a Buddha. So, too, do a few sūtras from the *Āgama*s translated about this time: see note 7 above. See also Kajiyama, "Women in Buddhism," *The Eastern Buddhist* (new series) 15 (1982):55–58. Thus, in some of the literature *first translated* into Chinese in the fourth/fifth centuries we come full circle *back* to the old ideas vanquished already in more forward-looking Mahāyāna sūtras such as the *Lotus, Vimalakīrti, Śrīmālādevī* and many others. The old ideas did not die.

22. GSC, p. 329.b.29–c.2.

23. *Bi-qiu-ni-chuan* (BQNC) T2063, p. 935.c.28; 936.a.23. See Zürcher, *Buddhist Conquest*, 1:109–10.

24. Dharmamitra's biography in GSC, p. 343.a.2–3.

25. BQNC, p. 940.b.11–14.

26. BQNC, p. 940.b.9–11.

27. BQNC, p. 938.b.16–18.

28. Zürcher, *Buddhist Conquest*, 1:159.

29. BQNC was composed by the monk Bao-chang about 516 C.E. The text has been translated into English: Jung-hsi Li, *Biographies of Buddhist Nuns, Pi-*

ch'iu-ni-ch'uan of Pao-chang (Osaka: Tohokai, 1981); K. A. A. Cissell, "The Pi-ch'iu-ni-ch'uan, Biographies of Famous Chinese Nuns from 317–516 C.E." (Ph.D. diss., University of Wisconsin, Madison, 1972).

30. The nuns' order was established with the help of foreign monks and a group of nuns from Śrī Laṅkā who thus established the Chinese order of nuns as the direct continuation of the Indian and Śrī Laṅkan order. The order of monks had been established in China much earlier. Yan Fo-tiao, who was ordained before 181 C.E., was the first known Chinese monk: *Chu-san-zang-ji-ji*, T2145, pp. 46.c.3, 50.a.6, 96.a.16; GSC, p. 324.c.4.

31. Cissell, "Biographies of Famous Chinese Nuns," p. 48. *The Gao Seng Chuan, Lives of Eminent Monks*, composed by Hui-Jiao about 530, is also a selective work. It includes monks renowned for various accomplishments and does not recount the lives of ordinary simple monks. But it is a *much* larger work than the BQNC and therefore provides more information about how the monks spent their time than we can extract about the nuns from Bao-chang's work. This is of course a vivid demonstration of the fact that men's activities were given far more attention than were women's, even within a Buddhist community whose doctrines were essentially egalitarian.

32. The nuns' and the monks' political influence was sometimes thought scandalous. In 389 critics accused them of forming a clique with some of the lesser women at court and trying to sway political events: Zürcher, *Buddhist Conquest*, 1:153.

33. Li, *Biographies*, p. 10. Also Zürcher, *Buddhist Conquest*, 1:105–10. Associations with monks were also eagerly pursued by the Chinese upper classes in the fourth/fifth centuries, and they were established as familiars in the palace and in noble homes before the nuns were; Zürcher, *Buddhist Conquest*, 1:81–179. Nonetheless, the special prominence of nuns at the southern court is unmistakable.

34. Biography in BQNC, pp. 936.c.19–937a.6. Cissell, "Biographies of Famous Chinese Nuns," pp. 166–69; Li, *Biographies*, pp. 45–47; Zürcher, *Buddhist Conquest*, 1:153–54.

35. Biographies in BQNC, pp. 941.a.8–b.12. Cissell, "Biographies of Famous Chinese Nuns," pp. 90 and 208–12; Li, *Biographies*, pp. 80–83.

36. BQNC, p. 936.a.27–b.10; Cissell, "Biographies of Famous Chinese Nuns," pp. 159–61; Li, *Biographies*, pp. 40–41. Dao-xing is one of the few nuns in the BQNC who in the fourth century remained at her convent in the north despite the social and political chaos which overwhelmed the land at frequent intervals. Her precise dates are not given; she was active in the latter part of the fourth century. Luoyang was one of the two ancient capitals of northern China, an older city than Jiankang. It was destroyed by Xiung-nu (Hun) armies in 311 and remained a spoil of war throughout the century as invaders and dynasties came and went.

37. BQNC, p. 937.a.7–17; Cissell, "Biographies of Famous Chinese Nuns," pp. 169–70; Li, *Biographies*, pp. 47–48. Dao-yi's nephew, Hui-yuan, was one of the most famous monks of the fourth century. He founded a monastery on

Mt. Lu, in the middle Yangzi region, far from Jiankang. It became a famous center of Buddhist learning, translation activity and meditation practice during Hui-yuan's lifetime.

38. This figure probably does not give an accurate picture of how intensively the *Lotus* was studied, or the other sūtras for that matter. We do not have complete information on all the sūtras which were known to the nuns. Bao-chang often says, in the biographies, that such and such a nun was very learned in Buddhist scriptures, without naming which texts she knew. Undoubtedly no information was available to him in most cases for nuns who died long before his birth. He compiled his information from epitaph eulogies, and interviewed people who knew the traditions connected with the nuns, sometimes even people who had known the women personally. Often the information gleaned was spotty. BQNC, p. 934.b.26–27, Bao-chang's introduction to the Biographies. It should be observed also that some of the nuns are said to have *chanted* the *Lotus*, especially the Guan-yin chapter of the *Lotus*. Even today rapid chanting of sections of the *Lotus* as part of the morning and evening liturgies in Buddhist monasteries and convents is practiced. The monks and nuns in many cases learn the passages by rote, and may or may not have real understanding of what they are chanting. The chanting itself is a meritorious religious act. This may have been the case with some of the nuns in the BQNC; it is impossible to be sure.

39. BQNC, p. 942.c.11; 947.a.11.

40. BQNC, p. 940.b.22–c.9; Cissell, "Biographies of Famous Chinese Nuns," pp. 203–05; Li, *Biographies*, pp. 76–77.

41. The enigmatic western missionary, Kālayaśas, is credited with the translation of the *Sūtra on the Meditation on Amitāyur-Buddha*, T365, translated between 424 and 442 in the Jiankang region. Dharmamitra, working at exactly the same time and in the same area, translated the *Sūtras on the Meditation on Ākāśagarbha-bodhisattva* and on *Samantabhadra-bodhisattva*, T409 and T277. These three are all Mahāyāna visualization sūtras. Dharmamitra also translated a text called the *Summary Method of Using the Sūtra on the Five Doors*, T619; this text teaches classical Buddhist mindfulness exercises, etc.—it is an essentially Hīnayāna work with some Mahāyāna additions.

42. BQNC, pp. 939.c.6–940.a.3; Cissell, "Biographies of Famous Chinese Nuns," pp. 194–97; Li, *Biographies*, pp. 68–70.

43. BQNC, p. 940.a.4–18; Cissell, "Biographies of Famous Chinese Nuns," pp. 197–99; Li, *Biographies*, pp. 71–72. The Bamboo Forest convent was one of the few establishments for nuns which was located in the mountains, not in a city.

44. Han Shan and Shi-de were two Buddhist eccentrics of the Tang Dynasty (late eighth-early ninth centuries) who looked to the world like two fools but were really enlightened *bodhisattva*s. Their sometime companion, Feng-gan, was often accompanied by a tame tiger; the two of them were also hidden masters. See Cyril Birch, ed., *Anthology of Chinese Literature* (New York: Grove Press, 1965), 1:194–96 for the story. As can be seen from this bi-

ography, the BQNC incorporates wonders and mythical elements in some of the records. It is hagiography, rather than what Westerners think of as biography.

45. BQNC, p. 935.a.6–25; Cissell, "Biographies of Famous Chinese Nuns," pp. 143–46; Li, *Biographies*, pp. 28–31.

46. *San-cong* is usually interpreted as a woman's obedience to the *wishes* of her father before she marries, her husband after, and her son in her old age. The expression actually has a somewhat different meaning, according to Marina Sung, "The Chinese *Lieh-nü* Tradition," in *Women in China*, ed. R. Guisso and S. Johanneson (Youngstown, N.Y.: Philo Press, 1981), p. 69, note 30. It really means a woman must be contented with the social rank of father, husband and son, for she has none independently. This is not as rankling as the notion of obedience to the commands of males, but it still means that a proper woman in ancient China was a dependent person, quite incapable legally and morally of existing on her own. An Ling-shou was arguing for the right to do just that. It is interesting to note that a Buddhist sūtra translated into Chinese during the period under discussion in this essay (but a hundred years after An Ling-shou's argument with her father) addresses a similar question. The *Strīvivartavyākaraṇā–sūtra* T564, translated by Dharmamitra in 424 or 441, asserts that a married woman who has genuinely committed herself to the religious life need not ask her husband for permission before becoming a nun. This was contrary to common practice in India at the time, too. There was a touch of radicalism in Buddhism after all. See T564, p. 920.a.1–16.

47. R. W. Guisso, "Thunder Over the Lake: the Five Classics and the Perception of Woman in Early China," in *Women in China*, Guisso and Johannesen, pp. 47–61; Sung, "Chinese *Lieh-nü* Tradition," pp. 63–74.

48. Guisso, "Thunder," p. 58; Teng Ssu-yü, *Yen Chih-t'ui, Family Instructions for the Yen Clan (Yen-shih chia-hsün)* (Leiden: E. J. Brill, 1968), pp. 18–20.

49. Teng, *Yen Chih-t'ui*, p. 19.

50. Sung, "Chinese *Lieh-nü* Tradition," pp. 70–71, 73.

51. J. Needham, *Science and Civilization in China*, vol. 5, part 3 (Cambridge: Cambridge University Press, 1974), pp. 37–39; J. R. Ware, *Alchemy, Medicine, Religion in the China of A.D. 320: the Nei P'ien of Ko Hung (Pao-p'u-tzu)* (Cambridge, Mass.: M. I. T. Press, 1966), pp. 264–65; M. Strickmann, "On the Alchemy of T'ao Hung-ching," in *Facets of Taoism*, ed. H. Welch and A. Seidel (New Haven and London: Yale University Press, 1979), pp. 164–92.

52. Sung, "Chinese *Lieh-nü* Tradition," pp. 72–73.

53. There were women who were prominent in Daoist circles at this period, and there were also many female shamans who were leaders of various popular cults. Neither Daoists nor Buddhists were friendly to the popular cults, and certainly the Confucianists were not. Female shamans have been common in China from the beginning of historical times until recently. They usually belonged to families of shamans. Such women were often of the lower classes, were not literate and lived in villages away from the great cities; a few had close connections with Daoism. R. A. Stein, "Religious Taoism and Pop-

ular Religion from the Second to Seventh Centuries," in *Facets of Taoism*, Welch and Seidel, pp. 54–81; L. Thompson, *The Chinese Way in Religion* (Encino, California: Dickenson Publishing Co., 1973), pp. 36–38.

54. In the *Perfection of Wisdom in 8,000 Lines*, the metaphors used to describe the *bodhisattva* show that s/he incorporates both male and female characteristics: the *bodhisattva* on the verge of enlightenment is like a pregnant woman about to give birth; the *bodhisattva* who has renounced personal happiness is like a mother caring for her only child without becoming exhausted; the *bodhisattva* pondering the perfection of wisdom is like a lover preoccupied with thoughts about the woman he is to meet who has not yet arrived. See E. Conze, *The Perfection of Wisdom in 8,000 Lines* (Bolinas: Four Seasons Foundation, 1973); J. Macy, "Perfection of Wisdom: Mother of All Buddhas," in *Beyond Androcentrism*, ed. R. Gross (Missoula: Scholars Press, 1977).

55. Zhi-yi founded the *Tiantai* school in the sixth century, in the mountainous area southeast of Nanjing. His commentaries on the *Lotus Sūtra* assert that women can be Buddhas. See Paul, *Women in Buddhism*, p. 282. The *Chan* school appeared first in north China in the sixth century near Luoyang. Not many women are encountered in *Chan* literature, but those who are, are the full equals of men. See Levering, "The Dragon Girl . . . ," *JIABS* 5 (1982): 27–30, the story of the Abbess of Mo-shan.

56. The Chinese Buddhist nuns of the early medieval period seem to have enjoyed a degree of power and influence far beyond any that Indian Buddhist nuns ever experienced. But in China too the golden age did not last. For further discussions of the impact of Buddhism and of the nuns as examples on the lives of Chinese women, see K. A. Tsai, "The Chinese Buddhist Monastic Order for Women: The First Two Centuries," in *Women in China*, Guisso and Johannesen, pp. 1–20; N. Schuster, " Women in Buddhism" in *Women in World Religions*, ed. Arvind Sharma (St. Lucia: University of Queensland Press) (forthcoming).

PART II

Social Transformation, the Role of Women and Traditional Religious Institutions

Chapter Six

The Magdalen: Reflections on the Image of the Saint and Sinner in Christian Art

Jane Dillenberger

Who was Mary Magdalen? Two contemporary theologians provide contrasting interpretations: the first dubs her "sinner" and "bride," and writes,

> The theme of the repentant harlot in love with Christ and become his bride was given a new dimension on account of a page of the Gospel and a happy historical error: The Gospel text in question is the moving pericope of Saint Luke, chapter 7, verses 36–50. We read there how Jesus, a guest of the Pharisee Simon, is visited by a woman who is a notorious sinner in the Town. . . . She weeps and pours out perfume on the feet of the Lord. The Pharisee reproaches Jesus for allowing her to do this. But the Master defends her, forgives her, and praises her. She is not named, but Latin tradition, as a result of a confusion in texts and names, identifies her with Mary of Magdala, out of whom Jesus cast seven demons (Luke 8:2), and with Mary, the sister of Martha and Lazarus (John

> 11:4–43). In this way, the sinner converted in the house of Simon became Mary Magdalen, and all that is said about the other two Marys is attributed to her. This is indeed a happy mistake![1]

Another theologian, Elisabeth Moltmann-Wendel, considers the conflation of these texts "as the greatest historical falsification of the West." She writes that

> The portrait of the Magdalene was constructed by men, and served to kindle male fantasies . . . .Anyone who loves the biblical Mary Magdalene and compares her with the "Christian" Mary Magdalene, must get very angry. . . .At the expense of women a provocative imaginary picture—scintillating, moving and dangerous—had been created by the patriarchal church.[2]

Wendel rejects the traditional identification and insists on resurrecting the true Mary of Magdala, who suffered from a serious mental illness, became the leader and spokesperson of the women about Jesus, encountered the risen Jesus, was the first apostle, and was the first woman preacher—this latter, according to legend, not scripture.

A more positive interpretation from the feminist perspective is given by Marina Warner who writes "Together the Virgin and the Magdalene form a diptych of Christian patriarchy's idea of women." The Church venerates two ideals of the feminine—consecrated chastity in the Virgin Mary and regenerate sexuality in the Magdalene. Mary the Mother of Jesus as pictured in the Gospels was transmuted by the Church into an ideal of sinless perfection and purity whereas the harlot saint reflects "one of the most attractive features of Catholic Christianity—the doctrine that no one, except Satan, is beyond the reach of grace."[3]

The identity of Mary Magdalen is indeed obscure in scripture: Luke recounts that an unnamed woman entered the house of the pharisee Simon, and while Jesus dined, she knelt, washing his feet with her tears and drying them with her hair. When the pharisee objected that Jesus allowed a sinner to touch him, Jesus calls attention to her ablutions and anointing with oil, saying, "her sins which are many, are forgiven, for she loved much" (Luke 7:47). Mark's account of the events that followed the crucifixion refers to Mary Magdalen who with two other Marys bought spices and went early to the tomb to anoint the body of Jesus (Mark 16:1). Mark also says that the risen Christ appeared first to Mary Magdalen "Out of whom he had cast seven devils" (Mark 16:9).

These scriptural passages provided the incomplete but suggestive data from which the image of Mary Magdalen emerged. Though none of the accounts state, or infer, that the casting out of the devils, or the allegation "sinner" by the pharisee Simon referred specifically to the Magdalen's having been a prostitute, it is as penitent whore that she is exalted in Christian theology and art.

Whether the changes in the Magdalen's imagery can be linked with changes in the economic, domestic, and political realms, or whether they relate to the changing status of women, are questions to be answered by those with extensive historical knowledge in those fields. This study presents such data, with speculations derived from the field of art history, a field closely allied with theology and church history during the periods discussed. It is hoped that historians of the role of women and those working in other disciplines may find material herein which will help them in drawing further conclusions in their own areas of interest.

The main attribute of the Magdalen is the "alabaster jar of very expensive ointment" (Matt.26:7). When represented as a devotional figure, or as a patron saint, the Magdalen is often richly and elegantly attired. According to the *Golden Legend* which recorded the lives of the saints, the Magdalen was of wealthy and noble lineage and thus artists often show her in the most chic attire worn by the ladies of their own day.

The Magdalen as Symbol of Resurrection

The earliest known representation of the Magdalen was in an ancient Christian baptistery in the remote frontier town of Dura Europos, Syria. There, in 1931–32, three buildings were excavated, an early Christian baptistery, a synagogue, and a Mithridates temple, all immensely important because of their early date and because all were decorated with works of art with religious imagery. As the earliest datable Christian art, these paintings from about 230 A.D. in the Christian baptistery, though crude, are of great significance. They represent the Good Shepherd, Adam and Eve, Christ healing the paralytic, Christ and Peter walking on the water, and most important for our purposes, the Marys at the tomb[4] (Plate 1). The first of these, the Magdalen and another Mary, are all that remain out of a group of five women in the original; they are depicted with each holding a torch in her right hand and a bowl of ointment in her left; the corner of the tomb is visible just ahead of them. We can discern little information beyond noting the possibly elegant dresses and long veils of these two clearly remaining Marys and their postures which, though close

Figure 1. *Three Marys at the Tomb: Christian Baptistery*, Dura Europos Collection, Yale University Art Gallery. (Permission Yale University Art Gallery.)

to the early Christian gesture of prayer, look oddly informal. Yet this fragment is strangely moving. It should be noted that the other subjects—Christ healing and his miracles—are rendered with awkward and sketchy contours presented as mere outlines of small figures. But the painter of the Marys fresco aspired to something more than representing signs and symbols. The Magdalen and the other Mary have a kind of presence in their larger scale, in the volume suggested by the painted dress and veils, and in their ceremonial gestures as they hold the torches and ointment boxes.

In this earliest extant dated representation of Mary Magdalen, she is symbolic of the resurrection in the elliptical visual language of early Christian art. Mary Magdalen was the first to see the risen Jesus, and having been directed by him to tell the brethren, there is scriptural basis for one facet of her role, as apostle to the apostles,[5] as Augustine was to describe her.

The Magdalen as Symbol of the Subjugation of Sin to Christ

Another work of art depicting the Magdalen from a very early period, and one which also has been greatly damaged by the ravages of time, is the famous Ruthwell Cross. This free-standing cross was carved in seventh-century England and has on it a number of reliefs and inscriptions. The two largest of these are on the front and back respectively, and are of Christ standing on the beasts and Mary Magdalen wiping the feet of Jesus with her hair. Even in its damaged state which makes the reading of these two reliefs difficult, the formal relationship of the two is clear: in one Christ stands over the beasts symbolizing the subjugation of the demonic; in the other Mary Magdalen crouches at the feet of Christ wiping his feet with her hair, symbolic of the submission of the sinner to Christ. Meyer Schapiro has pointed out that in time Mary Magdalen became the model of female asceticism and penitence and remarks that the legend about her retirement to the desert for thirty years was known in England as early as the seventh century. He notes the common English institution of the double monastery, often under the rule of an abbess, and that "the importance of female ascetics in England perhaps inspired the elaboration of the legend of the Magdalen as an imposing prototype."[6]

During the medieval period cults of the saints flourished. Jean LeClercq writes that in the eleventh century there was a sort of Magdalenian ferment, which he calls a

> "Magdalen boom" in spiritual writings particularly in hagiography but also . . . in formulas for private prayer. The legends and liturgical texts originated and spread from a few important abbeys, especially Vezelay, Cluny, Fleury. The movement spread from France to Italy and even to Rome . . . with the result that the feast of Mary Magdalen (July 22) was given increasing prominence on liturgical calendars.[7]

Victor Saxer[8] tabulated the cults of Mary Magdalen and records only 33 locations in the eighth to the tenth centuries, but 80 by the eleventh century; 116 between 1100 and 1146 (the time of the second Crusade), 125 by 1199, 196 in the period of 1279–1399, and a gradual dropping off thereafter.

In the thirteenth century Jacobus da Varagine (1230–1298) wrote a digest of the vast compilations of legendary lives of the saints. His digest, written in Latin, was called the *Legenda Aurea* (*Golden Legend*) which became a medieval best-seller, circulated and copied repeatedly. The legend of Mary Magdalen was recorded under her feast day July 22. Here we read,

> Mary Magdalene was born of parents who were of noble station, and came of royal lineage. . . . Together with her brother Lazarus and her sister Martha, she was possessor of the fortified town of Magdala; near Genezareth, of Bethany and of a large section of Jerusalem itself. . . .[9]

The account goes on to tell the life of the saint interweaving scriptural incidents with greatly elaborated accounts of her own miracles performed, and of her thirty-year penitence in a desert cave. The *Golden Legend* also refers to Mary Magdalen as the apostle to the apostles.

There is a curious discrepancy between the literary and liturgical evidence of the medieval Magdalenian ferment and the evidence from the visual arts. There are relatively few extant works of art from the medieval era depicting the saint. Even at Vezelay, in her own church, Sainte Madeleine, where a relic of the saint is venerated, there are only minor representations of her. Even taking into account that the Romanesque and Gothic churches were decorated by carvings having vast programs which favored schemes over single episodes or figures, it seems strange that we have no single memorable Magdalen from the medieval "Magdalen boom." She was represented in scenes of the raising of Lazarus, the crucifixion, the Noli me Tangere, and often in the pietà scenes, but no single image has captured the imaginations of believers and scholars, lifting that image into general familiarity.

The Magdalen as Symbol of Human Grief over Human Loss

By the mid-fifteenth century, however, when the cults began to decline in numbers, we have a memorable image of the Magdalen in the famous *Avignon Pietà* (Plate 2) or *Lamentation over the Dead Christ*, now in the Louvre (c. 1460). Here we see the red-cloaked sorrowing Magdalen kneeling while the body of Christ lies across the knees of Mary the Mother. The mood of this work communicates a sense of a cataclysmic event of universal importance. Each detail speaks the epic tragedy—the emptied Mary the Mother, white and silent, garbed as a nun; St. John with bowed head and brooding face; the Donor, his face a solemn mask, though he is not truly present at the event; and finally the Magdalen whose sloping body hangs over the Christ. With one hand she wipes her own tears with the convoluted fold of drapery, while with the other she holds her attribute, an ointment jar, which is charmingly decorated.

The sense of a grief almost beyond human bearing, yet a grief suffered with the knowledge that the tragedy has ultimate significance, is the mood of much of the art in the period toward the end of the fifteenth and early decades of the sixteenth century. The Magdalen became one of the principal vehicles for this passion.

Donatello's extraordinary sculpture of the saint (Plate 3) brings before our eyes and our consciousness a vision of a once beautiful woman whose flesh has been so subdued to the spirit that little of it remains on the gaunt frame: suffering and deprivation are written upon the face, which we at first find as hard to look upon as watching one who is dying. Yet as we enter into her being, her selflessness melts our defenses: she is wholly absorbed in another realm. Her stance shows a touching uncertainty, almost a hesitation as she steps forward. But what the Magdalen lacks in physical force is more than balanced by the spiritual power of her ravaged face and tender hands. She might have been a woman of Dachau or Buchenwald, and there we could have found her twentieth-century antetype, but having said that, we are again arrested by the profundity of her essential being. The Magdalen embodies infinitely more than a courageous and noble endurance of suffering. With incredible sensitivity the artist shaped her hands to express both pleading and acceptance, the central Christian experience of faith and grace.[10]

Donatello's sculpture *Mary Magdalen* has always been known as the "Penitent Magdalen," but it suggests another episode in the life of the saint elaborated in legends. The *Golden Legend* relates how Mary,

Figure 2. *Pietà d'Avignon*, Eugueuaud Quarton, c. 1460, Louvre, Paris. (Permission Cliché des Musées Nationaux—Paris.)

Figure 3. *Mary Magdalen*, Donatello, Duomo, Opera, Florence, Italy. (Permission SCALA/Art Resource, New York.)

Martha, Lazarus and two other Marys were put in a rudderless boat which was washed up on the shores of Provence in southern France. The Magdalen preached in that area, and then for thirty years lived in a cave in Sainte Baume in grim austerity as a hermit. Legend relates that at the canonical hours angels visited her and bore her heavenwards in ecstasy; "Whyth aungelys handys she uplyfted was" as Osbert Bokenham wrote in his *Legends of Hooly Wummen.*[11] Bokenham (1393–1447) was an Augustinian friar and Doctor of Divinity and patron of literature in East Anglia in the early fifteenth century. It is this vision of the Magdalen who levitates in the heavens surrounded by angels, that the German sculptor Tilman Riemenschneider represented. Like Donatello's *Mary Magdalen,* she is clothed only in her own hair! The Magdalen's flesh and face are not gaunt and wasted but have a lustrous full rotundity. She embodies the German and northern type of femininity—a very small bony frame with sloping shoulders, small high breasts and a pronounced protruding abdomen. Plump rounded arms and legs taper, and both feet and hands are tiny, narrow and delicate. By contrast Donatello's *Mary Magdalen* has a large skeletal frame, large and beautiful hands and feet. She is a classical Venus whose self-denial has ravaged flesh and muscle, leaving only the gaunt frame.

Donatello's *Mary Magdalen* is prophetic of the religious fervor which was to sweep Florence at the end of the century. Stirred by the preaching of the fiery priest and reformer, Savonarola, the sophisticated and luxury-loving people of Florence repented of their excesses and extravagances. For a time they submitted to the leadership of the Dominican monk in civil as well as in moral and religious matters. Savonarola's sermons which thundered from the pulpit of the Cathedral of Florence, were heard by two of Florence's most gifted artists, Botticelli and Michelangelo. Both artists were influenced in their own way by Savonarola's cry for repentance and amendment of life.

THE MAGDALEN AS SYMBOL OF THE ERRING CHURCH

Botticelli was fifty-two in 1497 when Savonarola was the virtual dictator of Florence; he had already painted decorations for the town hall of Florence and frescoes for the villa of Lorenzo the Magnificent, and for the Sistine Chapel in Rome. In his younger years Botticelli depicted the classical myths such as the *Birth of Venus* with lyric grace, poetry, and a sense of nostalgia. His early religious subjects—such as the lovely Madonnas holding a plump Christ Child—emanate a different spirit from his later works, which show a dramatic intensity reflecting a breathtaking religious fervor.

In Botticelli's *Pietà* (Direktion der Bayerischen Staatsgemäldesammlungen, Munich) (Plate 4) the time of this world is collapsed, as the mourners about the body of Christ include not only the three Marys, and John the beloved disciple (into whose hands Mary the Mother had been committed), but also St. Jerome who lived many years later and who is seen to the left holding a stone to his bared chest, and St. Paul whose conversion came after the event and who is depicted holding a sword. St. Peter stands to the right, and also a mysterious figure, perhaps the traitorous Judas, holding the nails in hand and shrinking from the sight of them. The figure which most interests us, however, is that of the Magdalen who kneels and with a swooping, ballet-like grace clasps the head of the dead Christ against her own cheeks. Botticelli's Christ is a beardless, youthful Adonis whose beautiful body describes a graceful arc. The winding cloth beneath his body and the veil of the Magdalen create rhythmic arpeggios in the minor mode. The rhythm of these accelerates at the point where in unutterable grief the Magdalen's embrace encompasses the head of Christ.

Two other works by Botticelli from the time of political and religious upheaval in Florence are the *Magdalene at the Foot of the Cross*, (Fogg Art Museum, Harvard University) (Plate 5) and the series of predella panels with illustrations of the life of the Magdalen (Johnson Collection, Philadelphia). The first is a visionary nightmarish scene; it shows the dead Christ on a cross on a hill outside the city of Florence: on the left in the skies, the forces of evil are in combat with the heavenly hosts. Below at the right of the cross, St. Michael raises a sword above the serpent (the devil) which he holds in his left hand. The only living human being in this painting is the Magdalen who clings desperately to the foot of the cross, her red cloak and hair rippling about her recumbent figure. But she is present not as an historic personage, but—and this may surprise twentieth-century lay persons—as an image of the Church. The harlot who turns from her sins in penitence and who through the love of Christ is forgiven, is an image of the Church whose excesses and errors will be forgiven when rooted in the love of Christ.

Botticelli's *Magdalene at the Foot of the Cross* reflects the intensity of emotion that dominated Florence during the brief period at the end of the fifteenth century when the fanatical priest Savonarola headed the Florentine government. In fiery sermons Savonarola attacked the

Figure 4. *Pietà*, Botticelli. (Permission Direktion der Bayerischen Staatsgemäldesammlungen, Munich.)

Figure 5. *Magdalene at the Foot of the Cross*, Botticelli, Fogg Art Museum, Harvard University. (Courtesy of the Fogg Art Museum, Harvard University.)

worldly and luxurious living of the Florentines, and organized the burning of books and works of art, the "vanities," in the city square as public acts of cleansing. Vasari reports that Botticelli was one of Savonarola's supporters—*Piagnoni*, or weepers (for many wept at Savonarola's sermons).[12] Botticelli depicted the Magdalen, as a weeper, clinging to the foot of the cross. The Church which Savonarola had preached against with such fervor is symbolized by the repentant and forgiven whore in Botticelli's painting. Savonarola's reforms were moral, political, and economic, not theological, as was the case with Luther's teachings of two decades later. Yet his rule was an evidence of the impulses toward reform already present before the time of Luther. Luther himself referred to Savonarola as a saint.

The beautiful little predella panel by Botticelli (Plate 6) of the last hours of the Magdalen does not display the same mood as does his crucifixion scene with its vision fueled by the deep spiritual anxieties experienced by the artist. The predella panel has a double scene which shows the Magdalen receiving her last communion, in the distance (at the left) she is about to be lifted into the heavens by two angels. The little painting resonates with a kind of crystalline, spiritual content. The body of the Magdalen seems to have lost all physicality: her flame-like hair flows about her as she kneels in a luminous empty room before the bishop who bends over her with the sacrament: in the landscape behind, her elevation is witnessed by a priest. Though the two events represented are both legendary, Botticelli imbues them with a visionary character touched with ecstasy. Whereas the *Magdalene at the Foot of the Cross* expresses "the mood of chiliasm of the end of the world [which] pervaded the time about the year 1500"[13] the little painting of the Magdalen's last hours affirms the transcending power of faith. Both paintings depict supernatural occurrences, and the vehicle for their expression is the figure of the Magdalen, who in the one is the Church Incarnate, and in the other is the soul of the individual sinner who in penitence and faith turns to God.

The Magdalen of the famous Issenheim Altarpiece, *La Madelaine*, (Plate 7) comes from a slightly later time, about 1515, but her figure and those of the others in this magnificent altarpiece are characterized also by a heightened intensity of emotion. The enormous figure of Christ looms up before us, his body stretched upon a roughhewn cross, the tension of his torso and his weight causing the great crossbeam to bend. His fingers claw stiffly at the empty air, and his knees buckle and the anklebones are riven from their sockets as the weight of the great body is pressed down upon them. At our right John the Baptist stands stiffly before us, with the scriptures in one hand, and

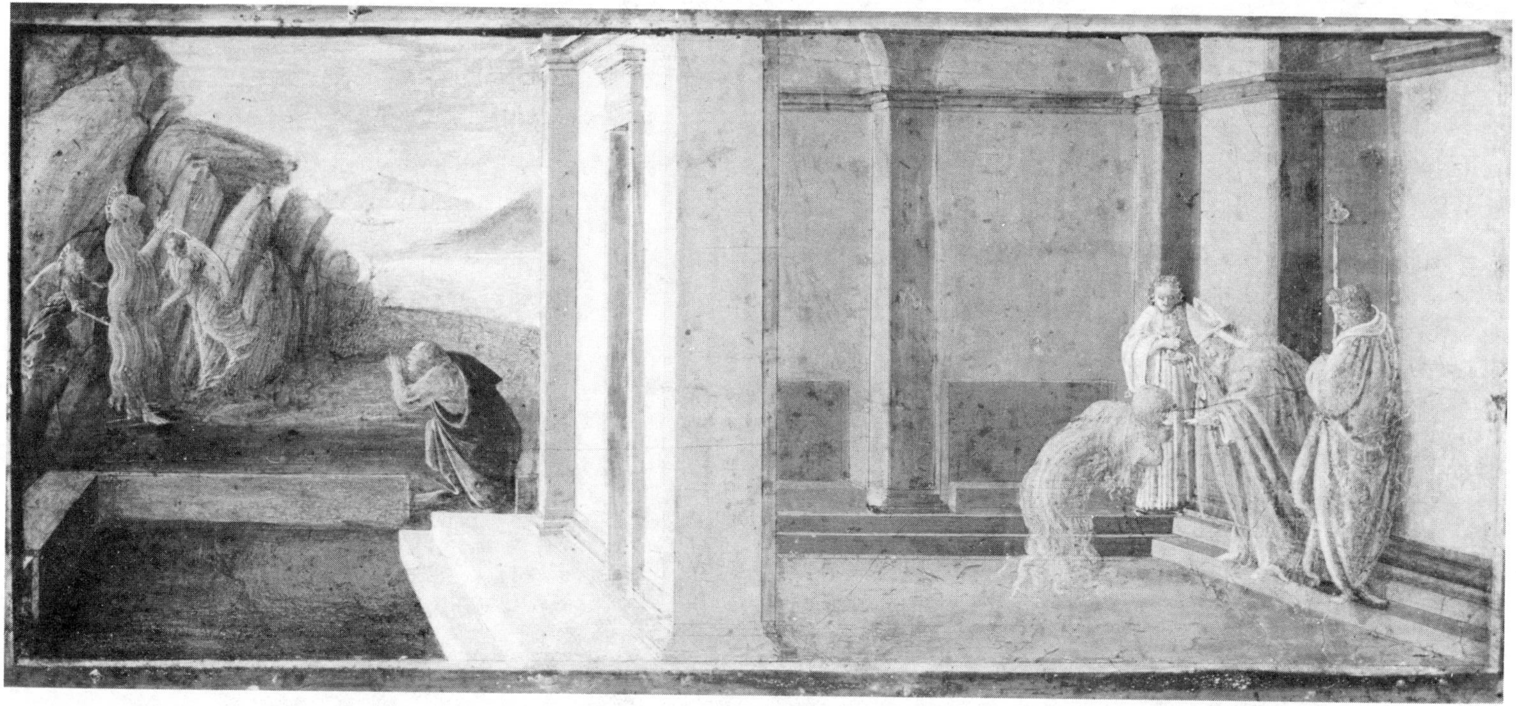

Figure 6. *Last Moments of the Magdalene*, Botticelli, Philadelphia Museum of Art. (Courtesy of the John G. Johnson Collection, Philadelphia.)

Figure 7. *La Madelaine*, Grünewald, from the Issenheim altarpiece. (Permission Musée d'Unterlinden, Colmar.)

with the other, points to the crucified. At the left of the cross, John the beloved disciple supports in his arms Mary the Mother who has been committed to his care. The tiny impassioned figure at the foot of the cross is the Magdalen. Her body is pressed backward in an anguished arc. Her interlaced fingers are locked tensely together. The painful upward thrust of her head exposes the quivering cheeks and pitiable chin in outline against the bleak landscape. Her cascading hair seems to vibrate with the grief that racks the small body. True to an ancient tradition, Grünewald shows the Magdalen as experiencing sorrow in openly physical terms whereas Mary the Mother grieves more inwardly.

Extremes of emotional expression are characteristic of the works of art with the Magdalen from the period before and after the year fifteen hundred. Parenthetically, and paradoxically, it should be noted that during the same period we have the creation of many of the great classical works of the high Renaissance—Leonardo's *Last Supper*, Michelangelo's *Pietà* for St. Peter's, and Raphael's early Roman Madonnas. The emotional restraint and classical balance of these masterpieces are characteristic of the dominating mood of the high Renaissance. Yet in the art of Donatello and Botticelli, and northern artists such as Riemenschneider and Cranach, Dürer, Baldung and Grünewald, ecstasy, fantasy, mysticism, and a highly charged emotionalism hold sway.

The unrest which would erupt into the Protestant Reformation was already in evidence in sporadic outbreaks such as Savonarola's Florentine republic. Furthermore great anxiety preceded the turning of the year 1500; predictions and signs abounded and apprehension that the end of the world was about to occur prevailed. Artistic expression, always sensitive to the tremors within society, mirrored these anxieties. Is it any wonder that the Magdalen, the repentant sinner, forgiven by Jesus Christ himself, would be the saint whose suffering and exaltation was repeatedly represented? By the late sixteenth and early seventeenth century the repentant Peter is also represented in art. Why was it that a woman saint, rather than the male saint, was used as the prime symbolic image for this period? Though the answer lies outside the realms of art history, one might speculate that in the period around 1500, the imagery of women still reflected the medieval symbolism in which woman is either the image of virgin purity, or the evil seductress who leads men to their ruin. The Magdalen is the *reformed* seductress, a wonderfully human image of repentance and amendment of life. The painters, as well as most of the patrons, were, of course, men.

THE MAGDALEN AS SYMBOL OF CONTEMPLATIVE LIFE

With the seventeenth century a new image of the Magdalen appears. She is represented as being deep in thought, and becomes the symbol of the contemplative life. Her role as contemplative stems from the story of Martha and Mary, beginning at Luke 10:38, when Mary "who sat at the Lord's feet and listened to his teaching" is contrasted with Martha who "was distracted with much serving." A fourteenth-century commentator, called the Pseudo-Bonaventura, wrote "You must know that the saints say that these two sisters represent the two lives, the active and contemplative . . . the deed and the intellect."[14]

The Magdalen represented by the French painter Georges de la Tour (Plate 8) is contemplative, "Searching for solitude of mind and attending only to God."[15] She is seated at a table in a dark chamber illumined only by a candle which is hidden from us but whose flame is seen at the periphery of the skull on which the Magdalen rests a large and graceful hand. Her other hand supports her chin as she gazes concentratedly not at the skull, but at its reflection in the mirror before her. The skull reflected in the mirror has a sharp-focus realism: it is the most detailed image in the whole painting. It compels our attention as well as the Magdalen's, and we note that the skull is in profile just as the Magdalen is—that it presents an eerie Xray in reverse of the lovely, living saint. The light touches her nostrils and the corner of her mouth, and plays across her wrist and the soft folds of her white sleeve. It is an image of silence, of a soul withdrawn into the depths of meditation. What image could contrast more vividly with the agony of the witness of the crucifixion in Grünewald's painting or the ecstatic elevation of the saint in Riemenschneider's carving?

Another interpretation of the contemplative versus the active life, and a curious one, is in the painting by Velazquez in The National Gallery in London (Plate 9). In the foreground, we see an elderly woman chiding a young woman who looks resentfully at us as she continues her task of mashing garlic in a mortar: four fish, two eggs and other objects on the table are painted with a surrealist attention to detail. But the real event occurs in the distance in a room which we see through an opening in the wall: there Christ is seated, his hand raised as he addresses Martha who stands expostulating, and Mary who is seated at her Lord's feet. Martha appears elderly and veiled and may be the same person we see at the left in the foreground. Experts do not identify the ruddy-cheeked servant girl at her side as Mary. The juxtaposition of the vivid kitchen scene and the Biblical

Figure 8. *Repentant Magdalen*, Georges de La Tour. (Permission National Gallery of Art, Washington, D.C., Ailsa Mellon Bruce Fund, 1974.)

Figure 9. *Kitchen Scene with Christ in the House of Martha and Mary*, Velazquez. (Reproduced by courtesy of the Trustees, The Na-

event, which is so small and so distant, gives the picture an arresting and puzzling character. Some of the unresolved questions of interpretation about this work are undoubtedly due to the fact that this is a very early picture by Velazquez, and that the elements borrowed from or influenced by other artists are imperfectly integrated into the whole conception.[16] Still, for the purposes of this article, the painting's interpretation of the theme of the active and contemplative life is to be noted.

The Magdalen as Symbol of Penance

The seventeenth century might be called the Magdalen's century. The Vatican catalogue notes the popularity of the theme at this time, and that the Magdalen even inspired an ode written by Cardinal Maffeo Barberini which was published in Paris in 1618.[17] Though other events of her life—Biblical and Apocryphal—were repeatedly represented, the most frequent subject was the penitent Magdalen. The Spanish artist El Greco painted many versions of this subject in the last years of the sixteenth century and the early years of the seventeenth century. In his painting *The Penitent Magdalene* (Plate 10) (Nelson-Atkins Museum of Art, Kansas City), El Greco represents the Magdalen before a rocky cave-like form which cuts down diagonally behind the figure allowing us to see a patch of turbulent sky and clouds illumined by an unnatural light. Perhaps kneeling in prayer, the Magdalen looks upward, her great eyes highlighted and shining with tears. Just behind her at our right we see a small glass vessel, her attribute, the ointment jar, and a skull. Like the skull in Georges de la Tour's painting, it is a symbol associated with penitence and the renunciation of all earthly possessions. It is a "Mememto Mori" ("Remember Death") and is a reminder of the transience of all earthly things. At the time of the Council of Trent, Roman Catholicism reaffirmed the sacraments, penance being one of these. Thus we find in the art of El Greco many pictures of both the penitent Peter weeping over his denial, and of the Magdalen who weeps over her sins.

The feminist theologian Elisabeth Moltmann-Wendel criticized these representations of the Magdalen as sinner as being sexist and asked "What is left of the great male sinner? . . .What would our tradition look like if it had made Peter a converted pimp?"[18] She is apparently not aware of the tradition in art in regard to Peter's denial and his repentance, both repeatedly represented. El Greco at different times did five paintings of *St. Peter in Tears*, many of them with the same posture and general format of his *Penitent Magdalen* paint-

Figure 10. *The Penitent Magdalene*, El Greco. (Courtesy of The Nelson-Atkins Museum of art, Kansas City, Missouri [Nelson Fund].)

ings. For Protestants of the time, Peter was the Apostle who denied Christ whereas for Roman Catholics, and El Greco, Saint Peter was the first pope and the tears shed after his repentance became a symbol of the sacrament of confession.

Far in the background to the right in *St. Peter in Tears* is a scene linking him to the Magdalen:

> An angel sits on the empty sepulcher of Christ, while Mary Magdalen, carrying a jar of spices she brought to anoint the body of the Messiah, hurries away to tell Peter of Christ's resurrection . . . the empty sepulcher suggests the idea of the Resurrection as the foundation for faith and hope.[19]

It is of no small interest that Luther also linked Mary Magdalen and Peter, not as penitents, however, but as sinners who received grace: "St. Peter, St. Paul, St. Mary Magdalene are examples" wrote Luther "to strengthen our trust in God and our faith, by reason of the great grace bestowed on them without their worthiness, for the comforting of all men." In another of his writings he again emphasizes faith and grace rather than her penitence: Jesus "also absolves Mary Magdalene because of her faith, for His words are, 'Go in peace; your faith has saved you!'"[20]

The beautiful painting of the *Penitent Magdalen* by Guercino (1591–1666) could be seen on the other side of a seventeenth-century scale which runs from the silence and annihilation of self of the Georges de la Tour paintings through many shades of emotional content to this comely grieving Magdalen. She gazes tearfully upon the instruments of the passion shown to her by the two angels at the tomb of Jesus. It is the moment before she turns around to find Jesus standing there; the blue sky and the lightening horizon suggest the coming of the dawn and of her savior. The Magdalen's plum-colored robe falls in large sculptural folds about her kneeling figure; her white gown has slipped away from the shoulder, the arm and the breast; her disordered hair falls caressingly across her flesh; her head tilts to one side and she clasps lovely hands as she gazes upon a great nail held up to her by one of the angels.

Guercino has skillfully controlled the source of light so that it gleams upon her arm and breast, her eyelids and nostrils, upon the underside of the angels' entirely believable wings, and finally upon the crown of thorns laid upon the abandoned winding sheet of Christ. The emotional impact of the Magdalen's beauty and her grief are heightened by the rich sensuality of her flesh. Yet, in addition to these observable characteristics, it is of interest to note that the catalogue of the *Vatican Collections: The Papacy and Art* states that in this painting, "the subject is given a somewhat moralistic, typically post-Tridentine interpretation," and it goes on to paraphrase G. Passeri's description, written in 1772, saying that Mary Magdalen

> kneels on the hard ground and laments her faults while one of the angels assisting in her penitence presents her with the nails with which Christ was crucified: the other points to heaven to indicate the true hope for her salvation.[21]

Other episodes in the life of the Magdalen are also frequently depicted during the seventeenth century, such as the *Noli Me Tangere* by Rubens's studio (the Fine Arts Museum of San Francisco), and again in the *Ecstasy of Saint Mary Magdalen* by the Spanish painter Ribera. In Ribera's painting, rather than expressing the supernatural by the other-worldliness of the saint, the artist portrays a lovely, sad young woman surrounded by plump playful putti who accompany her melodramatic "translation." Her soulful gaze upward appeals to sentiment and elicits our easy identification with her, but has little of the transcending power of Riemenschneider's sculpture of the same subject.

Several of the penitent Magdalens of this study as well as many other examples come from the early seventeenth century and are contemporaneous with a poem on the saint by an English writer, Thomas Robinson. It is titled "The Life and Death of Mary Magdalen."[22] This poem from about 1620 is thought to be the last about the saint in English. In two parts and highly allegorical, the first is about her "death to sinne," and the second about her "life in righteousness." The existence of this sentimental and allegorical poem is noted because it coincides with an overwhelming number of works of art devoted to the saint in the seventeenth century. Also its English provenance is of interest, for though the English Protestant clerics who formed the Anglican *Book of Common Prayer* on the basis of Roman Catholic liturgies severely limited the Common of the Saints, Mary Magdalen was included. However, she was not included in the American *Book of Common Prayer* ratified in 1789. It is to be remarked with approval and puzzlement that after almost 200 years in limbo, Mary Magdalen made a comeback and in the recent Episcopal prayer book she has regained her ancient appointed feast day, July 22.

The ubiquity of the Magdalen in seventeenth-century art in Roman Catholic Europe can be related, certainly in part, to the effects of the Council of Trent and its reaffirmation of dogmas and teachings of the Church. Roman Catholicism exalted the cult of the saints, and the saints of the seventeenth century are depicted in states of transport and aspiration, and embody a "painful effort to escape from human nature and to become absorbed in God."[23] Roman Catholicism reaffirmed all the sacraments (the reformers eventually retained only baptism and the eucharist), chief among them penance. As Emile Mâle remarked,

> For this reason the image of Mary Magdalen recurs frequently in the seventeenth century. . . . Beauty consuming itself like incense burned before God in solitude far from the eyes of men became the most stirring image of penance conceivable.[24]

THE MAGDALEN AS SYMBOL OF GRIEF, OF MYSTIC DEPTH AND INTENSITY

We have discussed in detail the two historic moments when the image of Mary Magdalen was vividly represented in painting and sculpture: first, right before and after the year 1500, and second, during the seventeenth century. What remains to be considered is the contemporary image of this figure.

In the twentieth century, the prodigious Picasso created perhaps the most memorable image of the Magdalen. She appears in a series of drawings of the crucifixion done by the artist in 1927 and 1929,[25] all of which are related to a small but very important painting of the subject completed early in 1930. The crucifixion appears unexpectedly within the work of the artist, whose large output up to that time had been concerned with persons, places, and things taken from the visual data that he saw about him. It should be noted that the drawings are all small spontaneous studies, showing the artist thinking through what he wants to do and how he wants to do it—experimenting, erasing, trying it another way. The drawings are private utterances, and in viewing them we are, as it were, watching the workings of his mind: even the culminating painting has something of this private character. It is to be noted that Picasso kept the painting in his own possession, along with a group of other works dubbed "Picasso's Picassos," all of which had special significance to the artist himself.

The first known (that is, published) drawing (Plate 11) is dated 1927; it bears the evidence of numerous erasures and revisions of form. The iconography, that is the reading of the images, begins with Christ. His small head encircled by a crown of thorns and set in an egg-shaped halo is in the center of the upper part of the composition. His bulbous arms stretch the length and breadth of a wide crossbeam, the hand at our right being palm up, and with a large ovoid nail at its center. Several figures merge into each other at the left side of the corpus, and at the right, a horseman with a two-pronged lance is about to plunge it into the side of Christ, while holding a shield in the other hand.

The most astonishing figure in this drawing is, however, the female one who bends backwards at the foot of the cross, achieving an extraordinary posture; her head falls back, the hair falls down toward her curved buttocks, and her massive ankles and feet. Her inflated arms reach upward imploringly, and the acrobatic curve of the body causes the breasts to be seen in profile against the foot of the cross. This is the Magdalen.

Picasso's Magdalen is related to the great early sixteenth-century representation of this Mary in Grünewald's *La Madelaine* (Plate 7) in which may be seen the small, but passionately-arched body of the Magdalen kneeling at the foot of the cross, her head pressed back, her interlaced fingers raised toward the body of the crucified. Her body is

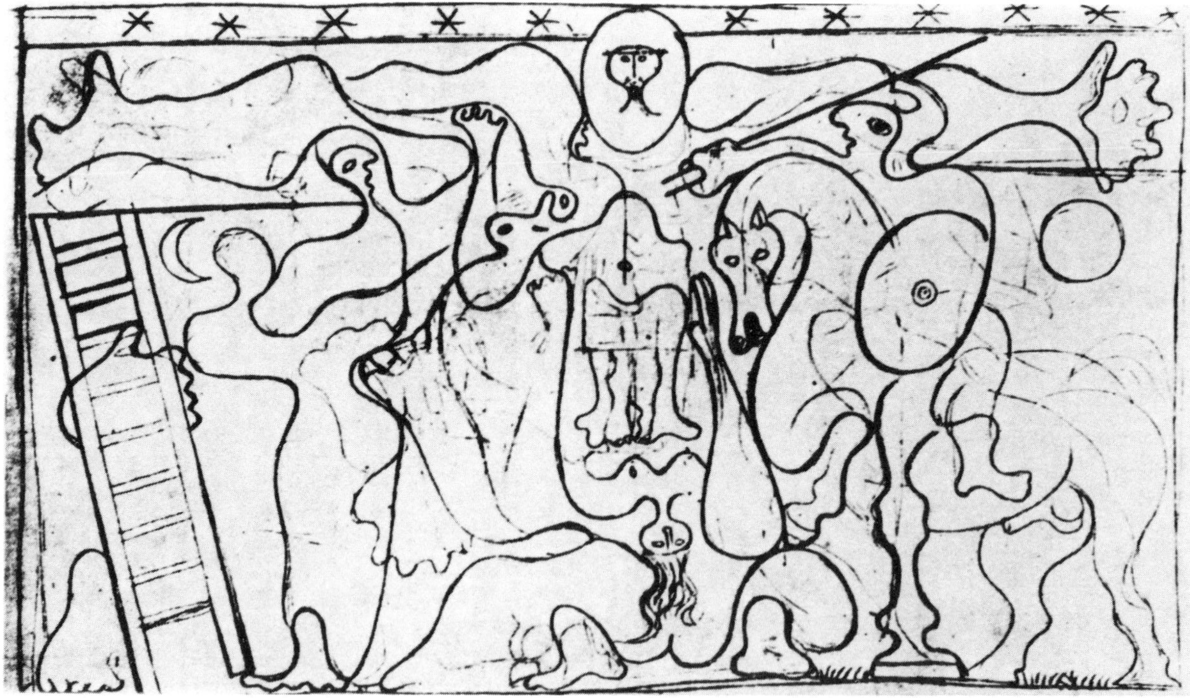

Figure 11. *Crucifixion*, drawing, Picasso, 1927. In *Cahiers d'Art*, No. 2:49-54. (Permission V.A.G.A., New York/S.P.A.D.E.M., Paris, 1984.)

tilted tensely backward in a "sprung" position. Picasso has taken this figure, rotated it so that her back is to us, and drawn her head down even further than did Grünewald.

Two years later Picasso returned to the crucifixion subject and this same figure in a series of extraordinary drawings. On the sheet dated May 25, 1929, we see a series of studies, also of this bent-sprung female figure (Plate 12). Again the arms reach upward and the head

Figure 12. *Studies for the Crucifixion*, drawing, Picasso, June 8, 1929. In *Cahiers d'Art*, No. 3-10, 1938. (Permission V.A.G.A., New York/S.P.A.D.E.M., Paris, 1984.)

falls backward: tubular legs and feet curve in unarticulated contours across the sheet. The breasts remain recognizable, but increasingly their contours serve a design function rather than a descriptive function. The four extra studies of the face rearrange the human features in willful, playful ways. Another page dated the next day has two studies of this figure and shows a further departure from the natural bodily proportions and relationships. The impulse to design is uppermost, creating a complex of lines bearing only some suggestive clues which relate, often in an abrasive way, to our experience of our own bodies.

Whereas the May 25th page shows the artist's hand, the servant of a mind groping for a visual image to express an idea, the May 26th page shows the image clearly possessed by that mind, and now elaborated consciously as a design. A more exaggerated contortion of the figure is depicted, bringing the nose to the pubic-anal zone. The lines are more purposeful; the elaboration of details like the carefully drawn fingernails and toenails, the reiterated curves which are read as hair or eyelashes, as blades of grass or as contours of the rib-cage, are all rendered with a masterful sense for pattern. A tight, small self-complete study at the lower left shows Picasso working with elements which vestigially relate to the human physiognomy and the breasts in particular, but these forms are displaced and designed so freely that they read first as a vivid black and white design, and only secondarily as nose, hair, mouth, eyes.

What are we to make of these willful, violent distortions of the human body, of the Magdalen's body and face, particularly when we view Picasso's works in the context of the great works of religious art of the past? In the 1927 drawing the Magdalen is primal woman, overcome by sorrow. "Beside herself with grief" is a popular epithet, here literally true. Despite the brevity of the linear delineation, it is not an ideogram, or a diagram. It is a visual image of woman emitting the primal scream. It is the *woman* who screams, elemental woman whose sexuality is affirmed even in anguish. Is it a "religious" work of art? For most viewers, this question which may not have arisen before, will come forcedly to mind in regard to this work by Picasso. What was his intention? Picasso himself spoke of the mystery of the creation of works of art:

> How can you expect an onlooker to live in a picture of mine as I lived it? A picture comes to me from miles away: who is to say how far away I sensed it, saw it, painted it, and yet the next day I can't see what I've done myself. How can anyone enter into my

> dreams, my instincts, my desires, my thoughts, which have taken a long time to mature and to come out into the daylight, and above all grasp from them what I have been about—perhaps against my own will?[26]

Picasso's dreams, instincts, desires, and thoughts have been those of the age in which we live. His oeuvre both expresses and has shaped our own seeing and being.

The fact that Picasso studied the famous Issenheim Altarpiece, transforming and retransforming its images, is to be noted. Grünewald's painting of the crucifixion speaks the language of ultimate meaning for the early sixteenth century, Picasso's works, for the twentieth century between two world wars.

We have seen that at two periods of momentous change in western history images of the Magdalen multiplied and were the bearers of meanings related to these changes. First, in the period around the year 1500 when there was much unrest in the church and outside of it, and chiliastic anxieties about the imminent end of the world abounded, the Magdalen was represented either as immersed in this world, as an archetype of suffering, or as escaping this world, in a mystical or ecstatic transport.

In the seventeenth century, the Magdalen had a multiplicity of roles when in art—for counter-Reformation churches—she became foremost in the pantheon of saints whose example was put before the faithful. She was depicted in scenes of the crucifixion, deposition, lamentation, the raising of Lazarus, the feast in the house of Simon the "Noli Me Tangere"—all of her Biblical appearances. But most frequently she is the penitent sinner whose travail of spirit was intended to strengthen worshipers in their belief and spur them to emulation. A scroll held by a Magdalen of an earlier period had a Latin inscription which translates,

> There is no need to despair, even
> For you who have lingered in sin;
> Ready yourselves anew for God
> Because of my example.[27]

We return to our original query, who is Mary Magdalen? In religious art, her image and the meaning borne by that image, have changed with each era. She symbolized the resurrection (Dura Europos), the subjugation of sin and the demonic (the Ruthwell Cross), human grief over human loss (Grünewald), the erring Church (Botticelli), mystical transport (Riemenschneider), the contemplative life

(Roger van der Weyden and Georges de la Tour), the sacrament of penance (Donatello, El Greco, Guercino), and finally with Picasso, a grief of mythic depth and intensity.

There is no Biblical figure other than the Magdalen who has borne a comparable breadth of humanity in all its many facets. Henry Adams thought that the Virgin was the greatest force the Western world had ever felt, and that it was her power that built the great cathedrals.[28] Her power was great but her humanity was narrowed by the Roman Church, and she was largely ignored by western Protestantism. By contrast the Magdalen was all that was female, and all that was human. She was the apostle to the apostles, and perhaps is still available to both women and men today.[29]

Notes

1. Jean LeClercq, *Monks on Marriage: A Twelfth Century View* (New York: Seabury Press, 1982), pp. 92–93.
2. Elisabeth Moltmann-Wendel, *The Women Around Jesus* (London: SCM Press, 1982), pp. 66–67, 82.
3. Marina Warner, *Alone of her Sex: The Myth and Cult of the Virgin Mary* (New York: Alfred A. Knopf, 1976), pp. 234–35.
4. Kurt Weitzmann, ed., *Age of Spirituality: Late Antique and Early Christian Art, Third to Seventh Century* (New York: Metropolitan Museum of Art, 1979), pp. 404–405.
5. See also Jacobus de Varagine, *The Golden Legend*, translated and adapted by Granger Ryan (London: Longmans, Green and Co., 1941), 2:357.
6. Meyer Schapiro, *Late Antique, Early Christian and Medieval Art* (New York: George Braziller, 1979), p. 164.
7. LeClercq, *Monks on Marriage*, p. 94.
8. Victor Saxer, *Le Culte de Marie Magdalene en Occident des Origines a la fin du Moyen Age* (Paris: Clavreuil, 1959), p. 182.
9. Jacobus de Varagine, *The Golden Legend*, 2:357.
10. Jane Dillenberger, *Style and Content in Christian Art* (Nashville: Abingdon Press, 1965).
11. Osbern Bokenham, *Legends of hooly wummen. Edited from M.S. Arundel 327* (London: published for the Early English Text Society, 1938).
12. Giorgio Vasari, *Lives of the Most Eminent Painters, Sculptors and Architects* (New York: The Modern Library, 1959), p. 159.
13. Otto Benesch, *The Art of the Renaissance in Northern Europe* (Cambridge: Harvard University Press, 1947), p. 10.
14. *Meditations on the Life of Christ: An Illustrated Manuscript of the Fourteenth Century*, trans. I. Ragusa and R. B. Green (Princeton: Princeton University Press, 1961), p. 246.
15. Ibid.

16. Neil Maclaren, *The Spanish School* (London: National Gallery, 1952), pp. 74–75.

17. *The Vatican Collections: The Papacy and Art* (New York: Metropolitan Museum of Art, 1983), p. 164.

18. Moltmann-Wendel, *The Women Around Jesus*, pp. 66–67.

19. *El Greco of Toledo*, exhibition catalogue by William B. Jordan (New York: New York Graphic Society, 1982), p. 234.

20. Jaroslav Pelikan, ed., *Luther's Works* (St. Louis: Concordia Publishing House, 1956), 21:323.

21. *Vatican Collections*, p. 164.

22. Thomas Robinson, *The Life and Death of Mary Magdalen: a Legendary Poem in Two Parts, about A.D. 1620* (London: Trench Trubner & Co., 1899).

23. Emile Mâle, *Religious Art from the Twelfth to the Eighteenth Century* (New York: Pantheon Books, 1949), p. 178.

24. Ibid., p. 172.

25. For plates showing this series see Jane Dillenberger, "Picasso's Crucifixion" in *Humanities, Religion and the Arts Tomorrow*, Howard Hunter, ed. (New York: Holt, Rinehart and Winston, 1972).

26. Herschel B. Chipp, *Theories of Modern Art* (Berkeley: University of California Press, 1968), p. 272.

27. Anna Jameson, *Sacred and Legendary Art* (London: Longmans, Green and Co., 1866), 1:352.

28. Henry Adams, *The Education of Henry Adams* (Boston: Houghton Mifflin Co., 1918), p. 388.

29. Elizabeth Schussler Fiorenza, *In Memory of Her* (New York: Crossroads Press, 1983)—an excellent study by a distinguished Biblical scholar which includes a discussion of the role of Mary Magdalen.

CHAPTER SEVEN

Women and Islamic Art

WALTER B. DENNY

The task of discussing the depiction in the imagery of Islamic art of the role of women in Islamic society and culture is an unusually difficult one, for two separate but complementary reasons. The first is the extremely tenuous nature of the status of art itself in Islamic society and culture. The second is the problematic nature of defining the role of women in Islamic society and culture. Both of these questions arise from the traditional interpretation of Islamic religious beliefs, and both of them are of special concern in our own times due to the conflict between what might be called the "liberal" element in Islamic thought, which seeks reconciliation between traditional beliefs and the exigencies of social, economic, technological, and political change, and the "conservative" element, which seeks to secure and maintain traditional beliefs in a state protected from these same exigencies. The problem is compounded when it is examined by an individual of predominately Western cultural and intellectual upbringing, and there are some who would maintain that under all of these circumstances the task being undertaken in this essay is impossible to execute in an appropriate manner. Keeping in mind, that a "value-free" assessment of this question is probably beyond mortal abilities, and that the author of these words is not a practicing Muslim, we turn to the task at hand. Our purpose is threefold: to examine the image of women as they appear over the centuries in various media of Islamic art; to examine the role of women as creators of Islamic art; and to see what insights these matters bring to the overall question of the social and cultural role of women of the Islamic world in a period of dramatic change and pressure for change.[1]

Before starting to examine the evidence—works of art which cast light upon the role of women in society—we should however mention the major differences of opinion that surround the two subjects of our essay, the role of art and the role of women in Islamic culture and society.

Taswir—representational art—occupies a tenuous place in Islamic custom because a preponderance of traditional Islamic belief holds that representation of human or animal forms in art is sinful.[2] Moreover, there are in the Islamic Traditions (*Hadith*), canon law (*shari'a*), and in the revealed Word of God (*Qur'ān*) numerous direct or indirect strictures against the enjoyment of precious and beautiful things, which in and of themselves militate against any kind of art.[3] The reasons for this state of affairs have been discussed by many historians and theologians, and it would be superfluous to repeat them here.[4] It suffices to say that Islam as a religion is essentially puritanical in outlook, and that it holds in common with its sister religion, Judaism, a deeply-held suspicion of artistic imagery as potential idolatry, an idolatry which Islam confronted for centuries at close range in the iconodulism of eastern Christianity. Figural art does exist in Islam, to be sure, but always in a state of tension with the strict interpretation of scripture, and thus it has been unusually prone over time to vandalism and destruction.[5] Figural imagery in Islamic art has been associated primarily with the art of the royal court in Islamic society and secondarily with the art of the urban middle class, but its fortunes have fluctuated over time as changes in scriptural interpretation, the degree of religious control over society, and the proximity and power of non-Islamic and anti-Islamic tendencies have taken place. There has emerged in recent times a revisionist interpretation of the acceptability of taswir which represents the liberal tendencies in Islam alluded to above.[6] Whether it rises above the status of ingenious casuistry remains to be seen. The fact remains that over all Islamic figural art and figural representations there rests the shadow of that Islamic tradition which states that on Judgement Day artists will be asked by God to breathe life into their human and animal creations, and upon failing to do so, will be condemned forever to hell.[7]

The position of women in Islamic society would seem at first glance to be considerably less ambiguous than that of art in Islamic culture. The Qur'ān and the Traditions contain numerous guidelines for social conduct, and they provide therefore an abundance of information on the proper legal role and status of women in society. That status, when compared to the present-day legal status of women in some of the more prosperous and liberal nations of the West, would appear to be considerably lower, in a Western view, than the status of men. According to both religious law and traditional social practice, Islamic women are relegated to a secondary role in matters of religion, economic life, politics, and intellectual and artistic life in many of the Islamic countries of the world today.[8] Once again there is a basic conflict between conservative and liberal interpretations of Islam, a conflict whose importance within Islamic society shows every sign of increasing as the pressure from external forces alluded to above becomes stronger and stronger. This conflict exists not only on an overt political level—the struggle between secular and religious elements in Islamic society has existed for fourteen centuries, after all—but on a theological level as well, as attempts, generally not very successful, have been made to re-interpret the Traditions, the Law, and the Word.[9] Here, the task of the Islamic liberal is infinitely more difficult than it is in the matter of the role of figural art, and the opposition from traditional Islam, religious and social, is far more vigorous and widespread.

All of this having been said, then, it remains to note that these situations are far from monolithic, and that exceptions to them abound in every part of the Islamic world. There is no question that the coming of Islam improved the status of women in the Arab world in some respects. Although the role of women is, by Western standards, strictly circumscribed, there have been important instances in Islamic history of women succeeding in everything from political life to military campaigns.[10] And although art, and especially figural art, is subject to disapproval from those tending toward a strict interpretation of Islamic rules, figural painting and sculpture do exist throughout the history of Islamic art.

When figural art appears in Islam, it appears in a number of ways. What we refer to as "Islamic painting" consists predominately of Islamic book illustration, and thus Islamic painting is heavily dependent on textual sources; portraiture, history painting, and genre paintings are distinctly subsidiary notions in Islamic painting where they exist at all. For this reason, examination of the role of women as revealed in Islamic painting may be closely allied with the concepts of such roles as developed in poetry and prose texts. Figural images also appear in what we sometimes call the decorative arts—pottery, woodwork, ivory, metalwork, textiles and carpets, and architectural decoration of all sorts, whether carved, moulded, or painted. Figural imagery also appears as a prominent part of Islamic royal art; the imagery of works of art created for the opulent and pleasure-loving (and hence basically non-religious) ambience of the Islamic secular courts tends to focus on the pleasures and power of those courts. Accordingly, the appearance of women in Islamic royal art occurs in proximity to its prevalent themes of hunting, battle, drinking, music, dancing, sport, and other diversions of royalty.[11] All of this gives us a somewhat limited stage on which to array our evidence, and we must not make the mistaken assumption that "what we have is all there was." To the extent that art *is* a mirror of a culture, no matter how poorly art may be regarded within that culture, the evidence we are about to examine says some important things about Islamic culture. Any warps and flaws in the mirror itself will affect the overall accuracy and usefulness of our findings, but it is our belief that the mirror is sufficiently dependable to give us a useful, if somewhat limited, picture of our subject.

We have developed the topics to be discussed here simply by taking a census of several thousand works of Islamic art in which women are depicted, and then extrapolating from this mass of data a series of themes, whose recurrence in many different times, places, media, and social levels lends some importance to them.

WOMAN AS PLEASURE

One of the most widespread types of representation of women in Islamic art, which is found from the earliest stages in its development down to the nineteenth century, is the image of woman as the provider of pleasure to men. The early frescoes of Qusayr ʿAmra and the stucco statues from Khirbat al-Mafjar, two of the most important eighth-century Umayyad palace complexes, are replete with images of women, either nude or semi-nude, cast as bath entertainers, dancers or servants.[12] The image of dancing women in Islamic art, carrying with it the iconography of the Sasanian goddess of fertility, Anahita, is an all-pervasive one.[13] Dancing figures serve wine from jars in frescoes from ʿAbbasid Samarra in the ninth century, and by the tenth century the image of dancing women begins to become important in Fatimid art in Egypt.[14] (Figure 13). The theme appears in the art of Umayyad Spain, Seljuk Iran, and in later times becomes a

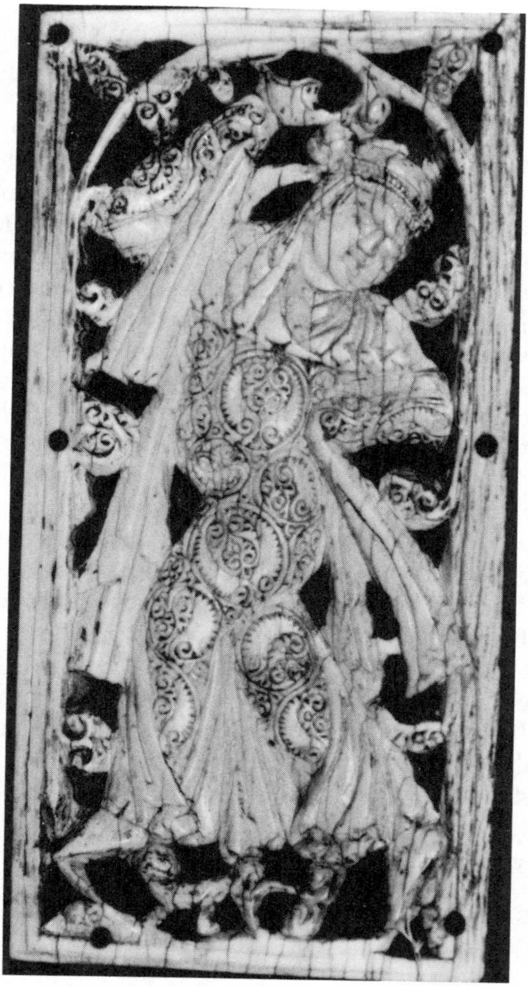

Figure 13. A Dancing Woman
Carved Ivory, Egypt (Cairo), XI century
Museo Nazionale (Bargello), Florence

stock image in the art of the Ottoman, Mughal, and Safavid empires.[15] In Islamic art dancing women are not depicted as goddesses or other-worldly figures, but as servants, either explicitly or by strong implication the servants of men; the frequency with which they are also shown pouring or carrying wine, or in the company of birds symbolizing lust or fertility,[16] leaves little doubt that their depiction in art serves as a sort of *dopplegänger* to their actual court role—providing entertainment and sexual pleasure to men is their purpose in both life and art.

The surviving examples of this type of imagery are overtly erotic only quite rarely, however. In contrast to the numerous Orientalist portrayals of Islamic women, where nudity, sexuality and the feminine libido are often strongly emphasized, in the Islamic world the theme of woman as the pleasure-giving servant of man is usually stated with more reserve.[17] It is as if in Islamic art the confusion of the work of art with the subject depicted is to be avoided at all costs, in marked contrast to Byzantine iconodulism, or to the manner in which sexual sublimation and voyeurism have been woven into the history of European art, especially since the fifteenth century.[18] Whether the woman courtier, who dances, sings, plays a musical instrument, or brings wine and food to her master, is only one more accoutrement of that complex of power-images defining the conventional Islamic *Prachtkunst*,[19] or whether this image aroused any specifically erotic feeling in its viewers in past times, are of course matters for conjecture. But the nature of the images themselves suggests that frequently the image of woman as the pleasure-giving servant of man becomes a formula, and that the significance we attach to this type of image must be understood in this light. If the name of God, repeated endlessly in pious formulae in the wall decorations of a great Muslim secular palace such as the Alhambra, eventually attains through repetition the iconographic significance of apotropaic wallpaper, so by its repetition, through the centuries does the image of the pleasure-giving woman become a conventional symbol of the Islamic court, as well as the symbol of the subject status of such women.[20]

WOMAN AS LOVER

Islamic literature abounds in lyric and narrative poetry about love, and the themes of love and lovers are found in Islamic music and verse from the Pillars of Hercules to far beyond the Oxus and Indus. Since so many of these popular narrative poetic works were illustrated (one thinks immediately of Khusrau and Shirin, Bahram and Fitna, Ardashir and Gulnar, Layla and Majnun, Bayad and Rayad, Humay and Humayun, Varga and Gulshah), the images of woman in love, and of woman as lover, are frequent ones in the history of Islamic art. Here the relation between image and text is very important, and it becomes a matter of some interest whether on occasion any real divergence in meaning between the two may exist. Woman in lyric poetry frequently takes the initiative in love; in Jami's *Yusuf and Zulayka*, the latter, an Egyptian noblewoman, falls in love at first sight with the slave Yusuf, and, in an auction scene at least as riveting as any real-life drama at Sotheby's or Christies, buys him for her own, and subsequently attempts to seduce him.[21] In Firdausi's *Shah-nameh*, two famous cases of bold women lead to romance. Tahmina, the daughter of a king in whose house the hero Rustam is visiting, comes into the hero's bedroom in the middle of the night. Their brief affair leads to the birth of Suhrab and eventually to one of the most tragic episodes of the epic, as the father unknowingly kills his son in combat. Gulnar the slave-girl is a more resourceful woman, using a rope to climb over the wall in order to join her lover Ardashir.

When the fifteenth-century artist of the Fogg's "Tahmina and Rustam" (Figure 14) painted his heroine coming to Rustam's chamber, she was shown in a pose of exquisite modesty and restraint:

> At noon of night, while Phosphor crossed the sky,
> There came mysterious whispers, Rustam's door
> Was softly opened, and a slave who bare
> A taper of savouring of ambergris
> Walked stately toward the drunken sleeper's couch.
> Behind the slave there was a moon-faced girl
> Sun-bright, all scent and hue, with arching eyebrows
> And locks that hung in tresses lasso-like
> In stature like a lofty cypress-tree
> With cheeks carnelians of Yaman in colour
> And mouth as straitened as a lover's heart.
> All soul was she and keen of intellect,
> Thou wouldst have said: "She is not of the earth."[22]

The great Tabriz master Mir Musawwir showed Gulnar, her rope still hanging over the wall in the left background, comfortably snuggled up with her royal lover[23] (Figure 15). As Oleg Grabar and Sheila Blair have pointed out in their study of *Shah-nameh* images,[24] significance can be attached to the choice of which poetic images are to be illustrated with visual images, and the frequent choice of these poetic episodes as the subjects for painters is indicative of their great popularity in the courtly milieu.

The stories of women in love do not therefore invariably depict women in a passive role. While the beautiful Layla, the heroine of Nizami's famous romance *Layla and Majnun*, is generally the victim of the tumultuous events which surround her,[25] the same cannot be

Figure 14. Tahmina Comes to Rustam's Chamber, from a *Shah-nameh* MS
Colors on paper, Iran (Herat), ca. 1435
Courtesy of the Fogg Art Museum, Harvard University
Gift of Mrs. Elsie Cabot Forbes, Mrs. Eric Schroeder, and the Annie S. Coburn Fund

Figure 15. Gulnar Comes to Ardashir's Chamber, from a *Shah-nameh* MS
Colors on paper, Iran (Tabriz), 1528
Painted by Mir Musavvir

said of Fitna, lover of the hunter Bahram Gur, in Nizami's *Haft Paykar*. Unseated from her camel and banished from her lover's side for having made pert and impertinent remarks about his prowess as a bowman (she belittled a great feat of marksmanship by pointing out that Bahram simply practiced a great deal), she bought a young calf and daily carried it up a steep flight of steps until it grew into a large cow. When she carried the cow up the palace stairs and presented it to an astonished Bahram Gur, the ruler wondered how she could do such a thing; her reply was that "practice makes perfect."[26] The seventeenth-century painter Muhammad Zaman, who added Italianesque miniatures of his own to the great sixteenth-century Nizami manuscript that had been made for Shah Tahmasp, chose to depict Fitna wearing a diaphanous dress over a pair of striped trousers; his sturdy heroine, back to the viewer, mounts the palace steps with ease (Figure 16). The fact that this episode should have been chosen for addition to a great sixteenth-century manuscript by a seventeenth-century painter calls up some interesting speculations about both the interest in the poetic episode and the mode of representation, including the European-influenced style with its use of drapery to reveal the human body rather than conceal it. It certainly demonstrates that the image of a clever and resourceful woman was consonant with court taste.[27]

WOMAN AS MORAL EXAMPLE

In a society where God-given rules concerning moral conduct abound, as they do in traditional Islamic society, there are many strictures that dictate the behavior of the sexes in strictly-defined roles. The separation of social roles by sex is naturally reflected in artistic imagery, in a manner which ranges from simple genre-painting to what we might call deliberate moral didacticism.

In the latter realm, paintings which attempt to define proper conduct for women are generally linked with didactic texts of one sort or another. The exemplary behavior of the mother of the Prophet, for example, or that of the Prophet's daughter Fatima, is reflected by the presence of their images, replete with veils, in the late sixteenth-century Ottoman Turkish manuscript of the *Siyar-i Nabi* by Darir.[28] In this context, holy women are shown in symbolic form as the companions or family of the Prophet, but their role in the action of the paintings or the narrative itself is minimal. Another artistic commentary on the conduct and social role of women of a more proscriptive sort is seen in the choice of poetic images for illustration in a manuscript of Mir Haydar's *Miraj-nameh*, the story of the Prophet's visits to heaven and hell, as executed by an unknown artist in Herat around 1436.[29] The artist of this manuscript seems to have had few qualms about depicting the Prophet's face, or that of holy women; on folio 51 *recto* Muhammad is shown encountering the pious wife of his companion Talha in company with three *huris* in paradise, and all figures are shown unveiled (Figure 17). The depiction of such *huris*, those per-

Figure 16. Fitna Carries the Cow to Bahram, from a *Khamseh* MS
Colors on paper, Iran (Isfahan), ca. 1676
Attributed to Muhammad Zaman
By permission of the British Library, London

Figure 17. The Prophet Muhammad and the Pious Woman, from a *Miraj-nameh*
Colors on paper, Iran (Herat), ca. 1435
By permission of the Bibliothèque nationale, Paris

petually chaste female inhabitants of paradise, is not confined to manuscripts of religious narrative, and in the sixteenth-century winged angelic figures of this type, wearing the traditional feathered headdress, became a standard part of the repertoire of imagery in Ottoman Turkish album painting, sometimes depicted with wine-bottles, wine-cups, and occasionally even in what looks suspiciously like a semi-intoxicated state[30] (Figure 18).

But if the artist of the Herat manuscript of the *Miraj-nameh* appears to have been working in an atmosphere of artistic liberalism, his comments on the proper social role of women give a more conservative impression. When the Prophet visits hell, he views the infernal tortures of numerous categories of sinners, among which are shameless women (who let their hair be seen by strangers), women of "disreputable behavior" (who mock their husbands or leave the house without their permission), and adulterous women (who compounded their felony by misrepresenting their illegitimate children as legitimate in order to usurp an inheritance). All of these women are shown in graphic depictions of infernal punishment replete with demons, flames, and various sorts of torture. However, it must be noted that these punishments meted out to women are less sadistic and ingenious than those reserved for men who embezzle the inheritance of orphans, or even for those masculine sinners whose errors were those of omission rather than of commission.[31]

The presence of women in illustrations of religious manuscripts in

Figure 18. A *peri* or angelic figure reclining, from a royal album
Ink on paper, Turkey (Istanbul), ca. 1570
Topkapi Palace Museum Library, Istanbul

Islam is a relatively infrequent occurence, but then again so are illustrated religious manuscripts themselves. Nevertheless, especially in manuscripts with a decidedly heterodox bent, it is possible to see women depicted in a highly sympathetic fashion. The lovely painting of the infant 'Isa (Jesus) with his mother found in a Turkish manuscript of the *Fal-nameh*, for example, shows the mother and child, together with a sugar-cone and a guardian angel, in a landscape (Figure 19). It reminds us of the European depictions of the Rest on the Flight into Egypt, while also calling up the universally acceptable theme of nurturing motherhood. In another illustration from the same manuscript, the Expulsion from Paradise, the same artist, completely untroubled by orthodox Islamic strictures against representation of the human form, shows Adam and Eve, wearing charming little kilts fashioned from leaves, as they stand outside the doors of paradise (Figure 20). If one recalls the agony of this moment in Masaccio's fifteenth-century Brancacci Chapel frescoes in Florence, the contrast is remarkable; the painter has given us no concept of either sin or grief, presenting instead a "no-fault" depiction of the event. There is no special blame on Eve, and the Archangel Gabriel, instead of expelling the Primal Parents with a great sword or a dramatic gesture, merely peeks around the door of paradise as a spectator. Whatever such an image as this represents in its narrower or broader theological meaning, the image per se does not project to either Westerner or Easterner a particularly unpleasant or negative image of women.

The other group of images which shows woman's proper moral and social role may be termed in a general sense "genre images." As used in the history of Western art, the term "genre painting" refers to images of everyday life, with or without ulterior symbolism; especially in Holland and France in the seventeenth century it became a highly developed art form.[32] In Islamic art, such genre elements are incorporated into narrative paintings as background adjuncts, or scene-setters, to the main subject of the painting; here, as in European painting, the setting sometimes becomes the main focus of interest while the ostensible subject may be relegated to a minor part of the pictorial image.[33] Genre aspects of imagery occur in virtually all periods of Islamic painting from which we have surviving examples. In the Fatimid ceiling decoration of the Palatine Chapel at Palermo we see scenes of everyday life such as a game of chess or a meeting at the water-fountain;[34] in the earliest Persian manuscript to survive, the thirteenth-century *Romance of Varqa and Gulshah*, the first miniature depicts an urban bazaar, with an apothecary, a money-changer, a baker and a butcher[35] (Figure 21). The greatest of Baghdad painters

Figure 19. Mary and Jesus, from a *Fal-nameh* manuscript
Colors on paper, Turkey (Istanbul), late XVI century
Topkapi Palace Museum Library, Istanbul

of the same century, Yahya b. al-Wasiti, who illustrated a celebrated manuscript of Hariri's picaresque adventure story known as the *Assemblies*, depicted numerous genre scenes, including a well-known image of village life. Here one sees a woman spinning wool and other

Figure 20. Adam and Eve expelled from paradise, from a *Fal-nameh* MS
Colors on paper, Turkey (Istanbul), late XVI century
Topkapi Palace Museum Library, Istanbul

women performing their traditional functions (Figure 22). Another scene from the same manuscript shows a service in a mosque, with women shown in the rear of the building or in a gallery, apart from the men (Figure 23). Yahya also shows women mourners in a village

Figure 21. Urban genre scene, from a *Varqa and Gulshah* MS
Colors on paper, Iran (?), XIII century
Topkapi Palace Museum Library, Istanbul

funeral, and other scenes of the participation of women in the everyday life of nomadic encampment and rural village, as well as that of the urban milieu.[36]

Genre elements of this sort in Islamic painting are legion, and one must assume that such paintings constitute accurate reflections of

Figure 22. Village genre scene, from a *Maqamat* MS
Colors on paper, Iraq (Baghdad), ca. 1237
Painted by Yahya ibn al-Wasiti
By permission of the Bibliothèque nationale, Paris

widely held social values and norms. In a famous painting now in the Fogg Museum, the sixteenth-century painter Mir Sayyid Ali showed an episode from Nizami's *Layla and Majnun*, in which Layla's father arranges her betrothal to a man named b. Salam (Figure 24). The main

Figure 23. Scene in a mosque, from a *Maqamat* MS
Colors on paper, Iraq (Baghdad), ca. 1237
Painted by Yahya ibn al-Wasiti
By permission of the Bibliothèque nationale, Paris

action of the scene, which occurs in the tent at the bottom of the composition, is of relatively little importance for the painter, who uses the theme as a pretext to depict for his sophisticated court clientele the entire panoply of activities of the nomadic encampment. Women are shown feeding animals, nursing children, spinning yarn, washing clothes, and milking goats—in short, all of the multifarious activities which even today are performed in the encampment by nomadic

Figure 24. Scene in an encampment, from a *Khamseh* MS
Colors on paper, Iran (Tabriz), ca. 1540
Painted by Mir Sayyid Ali
Courtesy of the Fogg Art Museum, Harvard University
Gift of John Goelet; formerly collection of Louis J. Cartier

women.[37] A manuscript of the *Khamseh* of the poet Ataʿi in the Walters Art Gallery is noteworthy for its accurate depiction, only broadly related to the accompanying text, of women involved in the spinning of yarn and the weaving of textiles (Figure 25). Perhaps reflecting the rather loose morals of the eighteenth-century Ottoman milieu, other illustrations in the manuscript show activities of the harem in an almost Chaucerian fashion.[38] Of course, outright pornography and blatant eroticism exist in Islam as they do in the art of every culture, but these images in Islamic art, especially the rare pornographic epi-

Figure 25. Women weaving, from a *Khamseh* MS
Colors on paper, Turkey (Istanbul), XVIII century
Courtesy of the Walters Art Gallery, Baltimore

sodes, also share with their counterparts in other cultures the essential ingredient of boredom.

The role that women play in Islamic family life necessarily demands that they be prominent in certain Islamic rites of passage, especially that often extravagant manifestation of conspicious consumption, the traditional wedding. Islamic paintings do at times show the circumstances and events surrounding birth, weddings, circumcisions, and other celebrations in Islamic society in which women participate, including pilgrimages, royal audiences, and the performance of the Shi'ite Passion Play.[39] The generally pejorative Islamic view of Western women is a subject discussed by this author in another context,[40] but Islamic art also demonstrates a curiosity about the role of women in other Eastern societies. In a manuscript of Juvaini's *History of the World Conqueror* executed in Herat in 1436, the Mongol Khan Mangu is shown receiving a foreign ambassador; what is unusual about this depiction is that three of the Khan's wives, without veils, are shown attending the ceremony, a comment perhaps on the unusual customs and mores of the Mongols[41] (Figure 26).

WOMEN AS HEROES AND PERSONIFICATIONS

In Western art, even at times when the societal role of women has been severely proscribed, women have served as symbols and personifications of positive values (Liberty, Victory, Wisdom, Justice, Charity, Love) in both political and religious contexts. The use of such personifications in Islamic art is quite rare, but it does occur at times. There is some debate on the actual meaning of the sculptural female heads which formerly adorned the great west portal of the hospital of Turan Melek at Divriği in Asia Minor (Figure 27): are these to be considered as donor portraits of the wife of Ahmed Shah Mengüchük, or are they instead personifications, possibly of the sun and the moon?[42] The tradition of women as astrological symbols has a Graeco-Christian heritage in the Middle East and appears in Islamic painting as early as the beginning of the eleventh century, as the well-known illustrations of Virgo and Andromeda in the Bodleian manuscript of al-Sufi's *Treatise on the Fixed Stars* demonstrate.[43]

An altogether more prevalent use of the image of woman as personification and as heroic figure is seen in the curious Iranian practice of including as part of a sort of frontispiece for manuscripts of the *Shah-nameh* or *Book of Kings* the representation of the enthronement of Solomon and Belkis, the Queen of Sheba.[44] A sixteenth-century Shiraz depiction of Belkis enthroned, long since separated from its

وخت به بر استد · وبادشاه جهان دار بر مرقفاه تخت بدذار مؤید وکامکار
نسته · وبادشاهزادکان جون ابواره منظفردحذمت بر میان مهر دریش مهر
آسمان عظمت واقتدار بسته · وخواتین بریسار هرک با مایه حسن و ملاحت آ
باز از فرط طراوت ونضارت جون از هار دار لطافت وبطافت مانند

Figure 26. Mangu Khan Receives Envoys, from a *Tarikh-i Jahan-Gusha*
Colors on paper, Iran (Herat), ca. 1436
Courtesy of the Worcester Art Museum
Jerome Wheelock Fund

Figure 27. Damaged sculpture of a female head
Portal of the Hospital of Turan Melek, ca. 1220-1230
Divrigi, Turkey

manuscript, shows the queen seated on a throne, surrounded by the beasts of the earth as her court (Figure 28). Belkis's reputation in Islamic culture as a wise and competent ruler is well established, but there is still some question as to why this queen plays such a role in an illustration accompanying the text of the *Book of Kings*. Clearly, there was room in Islamic culture for positive and powerful female personifications.

Figure 28. Belkis, Queen of Sheba, Enthroned, from a *Shah-nameh* MS
Colors on paper, Iran (Shiraz), ca. 1560-1570
Courtesy of the Museum of Fine Arts, Springfield, Massachusetts
Gift of Mrs. Roselle L. Shields

WOMEN IN CONTEMPORARY ISLAMIC ART

As we remarked at the outset, the traditional Islamic view of women, in both its religious and its social sense, is coming into conflict with various internal and external forces in the twentieth century. The institution of various forms of "Islamic Socialism," the imposition on Islamic societies of a colonial superstructure of Westernized institutions and values, and the curious metamorphoses of Islamic society under Soviet domination in Central Asia have all had their effect on contemporary art from Islamic lands. Contemporary Islamic art is very little known in the West—there are few publications, few exhibitions, only one major private collection, almost no examples in public collections. Because of this paucity of source material, our comments on the imagery of women in contemporary Islamic art will be of necessity both general and brief.[45]

Islamic art under the influence of European traditions has often adopted wholesale European types of representation of women. Ottoman "orientalist" painters even adopted the European concept of Islamic women in their work.[46] On the other hand, a rather affecting example of borrowing can be seen in the Turkish painter Zeki İzer's "The Road to Revolution" of 1933, in which the Turkish nation is personified by a female figure borrowed without any embarassment whatsoever from the famous "Liberty at the Barricades" by Eugène Delacroix[47] (Figure 29). The role of women in national struggles of liberation throughout this century has resulted in works of art memorializing their accomplishment. Turkish art has been the most active in this vein; as early as 1933 the painter Halil Dikmen, in his "Village Women Carrying Ammunition in the War of Independence" portrayed the heroism of women in the national struggle. The Palestinian cause has in its poster art emphasized the role of the male warrior; there is also traditional sentimentalism in the depiction of women in such images as that of the Iraqi Battul el-Fukaiki in her "The Land of the Sad Oranges" (Figure 30), inspired by a short story of the Palestinian writer Ghassan Kanafani.[48] In general, contemporary artists in Islamic countries, even those with pronounced socialist or left-leaning political views, seem to have relied on the traditional means of genre-painting, and upon the sympathetic portrayal of urban and rural struggles designed to overcome poverty, disease, sorrow, and traditional social repression of women.

The major exception to this in the Islamic world today is the painting of the Islamic republics of the Soviet Union. Of course the normal course of things dictates that public exposure of works of art is given

Figure 29. "Inkilap Yolu" ("Road to Revolution")
Oil on canvas, Turkey, ca. 1933
Painted by Zeki Faik Izer
Courtesy of the Painting and Sculpture Museum, Istanbul

only to those images reflecting the accepted governmental canons of style and subject, but it appears that "underground painting" of the type found in the Slavic republics of the U.S.S.R. is very limited in Central Asia, if it exists at all. If we are to judge by the works exposed in Soviet museums and published by Soviet presses, the art of Soviet Central Asia takes a "positive" view of the need for social advancement of women and implicitly or explicitly criticizes traditional religious and social strictures in this regard. For example, Chary Amangeldyev's triptych "Towards Light," painted in 1970, takes as its subject the status of women in the Türkmen S.S.R. The first panel, entitled "The Past," shows a veiled woman inside a traditional yurt dwelling, covered with a chador shawl and sheltering her young daughter. The second panel, from which the entire work gets its title, shows women, books under their arms, going off to school and to work, striding purposefully toward the left. The third panel, entitled "The Future" (Figure 31), shows an assertive young woman, obvi-

Figure 30. "Land of the Sad Oranges," detail
Oil on canvas
Painted by Battul el-Fukaiki
Museum of Fine Arts, Baghdad

ously the child from the first panel, clad in a brilliantly-colored dress, as "an emancipated member of contemporary society enjoying equal status with men."[49]

The optimistic, colorful, and direct depictions of Central Asian

Figure 31. "The Future," from a triptych entitled "Towards Light"
Oil on canvas, Turkmen S.S.R., 1970
Painted by Chary Amangeldyev
Art Museum, Ashkabad

woman in modern Soviet art include such works as Rakhim Akhmedov's 1962 "Portrait of a Woman," in which a brilliantly attired woman aggressively confronts the viewer, or the Tatar artist Kharis Yakupov's "Portrait of the Pig-tender M. Galiullina" of 1961.[50] Of a slightly more introspective mood are works such as D. Bairamov's 1972 "Plane Trees" or V. Bobrykin's "Yak Breeders" of the same year.[51] All of these works demonstrate the "proper" stylistic and ideological attitudes expected of officially sanctioned Soviet art today, and they reflect an official attitude on the status of women which may or may not be at variance with popular attitudes.[52]

WOMEN ARTISTS IN ISLAMIC SOCIETY

In traditional Islamic society we very rarely encounter the name of the artist attached to works of art. With the exception of a few very talented artists, Islamic artists seem in general to have acted anonymously, due in part to the lack of differentiation of the artist's role from that of other craft workers, and in part to the lack of a theoretical or critical literature about art. Given the usual anonymity of the artist in Islamic society and the general exclusion of women from the organized crafts and arts in Islamic society, the establishment of a body of historical artistic work by Islamic women artists, even were it supposed to exist, would be an impossible task. However, there are entire areas of artistic production in Islamic society, usually ignored to be sure by historians of art, in which women were by social definition the major artistic practitioners. Since art historians prefer to labor where there exist written sources of some sort, even if they don't cast light on artists' names, until recently very little attention has been paid to the study of art forms which certainly must rank socially, economically, and aesthetically among the most original and distinctive artistic produces of Islamic culture. These are the village and nomadic arts of rug-weaving and the urban and rural arts of embroidery, which are almost never associated with the name of a particular artist and are difficult to date, difficult to interpret symbolically, bereft of written documentation, but often incredibly powerful in their visual effects. In most Islamic societies these forms are also the exclusive product of women artists.

The most studied group of Islamic traditional rugs is that produced by women from the various Türkmen tribes of Central Asia and northeast Iran. Works by Western scholars, stimulated by the keen interest of collectors and the phenomenal performance of such rugs on the art market, have established a technical basis for determining the tribal origins of these rugs,[53] while the works of the Soviet anthropologist V. Moshkova have established a basis, however hotly debated, for the discussion of their symbolism.[54] The enormous surge of publications about these works of art in recent years and the growing cooperation among art historians, textile specialists, anthropologists, and historians, have begun to shed light on the traditional rug weavings of the nomadic and village peoples of Anatolia, the Balkans, Iran, the Caucasus, and Central Asia.[55] Even more recently, the domestic embroideries of Islamic peoples from Morocco to Central Asia have been subjected to scholarly attention, and important exhibitions have been mounted.[56] However much these forms have been neglected by traditionally trained historians of Islamic art, there can be no question that in the West today the most popular works of art from the Islamic world are the products of women artists.

Women and Islamic Art

When we look at the role of women as artists and subjects in Islamic art in the context of this volume, we should not be prepared for surprises. Implicit in the role of Islamic art as servitor to social values, rather than as molder of those values, is the expectation that Islamic art will confirm what we already know, and underline what we already hypothesize. And yet because the visual image often communicates more effectively than the written word, this overview of the role of women in Islamic art should caution us to avoid overbroad generalities about Islamic society as a whole; to every rule we posit there are significant exceptions, and for every pattern there are anomalous elements. The richness and diversity of representation of women, both in style and in subject, are merely the reflection of similar diversity within the complex matrix of Islamic society. And in the mirror of Islamic art we see reflections not only of the overpowering force of tradition but also of the equally venerable forces which in an era of rapid social change in the Islamic world now point toward an uncertain but dynamic future.

Notes

1. I owe to two colleagues particular thanks for help in this paper: Yvonne Haddad, who suggested the topic, and Anne Mochon, who sparked my interest in this subject some years ago. The original presentation included thirty–three pairs of slides as illustrations; this number has been greatly reduced for publication of this paper. Thanks go to all institutions and collec-

tors who generously granted permission to publish these illustrations, and to the colleagues who facilitated the difficult process of obtaining photographs for publication.

2. See the article "Taswir" in *Encyclopedia of Islam*; also Thomas W. Arnold, *Painting in Islam* (New York: Dover, 1965); Oleg Grabar, *The Formation of Islamic Art* (New Haven: Yale University Press, 1973).

3. See A. J. Arberry, *Aspects of Islamic Civilization* (London: Allen & Unwin, 1964), Chap. 3 ("The Sunna and the Successors"), for an overview of the early Islamic attitude toward earthly possessions.

4. See "The Attitude of the Theologians of Islam towards Painting," chap. 1 in Arnold, *Painting in Islam*.

5. See my article "Contradiction and Consistency in Islamic Art," in *The Islamic Impact*, Yvonne Y. Haddad, Byron Haines, and Ellison Findly, eds. (Syracuse: Syracuse University Press, 1984), pp. 138ff.

6. See Ahmad Muhammad Isa, "Muslims and Taswir" in *Fine Arts in Islamic Civilization*, M. Beg, ed. (Kuala Lumpur: Published by the author, 1981), pp. 41–68.

7. Arnold, *Painting in Islam*, p. 5.

8. Among the many excellent publications dealing with women in the contemporary Islamic world, see Lois Beck and Nikki Keddi, eds., *Women in the Islamic World* (Cambridge: Harvard University Press, 1978).

9. A positive view on the impact of Qur'anic revelation on the status of women is seen in Fazlur Rahman, *Islam* (Garden City, NY: Doubleday, 1968), p. 35.

10. See, for example, Bahriye Üçok's discussion of women rulers in Islam, *Islâm Devletlerinde Kadin Hukumdarlar* (Ankara: Turkish Historical Association, 1965).

11. See "Islamic Secular Art: Palace and City," chap. 6 in Grabar, *Islamic Art*.

12. See Richard Ettinghausen, *Arab Painting* (Geneva: Skira, 1962), p. 32.

13. Ibid.

14. Grabar, *Islamic Art*, illus. 91; Esin Atil, *Art of the Arab World* (Washington, D.C.: Smithsonian Institution, 1975), no. 16, pp. 44–45.

15. See, for example, Stuart C. Welch, *Persian Painting* (New York: Braziller, 1976), pp. 62–63; also his *Anvari's Divan* (New York: Metropolitan Museum of Art, 1983), pp. 101–103; and Nurhan Atasoy and Filiz Çağman, *Turkish Miniature Painting* (İstanbul: R.C.D. Cultural Institute, 1974), plate 50.

16. Grabar, *Islamic Art*, illus. 99; Kurt Erdmann, *Die Kunst Irans zur Zeit Sasaniden* (Berlin: Kupferberg, 1969), illus. 80.

17. See my article "Orientalism in European Art" *The Muslim World* 73 (1983).

18. See Kenneth Clark, *The Nude* (Garden City, NY: Doubleday, 1956).

19. Grabar, *Islamic Art*, pp. 156–57.

20. See Oleg Grabar, *The Alhambra* (London: Allen Lane, 1978), pp. 132–35.

21. Cf. Jami, *Yusuf and Zulaika*, trans. and ed. David Pendlebury (London: Octagon Press, 1982).

22. From A. G. Warner and F. Warner, eds., *The Sháhnáma of Firdausi* (London: Routledge & Kegan Paul, 1906), 2:123.

23. See Stuart C. Welch, *A King's Book of Kings* (New York: Metropolitan Museum of Art, 1972), pp. 168–71.

24. See Oleg Grabar and Sheila Blair, *Epic Images and Contemporary History* (Chicago: University of Chicago Press, 1980).

25. See Laurence Binyon, *The Poems of Nizami* (London: The Studio, 1928).

26. See Basil W. Robinson, *Persian Miniature Painting* (London: Victoria and Albert Museum, 1967), illus. 43.

27. Eleanor Sims has recently completed an exhaustive study of Muhammad Zaman, which has not yet appeared in print. See also Ivan Stchoukine, *Les peintures des manuscrits de Shah ʿAbbas Ier a la fin des Safavis* (Paris: Geuthner, 1964), pp. 60–61.

28. The broader question of the representation of women in Islamic religious art is touched upon in several works, including Wiebke Walther, *Women in Islam* (Montclair, NJ: Abner Schram, 1981), which is an excellent source of images of woman in Islamic art in general; see also Malik Aksel, *Religious Pictures in Turkish Art* (Istanbul: Elif, 1967); and Sarwat Okasha,*The Muslim Painter and the Divine* (London: Park Lane, 1981).

29. See Marie-Rose Séguy, *The Miraculous Journey of Mahomet* (New York: Braziller, 1977), for reproductions of all of the miniatures in this volume and a curious discussion of the style, iconography and text.

30. See Ivan Stchoukine, *La Peinture Turque* (Paris: Geuthner, 1971), vol. 2, plates xvii, xix.

31. Séguy, *Miraculous Journey*, plates 43, 50, 51, 53, 52, and 56.

32. See *Pictures of Everyday Life: Genre Painting in Europe, 1500-1900* introduction by Gordon Bailey Washburn (Pittsburgh: Carnegie Institute, 1954).

33. The pretextual nature of the titles of many seventeenth-century paintings, such as the mythological and religious subjects placed in landscapes by Lorrain and Poussin, comes immediately to mind.

34. Ettinghausen, *Arab Painting*, pp. 44–50.

35. See Souren Melikian, *Le Roman de Varge et Golšah* (Paris: *Arts Asiatiques* XXII, 1970), p. 214.

36. Ettinghausen, *Arab Painting*, pp. 104–24.

37. See S. C. Welch, *Wonders of the Age* (Cambridge, MA: Fogg Art Museum, 1979), pp. 178-79.

38. See Günsel Renda, "An Illustrated 18th-century Ottoman Hamse in the Walters Art Gallery," in *The Journal of the Walters Art Gallery* 39 (1981):15–32.

39. See G. E. von Grünebaum, *Muhammadan Festivals* (London: Curzon, 1976).

40. See note 17 above.

41. See W. Denny, *The Garden in the Arts of Islam* (South Hadley, MA: Mount Holyoke College Art Museum, 1980), p. 23.

42. Information kindly furnished me by Doğan Kuban of İstanbul of Technical University.

43. See Ettinghausen, *Arab Painting*, pp. 50–53.

44. See Arnold, *Painting in Islam*, p. 108.

45. See the material in Walther, *Women in Islam* (note 28 above).

46. See the material on Osman Hamdi cited in my article mentioned in note 17 above.

47. See Gültekin Elibal, *Atatürk ve Resim-Heykel* (İstanbul: İs Bankasi, 1972), after p. 184.

48. See Walther, *Women in Islam*, fig. 137.

49. See *Art in the Soviet Union*, compiled and introduced by Oleg Sopotinsky (Leningrad: Aurora, 1978), pp. 328–30, 372.

50. Ibid., pp. 264, 262, respectively.

51. Ibid., pp. 357–358.

52. Ibid., pp. 1-17.

53. See Louise W. Mackie and Jon Thompson, eds., *Turkmen: Tribal Carpets and Traditions* (Washington, D. C.: The Textile Museum, 1980). See also Jon Thompson, *Carpet Magic* (London: Barbican Gallery, 1983).

54. V. G. Moshkova and A. S. Morosova, *Kovr Narodov Sredneii Azii* (Carpets of the Peoples of Central Asia) (Tashkent, Fan, 1970).

55. The extensive bibliography of recent publications on village and nomadic rugs includes both useful publications and a fair portion of outright misinformation. A good starting point for bibliography would be the short bibliographies in Walter Denny, *Oriental Rugs* (New York: Cooper-Hewitt Museum, 1978) and Jon Thompson, *Carpet Magic* (see note 53 above).

56. See the bibliography in David Black and Clive Loveless, *Embroidered Flowers from Thrace to Tartary* (London: David Black Oriental Carpets, 1981).

Chapter Eight

Hindu Paradigms of Women: Images and Values

Sandra P. Robinson

Hindu attitudes toward women present striking contrasts. Hindus who entrust to a woman the political leadership of India are simultaneously familiar with the history of religious practices which at times consigned women to death.[1] Marked contrasts are found in the area of religious roles as well. While Hindu women are largely disenfranchised from priestly rites, they persistently maintain their own traditions of religious observances, performing rites which have been handed down from mother to daughter for many generations. This essay identifies two cultural constructs of the feminine which coexist in Hinduism, and explores some implications of women's observances in devotional Hindu traditions.

In approaching the general theme of women, religion and social change as it pertains to Hinduism, one encounters many symbolic configurations, some of which may serve as paradigms[2] for understanding ways in which idealized Indian portrayals of femininity have intersected with specific religious roles of women in Hindu society. Some images, such as that of the auspicious, life-giving Hindu wife and mother, have prevailed as undisputed conventions, while other images, like that of the newly widowed Hindu woman whose devotion to her dead husband traditionally called for life-denying acts, culminating for some in ritual self-sacrifice known as *satī*, have been touchstones for major controversy and reform within Hindu society.

The non-indigenous term "Hinduism" refers to a composite of religious traditions in which diverse philosophical, sectarian and cultic movements are loosely associated. The organizing principle for their association consists in the acceptance, to a greater or lesser degree, of Vedic literature[3] as the repository of an authoritative scriptural wisdom which is seen as ultimate and eternal. Adhering to this rather flexible criterion are numerous religions, most of which are conventionally categorized as "brahmanic" or "non-brahmanic." Brahmanic Hinduism is a Sanskrit-based priestly tradition emphasizing formal ritual. Although as a religious tradition brahmanic Hinduism has received patronage from members of all castes, brahmanic worship has been maintained in the custody of *purohits* (ritual officiants) belonging to the highest ranked caste, the brahmans.[4] Non-brahmanic Hinduism, expressed through regional languages, is a composite of diverse devotional practices emphasizing modes of worship which either deemphasize or obviate the priestly role. This general categorization bears critical significance with regard to religious roles of Hindu women in that historically, brahmanic Hinduism has tended to objectify and exclude women, whereas non-brahmanic Hindu traditions have tended to provide for full recognition and active participation by women.

A BRAHMANIC PARADIGM

In the culture of Hinduism, central symbolic configurations relating to women may be found in several cultural domains, the richest sources of images of women including the expressive genres of myth, epic literature and social history. While mythic and epic images provide models *for* social values, they also reflect models *of* society.[5] Among the many symbolic traditions which characterize brahmanic Hinduism, three configurations are, when juxtaposed, particularly useful in elucidating images and evaluations of women. The first is a configuration surrounding Hindu goddesses; the second relates to epic heroines; and the third concerns roles of human female worshippers. The more conceptual and literary issues to be considered include first, the position of goddesses in the Hindu pantheon and the ideological implications of their relations to male deities; and, second, the enduring use of epic heroines as role models for Hindu women. While the former portray dimensions of femininity which are seen as revelatory, the latter depict models of womanly roles which are regarded as exemplary. Our initial interest lies at that point where these two paradigmatic segments intersect—where the cultural construct of a transcendent feminine nature reflects and informs social models for womanly conduct; where that which is believed to be revealed through the immortals finds relevance in the lives of mortals. But there are additional issues, rather more dense in consequence, which grow out of brahmanic social institutions that developed during the course of Indian history. These, too, contribute to the brahmanic paradigm and warrant consideration here.

Goddesses and "Feminine Nature"

The first symbolic configuration, that of feminine nature revealed, grows out of the symbolism of Hindu goddesses. Their positions in the Hindu pantheon and the nature of their interactions with male deities present an ideological construct of the feminine as powerful but subordinate. The tension in this construct is partially resolved in that feminine power in its two major kinds of vehicles—the Devī or "Great Goddess" in forms such as Durgā, on the one hand, and numerous "consort" goddesses such as Lakṣmī on the other—is in the first case ambiguously derived from masculine power and in the second case subordinated to it. Some goddesses, as will be seen in the case of Pārvatī, participate fully in both realms.

The Hindu pantheon includes vast numbers of gods and goddesses, each of whom is understood to be a manifestation of the universal principle known as *brahman*. Their transformative aspects and mythic interdependencies illustrate that even the sectarian, quasi-monotheistic godheads Śiva and Viṣṇu are ultimately conceived as alternate forms of a single unity. Gender is a central factor both in the organization of the Hindu pantheon and in the allocation of traits among the deities.

Deities, like virtually all kinds of phenomena, are classified by Hindu thought into binary pairs symbolized by the imagery of male and female. By brahmanic convention, the male/female opposition generally conforms to high/low and right/left symbolisms.[6] However, the Hindu mythological designation of gender is not absolute; most if not all of the Hindu deities are regarded as androgynous in certain of their manifestations.[7] The androgynous forms are used as symbolic devices for expressing the theistic concept of ultimate unity in the two as one. Like male gods in the Hindu pantheon, female deities are associated with specific attributes and symbols reflecting their ascribed functions. Hindus generally believe that the principle of energy consists in the feminine, and that every male deity is activated by the *śakti* or dynamism of his female consort. Her role is not merely supportive; it is enabling. The numerous consort goddesses ultimately manifest the preeminent goddess herself, the Devī, as primary embodiment of *śakti*.

The Devī is more than the wife and mother of the gods, and she is worshipped for purposes which go beyond uxorial support and maternal succor. As Kālī the Devī governs time and unleashes destruction; as Māyā she arbitrates reality and illusion. In differentiated forms she afflicts and heals, provides and withholds, rewards and punishes. The sovereign and juridical aspects of the Devī's domain prevail essentially independently of her mythic relations to masculine forms of divinity, while her reproductive and nurturing aspects not only presuppose the Devī's relationships with male deities, but take such relationships as defining characteristics. The narrow mandate implied in the common generic use of "Mother Goddess"[8] signifies an interpretative disjunction between functions performed and traits acknowledged. The honorific element in the capitalization of the term accompanies the devalorization of the Devī as if in symbolic compensation.

The paradigmatic significance of Hindu goddesses may be suggested by a brief outline of the three prominent deities, Durgā, Pārvatī and Lakṣmī. In the Bengali-speaking region of South Asia, the goddess Durgā occupies a central position as the deity whose annual festival is most widely and elaborately celebrated. Durgā is the Devī in her aspect as slayer of the buffalo-demon, Mahiṣāsur. She is believed to encompass the other forms of female divinity. In the encompassing form of Durgā, the Devī originated as a composite of the powerful attributes of numerous male divinities, but she is said to wield definitive power independently.

The myth of Durgā as related in the Mārkaṇḍeya Purāṇa[9] describes her origin as occasioned by a crisis among the great gods who found themselves incapable of defeating the demons. Consequently, the gods resolved to combine forces by contributing their respective energies to a common purpose. They created the supremely powerful goddess Durgā, who appeared mightily and resiliently with eight arms, each hand holding a weapon or attribute of one of the donor gods. Seated on her lion mount, she vanquished the enemies of the gods, dealing a final blow to the buffalo–demon (see Figure 32). Her

Figure 32. Image of the Hindu goddess Durgā slaying the buffalo demon. (This and all following illustrations for this article were taken by Sandra P. Robinson in Calcutta, West Bengal, India, in 1977.)

promise to mortals was that she would reappear to ensure victory to all who worship her in her autumnal festival.

Although Durgā is portrayed as an omnipotent goddess, her power is derived from the gods whose collective force she manifests, but whose very forces are empowered by the feminine principle of energy or *śakti*. In this sense Durgā represents a reversion to type, reifying the energy which ultimately devolves upon the gods from the feminine wellsprings of dynamism. The Durgā myth, in fact, places male deities in the role of power source, even though prevalent associations of energy with the feminine distinctly predate the myth.[10] This myth demonstrates that in the brahmanic paradigm femininity is designated to be intrinsically powerful but positionally subordinate; what was primary source has become secondary synthesis. Since the Hindu concept of nature (*prakṛti*) as female represents raw energy, it would appear that to be harnessed as power for cultural use, the undifferentiated energy or *śakti* must be channeled through and actualized in refineries corresponding to the Hindu concept of form or personhood (*puruṣa*) as male; the feminine in nature is tamed by the masculine culture.

Whereas the Durgā myth points to broader implications of the brahmanic conception of feminine energy, myths of consort goddesses such as Pārvatī and Lakṣmī express power configurations inherent in mythological relationships between male and female Hindu deities. The term "consort" is problematic. Wendy D. O'Flaherty observes that although the term literally refers to a partner or spouse, its usage commonly implies that the consort is "a mere appendage, far inferior in power and status to his or her spouse."[11] Hindu goddesses relate to male mythic figures in two major ways. Where the Devī retains a dominant position, she is paired with a male figure unambiguously subordinate to her and belonging to a separate hierarchical domain, with the male husband figure serving as her guard or lieutenant. More commonly, however, the female consort relates to a dominant male figure as will be seen in the cases of Pārvatī and Lakṣmī. Lawrence Babb points to a revealing pattern in the two kinds of relationship, concluding that "when the feminine dominates the masculine the pair is sinister; when male dominates female the pair is benign."[12]

The goddess Pārvatī is both a form of the Devī and a consort of the great god Śiva. Mythologically she represents anthropomorphic aspects of the Devī and functions in a generally benign manner. What wrath she does exhibit is usually portrayed through imagery within the range of human emotions, such as wifely jealousy and anger. Superhuman rage conventionally requires her transformation into Kālī or another form of the goddess in her fierce aspect. Pārvatī's name means "daughter of the mountain," referring to her identity as child of the anthropomorphized Himālaya mountains and her association with elemental, chthonic energy. Iconographically Pārvatī most often appears as the matron consort of Śiva. She is not a geneatrix, but is mother by adoption to the six-headed Skanda, military general of the gods, and to the prominent elephant-headed Gaṇeśa, remover of obstacles. In Hindu myths Pārvatī goes through the fluctuating fortunes of domestic life, emerging as authoritative in connubial dialogues with Śiva on the mysteries of life and sexuality.

Pārvatī's relationship with Śiva is ambiguous in that she can be seen either as his appendage or as his controller.[13] She actualizes the ambivalence implicit in the identity of the consort. Through these dual aspects, Pārvatī employs her illusory (*māyā*) and transformative capacities and can be seen to mediate three levels or modes of being: the deific, the heroic and the mortal. As deity she is Devī and consort; as heroine she is *satī* (see below); in addition, she frequently assumes the role of a mortal by becoming incarnate in a manner characteristically attributed to Hindu deities. O'Flaherty finds this multiplicity of forms to be significant in that Pārvatī thus becomes a pivotal figure, serving as "the focal point of transition between male-dominated and female-dominated hierogamies."[14]

If Durgā represents ambiguously derived power and Pārvatī ambiguously subordinated power, Lakṣmī represents clarity in both function and status: she exercises her own independent mandate as a goddess with a specific functional domain, and simultaneously she is fully incorporated in the cult of Viṣṇu as the major consort of the great god. In this sense Lakṣmī can be seen as an uncompromised symbol of the brahmanic view of femininity; she possesses independent and full power while being fully dependent and subordinate to her male lord.

Lakṣmī is the Hindu goddess of wealth and prosperity. Whether or not she is cultically descended from the apparent goddess figures found in Indus Valley excavations,[15] she is symbolically linked to the feminine Vedic personification of fertility and abundance, Aditi. As goddess of fortune, Lakṣmī has both auspicious and inauspicious forms, the latter designated by a negative prefix as Alakṣmī. Lakṣmī is portrayed iconographically as a beautiful, buxom woman seated on a lotus, and is associated with symbols found in the worship of Viṣṇu, such as the mace and the discus. Her attributes as consort are described in the *Viṣṇu Purāṇa* using her epithet "Srī":

> Srī, the bride of Vishṇu, the mother of the world, is eternal, imperishable; in like manner he is all-pervading, so also is she, oh best of Brahmans, omnipresent. Vishṇu is meaning; she is speech. Hari [Viṣṇu] is polity . . .; she is prudence. . . .Vishṇu is understanding; she is [concrete] intellect. He is righteousness; she is devotion. He is the creator; she is creation. . . .He is sacrifice; she is sacrificial donation. . . .Govinda [Viṣṇu] is the ocean, Lakshmī its shore. . . .[16]

The objectified nature of the feminine is clearly presented here. Lakṣmī is viewed as the concrete complement of Viṣṇu, created by him and serving as the gift of his sacrifice. The same passage continues, however, with additional images, some of which illustrate Lakṣmī's role as the *śakti* or dynamic energy of Viṣṇu even as she remains subordinate:

> Lakshmī is the light: and Hari [Viṣṇu], who is all, and lord of all, the lamp. She, the mother of the world, is the creeping vine; and Vishṇu the tree round which she clings. She is the night; the god who is armed with the mace and discus is the day. . . . Govinda [Viṣṇu] is love; and Lakshmī, his gentle spouse, is pleasure. But why thus diffusely enumerate their presence:—it is enough to say, in a word, that of gods, animals and men, Hari is all that is called male; Lakshmī is all that is termed female: there is nothing else than they.[17]

The understanding of roles depicted here exemplifies the broader Hindu view of gender-specific attributes, and the text leaves no question but that these images of feminine nature are to be applied paradigmatically.

The Wifely Ideal

The second symbolic configuration, that of the exemplary woman, emerges from the roles of epic heroines as behavior models for women. Whereas only selected elements of goddess imagery are considered appropriate as models—the prescriptive thrust of the myths being revelatory rather than exemplary—the prevalent message in epic portrayals of women is precisely that the character of epic heroines should be aspired to by all virtuous Hindu women.

The *Mahābhārata* story of Sāvitrī,[18] whose persistent devotion brought about the resuscitation of her dead husband, illustrates the conventional Hindu concept of women as possessors of life-giving virtue; their explicit primary duty is faithful service to their husbands as their lords. In the epics as well as in the scriptural *śastra* texts, wives are enjoined to worship their husbands as gods and to identify entirely with the identities and interests of their families. Sāvitrī embodies the ideal of the *satī*, the faithful wife who avoids inauspicious widowhood by risking or sacrificing her own life in order to enhance her husband's karmic destiny.[19] However, she achieves the state of *satī* inversely; instead of joining her husband in death, she causes her husband to rejoin her in life. For this reason Sāvitrī is associated with the auspicious, positive role of the ideal wife.

The exemplary character of Sāvitrī is usefully seen in relation to two other prominent female figures in Hindu mythology. One is the goddess/heroine Satī, wife of Śiva, whose paradigmatic act of self-sacrifice represents wifely virtue *in extremis*, and by whose name, which means "virtue," the institution of *satī* is designated. The second is the heroine Sītā, wife of Rāma, whose persevering virtue is tested through extraordinary adversity. Their roles, too, are auspicious, but the emphasis in their stories is on the suffering of indignities and the exhibition of willingness to die for the sake of virtue, in contrast to Sāvitrī's direct victory over death.

Briefly, Satī is described in *purāṇa* myths[20] as the daughter of Dakṣa and wife of Śiva. Satī suffers an intolerable insult when her father spurns Śiva by denying him a proper share in his grand sacrifice. Satī consequently becomes enraged and enters into the fire, avenging her husband's honor by committing suicide; she is then reborn as Pārvatī. In the aftermath her body is dismembered, and the sites where her body parts fall become "energized" as pilgrimage centers throughout the subcontinent.

The *Rāmāyaṇa* heroine Sītā is associated with images of fertility. The name "Sītā" means "furrow," and she undergoes an apotheosis to become identified with Lakṣmī, goddess of wealth and increase. Sītā is portrayed as the ideal wife in that she remains dutiful to her husband Rāma throughout her long exile from him following her abduction by the demon Rāvaṇa.[21] The struggle between Rāma and Rāvaṇa is the central theme of the epic, and Sītā's role is pivotal as "the subtle provocatrice"[22] motivating Rāma's heroism.

Sītā is twice victimized, once in the abduction and extended captivity, and again when rescued and faced with the need to prove to Rāma that she has remained pure and faithful to him. Her suffering culminates in a self-imposed trial by ordeal wherein she steps into a sacrificial fire. Because the virtue of her intentions is intact, she emerges unscathed. By redeeming her virtue in this manner, Sītā risks death in order to protect the reputation of her husband.

The paradigmatic statement on the ideal wife seen in the examples of the epic heroines Sāvitrī, Satī and Sītā articulates and applies the construct of the feminine found in myths of the goddesses Durgā, Pārvatī and Lakṣmī. The significance of the paradigmatic images discussed here is apparent not only in the realm of ideology, but also in the arena of social history. Accordingly, the third genre contributing to the brahmanic construct of women's roles is found in *praxis*, in the history of religious practices undertaken by Hindu women within the brahmanic tradition.

The "Value of Women"[23]

Because of the overriding importance of marriage as culturally mandated in the lives of Hindu women, it is not surprising that throughout Indian history up to the modern period, the most consequential developments in brahmanic practices relating to women have centered on women's marital status. (In brahmanic thought, unmarried women seem to have been viewed as anomalous and therefore invisible.) Here is found our third symbolic construct, that of the value of women. In the extreme, brahmanic religion in effect sanctioned institutions which included female infanticide in the face of the dowry system, a ban on widow remarriage, and the practice of *satī*, popularly known as widow immolation.

During the earliest period of Indo-European civilization in South Asia prior to 600 B.C., Vedic religion allowed some active participation by women. Socially, widows were allowed to remarry, though generally this was to be done within the extended family. However, following the brahmanic synthesis by the second century A.D., the codifications of the *smṛti* scriptural traditions placed firm restrictions on the activity of women.

In particular, the *dharmaśātras* excluded women from the core of ritual, and firmly fixed their social status in a manner exemplified by some of the most frequently quoted textual excerpts from the "Laws of Manu":

> By a girl, by a young woman, or even by an aged one, nothing must be done independently, even in her own house.
>
> In childhood a female must be subject to her father, in youth to her husband, when her lord is dead to her sons; a woman must never be independent. . . .
>
> Her father protects (her) in childhood, her husband protects (her)

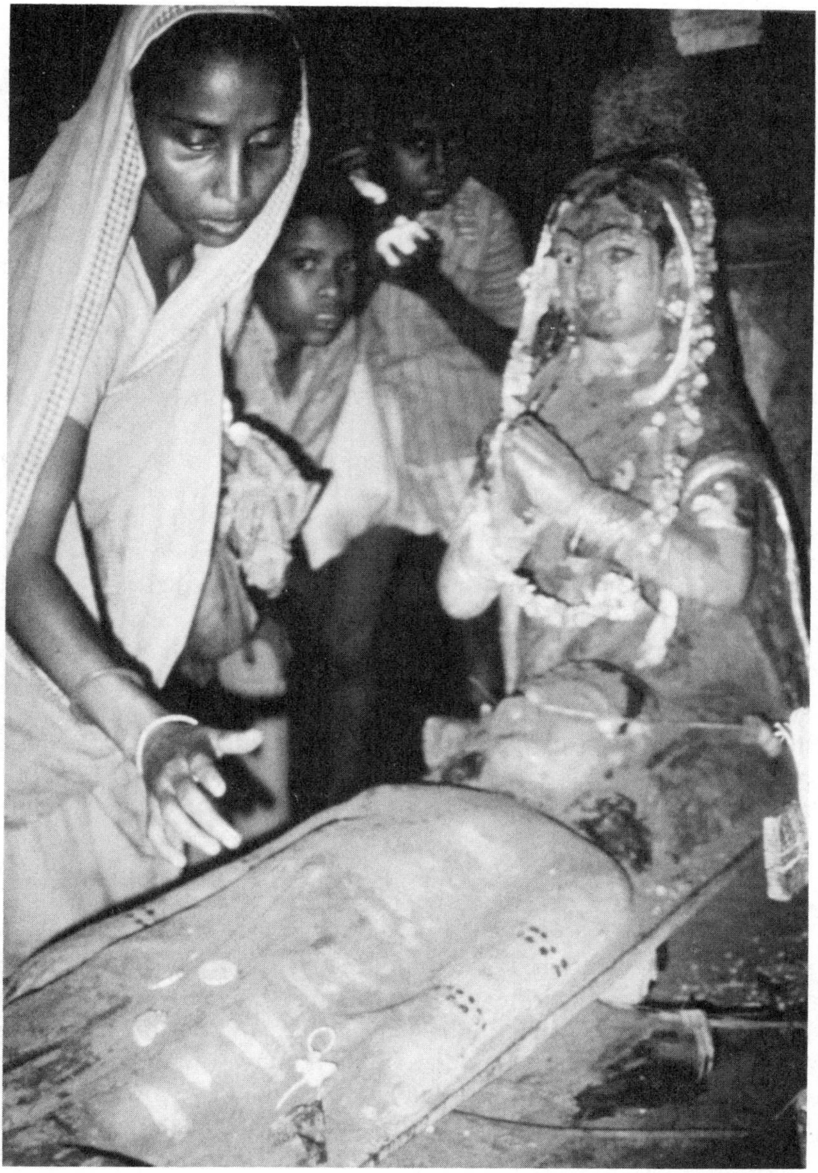

Figure 33. Hindu woman paying respect to an image of the epic heroine Sāvitrī whose devotion resurrected her husband.

in youth, and her sons protect (her) in old age; a woman is never fit for independence.

Reprehensible is the father who gives not (his daughter in marriage) at the proper time; reprehensible is the husband who approaches not (his wife in due season), and reprehensible is the son who does not protect his mother after her husband has died. . . .

Though destitute of virtue, or seeking pleasure (elsewhere), or devoid of good qualities, (yet) a husband must be constantly worshipped as a god by a faithful wife.

(*Manusmṛti*, V, 147–8; IX, 3–4; V, 154)[24]

The reasons for this disenfranchisement seem to reside in the general effort by priestly interests of the period to synthesize and codify a clear system of social tenets in order to consolidate Hindu society and arrest the increasing encroachment of popular heterodox movements such as Buddhism and Jainism. It is arguable that such a general effort required the codified subordination of women, but in fact the leading schools of thought took this course. The code of Manu and others like it generally governed values and guided conduct throughout the classical and middle periods of Indian history from the fourth through the eighteenth centuries A.D. Many Hindus complain that it continues to have significant impact even today.[25] In the eleventh century, India saw the start of the establishment of Muslim rule, bringing with it ideas on the suppression of women which may well have reinforced, but except on specific issues[26] certainly did not counter, the stringencies already endemic to Hinduism.

Perhaps more consequentially, however, there were economic institutions current in India which implemented the devaluation of women. At the center was the institution of the dowry. Critical religious observances were predicated on the dowry which, together with the traditional brahmanic prohibition on widow remarriage, underwrote a tragic history of female infanticide and widow self-immolation. These realities inspired derivative forms of symbolic life-denial as well, so that in addition to those women who were denied life itself, many more experienced what by all objective, even indigenous, standards must be regarded as a significantly compromised quality of life.

The practice of female infanticide seems to have arisen during the middle period of Indian history between the thirteenth and eighteenth centuries. It took a variety of forms ranging from the outright killing of newborn female infants by methods such as umbilical cord strangulation, opium on the mother's or nurse's breast, or drowning in the Ganges River, to more protracted practices of neglect or withholding of nourishment or medication.[27] Although common in certain parts of India, perhaps most notably Rajasthan and Bengal, infanticide was not the dominant norm, and wherever it was current it aroused indigenous opposition.

In part concurrently, the practice of *satī* was widely held as an idealized expression of wifely devotion in late middle period India, eventually culminating later in the nineteenth century. According to this custom, a newly widowed wife of any age was expected to join her husband in death by stepping onto his funeral pyre just before his body was cremated. The act of *satī* was replete with symbolisms of ritual sacrifice (that is, marking, anointing), and the courageous *satī* was believed to be blessed by her virtue. *Satī* seems to have begun among warrior castes in northwestern India where women went to such lengths to avoid falling captive to the enemy. If following one's husband into death on the battlefield began as an expedient, it in time become rationalized as a virtue and was associated with spiritual benefits. The practice then spread to other communities. Reports of incidents[28] indicate that *satī* at times was indeed undertaken voluntarily by the grief-stricken wife as a religious sacrifice, whether against the protest of relatives or with their encouragement; but at other times it was tantamount to murder. In the vulnerable, impressionable condition of grief, some women were persuaded or forced to perform the rite.

It should be acknowledged that by subjective standards from within the apologetic sector of pre-reformed brahmanic culture, infanticide and *satī* were viewed as compromises worth making for religious reasons. Both were seen as legitimate modes of sacrifice consistent with Hindu themes of renunciation more generally, and *satī* represented the penultimate expression of wifely virtue.[29] A wife's highest duty was to keep her husband alive and well. This earthly responsibility reflected the mythological association of transcendental power with the feminine. In addition, the institution of the dowry rendered remarriage of widows impractical. Philosophically and economically, a woman was believed to have no viable reason to live without her husband. If she were to live, a widow was traditionally expected to shave her head and wear only a plain white sari; to dispose of her ornaments; to avoid attending auspicious occasions; to eat no more than one spare meal a day. More than simply reflecting general modes of Hindu renunciation, such practices, specific to women, symbolically approximated death.

It must be emphasized that through the history of female infanticide and *satī*, many Hindus vehemently opposed the practices. Even before the modern period there were alternative traditions which inveighed against infanticide, holding that even the transgression of abortion was as grievous as that of killing a brahman.

The three symbolic configurations identified and discussed here are additionally suggestive when brought together, and their symbolic interactions may now be summarized. How does the goddess relate to the heroine, and how do these figures relate to women in the history of Hinduism? Brahmanic Hinduism presents an ideological construct of femininity which centers on subordination and the control, by appropriation or deflection, of raw feminine energy. The same values have applied to the lives of women in the purview of this religious tradition.

At the core of feminine nature as revealed in Hindu mythological constructs, the interaction between power (*śakti*) and subordination leads to a view of the feminine as preeminently enabling. The consort goddesses sign over their powers to male divinities; the Devī derives her powers from male divinities in order to fight her battles even as she is the source of their powers. The consorts are subordinate by hierarchical arrangement; the Devī is so by her derivative qualities, ambiguously derivative though they be. Therefore, femininity is portrayed to have no independent legitimacy. It follows, perversely though logically, that the institution of infanticide in its diverse economic and cultural aspects should have coincided with such an ideology. The spirit of the dowry is also reflected in this paradigm of dependent status conjoined with enabling power. With regard to women in brahmanic religion, the logic of mythological devalorization parallels the logic of economic devaluation.

To conclude this discussion of the brahmanic paradigm of women, the close relation of the construct of the exemplary heroine to the other paradigmatic segments illustrates that mythic goddess, epic heroine and mortal *satī* are not mutually exclusive entities in brahmanic conceptualization. Instead, these images overlap and merge in specific figures. Goddesses often appear as heroines; charismatic human women are at times transformed into legendary figures of epic proportion and, alongside associative paths conventional to Hindu thought, are on occasion approximated even to the Devī herself. *Satī* becomes a paradigmatic state of mind—an attitude incorporating images of life-giving power and enabling virtue, and a code prescribing self-sacrifice without complaint.

A Paradigm of Women in Devotional Hinduism

Alongside brahmanic Hinduism, devotional Hindu traditions present an alternative understanding of femininity and allow for more active religious roles on the part of women. In the daily lives of Hindus, devotional expressions by both men and women are the most prominent and visible of all religious practices which occur. Central features of devotional worship include the reverence of images as meditational aids, the offering of hospitality rites to deities invoked in those images, the presentation of food and other offerings to the deities, the conduct of pilgrimage to temples and other sacred sites, the observance of song and dance vigils, and the performance of other diverse gestures of servitude. All such acts are to be performed in a mood of devotion (*bhakti*). There are many schools of thought within *bhakti* traditions, and no definitive codification of doctrine is acknowledged by all of the schools. Generally, however, devotional religion is predicated on a direct relationship between worshipper and deity, with the devotee appealing directly to the deity in a modality of praise, petition, persuasion or gratitude.

Devotional practices in India are essentially pre-brahmanic, dating probably from a time prior to the arrival of Indo-Europeans on the subcontinent during the second millenium B.C. No clear chronology is available for the origins of specific devotional practices among the indigenous population because of the paucity of early textual documentation of non-Vedic traditions. Institutionalized devotional innovations such as the building of temples with permanently installed images, and the concomitant worship of divine consorts, are known to have been established during the early classical period between the fourth and sixth centuries A.D.[30] It may be safely assumed that many modes of devotional worship in India significantly antedated this period of institutionalization. The elaboration of devotional themes in *bhakti* religion and literature continued through the middle period of Indian history from the thirteenth through the eighteenth centuries A.D., concurrently with the growth of the brahmanic practices mentioned above.

Hindu devotionalism is not only essentially pre-brahmanic but also largely extra-brahmanic, requiring no priestly mediation between deity and devotee. However, many devotional observances occur in tandem with brahmanical ritual, separated often only by content, personae, location, sequence, or symbolic demarcations. Other devotional practices take place in formats quite apart from brahmanic contexts. Hindu women perform rites in both settings; some women's practices are adjunct to brahmanism and others are independent of brahmanic influence.

Devotional Roles of Women

Taking field observations from the region of Bengal to illustrate details of such configurations, women participate in devotional Bengali Hinduism in at least three major contexts, each of which is considered below. First, women along with men engage in mainstreamed acts of devotion addressed both to brahmanic deities and to popular regional cult figures. Such acts may be seen as generic to Hinduism, though not unique to it. These acts are thematically related to brahmanism even though they represent a different historical tradition popularly known as the "*bhakti* movement." Women's involvement in mainstream devotional Hinduism is distinguished from men's involvement, then, neither textually nor contextually. Secondly, women perform devotional acts which are separate from but coordinate with brahmanic festivals. Here, too, the deities addressed include both brahmanic and regional figures. These practices are known as "*strī-ācār*" or "wives' rites" and represent, in effect, a text of women's devotionalism in a context of the institutional male-dominated Hindu establishment. Thirdly, women carry on devotional practices developed around specific vows (*vrata*) which traditionally have been observed exclusively by women. The deities to whom the vows are addressed include brahmanic, regional and local gods and goddesses. Among several categories of vows, those performed exclusively by women include two subsets. The first, *śāstrīya vratas* (*śāstric* vows), grow out of traditions of generic *bhakti* and *strī-ācār*, thereby bearing marks of coordinate brahmanic Hinduism. The second, *jyoṣit vratas* (folk vows), reveal no more than a superficial linkage to brahmanical elements. *Jyoṣit vratas* are at the farthest remove from brahmanic religion textually and contextually.

Symbolic configurations found in women's devotionalism include primary as well as secondary constructs. Configurations such as those in *jyoṣit vratas* which emanate from practices "indigenous" to and exclusive to women, originating from women's concerns and reflecting women's evaluations of themselves, may be thought of as primary. Mixed configurations which show the incursion of brahmanic elements (for example, Sanskrit *mantras* or prayers), or which yield to structures, interests or values of the brahmanic establishment, or which reflect a mixture of male-dominated constructs and women's primary constructs, may be thought of as secondary. Before turning to women's own expressions within Bengali Hinduism and a paradigm suggested therein, the secondary configurations will be considered. Since most devotional practices are mixed, the primary/secondary distinction is best viewed not as a typology but as a continuum.

Women have virtually always been free to participate fully in the first category of wide-ranging generic devotional practices current in non-brahmanic Bengali Hinduism. Women frequently lead song vigils and devotional recitations in temples as well as homes. They figure prominently in pilgrimage activities, some of which include the performance of austerities of varying degrees of rigor, such as fasting, circumambulating shrines and temples, carrying pots of water or pots of burning coals along prescribed paths, or fulfilling special provisions of personal vows. Although the most vigorous athletic austerities tend to be reserved for men in popular Bengali festivals such as the *Śiva gājan*, the *Dharmapūjā* and the *Manaṣāpūjā*, coordinate austerities performed by women are viewed by Hindus as symbolically and functionally equivalent. By extension the ideological statement regarding women suggested in mainstream devotional Hinduism implies that in their religious roles, women are functionally equivalent to men.

This is not true, however, in the case of the second contextual category of devotional practices which coincide with brahmanic institutions; there, sex-linked religious functions prevail. Although women are excluded from officiating in priestly rites, regardless of caste, they often do more than play supportive roles even in the arena of active worship. The ritual status of a brahman woman approximates that of a man or woman of any of the lower castes, the important exception being the brahman woman's access to a significant share of derived ritual status through marriage. Where sponsorship of brahmanic rites is concerned, women routinely serve roles supportive to their husbands' roles as sponsors by preparing food offerings in certain circumstances and by organizing the social activities that inevitably surround domestic and temple worship.

In addition to such tasks, women perform their own ceremonies which sometimes occur in tandem with brahmanic observances. These practices are seen by the priestly establishment as residual, extrinsic, supplemental, "behind-the-scenes" activities; at most they have the status of being "riders" to the main events. Women, however, view their practices as important, consequential elements of a distinctive tradition. Women's ceremonies or *strī-ācār* are usually separated temporally or spatially from the titular rites. For example, in Bengal following the grand autumnal *Durgāpūjā* celebrations, once the brahman *purohit* (priest) has concluded the formal worship, women customarily approach the image of the goddess Durgā to place food on her lips as a gesture of farewell before the image is taken away for immersion in a pond or tank (see Figure 34). A psychodrama of reluctant departure accompanies this activity, inasmuch as the goddess has come only to go home again; there are wailing laments which explicitly replicate and anticipate the farewells of young brides as they leave their own families to return to their husbands' family homes. Such affairs of women have no place in the formal ritual agenda.

It is pertinent to compare the two classes of women's rites described thus far. Both represent dimensions of devotional religion, but in the case of generic bhakti devotionalism there is no major distinction between what women and men do in expressing devotional worship. Neither actions, gestures nor utterances are gender-specific. Since persons of both sexes participate together in devotional wor-

Figure 34. Hindu women feeding the image of Durgā after priestly rites have been concluded.

ship, the tradition links men and women contextually as well as substantively. By constrast, in the case of *strī-ācār* the women's practices are distinctly and substantively different from the coincident practices belonging to the male-dominated brahmanic establishment. By definition and symbolic articulation, what women do is "radically other." Priests recite codified mantras while women sing improvised laments; to reverse these roles would be traditionally unthinkable in one case (women reciting mantras) and laughable in the other (priests wailing laments). The content of women's devotional expressions retains its integrity here; the only link between the brahmanic and the women's rites is contextual.

Women's Rites

Moving away from the two secondary constructs of women in Hindu devotionalism where women are distinct from men in identity but equivalent to men in function, we now focus attention on the third construct of women's primary configurations as seen in the *vrata* tradition. In these observed configurations one finds a paradigm which may be juxtaposed with the brahmanic paradigm of women and which yields an alternative interpretation of the position of women in Hinduism.

Vratas are domestic rites which Hindu women perform in the fulfillment of specific desires. These rites are consistent with traditions of sacrifice, asceticism and penance pervasive in Hinduism more generally. The class of *vratas* discussed here belongs to the broad and important category of *vratas* or vows in that, by tradition, *vratas* in this class are performed exclusively by women. Since *vratas* vary greatly in different regions of India, this discussion refers specifically to the Bengali-speaking region of South Asia, although it should be remembered that as above, many of the practices have cognate but not necessarily identical forms elsewhere in India.

As a class of religious rites *vratas* are more comprehensive than "vows" are understood to be in western traditions. Hindu vows encompass much of the votive range of devotionalism. The element of promise, whereby the devotee commits herself to perform an act of worship, may be subsumed in *vratas* under any of several arrangements, including pragmatic contingency agreements in which the devotee promises conditionally to fulfill the vows provided the divine blessing requested transpires first.

The performance of a women's *vrata* follows a procedural format which includes four basic elements: 1) the performance of rites (*ācār*);

2) the chanting of verses (*chaddas*) which comment on the rite or entreat the deity to come forth; 3) the drawing of rice-powder diagrams (*alpanas*) depicting that which is desired; and 4) the recitation of stories (*katha*) which serve as mythical precedents for the rites and explain the purposes of the *vrata*. Although each of these elements may be performed independently of the *vrata* context, they are transformed from ordinary cultural expressions to putatively efficacious religious expressions when two or more are performed conjointly as parts of *vrata* observances. *Vratas* may be categorized according to calendrical fixedness, theistic reference, purpose, condition of the performer, or other such criteria. What is most significant about the *vrata* tradition is that women perform the observances entirely by themselves without priestly sanction or interference. The *vrata* tradition constitutes an alternative to brahmanism for women, since as noted, women have been generally disenfranchised in post-Vedic brahmanic ritual.

Women perform *vratas* in order to gain and maintain domestic welfare, health and prosperity. Each *vrata* is believed to serve a special function or provide a special benefit, and the vow is undertaken voluntarily for that reason. In addition, there are *vratas* which are performed for all purposes, but even these have some specialized claims attached to them. Some *vratas* are intended for unmarried girls to perform in order to get god-like husbands or benevolent in-laws; others are intended for married women to perform in order to have sons, to preserve the health and safety of husbands and children, to help children pass school exams or husbands prosper in their careers. Still others, few in number, are intended for widows to perform in hopes of better luck in the next life. Otherwise widows may perform those wifely *vratas* which are considered not inappropriate.

It seems clear, therefore, that while *vratas* are *of* women and *by* women, they are not *for* women. Those who perform *vratas* invariably explain that the benefits they gain are derivative. For this reason Hindu feminists generally have not supported the preservation of this women's tradition, even though many appreciate the *vrata* as an outpouring of creativity by women. *Vratas* are a religiously important form of action-meditation whereby one symbolically depicts one's desire in order to realize it. Through force of will rather than by magic, the *vrata* devotee seeks actively, to paraphrase Shelley, "to create that which she contemplates."[31] Handed down from mothers to daughters, *vratas* teach lessons which have idealistic and practical dimensions and are regarded as ethical and efficient.

Before considering one *vrata* in symbolic and historical detail, the basic format of the *vrata* story warrants comment. The *vrata* story (*katha*) explains the origin and justification for the rite. A typical story takes place in a domestic scenario with humans and deities as actors. The human protagonist is inevitably female. The sequential pattern of the story involves a predicament; intervention providing advice that the *vrata* should be performed and describing how it is to be done; the paradigmatic performance of the *vrata*; the ensuing solution to the predicament; and the charge that the practice be continued. The stories are usually situated in kitchens, bazaars, at weddings, or in gardens or courtyards. Common predicaments reflect women's work: cooking utensils may be broken and then, because of the *vrata*, restored; similarly, food spilled or consumed may be replenished; riddles posed and answered; deities disguised and recognized; and drowned persons revived. Such motifs occur throughout Bengali folklore, but the thematic range of subjects common to *vratas* is consistent with the women's perspectives from which they are told. The *vrata* stories elaborate upon women's traditional concerns, basic responsibilities and existential frustrations. Such motifs are to be found below in the discussion of the *Itu vrata*.

The contextual configuration of the *vrata* is one in which a woman is both sponsor and officiant of the rite, both protagonist and teller of the story. In the narrative, her primary relationship is with the goddess or god; she interacts with men initially by placing herself in the role of victim, but subsequently she transforms herself into the spiritual mentor or provider for men. She demonstrates sororal loyalty to other women. The dignity inherent in women is palpable in the images presented.

If a single paradigm may be drawn from segments of the devotional traditions discussed here, that complex paradigm reflects Hindu women as separate from men, but equivalent to them rather than subordinate in religious status. Women have control over their own domain and acquire influence in matters more general. In the *vrata* stories women usually remain mortal, but earn special power by virtue of cleverness. Women are shown to be perceptive in understanding the message revealed by the deity and obedient in following the deity's instructions. The power gained may reflect the principle of *śakti*, but that power is acquired through heroic labors. Since the power is used for the welfare of others, the woman in Hindu devotionalism retains the enabling function attributed to her by the brahmanic tradition. The spirit of renunciation also appears in devotional expressions, and may be cast in the imagery of *satī* in the sense of the ideal of a self-sacrificing attitude; however, the message, the model and the value are in distinct contrast to those found in the brahmanic paradigm.

Women, Men and the Itu Vrata

As one of the more popular practices currently observed in West Bengal, the *Itu vrata* illustrates salient dimensions of women's religiosity in Hindu devotionalism. In addition, settings in which this *vrata* is performed point to male attempts to appropriate elements of a tradition previously within the exclusive domain of women.

"Itu" is a familiarized Bengali form of the Sanskrit name "Mitra," Mitra being a Vedic male deity associated with the sun god Sūrya and his daughter Sāvitrī (after whom the epic heroine is named). Devotional worship of Itu takes place currently in three basic forms: in its original form as a women's *vrata* in both folk (*jyoṣit*) and literary (śāstrīya) rescensions; as a private *pūjā* involving conventional worship with offerings; and as a public community *pūjā* with broad-based sponsorship and diversified purposes. In the *pūjā* formats a brahman priest or *purohit* officiates. The original *vrata* form corresponds to the third context of devotionalism identified in the preceding section as exclusive to women; the *pūjā* forms are associated with the first category of generic Hindu devotionalism.

The distinction among the three forms of the *Itu vrata* is significant because the *pūjā* forms represent an incursion of the brahmanic establishment into the domain of women's Hindu observances. Such an incursion takes place in one of two ways: as the full appropriation of the *Itu vrata* adapted to new priorities which are largely male-defined, or as the partial incorporation of elements of the *Itu vrata* into the traditional brahmanic *Mitrapūjā* ritual. The latter is the more common, and evidence of it may be found in brahmanic *pūjā* manuals.[32] As for the former, it will be seen that brahman *purohits*, necessarily male, are currently performing certain women's *vratas*, including the Itu, for modern women clients who prefer to pay for this service at the temple rather than to perform the time-consuming observances at home. It is in the *purohits'* interests to earn fees for these services. Many women also enjoy the brahmanic prestige that accompanies such arrangements. Such prestige accords with conventional modes of upward mobility through "Sanskritization."[33] Beyond this formalized, professional appropriation, it will also be seen that in one observed case, low-caste men have appropriated in full the women's institution of the *Itu vrata*, performing it for the stated purpose of demonstrating their virility and machismo. They have radically adjusted the *ācār* or practices of the *vrata* to conform to their purpose.

The *Itu vrata* is traditionally performed by married women for the enhancement of family health and welfare, and by unmarried girls in anticipation of their future family interests; widows are not expected to perform this vow. The *vrata* is observed at midmorning every Sunday throughout the month of Agrahayan (late November through early December), with initial rites on the eve of the first day of the month and terminal rites at the end of the month. The *Itu* rite centers around the planting of seeds and grains and the subsequent germination of sprouts which are said to symbolize the devotee's wish for healthy children and domestic prosperity. The rite is also believed to be of help in curing blindness, reflecting a motif widely associated with myths of the sun. However, the vow itself is not believed to have automatic efficacy to ensure those blessings; the sincerity of the devotee's intention in fulfilling the vow is a determining factor on its successful culmination.

Like other *vratas*, the *Itu vrata* has a four-part structure including rites, verse recitations, pictorial diagrams and a *vrata* story. The ritual procedure generally followed for the *Itu vrata*, allowing for localized variations, begins with the devotees gathering in a domestic courtyard and making preparations for small plantings. Each vowtaker mixes soil with a bit of cow dung as fertilizer in a small earthen pot which she has decorated with red and white paint. She then places a prescribed number of seeds and grains in the pot; usually the number is five or eight of each (see Figure 35). Devotees refer to this act as planting the "sun's crop" ("*raviśaśya*"). Every Sunday the vowtakers pour water into their respective pots from water taken from a common, large, full pitcher. During the germination period food offerings are given to Itu, who may be represented in the image of a large, round, brightly colored pot with a face painted on its side. Many of the offerings are made of milk, flour, new fruits and new molasses of the season. These offerings are called "Itu's food cravings" (*Itur sādh*) as in pregnancy. After food offerings have been presented to Itu during each observance, the *prasād* (blessed leavings) are eaten by the women in attendance. Unlike the *prasād* of other ceremonies, this may not be given to men.

Verses recited during a *vrata* provide the best textual index to the degree to which the rite has been brahmanized. Where a vernacular rhyme is recited by the female ritual performers, the *vrata* is likely to have retained its original structure; where a Sanskrit mantra (prayer

Figure 35. The Hindu women's folk practice of tending germinating plants in the *Itu vrata*.

formula) is recited, usually by a priestly officiant, the *vrata* is likely to have been brahmanized. A typical recitation in the traditional form of the *Itu vrata*, chanted by women, is this simple Bengali utterance: "I put eight seeds and eight grains in the Itu pot; I hear the Itu story with full concentration; Itu gives us all good lives and prosperity." By contrast, in its brahmanized form the Itu observance includes the priest's recitation in Sanskrit of prescribed *mantras* within the fixed format of a conventional brahmanic *pūjā*. The *mantras* consist of formal epithets praising various forms of the solar godhead, culminating in stylized praise of the sun Sūrya as giver of light, cleanser of sins and, above all, source of all life, who appears radiant with his solar retinue. Such recitations introduce the brahmanic preoccupation with purity into the symbolic configuration of Itu. As Sūrya, Itu has a retinue including his female consorts Sanjnā ("Definition") and Chāyā ("Shadow"). The significance of these consorts is considered below.

The *alpana* or pictorial diagram associated with the *Itu vrata* may include any of several decorative motifs intended to attract the deity to attend the observances. Common *alpana* motifs, used both purposively and ornamentally, include lotus blossoms; creepers or vines; trees and plants; rivers and village scenes; birds, fish and other animals; anthropomorphic figures; and astronomical bodies.[34] These designs are drawn along with purposive sketches of ornaments, furnishings or symbols of other objects desired as a result of performing the *vrata*. The *Itu vrata alpanas* reflect such stock motifs without unique or special features. They are drawn for the conventional purpose of providing a "seat" for the large pot representing Itu. For this particular vrata, the *alpana* is deemphasized in favor of focusing on the decorative painting of the little clay pots which are distinctive in this rite.

The story (*katha*) for the *Itu vrata* has regional variants within Bengal,[35] but a general synopsis is given here:

The Story of the Itu Vrata

> There was once a poor brahman who lived with his wife and two daughters, Umna and Jumna. Umna was named after a sacred mountain: Jumna was named after a sacred river. One day the hungry brahman was angered to find that his wife, after cooking, had not saved all of the sweetmeats for him to eat. She instead had given each of her daughters one of the delicacies. Enraged, the greedy brahman took his daughters into the jungle and abandoned them.
>
> Throughout a long night in the jungle Umna and Jumna faced a series of crises. They were attacked by ferocious animals and by threatening ghosts. But despite their fatigue and hunger, they survived and managed to escape. Morning found them weeping.
>
> In the morning mist, celestial female spirits known as *apsaras* appeared before them and advised them to perform the *vrata* for Itu so that they might return home and their family never again want for food. One of the *apsaras* taught the girls all of the proper procedures for performing the vow. She told them to bathe and then to fill little clay pots with soil; to plant seeds of five different

Figure 36. A Hindu woman reading text of the *Itu vrata* story without priestly assistance at home.

plants in each pot along with grains; to water the plantings each Sunday with water from a large pitcher of Ganges River water; to cover the little pots with clay saucers while awaiting germination; and to concentrate on Itu as the source of life and fertility.

Having learned the procedure, Umna and Jumna prepared to do the *vrata*. Accordingly, they went to a pond to bathe. However, the pond was dry. The *apsaras* then gave each of the girls a ring made of *durva* grass. When they tossed the rings into the empty pond, the pond suddenly became full. Umna and Jumna then performed the *Itu vrata* on the bank of the pond. Itu was pleased and blessed them with the promise of health and prosperity. The fields became filled with crops.

On the way home, as they were gathering spinach leaves, Umna and Jumna discovered a golden pitcher. The pitcher had on it the image of a man's face—the man who resided in the pond. Jumna hid the pitcher in her sāri and the girls continued on their way home to see their mother. Their mother was delighted to see them, but their father cursed the return of his daughters. He took the golden-faced pitcher and threw it in anger, but the pitcher returned like a boomerang.

The girls then performed the *Itu vrata* at home as the *apsaras* had taught them to do. In time their mother gave birth to a handsome son. Meanwhile their father became rich and prosperous.

One day a thirsty rājā came to the brahman's house and asked for water to drink. Jumna gave him a very small pot of water, but the rājā was surprised to find that the tiny pot supplied enough water for his full entourage. The rājā and his chief minister married Jumna and Umna forthwith, and all lived happily from that time, spreading the fame of the *Itu vrata*.

The rags-to-riches theme matches the naive tone of this story; yet in its ritual setting the story functions more as a myth than as a fairy tale. The wishes and fantasies of poor Bengali village girls dominate the surface content of this *vrata* story, but at a deeper level the story offers a compelling statement on women's views of gender relations and on the powers believed inherent in the performing of women's rites.

The precipitating event in the story is not only the brahman wife's provoking her husband's greed. It is also a matter of her breaking the convention of traditional Hindu society which calls for men to be fed first. The mother is loyal to her daughters, and together with the *apsaras*, they constitute a feminine alliance in opposition to the oppressive masculine establishment represented by the father. But they do so by affiliating with the constructive powers of the sun god Itu who may be seen either as male or as transcendentally androgynous.

From textual evidence of variants of this story it is apparent that Umna and Jumna represent the two wives of Sūrya, the Hindu sun divinity.[36] Umna is the wife Chāyā, which means "shadow," and Jumna is the wife Sanjnā, which means "defined image" or "consciousness." Devotees who perform the *vrata* comment that the germination process requires shade just as the sprouts require sunlight. Significantly, these enabling agents are portrayed as feminine characters in the story.

In the resolution of the *vrata* story the Itu pitcher is patently a symbol of fertility; held under Jumna's sāri, it is associated sympathetically with the mother's conceiving a son and its presence in the household is accompanied by numerous transformations resulting in increase, fructification, wealth and prosperity. Because the pitcher is ever full, it becomes the signal means by which Umna and Jumna gain prominent husbands.

The condition of the sisters is transformed from passivity to activity and thereby from hunger to fulfillment. In this initiatory scenario they gain saving knowledge, and are rewarded for prevailing heroically in their ordeals. Values taught through this story include sororal loyalty, bravery, commitment and faithfulness. However, it is evidence of the social context that Umna and Jumna begin as dependents of their father and end as dependents of their husbands. Their net gain is that the father is known to be malevolent and their husbands are presumed—but only presumed—to be benevolent, if not by disposition then out of respect for the women's powers gained through their worship of Itu. These powers constitute their dowries.

In the performance of the Itu and other *vratas*, traditionally it is women who function both as sacrifiers, or sponsors of the rite, and as sacrificers, or officiants of the rite.[37] Unlike brahmanic ritual in which a priest is required (and only a male brahman may serve as priest), in this tradition of women's devotionalism the woman is the quasi-priestly ministrant. It is she who recites the story which in itself represents archaic, collective female authorship. The mythical and ritual motifs of the *vrata* articulate religious conceptions of, and express the self-awareness of, Hindu women in traditional Bengali society.

The paradigmatic configuration resulting from Hindu devotionalism differs from the brahmanic paradigm not so much in terms of the analysis of givens as in the interpretation of possibilities. In both, women are powerful but subordinate, but in the women's traditions their powers are used directly and resourcefully and their subordination is reduced, in effect, to a symbolic level. Instead of consigning their powers and efficacy to male agents as brahmanic consort goddesses do, women in devotional Hinduism exercise their powers themselves for purposes they themselves choose. The purposes in the end do reflect values of self-sacrifice, but the selflessness involved in performing rites for one's family welfare proceeds from a posture of efficacy and confidence, which differs fundamentally from the comparatively diffident and deferential statement of self-denial expressed by the act of *satī*, heroic though the idealized *satī* may be considered to be.[38]

The *Itu vrata* is no longer performed exclusively by women. The traditional priestly disdain for *vratas* as a collection of trivial women's customs has recently given way to priestly appropriation of the practices. For example, during the 1960s, an increasing number of temple *purohits* (priests) at Calcutta's prominent Kalighat temple began to offer their services to women clients who wished to have any of several *vratas* performed in the temple setting for reasons of convenience and prestige.

The *purohits* perform the *vratas* in the manner of a conventional *pūjā* (worship with offerings), but essential components of the *vrata* are retained. Figure 37 (1971) shows a woman listening to the *Itu vrata* story as read by the temple priest she has engaged to perform the rite. She holds a flower in her cupped hands, and maintains devotional concentration as she hears the story. The *alpana* (diagram) and *chadda* (jingle) are usually omitted in this kind of temple observance, but the *katha* (story) and the *ācār* (rite) are performed by the male priest.

The modern arrangement is advantageous to temple priests in that they earn fees for their services as they do for other rites they perform in the temple. Their clientele may be expanded as well, with *vrata* clients returning to them to have other Hindu observances performed. The women in turn are spared the time-consuming preparations for the *vrata*, the gathering of apparatus and making advance arrangements. In addition, they see the temple venue as a form of legitimation or upward mobility for the *vrata*; the *Itu vrata* is Sanskritized by virtue of the context in which it is performed.

In a separate and more distinctive development, certain men in Calcutta in recent decades have fully appropriated the *Itu vrata*, adapting it to their own purposes. In North Calcutta, an annual Gym-

Figure 37. A modern Hindu woman listening to a priest read the *Itu vrata* story at the Kalighat Temple in Calcutta.

nasium is held on a public street in front of a temple dedicated to Itu. The athletic feats performed by men on this occasion are known as the "Itu vrata." Activities include physical fitness demonstrations, athletic stunts and trapeze drills. The name of the deity, the *vrata* heritage, and the votive structure are consistent with the traditional *Itu vrata*. However, the rite (ācār) of planting is performed in an abbreviated manner by the male priest. The story (*katha*) of the *vrata* is dramatically reduced, and its reading by the priest becomes perfunctory. The diagram (*alpana*) and jingle (*chadda*) are, of course, absent. Most importantly, women are excluded from the observances.

The history of this baroque adaptation of a women's tradition dates from the late 1930s when two young men belonging to the low-ranked fisherman caste found themselves ridiculed by friends because neither had begotten a child after each had been married for more than four months. The two learned that they were to be mocked publicly by the erection of a Karttik image in front of their houses and the performance of a "Karttik *vrata*." (In Hindu mythology, Karttik is the son of Śiva associated with masculine prowess and virility.) Since this would ruin their social reputations they resolved to preempt their rivals by staging another rite on the same day, beginning earlier. The alternative was the *Itu vrata*. Their motives in making a display of machismo are apparent from these circumstances. The local tradition grew, and a small permanent temple to Itu was subsequently built on the site of the men's *Itu vrata* in North Calcutta.

Although this last instance of male appropriation of a women's rite is exceptional, the more general pattern of priestly involvement in the tradition suggests that significant changes are likely to continue, leading toward increased mainstreaming and brahmanization of women's *vratas*.

The two paradigms presented here point to two distinctive constructs of femininity that coincide and coexist in Hindu traditions. For each, interpretive sources of imagery have been found in literary referents and in social roles with message, model and value taken into account. In the brahmanic construct of the feminine, women are seen as custodians of virtue whose life-giving energy, when tamed, enables all action. Simultaneously, women are subordinate to male agents of the very action women empower. In code and practice, women are symbolically devalorized and economically devalued, self-sacrifice being the destiny of their virtue. By contrast, the alternative paradigm suggested by devotional Hindu traditions, here drawn from Bengali expressions, presents a view of women as efficacious agents of action whose religious domain retains self-legitimating integrity and value. Where self-denial is found, it is not gender-specific and therefore reflects a more general Hindu value of renunciative generosity. While Hindu women remain socially subordinate to men, women's devotional traditions are religiously coordinate with those of the male brahmanic establishment. Women's rites seem, in select circumstances, increasingly subject to male appropriation. The devotionalism of Hindu women is expressed through diverse, generative acts in an unmediated religious voice.

Notes

1. Mrs. Indira Gandhi was Prime Minister of India at the time of this writing. The historically important practices alluded to here include the institutions of the dowry, female infanticide, restrictions on widow remarriage, and the self-immolation of widows. Each of these practices has been unequivocally condemned by the Government of India, and contemporary Hindus generally dissociate themselves from these historical legacies. Infanticide and

widow immolation are virtually extinct; the values surrounding dowry transactions and widow remarriage have been slower to change. See *Status of Women in India: A Synopsis of the Report of the National Committee on the Status of Women* (New Delhi: Indian Council of Social Science Research, 1975).

2. "Paradigm" is used here simply to denote interpretative matrices in the traditions discussed. The images which form the paradigms are indigenous expressions drawn from myth, literature and social history. This usage is consistent with the classical, non-technical meaning of the term, and differs from technical applications current among those whose projects involve the exegesis of methods. In terms of Kuhnian categories (Thomas S. Kuhn, *The Structure of Scientific Revolutions*, 2nd ed. [Chicago: University of Chicago Press, 1970], and "Second Thoughts on Paradigms," in Frederick Suppe, ed., *The Structure of Scientific Theories* [Urbana: University of Illinois Press, 1974], pp. 459–82), the configurations discussed here may at most be likened loosely to "partial paradigms" or "exemplars" having to do with Hindu interpretations of womanhood, with the indigenous broader *weltanschauungen* of brahmanic and devotional Hinduism as "global paradigms," each reflecting its respective "theory" within the context of Indian religions. Kuhn's internal criteria for paradigmatic structure are reflected in the symbolic configurations used here: goddess configurations reflect "shared symbolic generalizations"; exemplary heroine configurations reflect "shared models," and sacrificial victimization configurations reflect "shared values" of the Hindu traditions discussed. (See Richard H. Wells and J. Steven Picou, *American Sociology: Theoretical and Methodological Structure* [Washington, D.C.: University Press of America, 1981], p. 12.)

3. Vedic literature represents a textual tradition in Sanskrit dating from the second millenium B.C. The literature centers on the *Vedas* (c. 1200-800 B.C.), consisting of four collections of hymns praising early Indo-European deities. Subsequent Vedic literature composed approximately between the eighth and fourth centuries B.C. includes the *Brāhmaṇas* (compendia of ritual commentaries on the *Vedas*), *Āraṇyakas* (esoteric elaborations on the *Vedas*), and *Upaniṣads* (speculative teachings based on the *Vedas*). This literature is believed to be "revealed" (*śruti*) and is traditionally regarded as the ultimate authority on all matters. Since Hinduism is neither a monotheistic nor a founded religion, the *Vedas* occupy a central position in Hinduism analogous to that occupied elsewhere by a supreme deity, a prophet or a founder.

Subsequent literature claiming penultimate authority as "remembered" tradition (*smṛti*) includes the two great epics of the *Mahābhārata* and *Rāmāyaṇa*, completed between the sixth and fourth centuries B.C.; the *sūtras* (aphoristic teachings) and *śāstras* (instructional treatises) dating from as early as the third century B.C.; and *Purāṇas* (mythological traditions) beginning between the fourth and sixth centuries A.D. The textual basis of Hinduism also includes numerous schools of commentary on each of the genres mentioned. See J.N. Farquhar, *An Outline of the Religious Literature of India* (Oxford: Oxford University Press, 1920).

4. The four general caste categories *varṇa* include *brahmans*, associated tra-

ditionally with religious authority and education, *kṣatriyas*, associated with royal or political authority, *vaiśyas*, associated with production and mercantile activity, and *śūdras*, associated with services which are ranked in terms of relative "cleanness." Below the four castes are others, traditionally considered "untouchable." Hindus belong to specific caste groups (*jāti*) which are hereditary, endogamous and commensal; each *jāti* is ranked within one of the four (*varṇas*). The caste system is maintained by consensual adherence to principles of hierarchy and purity/pollution. Although caste discrimination is illegal, caste customs persist to varying degrees in contemporary Hindu society. There is no real correlation between ascribed, *jāti-linked* occupations and actual occupations.

5. Clifford Geertz, "Religion as a Cultural System" in Michael Banton, ed., *Anthropological Approaches to the Study of Religion* (London: Tavistock Publications, 1966), pp. 1–46; see pp. 7ff.

6. For example, see E. F. Beck, "The Right-Left Division of South Indian Society," *Journal of Asian Studies* 29 (1970):783–84.

7. See Mircea Eliade, *The Two and the One* (New York: Harper and Row, 1965), especially the essay, "Mephistopheles and the Androgyne. . . ," pp. 78-124, *passim*. An illustration of the androgynous Śiva can be found in Heinz Mode, *The Woman in Indian Art* (New York: McGraw-Hill, 1970), plate 9.

8. For examples of this usage, see Narendra Nath Bhattacharyya, *The Indian Mother Goddess*, 2nd rev. ed. (Columbia, Missouri: South Asia Books, 1977), and M. C. P. Srivastava, *Mother Goddess in Indian Art, Archaeology and Literature* (Delhi: Agam Kala Prakashan, 1979).

9. F. Eden Pargiter, tr., *The Mārkaṇḍeya Purāṇa* in *Bibliotheca Indica* series, 2 vols. (Calcutta: The Asiatic Society, 1904; repr. ed., Delhi: Indological Book House, 1969). The myth of Durgā is told in the "Devī-Māhātmya" section of the text, Cantos 82–92 of the 1969 edition

10. See P. V. Kane, History of *Dharmaśāstra*, 5 vols., 2nd rev. ed. (Poona: Bhandarkar Oriental Research Institute, 1962); vol. 5, part 2, pp. 1041ff. According to Pargiter (see note 9 above, p. xiv) the *Mārkaṇḍeya Puraṇa* is thought to have been composed certainly prior to the tenth century and perhaps as early as the fifth century A.D. Wendy Doniger O'Flaherty suggests that the "*Devī-Māhātmya*" was probably interpolated into this *purāṇa* between the fifth and seventh centuries A.D. (*Women, Androgynes, and Other Mythical Beasts* [Chicago: University of Chicago Press, 1980], p. 81).

11. O'Flaherty, *Women, Androgynes, and Other Mythical Beasts*, p. 78. The brief comments on Pārvatī given here are based on one thread of argument within O'Flaherty's excellent interpretation of Pārvatī, in ibid., Chaps. 4, 5 and *passim*.

12. Lawrence A. Babb, "Marriage and Malevolence: The Uses of Sexual Opposition in a Hindu Pantheon," *Ethnology* 9 (1970):142.

13. O'Flaherty, *Women, Androgynes, and Other Mythical Beasts*, p. 121.

14. Ibid., p. 92.

15. Mortimer Wheeler, *Civilizations of the Indus Valley and Beyond* (New York: McGraw-Hill, 1966), *passim*. The figures in question have been widely

assumed to be "mother" goddesses created for ritual use; see note 8 above.

16. H. H. Wilson, tr., *The Vishnu-Purāṇa*, 3rd ed. (Calcutta: Punthi Pustak, 1961), pp. 52–53.

17.Ibid., p. 53.

18. J. A. B. Buitenen, tr., *Mahābhārata*, 3 vols. (Chicago: University of Chicago Press, 1974-1978); 2:760-78. For a discussion of Sāvitrī and other Indian epic heroines see Prabhati Mukherjee, *Hindu Women: Normative Models* (New Delhi: Orient Longmans, 1978).

19. Karmic destiny refers to the Hindu principle of *karma* which holds that one's destiny is determined by one's cumulative conduct, and that this process continues through future lives resulting from the transmigration of the soul. Religious Hindus seek release (*mokṣa*) from this chain of rebirths.

20. For example, see K. R. van Kooij, tr., *Worship of the Goddess according to the Kālikāpurāṇa*, part 1 (Leiden: E. J. Brill, 1972), pp. 120, 134–35. See also H. H. Wilson, *The Vishnu-Purāṇa*, pp. 56–60. A popular summary of the story can be found in Heinrich Zimmer, *The King and the Corpse*, ed. Joseph Campbell (posthumously) (New York: Bollingen, 1948), Part II.

21. See Hari Prasad Shastri, tr., *Rāmāyaṇa*, 3 vols. (London: Shantidarsan, 1962).

22. Cornelia Dimmitt, "Sītā: Fertility Goddess and Śakti," in John Stratton Hawley and Donna Marie Wulff, eds., *The Divine Consort: Rādhā and the Goddesses of India* (Berkeley: Graduate Theological Union, 1982), pp. 210–23; p. 220.

23. This term is used by Shirley Lindenbaum in an article on economic issues in an anthropology of Islamic Bengal (Bangladesh). See "The Value of Women," in John R. McLane, ed., *Bengal in the Nineteenth and Twentieth Centuries* (East Lansing: Michigan State University Center for Asian Studies, 1975), pp. 75-83. For a general history of issues discussed in this section see A. S. Altekar, *The Position of Women in Hindu Civilization*, 2nd ed. (repr.) (Delhi: Motilal Banarsidass, 1962). For bibliographies see Carol Sakala, *Women of South Asia: A Guide to Resources* (New York: Kraus International Publications, 1981) and Maureen L. P. Patterson, in collaboration with William G. Alspaugh, *South Asian Civilizations: A Bibliographic Synthesis* (Chicago: University of Chicago Press, 1981), *passim*.

24. G. Bühler, tr., *The Laws of Manu* (London: Oxford University Press, 1886); V, 147-48; IX, 3–4; V, 154; parentheses in verse are translator's. See also R. M. Das, *Women in Manu and His Seven Commentators* (Varanasi: Kanchana Pub., 1962).

25. Such complaints address the persistence of attitudes; the codes themselves have long been supplanted by modern Hindu codes and also superseded by secular civil law. A recent history of the women's movement in twentieth-century India may be found in Jana Matson Everett, *Women and Social Change in India* (New York: St. Martin's Press, 1979).

26. This point is a matter of interpretation, but may stand without holding Islam culpable for Indian misogyny. An example of one issue in which Islam was more liberal than Hinduism was that of women's inheritance rights.

27. Specific accounts of incidents of infanticide may be found in polemical treatises of the colonial period, e.g., James Peggs, *India's Cries to British Humanity* (London: Simpkin and Marsball, 1832). For a recent historical analysis of the institution see Lalita Panigrahi, *British Social Policy and Female Infanticide in India* (New Delhi: Munshiram Manoharlal, 1972), which contains a useful bibliography of primary sources including Parliamentary Papers.

28. See detailed accounts in the polemic by Peggs (see note 26 above) and in Edward Thompson, *Suttee: A Historical and Philosophical Enquiry into the Hindu Rite of Widow-Burning* (London: George Allen & Unwin, 1928).

29. For a discussion of the rationale for the view of *satī* as heroic, see Paul B. Courtright, "The British Civilizing Mission and the Controversy over Suttee," in Charles H. Long, ed., *The Primitive and the Civilized: The Locus of a Problem* (Macon, Georgia: Mercer University Press, forthcoming).

30. For an introduction to the historical context of these developments, see Romila Thapar, *A History of India*, vol. 1 (Baltimore: Penguin Books, 1966), pp. 136-41; 157–61 and *passim*.

31. ". . . to hope till hope creates/from its own wreck the thing it contemplates," Percy Bysshe Shelly, "Prometheus Unbound," Act IV.

32. E.g., Krishnachandra Smrititirtha and Ramdev Smrititirtha, eds., *Purohit Darpan*, 2 vols. (Calcutta: P.M. Bagchi, 1956), pp. 362–63.

33. See M.N. Srinivas, *Social Change in Modern India* (Berkeley: University of California Press, 1969).

34. This list of motifs was originally formulated in a popular Bengali work on the subject: Abanindranath Tagore, *Vaṅglar Vrata* (Bolpur: Viśvabharati Publications, 1919), pp. 75–76.

35. The synopsis given here is a composite summary of the account most current in West Bengal in 1977, when a twelve-month period of field research was conducted under the auspices of a Fulbright Faculty Research Award. The ritual data presented here was also collected during this period.

36. Krishnachandra Sm. and Ramdev Sm., *Purohit Darpan*, p. 363.

37. The terms "sacrifier" and "sacrificer" are used here following Henri Hubert and Marcel Mauss, *Sacrifice: Its Nature and Function*, trans. W. D. Halls (Chicago: University of Chicago Press, 1964).

38. See note 29 above.

CHAPTER NINE

Images and Roles of Women in Bengali Vaiṣṇava padāvalī kīrtan[1]

DONNA MARIE WULFF

It is commonly assumed that the social reforms affecting the condition of women that were carried out in India during the nineteenth century owed their primary or even sole inspiration to Western ideas.[2] From this premise it is easy to understand why pressure for these reforms would have grown in Bengal, the home of the British East India Company from the late seventeenth century and the locus of the first capital of the British Raj. Yet deviation from orthodoxy in eastern India has roots that go back much farther, and women of the region seem at times to have enjoyed a degree of respect and freedom unknown in most other areas of the north. Thus although the major impetus for change in the nineteenth century may have come from the West, indigenous or at least earlier patterns of thought and practice in eastern India quite possibly paved the way for the reforms of the modern period. A review of the evidence regarding religious conceptions and the status of women in Greater Bengal from ancient times will set the stage for our more detailed consideration of recurrent images and roles of women that emerge in the stories narrated by male and female singers of a major form of religious performance in contemporary Bengal, Vaiṣṇava *padāvalī kīrtan*. In looking at transcriptions from actual performances, we shall consider the possibility that women singers have positively influenced the direction of social change.

THEOLOGICAL CONCEPTIONS OF THE FEMININE IN BENGAL

Eastern India has played host to a series of unorthodox religious movements stretching back to Upaniṣadic times. As early as the sixth century B.C.E. the small riverine kingdoms in the eastern reaches of the Ganges Valley were proving hospitable to various heterodox teachings, including those of the Buddha and Mahāvīra.[3] Such receptivity was due at least in part to the fact that this region was geographically remote from the centers of Aryan culture to the west, and therefore relatively untouched by the Vedic sacrificial cultus and the concomitant brahmanical dominance in religious matters.[4] In addition to the early Buddhist and Jain communities, which grew up and continued to flourish there, the region saw the origin and development of tantric teachings and practices in both the Hindu and the Buddhist communities during the medieval period.[5] Unorthodox elements in the Bengali Vaiṣṇava movement inspired by Caitanya in the sixteenth century, which also flourished primarily in eastern India, are in large part a continuation of this tantric tradition.[6]

From the period of our earliest substantial evidence, that of the Pāla dynasty (ca. 750–1150 C.E.), female deities have played a major role in Bengali religious life.[7] The prevalence of images of goddesses of diverse types from approximately the seventh century of the common era demonstrates the popularity of goddess worship in the region.[8] In addition to images and reliefs in which the Goddess is the principal figure, we find numerous representations of pairs of divinities (usually Śiva and Devī in one of her forms; later also Krishna and Rādhā) and also of the androgynous Ardhanārīśvara, Śiva conceived as half male and half female.[9] Together with the iconographic evidence, moreover, we have abundant textual evidence of the worship of goddesses in Bengal, beginning with the *Devī Purāṇa*, which also advocates the worship of women especially in the form of young virgins.[10] From the *Gītagovinda* of Jayadeva, court poet of Lakṣmaṇa Sena of Bengal in the late twelfth century, there is likewise considerable textual and subsequently also iconographic evidence for the exaltation and worship of Rādhā, cowherd mistress of Krishna.[11]

Goddess worship was not confined to the Hindu segment of the population but became widespread among Buddhists as well. The goddess Tārā, for example, was worshipped among Buddhists in various areas of India from at least the sixth century C.E.[12] The antiquity of her worship in Bengal is suggested by the fact that the Buddhist grammarian Candragomī (c. fifth–sixth centuries C.E.) wrote a hymn of praise to her that was quite possibly inspired by the image of her at Candradvipa, where he is alleged to have settled.[13] The Chinese pilgrim Hsüan-tsang commented on the prevalence of the Tārā cult in Bengal in the first half of the seventh century.[14] That Tārā served as the banner or standard emblem of the Pāla kings is attested by the Nesari plates of the ruler Dharmapāla (ca. 770–810 A.D.).[15] The Buddhist cult of Tārā, itself almost certainly based on earlier forms of popular worship, in turn exerted considerable influence on subsequent Hindu conceptions and practices.[16]

In addition to the prevalence of female deities in Bengal from ancient times, there are other important religious conceptions, current especially in tantric circles, that have potential bearing on the question of the religious and social status of women. Chief among these is the view that the highest reality in the universe is androgynous.[17] We have seen one iconographic representation of this idea in the figure of Śiva as half male and half female. Theologically the female half of the polarity is expressed by the term *śakti,* the energy or power of divinity, and iconographically it is most often represented as a goddess consort of Śiva: Pārvatī or Umā, as her gentle aspect; Durgā or Kālī, as her ferocious one.[18] The triumph of the female half of the divine duality is symbolized in the image of the fierce Kālī: tongue lolling out, she wears a garland of bloody heads and a girdle of severed hands and stands on the body of her prostrate lover, inert except for a prominent erect phallus, who is interpreted as a mere corpse (*śava*) unless he is energized by her.[19]

Corresponding to the divine androgyny at the cosmic level, in the Śākta view, is a male-female polarity in the human sphere. Each man is a microcosm of the divine male, Śiva, and each women likewise contains within her the divine *śakti.* The more radical school of tantric practitioners used ritual sexual union as a means of realizing these potentialities. The Vaiṣṇava *sahajiyās* took over this fundamental conception and expressed it in their own terms, viewing human heterosexual love as a microcosmic version of the sublime union of Rādhā and Krishna.[20]

A distinct but equally important conception of the religious significance of woman evolved among orthodox Vaiṣṇavas.[21] Following the lead of the Vaiṣṇnava *purāṇas,* especially the *Bhāgavata* (c. 800 C.E.), in which the *gopīs,* the cowherd women beloved of Krishna, were portrayed as his most ardent devotees, writers of the Caitanya school put forth the view that the devotion of women represented the standard; male devotees were accordingly required to become female in their approach to divinity.[22] As we shall see, this view is of fundamental importance for the poetry and stories rendered in *kītan* performances.

WOMEN'S SOCIAL AND RELIGIOUS STATUS IN BENGAL

It has been possible to amass a considerable body of evidence for the popularity of goddess worship in Bengal, and for the prevalence of conceptions of reality and ideals of religious devotion in which the female is exalted over the male. Far more difficult, however, is the task of correlating such conceptions and practices with the actual social and religious status of women in the region. Unfortunately, the historical evidence is far too fragmentary to allow us to link prevailing conceptions of divinity among a certain group or in a given period with the actual social circumstances of women.[23] Furthermore, the evidence we have from the ancient and medieval periods is limited by and large to the elite strata of the population.[24] Yet as the general unorthodoxy of Bengal might suggest, some women of the region, contrary to the injunctions of *Manu* and other orthodox treatises on *dharma*,[25] have played and continue to play highly independent and significant social and religious roles.[26] It would appear that such women, by reinterpreting traditional religious images, have positively affected the process of social change.

Our evidence regarding the status of women in the ancient period (fourth–twelfth centuries) is especially meager. R. C. Majumdar, writing evidently of the upper classes, claims that women were educated, and that many were also probably literate.[27] He refers to contradictory evidence regarding the practice of secluding women known as *purdah*,[28] and he gives the *Bṛhaddharma Purāṇa* (c. 1250–1300 C.E.) as authority for the claim that "[i]n ancient Bengal, as in the rest of India, a woman had hardly any independent legal or social status. . . ."[29]

Majumdar likewise portrays the social position of widows as wholly unenviable. Viewed as inauspicious, they were rarely permitted to participate in rituals and ceremonies.[30] Again taking the *Bṛhaddharma Purāṇa* as his authority, Majumdar maintains with appropriate caution that widows were apparently encouraged to commit *satī* on their husbands' funeral pyres;[31] however, an alternative provision in the same passage, for doing so much later, with a cherished object of the husband,[32] suggests that the practice was by no means universal. Finally, Majumdar provides evidence of one area in which the legal injunctions in Bengal regarding widows were more liberal than those in other areas of India: the noted jurist Jīmutavāhana stipulated that a widow who had no son might inherit the entirety of her husband's property in accordance with what seemed to be fairly orthodox views of the status and function of a widow in society.[33]

Although still fragmentary, the accumulation of evidence from the medieval period (roughly thirteenth–eighteenth centuries) indicates a range of options available to women, especially of the upper classes, for assuming leadership roles. These opportunities were most abundant among the hill tribes to the north, where a remarkably egalitarian system seems to have prevailed: from the sixteenth to the eighteenth century, according to Sukumar Sen, women in this area were "the compeers of men in every sphere of life except perhaps the military."[34]

Even before the sixteenth century, we have evidence of one queen in eastern India who served highly successfully as regent during her husband's lifetime, Viśvāsadevī of Tirhut. In addition to her administrative abilities, she is known for having compiled a treatise on the worship of Gangā (the Ganges River conceived as Goddess),[35] and she commissioned the famous court poet Vidyāpati to compile a parallel treatise on the worship of Śiva.[36] In the late eighteenth century, we find another queen to the northeast who was likewise an able administrator and a patron of learning: Candraprabhā, the wife of Tāmradhvaja of Kachar, ruled her husband's kingdom when he was taken captive and later as the dowager queen before her son took over as king, and she successfully promoted the spread of Sanskrit culture in the kingdom.[37]

In addition to women rulers who were active patrons of literature, we have records of a number of women donors. Legendary among such women in Bengal was the zemindar Rāṇī Bhavānī, who is renowned for her prodigious charities. These included land donations to worthy brahmans and the founding of temples and temple endowments in such major pilgrimage centers as Banaras.[38] Women of families of far more modest means were also memorialized as donors. Kennedy claims that the Caitanya temple at Dhakkadaksin in Sylhet, the birthplace of Caitanya's father, was founded by a woman in Caitanya's family.[39]

We have noted the literary productivity and energetic patronage of several women rulers. Beginning in the late sixteenth century there were also—especially but not exclusively among the Vaiṣṇava community—a number of accomplished women poets and teachers whose Sanskrit and vernacular writings have survived. In the seventeenth-century *Bhaktiratnākara* of Narahari Cakravartī we find mention of Icchādevi, the wife of Rasikānanda, who wrote vernacular poetry in Bengali.[40] In the eighteenth century a significant number of women appear to have written at least on a small scale, but we have little historical evidence regarding these authors. Sen cites two sisters or cousins, of a Vaidya family from Faridpur, one of whom, Ānandamayī, assisted her uncle in composing a poem entitled *Harilīlā*.[41] Sen also mentions the renowned Sanskrit teacher Hatī Vidyālaṅkāra, of Sonai in West Burdwan, who likewise lived and taught in the eighteenth century. She had her own Sanskrit school and was, like the youthful Caitanya himself, "a match for the best Sanskrit pandits of the day."[42] Yet like Caitanya, too, it is as a Vaiṣṇava devotee that she is best remembered, for she retired to Brindavan at the end of her life and wrote devotional songs in Braj Bhāṣā that are still cherished today.[43] Finally, mention should be made of one prominent woman writer that Sen classifies as a non-Vaiṣṇava, Candrāvatī, daughter of Vaṃśīdāsa Cakravartī, a writer and singer of popular vernacular poetry in praise of Manasā, the snake goddess of Bengal. Yet although stray Manasā verses bearing her name suggest that she too wrote Manasāmaṅgal poetry, she also wrote a short Rāma poem for women to sing in marriage ceremonies. The few lines of the poem that have survived indicate the extreme poverty of her family; thus we may conclude that there were at least some learned and literary women among the lower classes.[44]

From such isolated examples of women authors, it is of course impossible to ascertain the extent to which women in general were educated or literate. Citing the *Caṇḍīmaṅgal* of Mukundarāma, a sixteenth-century work that provides a fairly detailed picture of the social circumstances at the time in Bengal, Dinesh Chandra Sen argues that even women of the lower castes in that period were receiving a fairly good education.[45] The Caitanya movement, with its great outpouring of Sanskrit and vernacular literature, appears to have served as a powerful stimulus to literacy; Kennedy cites as evidence for the increase in literacy among ordinary devotees, the large number of medieval manuscripts that have been found in quite humble homes, and he claims that many of these manuscripts were written by persons of low caste.[46] Although one may well doubt that literacy even among Vaiṣṇavas approached universality, Sukumar Sen's view that women of the leading Vaiṣṇava families were literate seems plausible in the light of the available evidence.[47]

The Vaiṣṇava community was singled out for special commendation in regard to literacy by two British writers of the first half of the nineteenth century. Hunter described a subsect of Vaiṣṇava women mendicants (*vairāgiṇīs*) who held a theory of women's independence and who were trained as teachers of women in order to propagate the sect's teachings. They were apparently so successful in that role that the British government proposed to establish a school for them so that they could be utilized in the general education of women.[48] William Adam, writing reports to the government on vernacular education in Bengal and Bihar in the 1830s, also noted that the only exception to the general conditions of illiteracy among ordinary women were found among the groups of mendicant Vaiṣṇavas.[49] It is striking that both these claims are made not of the Vaiṣṇavas as a whole, but of the mendicants among them.

We have seen that there were women rulers, patrons, and donors in medieval Bengal, as well as women writers and teachers. As we have noted, our evidence regarding the position of ordinary women is quite limited. Yet we are able to form a picture of a society that differs strikingly from the blueprint furnished by the contemporary treatises on *dharma*.[50] It is true that the practice of polygyny and the existence of a marked double standard indicate a situation of male dominance. Moreover, the magical practices described in texts of the period reveal an eagerness on the part of women to control their husbands that had no counterpart among the men.[51] Yet, as Raychaudhuri argues, the very existence of charms that "were meant to 'domesticate' the husband, who, ideally, should remain silent like a dead cow's head when the wife abused him" shows that women did not meekly fulfill the injunctions of the *dharma* texts to revere their husbands as gods.[52] Likewise calling into question the effectiveness of the ideal of wifely submission is the inclusion in a popular form of musical narrative (*pāñcālī*) of a set piece entitled "The Wives Malign Their Husbands," in which the women of the village contrast their husbands' faults with the virtues of the story's hero. According to Raychaudhuri, one rarely finds women being even mildly reproached for such lack of respect.[53] Thus, although the position of women in society appears to have been one of subordination and emotional insecurity, it was clearly not one of powerlessness.[54]

We have reviewed various strands of evidence regarding the social status of women in medieval Bengal. Likewise significant for our investigation is the question of women's religious status. As early as the Pāla period we find evidence of women teachers of Buddhist *tantra* in Eastern India,[55] and women *gurus* are also known to have played a significant role in the Sākta community.[56] Yet it is for the Vaiṣṇava movement inspired by Caitanya that we have the most impressive evidence: heirs to both Buddhist and Hindu tantric traditions, the Vaiṣṇavas have from the first honored women as religious leaders and teachers, and subsequently also as writers and performers of *kīrtan* songs.

Caitanya himself is depicted by his Bengali biographers as having had a characteristically ascetic position regarding women: he apparently saw them as distractions and enjoined his ascetic followers to avoid them.[57] Yet the biographical-hagiographical texts also indicate that certain women were held in great esteem by the early community. Among these were Śacī and Viṣṇupriyā, the mother and wife of Caitanya,[58] who have continued to be honored into the present century. Kennedy wrote of a shrine to these two women in Navadvip that was still popular among the women of the area.[59] Unlike Viṣṇupriyā, who apparently took no active part in the movement, Sītā and Jāhnavā, wives of Caitanya's two most prominent Navadvip disciples, assumed major leadership roles. The position of Jāhnavā was particularly exalted: greatly learned and endowed with a forceful personality, she appears to have been equal in status to the most prominent Vaiṣṇava leaders (*gosvāmīs*).[60] In the succeeding centuries a fair number of women, especially in the families of certain of the leading *gosvāmīs*, were likewise revered as spiritual teachers. The greatest such woman in the early seventeenth century was Hemalatā, the daughter of Śrīnivāsa, who was considered her father's spiritual successor.[61]

Women and kīrtan

We have seen evidence that there have been women writers in Sanskrit and Bengali in Eastern India from early medieval times and that it is among the Vaiṣṇavas that literary activity and literacy in general have been especially high. Much of what these women wrote was intended to be performed, and in the case of *kīrtan* we have evidence that there have been a significant number of women singers from fairly early times. Sen claims that in the late eighteenth century, when *kīrtan* was becoming fashionable in the cities, professional women *kīrtanīyās* were becoming influential. He gives the name of one woman singer Gaṅgāmaṇi, who was also a composer.[62] In my own research on *kīrtan*, I recorded and photographed several women singers currently performing in West Bengal.[63] In what follows, I shall draw on their performances, as well as those of men, in an exposition of the positive images of women found in those performances and of the interpretive roles assumed by men and women singers in relation to these images.

Although it is but a single element in a complex religious setting (see Figures 38 and 39), the musical form known as *kīrtan* or *padāvalī kīrtan*[64] provides a useful arena for exploring attitudes to women in Bengali religion from the time of Caitanya. It was a closely related form called *nāmasaṅkīrtan,* the communal chanting or singing of the names of Krishna and his beloved Rādhā, that was established by Caitanya as the central religious act of the Bengali Vaiṣṇava community. Both this communal form of singing and the more complex and demanding performance form that I am studying continue to be pervasive modes of devotion in Bengal today. There are as many as several hundred *kīrtanīyās* in West Bengal, who perform on a wide range of occasions, including Vaiṣṇava festivals, regional fairs, family celebrations, and *śrāddha* ceremonies for the dead. As I attended and reflected on their performances, which typically draw crowds of several

Figure 38. Bāsantī Chaudhurī meditates in preparation for a performance of *kathakatā*, a musical form closely related to *kīrtan,* in which stories from the *Bhāgavata Purāṇa* are narrated and elaborated upon.

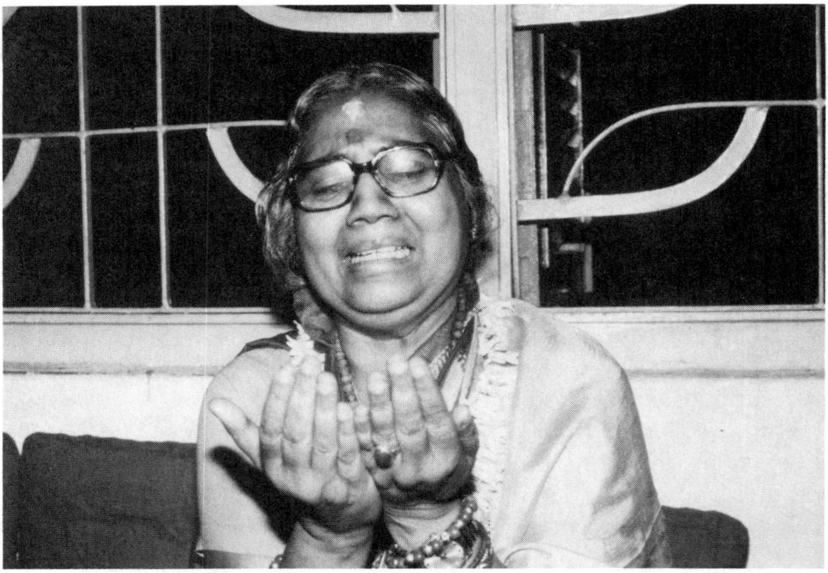

Figure 39. Bāsantī Chaudhurī in performance.

hundred, I came to realize that this form is not only characteristically Vaiṣṇava but also quintessentially Bengali in its elaborate cultivation and expression of religious emotion.[65]

A typical *kīrtan* performance, lasting approximately three or four hours, consists of a number of songs woven together into a narrative that centers on a phase in the love of Rādhā and Krishna or an event in the life of Caitanya. The songs are based on medieval poems in Bengali and Brajabuli,[66] which are expanded through additional lines commenting and reflecting on those of the original poems. In the course of the performance, the *kīrtanīyā*, assisted by several supporting singers with small brass hand cymbals and accompanied throughout by two or sometimes three drummers playing the elongated barrel-shaped *khols*,[67] spins out his story, the drums providing a continuous rhythmic backdrop even for the spoken portions that link the songs together. As the story unfolds, the *kīrtanīyā* expresses emotions not only through words and music, but also through dramatic gestures and dance, assuming now one role, now another, and drawing members of his troupe into the action at key points in the plot (see Figure 40). The drummers' role in generating and channeling excitement at various points in the drama is also crucial, and at one or two such points in the performance the *kīrtanīyā* may encourage the lead

Figure 40. Lalitā Devī dancing alone.

drummer to break into a vigorous solo. Audience members, too, do not remain passive, but participate in various ways. At moments of emotional intensity they may shout "Haribol!" or—in the case of the women—produce a characteristic high-pitched ululation with their tongues. Men and women alike feel free to express their grief by weeping openly during episodes of separation, and at the end of a performance one often sees members of the audience rising and singing a joyous *nāmasaṅkīrtan* with the performers (see Figure 41).

That the performance is for many a recreation of the events it portrays, rather than a simple retelling, is suggested by such emotional involvement as well as by the reverent gestures of some persons in the audience, who touch the *kīrtanīyā's* feet at the performance's conclusion (see Figure 42). Striking testimony to such immediacy of perception is also furnished by an incident that I witnessed in a highly dramatic rendering of an episode in Caitanya's life (see Figure 43). An elderly widow came forward during the performance and reached out to touch the *kīrtanīyā's* arm, and it was clear that her consolation was directed, not to the performer, but to Caitanya himself in his distress (see Figure 44).[68] Such immediacy of vision, clearly shared by many devotees, renders the performance a mode of worship, one that evokes, refines, and heightens the devotees' religious emotions.

Figure 41. Women members of the audience at a *kīrtan* performance.

In addition to narrative and dialogue, the spoken sections linking the songs together include extemporaneous commentary and spiritual exhortation, and it is thus to such portions of the transcriptions that we may look for clues about the meaning to the singers of specific elements in the stories. Because our interest is in the social and religious status of women, we shall focus on the portrayal of Rādhā and other female characters in the stories, and on the interpretations given by men and women singers of the nature and roles of women (see Figure 45).

The figure of Rādhā as portrayed by *kīrtanīyās* of both sexes is one of great strength (see Figure 46). The power and singlemindedness of her love for Krishna render her oblivious to the hardships through which she must pass on her way to meet him. In one episode she is described as wholly unaware of the scorching hot sand on her tender feet as she goes to the river, for her mind has preceded her to Krishna's side.[69] In another involving a nocturnal rendevous, she is likewise depicted as braving the thorns and snakes that block her path.[70] Her transcendence of all concern for her physical well-being is matched by her complete indifference to the scorn and abuse that will be heaped on her by her in-laws and other representatives of society's

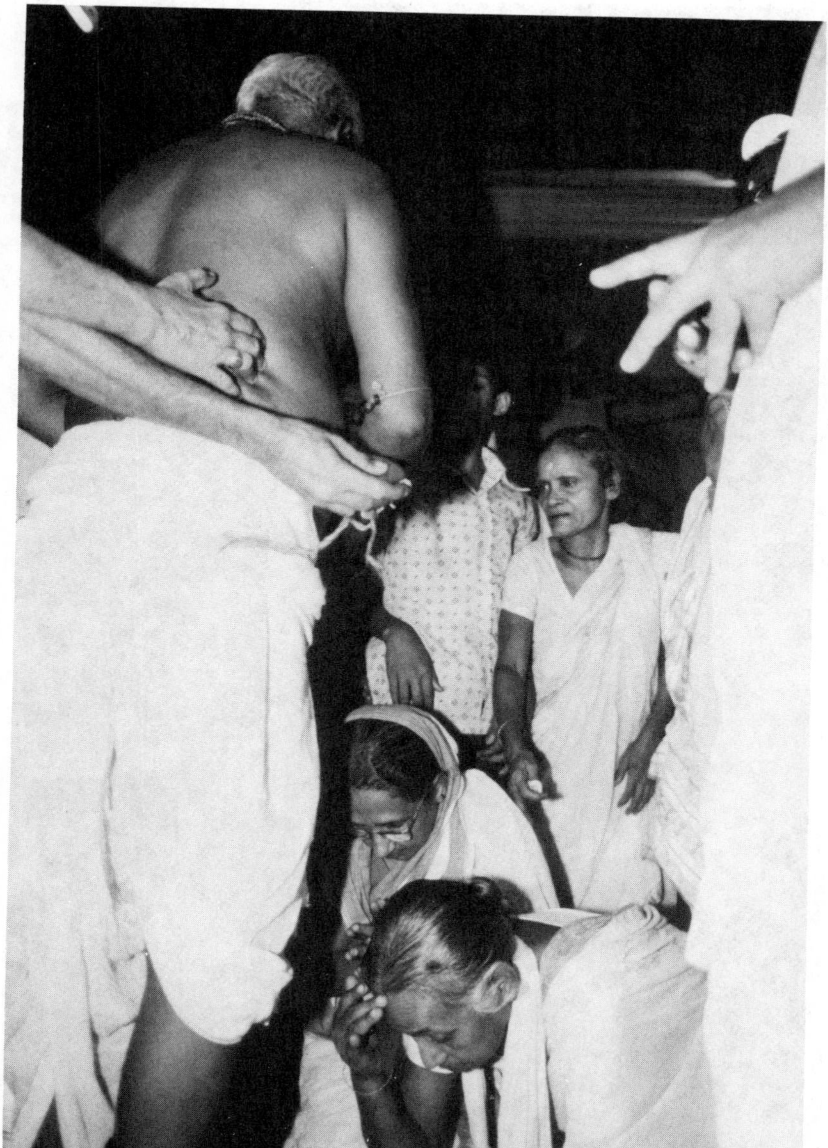

Figure 42. Women touching Nanda Kishor's feet after a performance.

Figure 43. A young woman affixes a floral crest to the head of Kānāi Sarkār during a performance.

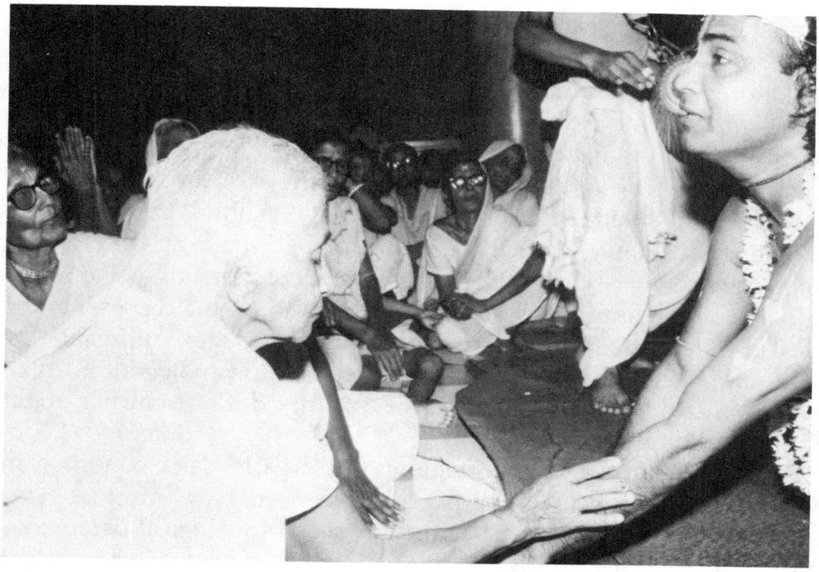

Figure 44. An elderly widow consoles Caitanya as portrayed by Kānāi Sarkār during a performance.

Figure 45. Rāmakrishna Dās in the role of a woman.

norms. Indeed, she is frequently compared to a *yogī* in her utter obliviousness to the external world.[71]

Not only do the singers portray Rādhā as a strong character in her own right, but they explicitly exalt her over Krishna. Such exaltation is especially prominent in stories woven around Rādhā's response to Krishna's fickleness.[72] In these episodes, the *kīrtanīyās* depict Rādhā's emotions in all their depth and subtlety, skillfully rendering the complex of jealousy, anger, hurt, and intense yearning that follows upon her discovery of Krishna's infidelity. Yet surprisingly, if one has in mind a model in which Krishna is God and Rādhā represents the ideal devotee, the singers portray Krishna as no less vulnerable: he pines and wastes away at Rādhā's rejection of his apologetic entreaties,[73] even threatening suicide if she will not desist from her anger and accept him once again.[74]

Rādhā's friends take advantage of Krishna's lovesick condition in order to make explicit comparisons between the two lovers, always, of course, at Krishna's expense. In a series of theological paradoxes, they highlight the wonder of Rādhā's inexplicable power over the Lord of the Universe.[75]

You charm the whole world—this I grant—
  Yet Rādhā's charm captivates you.

Figure 46. Lalitā Devī in a strong pose.

The worlds pay you homage—this I grant—
Yet a mere glimpse of Rādhā and your heart is lost.
Your songs and your flute attract the three worlds,
Yet Rādhā's speech puts all these to flight.
You pervade the world with fragrance—this I grant—
Yet our Rādhā's perfume steals away your heart.

The friends also point to the difference in their social status as a way of asserting Rādhā's superiority. Rādhā is a princess, whereas Krishna is only a cowherd, a simpleton who has not even learned to read or write, much less become acquainted with the ways of love.[76] All this abuse Krishna suffers in silence, thereby contributing to the impression of his vulnerability and ultimate powerlessness.

Especially through conversations between Krishna or Rādhā and her friends, the audience learns of numerous ways in which Krishna expresses his subservience to her. He refers to himself as a beggar in quest of Rādhā from all eternity,[77] and he respectfully entreats Brindā, the forest goddess, to intercede with her on his behalf. He declares that he is the humble servant of Rādhā's feet and he inscribes his pledge of servitude in a letter of indenture (*dāskhat*) that Brindā subsequently compels him to read.[78] He pleads with her, grasping her feet[79] and sometimes touching them with his forehead, thereby placing the highest part of his body in contact with the lowest, most polluted part of hers.[80] Rādhā's description of this last act emphasizes her disdain: she declares that she refused even to look at him when he bowed down before her; she knew that he did so only because she heard the sound of her anklets jingling as his crest touched her feet![81]

Certain of Krishna's statements to Rādhā have important theological implications. He testifies that she is his very life,[82] and elsewhere he uses a theological term to refer to her extraordinary power (*śakti*). She has been able to accomplish what no dyer can— she has changed his black eyes into ones that are red from weeping.[83] The theological implications of his utter infatuation with Rādhā are hinted at by her friends, as we saw in the poem translated above. Finally, the power of her name over him is given as a reason for its prevalent devotional use among Vaiṣṇavas, especially in Brindavan.[84]

Although Rādhā is the primary female figure who is exalted in the stories, her friends and Brindā, the forest goddess who serves as her messenger, are likewise represented as strong characters. In a refrain of a song used in at least two different episodes, Brindā is referred to as the proud messenger (*garavinī dūtī*)[85] as she sets out to meet

Krishna. The fact that Krishna relies on her to intercede for him likewise emphasizes her importance. Rādhā's friends, too, have dominant roles: they typically outwit Krishna, who concedes that he is always worsted by these *gopīs* and calls himself "Śyām the loser."[86] Further, he unhesitatingly obeys them when they tell him that he must address Rādhā as his *guru*, and he proceeds to give her his crest and his flute as a respectful offering (*guru-dakṣiṇā*) for the dancing lessons that she is about to give him.[87]

Such characterizations of Rādhā and her friends are made by both men and women singers. Yet when I compared the transcriptions of the tapes of the performances of the three women I recorded with those of men who narrated the same episodes, I found certain notable differences. First, the women singers seemed to take special delight in telling of Rādhā's triumph over Krishna, lingering with obvious pleasure over episodes in which he falls at her feet or is humiliated by her friends. Men made some of the same points, but somewhat more briefly, and they did not include so many in a single performance. Secondly, and more significantly, only the women drew general principles from such instances, interpreting Rādhā's superiority in relation to the positions of men and women in society. Let us consider examples of such generalization from each of the three women I recorded.

In her performance of the *rās līlā*, the story of Krishna's *rāsa* dance with Rādhā and the other cowherd women, the singer Krishnā Bisvās reflected on the fact that the women refrain from speaking first when they come out to meet Krishna. She had one of them say that if the heroine pleads with the hero, the heroine's self-respect (*ādar*) is lost, whereas if the hero pleads with the heroine, her honor is preserved.[88] The same point was made somewhat more elaborately by Lalitā Devī in her performance of *Kalahāntaritā*, the *pālā* that depicts Rādhā and Krishna separated in the aftermath of a lovers' quarrel (see Figures 38 and 39). In this episode Rādhā implores Brindā to go to Krishna, but not to make the first move, lest Rādhā's honor be lost. Brindā assures Rādhā that she, being a woman, knows exactly what to do to preserve a woman's honor. Brindā here comments at some length on Rādhā's proud sulking (*mān*), encouraging her to persist in her anger and specifying that *mān* is a distinctively woman's mode. When men become angry, she explains, women can easily dispel their anger, for men do not have the requisite firmness and perseverance. Women, on the contrary, are not so easy to win over. In the course of her commentary, the singer had Brindā shift from the term *nāyikā*, "heroine," to *nārījāti*, a generic term for women, indicating that she is referring not simply to Rādhā, but rather to women generally.[89]

In her portrayal of the *rāsa* dance, Krishnā Bisvās made another general point, this one of considerable significance for Vaiṣṇava devotion. She described Śiva as entranced by the dance and as coming down from his heavenly abode to Brindavan so that he might witness it. He is, however, denied entrance by the female gatekeeper. He tries dressing up as a woman, but is told that mere dress will not do; he will have to become a woman if he wishes to enter the sacred groves.[90] A similar point was made by Rādhārāṇī in the *pālā* called *Māthur*, which narrates the story of Brindā's coming to the city of Mathurā, where Krishna is ruling as king, to seek to convey to him a message from his beloved Rādhā, whom he has left utterly bereft and disconsolate. The messenger is told that she cannot enter the royal palace because she is a woman. She expresses surprise, having grown accustomed to the opposite restriction: on her Queen Rādhā's grove, she says, it is written that no men may enter.[91]

Both these stories refer to an important principle of Vaiṣṇava devotion that we have already noted: that the devotee, whether male or female, must assume a female mode of being in his or her devotional life. Rādhārāṇī explains that one may not "go in service (*sevā*) into Rādhā's grove" so long as the conceit of being a man (*puruṣatver abhimān*) remains.[92] Thus it is not Rādhā alone who is exalted, nor only the *gopīs*, but all women in relation to the ideal of the religious life.

A male singer whose performance of *Māthur* I recorded narrated the foregoing episode essentially as Rādhārāṇī did, but after stating that "in Brindavan it is men who are denied entrance," he simply left the point without further comment.[93] Rādhārāṇī, however, used the episode as an occasion for expounding her own feminist views. She drew a parallel between the women of Braj, who go out freely to meet Krishna, and the women of West Bengal, who move about without restriction in the outside world, doing the marketing, holding office jobs, and acting essentially like men in their indifference to social conventions (especially those introduced during the centuries of Muslim rule). Yet she did not stop with the assertion of women's equality, but went on to devalue men and, by implication, women's traditional work, which would, she claimed, now have to be taken over by the "worthless" men. As evidence for women's higher status, she noted the existence of train compartments reserved for women, and the fact that women indignantly order men out of these seats, whereas men meekly offer to help women and voluntarily surrender their own seats to them. She added that when men come home after work they have to endure their wives' abuse and abjectly apologize to them; she acknowledged, however, that this is possible only because it happens behind closed doors.[94]

Of greater interest to me than these extreme views, which may well have struck many men in the audience as laughable, is Rādhārāṇī's commentary on another occasion in which she redefined the nature of widowhood. The story she was narrating touches in passing on the issue of whether widows may attend a certain form of religious ceremony. Rather than responding to that narrower question, however, Rādhārāṇī raised the broader issue of who it is that should be considered a widow. A widow (*vidhabā*), she asserted, is one who does not have a devotional relation of love with Krishna, whether or not her earthly husband is alive. One who does not have such a relation with Krishna, then, regardless of her earthly marital status, is to be classed as a *sādhabā*, a married woman whose husband is still living.[95] I find this interpretation especially intriguing, for it gives the woman devotee of Krishna a status parallel in certain respects to that of the male renouncer, the *sannyāsī*, who has severed all ties with society and its categories.[96] There is, to be sure, an important difference: the exemption of the *sannyāsī* from social obligations has classical brahmanical sanction in the *dharma* texts, whereas Rādhārāṇī's interpretation of the woman devotee as exempt from the stigma of widowhood does not. Yet her position stands in a venerable tradition of devotional challenges to orthodoxy that stretch back at least to the time of the *Bhagavadgītā*,[97] and it may serve as important consolation to widows who hear it, liberating them to some degree from the stigma of their condition by replacing a largely negative self-image with a positive one.[98]

What are we to make of all this evidence? How do we interpret the strength and prominence of female figures, especially Rādhā, in the stories narrated by *kīrtanīyās*? First of all, it is clear that Rādhā's supremacy is being presented as something remarkable, as a reversal of what is expected; its power presupposes a situation of male dominance, both theologically and socially. It is because Krishna is viewed as the Lord of the universe that Rādhā's conquest of him inspires wonder, and it is also because wives are expected to touch their husbands' feet, and not the reverse, that his bowing down at her feet occasions astonishment and indeed awe.

Yet the fact that such positive religious images have been readily available to women in the Bengali Vaiṣṇava community from the medieval period to the present is itself noteworthy, especially given the long period of Muslim rule. Rādhā's exaltation over Krishna, the cleverness and pride of her friends, who serve as advisors and messengers, and the natural superiority of women as devotees are clearly presented in the stories narrated by both men and women singers, and the last of these is a cornerstone of Bengali Vaiṣṇava teaching.[99] Although it was only the women singers among those I recorded who drew out the feminist implications of the stories, these strong female images have a prominent place in the tradition. Thus women seeking to make such points need not, as women have had to do elsewhere, reject or radically rewrite the theology or dredge up half-forgotten images from the distant past. When Rādhārāṇī seeks an image for the independence of contemporary women, she turns to the cowherd women who went out freely to meet Krishna. Just as these *gopīs* defied social conventions in their eagerness, so women in contemporary Bengal must defy the social restrictions that are in part a legacy of Muslim domination if they are to move out freely into the world beyond the walls of the home.[100] Although the other two women singers that I recorded did not express such extreme views as Rādhārāṇī's, they likewise used the stories to highlight the independence of women and the superiority of the female mode of religious devotion.

What more general conclusions may we draw from the preceding study? We have seen that Bengal is an area in which female religious conceptions have been prevalent from ancient times.[101] Goddesses have been widely worshipped throughout Bengal by Hindus and Buddhists alike, and the region is also the birthplace of tantric conceptions of reality as an interplay of male and female principles. Together with such theological conceptions, we have noted the Vaiṣṇava view that female devotees represent the model for the religious life, and that men must assume a female identity in their devotional service to Rādhā and Krishna.

In addition to documenting the prevalence of strong female images and conceptions of deity in Bengal, we reviewed considerable evidence in support of the view that the social and religious status of women in the region has from ancient times been relatively high, especially in comparison to the status of women in other parts of North India. This correlation of religious conceptions and imagery with social structure and religious hierarchy is intriguing. Yet because of the preliminary nature of the foregoing survey, as well as the meager and fragmentary character of the historical evidence regarding women in all but the privileged classes, we must be cautious in interpreting these findings. Further research, for example, into the inscriptional evidence regarding women donors, as well as in the Sanskrit and

Bengali works by and about women, is necessary before we may draw broad conclusions. Here as elsewhere the relation between religious imagery and social structure is unclear. Do the religious images influence the social circumstances of women, as many writers assume, or do they rather reflect existing social circumstances? Or is the causal relation perhaps a reciprocal one? Alternatively, might the images not also serve as compensation for situations that would otherwise be intolerable for women?[102]

The complexity of the materials that we have surveyed makes any simple answer to these questions impossible. Indeed, in one specific regard, even my general initial hypothesis, that conceptions of deity as female and of femaleness as powerful would be positively correlated with relatively high social status among women, was challenged by my findings regarding literacy:[103] in the nineteenth century, female literacy among Śāktas, who worship the Goddess, was remarkably low. On the other hand, the relatively high degree of literacy among Vaiṣṇava women is striking. It is tempting to speculate that there may be a relation between this fact and the high regard for women as devotees in the Vaiṣṇava community, although the extraordinary outpouring of literature by the members of this community beginning in the sixteenth century is surely another important factor.

More evidence would be required to substantiate my general hypothesis. Yet it seems reasonable to suppose that the strong religious images of women in Bengal, such as those found in *kīrtan* performances, reflect something of the social conditions in the centuries prior to the period of Muslim domination. Contrariwise, images such as those presented in *kīrtan* appear to have had an effect on subsequent social conditions. Such images kept alive a vision of women's freedom through the latter centuries of Muslim rule, and they helped preserve women's dignity even when women were not the principal performers. The preservation and transmission of such images through a vital performance form have also rendered them accessible to reform-minded Bengalis in recent times. Thus the images of Rādhā and the other cowherd women, which have been central to Vaiṣṇava devotion from the time of Caitanya, could be revived in a social context by the neo-Vaiṣṇava movement of the late nineteenth century,[104] and they may well have contributed to the success of the reforms affecting women that likewise date from that time. Finally, it is difficult to estimate the extent of such influence, the uses to which we have seen the images put by women *kīrtanīyās* performing today testify to their continuing power to affect the attitudes and actions of women—if not also of men— in contemporary Bengal.

Notes

1. My research on *kīrtan* would not have been possible without the generous help of my research assistants both here and in Bengal. Nimai Biswas and the late Srabony Dey, both of Calcutta, transcribed dozens of tapes of *kīrtan* and other related performances, and Nimai also rendered invaluable assistance in making those tapes. In Santiniketan, Srinvanti Pal instructed me in the subtleties of medieval Bengali and Brajabuli. After my return from India, Aditi Lahiri and Rimli Bhattacharya discussed with me key portions of the transcriptions, and Rimli also waded through piles of transcriptions in search of material relevant to my present project. To each of them I am most grateful.

I would also like to thank David Pingree, Bimal Matilal, Joseph O'Connell, Tony Stewart, Robert Evans, Jack Hawley, Margaret Goldberg Henderson and Hitesranjan Sanyal for their invaluable comments and bibliographic suggestions as I worked on the historical portion of the article. Tony Stewart discussed with me several of the most relevant passages from the biographies of Caitanya, and Robert Evans ferreted out two important sources for me from the University of Chicago's library. A subsequent conversation with Bimal Matilal when he came to lecture at Brown University sharpened my thinking about the relations of the factors I discuss in the first part of the article. Finally, Jack Hawley, Margaret Henderson and Hitesranjan Sanyal commented helpfully on a completed draft; several of their suggestions have been incorporated into the present version.

2. For a discussion of the Unitarian influence on Rammohun Roy and other leaders of the Brahmo Samaj in the nineteenth century, see David Kopf, *The Brahmo Samaj and the Shaping of the Modern Indian Mind* (Princeton: Princeton University Press, 1979), pp. 3–41.

3. For a discussion of the basic teachings of the major heterodox schools, see A. L. Basham, *The Wonder That Was India*, 2nd ed. (New York: Hawthorn Books, 1963), pp. 258–300. For a summary of the historical background, see Trevor Ling, *The Buddha* (New York: Charles Scribner's Sons, 1973), pp. 37–83.

4. Manisha Roy makes a similar claim for Bengal throughout the ancient period. She points to the subsequent series of invasions—by the Pathans in the twelfth century, the Moghuls in the seventeenth and the British in the eighteenth—that profoundly affected Bengali society and culture. (*Bengali Women* [Chicago: University of Chicago, 1975], p. 3.)

5. The term tantric is used by a number of Western scholars to refer to a set of practices and conceptions taken up by both the Hindu and the Buddhist communities. The designation used by Buddhists to refer to the practices and

conceptions as they developed within the Buddhist community is Vajrayāna.

6. See Edward C. Dimock, Jr., *The Place of the Hidden Moon* (Chicago: University of Chicago, 1966), esp. pp. 35–40.

7. R. C. Majumdar, *History of Ancient Bengal* (Calcutta: G. Bharadwaj and Company, 1971), pp. 538, 546–67.

8. Ibid., pp. 546, 549.

9. Ibid., p. 547. From the Kushāna period (second-first centuries B.C.E.) there are also images of Viṣṇu flanked by two female figures identified by Majumdar as Lakṣmī and Sarasvatī (pp. 538–39); such images are reminiscent of the South Indian Śrī Vaiṣṇava images of Viṣṇu flanked by Śrī and Bhū.

10. This practice is referred to as Kumārī Pūjā. The *Devī Purāṇa* is thought to have been composed or compiled in Bengal in approximately the seventh century C.E. It is interesting to note that its views on caste are likewise revolutionary. (S. C. Banerji, *Tantra in Bengal* [Calcutta: Naya Prokash, 1978], pp. 214–15.)

11. See Barbara Stoler Miller, *Love Song of the Dark Lord: Jayadeva's Gītagovinda* (New York: Columbia University Press, 1977), pp. 26–37.

12. Narendra Nath Bhattacharyya, *History of the Śākta Religion* (Delhi: Munshiram Manoharlal, 1974), p. 68.

13. D. C. Sircar, *Studies in the Religious Life of Ancient and Medieval India* (Delhi: Motilal Banarsidass, 1971), p. 99.

14. Ibid.; Stephan Beyer, *The Cult of Tārā: Magic and Ritual in Tibet* (Berkeley: University of California, 1973), p. 8. This interpretation is based on the highly plausible assumption that "*to-lo* Bodhisattva" refers to Tārā. According to Beyer, it is not yet possible to say precisely when Tārā's cult originated in India (p. 6).

15. Sircar, *Studies*, p. 100.

16. Bhattacharyya, *Śākta Religion*, p. 68.

17. Such conceptions are not limited to the Hindu tradition; parallel in some respects to the Śiva-*śakti* notion discussed below is the Vajrayāna Buddhist conception of the marriage of the feminine *prajñā* (wisdom) with the masculine *upāya* (means to release). A significant difference between the two conceptions, however, is that for the Hindu it is the female principle that is the energizing force, whereas for the Buddhist it is the male principle. See Agehananda Bharati, *The Tantric Tradition* (London: Rider, 1965), pp. 200–27.

18. See Wendy Doniger O'Flaherty, "The Shifting Balance of Power in the Marriage of Śiva and Pārvatī," and Frédérique Apffel Marglin, "Types of Sexual Union and their Implicit Meanings," in John Stratton Hawley and Donna Marie Wulff, eds., *The Divine Consort: Rādhā and the Goddesses of India* (Berkeley: Berkeley Religious Studies Series, 1982). On Kālī, see David Kinsley, "Blood and Death out of Place: Reflections on the Goddess Kālī," in the same volume, as well as his *The Sword and the Flute—Kālī and Kṛṣṇa* (Berkeley: University of California Press, 1975).

19. Heinrich Zimmer, *Myths and Symbols in Indian Art and Civilization* (New York: Pantheon Books, 1946), pp. 205–207.

20. Dimock, *Hidden Moon*, p. 15.

21. See Ibid., pp. 13–18, for the distinction between orthodox and Sahajiyā Vaiṣṇavas.

22. Kṛṣṇadāsa Kavirāja, *Caitanyacaritāmṛta* 3.7, as cited in Melville T. Kennedy, *The Chaitanya Movement* (Calcutta: Association Press, 1925), p. 104; cf. pp. 111–12.

23. Majumdar, *Ancient Bengal*, p. 454.

24. Tapan Raychaudhuri, *Bengal under Akbar and Jahangir*, second impression with new introductory note (Delhi: Munshiram Manoharlal, 1969), pp. 5–6.

25. The verses most often quoted are *Manu* 5.148 and 9.3; see Georg Bühler, trans., *The Laws of Manu* (Oxford: Oxford University Press, 1886; reprint ed., Dehli: Motilal Bandarsidass, 1964).

26. On the status of women in contemporary Bengal, see the view expressed by Dimock in his highly perceptive Forward to Roy's *Bengali Women*, esp. p. x.

27. Majumdar, *Ancient Bengal*, p. 455. As evidence Majumdar cites the mention in Dhoyī's *Pavanadūta*, a lengthy Sanskrit court poem, of love letters written by women (p. 500, n. 144). One might well question the reliability of such a literary source as evidence for actual practice in a particular region, especially given the fact that the poem is modelled on Kālidāsa's *Meghadūta* and that the convention of a love-letter written by a heroine is common in classical Sanskrit literature.

28. Majumdar, *Ancient Bengal*, p. 456.

29. Ibid., p. 455; the passage in question is *Bṛhaddharma Purāṇa* 11.8–1–2, which "repeats the old dictum that the duty of a wife is to serve her husband and not to forsake [him] under any circumstances—she must not fast or perform any Vrata without his permission," pp. 455–56.

30. Ibid., p. 456; Majumdar cites no specific sources here.

31. Ibid., pp. 456–57.

32. *Bṛhaddharma Purāṇa* 2.8.10, as quoted in Majumdar, *Ancient Bengal*, p. 457.

33. Majumdar, *Ancient Bengal*, p. 456.

34. Sukumar Sen, "Great Hindu Women in East India," in Swami Madhavananda and Ramesh Chandra Majumdar, eds., *Great Women of India* (Almora, India: Advaita Ashrama, 1953), p. 369.

35. See Diana L. Eck, "Gaṅgā: The Goddess in Hindu Sacred Geography," in Hawley and Wulff, eds., *The Divine Consort*.

36. S. Sen, "Hindu Women," in Madhavananda and Majumdar, *Great Women*, p. 369.

37. It was also at her direction that Bhuvaneśvara Vācaspati wrote a Bengali verse rendering of the Nāradīya Purāṇa; Ibid., p. 370.

38. The estate in question is the Nātor estate in north Bengal; Ibid., pp. 371–72.

39. Kennedy, *Chaitanya Movement*, p. 182; unfortunately, Kennedy gives

neither the date nor any references to support this claim.

40. S. Sen, "Hindu Women," in Madhavananda and Majumdar, *Great Women*, pp. 374–75.

41. Ibid., p. 376.

42. Ibid.

43. Ibid., p. 377.

44. Ibid., pp. 375–76. I am puzzled by the apparent certainty with which Sen concludes that Candrāvatī was not a Vaiṣṇava, given the fact that her father's name, Vaṃśīdāsa, "servant of the flute," appears to be a Vaiṣṇava name. Moreover, Rāma, whose story is the subject of Candrāvatī's poem, is regarded as an avatar of Viṣṇu, along with Krishna, although he is not central to the devotion of the Bengal Vaiṣṇavas.

45. Dinesh Chandra Sen, *History of Bengali Language and Literature* (Calcutta: University of Calcutta, 1954), p. 507. This claim seems highly dubious, especially in the light of the general decline in female literacy under Muslim rule; see A. S. Altekar, *The Position of Women in Hindu Civilization*, 2nd ed. (Delhi: Motilal Banarsidass, 1956), pp. 23–25.

46. Kennedy, *Chaitanya Movement*, p. 83, citing D. C. Sen, *Bengali Language and Literature*, p. 598; the passage in question is found on pp. 507–508 of the edition I have cited.

47. S. Sen, "Hindu Women," in Madhavananda and Majumdar, *Great Women*, p. 375. Sen claims that some of these women knew Sanskrit and indeed wrote in both Sanskrit and Bengali, a fact that is attested by works in both languages that have survived. He notes that there may have been literary women outside the Vaiṣṇava community but points out that the evidence is sparse (p. 375).

48. Cited in R. L. Mitra, *Antiquities of Orissa*, 1:110, according to Kennedy, *Chaitanya Movement*, p. 86.

49. William Adam, *Adam's Reports on Vernacular Education in Bengal and Bihar, Submitted to Government in 1835, 1836 and 1838*. With a Brief View of Its Past and Present Condition, by the Rev. J. Long. (Calcutta: Home Secretariat Press, 1868), p. 133. Adam noted that zemindars generally educated their daughters at least minimally, so that they might be capable of managing their husbands' estates in the event of widowhood, and he also reported that some widows were educated for the same reason after the death of their husbands. Of the fifty or sixty principal zemindars in Nāṭor District, he noted, more than half were women (including widows) (pp. 131–33).

It is important to note that in traditional societies such as that of India, education is not synonymous with literacy, as the British tended to assume. See Altekar, *Position of Women*, p. 25.

50. The most authoritative such treatise in Bengal is the great *smṛti* text of *Raghunandan* (Raychaudhuri, *Bengal*, p. 173).

51. Although monogamy was the norm, taking more than one wife was an accepted practice, and men were not frowned upon for infidelity. Women, on the contrary, were subject to the strictest regulations regarding chastity; Raychaudhuri, *Bengal*, pp. 8–12.

52. Ibid., p. 11.
53. Ibid., p. 11, n. 5. The Bengali name of the piece is *Nārīganer Pati-nindā.*
54. Ibid., pp. 11–12. Raychaudhuri presents evidence from the *Caṇ ḍīmaṅgal* in support of his contention that husbands could not simply take their wives for granted.
55. S. Sen gives two examples from Orissa: Queen Lakṣmīnkarā and Cintā the *sahaja-yoginī*; "Hindu Women," in Madhavananda and Majumdar, *Great Women,* p. 373.
56. See, for example, Sir John Woodroffe, *Śakti and Śākta,* 8th ed. (Madras: Ganesh and Company, 1975), p. 344.
57. See Dimock, *Hidden Moon,* p. 45.
58. Ibid., p. 99; cf. the incident involving Kṛṣṇapriyā, who was termed "*bhakti* personified," that Dimock recounts on pp. 100–101. On Viṣṇupriyā, see also Kennedy, *Chaitanya Movement,* p. 86.
59. Kennedy, *Chaitanya Movement,* p. 181.
60. S. Sen, "Hindu Women," in Madhavananda and Majumdar, *Great Women,* p. 374; Dimock, *Hidden Moon,* pp. 96–98, 102. For her titles, see J. Helen Rowlands, *La Femme Bengalie dans la Littérature du Moyen–Age* (Paris: Adrien Maisonneuve, 1930), p. 210.
61. S. Sen, "Hindu Women," in Madhavananda and Majumdar, *Great Women,* p. 374; in addition to the family of Śrīnivāsa, Sen mentions those of Advaita, Nityānanda, and Śyāmānanda.
62. Ibid., p. 376. It is noteworthy that her father, Gopīmohan Cakravartī, of northeast Burdwan district, was not only one of the most famous *kīrtan* singers of his time but also well known for his song compositions.
63. Although the large majority of *kīrtan* troupes are found in West Bengal, there are also a number of troupes in Bangla Desh.
64. The term *kīrtan* comes from a verb root meaning "praise"; it is used in various parts of India to refer to devotional forms of vocal music, many of them communal in nature. The term *padāvalī* refers to the medieval poetry that constitutes the textual basis for the songs used in the performance form that I am studying.
65. For an illuminating discussion of the theology of the Bengali Vaiṣṇavas, see Edward C. Dimock, Jr., "Doctrine and Practice among the Vaiṣṇavas of Bengal," in Milton Singer, ed., *Krishna: Myths, Rites, and Attitudes* (Chicago: University of Chicago Press, 1966). For a somewhat fuller treatment of the devotional aesthetics of the movement, as found in the treatises of Rūpa Gosvāmī, see my *Drama as a Mode of Religious Realization: The Vidagdhamādhava of Rūpa Gosvāmī* (Chico, CA: Scholars Press, 1984), especially chap. 2.
66. See Sukumar Sen, *A History of Brajabuli Literature* (Calcutta: University of Calcutta, 1935).
67. See Figures 1–3.
68. Kānāi Sarkār, *Capal Gopāl Uddhār.* [For our purposes here, only the name of the performer and performance, respectively, will be noted. Succeeding citations will follow this form.].
69. Sanātan Gosvāmī, *Naukā Vilās.*

70. Nanda Kishor Dās, *Rūpābhisār*. Such imagery has classical antecedents; see Daniel H. H. Ingalls, tr., *An Anthology of Sanskrit Court Poetry* (Cambridge: Harvard University Press, 1965), p. 252, par. 3 for a general description of the type of woman called *abhisārikā*, literally, "one who ventures forth," that is, to meet her lover. Snakes and thorns are mentioned, in a somewhat different context, in verse 818, translated by Ingalls on p. 255.

71. E.g., in the famous poem "*Rādhār ki holo antare vyāthā*," attributed to Caṇḍidās, which forms the basis for a song that I learned from Pañcānan Dās in a course on *kīrtan* singing at Visva-Bharati University, Santiniketan, West Bengal. See my discussion of the image of Rādhā as a *yogī* in Rūpa's plays in my "A Sanskrit Portrait: Rādhā in the Plays of Rūpa Gosvāmī," in Hawley and Wulff, *Divine Consort*, pp. 28–29.

72. Episodes centering on this theme constitute a type called *mān*, a term the primary designation of which is the complex of Rādhā's emotions aroused by the suspicion or actuality of Krishna's infidelity. Subtypes of *mān* include *Kalahāntaritā*, the portrayal of Rādhā (and also Krishna) separated by a quarrel, and *Khaṇḍitā*, the portrayal of Rādhā as the "wounded" heroine.

73. Lalitā Devī, *Kalahāntaritā*.

74. Nanda Kishor Dās, *Kalahāntaritā*.

75. Nanda Kishor Dās, *Śrī Kṛṣṇer Pūrvarāg*.

76. Nanda Kishor Dās, *Kalahāntaritā*; Lalitā Devī, *Kalahāntaritā*; Nanda Kishor Dās, *Śrī Kṛṣṇer Pūrvarāg*.

77. Krishnā Bisvās, *Rāslīlā*; Lalitā Davī, *Kalahāntaritā*.

78. Nanda Kishor Dās, *Kalahāntaritā*; Lalitā Devī *Kalahāntaritā*. The theme of the letter of indenture was sounded by Krishnā Bisvās in her performance of *Rāslīlā*, and by Nārāyaṇ Rāy Gosvāmī and an unidentified male *kīrtanīyā* in their versions of *Māthur*.

79. Nanda Kishor Dās, *Kalahāntaritā*,

80. In his rendition of *Kalahāntaritā*, Nanda Kishor had Krishna instruct Rādhā to place her feet on his head, much as Jayadeva's Krishna tells her to do in the *Gītagovinda*. See the translation of the verse by Miller, *Love Song of the Dark Lord*, p. 113, vs.8.

81. Lalitā Devī, *Kalahāntaritā*.

82. Nanda Kishor Dās, *Kalahāntaritā*.

83. Nanda Kishor Das, *Kalahāntaritā*. The full phrase is *āścarya śakti*, "astonishing power."

84. Rādheśyām Dās, *Rāslīlā*; Rādhārāṇī, *Māthur*.

85. Lalitā Devī, *Kalahāntaritā*; Nārāyaṇ Rāy Gosvāmī, *Māthur*.

86. Rādheśyām Dās, *Rāslīlā*.

87. Krishnā Bisvās, *Rāslīlā*.

88. Krishnā Bisvās, *Rāslīlā*.

89. Lalitā Devī, *Kalahāntaritā*.

90. Krishnā Bisvās, *Rāslīlā*. On the treatment of the motif in the *rāslīlās* of Brindavan, see John Stratton Hawley, *At Play with Krishna: Pilgrimage Dramas from Brindavan* (Princeton: Princeton University Press, 1981), pp. 111, 160.

91. Rādhārāṇī, *Māthur*.

92. Rādhārāṇī, *Mālthur.*

93. Unidentified male *kīrtanīyā* performing *Māthur* in the compound of Baḍa Gosāin in Santipur.

94. Rādhārāṇī, *Māthur.*

95. Rādhārāṇī, *Dān Līlā.*

96. For the classical brahmanical view of the *sannyāsī,* see *Manu* 6.34–85.

97. See, for example, *Bhagavadgītā* 9.32.

98. On the duties of a widow, see *Manu* 5.156–162.

99. See Kennedy, *Chaitanya Movement,* p. 104.

100. See Mary J. H. Beech, "Factors Influencing the Recent Increase in Middle Class Female Labor Force Participation," in Richard L. Park, ed., *Patterns of Change in Modern Bengal* (East Lansing: Asian Studies Center, Michigan State University, 1979), pp. 193–201.

101. See Dimock's Forward to Roy's *Bengali Women,* in which he notes that "of all the forms that deity takes in Bengal, the goddess—'Mother'—is most prominent" (p. ix).

102. See the Comments of Norvin Hein in Hawley and Wulff, *Divine Consort,* pp. 116–24. Although he does not focus specifically on women's experience, he suggests that the erotic emotion of the communal *saṅkīrtan* singing may have served as a compensation for the oppression that resulted from Muslim rule (pp. 123–24).

103. I do not mean to suggest that literacy is an invariable concomitant of high social status, especially in a traditional society. Yet in British India, it seems to have been a key to financial independence; thus the differential findings for Vaiṣṇavas and Śāktas are striking.

104. See Kennedy, *Chaitanya Movement,* pp. 79–81.

CHAPTER TEN

*Sacred Paradoxes: Women and Religious Plurality in Nigeria**

ROSALIND I. J. HACKETT

For anyone familiar with black Africa's most populous country, to speak of the religious dimension of the Nigerian way of life is something of a truism. This religious dimension manifests itself not only through an underlying conviction of the influence of the divine in human affairs, but also through intense religious activity of a varied nature. Nigeria's religious plurality has proved to be a treasure trove for historians of religion, theologians and social scientists. Many areas are still relatively unexplored, notably the role of women in the process of religious growth and change.

From 1979 to date I have engaged in a study of the religious experience and diversity of one particular Nigerian town—Calabar, the capital of Cross River State in southeastern Nigeria.[1] This paper represents an attempt to describe and analyze women's religious worlds

* The research on which this article is based was supported by a research grant from the University of Calabar Senate Research Grants Committee.

in Calabar and to examine their different roles and functions across the religious spectrum. Although sacrificing depth, the survey approach is valuable in this context because it offers a more accurate portrayal of the religious situation as experienced by and affecting women. In reality women have an increasing range of religious options, and when not active participants, they may be passively influenced by a wide variety of religious attitudes through family, friends and work environments. While the primary objective of this study is to highlight the contemporary religious situation, some attention has been paid to historical foundations, as this will enhance our understanding of current phenomena and trends. The subject matter will be approached through a separate consideration of each of the major sectors of the religious spectrum. It should be remembered, however, that the religious activities of individual women are by no means limited to one particular religious type.

Traditional Religion

The area of traditional society and religion is both fascinating and ambiguous as far as women are concerned. Within this context women have been credited with great mystical powers and at the same time subjected to restrictive taboos and attitudes. For example, the Ekpe society, a religio-political organization or secret society first mentioned in the 1770s,[2] is believed to have been originally a women's society[3] and possibly imported to Calabar from Ekoi in the Cameroons.[4] At a later stage the men wrested it from the women and transformed it into an effective instrument of political authority. Eyo Okon Akak in his book *A Critique of Old Calabar History* disputes the claim that Ekpe was originally a women's society. He states that:

> the only women's secret society which was wrested in Efikland from the women by men is "Obon" as often reflected in its song: "obon ekedi idem iban"—that means the society (Obon) was originally a women's secret society. After this transfer the men injected certain charms which can harm any woman or non-member who happens to see the members in action. In most cases it is usually played during the night. The usual slogan when so played in the night is "okut akpa," meaning that, whosoever sees it dies.[5]

As the mythology goes, the transfer of power can be traced to a woman who in a romantic moment with her husband divulged the secrets of the society. Ever since that time women have not been

Figure 47. Woman in charge of traditional charms and medicines in Calabar market. She is also a prophetess at a local African independent church.

trusted to keep secrets, and it is for this reason that women are only initiated into the lower echelons of the Ekpe society up until today.[6] Some writers claim that as is the case of slaves and supercargoes, women were only admitted into the ranks of Ekpe at a later stage (probably around the end of the nineteenth and beginning of the twentieth centuries), as a result of economic pressures and changes. The society is believed to have been originally founded on the worship of a forest deity. "Ekpe" is an Efik word for "leopard" and is said to be a mysterious and invisible being inhabiting the forest, which is never seen, known or identified by women, whether members or not, and all other nonmembers of the cult. They may only hear its roar when it is brought to town for traditional ceremonies.[7]

The Efik conception of the deity has traditionally been understood in both male and female terms. "Ete Abasi" is the great father god who created the human race and is associated with the sky, while "Eka Abasi"—mother god—fashioned humankind in the womb and is therefore associated with the earth and procreation. This dual symbolism is also apparent in the Ndem cult. "Ndem Efik" is the Efik tutelary deity and is principally conceived of as a female water god, sometimes referred to as "Mammy Wata." In fact, out of the eight major representations of Ndem—in other words, those cited most frequently in libations and prayers—five of these are female.[8] Anansa has always been the most popular and prominent river goddess. A naval ship is named after her, the S. S. Anansa, which is based in Calabar. Ndem in general is believed to protect the people of Calabar and give blessings, fortune and children to those who consult her. Children born as a result of such consultations through the offering of sacrifices are known as "ndito ndem," the children of the deity. It is also possible for Ndem to possess children and adults in the course of their lives.

Women in particular may become immersed in the spiritual mysteries of Ndem and are known as "Iban Ndem" women of the Deity. Men who fall within this category are called "Iren Ndem" while ordinary male and female worshippers are "Mbon Ndem" or people of the Deity.[9] Priests and priestesses of the cult are called "Awa Ndem" and are responsible for sacrifices and consultations when needs arise. The Chief Priest or Priestess ("Oku Ndem") gains his or her status through prestige and experience. The current Oku Ndem is a woman and she performed the crowning of the Obong or King of Calabar in November 1982—an important political function which has always been reserved for the Ndem priesthood.

Cult members are reputedly fond of very emotional music, the color white, and cleanliness. The majority, according to Akak, are women who live in secluded rooms with signs in the form of *nsibidi* (secret writing) on the walls.[10] They use white chalk (*ndom*) to paint their faces and bodies white and wear knitted raffia rings around their necks, wrists and ankles. They are believed to have a special attraction for those who are fair-skinned, because such people are believed to have been sent by the deity to the world.[11]

The Efik belief in Ndem was once as great as the Roman cults of Neptune and Minerva, according to Akak.[12] However the situation was gradually eclipsed by the Ekpe cult, and by the start of the nineteenth century the priesthood had begun to lose much of its influence. There are no regular festivals of the Ndem cult, nonetheless recent events indicate that Ndem is still believed to be active in the life of Calabar. During the building of the new port, a series of accidents obliged the Ports Authority to offer sacrifices to Ndem. The death of the previous Obong of Calabar was (unofficially) attributed to his refusal to perform certain sacrifices to Ndem on moving to his new palace.

On a general societal level, patrilineal descent is preferred to matrilineal descent in Efik society, but in exceptional instances good connections on the mother's side may be preferable. For example, the Ambos claim that Eyo Honesty II, the great restorer of the Eyo clan, was elevated to the kingship because of his mother, who was an Ambo princess.[13] An Efik woman has always been able to become head of a sub-house or family but never head chief of a house and therefore never an Etubom or Obong. More recently women have been awarded chieftaincy titles, which are a mark of recognition for service to the community. Unlike Ibibio women, when Efik women marry they do not renounce their family rights in terms of property and inheritance. They are allowed to own land and this has meant that some Efik women have been able to attain independent economic status. This has had consequences for religious growth in Calabar as women have been instrumental in donating land to the churches, in particular to the Roman Catholic Church.

The Mission or Historic Churches

Anyone worshipping in the so-called mission or historic churches in Calabar today would observe that a majority of the worshippers, but only a minority of the church leaders or functionaries are female. However, a brief look at the history of the two main churches—the Presbyterian and Roman Catholic—would show the vital roles that

Figure 48. Women play key roles as mourners. Here they form part of the procession to mourn the late Obong of Calabar.

women missionaries played in the expansion and development of their respective churches. This situation, some would add, is highly reminiscent of Western Christianity. The Nigerian situation, and in particular that of Calabar, is rendered more complex by the interplay of African and Western Christian values, and more recently modern secular influences.

Let us return to the roots of the female Christian experience in Calabar. In the years following their arrival in Calabar in 1846, the Presbyterian missionaries reported their difficulty in gaining female converts. This was due to the reluctance of the Efik men to allow their wives to attend church meetings or school. Two young women were baptized in 1853, the same year as the first Efik male was converted —Esien Esien Ukpabio, who went on to become the first native teacher. Nonetheless, the growth of female worshippers and converts was noticeably slow until the year 1868.

A land dispute between Ikoneto and Okoyong towards the end of 1868 led to an outbreak of war. Duke Town and Creek Town sided with Ikoneto, and the Efik men had to leave for some weeks on the campaign.[14] During their absence, the attendance of women at church increased considerably. In his diary entry of Sunday 13 December 1868 the Reverend William Anderson recorded,

> an excellent turn-out of women today in church, both forenoon and afternoon. Hundreds of them were in church for the first time. The decorum they maintained was admirable.[15]

From then on women began to attend church in increasing numbers, some accompanied by a large retinue, although the missionaries never got used to the combination of fine apparel and bare heads and bare feet!

The early Presbyterian missionaries sought to abolish several customs which they believed were a threat to the basic dignity of women. The efforts of the missionaries culminated in the Hopkins Treaty of 1878 which Consul David Hopkins drew up on September 6 with the King and Chiefs of Duke Town.[16] The treaty consisted of fifteen articles in all, but we shall only mention those which specifically affected women.[17]

Article One: Twin Children and Twin-Mothers

> Whoever wilfully takes the life of a twin child or children shall be adjudged liable to the penalty of death . . . .Twin-mothers in future shall have full liberty to visit the town, and buy and sell in the

> markets, the same as any other women in the town, and they shall not be molested in any way. [The bearing of twins by a woman was considered to be unnatural and a bad omen in Efik society and many twin-mothers had taken refuge with their children in the missionary compounds.]

Article Two: Human Sacrifices

> While this referred to "anyone wilfully causing the death of another," it particularly concerned the wives and slaves of kings and nobles, who were obliged to accompany them to the grave on their journey to the next world.

Article Five: Ekpo Iquö, or the Stripping of Helpless Women in the Public Streets

> This abominable, disgraceful, and barbarous custom of allowing the young men of the town to take an Ekpe masquerade out, and seize, strip, and indecently assault any woman wearing a dress or cloth in the street, then exhibiting such dress or cloth hung upon a pole, or the tree in front of the Ekpe palaver-house, being so disgusting and revolting is now for ever abolished.

Article Six: Widows

> The custom of compelling widows to remain in seclusion for up to several years after the death of their husbands was abolished. A period of one month was permitted.

Conflicts with traditional authority occurred over these issues, but the missionaries had the support of the British flag behind them. In one instance, however, when a concession was made by King Archibong over suitable dress for women, an ensuing Ekpe order was passed insisting that only women whose husbands had purchased the full rights of Ekpe honors should dress as required by the missionaries. Women who defied the law were to be ostracized.

Another area of considerable tension was that of marriage. Any form of polygamy was condemned by the missionaries, and sanctions were enforced against the offenders. Some argue that this rigid attitude towards marriage led to the undermining of the social position of women and that the relative freedom and independence enjoyed by women in a polygamous setting turned into positions of dependence and subordination in the nuclear family context. In terms of education there also was certain unintended and questionable consequences.

The girls were initially prevented from attending school by the men and ever after that if there was a choice to be made it was the sons who received the education. An educational gap was therefore created between the sexes, and still exists to some extent today. Moreover, the type of education offered to women was of the role-determining variety; it consisted of training in needlework, housewifery, childcare and the scriptures.[18] This attitude still prevails today: the Presbyterians are constructing a hostel in Calabar to accommodate and train young girls coming into town for the first time. One of its aims will be to impart basic domestic skills to equip them to be good wives and mothers. However, many of the churches, notably the Roman Catholic Church, realize that since times are changing, there is a need to do away with discriminatory attitudes and instead to develop an educational system which produces professionally oriented women able to make their contribution to a modern, fast-developing Nigeria.[19]

At this point it is worthwhile to examine the careers of two exemplary women missionaries who believed fervently in the education and emancipation of women through the agency of Christianity. Mary Mitchell Slessor was born into a humble home in Aberdeen, Scotland on December 2, 1848. The family later moved to Dundee where life was hard, but Slessor's missionary inclinations grew and she eventually offered her services to the Foreign Mission Board of the United Presbyterian Church. She left Liverpool for Calabar on August 5, 1876 at the age of twenty-eight, travelling on a steamer where, as she remarked, "There are scores of casks, only one missionary." This, and the experience of having an alcoholic father, contributed to the war that she was later to wage against alcohol.[20]

Women missionaries, or "female agents" as they were known, were traditionally selected from middle-class, educated backgrounds. But it was a self-improved "mill-lassie" from Dundee, young Mary Slessor, who eventually arrived in Calabar. It is significant that she was escorted up to Mission Hill by Mrs. Sutherland, the missionary who was in charge of the school at the time and had been working tirelessly for twenty-seven years in the Calabar Mission. On her trips up river and into the forests, Mary Slessor had come to terms with the fact that few, if any, had ever seen a white women. She observed that the women were active in market trading as well as in the work of digging, planting and harvesting, but that culturally they were regarded as inferior beings who were subject to potential ostracism and rejection if infertile and to accusations of witchcraft at the death of their husbands. They had little authority in village affairs and could be flogged if they were outdoors at the time of an Ekpe procession.

Figure 49. The Presbyterian missionary Mary Slessor in 1911, holding one of the many twin babies she rescued.

They had to undergo a period of seclusion as part of the fattening ceremony before marriage. As widows they were subjected to periods of confinement and neglect, often lasting up to several years. Slave women had an even more insecure existence and could be taken as concubines at any time.

Slessor found the life-style at Mission House far too starchy for her liking. She soon mastered the language and was moving out to Efik settlements in the surrounding areas, displaying increasingly the ability, for which she became so well loved, to relate to people and understand and treat their problems. She eventually settled with the Okoyong people, renowned for their pride and fearlessness. Her courage and reputation grew daily as she intervened in disputes and confronted the chiefs and Ekpe authorities over what she considered to be the inhumane treatment of women and slaves. People not only were astounded that a woman could do such things, but they began to believe that she possessed certain supernatural powers, *ifot*. It was ironic that her successes, achieved through rebellious and eccentric ways, were eventually recognized in 1891 when Sir Claude Macdonald, the new Consul-General, appointed Mary Slessor as a Vice-Consul to the Okoyong people. She was to supervise the running of the native courts and prevent injustice and check abuses.[21] Slessor may not have realized it, but she was in fact the first woman to be appointed to such a post in the whole of the British Empire.

As Slessor made inroads into new territories, a new name for her began to travel along the bush paths—"Eka Kpukpro Owo" or Mother of All the Peoples. Towards the end of her life she had become consumed by the desire to see women granted more independence. She felt strongly that it would eliminate many of their problems and sufferings. In one of her Bibles, at the passage where St. Paul advocates the subjection of wives to husbands, she scribbled in the margin "Na! Na! Paul, laddie! This will no do!"[22]

When the barefoot, bareheaded missionary died on January 13, 1915, her energy and dynamism finally extinguished, she left behind four protegées, Martha Peacock, Beatrice Welsh, Mina Amess, and Agnes Arnot, who consolidated her work by setting up schools, outstations and a women's center at Arochukwu. The tributes to Mary Slessor's life and work came from many quarters. For Mr. Macgregor, Principal of Hope Waddell, Mary was "no ordinary woman."[23] James Luke had written to the *Record* in 1904 concerning the Aro expeditions: "Where the Church has failed, a single woman has stepped into the breach."[24] Mary Kingsley, the explorer, wrote of her, "The amount of good this very wonderful lady has done, no man can assess." More recently praise for Mary came from the lips of the Synod Moderator, Reverend Dr. Ude, as he laid the foundation stone of the new Mary Slessor Hostel on Mission Hill in Calabar in 1980. He described her not only as someone who was fearless but as a woman who "did the work of four men!"

Sister Mary Charles Walker was an Irish Sister of Charity renowned as an educator. She arrived in Calabar in October 1923 in response to an appeal by Bishop Shanahan for religious sisters. She was instrumental in setting up a whole range of educational institutions, from

Figure 50. The Slessor heritage lives on. Her adopted granddaughter, Jean Slessor, displays the centenary cloth produced to mark the arrival of Mary in 1876.

nursery schools to teacher training colleges. Like Mary Slessor she believed firmly in the importance of training native sisters. By 1926 she had gathered around her in the convent a small group of girls and teachers who had expressed the desire to become sisters.[25] This marked the origin of the native sisterhood of the Congregation of the Handmaids of the Holy Child Jesus. Sister Mary Charles left Nigeria in April 1934, having handed her work over to the sisters of the Holy Child Jesus and along with it the continued formation of the native sisters, which finally emerged as an autonomous indigenous religious congregation in 1959.[26] Charles, while perhaps not a figure of the same magnitude and character as the pioneering Mary Slessor, nonetheless left behind a legacy of educational and medical apostolates from which many people, particularly girls and women, have benefitted up to the present.

Despite the crucial pioneering work done by these early women missionaries and the appreciation of their role by subsequent generations in Calabar, the current role of women in the historic churches seems but a pale shadow of its former self. The Presbyterian Church of Nigeria is proud of its first woman minister, the Reverend Mbeke George Okore, ordained in 1982. But the majority of women are active at the congregational level only in the various women's associations, while a minority attain the status of elders usually after they have ceased child-bearing. A similar situation exists in the other churches of the type, women may become lay readers, lay preachers, lay presidents, and deaconesses, but rarely are they able (or are encouraged) to seek positions of higher authority and responsibility.There are cases of individual women breaking out of, while not abandoning completely, the official structures in order to give expression to their particular religious experiences and gifts. For example, in the Methodist Church "Ma Jekova" was renowned for her spiritual gifts. She used to receive Methodist members in her house for prayer and prescribe cures for their ills. Other women, while not abandoning their affiliation with the mission or historic churches, have taken the initiative to set up peripheral prayer and discussion groups in their own homes to complement the traditional activities of the churches. Alternatively the women's organizations within the churches provide a legitimate context in which women may come together not just for religious but also for social, economic and cultural purposes. It seems that women obtain more religious satisfaction from these organizations, where they are able to act independently according to their own needs, and be heard as a collective voice, than from the official, male-dominated forms of worship.

Figure 51. The Women's Fellowship at Efut Ekondo Presbyterian Church in Calabar.

The African Independent Churches

We now move on to the third major type of religious organization in Calabar, the African independent churches or "spiritual" churches as they are more popularly known. With respect to the interacting themes of women, religion and social change, the independent churches offer perhaps the most interesting and varied area of investigation. Within this milieu women may achieve full independence in religious activities and transcend traditional taboos and attitudes, while in contrast many of the historic churches perpetrate and reinforce sex stereotypes.

It is perhaps more appropriate to start with the most radical of possibilities that this type of religious organization offers to women, that of founding their own religious groups. Few women actually avail themselves of this opportunity—only six out of forty-seven distinct independent and indigenously created religious institutions in Calabar have women founders (12.7%). The reasons for this are not hard to discern and indeed stem from the socio-cultural attitudes and dearth of educational opportunities outlined above as well as the precedents established by the mission churches in terms of women's domestic and ecclesiastical roles. However, it is significant that a few women have utilized this particular channel of religious expression and thus important to examine some of these women leaders themselves and their churches.

Lucy Harriet Harrison was born in Creek Town, near Calabar, in 1900. She moved to Lagos with her husband and after the death of the latter she left the Catholic Church, of which she had been a member, and worshipped briefly in a spiritual church. She eventually formed a small prayer group in Lagos and as a result of a spiritual injunction that she must not marry again, "that she should go and preach and work no more," she initiated the Church of Christ, the Good Shepherd at Lagos in 1940.[27] After establishing the Church at Port Harcourt she later returned to Calabar to found the third branch in 1946 which became the headquarters of the church. Through the influence of the Most Spiritual Reverend Mother, or Big Mmama Prayer as she

Figure 52. The Blessed Spiritual Mother and Founder of the Holy Chapel of Miracles with the author.

became popularly known, the church developed its characteristic belief in faith-healing through prayer. The church grew relatively slowly and even today has no more than the original three branches and a few hundred members. It is significant that a male leader was appointed in the 1960s to be responsible for running the church, and at the death of the founder in March 1981, a man, Senior Apostle E. Etim, took over the affairs of the church.

Women are currently involved in the organization of the church but not at the highest levels. The Reverend Mother is ranked fourth in the hierarchy; women are appointed as elders as well as lay readers. There is also the office of the Shepherdess, which is reserved for a young girl. Women do not dominate in terms of membership.

The background of the founder of the Holy Chapel of Miracles is in some ways similar to that of Big Mmama Prayer. Now known as the Blessed Spiritual Mother and installed in Calabar as the spiritual head of the Holy Chapel of Miracles, she moved from Calabar to Oshogbo, Western Nigeria, in her youth. A midwife and staunch Catholic, she refused to believe a friend's prophecy that she was destined to do God's work. Despite the initial reluctance, she accepted her calling and founded the Chapel in 1947. She still maintains that the Church is a church from the East (of Nigeria) and that as the people from the East they are God's chosen people. The Calabar headquarters was established in 1956.

Asked about women and religion, she said that men have "strength in themselves" but that women have "great spiritual power."[28] She is fond of stating that women were "last at the cross and first at the tomb," and recounts with affection and enthusiasm the roles of the many Biblical women—Miriam, Deborah, Phoebe, Priscilla et al. The Blessed Spiritual Mother is in her seventies and is of a very gentle disposition. She is surrounded by men, both young and old, who revere her spiritual authority and play quite minimal supporting roles. Many of her clients are women who come for her special prayers in matters of infertility, sickness, domestic strife, and other family problems. Some may only attend the midweek prayer meetings and healing sessions or even visit secretly, preferring to retain their affiliation with the mission or historic churches. This type of fluid membership has militated against the expansion of the church.

The Church of God Lamentation of Jehovah is a small church in a remote part of Calabar distinguished not only by its name, but also by the fact that the founder, Prophetess Theresa Sunday U. Inyang, believes that only women can see visions and prophesy clearly. She herself is illiterate, engaged in trading and is married with children. The church began in 1976 as a result of the founder's religious experience and reflecting her varied religious background. Two years later another church, the Mount Olive Church of Christ, was formed in Calabar also by an Ibibio woman, Mrs. Maddie Raymond. A young woman, in contrast to the other women founders, she maintains that women are "spiritually equal if not more powerful, but out of fear believe themselves to be weaker souls."[29] Despite her religious initiative, she herself and the other women members tend to perform the largely spiritual and pastoral roles in the church, leaving the organizational responsibilities to the men, who alone can be ministers. Raymond's husband, who is a young lecturer at the University of Calabar, is playing an increasingly important role in the church, leaving his wife to deal, for example, with the Women's Fellowship. She sees this as an important aspect of her work, coaching women on how to be good wives and obedient to their husbands "because it is in the Bible." She herself was a civil servant in local government until her religious calling. She makes much use of her healing powers to solve women's problems and has plans to expand and develop her church by forming links with overseas churches.

One of the two other churches in Calabar known to have been founded by women is the Christ Holy Church, which is in fact a church of Ibo origin (Aba and Onitsha), whose founder, the Holy Prophetess of God (Odiono Obio), is not resident in Calabar. The church tends to attract illiterate Ibo women who do not feel at home in other churches. The second, the Temple of God Church, was founded in November 1982 as a result of female initiative and has grown fairly rapidly thanks to a donation of land from a local judge.

There is a general view (especially among men) that the independent churches deal primarily with women's problems and that the emotionalist character of the worship appeals particularly to women. Furthermore, the length of the services (anything from three to eight hours) is thought to be oriented towards the womenfolk who are believed to have plenty of time on their hands! Aye expresses strong views on the subject:

> These prayer houses draw more women and girls who, fickle as the wind and sentimental in their feminine constitution, occasionally fall a prey to corruption and immorality in the hands of unscrupulous men.[30]

There is some basis for these general observations. As mentioned earlier, one of the main attractions of the independent churches is their emphasis on healing. Given the pressures on women to perpetuate the lineage and the problems surrounding childbirth and rearing healthy children in a developing country whose medical facilities are still far from adequate, it is not surprising that women turn to these churches for total or supplementary support. We also should not ignore the supernatural beliefs or fears which surround conception and childbirth and which the independent churches treat as existential realities. It is not surprising that a survey conducted by Joseph Uyanga on "The Medical Role of Spiritual Healing Churches in Southeastern Nigeria," found that women were the predominant patients, with about 37% of the women—20% of the total patients—complaining of childbearing problems.[31] The Mount Zion Lighthouse Full Gospel Church in Calabar, for example, attracts many women due to its reputation for solving infertility problems.[32]

However, in general, independent church membership is fairly evenly balanced between men and women. In fact, in some of the major urban churches, with their complex bureaucratic and hierarchical structures, male attendance may be higher. Membership and attendance are far more complex than we have been able to demonstrate within the context of this article. Women in these churches are often hampered and restricted by the taboos surrounding menstruation and childbirth, which is why older women are more frequently seen in positions of authority. This fear of defilement of the sacred by women is demonstrated by the fact that the altar sanctuary is so frequently an all-male preserve. Congregational segregation is common, with separate doors for each sex.[33] Much attention is paid to the way women dress in church so that they do not distract male attention. In some churches men may pray for both male and female supplicants, whereas women may only pray for women.

Notwithstanding the restrictions, the independent churches do provide structures within which women may acquire and exercise power and responsibility. Women are usually barred from entering the highest echelons of the church hierarchy and their jurisdiction may be limited to other female members and the children. However, a prophetess or senior (usually older) female member (such as the matron of the church or the wife of a pastor, evangelist etc.) may command the respect of the whole group and influence (although often in an indirect way through divine revelation) the decision-making of the group. An interesting case in point here is that of a newly-formed church in Calabar, the Holy Face Healing Church. The leadership of this growing church is in the hands of the men, but spiritual authority is the domain of the women. All "spiritual people," that is visioners and prophetesses, are women or young girls. When in trance, they

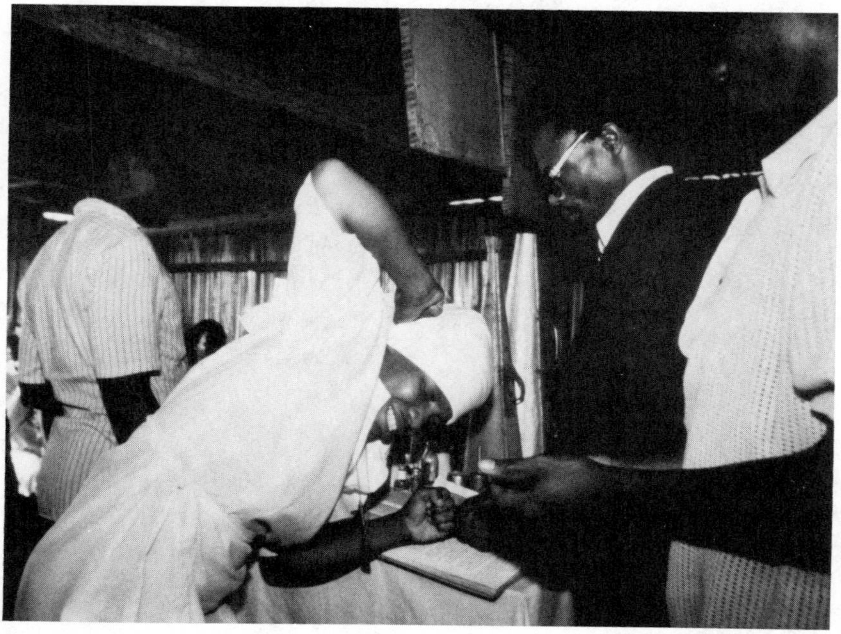

Figure 53. A prophetess in trance at the Holy Face Healing Church.

are able to manipulate and instruct the men to carry out certain (usually ritual) activities. Tensions are evident, for under normal circumstances no man would take such orders from a woman, and as leaders of the church the men feel obliged to try to demonstrate their authority over the female functionaries. However, it is the voice of the Spirit which has the last word under these circumstances and legitimates the symbolic and ritual reversal of the roles appropriate for each sex.

The latter example perhaps serves to illustrate, as we conclude this section, the type of opportunities which are available to women within the independent churches. Particularly for those women who have become "displaced persons" (childless, divorced, accused of witchcraft),

> The African independent churches with their small communities, offer them another social group in which they are known and accepted as persons, in which they become full citizens of the Kingdom of God, in which they can take initiatives and responsibilities, and in which they can acquire a social position independently from their situation at home.[34]

Figure 54. Female choristers at the Brotherhood of the Cross and Star.

Imported Sects and Movements

Our next major religious grouping, that of the imported sects and movements, is extremely heterogeneous and merits only some brief observations within this context. Evangelical and pentecostal groups, largely of American origin, are growing rapidly in popularity. They offer both men and women a training ground in Biblical literacy and organizational skills, and women may be very active as evangelists and even preachers. It is becoming common for women to form their own small prayer groups which are conducted in people's homes or local schools.[35] However, many of the more established organizations are conservative and fundamentalist in orientation and promote the image of women as inferior versions of God's creation, a viewpoint which many Nigerians find attractive and aligned with traditional attitudes. Evangelical associations such as the Deeper Life Christian Ministry, promoting a largely conservative Western Christian domestic ideology, run seminars on how to be a good, accommodating wife. In some of the older groups, such as the Faith Tabernacle, women are excluded from any responsibility and obliged to sit at the back of the church. In the Jehovah's Witnesses, women are instrumental in evangelism but are not allowed to preach God's word.

In the more Eastern and mysticism-related groups, where the emphasis is on esoteric knowledge, women are generally believed to have lower states of consciousness and not to possess mystical talents in the same way that men do. It is the men therefore, who are the largest consumers of occult, spiritualist and metaphysical literature, such as that produced by the Rosicrucians. Again new trends are emerging. A civil servant, A. Peter Akpan, has set up a group, "The Mystical Fellowship," to which he is trying to attract (with difficulty) female converts, since he believes in female mystical genius, citing the cases of Mary Baker Eddy and Madame Blavatsky.

Conclusion

Our examination of women's religious worlds in the town of Calabar has revealed both ambiguities and paradoxes. The extensive participation of women in their various religious groups and institutions is not matched by opportunities for leadership and authority. The general belief that women possess a capacity for great spiritual power is accompanied by the idea that women are weaker creatures with potentially evil tendencies which may pollute the sacred and "entice men away from the fulfilment of their spiritual role."[36]

Within the different spheres of religious activity and experience, women have, for the most part, been encouraged to take subordinate roles, their authority increasing as their social characteristics *qua* women decrease. Women have also been channelled into creating their own forms of religiosity and religious collectivities focusing on the "special burdens and sorrows of female life."[37] In this way women have benefitted from the channels of religious expression without challenging the basic social fabric, thereby preserving the ideology of male supremacy.

The time-honored images of women as mothers, teachers, healers and as specially concerned with the areas of birth and death even today find continuity and legitimation in Calabar's churches and religious groups. It is worth noting that one particular image—of the woman as being trustworthy—is receiving increasing support and implementation (women being appointed as church treasurers) in the fact of Nigeria's great social evils—bribery and corruption. On the whole, the various forms of religion in Calabar tend to validate the ordinary, rather than the extraordinary, concerns and calling of women.[38] While religious participation does allow women a temporary escape from their domestic duties and responsibilities and involvement in a different set of activities, there is no radical questioning of sex roles or power relationships, even in the independent churches where strong female leadership and participation provide an important alternative to male-dominated worship.

The effects of social change, notably improved educational opportunities for women, are being felt increasingly in the religious sphere. Women are no longer expected to adopt the religious affiliation of their husbands as in the past thus they have greater religious freedom and mobility. Women are gaining access to the same religious ideas and literature as men, evangelical, mystical and occult sources, as well as the other major areas of religious knowledge in both school and church. As female illiteracy recedes, women become able to receive the word directly and not through men. Traditional taboos and attitudes are showing signs of erosion as a result not only of modernization but also of the influence of the so-called foreign or Western-related churches which condemned the dehumanization of women, while often introducing negative images of their own making.

The fact remains, however, that for the majority of women in Calabar, religious activities and experience provide an alternative sense of worth and even redress for their problems and deprivation; but as long as women in Calabar and Nigeria as a whole do not press for leadership and direct expression of their religious and social initiatives, they must continue to accept male determination and manipulation of their roles and needs. Perhaps ironically it is Nigeria's political and church leaders who, in this time of social, cultural and economic upheaval, are calling for women to be more active in national and religious affairs. We end with the words of one such male observer, written in 1967 but still appropriate today:

> Efik women were not allowed at church by their men in the last century until the war with Okoyong in 1868 forced their hands. Today they are virtually the church everywhere in Calabar, and the upholders of the Christian tradition. Remove the women from the church and no church will exist in Efikland today.[39]

Notes

1. Calabar has an estimated population of around 200,000. There are three indigenous ethnic groups—the Efik (the largest), the Qua and the Efut, as well as the neighboring Ibibio and Ibo peoples. Most people belong to Christian-related groups. Islam is restricted to the migrant Northern peoples.

2. A.J.H. Latham, *Old Calabar: 1600–1891* (Oxford: Clarendon Press, 1973), p. 35.

3. P.A. Talbot, *Life in Southern Nigeria* (London: Macmillan, 1923), p. 162.

4. Ibid.

5. Eyo Okon Akak, *A Critique of Old Calabar History* (Calabar: Ikot Offiong Welfare Association, 1981), p. 67.

6. Ibid.

7. See E.U. Aye, *Old Calabar through the Centuries* (Calabar: Hope Waddell Press, 1967), p. 70, and E.O. Akak, *Efiks of Old Calabar*, vol. 3: *Culture and Superstitions* (Calabar: Akak & Sons, 1982), p. 288.

8. Interview with Emmanuel Nsan, Ekpenyong Idem (leader) of Nka Ekpenyong Nnuk, Calabar, 26 June 1983.

9. Akak, *Efiks of Old Calabar*, 3:293–94.

10. Ibid., 3:294.

11. Ibid., 3:295.

12. Ibid.

13. Report of the Enquiry into the dispute over the Obongship of Calabar, Official Document 17, Enugn 1964, p. 48.

14. Aye, *Old Calabar*, p. 124.

15. Ibid.

16. Akak, *Efiks of Old Calabar*, 3:346.

17. The articles are drawn from Akak, *Efiks of Old Calabar* 3:344–47.

18. Cf. Deborah Gaitskell, "Housewives, Maids or Mothers: Some Contradictions of Domesticity for Christian Women in Johannesburg, 1903–39," *Journal of African History* 24 (1983):241–56, who makes similar observations regarding the training of African women in Johannesburg: "Sewing . . . was

presented as an indispensable accomplishment for Christian womanhood. Perhaps this was partly a survival of the centrality of Western clothing as a sign of African conversion" (p. 245).

19. See *Golden Jubilee Magazine of the Holy Child Federated Alumnae, Cross River State Zone, 1930–1980* (Calabar: Holy Child Federated Alumnae, 1980). It was particularly through the agency of the Society of the Holy Child Jesus and the Handmaids of the Holy Child Jesus that this educational reorientation occurred.

20. M.O. Ogarekpe, comp., *Mary Slessor's Hundredth Anniversary Celebrations: A Short Biography for the Centenary Celebration by the Synod of the Presbyterian Church of Nigeria* (Calabar: Presbyterian Church of Nigeria, 1976), p. 5.

21. James Buchan, *The Expendable Mary Slessor* (Edinburgh: St. Andrew's Press, 1980), p. 138. This is the most recent and well-researched of the biographies on Mary Slessor.

22. Ibid., p. 195.

23. Ogarekpe, *A Short Biography*, p. 9.

24. Ibid.

25. See "The Handmaids of the Holy Child Jesus—Origin and Development," *Golden Jubilee Magazine*, p. 13.

26. Ibid., p. 14.

27. See Okorie Akuawanya, "Report on a Field Assignment to the Church of Christ, The Good Shepherd," University of Calabar, May 1982. See also unpublished field notes of Essien A. Offiong, 16 August, 8 and 28 November, 1981.

28. Interview with Blessed Spiritual Mother, Calabar, 29 March 1983.

29. Interview with Maddie Raymond, Calabar, 20 June 1983.

30. Aye, *Old Calabar*, p. 169.

31. Joseph Uyanga, "The Medical Role of Spiritual Healing Churches in Southeastern Nigeria," *Nigerian Behavioural Sciences Journal* 2, nos. 1–2 (1979):50.

32. In particular the Ikot Ekaidem branch, popularly known as "The Mount of Deliverance," run by the charismatic pastor Ezekiel Etokidem: see *Sunday Chronicle* (Calabar), 28 September 1980 and 21 September 1981.

33. This raises the issue of sacred space and the use of other symbolic mechanisms to differentiate roles on which there is not space here to elaborate. See Shirley Ardener, "Introduction: The Nature of Women in Society," in *Defining Females*, ed. Shirley Ardener (London: Croom Helm, 1978) pp. 32f.

34. Leny Lagerwerf, "Women in the Church," *Exchange* 12 (December 1975):48–49.

35. One such group, developed initially on the University of Calabar campus by a lecturer in English, Ebele Eko, has acquired considerable proportions through her fervent evangelism and tract distribution, and looks set to become an independent religious body—the Evangelistic Church of the Redeemed.

36. Carolyne Dennis, "Introduction to Section VIII: Religion and the Status of Women," in *Nigerian Women and Development*, ed. F. Adetowun Ogun-

sheye et al. (Ibadan: Editorial Committee on Conference on Nigerian Women and Development, University of Ibadan, 1982), p. 917.

37. Ibid.

38. See Nancy A. Falk and Rita M. Gross, eds., *Unspoken Worlds: Women's Religious Lives in Non-Western Cultures* (San Francisco: Harper & Row, 1980), p. xiv.

39. Aye, *Old Calabar*, p. 217.

PART III

Women, Religion and Revolution in the Modern World

CHAPTER ELEVEN

Islam, Women and Revolution in Twentieth-Century Arab Thought

YVONNE YAZBECK HADDAD

Throughout this century, the role, status and goals of women in the Arab world have been part and parcel of the revolutionary ethos that has permeated society as intellectual and political leaders have attempted to transform its institutions by implementing various plans of development and social change intended to achieve parity with the West. The prevalent image of the dominant West with its challenge to Islamic culture became an essential component of the ideological formulations appropriated as vehicles of change by various groups. In this endeavor, women have become the symbol of the transformation of society, thus gaining status as bearers and maintainers of cultural and religious values.[1]

The challenge of the West was intimately experienced at the turn of the century through European colonial occupation of most of the Arab world. The mandate system devised by the European countries after the First World War was justified on the basis of the teachings of Social Darwinism which gave European man "scientific" proof that he was at the acme of human evolution and that his civilization was the final stage in human achievement and progress.[2] The European powers assumed their "manifest destiny," what the British called the white man's burden and the French their civilizing mission, to prepare the Arabs for independence and full participation among the nations of the world. The superiority of western values was advocated in the new educational institutions established by the colonial governments and disseminated in the schools founded by Christian missionaries. Their curricula glorified western achievements, making it clear that what they saw as the decadence of the Arab world was the direct result of the "obscurantist" teachings of Islam. In the writings of western travelers, orientalists and missionaries, Islamic family law and regulations affecting the role and status of women were not only ridiculed as demeaning, but were also targeted as the cause of the backwardness of Muslim societies. Among the issues repeatedly raised were the education of women, veiling, seclusion, polygamy and easy divorce.[3]

This western challenge influenced Arab intellectuals, helping to generate a profound sense of dissatisfaction with the prevalent conditions and an awareness of the urgent necessity for radical change in order to restore society to prominence and strength. In the process, a variety of attitudes developed among some religious and political leaders. These ranged from agreement that social change is permissible in Islam to insistence that change itself is the essential nature of the religion which was revealed by God to order all aspects of human life in the world.[4] The argument for change was justified by the Qur'anic verse "God will not alter what is in people until they alter what is in themselves"(S. 13:12). While a consensus appears to have developed that change is necessary for the revitalization of society, there was no agreement on the method, purpose or dynamics of this change. Different ideologues posited various theories. Some advocated an ordered, evolutionary process of education that was to lead society to its desired goal, while others insisted on the need for revolutionary change designed to eradicate the failed existing system and replace it with one that is vibrant, capable of transforming the individual as well as the prevailing societal structures.[5] Thus the idea of social change was endowed with special positive characteristics, connotations and meanings and the "liberation of women" became the subject as well as the object of this change. This article will confine itself to an examination of some of the responses that fall under the rubric of revolutionary.

While Sunni Islam traditionally has frowned on revolution as disruptive to the social order, citing Qur'anic injunctions to obey God, the Prophet and those in positions of leadership,[6] revolutionaries of various allegiances in the twentieth century have idealized revolution as a positive agent in the transformation of society. They have perceived it as a necessary initial event that can revive society from its moribund state, setting in motion the forces of good that will generate wholesome attitudes, and preparing a moral and dedicated leadership willing to be the vanguard in the struggle to implement a worthy cause.[7] The revolutionary has been romanticized as one with a vision for a better world and a willingness to renounce personal comfort and material well-being in pursuit of a higher cause, that of a better life for the community.

Twentieth-century revolutionary thought in the Arab world has developed around three ideologies that have dominated public discourse: the nationalist, the socialist and the Islamist. (Islamism is a scripturalist form of religious piety, affirming the relevance of the Qur'ān for everyday activity and insisting on its regulation of all aspects of life.) The fortunes of these ideologies have varied depending on the political power of their adherents, who at times found it necessary to cooperate with those espousing different visions. The prominence of one ideology over another has often been due to the failure of an opposing perspective to ease the deep dissatisfaction the Arab people have felt when their governments were unable to create conditions that would have given them a sense of vitality, dignity and worth.

Nationalist revolutionary thought was dominant from the turn of the century to the early fifties.[8] It is marked by the development of Arab national identity that initially fostered rebellion against Turkish rule. Its modernist and secularist ideology reflected the influence of British and French occupation forces who nurtured its institutions and supervised their implementation. While nationalist revolutionary thought attempted to replicate a European order in the various aspects of public life, its primary focus was the transformation of the political institutions of society. Concentrating on the writing of constitutions, the establishing of parliaments, the defining of the role of citizens and the eligibility of voters, and the holding of elections, its major concern was to restore sovereignty to the Arab people by freeing Arab countries from foreign dominance. The decline in the prevalence of its appeal came after the withdrawal of foreign troops from the various Arab countries and the institutionalization of its bureaucracies, and as a consequence of its inability to prevent in 1948 the establishment of the state of Israel in Palestine, "the heart of the Arab world."

The socialist revolutionaries assumed power through military coups d'etat[9] in the fifties in Syria, Egypt and Iraq (and later in Algeria, Yemen and Libya). They were heralded as the liberators of the Arab people from foreign domination since they ousted leaders who were perceived to be "lackeys of imperialism," so designated because of the loss of Palestine to the Israelis. While the socialists attempted to revolutionalize all aspects of public life, their primary concern was economic development and the welfare of society which they sought to bring about by centralizing all economic policies and power in the state. They achieved this goal through legislation nationalizing and appropriating private wealth as well as natural resources and means of production. They therefore were able to eliminate the economic power of the middle classes, which prospered under the nationalist governments, as well as economic dependency on the colonial powers, whose interests were maintained through the resident alien population. In time, however, the dominance and appeal of the socialist ideology and its support by the masses was eroded as a consequence of the devastating defeat the Arabs suffered at the hands of the Israelis in 1967.

The malaise that followed the defeat was relieved by what was perceived to be an Arab "victory" over Israel in the 1973 war. This shifted the allegiance of the masses to the Islamist revolutionaries,[10] whose main focus is the transformation of the social order into an Islamic system that adheres to the tenets of the Qur'ān. Their ideology affirms that it is only through the transformation of the Muslim individual within the family structure that society can be saved from annihilation at the hands of its enemies. Furthermore, preservation of the divinely ordained Islamic social system with its cultural distinctions is the only guarantee of liberation from the domination of alien norms and values.

All revolutionaries, whether nationalist, socialist or Islamist, have recognized and challenged the oppression of women in underdeveloped Arab societies. They have identified it as part of the general decline of the Arab world, due in large part to oppression by foreign governments, through their mismanagement of wealth, disregard for industrialization and concern for their own political survival and economic monopolies. All of them appear to have agreed that the prevailing condition of the Muslim woman is unacceptable and that her transformation is crucial to the transformation of society as a whole. Where they have not been in agreement is in their respective visions of the symbolic role the woman plays and the means through which these visions can be actualized in society. Thus in the liberal nationalist revolution the woman has been symbolized as competent wife and devoted mother, in the socialist revolution as a good producer and participant in national development, and in the Islamic revolution as the repository of ethical values.

In all of the discussions of the role and status of women one thing stands out. Regardless of ideological commitment, whether nationalist, socialist or Islamist, and regardless of the sex of the author, the liberation of women is seen within the context of the liberation of the whole society, liberation essential in bringing about a virtuous order. An article written in the 1950s by ʿAbd al-Ḥamīd Ḥamdī stated:

> . . .let my respected ladies allow me to say that we did not call for your liberation for its own sake [literally, "for the blackness of your eyes"] as the proverb says; rather, it was out of the desire to elevate the level of this nation and to place it in its respected place among the nations. We also knew that [the realization of our goals] would not be possible if women remained behind the walls of ignorance and outmoded customs, for no reason other than the [fact] that woman is the mother of the man and his first teacher.

Ḥamdī concludes, directly addressing women:

> It is your crucial duty to study your current condition carefully, and prepare an ideal plan to purify the factors of weakness that may have seeped into your renaissance. Your goal in your efforts must be the same goal we strove for the day we called for your liberation: to work for Egypt, not for men alone and not for women alone.[11]

The theme of cooperation between men and women for the betterment of society is a recurring one. Muḥammad ʿAmāra, a Nasserite considered to be a Muslim liberal with socialist leanings, saw Islam as "a revolution to liberate woman and elevate her that she may keep up with the man."[12] And ʿĀ'isha ʿAbd al-Raḥmān, contemporary Islamic scholar and Qur'ān exegete, writes:

> There is no way of avoiding more sacrifices except by ending forever this strange and imaginary enmity between woman and man, or between her and society. This cannot be accomplished by one side [alone]. Therefore be with [the woman] on the way, for she is your daughter, your sister, your life partner and your comrade. She is the mother of your children, and the maker of your future. Remember the sign of God in her and in you.[13]

Liberation of the woman is thus seen to be linked to destiny, a matter for the whole society rather than the personal interest in the individual. Consequently we will find it common for leaders of the Arab feminist movement, regardless of their ideological persuasion, to make statements disavowing any effort to pit female against male and to assure their readers and listeners that the goal is the liberation of the whole society, male and female.[14]

The impact of the West on Arab society during this century has manifested itself in all aspects of public life: political, economic, educational, cultural and social. While there has been a great deal of resistance from different groups to the variety of changes designed and/or implemented, nothing has generated as much emotion, discussion and controversy as efforts to "liberate women." Basic to the conflict is the heritage of social and cultural institutions in which men's honor, pride and dignity have been inextricably bound to the modesty and chastity of their women.[15] Consequently, any innovations that attempted to alter the traditional institutions and customs of society resulted in endless debates centering on the potential degeneration of women, once liberated, into sexual objects easily available to men.

These debates sent the various factions to the Qur'ān, the scripture of Islam, to the Ḥadīth, the teachings of the Prophet, and to the sharīʿa, Islamic law, to ferret out material designed to substantiate their opinions. Through this process, Muslim writers have produced a special genre of literature, defensive in nature, which extols the elevated and liberating role Islam has assigned to woman, giving her a high position that is superior to that allocated to her by Christianity, Judaism, Hinduism or any other religion or social order. The rights guaranteed her by Islam include her right to live, to be educated, to inherit, to keep her maiden name, to carry on her own business transactions and to maintain her wealth.[16]

From the beginning, both the content and the scope of the debate have been influenced by two important factors. On the one hand, all proposed changes are articulated and implemented in public, under the watchful eyes of outside observers (including those from the West) who have made their agenda and expectations clear. On the other hand, the perimeters of the proposed reforms have been bound by the fact that out of the one-hundred verses in the Qur'ān believed to be proscriptive or prescriptive in nature and not subject to change, eighty percent deal with issues relating to women such as polygamy, divorce and the relation of wife to husband.[17] This means that all proposed changes, regardless of their source, can only generate conflict since they trespass on the domain of revelation.

The enchantment with revolution was introduced by the champions of westernization among the elites of Arab society who accepted the colonial contention that Europe's strength and potency were a by-product of its civilization and value system initiated in the Renaissance, maintained by the elimination of bondage to religious hierarchies and institutions, and achieved by the French Revolution. Their unabashed fascination with western secularism and advocacy of the emulation of western social norms and customs were openly discussed in books, magazine articles and newspapers. One of the earliest champions of the liberation of women in Egypt in the late nineteenth century was Qāsim Amīn, a lawyer who came to be identified with the cause of women through the publication of two books.[18] His analysis served to identify those issues that have been seen over the years as most controversial for various Muslim ideologues, whether or not they advocate his goals. Arguments cited today continue to relate back to his commentary of over eighty years ago. Describing his perception of the need for change, he wrote:

> This is the disease which we must proceed to remedy; there is no medicine but that we teach our children about western civilization, its sources, branches and heritage. When the time comes—and we hope that it isn't too far off—the truth will be manifested before our eyes, shining brightly as the sun. Then we will know the value of western civilization and will realize that it is impossible to reform what is around us if it is not founded on modern scientific knowledge. . . . This is why we see that civilized countries regardless of race, language, nation or religion are similar in the form of government, administration, legal system, family structure, education, language, writing, architecture and roads, extending even to many simple customs such as dress, greetings and food. This is what leads us to cite Europeans as an example and urge that they be emulated, and it is for this that we have undertaken to call attention to European women.[19]

The westernization Qāsim Amīn advocated was not as comprehensive as may appear at first glance. He only sought to have women uncover their faces, not take off the veil; he asked that women be consulted about their marriage partners, but did not make them responsible for finding a husband; he called for restrictions in the practice of polygamy, but allowed it under certain circumstances. In order to elicit the support of males for his reforms, he showed that the primary beneficiary of the "liberation of woman" is the man. Thus the education of women was projected as a means of providing better wives for the new breed of educated westernized men as well as more knowledgeable mothers to fashion the new generation.

> It is impossible to raise successful men if they do not have mothers capable of preparing them for success. That is the noble profession which civilization has entrusted in the woman in our age. She undertakes her heavy load in all civilized countries where we see her giving birth to children, then fashioning them into men.[20]

In this Amīn made the progress or degradation of societies contingent, among other factors, on the condition of their women.

To deflect religious opposition to his scheme, Amīn cast the role of women in the context of the social realm, outside the sphere of religion:

> Yes, I come with an innovation, however, it is not the essence of Islam, rather it is of customs and methods of interaction in which it is good to seek perfection.[21]

These ideas had earlier been expounded through lectures at al-Azhar and the publication of a new exegesis of the Qur'ān by Muḥammad ʿAbduh and Rashīd Riḍā, the two renowned religious reformers of the twentieth century. They had reinterpreted those passages traditionally understood as restrictive to women, giving them a new meaning which became the foundation of Amīn's teachings.[22]

This did little to halt the vociferous attacks of the religious leaders, especially those of al-Azhar. They accused Amīn of proposing changes that would denigrate women, whose domain they saw as restricted to the home and whose primary function they thought to be the bearing of children. Polygamy and the exposure of women's faces were two of the key issues discussed by Amīn's contemporaries. Muḥammad Ḥassan al-Būlāqī published several articles (some even in the secular press that was supporting Amīn) justifying polygamy as necessary in order "to increase progeny and populate the nation by those who affirm the unicity of God [Muslims]." He argued against uncovering the face, insisting that "It is incumbent to cover even the hands . . . to stay at home and not to go out unless for a need. . . ."[23]

Amīn also was attacked by such political leaders as Muṣṭafā Kāmil, a nationalist leader who found the call for the uncovering of the face highly objectionable since it led to "public exposure" of women. He denounced the attempt to imitate western women, reportedly saying

> Each nation has its own civilization. It is not fitting that we become monkeys who blindly emulate the foreigners. We have to preserve what is good in our character and not take [anything] from the West except its virtues.[24]

While there appears to have been little opposition to the education of women, the content of that education was debated, with traditional Muslims insisting that woman's education should be restricted to the study of religion, reading, writing, geography, history and mathematics. Some deemed her study of foreign languages "a waste of time"; others warned that any changes instituted would only give pleasure to those foreigners, mostly Christians, who seek to destroy Islám by changing its tenets.[25]

The secular Egyptian press of the time: *al-Ahrām, al-Mū'ayyid, al-Muqtaṭaf, al-Liwā', al-Hilāl* and *al-Muqaṭṭam*, as well as *al-Manār* (published by Rashīd Riḍa), championed Amīn's cause by allowing extensive coverage of the debate and publishing articles supporting the education of women and the removal of the veil. The authors of the various articles appear to have perceived the liberation of women as part of the general call for the liberation of the whole society, a call for equality, democracy and independence.[26]

Several factors helped accelerate woman's emancipation in various Arab countries. In the first place, the presence of European resident aliens provided a model for the trend-setters among the upper classes, many of whom appropriated European values and definitions of liberation. It also spurred the active participation of women from all walks of life in the political protest against foreign occupation in 1919 in Cairo, Jerusalem and Damascus. In Syria, Palestine and Algeria women also died fighting for their country.[27] Secondly, the education of women became public and universal (and consequently available to women from the peasant and working classes) after the Arab countries became independent, preparing women for new positions in society. The third and most important factor in the movement for women's emancipation appears to have been the willingness of various governments to legislate change despite religious and political opposition. In this case, discussion of the role of women became the occasion on which different political, economic and social theories were articulated, debated and implemented, and the arena in which men sought to demonstrate their own power and the vulnerability of their opponents.

This led various governments eventually to co-opt the feminist movements and absorb them as agencies in their bureaucracy, generally attached to the ministry of social affairs. Thus women became the center of attention, as programs for women, now supported with funds and personnel by those in power, continued to seek to transform them into "new beings." By 1975, when the year of the woman was celebrated, fifteen out of twenty-one Arab countries[28] had an official feminist movement as part of their government programs. In the process, the feminist movement ceased to be a voluntary organization led by women of leisure, a benevolent activity to help elevate the less fortunate. Now, supported by the political leadership, it concentrates on modernizing the masses and integrating the rural people into city life through new legislation, literacy campaigns (a 1977 U.N. survey shows that twenty-million out of twenty-four-million Arab mothers were illiterate), child care, health programs, the teaching of crafts and homemaking.[29]

The role and status of the Arab woman has undergone tremendous change since Qāsim Amīn called for her liberation. During this time, her cause has been championed by many and maligned by others. She herself has assumed new positions, participating more fully in various aspects of public life and the record of her achievement is a source of pride for the community. She is the lawyer, the doctor, the engineer, the cabinet minister, the ambassador, the judge, the police officer, the paratrooper as well as the nurse, the teacher and the social worker. Of significant note is her willingness to assume new roles and break new barriers contributing to the collective effort. While it is true that from early on the liberation of women has been championed by men, the fact is that it is the women who brought it about, the women who were willing "to go out," to put their reputation on the line, and to risk accusations and insinuations of bad moral conduct, in a society committed to the ideal of chastity and modesty as the highest virtue. For, even Qāsim Amīn's wife reportedly condemned his ideas for the liberation of women as dangerous and not based on a "solid foundation," and it took a long time before many of them were implemented.[30] It was twenty years after he published his book that Hudā Shaʿrāwī and Ceza Nabrāwī finally had the courage to take off their veils in public.

The socialist regimes that assumed power in the fifties focused special attention on the role of woman and her intellectual, social, political and economic development. Through legislation they altered the sharīʿa laws that governed her life in such areas as the age of marriage, polygamy and divorce. They attempted to give women voting rights and access to all aspects of public life. A Syrian Baʿth party statement declared that

> total popular democratic participation shall remain truncated as long as woman is distant from the public life of society. The liberation of the Arab woman is a democratic as well as a human necessity. . . . The liberation of woman is at the forefront of the tasks of the rational socialist revolution. The construction of the mod-

ern liberated democratic society is not complete or whole if it does not address the question of woman's liberation.[31]

In speeches, articles, books and various media programs, the socialist rhetoric portrayed the woman as the symbol of the progress of the nation. Her involvement in the world around her and her contribution to the community was to be equal to that of the man—in labor, in the democratic institutions being developed and in the socialist transformation of society. Her participation was crucial beyond its symbolic value; it became imperative because of her unique role in raising the new generation, the future socialists that were to carry the society into a better future. "The backwardness of the Arab woman in the economic, social and cultural fields is now one of the most serious obstructions in the path of the modern Arab renaissance."[32] Consequently the "liberation of woman" was placed at the top of the goals of the national socialist revolution, with various governments taking control of women's activities.[33]

Needless to say, this did not sit well with the religious leaders. To them, the social structures that governed the role and activities of women were in the domain of religion.[34] The "liberation of women" became a major issue of controversy between those who accepted the traditional definitions of women as articulated in the Qur'ān, the Ḥadīth and the sharīʿa and those who sought a new vision of society, one compatible with the modern world. Even the secularists among the nationalists found it necessary to justify their ideas by reinterpreting the teachings of the Qur'ān and the sayings of the Prophet Muhammad. This trend continued during the ascendancy of socialist revolutionary thought (except for the few Marxists who debated issues without reference to religious doctrines).[35] In all these debates the issues at stake were whether proposed changes were consistent with the Qur'ān or deviations of alien origin; whether women in public places could still be respectable or were objects of temptation for lustful males, consequently undermining the virtuous society; and, finally, whether the changes implemented were bringing about the desired goals of a progressive society.

A survey of articles on women in *Minbar al-Islām*, the official religious organ published by the Nasserite regime, is very instructive. Every issue printed in 1963 had a report on the progress of Muslim women in Muslim or largely Muslim countries, in Libya, Malaysia, Tunisia, Morocco, Senegal, Nigeria, and so forth. They highlighted the achievements of these women, especially in professions previously restricted to men such as those of doctors, lawyers, judges, ministers of government, legislators, diplomats and preachers. One Moroccan woman was even reported to be giving *fatwās*, legal Islamic opinions on various matters. Yet, while highlighting the goals the Egyptian government espoused in reports about the gains Muslim women had made in other countries, the government-controlled press published articles arguing against such developments in Egypt itself.[36] This apparent contradiction is not necessarily a schizophrenic response to societal pressures. Rather, it points to the most vulnerable issue on which most reformers, whether nationalist or socialist, finally faltered. Their attempts at social engineering tampered with what turned out to be the most important of all traditional values, the role of women.

The early resistance to the social change advocated by the nationalists and socialists came from traditional Muslim circles led by religious leaders from al-Azhar. While some of them objected generally to any idea of change, asserting that the message of the Qur'ān is eternal and valid for all time and place, their basic objection was to ascribing matters relating to women that are specifically addressed by the Qur'ān or the Ḥadīth and the sharīʿa to customs, thus making them open to new interpretation and innovation. What they objected to most vehemently was not the right to education, or the question of equality, but what they viewed as a threat to that which is central to the survival of an Islamic order: the modesty of women which is considered the key to public morality.

The contemporary vision advocated by Muslim traditionalists and revolutionaries perceives women's role as determined by the biological functions of her gender. Not only is she created to be pregnant[37] but more specifically all her roles are defined by her relations to the men in her life. She is rarely depicted as an independent person in her own right. Typical of this genre of literature is the following passage from a professor in Saudi Arabia, writing in the 1980s:

> [The woman] is a mother who nurtures her children forming men, a wife who beautifies life with her beloved smile, her tender touch soothing the ruggedness of the road and her expressive word easing the pressures of work, a sister who shares the bitter and the sweet with her family, and a daughter who fills the home with wholesomeness and beauty and is the delight of her parents.

Thus is created the ideal of a self-sacrificing individual whose existence is fulfilled only in the service of others and whose joy is completed by making others happy.[38]

Another feature of Islamist literature is that it envisions a very restricted public access for women. Several authors articulate what might be called an Islamist domino theory which sees all problems in the world, whether political, economic or social, to be initiated by woman's access to public places. Some feel that even uncovering her face will lead to underdevelopment, economic recession or even depression.[39] Work outside the home is considered degrading, often portrayed as the equivalent of prostitution (they do allow for women educators and doctors to care for other women), while the roles of housewife and mother are elevated to the highest possible degree. The superiority of the Islamic system has been increasingly documented by countless reports about western promiscuity, pornography, the rise in the number of illegitimate children and the abuse of western women. In this literature domesticity is shrouded with a special mystique, a profession designed by God himself for the glory of woman. The contrast is depicted in clear language.[40] In the Islamic system she is

> a guardian of her huband's affairs, an educator and nurturer of her children, a queen crowned in her kingdom and her home, not [one who follows a] profession chosen by the West debasing women, which allows her to earn her livelihood after she is robbed of her humanity . . . . [There] she is either the secretary for the entertainment [of her boss], or the show girl in bars and dance halls, or the model that displays her allurement to shoppers, or the worker in the factory.[41]

For a few, the working woman is an unnatural phenomenon. A recent publication distributed by Jordan's Ministry of Education (reportedly controlled by the Muslim Brotherhood) warns about the imminent appearance of "the third sex." It claims that European scientists have noted a decrease in the number of children born to working women. "It was presumed that this decrease was by choice under the pressure of necessity and the [desire] for stability in the work [situation]." However, according to the author it was found that this is a new form of sterility that is impervious to treatment. Scientists now presume

> that it is a change occurring in the being of the working woman as a consequence of her physical, intellectual and emotional distance from matters of motherhood and her attempt to become equal to the man, sharing with him the arena of work.

Thus the author concludes that the scientists are ready to declare the imminent appearance of "the third sex" in whom femininity is a recessive characteristic.[42]

The voluminous material being produced by advocates of an Islamic order might appear as reiterations of hackneyed arguments formulated at the beginning of the century and voiced repeatedly thereafter. While this may be true for descriptions of the virtues of domesticity and seclusion and for some of the discussions on authenticity, a substantial part of the recent material is colored by two new and dominant themes. The first links the liberation of woman to the "Judeo-Christian conspiracy" to undermine Islam. The second affirms unequivocally that the model (America) advocated by the reformers at the beginning of the century has proven to be corrupt and a total failure.

Among the advocates of Islamic revolution there is a growing concensus that ascribes the ills that have befallen the Arab world to outside forces: they are seen as a direct result of the long-standing hatred western Christians have harbored for Islam. This hatred Muslims see as epitomized in what is called the mentality of the Crusades, which manifests itself in colonial occupation and the activities of Christian missionaries and continues today in the support the West gives to the forces of Zionism. The colonial occupation is increasingly being depicted as not merely a means of harnessing human and economic resources in the service of the European economy and for the welfare of its society, or to insure markets for western products; rather, colonialism is understood as proceeding from religious motivations, a phase in the ongoing plot to destroy Islam.

In fact, several authors have identified westernized Muslims as part of the Judeo-Christian

> strategy to raise advocates from among the Muslims who call for the destruction of religion, of morality and tradition, to place them [the westernized] in positions of leadership and guidance so that Crusaderism and Zionism may hide behind them and Muslims may be duped by their words [believing] that they are Muslims [seeking] revival.[43]

This is seen as a persistent conspiracy evident even at the time of the Prophet Muḥammad, as revealed in the warning of the Qur'ān: "The Jews and the Christians will not accept you until you follow their religion" (S. 2:120) and "They will persist in fighting you until they turn you from your religion if they have the ability to do so" (S. 2:217).

The liberation of women is viewed as an integral part of the Crusader-Zionist conspiracy. Muḥammad Quṭb, whose writings are widely read and assimilated by a growing number of the Arab Muslim population today, identifies the liberation of women as one of five characteristics of contemporary society which demonstrate that the Arab world has deviated from the teachings of Islam.[44] The liberation of the Muslim woman

> is the most malicious means used by Crusader imperialism to destroy the Muslim entity in an effort to uproot it. By itself, it was guaranteed to disseminate moral, intellectual and religious disintegration among the Muslim people which all other means combined would have failed to achieve. . . . when the woman goes out naked into the street displaying her allurement to every seeker, arousing animal desire in the man, then there is no Islam, no religion, no doctrine . . . no bonding in public morality, no resistance. In this [situation] Crusading imperialism finds the opportunity to aim its blow.[45]

The liberation of women is seen as part of the missionary conspiracy to destroy Islam, using its own people to uproot it from within. The missionary objective is now understood as having been designed: to raise doubts about the adequacy of Islam as a way of life and to convince the Muslims that it is the cause of their decline; and to separate Muslims from their morality and values, so that they can be absorbed in the orbit of western civilization.[46] Towards these ends Christians accorded the liberation of women a central place in their strategy. At the Lucknow Conference of 1911 the missionaries targeted women and their social development as the second point on the agenda, while at their follow-up meeting in Cairo, the seventh and eighth points were concerned with Muslim women and their development.[47]

The missionaries are accused of wanting to liberate the woman not to promote the elevation of society but in order to contribute to its degradation and corruption.

> When they "educated" her, they taught her knowledge and mastery of corruption, a corruption based on "principles," educational principles at times, psychological, sociological or intellectual principles at other times . . . [but] at all times [principles of] corruption.[48]

Western missionary education comes under severe criticism because it used women to undermine Islam.

> Nothing is greater for [Christians] than to destroy the Muslim fortress from within, the forefront of which is the Muslim family. Their support comes from the woman who takes off the Islamic dress in missionary schools and learns about the life of nudity, the nudity of the spirit as well as that of the body.[49]

Etienne Lamme[?] is cited as proof of missionary intent to undermine. Lamme believed that the education of Muslim women in parochial schools run by nuns was the best means of destroying Islam; he reportedly said: "The education of girls in this manner is the only way to eradicate Islam by the hand of its own people."[50] Lamme supposedly also said that Christian education is a means by which a Muslim woman

> who is nurtured by a Christian hand knows how to overcome the man. When she conquers in this manner, it will be easy for her to influence her husband's beliefs and his Muslim sensibilities and to raise her children according to a religion, other than that of their father. In this we will have been very successful in our purpose to have the woman herself become the destroyer of Islam.[51]

Another westerner to come under serious attack is the well-known missionary Samuel Zwemer who is reported to have said such things as

> We have learned that there are other means besides the direct attack on Islam. . . . We must search for the crack in the wall and place the rifle. We know that the crack is in the heart of the women of Islam. It is the women who fashion the children of the Muslims.[52]

One proof cited to show that western education succeeded in its aims is the fact that Hudā Shaʿrāwī and Ceza Nabrāwī who, as mentioned above, dramatically cast off their veils in 1923, had both received a French education. Furthermore, Hudā Shaʿrāwī was the daughter of Muḥammad Sulṭān Bāshā who had been granted two medals by the British. He was initiated into the orders of Saint Michael and Saint George, sure indication he was an agent of the enemy, a traitor to the Arab cause.[53]

The most recent phase of the ongoing Judeo-Christian conspiracy to destroy the fabric of Islam is seen to be the current support of the West for the forces of Zionism. The impotence of the Arab countries in repeated military engagements with the Israelis and the ability of the state of Israel to annex land, deport inhabitants and impose its will without regard to international law, combined with the unquestioned and unrestrained support it enjoys from the United States, have lent credibility to the interpretation of Zionism as a menacing conspiracy. Material from The Protocols of the Elders of Zion,[54] reprinted in Arabic and quoted by various authors as proof of Jewish intentions, illustrates for the readers that the threat of Zionism is not in its military capabilities but in its perceived plan to destroy both Islam and Christianity by spreading teachings designed to debase humanity.[55]

Three Jewish thinkers (referred to by one author as "the three devils" and by another as "the satans among the Jews")[56] are cited as part of this global conspiracy: Emile Durkheim, "who claimed that the family is an artificial unit for which there is no necessity" and that "the original social order was one where women were commonly shared by males," Karl Marx, "who insisted that the woman must work [outside the home]," and Sigmund Freud, "who said that it is necessary for her to fulfill her role sexually without any restrictions."[57] From this vantage point, Zionism, in order to facilitate Jewish control of the world, is portrayed as seeking the destruction of the moral order by spreading subversive sociological and psychological theories in educational circles. As one author graphically says, they set these theories up as the gods of "economic, social and historical determinism."[58]

Part of the Zionist manipulation of society, in this view, comes through Jewish control over various modes of entertainment, as well as over the production of consumer goods, fostering style changes that "rob nations of their wealth." They dominate the fashion industry, producing clothing that "makes the woman nude and the man into a buffoon," raising the hemline above the knee to encourage immoral behavior. The final goal of the Zionists is to keep men preoccupied with women, away from faith and the fear of God. They have control over the music industry, writing songs with explicit and frank invitations to immorality and iniquity. They publish pornographic magazines advocating the mixing of sexes, which has resulted in the spread of veneral disease leading to the contamination of new born babies.[59]

The other theme emphasized in the recent Islamist literature is the failure of the American model. This is partly a response to what is seen as the American defeat in Vietnam and more recently in Iran, showing the vulnerability of the "mightiest nation in the world." Even more, however, failure of the American model is seen as epitomized in the feminist movement of the sixties and seventies with its "anti-male" bias and its "advocacy of free sex."[60] Feelings of disillusionment run deep precisely because the Arab feminist movement at the turn of the century built its case on the example of the modest American woman, working next to her husband to build a better future.[61] The model is no longer worthy of emulation. In fact the literature depicts America as currently afflicted with an epidemic of four plagues: narcotics, lawlessness, pornography and veneral disease.[62]

Recent events in the Middle East have focused western attention on the increasing commitment of a growing number of Muslims to Islamic identity. Given the growing conviction among Muslims that alternatives to the Islamic vision of the world are bound to lead to failure and social disintegration, adherence to Islam becomes an imperative. To do otherwise is a sure formula for defeat. This has been dismissed by many as a backward-looking return to traditional Islam. Few have bothered to analyze the ideology being proposed and the new world-view projected.

One of the most interesting features of contemporary Islamic literature is its theological formulation of what it means to be human, its concept of the world, of society and of history. Its vision of the individual is one of a responsible active agent of God, placed in the world for the purpose of managing, building and caring for it. This has become the foundation of an Islamic work ethic, rejecting the teachings of the classical Islamic theologians who portrayed man in a more passive role.[63] The theology of Islamic revolutionism is a progressive ideology for Islamic society that is optimistic, forward-looking and replete with confidence in human capabilities. It is a world-affirming vision grounded in the idea of human responsibility and perfectibility, with the committed believers ultimately seeking the redemption of the world. As man assumes his role as technocrat, making responsible use of the earth's resources, he helps shape destiny within the eternal laws God created for the world. Here the distinction between good works and labor disappears; work becomes similar to an act of worship, of obedience to God. Islam becomes the totality of life, affirming this world and the next, a life of work and prayer.[64]

This Islamic vision affirming the "vicegerency" of man on earth was advocated by the nationalists and modernists who were anxious to discard medieval beliefs in predestination which they had identified as the cause of decline in the Arab world. It was appropriated by Muslim socialists who expounded on its themes as inspired by their own agenda, and it has now been taken over by Islamists as the cornerstone of the accurate interpretation of the Islamic purpose of life. While there appears to be a growing consensus about the general validity of this perception, there are different ways of understanding the role that the woman plays in it. Only the socialists see her as full participant in every aspect of life (including all professions open to men). In all the ideologies we have been considering, woman is to assume her role as partner in a revolution that is aimed at transforming society. The Islamist vision, however, binds her to traditional views that restrict her area of competence to domesticity; her anatomy determines her destiny.

To the Muslim ideologist, woman's adherence to the precepts of religion has become a precondition for the survival of society. If women cease to be religious or refuse to adhere to the prescriptions of Islam, there can be no Islamic society. This is not only because women are now being projected as the repository of the value system in Islam, but primarily because of the profound belief that salvation is a corporate responsibility rather than a personal matter and that women are a key to its realization because of their innate capacity for sexual allurement. A good Muslim woman will not tempt men and lead them astray by appearing immodestly in public.[65] To ensure women's devotion to Islam is therefore the frontline of defense against the disintegration of society.

It is important to remember that this movement is being fostered in the midst of an urban revolution which can best be characterized as the "ruralization of the cities" brought about as millions of peasants migrate in search of education, employment and a better life. Modernization, westernization and accelerated social change have brought in their wake a massive disruption in the social order. The introduction of better health care in the rural areas has lowered mortality rates and increased fertility with a consequent growth in the population. The problem is exacerbated by the introduction of mechanized farming, which leaves hundreds of thousands of farmers unable to live off the land.

This ruralization of the cities has seriously altered the economic role of women in the family. In the rural setting they are full participants in such activities as planting, reaping and winnowing of the crops, raising poultry, and making dairy products. In the city they are unskilled and because they are generally illiterate their only avenue for economic contribution is in work outside the home as maids or factory workers. The Islamic revolution in confining them to the home is protecting them from exploitation, making men responsible for their upkeep. The Islamists thus are instilling traditional middle-class values, making it respectable for the woman to be confined to her domestic role and become economically dependent on the man. This view is validated by the Qur'anic verse "Men are in charge of women because God has made the one to excel over the other and because they spend of their wealth . . ." (S. 4:34), interpreted in such a way as to make men's leadership position contingent on their financial responsibility for women.

From this perspective putting on the veil becomes a symbol of status for the recently urbanized. But there are other reasons why women, some of them the granddaughters of those who ceremoniously took it off after the twenties, are wearing the veil.[66] Interviews I conducted between 1980 and 1984 with a number of Muslim women who have recently donned some form of head cover in Egypt, Jordan, Oman, Kuwait and the United States revealed a variety of purposes. The veil has become a useful cover for a multitude of reasons, acquiring in the process several symbolic meanings. The responses received to the question, "Why are you wearing a veil when women fought long to have it removed?" fell into the following categories:

Religious—an act of obedience to the will of God as a consequence of a profound religious experience which several women referred to as being "born again";

Psychological— an affirmation of authenticity, a return to the roots and a rejection of western norms (one woman talked about the "end of turmoil" and a "sense of peace");

Political—a sign of disenchantment with the prevailing political order;

Revolutionary— an identification with the Islamic revolutionary forces that affirm the necessity of the Islamization of society as the only means of its salvation;

Economic—a sign of affluence, of being a lady of leisure;

Cultural—a public affirmation of allegiance to chastity and modesty, of not being a sex object (especially among unmarried working women);

Demographic—a sign of being urbanized;

Practical—a means of reducing the amount to be spent on clothing, (some respondents claimed that others were receiving money from Libya and Saudi Arabia for the purpose);

Domestic—a way to keep the peace, since the males in the family insist on it.

It is also true that these practical reasons for veiling are undergirded by what is now a strong ideological position. The Islamists see themselves as the conscience of society, urging adoption of their modes of behavior while condemning deviations that they believe keep people from the worship of God.

There is evidence of a growing assertiveness on the part of many women which is based on the egalitarianism of the Qur'anic teaching. This affirms that although different in biology, role and function, women are equal before God and equally responsible for maintaining the moral order. Their equality is not granted as a gift from men out of benevolence, but is assumed as their God-given right affirmed repeatedly in the Qur'ān. In a society in social and economic flux, where education and technological training has provided avenues of social mobility, this egalitarianism also affirms the brotherhood of all believers. It cuts across class distinctions, making such common elements as ideological commitment and the profession of faith all important. For women, the outward manifestation of Islamic dress becomes in effect the initiation into a new sisterhood.

What we can see now is therefore a new generation of Muslim women, many of whom are not only educated in the liberal arts and sciences, but have also acquired an Islamic literacy—through study of the Qur'ān and the Ḥadīth—that their husbands who are actively working to build society through new careers in technology, are not able to attain. These women are taking as their models the founding mothers of Islam—the Prophet's wives ʿA'isha, Ḥafsa and Umm Salāma—as well as others of the early women believers who both participated actively in the struggles of the early Muslim community and helped keep the men accountable to the tenets of the faith.

With these early pioneers as examples, many modern women in the mode of Islamism view the role of women in society as redemptive, allowing them to reach out from the sanctity of the home to protect against moral degeneration and uphold the values that in the end will establish the "Kingdom of God" on earth. Ideologically Islam as revival accepts a new definition of woman as one who willingly assumes the task of redeeming society. It is clear, however, that despite her ability and right to be educated, to interpret scripture, and to actively guide the course of individual and social events, she is not seen as operating in the workplace. Islamism puts a special value on domesticity where, in the very acts of homemaking and raising children the woman becomes the repository of culture, religion and morality.

Thus by their own commitment to the faith women are able to hold men accountable to religious norms and to living lives of piety. At a time when affluence among certain classes is attainable, and the temptations for self-gratification are abundant, commitment to an Islamic order on the part of women helps keep men at home, safeguarding them from the temptations of excess money and freedom. And for the women themselves piety becomes a common and unifying bond among those who eschew the lures of modern society with its frivolous activities, consumer consumption and fadish trends. Life is now grounded in God, home and mosque, the last of which may serve to provide the one acceptable point of access for women to the public space which has been the domain of males. Islamism becomes therefore a kind of moral rearmament in which women are spearheading the construction of a new social order and playing active roles in the anticipated vindication of the Muslim people.

The feminist movement in the Arab world has struggled throughout this century to achieve the liberation of women. This liberation is not a goal in itself; it is not an exercise in self-indulgence or the beginning of a quest for self-fulfillment. It does not seek to cultivate an innate freedom of the individual to rebel, to protest or to define one's own identity. Rather, it has sought the development of a better society in an effort to effect an acceptable image of progress and parity with the West. From this vantage point, individual needs, quests and visions become an impediment to a corporate consensus of a unified, vibrant society.

There are certain characteristics that distinguish the Arab feminist movement from its counterpart in the West. To begin with, as noted above, it is not based on the concept of the liberation of the individual. Secondly, its most prominent advocates have been men who took up the cause of women, but found it necessary to convince others that the liberation of women was primarily in the interest of men since it produced better wives, homemakers, mothers and workers. In the third place, the movement has consistently been perceived as an integral part of the total effort to liberate society, whether from outmoded cultural norms, decadent social customs, or foreign domination. The leaders of the movement have consistently affirmed that it is part of the comprehensive liberation process of society. Finally, this movement in all its various manifestations has never advocated sexual liberation. In fact, from its inception, it has had to consistently disavow such a goal in order to survive.

Like their male counterparts, fathers, brothers and husbands, Arab women have participated in defining, initiating and supervising the change deemed necessary in order to maintain dignity and gain prominence in the modern world. A few have risen to positions of leadership as cabinet ministers, judges and directors of various government agencies. Others have crawled into foxholes and under barbed wire, have smuggled guns and bombs, aiding in the wars of liberation against colonial powers, reactionary regimes and forces considered to be impediments to the Islamic cause. Whether taking off the veil in the twenties or donning the Islamic dress of the eighties, taking up guns to participate in armed struggle or resigning from their jobs to devote themselves to the role of housewives, women have been defined to fit a range of symbolic categories appropriate to the system currently espoused and projected. Thus they have been modernized, revolutionized, radicalized, Islamized. In most cases their success in adaptation to these various roles has been due to the promotion, support, encouragement or supervision of male relatives. In no way, however, should this be seen as minimizing the achievements of those women who have responded in genuine commitment and who have often exposed themselves to public and private censure in their efforts to be at the vanguard of the change deemed necessary by the community of which they are such an integral part.

Notes

1. The current slogan in the Arab world advocating "borrowing technology but not ideology" from the West envisions the man as technocrat, building a modern industrialized nation, while the woman is the housewife safeguarding the Islamic nature of society by maintaining and transmitting its values. This is a new role for women, in line with the affirmation that male and female are equal but different. The traditionalist material written in the fifties and sixties is not as generous. For example,

> Men are the sole source of every accepted definition of good conduct whether for men or for women. Woman has never been a true source of anything to do with ethics or good character even though she brings up the children. The guidelines are provided by the male.

ʿAbbās Maḥmūd al-ʿAqqād, *al-Mar'a fī al-Qur'ān* (Cairo, 1959), p. 30.

2. For an elaboration on the civilizational confrontation see Yvonne Y. Haddad, "The Islamic Alternative," *The Link* 15, no. 4 (1982).

3. Ṣābir ʿAbd al-Raḥmān Ṭuʿayma, *al-Islām wa al-Thawra al-Ijtimāʿiyya* (Cairo: Maktabat Wahbi, 1978), pp. 495–98. Cf. Annie Von Sommer and Samuel Zwemer, *Our Moslem Sisters: A Cry of Need From the Land of Darkness, Interpreted by Those who Heard it* (New York: F.H. Revell Co., 1907).

4. For discussions of Islam and Social Change, see: Munīr Shafīq, *Al-Islām fī Maʿrakat al-Ḥaḍāra* (Beirut: Dār al-Kalima li 'l-Nashr, n.d.), pp. 115–21; cf.

Sayyid Quṭb, *Maʿrakat al-Islām wa 'l-Ra's Māliyya* (Beirut: Dār al-Shurūq, 1975), pp. 55–63; Muḥammad Kāmil Ḥittī, *Al-Qiyam al-Dīniyya wa 'l-Mujtamaʿ* (Cairo: Dār al-Maʿārif, 1974), pp. 209–21; Muḥammad ʿAmāra, *Al-Islām wa 'l-Thawra* (Cairo, Dār al-Thaqāfa al-Jadīda, 1979), pp. 28–71; Fatḥī Yakan, *Abjadiyyāt al-Taṣawwur al-Ḥarakī li 'l-ʿAmal al-Islāmī* (Beirut: Mu'assasat al-Risāla, 1981), pp. 81–100, 147–50. See also Muḥammad al-Bahī, *Al-Fikr al-Islāmī wa 'l-Mujtamaʿ al-Muʿāṣir* (Beirut: Dār al-Kitāb al-Islāmī, 1975), p. 26, where he writes,

> The message of heaven is a general revolution against evil in the cause of righteousness, against error and temptation, aiming at guidance. Those who believe in the message of God are the soldiers of the divine revolution which they nourish with their wealth and themselves.

5. The early reformers Muḥammad ʿAbduh and Jamāl al-Dīn al-Afghānī published *al-ʿUrwa al-Wuthqā* which advocated change and revolution against foreign oppression. ʿAbduh appears to have vacillated between the advocacy of gradual change and the call to revolution as the best means of achieving the revitalization of Islam. His zeal appears to have heightened during the ʿUrābī nationalist revolution in Egypt in 1882 and to have waned following his arrest and deportation by the British. Al-Afghānī, on the other hand, was a more consistent advocate of radical change as the only solution. His arguments continue to provide the theoretical foundation for those seeking revolutionary change. Cf. Muḥammad ʿAmāra, *Al-Aʿmāl al-Kāmila li 'l-Imām Muḥammad ʿAbdu* (Beirut: al-Mu'assasa al-ʿArabiyya li 'l-Dirāsāt wa 'l-Nashr, 1972), 1:21–24; cf. Muḥammad ʿAmāra, *Tajdīd al-Fikr al-Islāmī* (Cairo: Dār al-Hilāl, 1977), pp. 138–63.

6. See, for example, Ḥasan Ismāʿīl al-Huḍaybī, *Duʿāt lā Quḍāt* (Cairo: Dār al-Tibāʿa wa 'l-Nashr al-Islāmiyya, 1977).

7. ʿAmāra, *Al-Islām wa 'l-Thawra*, p. 142. See also Ṣābir ʿAbd al-Raḥmān Tuʿayma, *Irādat al-Taghyīr fī 'l-Islām* (Cairo: Maktabat al-Qāhira al-Ḥadītha, 1968), p. 287 who writes:

> Revolution in Islam is that perpetual, dynamic and constant renewal in the life of the Islamic society for the purpose of making it wealthy and advanced.

Advocates of Islamic revolution believe that even in the West religion continues to play an important function in the ideology.

> The renaissance of Europe was not a revolt against religion. Its success comes from its being grounded in a correct understanding of the role of religion in European society, after it was purified from the accretions of the ages of darkness. The source of its failure and the initiation of its final dissolution is its estrangement from this concept and its negligence of religion as an active ingredient in effecting a balance in the private and public life of people.

Its original impetus was not a revolution against religion but was aimed at the power of the church and the pope.

ʿAwn al-Sharīf Qāsim, *Al-Islām wa 'l-Thawra al-Ḥadāriyya* (Beirut: Dār al-Qalam, 1980), p. 99. Cf. Yvonne Yazbeck Haddad, "The Qur'anic Justification for an Islamic Revolution: The View of Sayyid Quṭb," *Middle East Journal* 37 (1983):14–29.

8. For background information see Ra'īf Khūrī, *Modern Arab Thought: Channels of the French Revolution to the Arab East*, trans. Iḥsān ʿAbbās, ed. Charles Issawi (Princeton: The Kingston Press, 1983); cf. Albert Hourani, *Arabic Thought in the Liberal Age 1798–1939* (London: Oxford University Press, 1970); and Hisham Sharabi, *Arab Intellectuals and the West* (Baltimore: The Johns Hopkins Press, 1970).

9. For translations of socialist ideologies see Kemal H. Karpat, ed., *Political and Social Thought in the Contemporary Middle East* (New York: Frederick A. Praeger, 1968), pp. 115–219; cf. John J. Donohue and John L. Esposito, eds., *Islam in Transition: Muslim Perspectives* (New York: Oxford University Press, 1982), pp. 98–137.

10. For a discussion of the influence of the 1973 Arab-Israeli war on Islamic revival see Yvonne Yazbeck Haddad, *Contemporary Islam and the Challenge of History* (Albany: State University of New York Press, 1982), pp. 33–45.

11. ʿAbd al-Ḥamīd Ḥamdī, "Al-Yawm Jā'a Dawrukun," *Bint al-Nīl*, no. 7 (June 1946), p. 4.

12. ʿAmāra, *Al-Islām wa 'l-Thawra*, p. 70.

13. ʿĀ'isha ʿAbd al-Raḥmān, *Al-Mafhūm al-Islāmī li Taḥrīr al-Mar'a* (Umm Durmān, n.d.), p. 15.

14. See, for example, Durriya Shafīq, *Al-Mar'a al-Miṣriyya* (Cairo: Dār al-Maʿārif, 1955), pp. 255–56 where she writes,

> We had organized marches, held conferences, distributed pamphlets, trained scouts, occupied the parliament. There was nothing left but for women to fight with the men in a civil war, a thought we never contemplated, naturally. For our fathers, brothers, husbands and sons are not our enemies no matter what they do and no matter how fast they hold to obsolete tradition.

See also Nuhād Ḥanbalī, "ʿAṣr al-Rajul wa 'l-Mar'a Maʿan," *Al-Mar'a al-ʿArabiyya* 79 (May 1975):49; she writes: "We . . . want this age to be for male and female together, building together and working together." See also Emily Naffāʿ, former secretary general of the Arab Woman's League in Jordan. "We believe that the cause of women is important to the whole society. From our experience we have learned that there are some men who are more supportive [of our cause] than some women." "Liqāʿ maʿ al-Sayyida Emily Naffaʿ," *Al-Mar'a al-ʿArabiyya* 77 (May 1975):12.

See also Jehan al-Sadāt where she is quoted as having said,

> It is not a battle against man; it is not a desire to be better; it is a yearning for participating, for self-realization, for fulfillment. . . . It

> is extremely important that we direct our energies where they would be most useful; not waste them in hysterical cries for revolutionizing—the man-woman relationship. It is important to realize and to prove to all that we are partners, not competitors in the struggle for a better world; that we complement not contradict one another.

Kay Camp, ed., *Listen to the Women for a Change* (Geneva: Women's International League for Peace and Freedom, [1975]), p. 41.

15. Peter C. Dodd, "Family Honor and the Forces of Change in Arab Society," *International Journal of Middle East Studies* 4 (1973):40–54.

16. Muḥammad ʿAṭiyya Al-Abrāshī, *Makānat al-Mar'a fī 'l-Islām* (Cairo: Dār al-Maʿārif, 1970), pp. 7–35. Cf. Al-Bahī al-Khūlī, *Al-Islām wa Qaḍāya al-Mar'a al-Muʿāṣira* (Kuwait: Dār al-Tawzīʿ wa 'l-Nashr, 1970), pp. 10–27; Abū Raḍwān Zaghlūl b. al-Sanūsī, *Al-Mar'a bayn al-Hijāb wa 'l-Sufūr* (Beirut: Dār al-Qalam, 1967), pp. 13–16; Muḥammad ʿIzzat Darwaza, *Al-Mar'a fī 'l-Qur'ān wa 'l-Sunna* (Beirut: Dār al-Fikr, 1967), pp. 15ff; and Ibrāhīm Zayd al-Kaylānī, "Makānat al-Mar'a fī 'l-Islām" in *Risālat al-Muʿallim* [special issue celebrating the fifteenth Islamic century] (Amman: Wazārat al-Tarbiya wa 'l-Taʿlīm, 1982), pp. 142–47.

17. Muhammad Fazl-ur-Rahman Ansari, *The Qur'anic Foundations and Structure of Muslim Society*, 2 vols. (Karachi: Zubair Printing Press, n.d.).

18. Qāsim Amīn, *Taḥrīr al-Mar'a*, reprint ed. (Cairo: Dār al-Maʿārif, 1970). Qāsim Amin, *Al-Mar'a al-Jadīda* (Cairo: Dār al-Maʿārif, 1905).

19. Amīn, *Al-Mar'a al-Jadīda* as quoted by Muḥammad ʿAbd al-Ḥakīm and Maḥmūd Muḥammad al-Jawharī, *Al-Akhawāt al-Muslimāt wa Binā' al-Usra al-Qur'āniyya* (Alexandria: Dār al-Daʿwa, 1980), pp. 250–51.

20. Amīn, *Taḥrīr al-Mar'a*, pp. 131–32.

21. Amīn, *Taḥrīr al-Mar'a*, p. 31.

22. ʿAmāra, *Al-Aʿmāl al-Kāmila*, 1:21–24.

23. Mukhtār al-Tuhāmī, *Thalāth Maʿārik Fikriyya* (Cairo: Dār Ma'mūn li 'l-Ṭibāʿa, 1976), p. 19.

24. Khayyāl and al-Jawharī, *Al-Akhawāt al-Muslimāt*, p. 216.

25. Tuhāmī, *Thalāth Maʿārik*, pp. 19–30.

26. Ibid., p. 47.

27. See, for example, David C. Gordon, *Women of Algeria: An Essay on Change* (Cambridge: Harvard University Press, 1968); Aziza Hussein, "The Role of Women in Social Reform in Egypt," *Middle East Journal* 7, no. 4 (1953):440–50. ʿAbd al-Ḥamīd Fāyid, *Al-Mar'a fī 'l-Ḥayāt al-ʿArabiyya* (Beirut: Jāmiʿat Beirut al-ʿArabiyya, 1975).

28. Two conferences were held during the Year of the Woman. The one in Cairo (1974), sponsored by al-Azhar, focused on the role and status of the women in the Muslim family. The Beirut conference (1975) was sponsored by the Lebanese Woman's Council and dealt with the role and status of the Arab woman as legislated by various Arab governments. For details see *Makānat al-Mar'a fī 'l-Usra al-Islāmiyya* (Cairo: Jāmiʿat al-Azhar, [1977]) and al-Majils al-Nisāʾī al-Lubnāni, *Al-Mar'a fī 'l-Qawānīn al-ʿArabiyya* (Beirut, 1975).

29. Nabīla al-Razzāz, *Mushārakat al-Mar'a fī 'l-Ḥayāt al-ʿĀmma fī Sūriyya*

(Damascus: Manshūrāt Wazārat al-Thaqāfa wa 'l-Irahād al-Qawmī, 1975); cf. Amal Sharqi, *The Progress of Women in Iraq* (London: The Iraqi Cultural Center, 1978); and Ismāʿīl Ḥassan ʿAbd al-Bārī, *Al-Mar'a wa 'l-Tanmiya fī Miṣr* (Cairo: Dār al-Maʿārif, 1979).

30. Khayyāl and al-Jawharī, *Al-Akhawāt al-Muslimāt*, p. 253. The authors also report that Qāsim Amīn changed his mind in 1906.

31. Al-Razzāz, *Mushārakat al-Mar'a*, p. 8. The Iraqi Baʿth party in its 1974 meeting declared that "The backwardness of Arab women in the economic, social and cultural fields is now one of the most serious obstructions in the path of the modern Arab renaissance." Sharqi, *The Progress of Women*, p. 6. Cf. Ṣafā' al-Ḥāfiz, "Fī Ḍaw' Qānūn al-Usra fī Jumhūriyat al-Yaman al-Dimuqrāṭiyya—Baʿḍ al-Mabādiʿ al-Asāsīyya li Qānūn al-Usra fī 'l-Mujtamaʿ al-Ishtirākī," *Al- Thaqāfa al-Jadīda* 7 (October 1975):45–61; and Ilham Nasr, "Society Restricts Them, While They Strain to Attain Sensitive Positions," *Al-Anwar* (Beirut, April 15, 1980), p. 10 as translated in *Near East/North Africa Report*, no. 2126, 3 June 1980, p. 66.

32. Amal Sharqi, *The Progress of Women in Iraq*, p. 5. She goes on to say on p. 8 that "The emancipation of women had to be achieved through their education, their full participation in the production process, the improvement of their legal position, and the elimination of social prejudice."

33. See for example "As leader of social change in all fields, the Arab Baath Socialist Party assumes the direct and full responsibility for the emancipation of women." Sharqi, *The Progress*, p. 6. In an address to the Third Conference of the Woman's Union on April 17, 1971, Ṣaddām Ḥusayn, president of Iraq, said,

> Woman represents half of society, if the woman is not free, aware and educated, our society will persist in retardation and lack of freedom. . . . Freedom is built on awareness, on knowledge and the understanding of the rational characteristics, commitment for the welfare of the masses, the assuming of the struggle against imperialism and zionism, and for the realization of the national goals. This freedom is capable of unleashing woman's capacities toward the correct direction—to build a free, strong, united and progressive nation.

Ṣaddām Ḥusayn, *Muqtaṭafāt min Aḥādīth Ṣaddām Ḥusayn* (Beirut: Dār al-Ṭalī'a, 1980), p. 15. For discussions on working women and their problems see: Ṭalʿat al-Rifāʿī, "Ḥawl Mashākil al-Mar'a al-ʿĀmila," *Minbar al-Islām* 22, no. 12 (1965):120–21; Ṭalʿāt Al-Rifāʿī, "*Al-Mar'a* wa Mayādīn al-ʿAmāl," *Minbar al-Islām* 22, no. 10 (1965):115–16; Inʿām Sayyid ʿAbd al-Jawād, "Tanshiʿat al-Aṭfāl Lada al-Mar'a al-ʿĀmila wa ghayr al-ʿĀmila," *Al-Majalla al-Ijtimāʿiyya al-Qawmiyya* 12, nos. 2 & 3 (September 1975):264–68.

34. See for example Nabīl Samalūṭī, *Al-Dīn wa 'l-Binā' al-ʿĀ'ilī* (Jidda: Dār al-Shurūq, 1981), p. 195 where he affirms

> Islam is concerned in an obvious manner with the structure of the family (how is it built, the systems that form it such as engagement, marriage, family relations, the exposition of the rights of the chil-

> dren and the rights of each of the partners, how they face family problems, how they dissolve the marriage if family life becomes impossible, how inheritance is distributed . . .).

35. See, for example, Nawāl al-Saʿdāwī, *Al-Mar'a wa 'l-Siraʿ al-Nafsī* (Beirut: al-Mu'assasa al-ʿArabiyya li 'l-Dirāsāt wa 'l-Nashr, 1977), Nawāl al-Saʿdāwī, *Al-Unthā Hiya al-Aṣl* (Beirut: al-Mu'assasa al-ʿArabiyya li 'l-Dirāsāt wa 'l-Nashr, 1974).

36. Najāt Aḥmad al-Zinnīrī, "Al-Mar'a al-Tunisiyya," *Minbar al-Islām* 21, 4 (September 1963): 198–200, talks about laws legislated in Tunisia for the benefit of women giving women the right to divorce, etc. The article then lists all the professions women entered including becoming a member of parliament, of the diplomatic corps, etc. The same issue includes an article by ʿAbdulla al-ʿAzāzī, "Hal Qasā al-Islām fī ʿUqūbat al-Zinā" (116–18) in which he attacks the fashionable woman who by her dress sends "a loud call to men" but her call will not be heeded because "she is degraded, . . . she has become worthless." For more examples, see other issues of the same magazine.

37. Do not be tempted by the arguments for birth control; it destroys the large family and puts an end to its bonds. It destroys the courage of its members and kills their resistance. It gives a woman free time which necessitates her search for something to fill it with. Lured by the temptation to make money, she goes out to the factory, the working place, the street and the house of ill repute. Then everything else follows. A war is declared between man and woman to ask for equality in freedom, in economic independence. . . .

Najīb ʿAmāra, *Al-Usra al-Muthlā* (Cairo, 1979), p. 276; cf. Aḥmad Muḥammad al-ʿAssāl, *Al-Islām wa Binā' al-Mujtamaʿ* (Kuwait: Dār al-Qalam, 1977), p. 213 where he lists the ability to bear children as one of the requirements of a wife quoting the Prophet's saying, "Marry the loving, the one who bears children, for I am making you more numerous than other nations on the Day of Resurrection." In an article published in *al-Ahrām* July 6, 1899, Muḥammad ʿAbd al-Rāziq al-Damanhūrī of Al-Azhar wrote against Amīn,

> The woman gets pregnant, then gives birth, then raises her children—this is the most prominent natural situation of woman—then as soon as she passes this period and she is plagued by another pregnancy which doubles her suffering and her burdens. This is how she passes her life between pregnancies, child birth and rearing.

As quoted by al-Tuhāmī, *Thalāth Maʿārik Fikriyya*, p. 26.

38. ʿAbd al-Raḥmān ʿAmīra, *Nisā' Anzala Allah Fihinna Qur'an*. (Riyad: Dār al-Linā', 1981), p. 9.

39. First we condone female public exposure; next dating and easy mixing; next, pre-marital "games"; next, extramarital relations and open marriages; next, the elevation of open homosexuality to an acceptable normal status; and next, uni-sex marriages. Where, and

> when, shall we stop? . . . The result: Broken laws, blood relations torn apart, deep dissatisfaction, a criminal climate, a disquieting sense of insecurity, fear and mutual mistrust, wide-spread corruption, irresponsible strikes, uncontrolled inflation, more frequent cases of rape, and the threat of depression and bankruptcy.

Muhammad Abdul-Rauf, *The Islamic View of Women and the Family* (New York, Robert Speller and Sons, 1977), p. 35. Cf. ʿAmāra, *al-Usra*, p. 298; and Ramḍūn, *Khatar al-Tabarruj*, pp. 80ff, where he posits a "domain theory" that begins with the temptation on seeing a woman who is wearing make-up. This leads to adultery, to the disintegration of the family, to prostitution, to economic decline, to decline in progeny (women don't want to ruin their bodies), homosexuality, oppression of children, the suffering of both males and females, the degradation of women and, finally, the total moral collapse.

40. ʿAbd al-Bāqī Ramḍūn, *Khaṭar al-Tabarruj wa 'l-Ikhtilāṭ* (Beirut: Ma'ussasat al-Risāla, 1974), in which one chapter is entitled: "Woman's Work outside the Home is a Crime against her and a Danger to her Life." In a later chapter, "Comparing Two Cultures," he provides a chart outlining the differences between the "Islamic Society" and the "Fixed Society." The Islamic society is described as "based on the cooperative bonding of families, whose progeny is legitimate, providing for physical and spiritual needs, supervised by divine values where the individual is a servant of God [upholding His laws] and is secure." The contrast is to "disintegrated individualistic society that is illegitimate [children not knowing who their father is], materialistic, worldly, weak in spirit, supervised by materialist values, a slave to desires, lust, money, alcohol, and Satan, and insecure in its most basic needs," p. 179. Cf. al-ʿAssāl, *Al-Islām*, p. 210, where he notes that women through sacrificing for the husband are victorious over selfishness. When they have a child, their compassion eradicates all lingering feelings of selfishness.

41. ʿAbd al-Raḥmān ʿAmīra, *Nisā' Anzala*, p. 17. Cf. Nabīl Samalūṭī, *Al-Dīn wa 'l-Binā' al-ʿĀ'ilī*, p. 204, where he notes that a woman should not leave her house except in cases of necessity and only after receiving permission from her husband.

42. Al-Kaylānī, *Makānat al-Mar'a*, pp. 159–61. He attributes the report to ʿĀ'isha ʿAbd al-Raḥmān who wrote about the phenomenon in *Al-Ahrām*. Sayyid Quṭb wrote about it in his book *Al-Islām wa Mushkilāt al-Haḍāra* on which Kaylānī's piece is based. For a discussion of the problems that afflict society whose women work outside the home, see ʿAbd al-Ghanī ʿAbbūd, *Al-Usra al-Muslima wa 'l-Usra al-Muʿāṣira* ([Cairo]: Dār al-Fikr al-ʿArabī, 1979), pp. 139ff.; also Abū al-Aʿlā al-Mawdūdī, *Mabādi' al-Islām* (Cairo: Dār al-Anṣār, 1977), p. 143–44, and ʿAbbās Maḥmūd al-ʿAqqād, *Al-Falsafa al-Qur'āniyya* (Cairo: Dār al-Islām, 1973), pp. 46–47.

43. Muḥammad Quṭb, *Maʿrakat al-Taqalīd*, p. 171; Muḥammad Fāḍil al-Jamālī, *Daʿwa ilā al-Islām* (Beirut: Dār al-Kitāb al-Lubnānī, 1963), p. 199; Anwar al-Jundī, *Al-Tarbiya wa Binā' al-Ajyāl* (Beirut: Dār al-Kitāb al-Lubnānī, 1975), p. 12. Muḥammad Jalāl Kishk, *al-Ghazū al-Fikrī* (Cairo: Al-Dar al-Qawmiyya li

'l-Ṭibā'a, 1966), p. 2; Muḥammad al-Bahī, *Al-Fikr al-Islāmī al-Ḥadīth wa Ṣilathu bi 'l-Isti'mār al-Gharbī* (Cairo: Maktabat Wahbe, 1975), p. 178; 'Abbūd *al-Usra al-Muslima* (n.p., 1979), pp. 127–28; 'Alī 'Adb al-Ḥalīm Maḥmūd *Al-Ghazū al-Fikrī wa Atharuhu fī 'l-Mujtama' al-Islāmī al-Mu'āṣir* (Kuwait: Dār al-Buḥūth al-'Ilmiyya, 1979), pp. 167ff; Ṣābir Ṭu'ayma, *Al-Islām wa 'Ālamuna al-Mu'āṣir: Dirāsa fī 'l-Da'wa wa 'l-Du'āt* (Riyad: Maktabat al-Ma'ārif, 1981), p. 25. At the turn of the century Qāsim Amīn was accused of helping destroy Islam from within by his call for the "liberation of woman." G. W. J. Drewes, "The Beginning of the Emancipation of Women in the Arab World" in *Nederlands-Arabische Kring, 1955–1965: Eight Studies Marking Its First Decade* (Leiden: E. J. Brill, 1966), p. 54.

44. The other four are: (1) advanced knowledge that will lead humanity away from God; (2) man's arrogance vis-à-vis the Creator, as he is enthralled by the products of knowledge and material progress which lead him to think that he does not need God, or that he is God; (3) scientific theories that lead people to deviate in all aspects of life, especially the social, psychological and economic areas; and (4) seduction by progress. Muḥammad Quṭb, *Jāhiliyyat al-Qarn al-'Ishrīn* (Cairo: Dār al-Shurūq, 1980), p. 52.

45. Muḥammad Quṭb, *Hal Naḥnu Muslimūn* (Cairo: Dār al-Shurūq, 1980); Ṭu'ayma, *Al-Islām wa 'Alamunā al-Mu'āsir*, p. 25; and Mahdiyya al-Zamīlī, *Libās al-Mar'a wa Zīnatuha* (Amman: Dār al-Furqān li 'l-Nashr wa 'l-Tawzī', 1982), p. 39.

46. Khayyāl and al-Jawharī, *Al-Akhawāt al-Muslimāt*, p. 226.

47. Quṭb, *Hal Naḥnu*, p. 178. The actual text of the Lucknow meeting reads: "That the aid of Christian women is urgently needed for the evangelization and uplifting of Mohammedan women who, with their little children, constitute the larger part of the Moslem world." Annie Van Sommer and Samuel M. Zwemer, *Daylight in the Harem* (Edinburgh and London: Oliphant, Anderson and Ferrier, 1911), pp. 213ff.

48. Ibid.

49. Kayyāl and al-Jawharī, *Al-Akhawāt al-Muslimāt*, p. 225.

50. Ibid.

51. Ibid., p. 226.

52. Ibid., p. 227.

53. Ibid., p. 256; al-'Assāl, *Al-Islām*, pp. 187, 190.

54. Quṭb, *Ma'rakat*, p. 167; see Norman Cohn, *Warrant for Genocide* (Chico, CA: Scholars Press, 1981)

55. Quṭb, *Jāhiliyyat*, p. 155; Ramḍūn, *Khaṭar al-Tabarruj*, pp. 188–99.

56. Quṭb, *Jāhiliyyat*, p. 156.

57. Khayyāl and al-Jawharī, *Al-Akhawāt al-Muslimāt*, p. 126.

58. Quṭb, *Jāhiliyyat*, p. 71.

59. Khayyāl and al-Jawharī, *Al-Akhawāt al-Muslimāt*, pp. 216–18. They report that the tenth protocol says, "If we convey to each person the idea of the importance of his individuality, we shall destroy family life among the goyim—the non-Jews." Najīb 'Amāra describes what he calls a war between men and women over issues of equality in freedom and economic independence.

Over the objections of men, the development of Islamic societies is tied to the demands of women. This is inspired by international Zionism, he says, which regulates advertising. Life will soon be controlled by sex. The next generation will be raised on these principles of "gender integration, distracted or in desperate restlessness that the Jews may realize . . . their control and those who fight them will suffer a devastating defeat from which they will not recover." ʿAmāra, *Al-Ursa*, p. 276.

60. The western sense of morality is perceived as different from that designed by God; Westerners consider a moral person anyone who does not cheat or lie, a person who is honest and faithful, who had good intentions and works for the service of the nation. They do not consider sex as related to morality; Quṭb, *Jāhiliyyat*, p. 149. Another author portrays western women as fulfilling their sexual desire without a need for a husband or for children. The West attacks any religion that calls for modesty and virginity. They do not distinguish between a good woman and a loose one (dancers and singers are treated with respect). They have clinics for abortion, clubs for nudity. They have beauty contests for the best breast or legs, and pornography is rampant. They allow for a trial period prior to marriage and practice wife swapping; Khayyal and al-Jawharī, *al-Akhawāt al-Muslimāt*, p. 231. Three ideas depicted as crimes have brought disintegration to western society: (1) equality of women and men (2) the mixing of the sexes (3) the working woman and her economic independence. "It is criminal to expect from a woman what she is not capable of doing [being equal to the man]"; al-ʿAssāl, *Al-Islām*, pp. 172–77. These western evils have had a pervasive influence on the Muslim family. The child "is raised in corruption in the family from infancy and is inculcated by his mother and father in the trends and customs of effeminacy and wantoness . . . by his mother who has no other exemplar [except] actresses, fashion models and singers. The uncontested reality is that the woman in the Muslim East has become the messenger of corruption wherever she goes. At home, she corrupts the young, impedes her husband from righteous deeds and noble goals; nothing satisfies her except that he should fill her handbag with bank notes that she may fritter them away on pleasure and adornment. . . . She does not understand her relationship to her husband except as a cow to the bull. She is in society as an agent of allurement and enticement spreading corruption in every direction by being spoiled and through her nakedness. . . . The influence of this is reflected in the character of young men who have become transformed into young animals in the form of humans dispersed on the crossroads of avenues and roads of the city devouring with their hungry eyes the bodies of half naked women as they pass by." Khayyāl and al-Jawharī, *Al-Akhawāt al-Muslimāt*, p. 219.

61. Qāsim Amīn wrote: "As for the nations that have progressed to a high level of civilization we see the women elevated little by little from their previous degradation. They have narrowed the distance that used to separate them from the men. . . . The American woman is at the forefront." *Taḥrīr al-Mar'a*, p. 34. In a later passage, he noted, "Of things witnessed in which there is no argument [is the fact] that the women of America among all

women in the world, have the greatest amount of freedom. They mix the most with men. Even the women in their youth receive their education with men in one school. The girl sits next to the boy to receive knowledge and despite this, those knowledgeable about America say that its women are the most chaste and are more moral than others. They ascribe their virtue to the great extent of mixing among the two sexes, male and female, at all stages of life," p. 101.

62. ʿAmāra, *Al-Usra al-Muthlā*, p. 298.

63. For a more progressive view of the role of woman as active agent, see Muḥammad ʿAzīz al-Ḥabābī, *Al-Shakhṣāniyya al-Islāmiyya* (Cairo: Dār al-Maʿārif, 1969), pp. 93ff.

64. "This is the revolution of Islam: Islam the revolution in the social arenas. . . . It sees wealth as belonging to God. . . . From Him it proceeds and overflows. . . . It decrees that work is its [Islam's] specialized means of acquisition," ʿAmāra, *Al-Islām wa 'l-Thawra*, p. 64.

65. See, for example, the passage in Ramḍūn, *Khaṭar al-Tabarruj*, pp. 80ff., referred to above, note 39.

66. John Alden Williams, "Veiling in Egypt as a Political and Social Phenomenon," in *Islam and Development*, John L. Esposito, ed. (Syracuse: Syracuse University Press, 1980), pp. 74–75. See also Nesta Ramazani, "The Veil— Piety or Protest," *Journal of South Asian and Middle Eastern Studies* 7, no. 2 (1983):20–36; Lois Lamya' al-Faruqi, "Islamic Traditions and the Feminist Movement: Confrontation or Cooperation," *Islamic Quarterly* 27, no. 3 (1983):132–39.

Chapter Twelve

Woman's Place and the Place of Women in the Iranian Revolution

William R. Darrow

Popular western consensus sees an unchanging and uncompromising 'fundamentalism' in the Iranian revolution that refuses to recognize, let alone adjust to, 'modernity'. The informed observer, on the other hand, can discern development and change rather than atavism and regression in both the ideological underpinnings and actual policies implemented by the current clergy-dominated Iranian revolutionary regime. The post-revolutionary constitution of the Islamic Republic of Iran, ratified in December of 1979, when read with the earlier positions taken by the clergy in mind, is a remarkable index of the change in their attitudes, even as it secures them in power. In 1906 when Iran drafted its first constitution, which established a parliament and limited the monarchy, the clergy played a significant role in its writing. However, by the end of that decade most of them had moved into opposing the idea of constitutionalism; now flushed with victory, they have written one. In 1924 during the height of popular support for a republic, the majority of the clergy were monarchists; now, they have abolished the monarchy and established an Islamic republic with the clergy as the effective rulers. In 1963 under the leadership of Khomeini, the clergy generally opposed the enfranchisement of women; in 1979, women cast their ballots to ratify the constitution of the republic and have continued to retain the right to vote under the current regime.

When approaching an issue as volatile as that of the place of women in revolutionary Iran it is important to recognize those aspects that are new in the society's perceptions rather than to assume a constant presence of a timeless system of the oppression of women. On the one hand, for those who stand as critics of what has occurred under the new leadership, recognition of the new bases for oppression, the new disguises of power, is vital if their opposition is to be effective. On the other hand, those of us who are more or less disinterested observers can more fully understand events and more closely read the ideology if we can see what is new and different in the formulation of ideas concerning the place of women in revolutionary Iran. The impetus to be able to do so is increased when we recognize that a large portion of Iranian women have given their real assent to this formulation.

This article examines in two parts the ideology of the Islamic woman as it has evolved in revolutionary Iran. In the first we shall briefly examine the sources of some of the central themes of that ideology. In the second we shall consider how the ideological formulations have been implemented as policy by the new regime. We will thus recognize what a society based on this ideology has evolved into and what the very question of the place of women in that society has become.

I.

Two portions of the 1979 Iranian constitution specifically deal with the place of woman in the ideal Islamic society which the constitution seeks to establish. The first is in the introduction which focuses on the historical background and ideology of the revolution. Following two sections dealing with the leadership role of the clergy and the spiritual goal of economic life, and preceding one on the role of the army, is a section entitled "Women in the Constitution" which reads:

> In the creation of Islamic social institutions, all the human forces that up to now had served the multifaceted foreign exploitation of our country are to regain their true identity and human rights. As part of this process, it is only natural that women should enjoy greater rights, since they suffered greater oppression under the despotic regime.

Iranian constitution

> The family is the fundamental unit of society and the main institution for the growth and advancement of the human being. Agreement of faith and ideals is the main consideration in the establishment of a family, for the family provides the primary basis for the human's development and growth. It is the duty of Islamic government to provide the necessary facilities for the attainment of this goal. This view of the family unit delivers woman from being regarded as an object or as an instrument in the service of consumerism and exploitation. Not only does woman recover thereby her momentous and precious foundation of motherhood, rearing alert and active human beings, she also becomes the fellow struggler of man in all the different areas of life. Given the weighty responsibilities that woman thus assumes, she is accorded in Islam great value and nobility.

The second portion of the constitution that deals with women is Article 21 which spells out the role of the government in achieving the place for women envisioned in the introduction.

> The government must assure the rights of women in all respects, in conformity with Islamic criteria, and accomplish the following goals: a) create a favorable environment for the growth of woman's personality and the restoration of her rights, material and intellectual; b) the protection of mothers, particularly during pregnancy and child-rearing and the protection of children without guardians; c) the creation of a competent court to protect and preserve the family; d) the provision of special insurance for widows and aged and destitute women; e) the granting of guardianship of children to their mothers whenever suitable in order to protect the interests of the children, in the absence of a legal guardian.[1]

Several features of these two sections of the constitution should be noted. First, women require special attention; there is no equivalent section on men. They are implicitly identified as being a profession and envisioned as a separate institution in society like the army and the clergy. Moreover, women are singled out by the constitution because they suffered the most under the previous regime. How have they suffered? They were separated from their "true identities" and were made into objects at the service of a Westernized consumerist and exploitative society. They were seduced into doing so because their identities were (and presumably are) particularly vulnerable. Behind this explicit image of women is a more subtle metaphorical connection between the nation as a whole and women. Women are the nation's vulnerable half, and are thus regarded as both a cause and a symptom of the exploitation and dependency of Iran under the previous regime. The nation is like a woman at the mercy of more powerful outside forces. At the same time the nation is also betrayed by its women who are most easily seduced by these outside exploitative forces. The interaction of concepts of the dependency, weakness and vulnerability of the nation as a whole and of its women is a powerful connection of metaphors and stands behind the special attention the constitution devotes to women.[2]

Woman has a true identity, a personality, but it is not a strong one for she is easily distracted. Therefore a new society must be built to prevent such distraction, a society that must be founded on the strong family unit. This highlighting of the family and the placing of the woman at its center may seem so utterly traditional to the outsider that we do not recognize some interesting nuances of the position, three of which are worth noting. First, the family is marked as the center for nurturing the young, presenting the nuclear family as the fundamental unit of society rather than the traditional extended family. While this contrast is not made explicit, the weight of the image points in this direction.[3] Second, the mother's role in this process is significant. It should be recognized that this marking and protection of the mother's role has deep traditional sources in Iranian and Mediterranean cultures. The mother has always played a central role as nurturer and socializer of her children. But there is at least an implication in the constitution of a decline in the traditional power of the father. The ambiguous clause that allows women guardianship of their children under certain circumstances points to such a decline. The question of guardianship of minor children after the end of a marriage has been one of the most heated issues in Iranian family law debates in the last decades. Following general Islamic precepts the policy has been that sons after the age of two and girls after the age of seven were awarded to the father and his family. This policy in fact seems to have continued after the revolution, signifying little change. Finally, what is new is that family life has become a major arena for the establishment of a revolutionary society, and woman's role as mother within it is freighted with social significance. The family sphere is part of a larger process of revolutionary struggle.

The bases for the constitution's elaboration of an ideology can be found in the thought of two pre-revolutionary Muslim thinkers: ʿAlī Sharīʿatī (d. 1977) and Murteza Mutahhari (d. 1979). Sharīʿatī was the leading radical religious ideologue of the Iranian revolution. Raised in a religious family he completed his education in Paris in sociology. His success lay in his ability to infuse the Shiʿite tradition, and especially the exemplars of that tradition, with a dialectical logic that addressed in a remarkably effective way the dilemmas of educated but displaced Iranian youth. His reappropriation of his tradition inspired a vision of social justice which Shiʿism, if correctly manifested, could embody. His thought inspired the younger generation still attached to its religious heritage, but impatient with the formulations and stances of the traditional clergy. His lectures both in Mashad and in Tehran during the shah's regime were extremely popular which led to his persecution by the government and his exile to London in 1977 where he died. Since the revolution the fortunes of his ideological legacy within Iran have varied widely. He was generally seen as one of the most important intellectual sources of the revolution, but also condemned by the clergy since his thought provided the basis for opposition groups that confronted the clergy-dominated regime.

Sharīʿatī addressed the question of the place of women in one of his tracts, *Fatimah is Fatimah.*[4] It is typical of his way of thinking that he sought to infuse the figure of Fatimah, daughter of the Prophet and wife of the first Imam ʿAlī, with relevance for the dilemmas of the contemporary Iranian women. For Sharīʿatī the Iranian woman of today is caught between two equally unattractive alternatives: that of being a blind captive of her religious heritage or of taking on the meaningless façade of a modern westernized woman. To him neither of these is a satisfactory alternative. While blind unthinking adherence to the dead hand of religious tradition is unacceptable fanaticism, the adopting of the façade of westernization plays into the hands of imperialist exploitation since the woman becomes a sex object who distracts herself and her mate from a clear recognition of the forces of exploitation. The westernized woman as the quintessential consumer is victim to capitalism's fundamental need to encourage consumption to guarantee its own survival. Beyond these two alternatives, Sharīʿatī projected a new identity that must be forged for contemporary Iranian women, and for this Fatimah provided the model.

Fatimah was born as the last daughter to the prophet Muḥammad in a world which still only valued sons.[5] But it was a world whose values were in revolution as a result of the prophet's revelation. Fatimah's very existence at a time when woman's status was being raised by divine revelation is already significant. She is a symbol of all the dimensions of being a woman. She is a daughter, loving and faithful to her father, in fact 'the mother of her father' who cared for her father after the death of her mother. She is a wife to ʿAlī, sharing with him poverty and defeat. She is a mother of two sons, Hasan and Hussein, and is the link between the prophecy of her father and the imamate of her husband and sons. She is also a strong woman who fights for her husband's legitimate succession to the leadership of the Muslim community and for her own rights against tyranny. Her struggle against the prevalent forces of tyranny fails and the theme of the innocent sufferer is a constant one in her biography, as it always is in Shiʿite hagiography. But for Sharīʿatī the fundamental point is that Fatimah is Fatimah who became truly and completely herself and in this is a model and a guide for all women. The three other great women of Islam, Mary the mother of Jesus, Pharoah's daughter who cared for Moses, and Muḥammad's wife, Khadijah, were great but *only* in virtue of the role they played toward their men. According to Sharīʿatī's sense of dialectic Fatimah played all these roles and transcended them as well. In this lies her power.

This image of Fatimah implies several things. First, Shiʿite Islam has found a dynamic role model for Muslim women. The anniversary of Fatimah's death has become Iranian Women's Day since the revolution replacing International Women's Day, which had been celebrated under the shah. (It may also be of interest that Sharīʿatī is buried next to the grave believed to be that of Fatimah.) Second, it is within the family context, specifically in her relations with her male relatives, that Fatimah is defined, though Sharīʿatī, true to his dialectical sense, wants us to see that she has transcended this context. Finally, there exists no inherent tension between her role within the family and her role as a fighter for justice and against tyranny. The two roles are complementary.

Murteza Mutahhari was one of the most significant thinkers among the Iranian clergy and a close associate of Khomeini. If ʿAlī Sharīʿatī marked the forging of a new discourse that enlivens the religious tradition and motivates political action, Murteza Mutahhari represented a union of traditional theological discourse with radical analysis of Iranian society and Western civilization. ʿAlī Sharīʿatī and Murteza Mutahhari collaborated in establishing religious educational institutions in Tehran during the shah's reign. After the revolution Murteza Mutahhari played a significant role as an ideologue until his assassination in 1979. Mutahhari addressed the question of the rights of women in his *The System of the Rights of Woman in Islam*. This was originally written in 1974 for one of Iran's leading women's magazines that championed women's rights and had accused Islam of considering women inferior. The bulk of the book exposits and extols features of traditional Islamic family law including dower, marriage, divorce and inheritance. It begins with a consideration of the special status of the familial sphere in society.[6] The familial world contrasts with civil society, the latter including all aspects of economic, cultural, social and political life. Civil society is the product of the arena for human activity. Islam has always acknowledged that in civil society men and women are of completely equal value. The West has only affirmed the equality of men and women in the past century when it was recognized that in doing so women could provide a cheap source of labor for the capitalist system to exploit.

For Mutahhari the case of the familial sphere is different. The family is a natural institution rather than a cultural one. It is in the family sphere that the natural differences of men and women come to the fore, where sexual activity, that constant threat to the harmony of civil society, must be restricted. As a religion Islam is completely in conformity with what is natural, having established the rules of the family sphere with full awareness of the natural differences between men and women. The effectiveness of Muslim family law is that it conforms with nature. Women by nature are more emotional than rational, and have a stronger sexual drive. But women are more capable than men of controlling their sexual drive since their emotional nature provides the desire for love as a natural curb to sexual desire. In addition, women find the task of motherhood as the most satisfying. These differences between men and women do not imply the superiority of one sex over the other. In fact, the family sphere is not simply the "women's sphere." Rather it is the one specific and special area where the two sexes can safely and productively meet because its rules control and direct the natural tendencies of each sex into the possibility of balanced and complementary interaction.

Mutahhari recognizes that certain implications of the structure of the Islamic family sphere carry over into civil society, but nothing should prevent women from functioning as equal players in civil society once their tasks as mothers have been fulfilled. The rub is that it is largely in a sex-segregated civil society that women should function. Women can take part in all areas of civil life, except war and judicial decision making (where their emotional natures would hinder their effectiveness). In all other areas women can participate (and Mutahhari appears to have at least implicity included the rest of the political arena), but this participation is in a system that establishes a segregated civil society, one male and one female. Women serve women in the educational, medical, service and economic spheres and men serve men. Interaction of the sexes which is inevitably fraught with all the natural problems familial law seeks to control are kept to a strict minimum in this segregated civil society. The requirements of modesty in dress and demeanor placed on women in civil society are absolutely necessary if this dual society is to function.

The analyses of ʿAlī Sharīʿatī and Murteza Mutahhari are thus quite

dual society

different, but they both stand behind the formulations of the constitution of 1979. The affirmation of the importance of the family sphere and of women's particular role in it is common to both thinkers. They both assume an essential identity for woman, and the potential vulnerability of that identity to seduction. For Murteza Mutahhari women's vulnerability is basically sexual and he accepts the traditional notion that women are inevitably a source of discord in areas where men and women interact. ʿAlī Sharīʿatī does not focus on female sexuality, but confirms woman's vulnerability to empty fads in a consumer society, although she is not condemned to that by biology. Both recognize the need to construct special protections for and walls around woman. But for neither is woman restricted to the family role; she can be an actor in civil society, with some restrictions made necessary by her nature. In both the family and civil society she can be a crucial participant in the revolutionary struggle.

II.

Such are the ideological foundations for the vision enshrined in the 1979 constitution of the place of woman in an Islamic society. Is this the vision that women fought for in the 1978–1979 revolution? This is a complicated question. To answer it we must be attuned both to important changes in the flow of ideas and events in Iran since 1979 and the differences in class and social status of those involved. Women from the educated elite have often played a crucial protest role in periods of unrest in recent Iranian history.[7] The story of the active participation of women in the revolution of 1978–1979 continues a long tradition of the intervention of upper class and middle class women in political affairs at times of crisis. Those women who participated in the major demonstrations of the fall of 1978 were drawn from the urban educated middle class. These were women who were likely to have discarded the use of the chador, the traditional Iranian cloth covering the body, but who were willing to put it on again as a symbol of protest against what was seen to be an oppressive and alien regime. In fact, use of the chador by this class of women had been on the increase in the period preceding the revolution. Once the revolution was underway, under the direction of the clergy who provided the organizational backbone, it was only by wearing the chador that women could participate since the clergy required it.

Urban women from the lower strata who had always worn the chador certainly supported the revolution, but were less likely to demonstrate or play active roles outside their homes except by providing a support network for the dissemination of news and information. On the other hand, men who were active were drawn from both the middle and lower classes of urban society as well as from some nearby villages. Active participation by women from these latter two strata appears to have been rare. In short, those women most active in the actual revolutionary struggle were from the middle class and upper class educated strata of society, were accustomed to the relative independence accorded them through the changes in Iranian society initiated under the shah, but were now disgusted with the shah's regime.

A month after the revolution in March 1979 on the eve of International Women's Day, Khomeini issued a proclamation insisting on the use of the modest dress (that is, the chador) by working women. This was met with a protest demonstration of about 5,000 women that gained international attention. (The counterprotest of 100,000 people against these women was hardly noted.) The original protest eventually did lead to the softening of the request. It was precisely the strata of middle class women most active in the revolution that was alienated by this move. The chador which had been willingly taken on as a sign of protest against the shah's regime had changed its signification to being a mark of the new social order and the special status of women in that order. While the initial moves of March 1979 were met with resistence, more informal forces have now been successful in imposing the wearing of the chador in public. The harassment suffered by women from men in the streets provided an effective means of enforcement. In addition women were increasingly excluded from civil society and the working place. For example no women now teach at Tehran University, reopened in the fall of 1983. Only ten percent of the 4,000 students are women. (Before the revolution forty-three percent of the University's 23,000 students were women.) They sit in divided classrooms where men and women are forbidden to talk to one another; to do so would be to commit an anti-revolutionary act.[8] Rather than the sex-segregated society envisioned by Murteza Mutahhari, the revolution has meant the increasingly systematic exclusion of women from areas outside the home.

Demonstrations in December 1979 and July 1980 by a smaller number of women still protesting the insistence on the use of the chador were not joined by other opposition groups. These groups apparently have never considered the question of women's rights as a separate or separable issue in their opposition to the clergy dominance of power that emerged as the main post-revolutionary political reality within Iran. Since 1980 the increasing harshness and repression of the

Islamic Republic, the lack of interest in the separate issue of women by opposition forces and the departure of a significant portion of opponents of the regime, have resulted in little sign of protest by women on behalf of women's rights inside Iran. In fact the image of the new Iranian woman cultivated by the regime, wearing a chador because it saves having to go to the hairdresser and is the best way to hide an automatic weapon, seems to have been embraced by a good portion of Iranian women from all classes, providing them with a meaningful symbol of authentic feminine identity.

There are two implications of this development that appear to be relevant for our considerations of the role of women in social change. First, we can recognize that it is only as a result of the events of March 1979 that the question of women emerged as an independent issue in the climate of revolutionary Iran. Until that time women were primarily pawns in the larger political struggles of recent Iranian history. Unveiled they were to be the mark of successful modernization. Veiled they were to be the mark of the continuity of traditional values. Both Reza Shah and his son deliberately sought to take on the mantle of supporters of women's rights. This began with Reza Shah's encouragement of education for girls and the abolition of the chador in 1936. The Family Protection Acts of 1967 and 1975 did go part of the way toward altering some of the most severe legal impediments to women in the areas of marriage and divorce. (These acts were repealed in August of 1979 and the family courts they established were replaced by special civil courts.)

The ideology of the revolution in one sense continues this strategy by its special marking of the place of women. Women do not themselves address the issue of their place. Rather the image of the revolutionary woman, of Fatimah, is yet another ideal imposed upon Iranian women. Continuity of traditional attitudes and cooptation of women remains the order of the day. At the same time the clergy's successful implementation of the Islamic revolutionary ideological vision into a social reality has fundamentally changed the context in which women function. For the first time it established the possibility for the articulation of an independent and self-sufficient feminist movement in which women speak for themselves and define themselves as women in the face of a deliberate policy of suppression.

Our second point has to do with the emergence of women's opposition to the Khomeini regime. Outside Iran one can see the emergence of women's voices protesting developments within Iran; their inspiration at times lies in the less oppressive vision of ʿAlī Sharīʿatī, but more often represents a fundamental rejection of Islam as hopelessly oppressive. It should be emphasized that this is still a small minority of the exile population and that they are by no means united.

Within Iran, from the available information that can be gleaned, the situation is different. The ideological image of the new Muslim woman seems still to have many adherents among women of all strata of society. Its effectiveness in combining traditional values and a radical critique of alternative feminine identities seems quite striking. Four women now sit in the Parliament quite consciously as representatives and embodiments of this vision. They include the daughter of one of the leading ideologues of the revolution and the widow of the assassinated president. Their sometimes critical voices are recognized as authoritative spokespersons for women and they have denounced some of the excesses in the social policies of the regime regarding women, especially the increasing de facto restrictions on women in the work place. These criticisms do not question the basic goals or vision of the revolution or the specific place of women in it. In general, the question of women's rights has ceased to be a public issue within Iran, precisely in a context when an outsider might have expected it to be a major issue. Among supporters of the regime it cannot be an issue since the image of the new Muslim woman holds the day. One can argue about the specific implications of that image, but a widespread consensus limits the issues that need to be further defined. In addition, questions of women's rights are often identified with the special interests of the middle class woman, the most suspect strata of revolutionary society.

Women's rights as perceived in the West also seem not to be an issue among the opponents of the regime within Iran, either those inspired by Muslim or by leftist ideology, since raising it would dissipate revolutionary energy. The question of the status of women may be a legitimate cause for opposition to the existing regime among these groups, but a concentration on this issue at the expense of others has not emerged. In short, the image of the modern Muslim woman, veiled, mother, and revolutionary, holds the day in Iran and is likely to do so for the foreseeable future.

Does contemporary Iran confirm the thesis that women participate in public life more fully during periods of social crisis when the community stability and integration that is the purview of women is most deeply threatened? Two concluding comments seem appropriate. First, the nature of participation must be defined. We recognized that actual participation of women in the revolutionary process was primarily a feature of a well-defined social strata. Women from other strata of society did not overtly act. Defining participation of women in public life must thus always pay attention to class factors. In addition, what constitutes participation also must be defined. Demonstrating, on the one hand, and remaining at home while providing a network for information, on the other, are both modes of participation. Their appropriateness for individuals is defined by class differences. Second, social and cultural change are interfused. The actual meaning and content of images of community stability and integration, which does seem to be the purview of women, are in constant flux and transformation. Sometimes new ones are forged that appear to the outsider as alien or repugnant. The image of the veiled revolutionary woman was not statically available before or during the revolution; rather, it is a product of the revolution and one which seems to continue to evoke broad assent and provide meaning and integration in the face of great hardships and suffering.[9]

NOTES

1. My own translation based upon those of Hamid Algar, *The Constitution of the Islamic Republic of Iran* (Berkeley, CA: Mizan Press, 1980) and Rouhollah K. Ramazani, "Document Constitution of the Islamic Republic of Iran," *Middle East Journal* 34 (1980): 181–204.

2. For an illuminating article on the role of the metaphor of the feminine in revolutionary discourse see Gustav Thaiss, "The Conceptualization of Social Change Through Metaphor," *Journal of Asian and African Studies* 13, nos. 1–2 (1978): 1–13.

3. For a discussion of the idea of the family in Islam cf. John H. Chamberlane, "The Family in Islam," *Numen* 15 (1968):119–41 and H.S. Karmi, "The Family as a Developing Social Group in Islam," *Asian Affairs* 62, no. 1 (N.S. 6) (1975):61–68. For recognition of the decline of the patriarchal extended family see J. N. D. Anderson, "The Eclipse of the Patriarchal Family In Contemporary Islamic Law" in *Family Law in Asia and Africa*, J. N. D. Anderson, ed. (London: George Allen and Unwin, 1968).

4. *Ali Shariati's Fatima is Fatima*, trans. Laleh Bakhtiar (Tehran: The Shariati Foundation [1980]). I have not been able to obtain the Persian text of this work. For an introduction to ʿAlī Sharīʿatī's significance and thought, cf. Ervand Abrahamian, "Ali Shariʿati: Ideologue of the Iranian Revolution," *MERIP Reports* 102 (January 1982):24–28; Shahrough Akhavi, "Shariati's Social Thought" in *Religion and Politics in Iran*, Nikki R. Keddie, ed. (New Haven: Yale University Press, 1983), pp. 125–44. For a fuller treatment of Sharīʿatī's position in *Fatimah is Fatimah* cf. Adele K. Ferdows, "Women and the Islamic Revolution," *International Journal of Middle East Studies* 15 (1983):283–98.

5. There is uncertainty as to the birth order of Muḥammad's children. ʿAlī Sharīʿatī considers Fatimah the youngest child, born most significantly after the death of the two sons of Muḥammad.

6. Murteza Mutahhari, *Niẓām-i huqūq-i zan dar Islām* (Tehran, 1353 A.H. [solar] 1974 C.E.). There is a useful summary of the introductory portion of this work by Mina Modares entitled "Women and Shi'ism in Iran" in *m/f: a Feminist Journal* 5–6 (1981): 61–81. This article also contains a less full summary of ʿAlī Sharīʿatī's *Fatimah is Fatimah.* Modares's piece is quoted verbatum without explicit citation by Nahid Yeganeh in her essay entitled "Women's Struggles in the Islamic Republic of Iran" in Azar Tabari and Nahid Yeganeh, eds., *In the Shadow of Islam* (London: Zed Press, 1982). A briefer summary of Mutahhari's views is also available in a pamphlet *Sexual Ethics in Islam and in the Western World,* trans. and ed. Muhammad Khurshid Ali (Albany, CA: Moslem Student Association [Persian Speaking Group], n.d.).

7. For a history of the movement for women's rights under the Pahlavi dynasty cf. the work by Badr al-Mulūk Bāmdād (Badr ol-Moluk Bamdad), *From Darkness Into Light: Women's Emancipation in Iran, 1905–1911,* ed. and trans. F.R.C. Bagley (Hicksville, NY: Exposition Press, 1977) and Eliz Sansarian, *The Woman's Rights Movement in Iran: Mutiny, Appeasement and Repression, from 1900 to Khomeini* (New York: Praeger, 1982). For the role of women in the Constitutional Revolution cf. Mangol Bayat-Philipp, "Women and Revolution, 1905–1911" in *Women in the Muslim World,* L. Beck and N. Keddie, eds. (Cambridge: Harvard University Press, 1978), pp. 295–308. For a general survey of changes in the status of women under the Pahlavi dynasty cf. Michael M.J. Fischer, "On Changing the Concept and Position of Persian Women" and Behnaz Pakizegi, "Legal and Social Positions of Iranian Women" in Ibid., pp. 189–215 and pp. 216–26, and Shala Haeri, "Women, Law and Social Change in Iran" in *Women in Contemporary Muslim Societies,* Jane I. Smith, ed. (Cranbury, NY: Associated University Presses, 1978), pp. 209–34.

8. Accounts of the issue of women in post-revolutionary Iran are numerous. Useful ones include: Cheryl Benard, "Islam and Women: Some Reflections on the Experience of Iran," *Journal of South Asian and Middle Eastern Studies* 4 (1980):10–26; Mary Elaine Hegland, "Traditional Iranian Women and How they Cope," *Middle East Journal* 36 (1982):483–501; Guity Nashat, "Women in the Islamic Republic of Iran," *Iranian Studies* 8 (1980):165–94; Azar Tabari, "The Enigma of the Veiled Iranian Woman," *MERIP Reports* 103 (February 1982):22–27; Tabari and Yeganeh, *In the Shadow of Islam;* Sansarian, *The Woman's Rights Movement in Iran;* Guity Nashat, ed., *Women and Revolution in Iran* (Boulder, CO: Westview Press, 1983) and Shireen Mahdavi, "Women and the Shii Ulama in Iran," *Middle Eastern Studies* 19, no. 1 (1983):17–27. The statistics concerning Tehran University are taken from *The Sunday Times,* 23 October 1983 in a story by Amir Taheri.

9. I have profited from comments on an earlier draft of this paper by Kathryn Darrow, Lila Abu Lughod, Janet Bauer and Yasmin Mossavar-Rahmani. I am, of course, responsible for all errors of fact and interpretation.

CHAPTER THIRTEEN

Religious Aspects of Women's Role in the Nicaraguan Revolution

PAULINE TURNER

Developments in Nicaragua from 1965 to the present offer a unique opportunity for the study of the impact of religious ideology on women's participation in revolutionary social change.* The country has seen a basic shift in women's status with a consequent change in the participation in public affairs as well as a radical transformation of their self-image. The widespread and critically important involvement of Nicaraguan women in the 1979 overthrow of the Somoza dictatorship appears to have precipitated a fundamental reversal in attitudes towards women's religious, social, political and economic roles.

*An excellent annotated bibliography covering the political and social history of Nicaragua under the Somozas is John Booth, "Celebrating the Demise of Somocismo: Fifty Recent Sources on the Nicaraguan Revolution," *Latin American Research Review* 17 (1982):173–89. Other important general resources on the history of the revolutionary process and the reconstruction period are: Thomas Walker, ed., *Nicaragua in Revolution* (New York: Praeger, 1982); George Black, *Triumph of the People: The Sandinist Revolution in Nicaragua* (London: Zed Press, 1981); J. Booth, *The End and the Beginning: the Nicaraguan Revolution* (Colorado: Westview Press, 1982); and James D. Rudolph, *Nicaragua, A Country Study* (Washington, D.C.: American University, 1982).

It is too early to conclude at present whether this change is: temporary, dictated by prevalent revolutionary conditions; transitional to a yet new formulation that may develop; or permanent to be bureaucratized as the revolution consolidates its vision into institutions. This essay will therefore attempt to delineate (1) the extent of the breakdown in social cohesion that prevailed under the Somoza regime and its influence on women (2) the social and cultural transformation of Nicaraguan society during the revolutionary period that followed the insurrection, and (3) the contribution of Roman Catholicism as reinterpreted after Vatican II to the ideological legitimation of participation in social change as divinely mandated to help realize the "kingdom of God on earth."

A traditional Hispanic saying succinctly embodies the prevalent social mythology: "La mujer en la casa, el hombre en la calle" ("Woman in the home, man in the street"). This proverb encapsulates the strict division in roles assigned by sex that is prevalent throughout Latin America as well as in Nicaragua.[1] *La calle* as a metaphor for the world outside the home is considered the proper testing ground for men's masculinity but dangerously inappropriate for women. *La casa* expressed the ideal of the self-sacrificing wife dedicated to administering the home and the domestic economy, educating the children and, as an acceptable extension of this traditional family role to the public arena, working for charity and the Church.[2]

It was reinforced by the law of *patria potestas*, which recognized male domination over wife and children, legitimizing and reinforcing a patriarchal form of *machismo*. It legalized a pattern of strict controls over women's behavior in society and in the family.

But even if it were to be thought desirable, this image of the upper-class daughter of an overly-protective father becoming the loving wife and dutiful mother under the watchful eyes of a jealous spouse was for the majority of the population quite out of the question. The dominant ideology that envisioned the nuclear family in which women were materially and emotionally dependent on men and restricted after marriage to the home and to the care of children was completely contradicted by the actual situation of most women.[3] Outside the small middle and upper classes, as many as half of all families were headed by women who were solely dependent upon themselves for economic support and on the extended family for emotional support and other kinds of assistance, such as child care. Susan Ramirez-Horton observed:

> To be a poor woman in Nicaragua in the 1970's, after 30 or more years of dependent [capitalistic] development, meant to expect to

live to be about 50. To be poor and female meant a three out of ten chance of never attending school and becoming one of every two over the age of ten who remained functionally illiterate. To be poor also meant to end childhood and adolescence abruptly at or shortly after puberty with a first pregnancy, usually out of wedlock. To be a woman, age 34, meant having reached advanced middle age. In the rural areas such a woman could expect to be pregnant on an average of eight times, although only three or four children would still be alive. In the more urbanized department of Managua about half of the single mothers of comparable age could count on having three of five children alive. The vast majority would be matriarchs, probably not by choice, with responsibility for maintaining the household.[4]

The Family

The tradition of *machismo* maintained the belief that the measure of one's masculinity was enhanced by siring a large number of children by various women.[5] This pattern of behavior, aggravated by alcoholism and dismal poverty, gave rise to a high rate of paternal abandonment of families. Consequently, as many as fifty percent of all households were headed by single women.[6] The male had no sense of accountability and the woman had no way to claim financial support. This pattern of infidelity and desertion accounts for the high number (estimated at fifty percent) of couples living together without benefit of marriage.[7] A different pattern exists among the middle and upper classes where fewer wives are abandoned. Among that group men value the image of a good husband and father and are generally economically capable of maintaining a wife as well as one or two mistresses with their children.

Socio-economic Situation

Under this system Nicaraguan women suffered the most. They constituted 51% of the population, and in the 1960s and 1970s a high proportion of them formed the principal or only support for their families. The number of women in the Economically Active Population (EAP) grew from 14% in 1950 to 22% in 1970 to 29% by 1977. The high rate of working women in the salaried labor force in Nicaragua (the overall average of EAP women for Latin America for 1977 was 20%) did not include domestic workers or casual vendors. Statistics for these two categories indicated that 20% of Nicaraguan women were engaged in domestic labor, another 20% in vending, while 20%

were engaged in farming. Studies show that 50% of women over ten years of age and 86% of the women who headed families worked outside the home.[8]

The hallmarks of rural life were economic insecurity and social and family instability. The growth of the two cash crops—coffee and tobacco—in the 1950s resulted in the ruthless appropriation of land for large holdings, forcing many peasants (39% suffered this plight by 1978) off small traditional farms into the status of rural semi-proletariats. Seasonal work plus tenant farming or sharecropping on meager plots for subsistence crops yielded bare survival. Those totally dispossessed migrated to towns and urban *barrios* to find work. Between 1960 and 1977 the rural population declined from 60% to 48%, among these were large numbers of the single women heads of households. The number of urban women working in the commerce and service sector (mainly vending and domestic work) rose to 87%.[9]

In the urban areas, the opportunity developed for a growing number of young middle class women to attend school in the 1960s and 1970s. This enabled them to work outside the home—mainly for multinational corporations in clerical, office, and commercial positions—where they generally fared reasonably well.[10] The vast majority of female laborers, however, worked in the marginal sectors of the economy, in the least skilled, least secure, and lowest paid jobs. Characteristically, working conditions were poor—no social security, no work contract (particularly for domestic workers), no regulated work schedules, and always wages unequal to those of men.

LEGAL SITUATION

The Nicaraguan Constitution contained laws other than *patria potestas* that legalized men's domination and women's subordination in such areas as marriage, divorce, abortion, and rape. The prevailing double standard was enshrined in the legal grounds for divorce. The man could be charged with the crime of adultery only in cases of concubinage that involved his maintaining the other woman in the same household as his wife. The woman committed criminal adultery, a valid cause for divorce, if she had sexual relations even once outside the marriage.[11] Moreover, these law-supported traditions had a formidable enforcing agency in the dictatorship's custodians of "law and order," the National Guard. Once women transcended the boundaries of traditional roles, they were thought to deserve whatever abuse ensued. An instance of the very worst abuse visited on women by the National Guard came in connection with prostitution.

In the 1970s, as economic conditions worsened and unemployment grew, prostitution was reaching massive proportions. Some women workers

> found themselves obliged to walk the streets on weekends in search of a customer . . . . These women were submitted to the worst kind of abuses . . . repressed by special patrols of the National Guard who are reimbursed by brothel owners. They arrest these women, rob and rape them, and impose very stiff fines. Another kind of prostitution results from dealers in white women, people in charge of supplying the brothels with women . . . go into the countryside, to the mountainous regions where the population suffers from hunger, and recruit women supposedly to do housework in the city. They bring peasant girls thirteen and fourteen to work as "daughters of the house." These people use this cover to recruit young peasant girls, daughters of ruined peasants or of the agricultural proletariat, who are brought to the city and taken directly to the whorehouses . . . the madams of the houses of prostitution carry on their business together with the Guard and the Commanders of the barracks and the jails.[12]

Religious Life

In Nicaragua, as in much of Latin America, the dominant Roman Catholic Church played a strong historical role in legitimating the ideology that depicts women as the repositories of morality: spiritually strong, self-denying, and long-suffering. Women's role as divinely sanctioned effectively locked women into the pattern of obedient wife and ever-nurturing mother.[13] Enhanced by the cult of the Virgin Mary who is venerated as the symbol of the twin ideals of virgin and mother, this ideal resulted in a great ambivalence among women about their sexuality, leading to shame and self-denigration.[14] The Church's historical role in legitimating and reinforcing patriarchal domination encouraged *machismo.*[15] Consequently, when the revolution started, "Women participated massively in the Nicaraguan Revolution in roles more varied and significant than in any other 20th Century revolution."[16]

Women and the Overthrow of the Dictatorship: The War of Liberation

The prominence of women in Nicaragua's revolution was encouraged by the leadership of the Sandinista National Liberation Front

(FSLN). As far back as the period when Sandino waged guerrilla warfare against the United States Marines (1928–1933), positions of leadership were open to women.[17] By the 1960s a few women had already joined the FSLN—among them Gladys Baez and Doris Tijerino—and by the early 1970s the FSLN began active recruitment of women.[18]

Its announced goal from its founding in 1961 by former student activists Tomas Borge, Silvio Mayorga, and Carlos Fonseca Amador was equality and the emancipation of women.[19] Within the ranks of the guerrilla organization, women found morale-boosting discipline, respect, and advancement based on qualifications and merit, not on sex.[20]

OVERTHROWING THE DICTATORSHIP

Women's participation with the Sandinistas took more systematic and sustained form with the organizing in September 1977 of the *Asociación de Mujeres ante la Problematica Nacional* (AMPRONAC).[21] Encouraged by Jaime Wheelock of the Proletariat Tendency of the FSLN,[22] the well-educated but organizationally inexperienced women who founded AMPRONAC provided a major channel for the good intentions and individual actions of many women sympathizers who were already collaborating with the FSLN. Starting with sixty members, of varied social background and spanning different political ideologies, AMPRONAC grew to 8,000 by July of 1979. From the beginning, AMPRONAC women defined their objectives as:

1. Women's participation in the study and solution of national problems posed by the dictatorship;

2. Defense of the social, economic, and political rights of Nicaraguan women;

3. Defense of human rights in general.[23]

AMPRONAC organized groups in the other major cities and departments: Leon, Chinandega, Masaya, Esteli, Matagalpa. Through a variety of activities, they struggled for their objectives; they denounced the atrocities committed by Somoza's National Guard during the long years of martial law and state of seige (1974–1976). On one particularly important occasion, the group organized an unprecedented assembly attended by over one-thousand people condemning the disappearance of hundreds of peasants in the north. They occupied churches, held hunger strikes to demand the release of political prisoners, informed citizens of their rights, organized a variety of campaigns against repression, against rising food prices, and against increased taxes. AMPRONAC mobilized women across the nation by broadcasts as well as by a monthly bulletin "Voices of Women," in which the Association analyzed the current situation, providing a forum for expression.[24]

In the wake of the regime's assassination of the widely-admired journalist and opposition leader, Pedro Joaquin Chamorro, in January, 1978, AMPRONAC actively worked to organize more militant demonstrations and a general strike which coalesced the various sectors—bourgeoisie, workers, women, and guerrillas—in a commitment to overthrow the dictator and his government.[25]

In early 1978 the situation deteriorated nationally and pressure increased for AMPRONAC to become involved in the insurrection. AMPRONAC members engaged in a series of political seminars to clarify and determine their objectives. In addition to the initial three goals, the women now realized the need to oust Somoza and to exchange his kind of government, which they called *Somocismo*, for one that would focus on the people's interests. AMPRONAC's program included these specific demands: 1) a halt to repression, 2) freedom of organization, 3) freedom for political prisoners, 4) punishment of those responsible for crimes and outrages, 5) a halt to the rising cost of living, 6) an end to all discriminatory laws against women, 7) equal pay for equal work, and 8) an end to the commercialization of women.[26]

Following the National Guard's brutal termination of AMPRONAC's two-week occupation of the United States offices (protesting the "disappeared" individuals), many working-class women joined the group, precipitating a new self-definition. A split developed in the organization when the overwhelming majority voted for the involvement of women in national politics and in the effort to overthrow the dictatorship. Consequently, many upper and middle-class women resigned.

> Ampronac's growing base of support shifted . . . to the poorer women who were experiencing the repression more directly and hence were more ready to confront it in militant fashion.[27]

At this point, AMPRONAC opted to join the *Movimiento Pueblo Unido* (MPU), organized early in the summer of 1978 as a left-wing political coalition and mass insurrectionary front.[28] In the last year of struggle, the women of both the *campo* and the working-class *barrios* of the cities found their participation in the insurrection facilitated by

AMPRONAC's provision of infrastructural support. These women played a key role in building up the critically important Neighborhood Civil Defense Committees and setting the stage for the insurrectionary process that occupied the year leading up to Somoza's overthrow. They did so

> by organizing clandestine medical clinics in the hard–hit barrios, setting up food stocks and mangaging food distribution networks, establishing networks for secret information and emergency communication. As the fighting escalated, women guarded trenches, made bombs, delivered messages, and hid Sandinista fighters in their own homes.[29]

But women's participation went far beyond their work in the *barrios* and in the *campo*. By the time of victory, women constituted 30% of the membership of the FSLN. Of these, about half were involved in combat and half in other political and organizational tasks.[30]

The disappearance, imprisonment and torture of sons and daughters by the National Guard precipitated a determined response by the women to fulfill their traditional role as protectors of their offspring. To accomplish this, it became necessary for them to follow their children into the public realm. Once exposed to the "national problematic," and as their understanding of it grew, Nicaraguan women became concerned for all the children, indeed for all their oppressed compatriots.[31]

WOMEN AND THE REVOLUTIONARY PROCESS

The Sandinistas, who assumed leadership of Nicaragua in 1979, began to implement a series of political and economic programs that concentrated on building public-sector structures to provide for the basic human needs of the impoverished majority, while still maintaining a mixed economy with private property and a private business sector.

> Their primary commitment was to the poor, to a political and economic system which would end illiteracy, disease, malnutrition and slum housing and to a system which would bring political power to the workers and peasants.[32]

The structure developed by the FSLN to empower the workers and peasants politically was the mass organization, the basis for which had been laid during the latter years of the war of liberation. As key elements in the redistribution-of-power goals of the new popular democracy, each mass organization represented a particular popular sector or social organization. This included urban workers, rural laborers, armed forces, youth and neighborhood civil defense groups and women. Each group is commissioned to work for the defense of the revolution and to lobby for its particular interests. Each mass organization has membership in the government's legislative body, the Council of State.[33]

Within a month of assuming power, the Sandinista leadership fulfilled its pledge of 1967, by announcing the basic elements in its program for the emancipation of women. The Government of National Reconstruction (GRN) using law as an indispensable tool for social change, issued on August 21, 1979, *The Statute of Rights and Guarantees of Nicaraguans*. Functioning as a bill of rights, the statute laid out a foundation for women's equal treatment before the law. Its stipulations touch on personal, economic, and familial rights: 1) women's equality under the law; 2) the right to a job and equal pay, specifying that everyone, male or female, who is at least fourteen years of age, must be included on the payroll as a worker; and 3) women's equal rights within the family.[34] The last provision was an obvious revocation of the infamous *patria potestas* of the Somozan constitution.

On an earlier occasion, July 20, two other legal strictures, directed toward overcoming the abuse of women as sex objects, had been promulgated. These outlawed prostitution and forbade the use of women's bodies for commercial purposes by the media.[35] Clearly, these laws were an immediate response to the demands put forth by AMPRONAC in 1978. The second step in the government's program for women recognized the valuable contribution of women in the overthrow of the dictatorship, as well as the need for women to unite in overcoming their own oppression and exploitation.[36] The women of AMPRONAC were summoned to reconstitute themselves as a mass organization.

Symbolic of the new avenues the revolution had provided women to gain control over their lives, AMPRONAC changed its name to *Asociación de Mujeres Nicaraguenses 'Luisa Amanda Espinoza'* (AMNLAE). Named for the first Sandinista woman to die in combat, AMNLAE was honoring a fallen *compa* and signalling the combative spirit with which they were undertaking "the war of the women."[37]

As mandated by the government, AMNLAE undertook as overall goals 1) defense of the Sandinist Popular Revolution and 2) the task of critiquing the remainder of the laws touching on women's issues, creating new egalitarian laws to the full extent possible under the severe political and economic constraints of the country.[38] From its first year, AMNLAE experienced an uneasy tension in the double role required of it as a mass organization. Its main aim and the key to women's liberation, according to Gloria Carrion, a member of the executive, in October, 1979, "is to maintain the mobilization of women around the defense and consolidation of the revolution."[39] Others insisted that the twin issues of gender and class must be raised simultaneously.[40]

Undoubtedly, this tension fed into the decision by AMNLAE in the early months of its existence to undertake a critical self-study to determine what structures and methods would be most effective for a women's movement. The self-study concluded that AMNLAE had focused on organizing thousands of women to participate in social programs such as literacy and health campaigns but

> it did not arrange for its constituents to tackle their own problems on an ongoing basis, nor has it . . . encouraged them to group together to confront their everyday problems, in particular the topics of male violence, sexuality, and birth control.[41]

As AMNLAE moved, in the summer of 1981, to change its status from a mass organization to that of a broad-based women's political movement, it also stressed goals that emphasized women's problems in the workplace:

> 1) to promote fuller participation by means of women's caucuses in each of the critical sectors where women work, study, organize or care for their homes and children;[42] 2) to help women develop ideological and political clarity, to insure that women's issues are understood and taken seriously; and 3) to coordinate its work with other existing organizations such as the Ministry of Health and the Ministry of Welfare, being wary of over extension into areas of women's issues proper to these groups.

The Association retains a national structure and a representative on the Council of State.[43] Whether this will enable it to progress toward its most challenging goals, only time will tell.[44] The Sandinista political program from 1979 has aimed at placing qualified women in leadership roles; a substantial number have been appointed to highly-visible and important FSLN and government positions.[45] These include three women who have attained the highest rank in the revolutionary forces, that of *commandante*. They hold prominent posts in the FSLN. Letitia Herrera heads the Sandanista Defense Committee (SDC) Executive Secretariat; Doris Tijerino heads the Secretariat for External Relations; and Monica Baltadano heads the Secretariat for

Mass Organizations. In addition, Lea Guido, one of the founders of AMPRONAC, serves in the cabinet as Minister of Health.[46]

Women hold five of the fifteen heads of Departmental Leadership Committees for political work, and constitute almost all of the political *cadres* in those committees.[47] And although they make up half of the police force they are less than a quarter of the Sandinist Popular Army, which has seven all-women battalions. Only fifteen of 230 officers are women.[48] Furthermore, 47% of the territorial Sandinista Popular Militia entrusted with the defense of the revolution in neighborhood, community and work centers are women. AMNLAE itself had reached a membership of 50,000 by late 1982.[49]

Nevertheless, there is still no equality in work opportunities for women, who are 48% of the labor force and mostly single mothers in their thirties. Concentrated in the least skilled, lowest paid, most insecure sectors, much of women's work is casual, part-time self-employment. Unfortunately, these are areas in the private sector unaffected by new legislation on minimum wages and working conditions. According to AMNLAE analysts, women's economic exploitation is partly rooted in the distortions intrinsic to Nicaragua's dependent capitalist situation.

A program critical to AMNLAE's responsibility of integrating women into the revolution was the development of child-care centers, freeing women for production and social work. Presently there are twenty child development centers in the cities, twenty-two infant rural services, and seven rural infant cafeterias. Altogether these agencies provide for 3,368 children, which amounts to only .5% of the infant population between birth and five years.[50]

Since 1981 AMNLAE, as part of its shift in priorities from building the community "social wage" to organizing the workplace and within the mass organizations, has been bringing pressure, through the women's caucuses, on both unions and employers to respond to women's needs.[51] The Ministry of Social Welfare in conjunction with the CDS's and AMNLAE has attacked the women's unemployment problem through development of nearly one-hundred production collectives. Domestic workers have had perhaps the worst working conditions. A prime example of women who are not recognized or paid as "workers," domestics' pay was minimal even when combined at times with housing and food. These women were expected to work as many hours as demanded by employers. Due to union efforts, the limit of ten hours is now the daily maximum and the wage must exceed the current legal minimum.[52]

AMNLAE's major achievement is in the legal area: where it has been the vanguard in formulating legislation to be adopted by the Council of State. In an effort to make laws address the concrete needs and circumstances of the people, legislation touching women's lives was designed as an educational process. Discussion of proposed laws are held at each level of appropriate mass organization while legal research is conducted on the issues. Thus the legislative process is designed as a consciousness-raising experience. An example of this is the 1981 Law of Relations between Mothers, Fathers, and Children which attempts to strengthen the family and equalize relations between the spouses. The constitution declares that the family is the basic unit in society.[53] This counters both the law of *patria potestas* (with its symbolism of patriarchy) and the law of *machismo* assuring a complete equality of rights and obligations between men and women in family relations.

Another significant piece of legislation is The Food Law, passed by the Council in November, 1982. It is now illegal for a man to neglect his family responsibilities. It aims at ensuring that men make a full contribution to domestic labor and recognizes the extent to which domestic work is of value for both the family and the economy. Under this law, a person remains responsible for his or her family after the relationship is dissolved. Even unmarried couples, if they separate, are obliged to provide for their family.[54] A man who deserts his common-law wife is required to support her if for health reasons she cannot work.

Status and Role of Women in the Nicaraguan Church

Several Christian churches have participated in the revolutionary process; in Nicaragua, however, the Roman Catholic Church has been the major religious presence because of the Spanish cultural tradition and the fact that 86% of the population is Roman Catholic.[55] Before trying to assess the place of the Catholic religion in the motivation and ideological commitment that led Nicaraguan women to unprecedented involvement in revolution, it will be necessary to sketch the changes in Roman Catholicism itself between 1960 and the present.

Drawing from the personalist philosophy that was prominent in the late nineteenth and early twentieth century, the Second Vatican Council, called by Pope John XXIII in 1962, described the Church as "the people of God" and recognized the full and active status of all Catholics. Moreover, the Council insisted on the responsibility of Christians to work for a just and truly human society, for economic justice and political freedom in the world. The Council reinforced the "rediscovery" of the Bible and the revitalization of the liturgy that had marked early decades of this century. This shifted the emphasis from other worldly considerations urging Catholics to become involved in the effort to construct a world where justice, equality and human dignity are universally honored.[56]

The bishops of Latin America met in 1968 in Medellin, Colombia, to consider the application of the Council's resolutions to this portion of the Church. Pointing to the dependent situation of the continent, the bishops declared that the people were oppressed by "institutionalized violence" of internal and external colonial structures and denounced the unjust distribution of wealth and the victimization of the masses. The bishops proposed participating with the poor in their own liberation and recommended the use of the literacy process developed in the early 1960s by Brazilian Paulo Freire, commonly referred to as "conscienticization." With little dissent, the bishops redirected the Latin American Church towards concern for the identification with the poor, reversing their traditional alliance with the wealthy establishment.[57]

Furthermore, the bishops gave their support to the development of the so-called *communidades ecclesiales de base.* These base communities were made up of relatively small groups of committed Christians, gathered together to reflect upon their life in the light of the Gospel and search for ways to implement their faith by becoming involved in transforming the society around them.[58]

This trend in the Catholic Church found theological expression in "liberation theology" which grounded its reflection in the experience of the people and provided scriptural guidance for that experience. At the heart of this theology was belief in a liberating God at work in history freeing people from sin, both in its personal and social dimensions. Development of the notion of social sin highlighted the moral aspect of social structures and provided tools for critiquing the prevalent injustices of Latin American society. To many it seemed that

> Nicaragua presented a text-book case of what the new Theology of Liberation was all about: "a situation of injustice which may be described as one of institutionalized violence . . . revolutionary insurrection may be legitimate in the case of evident and prolonged tyranny which dangerously threatens the common good of the country."[59]

This reference to the legitimacy of revolutionary insurrection appeared in Pope Paul VI's encyclical "The Development of Peoples," which was directed at Latin America. Up to that point, Nicaraguan Catholics believed that the seemingly intrinsic link of Marxist atheism and violent revolution ruled out their participation in revolution. Pope Paul's statement opened up for those Christians, disillusioned with the possibility of reformist measures, the legitimacy of participating in the violent overthrow of the Somozan dictatorship.[60]

One year after Medellin, in 1969, in the middle of the Anastasio Somoza, Jr. dictatorship, the priests and religious of Nicaragua met to assess the situation of the Church.

> They found a conservative and divided hierarchy, distant from the people and without initiative. There were few diocesan priests, they had antiquated ideas, and they did not dialogue with the people. . . . Men and women religious were isolated in their schools. There were no communities in the parishes, very few people attended Mass, the liturgy had not been renewed. Parish priests were also distant from the people and too obviously concerned about their own economic well-being. The only exception to this picture were a small group of very dynamic diocesan priests and some communities of women religious who had begun to work on behalf of social progress.[61]

The priests and the hierarchy were aligned with a government hated by people.[62]

Meanwhile, those in the Church who responded favorably to Vatican II and Medellin experienced a significant renewal. Exemplary of this development was the base community of the *campesino* and monastic community founded at Solentiname by Padre Ernesto Cardenal, a Nicaraguan diocesan priest, in 1966,[63] which became famous for its art, poetry and especially for the development of a scripturally-based "liberation theology." Weekly reflections on the meaning of the Biblical texts and liturgical celebrations encouraged women to participate in this community where they were treated as equal, their dignity and personhood respected.

In the mid-1970s, the Solentiname community, which had initially espoused non-violence as the means for change in the social order, became radicalized by the increasing oppression and brutality of the National Guard. Nearly twenty members of the Solentiname community joined the insurrectionist effort of the FSLN, among them Ernesto Cardenal. They perceived this as the logical expression of their Christian faith. It is clear that the women who participated were very aware of the significance of their involvement, both as women and as Christians. They hoped that it would attract other women and Christians to the revolutionary cause.[64]

Another development in the Catholic church was instituted by the Capuchins who had been engaged in missionary work in Zelaya, Esteli and Nueva Segovia.[65] After Medellin, they began to promote Christian base communities throughout their mission territory. Faced with a shortage of priests, they delegated lay members to lead church groups. Called "Delegates of the Word," they were given instruction at central training centers, where they studied the scripture and prepared for leadership of their base communities. Their responsibilities included conducting "Celebrations of the Word" each Sunday (in which people dialogued about the application of the word of God to their daily lives) baptizing, performing marriages, anointing the sick, distributing Holy Communion, and acting as pastoral guides for their communities.[66]

> Now in the coastal and central regions of the country, we have 1000 communities led by Delegate couples, a husband and wife who share responsibility.[67]

The conscious intent of the Delegate program was to give voice to very marginal citizens in the spirit of Medellin. While no political impact was intended or foreseen by the Capuchins, Somoza's National Guard came to regard the Delegates as subversive and to harrass them. The Capuchins discovered that some of the delegates had made a Christian option to work against the regime. Having repulsed the Sandinistas because of their Marxist, irreligious arguments a few years earlier, these same Christians, much more sensitive to the meaning and implications of their Christianity, had come to sympathize and often collaborate with the FSLN. In turn, the Sandinistas had become more open to the Christian bases for political action. They found that those involved in the CEB were offering an interpretation of the scriptures which affirmed the right of the poor to create independent grass-roots organizations to defend their human dignity and rights. The Church thereby found itself at the heart of the class struggle.[68]

Another development took place in the mid-60s with the founding of the Institute for Human Advancement by progressive sectors of the Church. Employing the "conscienticization" process of Paulo Freire, this Christian group formed three mass-oriented organizations: The Movement for the Liberation of Women, The Federation of Rural Organizations, and the National Movement for Youth. Stressing literacy, popular education, critical thinking, and problem solving, the Institute had organized 300 peasant leagues and peasant unions by 1970. The organizing activity of the Institute is said to have helped buttress the FSLN's awareness of the need for mass mobilization and contributed significantly to the organized incorporation of the masses into the armed struggle in the late 1970s.[69]

Ecclesial base communities increased in the urban areas between 1968 and 1970. In Managua, starting with a pilot project in the San Pablo parish,[70] these communities, mostly located within parishes in the poorer eastern barrios, became a focus for political protest following the 1972 earthquake. When the government failed to help the poor the people came to see *Somocismo* as the structural sin of which Medellin had spoken.[71]

Women, too, came into the Christian movement. Monica Baltodano, who was a participant, writes:

> At an early period women in the Christian movement were more conscious than many in the *Frente Estudiante Revolucionario*. There were always scores of women in the Christian movement and they participated on the basis of a strong conviction. . . . Later, when the FSLN began working with the Christian movement, the fact that the women involved were really strong and had a high level of consciousness had an effect on the FSLN. Many of these women joined the FSLN.[72]

From Colonia Nicarao barrio, Norma Gallo, active in her CEB since 1965, reflected on the awareness which she and the women of her community gained through their double oppression and the need for women to break out of the tradition of *la casa* and to engage in all spheres of public life:

> We have a great problem here with the ideological struggle. Sometimes we actually believe that a woman was really meant to be shut within the walls of the home and should not leave it, that it's the place where she belongs. I've realized the opposite, that women have to be inserted in everything because we have been doubly exploited, we as women.[73]

Challenging this old ideology seems to have become possible through women's experience in the base community. This CEB, in what was an extraordinary departure within the church structures of that time, was composed mostly of very poor women, an excellent example of the process of development of the "Church born of the poor" and of "conscienticizing evangelization."[74] In the 1970s Norma Gallo and the other women in her CEB became involved in organizing AMPRONAC.

> Christian Base Communities held an assembly [in Las Palmas Church] to unite efforts and precisely to organize women. There

> had been a massacre in the countryside and this could only be denounced by the Church.[75]

Organizing women around the human rights violations against the *campesinos* marked the beginning of collaboration between the FSLN and the women of the CEBs and gave impetus to women to begin their own organization for insurrectionary activity.

Beginning in the fall of 1977, Norma Gallo and the other CEB women worked through AMPRONAC to organize neighborhood defense committees, set up safe houses, and perform the myriad other tasks required. In response to the high level of regime repression and violence in the mid-1970s, CEBs in general, like the ones in which Norma Gallo and Uriel Molina were involved, became key organizational and logistical resources for the guerrillas: raising money, stockpiling food and medical supplies for combat. Many clergy (by 1979, 85% of the clergy supported the insurrection) and laypersons previously reluctant to align themselves with the insurgents now did so. Church buildings served as sanctuaries for activists and for the FSLN. A few became revolutionary armories.[76]

Maryknoll sisters contributed to building up the Church of the poor by working as pastoral agents in Open 3 *barrio* in the Managuan suburbs and in the northern border area around Ocotal. Their work focuses on training leaders to teach and instruct their own people, lead the community in its own liturgy, and help popular religiosity to mature.[77] They also concentrated on community development work and Christian Youth clubs.

University students from the Christian Youth Movement founded by Jesuit Fernando Cardenal collaborated with the sisters in the youth clubs and reflection groups. Focusing their Bible study on issues underlining the dignity of poor people, the young people, in conjunction with other groups including a women's organization, undertook a series of political struggles between the *barrio* and the government. As a result of their participation in Christian renewal groups and community development projects, many of the young people went from being anti-Somoza to being Christian revolutionaries.[78]

In the Ocotal locale, Sisters Joan Uhlen and Pat Edmiston began work in the mid-1970s with weekend workshops for women. The aim of these workshops was to enable women to recognize their own worth by drawing them out of their timidity and fear and providing a community in which they could have an expanded role as dedicated Christians. Participants ranged

> from 16-year old girls just beginning to realize how few of their society's privileges are open to them to middle-aged women al-

> ready aware that their hard lives have been made more difficult simply because they are women.[79]

The sisters traveled throughout the region, holding courses in people's homes. In keeping with their goal to develop local leadership, they trained a group of forty lay women who collaborated in the conduct of the workshops. Courses emphasized reflection on Biblical themes such as: God's love for each person, the nature of early Christian communities, scriptural approach to the oppression of women, Christian guidelines for community practices of corporate prayer. The concluding session involved speaking of the activities and accomplishments of women in the world, discussion of improvements and goals for their own community, and planning for achieving these goals.[80] At the time of the writing of this report, January 1977, over 2,000 women had participated in the seminars.[81]

Another religious order that provided leadership for building up "the Church born of the poor" was the Society of Jesus. In 1968 with hierarchical support, the Jesuits created CEPA, (Centro de Educación y Promoción Agraria) a self-help program to assist peasants meet their daily needs with increased effectiveness. Working at first in the Corzao and Masaya areas and later in the region from Esteli to Leon, CEPA trained *campesino* leaders in appropriate agricultural techniques—but always in the context of Biblical reflection. Soon, in response to the social reality of the *campo*, the training began to include the social and political implications of the Gospel for those who worked the land. A "subversive" message began to circulate in the countryside in the comic book *Cristo, Campesino* published by CEPA:

> Each human being is important before God, and therefore has the right to the resources necessary to live in dignity . . . you have a right to the land.[82]

As a result, CEPA added to the training program components on problem-solving and political action. By the 1970s CEPA activists became increasingly committed to radical socio-political change. This development led the Jesuit-sponsored organization to sever official connections with the bishops; CEPA became an independent Christian organization.

As the documents of Vatican II and Medellin were studied in the Catholic schools, teachers became aware that their educational activities were reserved for the elite. In order to begin to implement the preferential option for the poor and inculcate concern for a just social order, many teachers urged their high school and university students to help voluntarily in the poor barrios. Thus, many students discovered the reality of the poor and began to search for some way to help. The growing activism of the students coincided with a second national pastoral meeting in 1971 at which the priests concluded that evangelization had to be aimed at conscienticization.[83]

Leadership in Christian renewal came not just from the Capuchins, Jesuits, and other religious order priests, but also from groups and individuals of the religious orders of women. In addition to the Maryknoll Sisters, the Sisters of the Assumption in the Managua parish of San Judas had been radicalized by events following the 1972 earthquake and were heavily involved in supporting their people in the revolutionary process. Individuals such as Sister Marta Frech of the Congregation of Missionaries of Charity, a teacher in Santa Teresita School, worked actively in the student movement until events forced her to flee to Matagalpa and the country. She then worked with the FSLN until the victory. Sister Maria Hartman of the Sisters of St. Agnes worked with the poor in the De Riguero *barrio*. Dorothy Wilson of Puerto Cabeza left a contemplative order in 1974 and started a religious community to work with the peasants in the Siuana area. There she collaborated with the FSLN finally leaving her religious order and joining the guerrilla ranks.

This, then, was the picture of the Catholic Church just before the final insurrection. The converging relationship of the FSLN and the base Church over the previous decade was based on a discovery of common areas of political concern, which led to fusion of action. It is of utmost importance to note that the openness to socialist or Sandinista movements by substantial minorities of the Church was not due, as some have insinuated, to a Marxist penetration of the Church. Rather, it appears that a few may have used elements of Marxist social analysis in their evaluation of the prevalent socio-economic conditions. They had been encouraged to take the plight of the poor seriously by the guidelines provided by Pope Paul VI. Finally, it was their experience of the Nicaraguan situation and their understanding of that reality that resulted in their despairing of capitalist development and its ability to substantially improve the lot of the poor.[84]

Even this brief survey of the emergence and growth of the base Church in Nicaragua in the 1960s and 1970s points to an incredible change in the role and status of women in that sector of the Church; their situation in the traditional sector remains static and unchanged. While there is a new approach to women in the base communities, one finds no evidence of a frontal attack on the church's historical role in legitimizing and reinforcing male domination. A radical critique and repudiation of the basically patriarchal ideology and structure of the traditional Roman Catholic Church still needs to be addressed.

Ideological Shifts in Nicaraguan Christianity, the Impact on Revolutionary Women

What, then, was the influence of the ideological shift within Roman Catholicism on the involvement of women in the Nicaraguan revolution? This shift, which itself deserves to be characterized as "revolutionary," touched every aspect of Catholic belief and practice, and was unquestionably a major catalyst in Nicaragua's revolutionary process.

First, and most importantly, there was a new understanding of the Church. While institutional elements of the Church still remained in place, these were now seen as secondary; the previously dominant hierarchial, pyramid image of the Church was replaced by the concept of "the people of God." Since in Nicaragua the bulk of the people were poor and marginalized, the Church took on a new preference for and identity with the poor. The laity began to see themselves as full members of the Church, meant to be actively responsible for the Church's own life and the fulfillment of its mission in the world.

This new view did not remain theoretical: in Nicaragua as throughout Latin America, it found expression in the base ecclesial communities, where women and men as laity, now experienced being the Church. Vatican II theology of the priesthood of the people combined with an acute shortage of ordained clergy provided the opportunity and need to implement this new vision. In the CEBs, the leaders were chosen by community approval. Formed through a training program often referred to as "conscienticizing evangelization," they were guided by a theologically-grounded sense of service to their people. Where the prevailing practice of designating a husband and wife team to share the delegate post was the norm, it reflected positively on the married state as equal in dignity and holiness to that of the religious state while demonstrating the egalitarian character of the Christian community.

One of the notions classically associated with the Church was "the kingdom of God." Modern Biblical study had made it clear that "the kingdom" was broader than the Church, that it did not refer exclusively or even primarily to the after-life, and that it coincided with the establishment of a situation of justice and peace among humans.[85] When Nicaraguans reflecting on their situation found not justice but deprivation and Somozan repression, they came to understand this situation as structured sin contrary to the human liberation willed for them by a loving God. Delegate leadership came to understand political change as central to the Christian's vocation because it was the key to improving the situation of the poor. It is the poor themselves who now determine the relevance of Christ's teachings to their situation. Brazilian theologian Leonardo Boff, himself deeply involved with the CEB movement, appraises their significance:

> The Christian Base Community is the place where the theological essence of the Church is realized and, at the same time, the practice of liberation of the poor by the poor themselves.[86]

Second, the new-found sense of being the people of God was increasingly honored and confirmed in people's liturgical experience. Instead of sacramental rites that had been understood as occasions when something happened to them, when they received something mysterious called "grace," the base communities now emphasized the Biblical word whose meaning and implications for life they discussed together, came to appreciate, and celebrated in their weekly liturgies.

Eucharistic liturgy in the CEBs, when made possible by the presence of an ordained priest, fed upon this evangelical awakening and became more a celebration of Christian Life that related to the concrete social and historical situation of the people. One cannot listen to the words and music of the "Credo" in the *Misa campesina* without catching some of this new spirit:

> I believe in you, companero
> . . . the worker Christ.
> You are reborn
> in every arm which is raised
> to defend the people
> against domination and exploitation.[87]

Third, if the people's liturgical life was revitalized, their devotional life that had often focused on Mary and on traditional saints now emphasized Christ and did so with new understanding. Liberation theologians were developing new insight into Christ as the risen liberator who continues to be present to the Christian people and who is identified with the poor and oppressed.[88] These concepts were quickly transmitted to the popular level. If the people of God are meant to carry on Jesus' own mission, and if scripture attests to the fact that women in early Christianity shared in all the key aspects of Jesus' mission of liberating the oppressed, it requires little imagination to see why women as well as men believed that their involvement in the revolution was a Christian undertaking.[89]

Accompanying this changed attitude towards Jesus Christ was a different understanding of his mother. No longer imaged as the tender maiden, the *purissima,* untouched by life and raised above ordinary women as the virgin/Mother, Mary now came to be viewed as a women of the poor, the strong, mature, committed women of the "Magnificat." As such, she carries a message of liberation to the world, proclaiming God's predilection for the poor and the fall of the oppressing rich. As the faithful believer who accompanied her son in the Pasch, she is both responsible for and supportive of Jesus in his revolutionary teaching and mission.[90]

Fourth, the post-Vatican II emphasis on responsibility and courage rather than obedience as patient acceptance of injustice helped free the conscience of many women and men in the base communities from the guilt they earlier might have felt in opposing exploitative officials and structures. It was the concrete misery of the oppressed, the concern felt for needy brothers and sisters, the profound conviction that God was at their side, that led them to opt for armed resistence.

Common struggle and the discovery of shared values and concern gave rise to a new kind of ecumenism, one which enabled the people of the Christian renewal movement to overcome supposedly insurmountable obstacles between Catholics and Protestants, between Christians and non-Christians working together for common goals. This very important and necessary development freed the CEBs from fears engendered by the heavy anti-communist propaganda of the Somoza government against the FSLN. Out of groups working together to bring about the revolution would come "an unusual and original blend of pragmatic Marxism and progressive Catholic thought."[91]

Without the impact that these radical shifts in religious understanding had on Nicaragua's Catholic women, the overthrow of Somoza might never have happened and the social revolution now taking place might never have been initiated.[92]

A cautionary word: the overthrow of Somoza did not mean the disappearance of all elements of domination and oppression in society or in the Church. Wealthy oligarchs have not taken kindly to the redistribution of wealth and opportunity and some of the bishops disapprove of base ecclesial communities and of the initiatives taken by lay women and men. The powerful backlash by conservative elements in both society and Church has tended to ally itself with the counter-revolutionary forces now trying, with financial and military backing from the United States, to topple the Nicaraguan government and to reverse the revolution. The recent gains and new-found status of Nicaraguan women are still in jeopardy.

Notes

1. Elsa Chaney, *Supermadre* (Austin: University of Texas Press, 1979), pp. 40–43; Susan Ramirez-Horton, "The Role of Women in the Nicaraguan Revolution," in Walker, *Nicaragua in Revolution*, p. 147; Evelyn Stevens, "Marianismo: the Other Face of Machismo," in Ann Pescatello, ed., *Female and Male in Latin America* (Pittsburgh: University of Pittsburgh Press, 1973), pp. 89–101; Helen Shapiro, "The Many Realities," *NACLA Report on the Americas* 14 (1980):3–13. Recent works focusing on Women in the Nicaraguan Revolution include: Norma Stoltz Chinchilla, "Women in Revolutionary Movements: The Case of Nicaragua," *Revolution in Central America* [publication of the Stanford Central American Action Network] (Boulder: Westview Press, 1983); Jane Deighton, Rossana Horsley, Sara Stewart, and Cathy Cain, *Sweet Ramparts: Women in Revolutionary Nicaragua* (London: War on Want and the Nicaraguan Solidarity Campaign, 1983); Paula Diebold de Cruz and Mayra Pasos de Rappauoli, *Informe sobre el papel de la mujer en el desarrollo economico de Nicaragua* (Managua: U.S. Agency for International Development, November 1975); Elizabeth Maier, *Nicaragua, La Mujer en la Revolucion* (Mexico City: Ediciones de Cultura Popular, 1980); Susan Ramirez-Horton, "The Role of Women," in Walker, *Nicaragua in Revolution*; Margaret Randall, *Sandino's Daughters* (Vancouver: New Star Books, 1981); Doris Tijerino, *Inside the Nicaraguan Revolution* (Vancouver: New Star Books, 1978).

2. Ramirez-Horton, "The Role of Women," in Walker, *Nicaragua in Revolution*, p. 101, Black, *Triumph of the People*, p. 323.

3. Chaney, *Supermadre*, pp. 40–43.

4. Ramirez-Horton, "The Role of Women," in Walker, *Nicaragua in Revolution*, p. 147; Tijerino, *Inside the Nicaraguan Revolution*, describes the conditions of Nicaraguan women in the 1970s in graphic, compelling fashion.

5. *Envio* (publication of the Instituto Historico Centroamericano, Managua) 3 (July 1983):3c.

6. Diebold de Cruz and Pasos de Rappauoli, *Informe sobre el papel de la mujer*, p. 8.

7. *Envio* 3 (July 1983):3c.

8. Norma Stoltz Chinchilla, "Women in Revolutionary Movements," *Revolution in Central America*, pp. 422–34.

9. Deighton et al., *Sweet Ramparts*, pp. 90, 93.

10. Chinchilla, "Women in Revolutionary Movements," *Revolution in Central America*, p. 429.

11. Deighton et al., *Sweet Ramparts*, p. 128.

12. Tijerino, *Inside the Nicaraguan Revolution*, pp. 107–108.

13. Shapiro, "The Many Realities," *NACLA Report on the Americas* 14 (1980):4.

14. Deighton et al., *Sweet Ramparts*, pp. 146–47.

15. Chaney, *Supermadre*, pp. 40–43; P. Turner, "Patriarchal Sexism: Liberation Theology's Critique," *At the Crossroads* (Worcester, MA: Worcester Connection, 1983).

16. Chinchilla, "Women in Revolutionary Movements," *Revolution in Central America*, p. 422.

17. Black, *Triumph of the People*, p. 21: "numerous women joined Sandino's army. . . . Sandino's wife, Blanca Arauz . . . took charge of communications."

18. The FSLN had issued a critique of women's situation in a platform statement in 1967: "Unequal wages, a double workload (inside and outside the home), isolation from political and social participation, fundamentally in rural areas, use as a sexual object, prostitutes, exploitation of women in the media, etc. and to complete the picture, legal discrimination." *Envio* 3 (July 1983):4c.

19. All three had begun their political activity while high school students in the northern mountain city of Matagalpa; later, in Managua as university students, Fonseca and Borge were arrested for conspiracy in the plot that resulted in poet Rigoberto Lopez's assassination of Somoza Garcia in 1955. Early history of the FSLN is related in "Guerrilla War—People's War," Black, *Triumph of the People*, pp. 75–99.

20. Chinchilla, "Women in Revolutionary Movements," *Revolution in Central America*, p. 429.

21. Ibid., p. 416. Many of the young women who joined the struggle early had followed in the footsteps of brothers, while others were recruited through the Sandinista-connected student association. Other women later became committed and integrated into the struggle because of growing repression visited on their sons and daughters. Joseph Collins points out that as he moved throughout the countryside and talked to innumerable government and peasant leaders he was struck by the "deeply religious purpose so many expressed" as they described "how their commitment was sparked in Catholic study groups where as teenagers they met with friends to discuss the Bible and reflect on the relevancy of Jesus' teaching in a society of gross injustice and misery," *What Difference Could a Revolution Make*? (San Francisco: Institute for Food and Development Policy, 1982), p. 24. See also Randall, *Sandino's Daughters*, pp. 1–34; where she gives a history of the development of AMPRONAC.

22. Randall, *Sandino's Daughters*, p. 2. Lea Guido, an FSLN member, states that in April of 1977 she received a note from Jaime Wheelock of the Proletarian Tendency in which "he suggested we organize a work commission to look at women's problems and work toward the creation of a broad-based women's association."

23. "Nicaraguan Women: Struggle for a New Homeland," *Lucha* [published by New York Circus] 3, no. 2 (1979). Also discussed in Ramirez-Horton, "The Role of Women," in Walker, *Nicaragua in Revolution*, pp. 150–52; Black, *Triumph of the People*, p. 324.

24. A first-hand account of the development and activities is given by Mayra Passos de Rappauoli, "Where are our campesino brothers? Let the murderers answer," in June H. Turner, ed., *Latin American Women: the Meek Speak Out* (Silver Spring, Maryland: International Educational Development, 1980).

25. Black, *Triumph of the People*, p. 120.

26. *Lucha* 3, no. 2 (1979):2–3.

27. Patricia Flynn, "Women Challenge the Myth," *Revolution in Central America*, p. 417; Deighton et al., *Sweet Ramparts*, p. 41.

28. Black, *Triumph of the People*, pp. 120–22; Ramirez-Horton, "The Role of Women," in Walker, *Nicaragua in Revolution*, p. 151.

29. Lynn Silver, "Nicaraguan Women Organize to Defend the Revolution," *Intercontinental Press*, 15 October 1979.

30. Black, *Triumph of the People*, p. 324; Randall, *Sandino's Daughters*, "The Commanders" consists of interviews with the three FSLN women who attained the rank of *Commandante*.

31. "But once they became involved, the traditional aspect of their motivation often transformed into its opposite," Chinchilla, "Women in Revolutionary Movements," *Revolution in Central America*, p. 428.

32. Black, *Triumph of the People*, p. 186.

33. For a discussion of the nature and structure of mass organizations, see Ibid., pp. 230–48; Walker, *Nicaragua in Revolution*, pp. 94–114 ("The Sandinist Mass Organizations"); Rudolph, *A Country Study*, pp. 150–64.

34. *Envio* 3 (July 1983):4c.

35. Ibid.

36. Paulo Freire, *The Pedagogy of the Oppressed*, trans. Myra B. Ramos (New York: Continuum, 1973). Freire's theory, much respected by Nicaragua's revolutionary government holds that the oppressed themselves must work to bring about their own liberation; women, therefore, come under this stricture.

37. Luisa Amanda Espinoza's story is told by those who knew her; Randall, *Sandino's Daughters*, pp. 24–33.

38. Deighton et al., *Sweet Ramparts*, p. 47; "The Legal Situation of Nicaraguan Women," *Barricada* (official FSLN newspaper), Managua, 23 March 1980.

39. Deighton et al., *Sweet Ramparts*, p. 43.

40. Ibid., p. 44.

41. Ibid., p. 47. To these topics should be added another sensitive one—abortion. Given the Roman Catholic religious outlook of the majority of the people, it is easy to understand the cautious attitude expressed by some AMNLAE leaders towards proposing legislation on this issue. AMNLAE along with other agencies is taking a very positive approach by promoting sexual education programs which demystify the outlook on sexuality (sometimes referred to as "the Virgin Mary complex") held by large numbers of women. Ibid., pp. 155–56.

42. For a fuller discussion of AMNLAE's self-critique, reasons for change, and the nature of new structures, see Deighton et al., *Sweet Ramparts*, pp.

47–49; Harry Fried "Nicaraguan Women Demand Rights," *The Guardian* 21, December 1981. By 1982, AMNLAE had organized 817 caucus groups with extensive increase planned.

43. Deighton et al., *Sweet Ramparts*, pp. 44–46; *Envio* 3 (July 1983):4c.

44. Deighton et al., *Sweet Ramparts*, p. 47, finds the lack of full autonomy from the FSLN a serious limitation for AMNLAE as a women's movement; on the other hand, AMNLAE may find considerable advantage in having the backing of the government to achieve its purposes.

45. Ibid., p. 22: "In general, the government follows the line that achieving positions of leadership is not a matter of affirmative action or formal mechanisms of promotion." Many of the women now in leadership positions had fought their way to acceptance in similar positions in the FSLN before the victory in 1979.

46. Randall, *Sandino's Daughters*, pp. 40–79.

47. Flynn, "Myth," *Revolution in Central America*, pp. 415–16; Deighton et al., *Sweet Ramparts*, pp. 50–59.

48. Ibid., pp. 52–59.

49. *Envio* 3 (July 1983):7c; Marian MacDonald, "Women in the Forefront of Nicaragua's Liberation," *The Guardian*, 19 June 1983, p. 13; Deighton et al., *Sweet Ramparts*, p. 29.

50. *Envio* 3 (July 1983):5c–6c.

51. Deighton et al., *Sweet Ramparts*, p. 72 ("Amnlae and the Unions"); *Envio* 3 (July 1983):4c–5c.

52. The Food Law is intended to come to grips with *machismo* and to eventually transform the sexual division of labor in the home. Deighton et al., *Sweet Ramparts*, pp. 129–31.

53. Ibid., p. 129; *Envio* 3 (July 1983):4c–5c.

54. Deighton et al., *Sweet Ramparts*, pp. 129–31.

55. *Status of Christianity Country Profile: Nicaragua*, Strategy Working Group of Lausanne Committee for World Evangelization and MARC, a ministry of World Vision, Monrovia, California.

56. Walter Abbot, ed., *The Documents of Vatican II* (New York: America Press, 1966). See especially "Constitution on the Church," "The Church in the World Today," "Constitution on Divine Revelation," "Constitution on the Sacred Liturgy," and "Decree on Ecumenism." Cf. also Donal Dorr, *Option for the Poor, A Hundred Years of Vatican Teaching* (Maryknoll, NY: Orbis, 1983).

57. Latin American Bishops, *The Church in the Present Day Transformation of Latin America in Light of the Council* [Medellin documents], 3rd. ed. (Washington, D.C.: NCCB Latin American Secretariat, 1979). Consulting Episcopal Commission on Latin America statement, "Christians in Central America: The Church of the Poor is Born," *LADOC* 14, no. 1 (September/October 1983):1–20.

58. For the description of an experience analogous to Nicaragua's, cf. J. B. Libanio, "Experience with the Base Ecclesial Communities in Brazil," *LADOC* 12, no. 2 (November/December 1981):1–20; cf. also Frei Betto, "The Church Born of the People," *LADOC* 12, no. 3 (January/February 1982):1–15.

59. Black, *Triumph of the People*, p. 317.

60. English translation of the encyclical in David O'Brien and Thomas Shannon, eds., *Renewing the Earth: Catholic Documents on Peace, Justice, and Liberation* (Garden City: Doubleday, 1977), pp. 313–51.

61. *Envio* 3 (July 1983):2b.

62. "The Catholic Church in Nicaragua," Report of the Catholic Press Association, 1963, p. 18.

63. See Part I, "Solentiname," pp. 39–120 in Margaret Randall, *Christians in the Nicaraguan Revolution* (Vancouver: New Star Books, 1983); also "Ernesto Cardenal, Minister of Culture," in Teofilo Cabestrero, *Ministers of God, Ministers of the People* (Maryknoll, NY: Orbis, 1983); also the four volumes of E. Cardenal, *The Gospel in Solentiname* (Maryknoll, NY: Orbis, 1982), an invaluable record of the developing "liberation theology."

64. Black, *Triumph of the People*, pp. 103, 317. Of the twenty members who joined the FSLN, three were women.

65. These are the rural areas where the base Church of the poor flourished in the late 1960s. Cf. M. Dodson and T. Montgomery, "The Churches in the Revolution" in Walker, *Nicaragua in Revolution*.

66. Ibid., pp. 170–73; Arthur Cooney, "Conscienticization as Integral to Evangelization in Nicaragua," (Master's thesis, St. Francis Seminary School of Pastoral Ministry [Milwaukee], April, 1977); Gregorio Smutko, "Cristanos de la Costa Atlantica en la Revolucion," *Nicarácua*, no. 5 (Managua: Revista del Ministerio de Cultura de Nicaragua, April–June, 1981), pp. 49–65.

67. J. Collins and F. Moore Lappe, *Now We Can Speak* (San Francisco: Institute for Food and Development Policy, 1980), p. 50.

68. Black, *Triumph of the People*, p. 318.

69. Walker, *Nicaragua in Revolution*, pp. 52–53; Phillip Berryman, *The Religious Roots of Rebellion* (Maryknoll, NY: Orbis, 1984), p. 59.

70. For Padre Molina's own account: Part II, "El Riguero" in Randall, *Christians*.

71. Dodson and Montgomery, "The Churches in Revolution," in Walker, *Nicaragua in Revolution*, pp. 165–66.

72. Randall, *Sandino's Daughters*, p. 66.

73. "Women and Christians in Nicaragua," *Lucha* 6, no. 5 (October, 1982).

74. A manual that describes concrete ways to approach conscienticizing evangelization is Gregorio Smutko, *La conscientizacion. Dinamicas y applicaciones* (Bogota: Ediciones Paulinas, 1978).

75. *Lucha* 6, no. 5 (October, 1982):32.

76. Booth, *The End and the Beginning*, p. 136; Black, *Triumph of the People*, pp. 319–20.

77. Jose Miguez Bonino, "Popular Piety in Latin America," *LADOC* 4, no. 5 (May/June, 1977):30–41.

78. The work of Maryknoll in Open 3 is described in Dodson and Montgomery, "The Churches in Revolution," in Walker, *Nicaragua in Revolution*. On Ocotal, see Patricia Jacobsen, "Weekend Workshops for Women" *Maryknoll Magazine* 71, no. 1 (January 1977):119–26. Also, Penny Lernoux, *Cry of the People* (New York: Penguin, 1982), pp. 181ff.

79. Jacobsen, "Weekend Workshops," *Maryknoll Magazine* 71, no. 1 (January 1977):26. Over 2000 women had participated in the seminars at the time of the report; forty lay women had been trained to assist with the Biblically-based and community-development-oriented courses.

80. Jacobsen, "Weekend Workshops," *Maryknoll Magazine* 71, no. 1 (January 1977):126.

81. Ibid.

82. Dodson and Montgomery, "The Churches in Revolution," in Walker, *Nicaragua in Revolution*, p. 170; Booth, *The End and the Beginning*, p. 134. CEPA's work is discussed in Joseph Collins, *What Difference Could a Revolution Make* (San Francisco: Institute for Food and Development Policy, 1982), pp. 24–25.

83. In addition to the Youth Club of Open 3, the Christian Revolutionary Movement, which was begun in 1971 by Jesuit Fernando Cardenal and Padre Molina, is described in Cabestrero, *Ministers*, p. 45–89. On Uriel Molina's association with students in El Riguero *barrio* cf. Randall, *Christians*, pp. 121–202. In Lappe and Collins, *Now We Can Speak*, young Nicaraguans speak of the beginnings of their involvement with the revolution sparked during high school days in study groups by reflection on the Bible and on the relevance of Jesus' teaching in a society of gross injustice and misery. Such reflection led them to work in community development with the poor. Two who testify to the impact of these origins on their own commitment are Caliche Borrios (p. 7) and Malena de Montes (p. 70). Young working people had their own organization, the Juventud Obrera Catolica (Young Catholic Workers) which emerged in 1970, one of the first with overlapping spiritual and class concerns. Cf. Black, *Triumph of the People*, p. 317.

84. Pope Paul VI's guidelines are in his apostolic letter "Octogesima adveniens," May 14, 1971 (*Acta Apostolicae Sedis* 63 [1971]:401–41). English translation in O'Brien and Shannon, *Renewing the Earth*, pp. 352–33; a commentary on the letter is in Dorr, *Option for the Poor*, chap. 8.

Margaret Crahan, in her excellent paper "Religion in Contemporary Nicaragua" (prepared in Latin American Studies Program, School of Advanced International Studies, John Hopkins University), argues that there has been no Marxist penetration in the openness of the Christian base movement to the Sandinistas. See also Black, *Triumph of the People*, pp. 316–23 ("The Dialogue between Marxists and Christians"). For Padre Fernando Cardenal's view of this issue, cf. Cabestrero, *Ministers*, pp. 75–78.

85. Cf. Norman Perrin, *Jesus and the Language of the Kingdom* (Philadelphia: Fortress, 1980).

86. Gustavo Gutierrez, "The Church and Liberation: Revolutionary Christianity," *Revolution in Central America*, p. 36.

87. Black, *Triumph of the People*, p. 170. *The Misa Campesina*, composed by Carlos Mejia Godoy, y el Taller de Sonida Popular, CBS Records, Costa Rica, 1977.

88. Jon Sobrino, *Christology at the Crossroads* (Maryknoll, NY: Orbis, 1978).

89. For an excellent critical study of women in early Christianity, see Elizabeth Schussler Fiorenza, *In Memory of Her* (New York: Crossroads, 1983).

90. Randall, *Christians*, p. 162; *LADOC* 11, no. 2 (November/December 1980):25–26; Ernesto Cardenal, *The Gospel in Solentiname*, 4:233–35.

91. Walker, *Nicaragua in Revolution*, p. 121.

92. Crahan, "Religion in Contemporary Nicaragua," gives a fine analysis of the contemporary situation; Teofilo Cabestrero, *Lo que hemos visto y oido* (Bilbao: Desclee de Brouwer, 1983), especially chaps. 5 and 6.

CHAPTER FOURTEEN

*Goddesses, Mothers, and Heroines: Hindu Women and the Feminine in the Early Nationalist Movement**

LOU RATTÉ

Rāma:
I have done all that a man should do to wipe out an intolerable insult at the hands of an enemy. I won you, Sītā. . . .But let it be known, if you please, that the great effort accomplished by means of . . . heroism. . .was not undertaken by me for your sake. I protected my own reputation and expunged completely the scandal and degradation which had been cast upon my own famous family line.

*Research for this article was initially undertaken under a grant from the Pembroke Center for Teaching and Research on Women at Brown University, 1982–83. I am indebted to participants in the Seminar on Gender and Politics, led by Joan Scott and Elizabeth Weed, for generating ideas on how to approach the study of gender representation in political movements; many of these ideas I have attempted to incorporate here. I also owe special thanks to Lawrence A. Babb of Amherst College for his helpful comments on an earlier version of this article.

> Sītā:
> Why do you speak such rough words, cruel to the ears, inappropriate to me, O Hero, like a common man to a common woman? . . . Have confidence in me. . . .My heart, which is under my control, is ever attached to you. . .Tiger among men, by giving way to anger like a trivial man you have made womankind preferable.
> from the *Rāmāyaṇa*[1]

In the great Hindu epic, the *Rāmāyaṇa*, known and loved throughout India, Sītā represents the ideal Hindu wife. She follows her husband, Rāma, into exile, endures the hardships of forest life, and remains chaste and faithful when she is captured by the demon, Rāvaṇa. When Sītā is finally rescued and she and Rāma are reunited, Rāma, the king, fearing that his subjects will think him weak and susceptible to the pull of emotion over duty, refuses to take her back. Sītā protests, professing her own virtue. She poses a perennial question: what is the relationship between social duty and private virtue? Beneath that question lies another: what, in Hindu culture, is the proper relationship between men and women?

These questions assumed renewed importance in the early years of the nationalist period in India, between 1800 and 1920, as changes generated by the imperial presence and the rise of organized nationalism threatened to dismantle the structure of traditional society which kept the lives of men and women separate. The questions were at least partially answered by men and women nationalists in Bengal, the seat of British power until 1911, and this paper explores the process through which these men and women attempted to accommodate to change. Both men and women nationalists invoked traditional sources to capture the changes in symbolic representations which linked the masculine and the feminine together, establishing complementarity in gender relations. For both men and women, symbolic representations were calls to action, but women's representations were equally aimed at supporting women's claim to act outside the domestic sphere in the wider social realm. While men sought to define social duty and private virtue in ways that sustained differences in social roles, women sought to dissolve the gender difference between duty and virtue and to legitimize their right to active participation in the nationalist struggle.

Hindu men for generations had proceeded through the educational system provided by the British imperial government and entered imperial service as junior administrators, lawyers, judges, and teachers. By the 1870s many were suffering from the threat of unemployment as the number of qualified graduates rose and the number of available positions remained the same. As they became more fully conscious of the way many of the British viewed them, those already employed realized that there was a ceiling to their upward mobility.

As a group, western-educated Hindus were not perceived by the British as unequals, but as effeminate babus who could ape the British in speech but were hardly capable of accepting responsibility in deciding their own or their country's affairs.[2] Under the conditions imposed by heightened racism and a tightening of imperial rule directed from Britain, which subordinated Indian interests to empire-wide concerns, the interests of the western-educated class of Hindu men were bound to clash with imperial interests.

To ease the situation a retired British official, sympathetic to the western-educated class, proposed a solution which pointed in the same direction toward which the Indians themselves had been tending.[3] Allan Octavian Hume advocated the formation of an organization which would provide educated Indians with a platform to discuss political questions, make their grievances known to government, and represent the interests of the mass of Indians who, due to their ignorance, could not speak for themselves. Out of Hume's efforts and the cooperation of educated Hindu men emerged the Indian National Congress in 1885. The Congress met annually every December from 1885 throughout the nationalist period, and its formation marks the beginning of the organized nationalist movement.

The Congress had a stormy history throughout the early nationalist period before the rise of Mohandas K. Gandhi.[4] The initial group of Congressmen were not anti-British, nor were they opposed to the continuation of imperial rule. They wanted reforms in the government, including their own greater participation in political decision-making. In the 1890s, however, they were joined by younger men who challenged the reliance on political reform. This group, led by B. G. Tilak from Maharashtra, called themselves Extremists, in contrast to the Moderates they opposed, and their goal was political independence. Taking history as his measure, Tilak asserted:

> There is no empire lost by a free grant of concession by the rulers to the ruled. History does not record any such event. Empires are lost by luxury, by being too much bureaucratic or overconfident or from other reasons. But an empire has never come to an end by the rulers conceding power to the ruled.[5]

In the course of his turbulent career Tilak worked out what, for India, he meant by the "other reasons" by which empires could be brought down.

In the 1890s and early 1900s secret societies espousing revolution began to form, and in 1905, in response to an official decision to partition Bengal province, a terrorist movement took shape with at least the tacit encouragement of the Extremists.[6] In 1907, at the annual Congress session, the difference between Moderates and Extremists resulted in a formal break; after much shoe-throwing, shouting, and exchange of verbal abuse, the Extremists walked out of Congress.

By 1910 the government had put down the terrorist movement, and in the second decade of the century Moderates and Extremists were reunited. By the end of the decade, they had moved in the direction of accepting non-violent means of confrontation and agreed on the goal of political freedom. This paved the way for the work of Gandhi.

The events sketched above usually are the focus of serious historical study of the early nationalist period. However, beneath the narrative of how western-educated Hindu men worked out their differences and mounted a nationalist campaign against British rule lies another narrative, which is the concern here. This other narrative addresses the questions of public duty and private virtue and the proper roles of men and women, as western-educated Hindus confronted those issues between 1880 and 1920.

Histories of nationalism which focus on confrontation with the British isolate as the primary actors western-educated Hindu men. These men played the leading role both in articulating the emerging nationalist message to the British and in making that message known to non-westernized Indians whose support was necessary if the goals were to be achieved. Mohandas K. Gandhi, the Mahatma, is usually credited with bringing to fruition the latter enterprise and with enlisting the support of Hindu women. However, there is a body of literature which shows that Hindu women were active in British Indian society during the earlier period,[7] and it was over the social and political roles of these women that questions of duty, virtue, and gender were initially posed.

From the beginnings of the implementation of imperial policy in the early 1800s to the early 1880s, Hindu women—the wives, daughters, mothers and sisters of the men gaining a western education—had remained outside British Indian society. Their lives were no doubt altered in innumerable ways by altered patterns of behavior in the men, but the changes could be accommodated and traditional patterns and relationships maintained. Though they remained invisible in British Indian society as actors, Hindu women were not entirely absent from the concerns of the westernizing men, nor from those of the British interest groups whose goal was to reform Indian society. Beginning with the agitation over the issue of whether to outlaw the practice of widow-burning in the 1820s, the condition of Indian, and primarily Hindu, women occupied what could be viewed as an inordinate amount of attention from Hindu and British men.

With the passing of the decree in 1828 which forbade the practice of *satī*, the imperial government initiated a reform movement which continued throughout the century. The premises of the movement were finally challenged by those nationalists who were not opposed to improvement in the lives of Hindu women but who set themselves against the assumptions upon which the reform program was based. Social reform, as Extremists understood it in the 1890s, was inseparable from the methods of political reform to which they were opposed; to accept either type of reform was implicitly to sanction British ideas of how government and society should be organized. Acceptance of the need for social reform, furthermore, would constitute tacit acceptance of the negative judgements of Hindu society and culture which had gained currency in the nineteenth century and to which western-educated Indians had subscribed.

The Extremists had a point. Christian missionaries, who played a role in influencing official opinion, and evangelical reformers within the British administration, had come to regard Hindu women, collectively, as the abject victims of a decadent, priest-ridden system. Hindu reformers had at least partially accepted these judgements. They agreed that Hindu women at present were abject victims, but they constructed a golden-age theory of history to show that such had not always been the case; in the past, they argued, Hindu women had been men's social equals and the religious system had been pure.[8]

Once agitation over the *satī* question had subsided, attention turned to such oppressive customs as child marriage, denial of education to women, and the enforced chastity of the Hindu widow. An effort was made to alter these customs by gaining agreement from within the Hindu community on raising the age of marriage, opening up educational opportunities to women, and allowing widows to remarry. Hindu reformers had hoped that the imperial government would help them secure reform by enacting legislation, but in the post-mutiny period (after 1857) the government had become less willing to interfere in custom, viewing such interference as cause for Indian unrest.[9] Reformers, as they gained access to administrative positions, attempted to initiate legislative reforms on their own and to propagandize the need for reform in orthodox communities. By 1880, on the question of social reform Hindu men of the western-educated class conceived their duty to be the introduction of progressive reforms into society. Hindu women had been all but deprived of their traditional virtue, for they labored under pernicious customs which reduced them to the condition of depravity. In reform ideology, men were active agents, women passively submissive.

Beginning in the 1880s, the hopes of educational reformers appeared to be realized. Secondary education had been made available to the women since 1854,[10] and the women who took advantage of the opportunities were the female relatives of western-educated men. Colleges, universities, and even professional schools had opened their doors to women, and in 1882 two women graduated from the University of Calcutta. Private tutoring had always been an option for westernized Hindus, and from 1882 on, increasing numbers of Hindu women emerged into British Indian society.

Some of these women had even received university and professional training abroad, and many were aided by British and foreign sympathizers who offered training, social space, colleagueship, and even money, encouraging Hindu women in the direction which had been set by reform ideology. Women who were the beneficiaries of education were to assume active roles in the effort to reform the condition of less fortunate Hindu women.[11] Their duty was clear. Their virtue was determined by their willingness to extend the range of reform. They were to be partners with the men who had understood the need for reform.

As long as the Moderates remained in control of Congress there was no contradiction between social reform aimed at improving the condition of women and political reform. Moderates had institutionalized the difference between the two by deciding that Congress should concern itself only with narrowly defined political issues, while a sister organization, the Social Conference, could treat social issues. Founded in 1889, the Social Conference debated many topics, but it gave predominant attention to reforms affecting women, and many women participated in its annual meetings. Women were not excluded from the political Congress, but their participation was minimal and men retained leadership positions.[12] As the Extremists emerged to challenge the whole reform mentality some form of confrontation was inevitable. It manifested itself in an attempt to imagine Hindu society as being capable of regeneration from within, without reliance on the British for support. What would such a society be like, and what would be the roles of men and women in it? In the new society, how would duty and virtue be defined?

The attempt at reconstituting Hindu society to present it as strong, historically continuous, and capable of self-regeneration became a conscious goal of nationalists, and entered into their attempts to forge an ideology when the Extremists emerged in the 1890s. The subsequent agitation over the partition of Bengal in the first decade of the twentieth century lent force and urgency to the attempt, as terrorist acts multiplied and revolutionary propagandists popularized their views in the Indian press.

Suprisingly, perhaps, many of the educated women who took up the peaceful goal of gradual social reform participated in revolutionary and even terrorist activities. Many women who had hitherto remained outside the culture of British India also declared themselves by their actions to be nationalists.

Women's motivation, insofar as it is recoverable, appears to have been both politically and economically inspired.[13] In accordance with the total boycott of the British goods and services which male leaders had declared, educated women began to use propagandistic techniques to urge other women to spin their own cloth, thus lessening dependency on foreign imports.[14] Many women whose names were unrecorded contributed their valuable ornaments to the National Fund established by the leaders of the boycott, and wives and daughters of prominent leaders made public gestures of support.[15] Female high school students agitated in their classrooms and a few young women committed terrorist acts. Others aided male terrorists by hiding weapons, passing messages, and offering refuge to men under suspicion. Some educated women produced propaganda in support of revolution, while the more moderate female leaders organized women in street processions and mass meetings, one of which brought together five hundred women in protest. When one of the leading male revolutionary propagandists was arrested in 1907, two hundred women, led by Lilabati Mitra, the wife of a male leader, marched to his mother's house with an address of appreciation.[16] Quite clearly, women did not feel themselves bound by the ideology of reform, which has assigned them the role of service to other women in the cause of social uplift. The very force and speed of historical circumstance were propelling women into action without regard to Moderate or, for that matter, Extremist gender ideology.

It is impossible to gauge to what extent women would have spontaneously participated in activities generated by the Bengal partition had there been no educated women leaders to provide skills in public speaking and organization. What is clear is that neither Extremists nor revolutionaries had thought of actively recruiting women. While this may appear surprising, there is an explanation for it which introduces us to the process of symbolic representation as nationalists engaged in it.

Both Extremists and revolutionaries—and they often merged during this period—had given attention to the ideological goal of imagining Hindu society as capable of self-regeneration. The society they wished to imagine included men and women, but models were drawn from traditional, timeless Hindu society. A cultural movement, begun in Bengal in the 1860s and continuing into the first decade of the new century, provided both the sources and much of the content of this attempt. In novels, dramas, and visual art, Bengalis were producing images of the changeless world of tradition, wherein men and women lived and worshipped according to age-old patterns.[17]

When authors attempted to deal with change in their literary productions, they examined only changes affecting men, while women remained in the traditional world, often serving to exemplify traditional virtues. The overall effect of the literary and artistic revival, especially when politicians borrowed its images, was to project an image of a well-ordered society which was organized according to gender divisions and which distinguished between the duty of men to uphold order and the virtue of women in doing so. Historical novels, a popular genre of the period, drew upon the same traditional materials but concentrated on those periods when peace had been threatened from without and Hindus had found within themselves the means to thwart the enemy.[18] Writers and speakers concerned primarily with religious experience had found within the multiple and various religious systems which constitute the vast complex of Hinduism the same evidence of strength and beauty; indeed, cultural revivalists, whatever their particular objectives, had declared that it was impossible to think of Hindu society and culture apart from religion. Religion, all agreed, permeated every corner of Hindu life. With such an attempt at traditionalizing both Hindu society and women's role in progress, it is hardly surprising that male leaders did not imagine that the women, whom they were relegating to the traditional world, would play an active part in the nationalist struggle. However, women did enter into nationalist ideology at the symbolic level, but they were preceded by the Hindu mother goddess. Her entrance marks the first attempt, initiated by men, to represent complementarity in gender relations in the changing society.

Hindu goddesses of mythological tradition and popular Hindu practice had suffered from the same ignominy visited on Hindu womanhood in the nineteenth century. Goddesses, especially in their sexual roles, had horrified the monotheistic and patriarchal British, and Hindu religious reformers, in their search for ways to present Hinduism as equal in philosophic depth and insight to Christianity, had relegated the goddesses to the ranks of ignorant superstition.[19] Interest in goddess traditions and goddess worship among westernized Hindus had begun to revive in the 1860s, due to the influence of a non-westernized and immensely appealing Hindu priest in Calcutta named Ramakrishna, who gathered around him a following of young western-educated men disillusioned with their condition.[20] It was not, however, until 1882, when the Bengali novelist, Bankim Chandra Chatterjee, employed the goddess traditions of rural Bengal in his reconstruction of a late eighteenth-century Bengali rebellion against foreign rule, that the goddess became a part of nationalist ideology; and it took the partition of Bengal to introduce her as an active force in regenerating India.

In Bankim's novel, *Anandamath*, the Bengali goddess Kālī, a sometimes sinister figure of destruction, garlanded with skulls but always a revelation of truth,[21] was identified with the country of Bengal. Bankim made the symbolic union in a song sung by the devotees of the goddess which, while addressed to the Mother, seemed to a potential recruit to be about the country. When questioned on this the devotee responded:

> We own no other mother. . . we think the land of birth to be no other than our mother herself. We have no mother, no father, no brother, no wife, no child, no hearth or home, we have only got the mother.[22]

Bankim, employing goddess mythology and the Puranic, or mythological, view of history, assigned Kālī the traditional role which mythology provided: she was the slayer of demons who inevitably arise in the course of the historical cycle, and her role was to restore the social order. To perform her historical function she demanded only that her devotees give her their total allegiance. As both the personification of the country and the historical process, Kālī, in Bankim's novel, stood as proof of the self-regenerative capacity in Hindu culture.

Though the novel was widely read in the intervening years when Congress was formed and factionalized, it took the Bengal partition for its revolutionary potential to be thoroughly explored. The man who did so was Aurobindo Ghose, educated in England from an early age, a classical scholar, and on his return to India in 1898 a committed revolutionary. Aurobindo worked as an English teacher in the princely state of Baroda, technically outside the domain of British rule, until 1905 when he went to Calcutta and became the force behind the revolutionary movement.

Before the move Aurobindo had made contact with secret revolutionary groups organizing in British India. In 1905, before the partition was announced, he had produced a tract modelled on *Anandamath,* which called for the organization of a secret society dedicated to the goddess and to the overthrow of British rule.[23] During the crisis over the partition his main work in Calcutta was as a revolutionary propagandist. Once partition had been announced, Aurobindo and others publicized his views in the press: Bankim was hailed as the seer of the nationalist movement; the force behind the movement was identified as the divine *śakti,* or energy, of the goddess; the form of address used in *Anandamath,* "Hail to the Mother!," was declared to be the mantra of the movement;[24] the British were depicted as the traditional demons of mythology, and British rule as *māyā,* or illusion; the male patriot was represented as a devotee of the goddess; and Mother Kālī was hailed as the movement's deity.

Why the invocation of the goddess and the politicization of her worship should have had the appeal that it did has puzzled historians.[25] It can perhaps be better understood if we examine a further elaboration of it in the Bengali press in 1908. In an article entitled, "The Worship of the Mother, the Country," the author stayed close to the notion of the goddess as she appears in mythology. He began by drawing the familiar picture of Kālī, with her garlands of skulls, engaged in a dance of destruction. As tens of thousands fell victim to her might, she called upon the people to purify themselves. In response, the author had the worshipper declare:

> We have understood that the Mother's seat will not be moved, and Shiva, who is under her feet, will not give up the form of a corpse, unless we can rip our breast open and offer up streams of blood to the lotus feet of the Mother. We are learning to burn selfishness, [and] self-pride. . . to ashes in order that the Mother may dance in our hearts; and that is why there is being a possibility of obtaining nectar as the result of the mother's worship. . . Fie on the birth of him who, being a son, has not worshipped the Mother!. . .Since everyone dies, die a noble death.[26]

Clearly, the mother here is the goddess, cast in her traditional role, but as *śakti,* or historical energy, her action is not inevitable. The cyclical return to order depends upon the character and action of devotees who must rid themselves of selfishness and pride, and the way provided is through offering themselves as the sacrifice.

Nectar in Hindu mythology is a regenerative fluid, and devotees will receive it through the transforming experience of heroic and sacrificial death. In the context of Kālī-worship the death imagined is a symbolic one referring to the conquest of the self, which is the goal of worship; in the context of the revolutionary movement, the meaning is more ambiguous. Traditional Bengali literature abounds with tales of death and regeneration, but revolutionary terrorists were confronting British steel. Whether physical or symbolic death was implied, the call to duty was clear, as were the virtues necessary to perform it, but the actors were to be men.

Is the union of devotee, patriot, and son significant? Does it exclude daughters? Aurobindo, who, if he did not write this piece certainly influenced it, worked with women, including foreign women, in his revolutionary council,[27] and these women were representative of others who sought to identify themselves with the nationalist struggle. While Aurobindo found such women useful as collaborators, it was the goddess who inspired him. As is clear from his writings, he was immensely moved by the terrifying potential in the figure of the Hindu goddess of destruction and willing to employ her to represent power in Hindu culture and historical process. Aubobindo's writings, however, do not provide evidence that he saw any connection between divine female power and the potential of human women for action.[28] He was not a feminist and, while seeking to give symbolic representation to men which drew upon the principle of complementarity between the sexes, did not recognize a need for finding ways to represent active women. His concerns were with the male patriot.

Although there is sufficient grounds for accusing revolutionary theorists of consciously excluding women's activities from their representations of patriots, there is general evidence from the period to show that the nationalists were somewhat confused about how to regard the newly active Hindu woman. As reform ideology came under attack, and nationalists turned to the dual attempt to represent Hindu society as capable of self-regeneration and the male patriot as deriving his motivation from Hindu sources, it was not at all clear what roles women should play, especially at the symbolic level.

Speaking in 1903 to an audience of male college students, Sarojini Naidu, a woman educated in English at home and abroad who was to emerge as a leading woman political and social activist in the years before 1920, declared that she was willing to lay down her life for the welfare of India.[29] The call to heroic death in the revolutionary struggle had not yet been made, and such statements as this were frequent in nationalist rhetoric. Coming from a woman, however, it points to the fact that she did not see her role as vicarious, but expected to be an active participant. Three years later, in 1906, appearing before the Theistic Society in Calcutta, she spoke of the "terrible individual responsibility of every human being for his [or her] own destiny"[30] and called upon the sons and daughters of India to live lives that would reflect the glory of their country. Although Sarojini Naidu had a brother who was a revolutionary and a father sympathetic to the cause, she herself was more drawn to the Moderate position, which still had the majority of adherents outside Bengal.[31] But in her efforts to define a role for women she drew upon some of the insights of Extremist and revolutionary ideology.

Speaking from the platform of the Social Conference, the Moderate organization dedicated to social reform, also in 1906, Sarojini addressed herself to the question of women's education. In tones which may reflect her awareness of British thinking on the "woman question," she argued that women needed education to equip them to be good mothers.[32] She introduced a discordant note, however; as she warmed to her subject, she accused the western-educated male audience of wanting to teach some things to women and deny them others. She cried:

> How, then, shall a man dare to deprive a human soul of its immemorial inheritance of liberty and life? And yet, my friends, man has so dared in the case of Indian women. That is why you men of India are to-day what you are. . . .[33]

And what they were, were men deprived of their inheritance, a reflection of the revolutionary notion implicit in the representation of the male patriot as devotee of the goddess, that men had deviated from the path of truth.

Sarojini Naidu was not alone in singling out western-educated men for attack over the issue of how much and what kind of education was available to women. A contemporary of hers, Saroj Nalini Dutt, a social reformer who worked with rural women in Bengal and herself a product of private tutoring in English in her westernized home, had similar ideas. Saroj Nalini had satisfied herself that village women did not fit the reform stereotype, but that they suffered from a lack of the kind of technological and practical help a modern education could provide. She wanted lantern slides and other modern technological aids brought to the villages. She observed that village women "may be illiterate. . . but they are by no means unenlightened" and she denied that they were not, "as generally believed, an inert mass impervious to progressive ideas and incapable of effort for self-improvement . . . ."[34] Rather, the cause of women's backwardness was the refusal of educated men who had reaped the benefits of education for themselves to extend those same benefits to women. The result, she declared, was that "The men have made a hopeless mess of everything. It is the women alone who can set things right now."[35]

The repeated invitations she received to speak to male audiences suggest that Sarojini Naidu's criticisms of western-educated men did not dampen their enthusiasm for listening to her.[36] Indeed, nationalists of all factions frequently engaged in self-criticism on their own over their struggles to work out a program of action and to revise their estimate of Hindu culture. Furthermore, many were attempting to disassociate themselves from reform assumptions about women, and women's own reconstructions of the image of village life aided in this effort. But the role of the active woman still posed problems, for women seemed not to favor the notion of complementarity that men espoused, but rather, the notion of autonomy. For reasons which may have had something to do with the politicization of goddess traditions and the implicit struggle waged between the male desire for complementarity and the female desire for autonomy, the Hindu mother was the first woman to be collectively rehabilitated.

As early as 1901, the religious leader Swami Vivekananda had declared to an American audience that whereas the West honored women as wives, Hindu society honored them as mothers. In grander terms, a writer in the liberal nationalist journal, *The Modern Review*, in 1910 contrasted the culture of the East to that of the West, asserting that in all the East the mother had been worshipped, but "Hindus alone of all the ancient peoples produced a worthy type of womanhood."[37] Foreigners sympathetic to the nationalist cause joined in this celebration of the Hindu mother, even to the extent of praising the Hindu widow, that much maligned figure of nineteenth-century reformers' thinking, as the embodiment of true virtue and cultural strength.[38]

Glorification of the Hindu mother may also have inspired a presentation of the Hindu goddess of her patriot devotee which appeared in the Bengali press at the same time as the one previously discussed. In this article, entitled "The Mother's Word," the Mother is made to speak to the foreigner:

> Stand still here and listen to my words; do not advance any further. You are guests, . . .One day each one of you assuming the aspect of robbers gave rise to great consternation in my peaceful cottage.
>
> Cruelly struck by your sword in the silent night, the decapi-

> tated heads of my heroic boys came to my breast crying "Mother, Mother" and obtained peace there, . . .The drops of blood of hundreds and hundreds of my sons are restlessly moving about in the waves. . . in the expectation of revenge. . . .You have by deceit, force and stratagems, looted all that I preserved, and have after calling my heroic sons robbers, proclaimed your own robbery as heroism in the history of the world, . . .Do not . . . make the blackness of your infamy more shining by coming like a shameless man to call me friend.[39]

There are a number of variations here which separate this mother from the traditional Kālī as revolutionaries imagined her. Though the peaceful cottage is a metaphor for the land, in recognition of Bankim's original symbolization, cottage and mother are distinguished from each other, and the mother is a domestic figure, no longer inhabiting the transcendent realm. She is no longer the agent of destruction, but rather of present regeneration, which she offers through the beast. The perpetrators of violence are now the evil and hypocritical foreigners who destroy what the mother preserves; and sons are no longer called upon to sacrifice themselves but only to exact the less well-defined revenge. The mother's weapon is no longer either the sword or the dance, but grief.

While the representations of the goddess as benevolent and nurturing are consistent with aspects of religious thought and mythological tradition, the deviation from the traditional picture of Kālī presents a neat correlation with the attention Hindu women activists had given to human mothers, whom they brought symbolically into the movement when sons had suffered. Revolutionary propagandists, concerned with motivating action through a call to religiously sanctioned behavior, may have been aware of the potential inherent in the symbolic representation of the human mother as sufferer; interestingly, in this representation the goddess plays no historical role other than that of preserver of the peaceful cottage, and attention is focused on the present moment rather than the mythic past.

If attention to the Hindu mother is to be taken seriously, new definitions of duty, virtue and gender appear to have been germinating in the early 1900s. The relationship of mother and son was being examined for what it could offer to the vision of a regenerated India; the duty to venerate the mother and to act was being assigned to the son, while uncomplicated virtue and cultural preservation were ascribed to the mother. Manhood was being defined as sonship, and womanhood as motherhood.

It is impossible to recover with certainty how educated and active women regarded the glorification of the Hindu mother. In the early days of partition women had contributed to the propaganda effort surrounding the invocation of the militant goddess,[40] and, as has been shown, leading women attempted, at least symbolically, to recruit other women through the appeal to human motherhood. Much later, in 1915, when the terrorist fervor had subsided, Sarojini's language still resonated with allusions to both divine and human mothers. Speaking once again at the Social Conference, she said of Indian women:

> . . .the women themselves, have begun to realize the cause of new spirit which is nothing but a renaissance of the old spirit which gave to India . . . those Savitrīs and Sītās.

Women, Sarojini claimed, relied on neither men nor government; rather on their own they were realizing:

> . . .their common womanhood. . . one question that has never changed since the beginning of time itself, and life itself, the duty of womanhood, the influence of womanhood, the sanctity of womanhood, the simple womanhood as the divinity of God upon earth, the responsibility of womanhood in shaping the divinity into daily life.[41]

There is, however, once again a jarring note in Sarojini's speech; women do not rely on men or government and do not find their inspiration from relationships formed in these quarters. Womanhood has an eternal quality to it, but it is also rooted in tradition. Its force is to be found in the classical heroines of epic tradition, who displayed their virtue in times of crisis.

In this apparently sentimental paean of praise to Hindu womanhood, Sarojini had actually managed to combine several often contradictory elements of nationalist thought about women. While omitting altogether the negative evaluation of the Hindu women characteristic of now outmoded reform thinking, she included the positive assessment of women's daily lives, with the obvious association with motherhood, and the tangential association of human motherhood with divinity. Also present was a reminder of the western-educated men's failings with regard to women's education, but it took a new form. Women were no longer held back by men's failings but had found sources of strength on their own. Traditional society was indeed capable of providing the impetus for regeneration, but not through a return to an idyllic and static past. Instead, the heroines entered as vital forces, embodying action.

It is possible at least to speculate, in the absence of additional supporting evidence, that women who played a political role during the Bengal partition and committed themselves to nationalist goals, found themselves at odds with the leadership of men who appeared to value them and their contributions only when they could be associated with motherhood. To see women only as exemplars of virtue in a traditional role did not accord with women's own conception of duty. Nor in their public roles did women desire to separate themselves from the goals of reform since many had discovered, as did Saroj Nalini, that Hindu women outside the pale of British Indian society were capable of improving themselves as its supporters.

Even in male-led organizations which favored the continuation of social reform, however, women with independent ideas encountered opposition. In 1910, Sarala Devi, a woman who had played a leading role in the revolutionary movement in Bengal and was a niece of the poet and nationalist Rabindranath Tagore, proposed to the Social Conference that she organize Indian women after the model of the YWCA, which she admired. Her goal was continued social reform. The male leadership of the Conference turned her down, and she wrote of the experience in the *Modern Review*:

> They are the so-called social reformers. They advertise themselves as champions of the weaker sex; equal opportunities for women, female education and female emancipation are some of their pet subjects of oratory at the annual show, . . . But woe to women if they venture to act for themselves. For the past few years man-manoeuvred women's meetings have been held in connection with the sessions of the Indian National Social Conference, . . .[When she proposed her plan] the avowed champions of the sex opposed it tooth and nail and issued a bull from Bombay discouraging the attempt and insisting on a man-manipulated meeting of women as usual.[42]

Did men view active women as simply a nuisance, or a threat? Undoubtedly the personalities of individuals helped determine how easy or how difficult cooperative effort would be. The liberal *Modern Review* found many occasions to praise socially and politically active women, often comparing them favorably to British women. In one article the author even praised Hindu society for the way it welcomed active Hindu women. Comparing the difficulties of the British suffragists to the active Hindu woman, he wrote, "as a social entity, both at home and in the business world, the woman of England still is nothing more than a helot." Another article, applying Hindu categories to

British women's experience, described the suffragists in their struggle against entrenched male power as "worthy followers of *shakti*."[43]

For many men, however, women undoubtedly posed a problem. As long as they stayed safely in the traditional world or in reform activities under male direction, they were admired, and their work could be viewed as a logical outgrowth of their nature as women.[44] When they moved over into politics, however, they were stepping into the male preserve, challenging the traditional division of labor which held the vision of the regenerated society intact. Men were understandably confused about the meaning of non-traditional behavior in women. An appropriate gender ideology adequate to explain and contain the changes women had experienced had not yet been formulated.

Sarojini Naidu, the far-seeing Moderate, provided an escape from confusion. She became a leading figure in the women's movement that developed in the second decade of the century, but she did not take advantage of the opportunities presented through association with the largely British-led organizations to mount a full-scale critique of male dominance. One British feminist resident in India, James Cousins, himself confused over Naidu's apparent lack of enthusiasm, accused her of perpetuating a "doormat" view of Hindu women in her writing.[45] He was unaware, however, of the playfulness and complexity of her thought and did not fully understand her commitment to the nationalist cause. Nor did he comprehend her ability to manipulate traditional symbols.

In 1915 Sarojini Naidu announced to an audience of young male nationalists that the ideals of Sītā and Savitrī, the classical heroines of epic tradition, were still alive, "because we [Indian women] have gathered a great deal of world experience, of high civilization, and growing responsibility."[46] Sītā, the chaste wife of Rāma, and Savitrī, who through her endurance rescues her husband from the dead, were to appear again and again in her speeches, and to them she assimilated the women of the day. The wives of indentured laborers became modern Savitrīs who "have followed their men to the gates of death, and have won back, by their indomitable love, the dehumanized soul of their men in the colonies abroad."[47] Kasturba Gandhi, the wife of the Mahatma, became a living Sītā who exemplified "the underlying spiritual ideals of love and service and sacrifice."[48] In January 1916, she asked an audience of women:

> Why are the names of Sītā, [and] Savitrī. . .so sacred and common-place in every household and the cause of inspiration?

. . . It is spiritual understanding and intellectual development that made them great. . . . No one can be greater than a good woman . . . .cooperation and help to suffering humanity are nation building works. . . .[49]

In linking "spiritual understanding" to "intellectual development" Sarojini eliminated the difference between the newly revalued traditional woman and the educated, activist woman, identifying both with the heroines. She even took on the role of Sītā for herself. Addressing a group of nationalist leaders, including the prominent Congressman, Motilal Nehru, when her fame was at its height and she was known throughout India and abroad as a leader in her own right, she said:

If I speak to you to-night it will not be as a politician, since, I say it over and over again, my woman's intelligence cannot grapple with the transcendent details of politics. I only understand the great abiding principles of patriotism which impelled each generation to give its own contribution of loving service to the Motherland. . . .[50]

Finally, speaking at the Congress session in December 1917, Sarojini identified herself and all Indian womanhood with Savitrī:

I am only a woman and I should like to say to you all, when your hour strikes, when you need torch-bearers in the darkness to lead you, when you want standard-bearers to up-hold your banner and when you die for want of faith, the womanhood of India will be with you as holders of your banner, and sustainers of your strength.[51]

By invoking the heroines to represent all Indian women, including the group of western-educated women whose behavior did not conform to traditional patterns, Sarojini Naidu provided nationalist society with a new view of gender which sanctioned non-traditional behavior through traditional references, but took account of the real ways in which women's lives had been changed. Hindu men had nothing to fear from the ideal of complementarity which the representation of the woman as heroine states; in fact, they had much to gain. Though the power attributed to women was symbolic, and even the modern Savitrīs could not restore life to a physically dead patriot, the capacity to restore spiritual vitality was real. Mahatma Gandhi, whose disciple Sarojini was later to become, experienced such power emanating from her. G. K. Gokhale, whom both Sarojini and Gandhi claimed as their political *guru* and a Moderate leader until his death in 1915, expressed his reaction to her when he spent some time with her in her father's house:

> You have given me new hope, new faith, new courage. To-night I shall rest. I shall sleep with a heart at peace.[52]

However great the personal charisma of Sarojini Naidu, it is important to remember that her attempts to ameliorate conflict between men and women were made toward the end of a period during which men and women of the educated class experienced considerable stress over women's new social roles. However much these new roles challenged the personal authority of individual men, they also were being taken up when attitudes toward reform were in the process of changing and the makers of ideology were intent on imagining Hindu society as imbued with power independent of British and western influence. Men, understandably, wanted to create an ideology which would not only inspire themselves and other men to act, but which would endow the male patriot with sufficient power and authority to succeed in what he undertook. Sharing power with women was acceptable if, as in the representations of both goddess and mother, powerful female figures played an inspirational role while remaining in the background, removed from the field of action. Women, however, looked for symbols that would include the desirable notion of complementarity while at the same time freeing women from domestic roles in order to make their active presence in the social and political realms both useful and necessary. In choosing the epic heroines women were fortunate in finding within their cultural and religious heritage a traditional symbol broad enough to encompass women's need for and experience of autonomy and involvement, and society's need to give clear meanings, traditionally justified, to the notions of duty and virtue.

Did Sarojini's use of the heroine tradition reflect the cultural truth contained in those traditions? The question is irrelevant. The tradition in the early twentieth century was a living tradition, and even men and women of the western-educated class, whom many have judged to be culturally alienated from their traditions, could find new meanings by engaging in the perennial Hindu practice of creating new syntheses. Was Sarojini Naidu a feminist? She was not a feminist according to the definition provided her by the British women who had come to India to work for improvement in women's condition in Hindu society. The social changes associated with the emergence of nationalism had already liberated Sarojini from the conditions that

British women found oppressive. As a contributor to nationalist ideology, however, she was an intellectual feminist, asserting through the invocation of traditional symbols that the new society could no longer carry old cultural baggage into the future.

When Rāma encountered Sītā after her rescue from Rāvaṇa, he denied that the rescue efforts had been undertaken for her sake, claiming that, instead, "I protected my own reputation and expunged completely the scandal and degradation which had been cast upon my own famous family line." It appears that western-educated men initially reacted in like fashion to the women who sought autonomy, but whom the men saw as products of their own benevolence. In response, the women, through Sarojini Naidu, echoed Sītā's response:

> Have confidence in me. . . .My heart, which is under my control, is ever attached to you. . . .

NOTES

1. From *The Rāmāyaṇa,* in Wendy Doniger O'Flaherty, *Hindu Myths* (Middlesex, England: Penguin Books, 1980), pp. 199–201.

2. For the influence of British racist attitudes on one important Indian nationalist see Susanne Hoeber Rudolph and Lloyd Rudolph, *Gandhi: The Traditional Roots of Charisma* (Chicago: University of Chicago Press, 1983).

3. On the founding of Congress see Leonard A. Gordon, *Bengal: The Nationalist Movement, 1876–1940* (New York: Columbia University Press, 1974), and Britton Martin, Jr., *New India, 1885* (Berkeley: University of California Press, 1969).

4. The literature on Indian nationalism and the history of Congress is voluminous. For a start see Daniel Argov, *Moderates and Extremists in the Indian Nationalist Movement, 1883–1920* (London: Asia Publishing House, 1967) and Gordon, *Bengal: The Nationalist Movement.*

5. [Bal Gangadhar Tilak], "His Writings and Speeches," in vol. 2 of *Sources of Indian Tradition,* 2 vols., William Theodore DeBary, ed. (New York: Columbia University Press, 1958), p. 169.

6. British officials claimed that the decision to partition the province was based on its unwieldy size and large population which made administration difficult. However, since the partition divided the province into Hindu and Muslim sections, many Indians took it as an attempt to divide and inspire hatred between the two largest religious communities. Furthermore, Hindus in Calcutta understood partition to be an attempt to localize the influence of Calcutta radicals. See Amales Tripathi, *The Extremist Challenge* (Bombay: Orient Longmans, 1967).

7. See especially Pratima Asthana, *Woman's Movement in India* (Delhi: Vikas Publishing House, 1974), and Manmohan Kaur, *Role of Women in the Freedom Movement, 1857–1947* (Delhi: Publishers Private, 1968).

8. As early as 1822 the orthodox reformer, Radhakanta Deb, had helped to produce a pamphlet for use in girls' schools which incorporated the golden-age theory. See *Stri Sikshavidhayaka (The Importance of Female Education; or Evidence in Favor of the Education of Hindoo Females from the Examples of Illustrious Women Both Ancient and Modern)* (Calcutta, 1882). Only the title of the pamphlet has been translated from the Bengali. In the early nationalist period Mahadev Govind Ranade was the leading exponent of similar views. See M. G. Ranade, *Religion and Social Reform: A Collection of Essays and Speeches*, collected by M. B. Kolesker (Bombay: Gopal Narayen, 1902). The centrality of concern for Hindu womanhood is reflected in reform literature and historical studies of reform. For a recent perspective which touches tangentially on the issue see David Kopf, *The Brahmo Samaj and the Shaping of the Modern Indian Mind* (Princeton: Princeton University Press, 1979).

9. The Mutiny, which broke out in 1857, was an uprising of sepoys (Indian soldiers in the Imperial Service) which spread from a garrison in northern India to Delhi and other areas. While most Indians remained loyal to the Raj, the British were badly frightened. For a study of the change in policy after 1857, see Francis G. Hutchins, *The Illusion of Permanence* (Princeton: Princeton University Press, 1967).

10. The Woods Despatch of 1854 gave official government approval to female secondary schools, thus allowing for the use of government funds. See J. A. Richey, *Selections from Educational Records, Part II, 1840–1859* (Calcutta: Government of India, 1922), p. 388.

11. The best early example is Pandita Ramabai Saraswati, a Brahmin woman who studied and travelled in England and America in the 1880s and whose later work in India was supported by an American foundation established for the purpose. See Clementine Butler, *Pandita Ramabai Saraswati* (New York: Fleming H. Revell Co., 1922).

12. In 1917 Congress elected its first woman president, Annie Besant, an Irish woman recently released from prison after having been charged with sedition. Besant came to India initially as a Theosophist but became involved in nationalist politics and supported the Moderate position as it was defined in the 1910s. The second female president was an Indian woman, Sarojini Naidu, elected in 1925.

13. See Kaur, "Origin and Growth of Extremist Women in Indian Politics 1900-1913," chap. 5 in *Role of Women in the Freedom Movement*.

14. Kaur, *Role of Women in the Freedom Movement*, pp. 96–97. Gandhi is usually credited with introducing the spinning wheel as both a symbol of protest and a serious attempt to encourage home manufacture. In the earlier period Bengalis had raised the cry of *Swadeshi* (own country) as a call to the manufacture of necessities in order to eliminate reliance on foreign imports. Women of the Tagore family were leaders in propagandizing this effort. For information on Sarala Devi, a niece of Tagore's, see Kaur, *Role of Women in the Freedom Movement*, pp. 103–107 and Jogesh C. Bagal, "Women in India's Freedom Movement," *The Modern Review*, June 1953.

15. It is worth noting that in India women's private wealth consists in their

ornaments, their access to landed property being limited by inheritance laws; hence, donating ornaments was an important and financially sacrificial gesture.

16. Lilabati Mitra was also the aunt of the revolutionary theorist, Aurobindo Ghose; see Bagal, "Women in India's Freedom Movement," *The Modern Review*, June 1953, p. 471. As the movement developed and women became more fully integrated into it, mothers of sons who had suffered continued to play a symbolic role. For instance, at the 1917 Congress, which elected Annie Besant, the mother of the Ali brothers—writers charged with sedition—was asked to preside, along with Besant and Sarojini Naidu, on the platform. See "Women Leaders at the Congress," *Stri Dharma* 1, no. 2 (Feb. 1918):17. At issue then was national unity, and the author in *Stri Dharma*, the journal of Women's Indian Association, stressed that the women represented the unity of Hindu, Muslim, and British in the nationalist cause.

17. Bankim Chandra Chatterjee and Rabindranath Tagore are the best known Bengali writers who engaged in the literary reconstruction of the traditional world. Oddly enough, an Irish woman, Margaret Noble, who took the name of Sister Nivedita when she came to India to devote herself to the service of Indian women and who is probably best known for her involvement in revolutionary politics, was instrumental in encouraging a renewed interest in painting, as well as in all artistic forms which embodied traditional values. For an introduction to the cultural complexity of this period see Stephen N. Hay, *Asian Ideas of East and West* (Cambridge: Harvard University Press, 1970). Also involved in cultural regeneration was Ananda Coomaraswamy, a Ceylonese Hindu who later became an internationally-known art historian and curator of Indian Art at the Museum of Fine Arts, Boston. For information on Coomaraswamy see Roger Lipsey, *Coomaraswamy: His Life and Work* (Princeton: Princeton University Press, 1977).

18. See Gordon, "Identity, History, Ideology: Romesh Chunder Dutt and Syeed Ameer Ali," chap. 2 in *Bengal: The Nationalist Movement, 1876–1940.*

19. See Ranade, "The Philosophy of Indian Theism," in *Religion and Social Reform: A Collection of Essays and Speeches*, p. 17. Ranade said, regarding the tribal and local origins of gods and goddesses, "It [the worship of goddesses] obtains still in this and other countries among people who cannot understand the universal harmony of nature's law as science discloses it." See also Ainslee Embree, "Bengal as the Image of India in the Late Eighteenth and Early Nineteenth Centuries: Notes towards the Definition of an Imperial Experience," in Marvin Davis, ed., *Bengal: Studies in Literature, Society and History* (Ann Arbor: Michigan Occasional Papers, 1976) and Knopf, *The Brahmo Samaj*.

20. See relevant passages in Kopf, *The Brahmo Samaj.*

21. For a recent study of Kālī worship as practiced in contemporary Bengal see David R. Kinsley, *The Sword and the Flute: Dark Visions of the Terrible and the Sublime in Hindu Mythology* (Berkeley: University of California Press, 1975).

22. Bankim Chandra Chatterjee, *Anandamath* (*The Abbey of Bliss*), quoted in

DeBary, *Sources of Indian Tradition* 2:158. There have been several full translations of the novel into English. See Chatterjee, *Anandamath*, trans. Aurobindo and Barindra Ghose (Calcutta, n.d.). Aurobindo began the translation in 1909 and his brother finished it a year later. The accepted date for publication of the first Bengali edition is 1882.

23. See Aurobindo Ghose, "Bhawani Mandir," reprinted in James Campbell Ker, *Political Trouble in India, 1907-1917* (Delhi: Government of India, 1917).

24. "Hail to the Mother" is a translation from the Bengali of "Bande Mataram." By the term "mantra" Aurobindo meant something more technical in Hindu thinking than what the word connotes in popular usage today. In an essay on Bankim, published in 1907, Aurobindo wrote:

> Among the Rishis of the later age we have at least realised that we must include the name of the man who gave us the reviving mantra which is creating a new India, the mantra "Bande Mataram." . . . A great and vivifying message had to be given to a nation or to humanity, and God has chosen this mouth on which to shape the words of the message. A momentous vision had to be revealed, and it is his eyes which the Almighty first unseals. The message which he has received, the vision which has been vouchsafed to him, he declares to the world with all the strength that is in him, and in one supreme moment of inspiration expresses it in words which have merely to be uttered to stir men's hearts and impel them to things which would have been impossible to them in ordinary moments. Those words are the mantra which he was born to reveal and of that mantra he is the seer.

Sri Aurobindo, *Bankim-Tilak-Dayananda* (Calcutta, 1947), pp. 7–8. The essay first appeared in Aurobindo's journal *Bande Mataram* on April 16, 1907.

25. See Tripathi, *The Extremist Challenge*.

26. "Desha-matrika Puja" ("The Worship of the Mother, the Country"), *Nayak*, Feb. 8, 1908, in "Report on Native Papers in Bengal, for the Week Ending the 15th Feb., 1908" (Confidential 7 of 1908), *Home Department Proceedings*, 1908 India Office Library.

27. Both Sarala Devi and Sister Nivedita (Margaret Noble) are reported to have been members of Aurobindo's Revolutionary Council at various times.

28. It should be mentioned here that students of goddess mythology in India as well as elsewhere caution readers against assuming that there is any immediate connection between religious conceptions of the divine as feminine and the status of women in society. Sudhir Kakar in *The Inner World: A Psycho-analytic Study of Childhood and Society in India* (Delhi: Oxford University Press, 1981) takes a generally accepted view, supported by Wendy Doniger O'Flaherty in *Women, Androgynes, and other Mythical Beasts* (Chicago: University of Chicago Press, 1980), that goddess mythology, originated by men, represents unconscious male collective experience.

29. Sarojini Naidu, *Speeches and Writings*, 3rd ed. (Madras: G.A. Nateson & Co., n.d.), p. 7.

30. Naidu, *Speeches and Writings*, p.9.

31. For biographical accounts of Sarojini Naidu see Tara Ali Baig, *Sarojini Naidu* (New Delhi: Publications Division, Ministry of Information and Broadcasting, Government of India, 1974) and Padmini Sengupta, *Sarojini Naidu: A Biography* (Bombay: Asia Publishing House, 1966). Baig notes that when Sarojini's father and brother were under suspicion for involvement in revolutionary activities, she wrote a letter to the press dissociating herself from them. Baig, *Sarojini Naidu*, p. 12.

32. Sarojini Naidu attended London University and Girton College, Cambridge, in the 1890s. She did not take a degree and spent much of her time in literary circles. Though little is known of her contacts with British women during this time, it is probable that she was exposed to the ideas and activities of British feminists.

33. Naidu, *Speeches and Writings*, pp. 12–13. Sarojini's years in England, between 1895 and 1898, had provided her with a basis for comparing the British and Indian educational systems. Much of what Indians were doing for the education of Indian women was borrowed from available British models which based the female curriculum on the supposed needs of women. A leading male educator of women, D.K. Karve, reminiscing about his efforts on behalf of Hindu women, said in 1913: "we hope to frame an optional course in which the goal will not be to prepare students for an examination, but to prepare them to be good wives, good mothers, and good neighbors": D.K. Karve, "My Twenty Years in the Cause of Indian Women, or A Short History of the Origin and Growth of the Hindu Widows Home and Cognate Institutions," paper read before a public meeting in Poona, 28 August 1913, *India Office Library Pamphlets*, P/T 196–209, p. 32.

34. G.S. Dutt, *A Woman of India: Being the Life of Saroj Nalini* (London: Hogarth Press, 1929), pp. 90, 96. Dutt wrote his eulogistic biography of his wife after her early death at the age of thirty-seven. He claimed to be quoting her, but by the time he was writing the connection between social action and women's traditional virtues had been made and become a part of nationalist ideology. His remarks, therefore, have to be viewed with some skepticism.

35. Dutt, *A Woman of India*, p. 99.

36. Sarojini Naidu occupied a special place in British Indian society throughout the first two decades of the twentieth century, largely because of the favorable reviews that her three volumes of published poetry received in the British press. These volumes came out in 1905, 1912, and 1917. For the British reaction see Arthur Symons, "Introduction," in Sarojini Naidu, *The Golden Threshold* (London: William Heinemann, 1906) and Edmund Gosse, "Introduction" in Sarojini Naidu, *The Bird of Time* (London: William Heinemann, 1912). The poems established her as the Nightingale of India, and gave her access to public platforms. As a public speaker, however, she devoted herself to the nationalist cause.

37. Satish Chandra Basu, "Female Education in Japan and in the United States of America," *The Modern Review* 3, no.4 (Oct. 1910).

38. See especially Sister Nivedita, "The Web of Indian Life," *The Complete Works of Sister Nivedita*, vol. 2 (Calcutta: Ananda Publishers, 1967). The work was first published in book form in 1904 and serialized in *The Modern Review* later in the decade. Margaret Noble had come to India in 1897 as a disciple of Vivekananda, taking the name Sister Nivedita when she joined his Ramakrishna Order. After his death in 1903 she severed her connections with the Order and devoted herself to nationalist politics. She became an influential exponent of the new view of Indian womanhood. See note 17 above.

39. "Mayer Vani," ("The Mother's Word"), *Yugantar*, Feb. 1, 1908, in "Report on Native Papers in Bengal, for the week ending the 1st Feb., 1908" (Confidential #5 of 1908), *Home Department Proceedings*, 1908, India Office Library.

40. Kaur, *Role of Women in the Freedom Movement*, pp. 96ff. Kaur mentions Kumudini Mitra who wrote propaganda for the Bengali magazine *Suprabat*. A representative piece, which may have been written by her, went as follows: "The mother can no longer be worshipped with fruits and flowers;/ The mother's hunger can no longer be appeased with words;/ Blood is wanted;/ Bands of followers are wanted with firm resolves." From *Home Political (Confidential) Proceeding*, nos. 7-10, December 1910, in Kaur, *Role of Women in the Freedom Movement*, n.6, p. 97.

41. Sarojini Naidu, *Speeches and Writings*, 2nd ed. (Madras: G.A. Nateson & Co., n.d.), p. 73.

42. Sarala Devi, "A Women's Movement," *The Modern Review* 10, no.4, (Oct. 1911).

43. Saint Nihal Singh, "The English Woman's Battle for the Ballot," *The Modern Review* 3 (Sept. 1910); and "Editor's Note," *The Modern Review* 3 (August 1910). *The Modern Review*, a liberal nationalist journal, played a major role in publicizing attitudes toward Hindu women which both glorified the achievements of active women and rehabilitated the image of the traditional woman.

44. Gandhi was later to adopt this attitude toward Indian women, welcoming them into the nationalist movement but claiming that their ability to contribute was derived from womanly ability to sacrifice for others.

45. Sengupta, *Sarojini Naidu: A Biography*, p. 69. Sengupta's biography gives an account of Sarojini's involvement in the feminist movement. See also Asthana, *Woman's Movement in India*, and Jana Matson Everett, *Women and Social Change in India* (New York: St. Martin's Press, 1979). For studies of British women's involvement see Geraldine H. Forbes, "Votes for Women: The Demand for Women's Franchise in India," in Vina Mazumdar, ed., *Symbols of Power* (Bombay: Allied Publishers, 1979); Barbara Ramusack, "Catalysts or Helpers? British Feminists, Indian Women's Rights, and Indian Independence," in Gail Minault, ed., *The Extended Family: Women and Political Participation in India and Pakistan* (Delhi, 1981); and Barbara Ramusack, "Women's Or-

ganizations and Social Change: The Age of Marriage Issue," in Naomi Black and Ann Cotrell, eds., *Women and World Change: Equity Issues in Development* (Beverly Hills: Sage Pub., 1981).

46. Naidu, *Speeches and Writings*, 2nd ed., p. 48.
47. Ibid., pp. 92–93.
48. Ibid., p. 20.
49. Ibid., pp. 76–77.
50. Ibid., p. 84.
51. Ibid., p. 185.
52. Ibid., p. 28.

CHAPTER FIFTEEN

The Soong Sisters and China's Revolutions, 1911–1936

MICHAEL E. LESTZ

A notable characteristic of the political thinking of many reform-minded intellectuals in early twentieth-century China was an inventive eclecticism. Leaders of political movements of both the left and right sought solutions to contemporary dilemmas not only in China's own long political and economic history but in the experience of the contemporary world. This was an unusual phenomenon in Chinese history and was in part the result of confidence-shattering conflicts with foreign powers that validated alternative approaches to the renovation of Chinese society. Perhaps in no other period in Chinese history were Chinese thinkers and politicians so captivated by the experience of foreign societies or so willing to propose radical solutions for the revival of the state. Rival ideas of reform and revolution that emerged first in the context of the historical experience of other societies were accepted with enthusiasm in China in the early decades of the twentieth century and were incorporated, sometimes in haphazard ways, into the ideologies and political programs forged by leading political thinkers.

The exceptional careers of Mayling and Chingling Soong epitomized in a striking way the manner in which this process of absorption and transformation of ideas could occur. Both women made major contributions to Chinese political life and practice. Both struggled to introduce new visions of femininity, novel modes of social organization, and a unique concept of political activism and morality. Drawing on their own distinctively bi-cultural upbringing and a strict Methodist faith, they created compelling and influential models for other Chinese of their generation. They worked energetically to alter the contours of China's political landscape and, despite the fact that their efforts were rarely harmoniously meshed, they succeeded, within their respective spheres of political activity, in establishing powerful identities in the normally androcentric world of Chinese politics.

ROOTS

The patriarch of the Soong family was an enterprising Hainanese named Charley Jones Soong, who came to America in 1875 to work in the shop of a relative who sold tea and silk in Boston. Influenced by a chance conversation with two of China's first exchange students to the United States (Wan Bing-chung and New Shan-chow—both members of the Chinese Educational Mission organized by Dr. Yung Wing), he decided to set off on his own to gain an American education in 1878.[1] After complicated adventures, Soong was adopted by a North Carolina family and ultimately received a degree from Trinity College in Wilmington.[2]

Soong's adoptive family were Southern Methodists and he was converted to their faith not long after his arrival in North Carolina. An article in the Wilmington Star in 1880 announced that in that year he had become: "the first Celestial that has submitted to the ordinance of baptism in North Carolina."[3] Charley Soong became a passionate believer in Methodism and was soon writing letters to his family in China that condemned idol worship and urged them to abandon the pantheon of Taoist and Buddhist folk deities.[4] Like Sun Yat-sen and many other late nineteenth-century intellectuals who spent long periods of time in America, he found Christianity an alluring substitute for the mix of religious beliefs and superstitious practices so prevalent in late Qing-village life.

First at Vanderbilt and then at Trinity College, Soong studied to enter the ministry. When he returned to China in 1886 it was to serve as a missionary near Shanghai. Dr. Young Allen who headed the missions of the Southern Methodist Church in southeast China was skeptical of native missionaries and plainly disliked Soong. In a patronizing report on Charley Soong's progress as a missionary, Allen wrote: "Soon [*sic*] will never become a Chinese scholar. At best he will be a de-nationalized Chinaman, discontented and unhappy unless he is paid far beyond his desserts."[5] Like many other leaders of the mission movement in China, Allen plainly preferred Chinese converts who applied the textual skills of Chinese scholarship to studies of the Scriptures and was impatient with Charley Soong's lack of docility and his unwillingness to work for the miserly wage normally allotted to native missionaries.[6] Soong deeply resented Allen's "one man power at Shanghai" and after several confining and unhappy years in the ministry, deserted it to join Shanghai's thriving business community.[7] Under Allen, Soong found that the treatment of Chinese by foreign co-religionists in China differed markedly from his experience in the warm and relatively democratic Methodist community of North Carolina.[8]

Although Allen's criticism of Soong was patronizing it was not entirely wrong. Charley Soong had been powerfully influenced and changed by his experiences in the United States. When he set up his own household in the Hongkew district of Shanghai, he built an elegant Western-styled mansion and furnished it throughout with heavy Victorian furniture. His three daughters attended a Shanghai Methodist school, learned English, studied the piano, and were raised in a manner that mirrored their father's own educational predelictions and the hybrid style of the Chinese elite of the treaty ports.[9] Soong's cultural preferences were also reflected in his rejection of Chinese cuisine. In preference to the delicacies of Shanghai cooking, he favored Southern specialties like roast chicken and gingerbread, and servants in the Soong household were specially trained to make these and other American dishes. In business, Soong capitalized on his knowledge of English to act as an agent for foreign firms importing flour-milling machinery, and rapidly establishing himself as a successful and well-connected compradore merchant.[10] His political sensibilities, too, showed a lingering fondness for America; he opposed the Qing monarchy and became an early adherent of the growing movement to replace it with a republican state.

Shortly after his return to China, Soong had married the daughter of an eminent Shanghai Christian family. Emily Hahn, an early biographer of the Soong sisters, has described Charley Soong's wife in the following terms:

> Her education and home training had made her a Christian of the evangelist type, with a strong belief in the efficacy of prayer and

> the abiding value of "good works" on the small, personal scale, the sort of thing which was soon to develop into social service.[11]

Prayer and a strict religiosity dominated the household, and as soon as the three Soong daughters were old enough, they were packed off to Wesleyan College in Georgia to continue their Methodist educations.

At Wesleyan, the Soong sisters were among the very few non-white students but they surmounted prevailing prejudices and played an active role in student life.[12] They also began to evince an interest in the politics of China and the problem of reform.

Soong Chingling, the second oldest daughter, in a theme which she published in a Wesleyan student literary magazine in 1911, criticized nepotism and dishonesty in Chinese political life and advocated study abroad, physical education, and Christian associations like the Y.M.C.A. as instruments of cultural renewal. She was critical of "strikes, riots, and political disturbances" and predicted that leadership by an enlightened elite of returned students would go far toward "lessening existing evils and reforming the lower classes."[13] Like many other intellectuals of her generation educated in the United States or in Europe, she was convinced that revolution would come from her own class, the "better class" of Chinese society. The ideal reformer was only a step away from the sort of missionary her father had been. In 1911, the implications of a broadly-based social revolution were as yet only dimly apprehended by the Chinese political avant garde, and the concerns of Soong Chingling's essay were echoed in other political treatises written by young, reform-minded intellectuals in the waning years of the Qing dynasty.[14]

In China, Charley Soong was playing a political role that was in keeping with his daughter's idealism. He was earnestly involved in the activities of Sun Yat-sen's revolutionary coalition in Shanghai and served as a banker and go-between to promote the organization's clandestine activities. After the collapse of the Qing dynasty in the winter of 1911, Sun Yat-sen appointed Soong to serve under him as the treasurer of the short–lived Chinese Railway Planning Commission created by Yuan Shikai's Beijing government.[15] Two of the Soong sisters, first the eldest, Ailing, and then Chingling, served as Sun's English-language secretaries during this time and when Sun Yat-sen was forced into exile by the Beijing regime in 1913, Soong Chingling and others followed him into exile in Japan.

During this depressing stage in the history of the revolutionary movement, the Chinese emigre community in Tokyo was a close-knit group bound together by its members' devotion to Sun's cause and by opposition to the Beijing government. Cloak-and-dagger missions to China, frantic attempts to raise funds, and unceasing efforts to win foreign support for the overthrow of Yuan Shikai characterized the movement in this phase of its existence. During this interlude of harried activity and uncertain political prospects, the relationship between Sun Yat-sen and Soong Chingling blossomed into a romance. In 1914, over the opposition of her father, Soong Chingling married Sun, who was nearly thirty years her senior, in Tokyo. In a disgruntled letter to a friend, that expressed Charley Soong's recognition that his daughters had become more independent-minded than he perhaps had hoped they would become, Soong wrote: "Don't send your children abroad. Nothing's good enough for them when they come home. They want to turn everything upside down. . . .Take my advice, keep your children at home."[16]

Soong Chingling and China's Social Revolution

For the eleven years before Sun's death in 1925, Soong Chingling was Sun Yat-sen's companion and aide but stood very much in the shadow of her famous husband. Most political wives in the Republican period were seldom seen and never heard. (Anthologies of Soong Chingling's speeches invariably begin with speeches given after 1925.) Although we know a great deal about Sun's activities during these years, little is known about the life of Soong Chingling. Only a few autobiographical fragments survive that provide a sense of her thinking and adventures during these troubled years in the history of the revolutionary movement.

During the early twenties, the Nationalist Party (Guomindang) that Sun Yat-sen led lacked a popular base and its leadership was forced to enter rickety and treacherous coalitions with local militarists and self-interested foreign powers to promote its revolution. Soong Chingling shared the perils of these years and in June, 1922 narrowly escaped death during a mutiny of warlord troops commanded by Chen Qiungming. In a rare autobiographical essay, she described her escape under the protection of troops still loyal to the Party:

> A rush of enemy troops flashed by, attempting to loot the Ministry of Finance and the Customs Superintendent's office. We picked our way through the crowd in the savage mob, finding ourselves at last in a small lane, safe so far from the looters. I was absolutely exhausted and begged the guards to shoot me. Instead

> they dragged me forward, one on each side supporting me. . . . Corpses lay about everywhere, some of the Party people and other of plain citizens. Their chests were caved in, their arms slashed, their legs severed. Once we saw two men squatting face to face under a roof. Closer observation revealed that they were dead, their eyes wide open. They must have been killed by stray bullets.[17]

She survived this perilous experience by disguising herself as a peasant and was led without incident to the gunboat on which her husband had taken refuge. The unreliability of warlord allies and the dangers of building the revolution on ramshackle coalitions that depended on their support must surely have made as strong and enduring an impression on Soong Chingling as it did on her husband and his followers. It was becoming cruelly apparent that reformist intellectuals of China's "better classes" and politically backward soldiers like General Chen could not make a success of China's revolution.[18]

During the early twenties, she and her husband shuttled between their home on Rue Moliere in the French Concession of Shanghai and Canton as Sun attempted to reconsolidate his revolutionary base. Soong Chingling played no public political role during this period, but it is clear that she was deeply sympathetic to the left wing of the Guomindang as it emerged in the years after 1924 and supported the growing sentiment within the Party for a political program of social revolution.[19]

During the early twenties, the Guomindang was undergoing a complicated evolution. The Bolshevik revolution and the spontaneous urban demonstrations that were China's response to the sell-out of Chinese interests at Versailles persuaded many Guomindang leaders that the Party could make a successful revolution in China only by first finding means to channel the unpredictable energies of the Chinese masses.[20] The consequence of this conclusion was that Party theoreticians began actively to explore means of broadening the Guomindang's base. In 1924, in what was to be a star-crossed *marriage de convenance*, a united-front was formed with the tiny Chinese Communist Party. Communists were admitted into the ranks of the Guomindang as individuals and the Party began to build new mass organizations designed to mobilize women, peasants, and workers.

Soong Chingling, who was twenty-five years younger than her husband, was of the same generation as many of the founding members of the Communist Party. She joined enthusiastically in the work of building a social revolution and remained committed to this goal even when the united front policy was disavowed by the Guomindang leadership.[21] In the intricate factional battles that developed following Sun's death in March 1925, she emerged from relative political obscurity to become a powerful voice on the left and began to play a significant role in the inner councils of the Party. She became closely allied with Wang Jingwei, Eugene Chen, and others of the Party left; was elected to the Central Executive Committee; and outspokenly opposed Chiang Kai-shek's increasingly obvious maneuveurs to succeed Sun Yat-sen as leader of the Guomindang.

She also began to speak out for the rights of women. A strong consciousness of the importance of women's rights was a conspicuous feature of the Left Guomindang's political program, and in the Party's campaigns against Northern warlords and in urban political work women activists energetically promoted feminism as a central component of revolution.[22] In two speeches written before the collapse of the united front in the spring of 1927, Soong Chingling addressed the role of women in China's revolution. She insisted that sexual equality was as important as the equality of classes and that women had a major role to play in defeating "feudalism" and tradition. In China's traditional society, she argued, women received educations suitable only to make them capable mothers and obedient wives. Now circumstances demanded that they play a role in the national revolution and stand on the same battle line with men.[23] In a speech titled "On Chinese Women's Rights Movement," she recalled witnessing the struggle of American women for voting rights and legal equality during her student days in the United States and insisted that the ideology of the Guomindang embodied a promise of universal rights.

This promise and other promises of the Left Guomindang were never fulfilled. In April 1927, Chiang Kai-shek dissolved the united front in a brutal purge of the left. Soong Chingling and many of her closest political associates were driven into opposition. After playing a brief role in the ill-fated government of left oppositionists created by Wang Jingwei in Wuhan, Soong Chingling fled secretly to the Soviet Union in July 1927. She believed, and this was a conviction she clung to consistently in subsequent years, that by jettisoning the mass movement and the doctrine of class struggle, Chiang Kai-shek had violated the ideals of Sun Yat-sen. Whether this was true was certainly debatable, but in an era in the history of the Guomindang during which virtually all of its politicians claimed to be orthodox disciples of the departed leader such an argument, even on the part of his widow, was almost obligatory. Shortly before Soong Chingling's departure for Russia, she issued a statement in which she reiterated her view of revolution. In it she wrote: "all revolution must be social revolution, based upon fundamental changes in society; otherwise it is not a revolution but a change in government."[24] For Soong Chingling, the ascension of Chiang Kai-shek to the leadership of the Party signified a retreat from the ideas which she, an independent-minded woman no longer constrained to keep the demure silence of a Chinese political wife, believed constituted the core of revolutionary activism.

During the two years Soong Chingling spent in the Soviet Union, conservatives in the Guomindang worked assiduously to deify Sun Yat-sen and to bend his inconsistent corpus of political writings to their own ends. Hu Shih, a liberal educator who opposed the new orthodoxies of the Nanjing government, rebuked this tendency in the following terms in 1928:

> out of the alliance between the Communist party and the Guomindang grew an absolute authoritarianism which has brought about the total loss of freedom of thought and opinion. You may now deny God but you may not criticize Sun Zhongshan (Sun Yat-sen). You need not go to church but must not fail to read the Zongli's Last Will and Testament nor to observe the weekly memorial service.[25]

An ironic by-product of this process of deification of Sun was that Soong Chingling's stature and position of moral authority grew higher in China. Like Krupskaya, Lenin's widow, Chingling represented an important link to the life of the party's founder and leader, and this permitted her, even in opposition to Nanjing and its politics, a political freedom and independence that would have been dangerous for other Chinese.

In 1929, Soong Chingling returned from the Soviet Union to participate in ceremonies that marked the opening of the enormous mausoleum built by the Guomindang for Sun Yat-sen outside the city of Nanjing. She announced publicly that her return was not to be interpreted as an affirmation of support for Chiang Kai-shek or the repressive policies of the Nanjing regime. In August 1929, in an open letter to Dai Jitao, a former secretary of her deceased husband and the leading ideologue for the Chiang clique in the Party, Soong Chingling hinted none too subtly at her real view of Chinese politics since 1927.[26] In the letter, she chided Dai for inviting her to play a role in the Nanjing government and accused him of forsaking his commitment to revolution. She was not, she wrote, "suitable for the life of a ward heeler (zhengke)" and went on to argue that: "A revolutionary is someone who is unhappy with the whole of the status quo and seeks to build a social system that will benefit everyone." The Guomindang of Chiang Kai-shek, she perceived, spared no effort in improving the appearance of Nanjiing and its various flashy public works projects, but the cost of this process of outward reform was the imposition of an internal tyranny that had taken the lives of thousands of able young people who might have helped to replace worn-out political credos and bring new life into the Party.[27]

Forthright condemnations of the Nanjing leadership were becoming increasingly rare in China by 1929. Although Chiang Kai-shek controlled only a few provinces in the lower Yangtze region, he was gradually expanding the activities of his internal security forces to quash dissent and discourage public debate of his government's policies. Soong Chingling, however, was invulnerable to such interference. By now her sister, Mayling, was the wife of Generalissimo Chiang and to attack someone who was both a relative *and* the widow of China's greatest revolutionary hero would have been politically unthinkable.

The relationship between Chiang Kai-shek and his outspoken sister-in-law was strained almost to the breaking point, however, when she became a founding member of the Chinese Human Rights Protection League in December 1932. This organization was created to promote the release of political prisoners, improve prison conditions, and provide legal aid for those incarcerated for political crimes, and the struggle for basic human rights in China. Branches of the organization were headed by some of China's most eminent intellectuals and the organization quickly became a "nail in the eye" of the Nanjing regime. Its active intervention on behalf of leftists and intellectuals arrested in crackdowns on dissent brought public notice to a sphere of activity the Guomindang wanted ignored.[28] On June 18, 1933, Yang Quan, the Secretary General of the Human Rights League and a leading figure in the Academia Sinica, was murdered in the French Concession, not far from Soong Chingling's residences, by Guomindang thugs. Even for those most prominent in Nationalist China, criticism had clearly become a hazardous enterprise.[29]

Despite these dangers, Soong Chingling remained selflessly devoted to the cause of social revolution and to a style of frank criticism that was discouraged or represssed by the reactionary elite of Nanjing. She continued to work for change in Shanghai and to speak out for the left throughout the years before the war. From the vague Methodist reformism of her youth, a reformism that associated change with the benevolent influence of the "better classes" on society at large, she had moved to an intellectual commitment to revolution that she shared with some of the best minds of her generation.

SOONG MAYLING AND REVOLUTION ON THE RIGHT

The youngest of the Soong daughters, Soong Mayling, like her oldest sister Chingling, was educated in the United States and was deeply influenced in her formative years by her experience in the South and at Wellesley College. Certainly no member of the Soong family was more "de-nationalized" as the result of time spent in America than the future Madame Chiang Kai-shek. While in the United States, she forgot whatever written Chinese she had learned, began speaking English with a distinctly Southern accent, and learned, as an adopted Georgian, to take umbrage whenever General Sherman was mentioned favorably.[30] Photographs of her taken as a college student show a young woman who, in the words of Emily Hahn, looked the part of the "perfect type of pre-war American college girl back in the days of banjos, fudge, and pennants on the wall."[31] When she returned to China in 1917 she was forced to relearn Chinese and, in a disgruntled letter to a friend, wrote that, "the only thing oriental about me is my face."[32] Unlike her father, who never quite escaped the burden of his impoverished past while in America, Soong Mayling, as the attractive daughter of a wealthy Shanghai family, felt perfectly at home with Wellesley and the life style of America's *haute bourgeoisie*.

Almost from the moment she returned to Shanghai, Soong Mayling was pursued by Chiang Kai-shek. Her family objected to the match however; Chiang was her senior by ten years, already married, and a Buddhist. He was also known to have led a dissolute life as a younger man in Shanghai, had a sometimes brutal disposition, and was said to be closely connected to gangsters of the Green Gang. Few strict Methodist parents anywhere in the world in 1917 would have found him an ideal husband for their daughter.

Chiang, however, persisted and as his star rose in the revolutionary movement, his suit seems to have won more favor from Soong Mayling's mother. (Charley Soong had died in 1918.) In December of 1927—by now Chiang was the leader of the most powerful faction of the purged Guomindang—the long-delayed marriage took place in Shanghai. Chiang Kai-shek agreed before the ceremony to convert to Methodism and the ceremony was performed by the secretary of the Shanghai Y.M.C.A.[33] The reception took place in the ballroom of Shanghai's Majestic Hotel, and the presence of many luminaries from the foreign diplomatic and business community of the city underlined the Guomindang's rejection of the strident anti-imperialism of the united front years and suggested the willingness of Nanjing's leaders to form expedient arrangements with foreign powers. A Shanghai reporter by snidely suggesting that there was a "methodism" in Chiang Kai-shek's "madness," captured another dimension of the wedding: Chiang was fully aware that his wedding established a useful bridge to the eight-million members of the American Methodist community.[34] The wedding was a public relations coup that served Chiang on many levels. It provided new legitimacy for his claim to be the anointed successor of Sun Yat-sen; it created at least the illusion that Chiang was renouncing his days as a xenophobe and baiter of imperialists, and it linked him to an elegant and cultured wife who could (and would) serve as a go-between in relations with the United States.

While a full account of Soong Mayling's activities as Nanjing's first lady, the "Missimo of China," is beyond the scope of this paper, it is possible to suggest some of the ways in which her background guided her approach to revolution and influenced her husband's political career. Unlike Soong Chingling, who by the 1930s shunned direct references to the family's Methodist faith, Soong Mayling continued to believe that evangelical reformism could be an important force in China's revolution.

One of the Guomindang's major experiments in mass mobilization in the thirties was the New Life Movement that was launched in the spring of 1934 from Chiang Kai-shek's military headquarters in Nanchang. Critics of New Life have argued that the movement was merely an attempt to force Chinese political life into the confining straitjacket of crude military rules.[35] While true in part, this analysis overlooks intriguing traces of something suspiciously akin to missionary reformism in the propaganda of New Life and even in the speeches of Chiang Kai-shek.

Although there is little evidence to suggest that these qualities of the movement can be directly attributed to the influence of Soong Mayling, there are passages in Chiang's speeches on the New Life movement that seem to resonate with another voice. Criticisms of China that were stock fixtures of both missionary tracts and the writings of returned students who found China wanting after their long sojourns in Europe or the United States are obvious characteristics, for example, of this excerpt of a speech given by Chiang at Nanchang when the New Life Movement was inaugurated in 1934:

> Why do we Chinese not live up to the standards of foreigners and why do they look upon us as a barbaric people? Everyone of us should examine himself and ask whether. . . [his compatriots] are

> as orderly, clean, and neat as foreigners in all matters? For example, are they [Chinese] as tidy in their dress, living habits, and behavior in classrooms and on the drill field as foreigners? Are people walking along the street as regulated as the foreigner who walks on the left side. Are our compatriots, like foreigners, capable of not spitting where they please? It is because our compatriots' lives are disorderly and they are unable to accomplish even these small things that foreigners can do that we are looked down upon and insulted as a race.[36]

What is arresting about this comparison of foreigners and Chinese is its defensiveness and willing deprecation of the bad habits of the masses. For Chiang Kai-shek, as for many missionaries, dirt and disorder were symbols of a grave social malady and provided evidence that twentieth-century Chinese civilization was inferior to that of the West.

In the same speech, Chiang Kai-shek suggested that his own life might be taken as a model for would-be reformers. He summarized the rigors of his own upbringing and made the following suggestion to his listeners:

> You should realize that the Chiang Kai-shek of today became what he is because when he was small he swept the ground, washed dishes, and cleaned chopsticks. If you want to accomplish an enterprise for the nation and to obtain an honor for the race and to become revolutionary leaders of China, you should emulate the example of Chiang Kai-shek. I hope that all of you can do this and create thousands and tens of thousands of Chiang Kai-sheks as future revolutionary leaders to make a contribution to our nation and race. A few last words: Please, take me as your model and with the greatest perseverance and resolve, implement New Life and go forward to accomplish China's revolution![37]

The leader might accept suggestions from his wife and others but there was no question about whom the people should imitate.

Madame Chiang Kai-shek repeated her husband's sentiments in her own speeches on the New Life movement. For her, Chiang Kai-shek combined "the courage of a soldier with the soul of a poet."[38] During the heyday of the movement, she acted as the director of the New Life Movement's women's department and promoted New Life through the Chinese Y.M.C.A. and the Officer's Moral Endeavor Society. In a 1935 speech she argued, in terms that were by now familiar to the captive audience toward whom the New Life Movement's propaganda was directed, that those who were "sloppy and careless about. . . personal appearance and general conduct. . . would also be untidy in thought."[39] For her, as for her husband, outward beauty was a precondition for inner spiritual change.

Madame Chiang's pronouncements on the status of women in China tended to parrot the warmed-over and by now outmoded Treaty Port reformism of the first two decades of the century. She argued that women should seek emancipation from ignorance and pit themselves against vice: "Their family life should be orderly, their houses clean, and they should work resolutely against gambling, smoking, drinking, extravagance, and other bad habits of life."[40] For Madame Chiang, as for her husband, social ills were identified with "bad habits" or disorderly behavior. Absent from her speeches on the question of feminism in China were any references to the relevance of this issue to the economic and social dilemmas then being faced by millions of Chinese.

If there was an all-too-obvious parallelism in the speeches of Soong Mayling and her husband on the behalf of the New Life Movement, it was certainly an outgrowth of her wholehearted and unqualified support for Chiang's party dictatorship.[41] Soong Mayling was content to sacrifice her opportunity to establish an independent political persona and operated instead as an attractive but clearly subordinate fixture in Chiang's entourage. Unlike her eldest sister, Soong Mayling never dared to move beyond the flaccid reformism of the Treaty Ports. She was a pioneer of sorts in twentieth-century Chinese history because of her energy and visibility, but she represented a political order that promised no fundamental changes in the role of women in society and that failed to see this issue in a framework that related the liberation of women to the society's other economic and social dilemmas. Unlike her sister, she never came to understand that the oppression of women in Chinese society was sustained by a substructure of economic and social values that had to be largely dismantled before meaningful change could occur. Class harmony, moral revival, and leadership by an enlightened elite were the tenets of her revolutionary faith, but such ideas, laudable as they may in part have been, failed to provoke basic challenges to the *status quo*. Missionary reformism and piety in a China wracked by civil war, famine, and foreign invasions missed the point and were positively harmful when offered as a substitute for more creative reform.

And yet, despite her inability to establish a political identity independent of that of her husband or his party, Madame Chiang Kai-shek did play a role with at least some important consequences for women during the Nanking decade. Her sheer visibility and work as an "America hand" for the Guomindang made her a player to be reckoned with on the political board in China before the war. Her talents as a linguist and interpreter of American ways made her an invaluable asset to a party led for the most part by male politicians with little experience of the world outside of China. In a political organization that was totally dominated by men, she was a woman who was obviously powerful as well as intellectually superior and better educated than many of the mediocrities to be found in her husband's inner circle of political advisers. Although the model of activity as a woman in public life that she established was something beyond the reach of most of her contemporaries, the very fact of her presence so close to the apex of the Nationalist Party's political hierarchy was valuable.

Conclusion

This brief descriptive summary of the careers of the Soong sisters suggests the sorts of dilemmas that confronted women in China in a century of revolution. Women were faced with ever-more sharply defined alternatives in Chinese political life. Soong Chingling's life was tied to the left's attempt to drastically alter definitions of self and society and to attain liberation, along a broad front, from the restraining structures of tradition and economic oppression. Like many other intellectuals of her generation she became progressively alienated from the Guomindang of Chiang Kai-shek and committed herself ultimately to the revolution led by the Communist Party.

For her younger sister, on the other hand, revolution signified an extrinsic and limited attack on the ills of society. Soong Mayling spoke often and even eloquently about democracy and economic reform but there was little in her political behavior to suggest that she had made an effort to convert her vaunted ideals into practice. Marriage to China's autocratic leader, even if Soong Mayling had had the inclination to help bring about basic reforms, was a role that left scant room for the emergence of a powerful and independent personality.

Notes

1. This mission was organized by Rong Hong (Yung Wing) who left an autobiographical account of his experiences in America in Yung Wing, *My Life in China and America* (New York: Henry Holt, 1909). A short biography of Rong Hong can be found in Arthur Hummel, *Eminent Chinese of the Ch'ing Period*

(Washington, D.C.: U.S. Government Printing House, 1943), pp. 402–405.

2. James Burke, *My Father in China* (New York: Farrar and Rinehart, 1942), p. 5. Burke's account of his father's experiences in China provides an unvarnished account of Charlie Soong's experiences in the United States. It was very unpopular in China and for a brief period of time in the 1940s Guomindang supporters in the United States facilitated its disappearance from library shelves. Two other useful biographical sources for the Soong family are Emily Hahn, *The Soong Sisters* (Garden City, New York: Doubleday Doran, 1940) and Elmer T. Clark, *The Chiangs of China* (New York: Abingdon-Cokesbury, 1944). Biographical sketches of the entire Soong family can also be found in Howard Boorman, *Biographical Dictionary of Republican China* (New York: Columbia University Press, 1970), 2:137–53. Illuminating descriptions of Charlie Soong's sojourn in the South can be found in Louis Moore "Recollections of 'Charlie Soong,'" *World Outlook*, August 1938 and in Fred T. Barnett, "The Romance of Charlie Soong, "*The Duke Divinity School Bulletin*, January 1942.

3. Burke, *My Father in China*, p. 6.

4. Ibid., p. 8.

5. Ibid., p. 14; Hahn, *The Soong Sisters*, p. 21. Bishop H. N. McTyeire of the Southern Methodist Church recommended Soong to Doctor Allen for mission work after discouraging him from studying medicine in the United States. McTyeire described Soong in the following terms in a letter to Allen dated July 8, 1885:

> But we thought better that the Chinaman that is in him should not all be worked out before he labors among the Chinese. Already he has "felt the easy chair"—and is not averse to the comforts of higher civilization. No fault of his.
>
> Let our young man, on whom we have bestowed labor, begin to labor. Throw him into the ranks: no side place.

Clarke, *The Chiangs of China*, p. 23.

6. For an account of Young J. Allen's long career in China, see Adrian Arthur Bennet, *"The Missionary Journalism in Nineteenth-Century China: Young Allen and the Early Wan-kuo Kung-Pao, 1868–1883"* (Ph.D. diss., University of California, Davis, 1970) and Warren A. Candler, *Young J. Allen: "The Man Who Seeded China"* (Nashville: Cokesbury Press, 1931). See also Young J. Allen, *The Diary of a Voyage to China, 1859–1860* (Atlanta: Emory University, 1943); Lin Lozhih [pseud. Young J. Allen], *Zhongxi quanxi luelun* ("A General Account of Chinese-Western Relations") (Shanghai: Meihua Press, 1876); and Young Allen, *The Gospel Liberating China: The Present Situation in China and Our Relation To It* (Shanghai: Mission Press, 1900).

7. Hahn, *The Soong Sisters*, p. 21.

8. Young J. Allen treated Soong as a "native preacher" rather than a missionary. The distinction was an important one. The salaries for Chinese clergy were a mere fraction of those of their American counterparts. Soong

received only $15.00 a month, which was ultimately insufficient to support his wife and children. Clark, *The Chiangs of China*, p. 31.

9. By the last decade of the nineteenth century, a thriving European city had grown up in the midst of Shanghai. The foreign zone of the city (the Concessions) was administered by the British and French and served as an important conduit for alien ideas and styles. A valuable but profoundly pro-foreign description of the development of Shanghai can be found in F. L. Hawks Pott, *A Short History of Shanghai* (Shanghai: Kelly and Walsh, 1928). For a scholarly treatment of the growth of Shanghai, see Rhoads Murphey, *Shanghai: Key to Modern China* (Cambridge: Harvard University Press, 1953).

10. Clark, *The Chiangs of China*, p. 33; Boorman, *Biographical Dictionary*, 2:142.

11. Hahn, *The Soong Sisters*, p. 26. Charley Soong's wife, Ni Kwei-tseng, was a descendant of a prominent Chinese official, Hsu Kuang-ch'i, who converted to Christianity in the early Ch'ing period. The following intriguing description of Hsu Kuang-ch'i's Christianity was recorded in a posthumous biography of Ni Kwei-tseng:

> Ever since the end of the Ming Dynasty, after Wen Ting-kung (Hsu) was converted to Christianity and began to respect the new education, *the family has maintained this tradition, treating their children in a manner absolutely free of sex prejudice*. (emphasis added)

Ibid., p. 22. For a biography of Hsu, see Hummel, *Eminent Chinese of the Ch'ing*, pp. 316–19.

12. The only other students of color were a few American Indians.

13. Printed originally in the Wesleyan College student literary magazine, November 1911. Reprinted in Hahn, *The Soong Sisters*, pp. 63–65.

14. Shanghai's radical community shared a strikingly similar view of revolution in 1911. For a description of Shanghai's radical circle before and just after the Revolution of 1911, see M. Lestz, "The Meaning of Revival: The Kuomintang 'New Right' and Party Building in Republican China, 1925-1936" (Ph.D. diss., Yale University, 1982), pp. 28–36.

15. This period in Sun's career is described in C. Martin Wilbur, *Sun Yat-sen: Frustrated Patriot* (New York: Columbia University Press, 1976), pp. 23–26.

16. Clark, *The Chiangs of China*, p. 58. Sun Yat-sen was already married at the time of the proposal and had three children.

17. The Chinese version of this text can be found in Sung Ch'ingling, *Sung Qinling zijuan ji yaniun* ("The autobiography of Sung Ch'ing-ling and her speeches") (Hong Kong: Huaguang Publishers, 1938). The translation here is from Hahn, p. 113.

18. For a biography of Chen, see Boorman, *Biographical Dictionary*,1:173–80.

19. Unfortunately, little information exists about Madame Sun's activities during the period of the United Front (1924-1927). I make this assumption on the basis of her speeches and comments on political matters made in the two years following her husband's death in March 1925.

20. This is clearly established by reference to the numerous articles on Marxism and social revolution published by major Guomindang theoreticians between 1919 and 1920 in the party's theoretical journal *Jianshe*. See Corinna Hana, *Sun Yat-sen's Parteiorgan Chien-she, (1919–1920)* (Weisbaden: Franz Steiner, 1978). See, too, James Gregor and Maria Chang, "Marxism, Sun Yat-sen, and the Concept of Imperialism," *Pacific Affairs*, 55, no. 1 (Spring 1982):54–72.

21. A translated anthology of some of Madame Sun's earliest political speeches that establishes this point can be found in Sung Qingling, *The Struggle for New China* (Beijing: Foreign Language Press, 1952), pp. 1–104. Chinese versions of these speeches (and others not translated in the English anthology) can be found in *Sung Qingling xuanji* (Hong Kong: Zhonghua Press, 1967).

22. Many conservative Guomindang leaders felt uneasy about the active role women organizers had begun to play in party affairs during the May 30th Movement and the Northern Expedition. This phenomenon was roundly denounced, for example, by the Guomindang propagandist Dai Jitao (with whom Madame Sun would have occasion to cross swords publicly in 1929) in a speech in a 1928 anthology of speeches entitled *Qingnian zhi lu* ("The path for youth") (Shanghai: Minzhi Press, 1928). Dai was critical not only of women who chose to play a political role but also of students. See Ibid., pp. 17–45. A rather different description of women and the role they played in the Northern Expedition can be found in Hsieh Ping-ying, *Autobiography of a Chinese Girl*, trans. Anor and Adet Lin (New York: John Day, 1940).

23. See "Funu yingdang canjia guoming geming" ("Women should participate in the national revolution"), a speech given on February 12, 1927, for an expression of this outlook. The Chinese text is in Sung Ch'ing-ling, *Sung Qingling Xuanji*, pp. 14–15.

24. "Lun zhongguo nuquan yundong" ("About the Chinese women's rights movement"), March 1927. in Ibid., pp. 17–19.

25. Hu's statement is translated and reproduced in Jerome B. Grieder, *Hu Shih and the Chinese Renaissance: Liberalism in the Chinese Revolution, 1917–1937* (Cambridge: Harvard University Press, 1970), p. 230.

26. See *Sung Qingling yisheng quanchi* ("Intriguing aspects of the life of Sung Qingling") (Hong Kong, 1977), pp. 15–18.

27. Ibid., p. 18.

28. An interesting description of Guomindang internal security efforts in the 1930s and Chiang Kai-shek's security chief, Dai Li, can be found in Shen Cui and Wen Qiang, *Dai Li qi ren* ("That person Dai Li") (Peking: Wenshi zilaio qubanshe, 1980).

29. For another description of the hazards of dissent, see Letsz, "The Meaning of Revival," pp. 233–53.

30. The following excerpt from Emily Hahn's biography of the Soong sisters reveals much about Sung Mayling's feelings for the South:

> One summer when the girls were at a northern summer school, the history tutor asked Mayling to describe Sherman's march through

> Georgia. Mayling said, "Pardon me, I am a Southerner and that subject is very painful to me. May I omit it?"

Hahn, *The Soong Sisters*, p. 63.

31. Ibid., p. 95
32. Ibid.
33. Chiang's converson took place ultimately in 1930.
34. Burke, *My Father in China*, p. 228.
35. Excellent descriptions of the New Life Movement and its aims can be found in Arik Dirlif, "The Ideological Foundations of the New Life Movement: A Study in Counterrevolution," *The Journal of Asian Studies*. 39, no.1 (August 1975):945–80, and in Samuel Chu, "The New Life Movement Before the Sino-Japanese Conflict," in Gilbert Chan, ed., *China At the Crossroads: Nationalists and Communists, 1927-1949* (Boulder, Colorado: Westview Press, 1980).
36. Excerpted from "Implementing the New Life Movement," *General Report of the New Life Movement for 1934* (Nanchang, 1935), pp. 80–85. A full translation of this speech and other writings by notable Guomindang figures of the late twenties and thirties will appear in a forthcoming volume edited and translated by Cheng P'ei-kai and myself to be titled: "The Voice of the Right in the Nanking Decade."
37. Ibid.
38. Sung Meiling, *War Messages and Other Selections* (Chungking: Free China Press, 1938), p. 271.
39. Ibid., p. 306.
40. Ibid., p. 312.
41. Ch'ien Tuan-sheng has commented on Chiang Kai-shek's relationship with his political followers in these terms:

> The Actonian axiom, power corrupts and absolute power corrupts [Chiang's] relationship with other men. In his anxiety to cling to power, more and more he mistrusts people who criticize him or even dare to differ with him. The men who work with him have to be first and last loyal to him personally. In the end he became the leader of a party of servile men but not a party of men and ideas, which were once the glory of the Reorganized Kuomintang.

In political terms, Chiang's expectations of Soong Mayling fit a similar mold. Ch'ien, *The Government and Politics of China* (Cambridge: Harvard University Press, 1950), p. 123.

PART IV

Women, Religion and the Transformation of Society in North America

CHAPTER SIXTEEN

Iroquois Religion and Women in Historical Perspective

ANNEMARIE SHIMONY

INTRODUCTION

The term "Iroquois" is broadly used to refer to a group of sixteen historically identifiable Native American peoples having cognate languages. Some of these peoples are now extinct, some have lost knowledge of their aboriginal language, and others still speak modern Iroquoian languages. Among these languages it has been determined that Cherokee is the most divergent, and it is estimated that the differentiation of Cherokee from the others dates from approximately 3500 to 4000 years ago.[1] Thus the Northern Iroquoian languages are more closely related to each other than they are to Cherokee, which represents the southern branch. In this article I shall confine the discussion to the Northern Iroquois, and more particularly yet, to the best known of the Iroquoian speakers, namely the members of the famous League of the Iroquois: the Mohawk, Oneida, Onondaga, Cayuga, and Seneca. These tribes, that once lived across most of the breadth of upper New York State, were joined in 1722 or 1723 by the Tuscarora, another Iroquoian-speaking people, and were thereafter known as the Six Nations.

Collectively this group is interesting for many reasons. First, they had developed and continue to retain a fascinating culture. Thanks to the most famous American ethnography, *League of the Ho-dé-no-sau-nee or Iroquois*, by Lewis Henry Morgan,[2] it is widely known that the Iroquois were a matrilineal society with a sophisticated political organization patterned essentially upon the social organization. Thus, the important involvement of women in Iroquois society and politics has long been emphasized. Second, the Iroquois played a significant role overall in American history, for they figured crucially in the colonial wars, the fur trade, and the American Revolution. Even the War of 1812 saw both the newly born nation and Great Britain vying for Iroquois allegiance, each side attempting to enlist Iroquois warriors to its own advantage. For at least two centuries, therefore, Iroquois chiefs had an opportunity to play off rivals in order to benefit from a balancing of powers, while Iroquois warriors gave force to these policies by backing threats with armed attacks on enemies. Third, and happily for the ethnohistorian, the Six Nations are a well documented people making it possible to infer about social changes from the time of contact to the present. In addition, there exists a rich literature on the Huron, an Iroquoian people who exhibited cultural patterns akin to those still seen among contemporary Iroquois.[3] The seventy-three volumes of the Jesuit Relations[4] from 1610 to 1791 are especially valuable in providing a fully documented date-line. By examining the social organization, the religion, and the status of women reported in the Jesuit Relations, one can appreciate the extent of cultural conservatism as well as cultural innovation since that time.

For purposes of analysis it is convenient to identify several historical periods: the pre-contact period; the early contact period, when European influence was still small; the colonial period, up to and including the American Revolution; the post-Revolutionary period of general dislocation, concluding with confinement on reservations; and the reservation period. The last should in turn be subdivided into that period when most Iroquois did indeed inhabit the reservations and the post-World War II period in which more and more people moved to urban areas as their primary place of residence. Since each of these periods presented the Iroquois with different problems, it is only natural that there should have been distinctive responses in social organization, religion, and the role of women. This article will trace some of the changing responses and will attempt to give structural and psychological explanations for the direction of the changes, particularly of those pertaining to women and their religious participation.

Pre-contact and Early Contact Periods

In the pre-contact period the general cultural patterns of the Northern Iroquoian society were already discernible. Horticulture and collecting were combined with fishing and hunting, and it is entirely probable that the prominent sex division of labor, whereby women planted and collected while men fished and hunted, already existed. The units of residence were extended families, presumably matrilocal, who inhabited longhouses in villages of about a thousand souls.[5] Although the individual villages were economically self-sufficient, they were probably united on a tribal level. Already there were tribal wars, giving the men an activity which was to become increasingly prominent after European contact in 1543. In particular, the desire for European trade goods and for control of the beaver trade, which flourished along the St. Lawrence River in the late sixteenth and seventeenth centuries, caused the Mohawk to attack the Iroquoians and Algonquians living there and may have been the impetus for the formation of the League of the Iroquois.[6] The French intervened just enough on the anti-Iroquois side to force the Mohawk to rely upon raids for trade goods, thus actively stimulating the pattern of warfare. It is also conjectured that the desire for the trade goods which finally reached the Hurons induced the Seneca to transform their warfare pattern from ceremonial to economic conflicts.[7] As a result, isolated communities were further transformed into potential confederacies. Trigger also conjectures that the Mohawk ended their military raids against the Montagnais-Algonquin-French alliance in the St. Lawrence Valley not from a fear of their combined strength, but more from a desire to establish a beaver monopoly of their own, comparable to that of their northern enemies, at the fledgling Dutch trading post at Fort Orange.[8] One can therefore surmise that the political acumen for which the Iroquois are celebrated was already in evidence at this time, approximately 1624 A.D.

The increasing demand for beaver pelts by Europeans and for guns by the Indians, as well as the shifting alliances by European powers with various tribes which the latter believed to be helpful to their aims, set off an exceedingly complicated chain of inter-tribal conflicts.[9] For the Iroquois these conflicts meant an enhancement of the male warrior complex, but also a devastation of the male population. When one adds the ravages of smallpox and other epidemic diseases introduced into the Northeast, the consequence was a depopulation of such magnitude that social change could not but occur. Male leaders died or were absent on the warpath, forcing women into prominence at home. And, to the extent that an increasing number of prisoners had to be adopted into the tribe in order to replace the lost warriors, a process in which the women made the decisions, women undoubtedly gained in power. As Trigger mentions, it was at this time, the seventeenth century, that the putative aboriginal matrilineal institutions of the Iroquois were enhanced.[10] Wallace talks of Iroquois society as one with characteristically sedentary women and mobile men—men who leave for war, roam to hunt, and journey on diplomatic missions—and just such a pattern emerged in this period.[11]

The fact that the Jesuit Relations did not describe women's political influence in terms as positive as was reported in later ethnographies may also indicate that the structural transformation of Iroquois society was just beginning, as one would expect from the foregoing analysis. It is of course possible that the Jesuits were not attuned to noticing female power, but since they reported quite accurately on other topics, that is a less plausible assumption.

The religious and ceremonial observances among the Huron in the early seventeenth century were also predominantly within the male domain. They emphasized obsequies for the dead, dream interpretation, and cures for supernaturally caused illness, for witchcraft and for the unrequited desires of one's own soul. These concerns for the problems of the living were prominent in the well known Huron winter festival, *ononharoia* ("the upsetting of the brain"), during which men and women ran through the villages as if demented and required that objects revealed in their dreams be guessed and presented to them. It was only in this way that the participants could "cast out their madness," and the sick person for whom the rite had been initiated could recover. Dreams which revealed the desires of the soul often had to be interpreted by shamans, for only they knew the true etiologies and cures. Since shamans among the Huron were always male—women with supernatural power confined themselves to divining[12]—one has an overall impression that men dominated the Huron religious observances. Women participated and were the objects of religious solicitude for they needed to have their dreams interpreted as much as men did, but they did not direct the activities. This impression is further reinforced by the absence of agricultural calendric rituals from the Huron observances. Tooker also noted that the primary focus of Huron—and, by extrapolation, of seventeenth-century Iroquois religion generally—was curing, and that the shift to the observances of the growing cycle came later.[13]

The most spectacular religious observance of the Huron was the Feast of the Dead, a re-interment in a communal grave of all those who had died in the preceding temporal interval (varying from eight to twelve years). Interestingly, it was the women who with seeming equanimity stripped the flesh from the semi-decomposed cadavers before they were re-buried, but otherwise the ritual was directed by the chiefs and Masters of the Feast.[14] Among the Iroquois today the religious society in charge of communal graves and of the welfare of the departed is considered to be a women's society and is led by two head ladies who organize the observances, but that was obviously not the case in the seventeenth century. Furthermore, because many personal illnesses were thought to derive from careless neglect of the dead, and because curing rituals, which were a male activity, were the remedy for such illnesses, these great Feasts of the Dead were classified as being in the male rather than in the female domain.

Finally, the Jesuit Relations state that Huron ceremonial life, particularly the transmission of mythological tales, was in the hands of old men.[15] It should be said, however, that in spite of the prestige and ritual importance of men, women did have a certain freedom of expression, particularly in their homes.[16] Though they did not seem to have had much influence over their sons, they educated their daughters, if only by example. Despite the disruptive wars and the Christian proselytizing (which was not particularly successful), one is led to infer that the culture was sufficiently immune to pressure to change that religious attitudes were transmitted as a matter of course. In fact, one measure of the unquestioned adherence to the cultural prescriptions of Iroquois religion was the difficulty the Jesuits encountered in their attempts at conversion. Iroquois society emphasizes conformity, and one who deviated from the norm was susceptible to being stigmatized as a witch, a crime punishable by death. As long as such beliefs remained there was no particular need to emphasize religious education. People had recourse to the curing societies and the shamans with complete confidence, and it should be no surprise that the Jesuit fathers were perceived in the light of these beliefs. Since the great epidemic of 1634–1640 coincided with the arrival of the missionaries, it was but a logical step to believe that they were the sorcerers who had brought on the disease. These beliefs deterred conversions, as did the conviction that the souls of the converted would congregate in a different place from that of the pagans, and no one wished to be separated from loved ones after death.

In summary, the European entry into the Northeast initiated many structural social changes which had profound consequences for women and for their political and religious influence. Certainly the involvement of the Iroquois raiding parties in larger and deadlier combats had a devastating effect on the male population. The beaver wars also widened the distance in time and space between men and women. Men were gone longer than on the previous hunting and raiding expeditions, and they roamed farther afield. Women left at home to cultivate also had to assume more responsibilities, and to the extent that they replaced the dead with captives, they played an enhanced political role. It is also said that the loss of so many senior warriors left the governance of the society more in the hands of the younger men and of the women who influenced them. The incipient matrilineal organization, which is hinted at in the earlier literature, became more pronounced during this period, and the Iroquois towns were clearly organized along matrilineal lines by the end of the seventeenth century.[17]

COLONIAL PERIOD

During the colonial period, from the early seventeenth century through the American Revolution, many of the aforementioned social transformations persisted among the Iroquois, despite radical changes in the political fortunes of the League. This was the era in which the Iroquois were reduced from courted allies and feared warriors to a neglected people. The major causes of this decline were the vagaries and the consequences of the fur trade, the sweeping epidemics, and the changing power relations of the Europeans and the American colonists, who ultimately deprived the Iroquois of most of their homelands.

As long as the Europeans competed with each other for furs, the Iroquois understood that it would be to their advantage to intensify the competition among the colonial powers by offering their allegiance first to one, then to another. On the European side there was also a jockeying to become the favorite trade partner. For example, the Dutch, and later the English, broke the French-Huron monopoly on the St. Lawrence River by offering to the Iroquois, particularly the Mohawk, more and better goods in exchange for the furs, and somewhat later by also being generous in trading guns and ammunition in Albany. The consequence of the accelerating trade was that the Iroquois became ever more dependent on European goods (as evidenced by the archaeological finds from sites of this period[18]) to such an extent that the various tribes also became embroiled in internecine competition. Rivalry occurred not only between the League and non-League tribes, but also among the members of the League. The League may well have been founded as a collective response to the fur trade, and its ideal was to maintain peace within the League and to wage effective war outside it. The realities of the situation in the seventeenth and eighteenth centuries precluded the full realization of these aims. Local conditions often differed, and communities were motivated to act in their own interest. Already by 1640, for example, a perceived scarcity of beaver in the Mohawk territory of eastern New York,[19] which was perhaps due to a siphoning off of furs by New England traders,[20] caused a scramble for control of those nations, routes, and territories which were crucial for the delivery of pelts. Within the League, the Mohawk at the eastern door and the Seneca at the western door acted competitively as much as cooperatively,[21] and an undercurrent of animosity persisted in spite of their alliance. Another illustration of intra-League tension was the smoldering Onondaga-Mohawk competition,[22] which in 1647 prompted the Onondaga to attempt a separate peace with the Huron, an initiative foiled only by the Mohawks' murder of a Huron embassy to the Onondaga.[23]

Iroquois military conquests of tribes outside the League escalated steadily from 1630 to 1680. During that time the Iroquois not only made frequent forays against the French, but attacked most of the surrounding tribes, including the Algonquin in the Ottawa valley, the Montagnais, the Abenaki, the Huron, the Mahican, the Sokoki, the Maliseet, the Ottawa, the Nipissing, the Petun, the Neutral, the Erie, the Susquehanna, and the Illinois. There were occasional large-scale attacks, as large as the thousand-man force which dispersed the Huron in 1649. Diplomacy in search of alliances to support such extensive military activity engaged much of the attention of the Iroquois at this time.

Warfare and diplomacy were male activities. Nevertheless, women were influential to the extent that they advised warriors, articulated the need for adoptees from among the prisoners taken in combat, and supplied the men with such provisions as corn and moccasins for their expeditions.[24] Furthermore, women played a role in the ritual aspects of warfare, a topic which requires special attention.

Although the warfare patterns changed during the colonial period from individual raids for revenge and prestige to campaigns intended to disperse entire tribes, it can nevertheless be assumed that the rituals, feasts, and songs which accompanied the departure of the warriors and their return with captives did not change very much, and continued to fulfill psychological needs that were both secular and sacred. Lafitau certainly gives the impression that, aside from the boasting and courage-enhancing character of these rites, they were "religious," particularly in the familiar Iroquois pattern of supplication to higher spirits and consequent expectation of favorable response.[25] Warriors would feast on dog, participate in a characteristic "striking stick" dance (recounting exploits and enlisting participants), sing personal war chants (also known as the warrior's death song—Adõwa), and prepare themselves for the rigors of the expedition. Then the warriors, flanked by their wives and children adorned in their finery, invoked the spirits to grant them a safe return. The men left the village, preceded by the chief singing his death song, and the women met them some way outside, provisioned them with food and divested them of unnecessary gear.[26]

The return of a warrior was also heavily ritualized. A messenger gave the death cry outside the village, alerting the population to his arrival, and entered to tell first of their own casualties and fatalities. A suitable period for mourning was then allowed to the bereaved, before the victories and successes would be recounted and the captives led into the village.[27] The severe tortures inflicted on the prisoners may have been a manifestation of the anxiety and the aggression of the torturers. The Jesuit Relations present evidence that the torturers had ambivalent attitudes toward their victims. On the one hand they were annoyed if the victim did not cry out, and feared that misfortune would result from his stoicism.[28] On the other hand, more exalted sentiments must also be recognized, for the captives were expected to dignify their own deaths and to bring honor to their tribe by stoically singing their death chants to the very end. Thus the mundane business of warfare was raised to a more religious level, thereby integrating the sacred and the secular realms. Had the situation been reversed, the torturers would have been no less stoic. No matter how courageous the warriors were, however, the many observances dedicated to emboldening them, strengthening their resolve, supplicating for their safe return, and expressing gratitude for their success gave testimony to a full realization of the mortality of man and of the dangers involved in expeditions to hostile territories.

It can be argued that on the European side the establishment of the Christian religion among the Iroquois was as much a consequence of politics and trade as of religious solicitude for the souls of the unbaptized. As individuals, the missionaries faced their labors in the New World with religious sincerity and courage, mindful of the interest of the Indians as they conceived it. But as members of powerful orders which were deeply involved in European politics, they were subject to forces often at odds with their individual convictions. Missions were used to infiltrate tribes and to establish French influence, either to acquire furs or to counteract the Dutch and English. To suggest that the flag followed the beaver, and the Church the flag, is not too far fetched. Governor Frontenac's oft-quoted, and somewhat unfair, comment to LaSalle in 1672 concerning the Jesuit missionaries, "to speak frankly to you, they think as much of the conversion of the beaver as of souls"[29] is testimony to the secular motivation of some of the missionary activity, and incidentally is also an indication that the economic and political rivalry between the pope and the French king had manifestations in the New World.

As long as the difference in power between the parties to an alliance was not too great, both could play for advantage, and the Iroquois, for their part, accepted the missions quite opportunistically. When they desired an alliance with one European power, they tolerated its missionaries, but as soon as the alliance no longer seemed necessary the missionaries could be expelled and the missions destroyed. Obviously, the missions were not desired primarily for instruction or conversion, but rather as instruments in the service of a political arrangement. The mission known as Sainte Marie, established among the Onondaga after the Iroquois-French peace of 1653 and abandoned with the resumption of hostilities in 1658, provides an early example of such behavior. The Seneca had initiated a rapproachement with the French, intending to neutralize them long enough to win a war against the Erie. The resultant peace emboldened the Jesuits to penetrate into the Onondaga villages. But after the Erie had been vanquished the peace deteriorated, and when the clerics learned that the mission was to be destroyed they left precipitously.[30] Similar scenarios occurred again and again during the period of inter-tribal wars.[31] To the extent that these on-again, off-again alliances, involving factions which disagreed on whether to retain the missionaries, were secular rather than religious matters, women were involved only in so far as they had political power by influencing the warriors or through the naming of peace chiefs (*sachems*).

Lafitau, the astute though opinionated observer of the early eighteenth-century Iroquois, not surprisingly depicted their warfare as "indispensible" to "one of their fundamental laws of being" rather than as a necessary response to troublesome neighbors.[32] The point is not that his assessment was false or that he failed to realize the extent to which war was motivated by a desire for trading privileges, or was incited by the colonial powers. Rather, it is one that one must suppose that the deepest concerns of the people revolved about the activity which engaged so much of their emotional life, regardless of the actual time spent in fighting. Men were the primary subjects of war-related rituals, but women had as much of a stake emotionally and objectively as did their sons, husbands, and fathers. Keeping the faith during this period reasonably emphasized safeguarding the lives of the warriors and honoring their deaths by mourning. During this period informal and private observances undoubtedly continued, which addressed themselves to personal curing and to preservation of individuals by means of dream-guessing and the supernaturally aided medicine societies. Nevertheless, the thesis I wish to suggest is that religious attention was very much focussed on matters related to the wars which the fur trade forced upon the Iroquois.

It is interesting to speculate just how much influence women had in persuading men to go to war during the period of the beaver wars and during the ensuing period of Iroquois involvement in European power struggles. In an earlier age women could suggest to a warrior that he might go on a raiding party and return with captives, either to avenge a previous loss or to replace a loss with an adoptee. Simultaneously, the raid provided the young warrior with an occasion to attain honor and make a name for himself, even in opposition to the wishes of the peace chiefs who might deem an attack unwise. But now that the nature of warfare had changed, and war was waged as a political action in pursuit of economic objectives and in alliances with colonial powers, the expeditions were less likely to have been initiated by women, even though increased military activity cost more lives and necessitated the adoption of more captives. As in earlier times women had an interest in the replacement of lost warriors, but the difference was that social and economic forces, not the prodding of individual women, became the determinants of war. Women were still influential through their spokesmen in councils (mostly warriors) and through their role of nominating peace chiefs. But despite the celebrated matriarchal character ascribed to Iroquois institutions, there were checks upon the nominations of a chief by the matron, for his own lineage and clan had to approve, and perhaps approval by the opposite moiety was also required, as is the case today.[33]

Even if one argues that the religious observances and the political decisions in the forefront of consciousness were tied into the warfare complex and were concerned with the fortune, welfare, and honor of men and nations, nevertheless women in their capacity as primary food producers must have been concerned about the success of their crops. For this reason they surely engaged in religious observances designed to assure an adequate harvest by bringing the supernatural and human powers into harmony. The early literature is not very helpful in identifying agricultural observances, but again that does not mean that they were absent. Tooker speculates that the type of feast (*enditeuhwa*) characterized as a thanksgiving feast, announcing and rejoicing in good fortune, may have been a calendric ceremony.[34] And Lafitau, while admitting that he did not specifically investigate agricultural religious festivals, does hint at them several times, mentioning offerings and formal speeches to the sun which were accompanied by feasting, chanting, and dancing in order to "make the wheat [*sic*] grow in their fields, [and] to cause them to have good hunting or good fishing."[35] He also indicates that these rites were accompanied by a drum and a rattle, which are characteristic of modern agricultural ceremonies. Furthermore, he alludes to a harvest "festival of binding together corn shocks," in which men uncharacteristically helped women in the fields.[36] He thinks it may have had some religious significance in the past, though again he admits that he had not tried to learn its peculiar features. Sentiments of supplication and thanksgiving are very much in evidence today in the traditional calendrical rites, and this lends credibility to the interpretation of Lafitau's report suggested here. To the extent that the observers were men, and food production was a feminine occupation, the documentation of calendric ceremonies may also have been sparser than that of the more spectacular warfare complex. On all counts it seems reasonable to infer that the agricultural rituals did exist in this period, though subsidiary in importance to those of the warfare complex, but as war and its implementation receded in importance later on, the agricultural ceremonies became more complex and central.

The political history of the Iroquois at the end of the seventeenth century and through much of the eighteenth still revolved about the fur trade. Since the competition between Britain and France persisted unabated, plunging them into four wars—King William's (1689–1697), Queen Anne's (1703–1713), King George's (1744–1748), and the French-Indian War (1756–1763)—the Iroquois were constantly importuned to help one side or the other, thereby bringing the wrath of the other upon them. On the other hand, colonial competition also gave the Iroquois some manipulative opportunities, and Wallace in particular depicts them as enjoying two generations of relative peace and tranquility.[37] It was at this time that villages were well built and unfortified, indicating confidence that secure times would continue. The agricultural output was plentiful, as evidenced by large cornfields and orchards, and the newly established trading posts contributed to the material wealth of the settlements. Furthermore, quantities of "presents" given to the Iroquois by the rival powers also improved their standard of living. Finally, the self-esteem of the warriors and the success of diplomatic initiatives are said to have made for high morale in general. Wallace stresses that the traditional religion at this time was able to provide "cognitive assurance and emotional support" to the entire population.[38] He describes a religious balance consisting of shamanistic curing rituals, rituals of mourning, and the annual round of ceremonies concerned with the growth of life-supporting products. As the emphasis shifted from war to reaping the benefits of relative peace and prosperity, concern with the war complex diminished while, in compensation, the calendric ceremonies were enhanced. And as the latter complex was enhanced, the women, who were primarily concerned with food production, must have felt some satisfaction.

With the fall of New France and the Treaty of Paris in 1763 the Iroquois entered a much more difficult period, since their old policy of pitting the French against the British was rendered obsolete. Iroquois control over trade also diminished, and the British were able to drive much harder bargains when buying pelts. In a last desperate effort to break British domination of the Ohio Valley the pro-French Western Seneca joined in Pontiac's Rebellion (1763–1764), but failure of the Rebellion placed all the Iroquois wholly under British jurisdiction, and as a consequence the Seneca were deprived of some lands along the Niagara River. Soon further lands became attractive to European settlers, and already in 1768, in the first Treaty of Ft. Stanwix, the Iroquois ceded their interests in the entire area south of the Ohio and Susquehanna Rivers. More serious for the immediate welfare of the Iroquois was the fact that not only the distant lands in which they roamed for beaver but their very homeland had begun attracting European settlers. Despite a royal proclamation of 1763 prohibiting settlement in lands west of the Appalachians, encroachment was now imminent.

A repercussion of the changed balance of power was the steady diminution of the independent action of warriors, diplomats, and hunters. By contrast, local concerns and women's activities continued along previous lines, and visitors were astonished by the standard of living in many of the villages. The balance of activities assigned to the male and the female spheres continued to tilt towards the latter, particularly since the production of staples for subsistence remained at a high level. Nevertheless, the Iroquois activities which ideally had high prestige may well have remained the male occupations, and the result was therefore an incipient demoralization more of men than of women.

The interwar years 1763–1775 saw the League subjected to numerous divergent pressures, both from interested missionary societies and from representatives of opposing political persuasions. On the British side the Northern Indian Superintendent, Sir William Johnson, lived among the Mohawk and labored ceaselessly to keep the League at peace and also firmly attached to the loyalist cause. Even though he died shortly before the outbreak of the Revolution, his policies were continued with considerable adroitness by his successor Guy Johnson (his nephew and son-in-law) and by the Mohawk war captain Joseph Brant (whose sister was not only Sir William's common-law wife but a clan matron exercising much influence later in the Revolution in keeping the Iroquois loyal to the British). On the other side the colonists' cause was most ably represented by the Reverend Samuel Kirkland, whose immense influence among the Oneida succeeded in attaching most of that nation to the rebels. These rivals convened councils at which they presented their respective requests in increasingly importunate terms, while offering extravagant bribes of liquor, guns, ammunition, vermilion war paint, ostrich feathers, wampum, trinkets, and other sundry articles to chiefs and their followers. Consequently, as in earlier wars the League's unanimity was undermined by local political and religious affiliations as well as by the eagerness of warriors to engage again in attacks and raids. By 1777 all but the Oneida had committed themselves to the service of the King. As a consequence the Americans retaliated by laying waste most of the lands of the pro-British tribes, while the British burnt the Oneida settlements. The destruction of villages and standing crops by the infamous Sullivan expedition in 1779 brought such suffering to the Indians that General Washington, who had ordered the expedition, is designated to this day in the religious recitations of the Longhouse as "the Destroyer of Villages." The Treaty of Paris in 1783 completely ignored the indigenous combatants, and the only reward for services to the King was a refuge in Canada to which they could emigrate.

The Reservation Period and the Good Message

Captain Joseph Brant led about two thousand people to the new tract of land in Canada, thereby substantially weakening the League by withdrawing about half of its political leaders and ritualists. For those Iroquois who remained behind in the newly independent nation the post-Revolutionary period was characterized by the disillusionment and humiliation of chiefs and their peoples, by enormous forced and fraudulent land sales and cessions, and by life on reservations where it was difficult to recreate a cultural existence predicated on the assumption (expressed by the war chief of the Mohawks at the end of the Revolution) that we "were a free People subject to no Power upon earth."[39] The dispiriting trends initiated during the inter-war years (1763–1775), and perhaps briefly interrupted by the military and diplomatic activity of the Revolution, recurred in earnest and in a very augmented form. As the various family groups settled on the reservations they were torn by competition between traditionalists and Christians, and by political factions which arose from resentment of and blame for the sale of lands. According to Wallace,[40] "Within a few years they [the reservations] were slums in the wilderness, displaying unacceptably high levels of drunkenness, of fighting and brawling, of instability of households, and of witchcraft accusations."

In the day-to-day business of making a living the women resumed the cultivation of the fields, and the men hunted in a very restricted manner on nearby territory and traded with whites, but the days of free-wheeling prestigious male occupations were over. The narrowing of traditional options which Iroquois society experienced because of the systematic loss of power and lands affected the occupations of men first and therefore must have been felt more keenly by them. If at the same time the religious rituals continued to tilt from those concerned with fighting toward the calendric observances, it would not be surprising that men might feel psychologically unsupported and as a consequence experience feelings of insecurity and anomie manifested by ailments which needed therapy. It is understandable, therefore, that there was an upsurge in shamanistic curing rituals which ministered to individuals, as well as an increase in the number of witchcraft accusations.

Wallace proposes a theory of revitalization movements according to which

> religious belief and practice always originate in situations of social and cultural stress and are, in fact, an effort on the part of the stress-laden to construct systems of dogma, myth, and ritual which are internally coherent as well as true descriptions of a world system and which thus will serve as guides to efficient action.[41]

This is his explanation for the success of millenarian and nativistic movements. The Iroquois were distressed and ready to receive a message of religious instructions from a suitable prophet. Their needs were answered by Handsome Lake (1735–1815), also known as the

Seneca Prophet, who held one of the peace chiefs' titles, had been a warrior in the Revolution, and was a signatory to the Treaty of Big Tree (1797). On June 15, 1799, after a two-hour trance, he reported the first of a series of communications transmitted to him by three supernatural beings during his altered state of consciousness. Subsequently he experienced further visions. The collected and codified instructions to him, together with some anecdotes and dicta, constitute the Code of Handsome Lake or *káiwi·yo·h,* the Good Message, or simply the Longhouse Religion. The message has been passed on orally from preacher to preacher and today constitutes a major part of the doctrine of the traditional religion of the conservative Iroquois.[42]

Handsome Lake was an innovator, preaching a religion which was a synthesis of the indigenous religion with a Christian admixture. The dominant Christian influence on Handsome Lake was that of the Quakers, some of whom lived in his village primarily to instruct the Indians in the practical arts necessary for making the transition to a European mode of livelihood rather than to proselytize, but who had held some religious discussions with the Iroquois, particularly with Handsome Lake's half-brother Cornplanter, the political leader of the community.

The Good Message preached an essentially moralistic ethic, forbidding certain sins, recommending repentance, and promising salvation if the prescriptions were followed but hellish tortures if they were transgressed. The sins which most concerned Handsome Lake were drunkenness, witchcraft, charms, and abortions, but he also condemned a long list of actions which would render a community disharmonious. In fact, the prohibitions could be read as a listing of the culturally disruptive forces at work in the demoralized reservation society.

On the positive side the Good Message admonished the Iroquois to maintain their traditional ceremonies, though it forbade the curing and masking complex (a prohibition which has been largely ignored). It also instructed the population to accept farming, house-building, and the raising of domestic animals, and to send twelve of their number to European schools. Thus, Handsome Lake can be seen as a culture broker, attempting to mediate between two different styles of life. Significant for the concerns of this paper is the fact that Handsome Lake advocated the use of the plow and male participation in agriculture, which can be seen as an upgrading of tasks previously assigned to females, as well as an accommodation to Quaker teaching and to modern times. Accommodation was to be kept within strict bounds, however, for *káiwi·yo·h* was pervasively a manifestation of ethnic identity.

The Longhouse Religion is to this day a viable church with several thousand adherents. Despite fear of its demise, it is today as lively as at the turn of the century, and there are eleven centers of worship on the various reservations. Bryan Wilson characterized this religion as an introversionist movement, by which he means a religion which perpetuates a tribal or native way of life, and which creates and retains a social system and a form of religious practice differing from those of the dominant culture.[43] A detailed description of the Longhouse way of life is beyond the scope of this article,[44] but it is appropriate to examine the role of women in the Longhouse and in related parts of the culture.

A cardinal principle among the Iroquois is that men and women must stand in a reciprocal relation to each other. This reciprocity is symbolized in many contexts: the "house" (place of worship) is divided on most ceremonial days into male and female sectors, there is a women's and a men's stove, and a women's and a men's door. Seating is by gender (except on those days when there is a moiety division of the clans). Furthermore, the sacred bowl game is played with women gambling against men at the seed-planting ceremony in order to make the plants grow. Male and female deacons, called faithkeepers, have equal status and must cooperate with each other in order to facilitate the running of the Longhouse ceremonies. Some ceremonies are scheduled and planned by men, but the majority (particularly the agricultural ones) are scheduled and planned by women.

The female faithkeepers are a particularly influential group in the retention of the religion. As both chiefs and their clan matrons have declined in power, the faithkeepers have taken over many of their functions and render religious and moral advice to members of the congregation. In this capacity, the head faithkeeper of each moiety is most important, but all other faithkeepers, both those who inherited their positions and those who gained them by merit, perform these services. Women are often firm advocates of the belief that political offices should be associated with the native religion. This was not always the case; and while there are still Christians among the peace chiefs, as the chiefs have come under pressure and have lost power in the secular realm, they and their matrons have frequently found a haven in the Longhouse. Often a clan matron who holds the validating wampum which invests a chief will insist that her chief be installed in the Longhouse, or at least with the traditional ceremony.

The women who are most influential in keeping the society traditional are the fortunetellers. (Some fortunetellers are male, but the majority now are female.) A fortuneteller functions largely in the religious domain, for her power comes directly from the Great Creator, and thus she can interpret occult signs and prescribe remedies for misfortune and illness. These prescriptions are always traditional in character, drawing either on Longhouse rituals (called "doings") or on native curing ceremonies (paradoxically, precisely those prohibited by Handsome Lake). Thus, a dance, a song, a lacrosse game, a thunder ceremony may be prescribed as a medicine or as an antidote to witchcraft. Contemporary traditional Iroquois, and many acculturated ones as well, feel that they cannot afford to neglect the advice of a fortuneteller. Neglect could bring ill fortune or even death not only to the transgresser, but to his or her matrilineal or bilateral family. There are many women ritualists attached to one or another of the curing societies, the most powerful of which is the Little Water Society. Women are often the dispensers of the traditional herbal cures, which also derive their efficacy from the Great Creator, particularly after they receive a supplicant's message by means of the sacred tobacco which many women grow.

Conservatism in Modern Times

It is interesting to inquire how an introversionist movement like the religion of Handsome Lake has been able to maintain itself for nearly two hundred years. When he first preached, his context was a matrilineal, probably matrilocal, rural village society with face-to-face interaction. Today, many of the Iroquois live in cities and are directly immersed in the individualistic mass society, and even those who remain on the reservations feel the impact of that society via employment patterns, automobiles, and the mass media. Fewer and fewer of the children learn Iroquois languages. As early as the post-Revolutionary period the political power of the peace chiefs among the Iroquois resident in the United States was undermined on many of the reservations by the corrupt sale of land; and on Six Nations Reserve in Ontario the Canadian government in 1924 transferred power over local affairs from the council of peace chiefs to an elected council. Both in the cities and on the reservations the Iroquois have come to depend to some extent upon the white-dominated government for services in health, education, and welfare. Yet, despite all these corrosive factors the Longhouse Religion seems to serve the needs of a large segment of the Iroquois population. It is evidently a complex matter to explain this phenomenon. The best that can be done here is to indicate briefly some of the factors in an intricate psychological and social dynamic.

Because of the special concerns of this study, the contribution of women to the maintenance of Iroquois traditions will be underlined, but without any intention of playing down the contributions of men.

Above all, the Good Message provides a coherent expression of ethnic identity. The sense of being an Iroquois is internalized by a child for many reasons—physical appearance, racial prejudice of the white community, and the ethnic self-identification of the people among whom the child grows up. For the purpose of morale it is obviously important that the self-identification be accompanied by feelings of pride and confidence. The Longhouse Religion provides an ideological justification for such positive feelings, for it spells out the special relation that the Iroquois have with the Great Creator and to the whole hierarchy of spirits, and it celebrates the Indian way of life in preference to that of the white men. To be sure, a positive attitude towards Iroquois identity can be achieved in other ways, via political-action groups, social clubs, and pan-Indian organizations. But none of these means has the coherence, structure of ideas, noble language, and historical associations that the Longhouse Religion can provide. Even Christian Iroquois, who do not literally believe in the preachings of Handsome Lake and perhaps feel some cultural superiority to them, nevertheless acknowledge that he is a source of inspiration for anyone who wishes to maintain Iroquois identity.

It was stated earlier in this paper that during the colonial period religious instruction was automatically part of child-rearing, and there was no need for a conscious effort to perpetuate traditions. Now, however, in the face of acculturative pressure, parents inculcate their children quite consciously. Inculcation is done much more by the mothers than by the fathers, largely because the latter are so often away from home. The efficacy of the inculcation can be seen in the fact that the Longhouses are as well attended now as they were thirty years ago, and many of those in attendance are young.

An important factor in the perpetuation of the traditional religion has been that the congregation is innovative and adaptive in the details of rituals while conservative in the overall ideology. Because the external conditions have changed—socially, economically, technologically—the Iroquois must accommodate, and they relax praxis (because things cannot be done exactly as they should) in order to continue the ideology. This sacrifice, however, is a serious one in the eyes of the Iroquois, for they are very "particular" about details and procedures. An omission or an error or a change requires that the practitioner address the situation and activate devices to counteract the disturbance. For example, tobacco may be dropped as compensation, or the Great Creator may be ritually informed that there has been a one-time occurrence and asked for forgiveness. Iroquois are so concerned with exact procedure (letter-perfect memory being an ideal) that they often attribute a ceremony's failure to accomplish its ends to a procedural error. But unpleasant as a change of procedure may be, the traditionalists know that substitutions must be made, and they do make them. They rationalize, "Our religion is a thing of the heart, not of paint and feathers." The women faithkeepers and fortunetellers are inventive about substitutions. For instance, lard is sometimes substituted for sunflower oil, canned salmon for fresh fish, beef for bear, chicken for eagle meat, nail polish for red paint, the telephone for human messengers, and women for men in some rituals (a practice unheard of in earlier times). Especially in the cities women are the communicators and facilitators, and they allocate to themselves leadership roles. Men do not seem to object, perhaps because heeding a woman in the role of matron or faithkeeper has long been a cultural trait. Thus religious and social change is effected though many small increments by both women and men.

Despite a general consensus concerning the necessity of the process just described, in particular cases it gives rise to problems. Women are resourceful in adapting their religious practices to modern times, but they are critical about changes made by other practitioners of either sex which they would not have made themselves. Consequently, they often revert to the pattern of ascribing failure or misfortune to a change in procedure or to an omission. Here is an example. The head lady of the *Giwe* Society (the Society for the Dead) wished to clean the graves in the cemetery by hand, as is traditional in the biannual communal ceremony, but one of the chiefs from the Longhouse wished to do it in a more efficient modern way. The head *Giwe* lady disapproved but ultimately acquiesced to the chief's proposal. Shortly thereafter the chief experienced misfortune in his family, and other members of the Longhouse community became ill or died. Why? Because the grave cleaning procedure had been violated.

What is the consequence of this paradoxical system of beliefs and behavior? Is it inimical to the perpetuation of the main lines of Iroquois religion and culture, or is it somehow beneficial? The assessment may depend on the point of view of the analyst, but as suggested elsewhere consideration of the modern structure of Iroquois religion (a structure dominated by *káiwi·yo·h* but buttressed by what might be called folk practices of curing and protection against witchcraft), has the consequence that an entrenchment of the main lines of the traditional religion occurs. For in the final analysis, what keeps the complex going? To a large extent a series of misfortunes. The practitioner attributes these to change of procedure, to neglect, or to evil deeds, but in any case corrective ritual must be performed. Thus, one has a mechanism which can be compared to a closed cybernetic system. A activates B, and B reacts on A. In other words, to keep the religion going one must make adjustments, but making adjustments brings problems. Where does one resolve these problems? One resolves them in the conservative domain of the fortuneteller, the faithkeeper, and the traditional ritualist. She, or he, prescribes a traditional ritual of a type which is culturally acceptable in the main, despite slight modifications made for the sake of feasibility. In this way micro-change results in macro-retention. We may conjecture, incidentally, that the eighteenth-century shift from religious rituals centering on warfare to those centering on agriculture, which we discussed earlier, conformed to the same pattern of micro-change and macro-retention, but we unfortunately do not have detailed documentary evidence to establish this conjecture definitively. What we can assert with some confidence is that women were as instrumental in that shift as they are in the shifts which are taking place now before our eyes, for women are both adamant and resourceful in "keeping the faith."

We shall conclude with some remarks about the retention of Iroquois culture on a secular level. There are many political activists, some of them Longhouse adherents and some not, who trade upon traditional symbols in order to revitalize the traditional culture. The Mohawk Workers, a group dedicated to activity designed to secure Iroquois rights and perpetuate traditions, consists largely of Iroquois who do not belong to the Longhouse (nor do all Mohawk). The organization is largely staffed by women, and indeed women have taken over many roles previously filled by men. There are also numerous women teachers who have reintroduced Iroquois languages and native cultural programs in the public schools. Not surprisingly, many of these women come from Longhouse families, for those are the most knowledgeable about the traditional culture. The effectiveness of these women should not be underestimated, for they have dedication and strength of character.

NOTES

1. Floyd G. Lounsbury, "Iroquoian Languages," *Northeast*, vol. 15 of *Handbook of North American Indians*, ed. Bruce G. Trigger (Washington, D.C.: Smithsonian Institution, 1978), p. 334.

2. Lewis H. Morgan, *League of the Ho-de-no-sau-nee or Iroquois* (Rochester: Sage and New York: M. H. Newman, 1851).

3. Elisabeth Tooker, *An Ethnography of the Huron Indians, 1615–1649*, Bureau of American Ethnology Bulletins, no. 190 (Washington, D.C.: U.S. Government Printing Office, 1964).

4. Reuben G. Thwaites, ed., *The Jesuit Relations and Allied Documents: Travel and Exploration of the Jesuit Missionaries in New France, 1610–1791*, 73 vols. (Cleveland: Burrows Brothers, 1896–1901).

5. Bruce G. Trigger, "Early Iroquoian Contacts with Europeans," *Northeast*, vol. 15 of *Handbook of North American Indians*, p. 344.

6. Tooker, *Ethnography of the Huron Indians*, p. 4.

7. Trigger, *Early Iroquoian Contacts*, p. 347.

8. Ibid., pp. 348–49.

9. Ibid., pp. 347–56.

10. Ibid., p. 356.

11. Anthony F. C. Wallace, *The Death and Rebirth of the Seneca* (New York: Alfred A. Knopf, 1970), p. 28.

12. Bruce G. Trigger, *The Huron: Farmers of the North* (New York and Chicago: Holt, Rinehart and Winston, 1969), p. 115.

13. Elisabeth Tooker, *The Iroquois Ceremonial of Midwinter* (Syracuse: Syracuse University Press, 1970), p. 83.

14. Trigger, *The Huron*, p. 108.

15. Thwaites, *The Jesuit Relations*, 10:49 quoted in Conrad E. Heidenreich, "Huron," *Northeast*, vol. 15 of *Handbook of North American Indians*, p. 372.

16. Trigger, *The Huron*, p. 84.

17. Joseph Francois Lafitau, *Customs of the American Indians Compared with the Customs of Primitive Times*, vol. 1, ed. William N. Fenton and Elizabeth L. Moore (Toronto: The Champlain Society, 1974).

18. James A. Tuck, "Iroquois Confederacy," *Scientific American* 224, no. 3 (1971):41.

19.George T. Hunt, *The Wars of the Iroquois: A Study in Intertribal Trade Relations*, 2nd ed. (Madison: University of Wisconsin Press, 1960), pp. 33–35.

20. Trigger, *Early Iroquoian Contacts*, p. 352.

21. Elisabeth Tooker, "The League of the Iroquois: Its History, Politics, and Ritual," *Northeast*, vol. 15 of *Handbook of North American Indians*, p. 430.

22. Hunt, *The Wars of the Iroquois*, p. 64.

23. Ibid., pp. 88–89. Trigger, *Early Iroquoian Contacts*, p. 355.

24. Martha C. Randle, "Iroquois Women, Then and Now," *Symposium on Local Diversity in Iroquois Culture*, Bureau of American Ethnology Bulletins, no. 149, ed. William N. Fenton (Washington, D.C.: Smithsonian Institution, 1951), p. 172.

25. Lafitau, *Customs of the American Indians*, 2 (1977):111–14.

26. Ibid., 114.

27. Ibid., 149.

28. Tooker, *Ethnography of the Huron Indians*, p. 33.

29. Hunt, *The Wars of the Iroquois*, p. 153.

30. Tooker, *The League of the Iroquois*, p. 431.
31. Ibid., pp. 431ff.
32. Lafitau, *Customs of the American Indians*, 2 (1977):99.
33. Ibid., 1 (1974):291–93.
34. Tooker, *Ethnography of the Huron Indians*, p. 75.
35. Lafitau, *Customs of the American Indians*, 1 (1974):149.
36. Ibid., 2 (1977):55.
37. Anthony F. C. Wallace, "Origin of the Longhouse Religion," *Northeast*, vol. 15 of *Handbook of North American Indians*, p. 442.
38. Ibid., p. 442.
39. Barbara Graymont, *The Iroquois in the American Revolution* (Syracuse: Syracuse Univesity Press, 1972), p. 260.
40. Wallace, *Origin of the Longhouse Religion*, p. 445.
41. Anthony F. C. Wallace, *Religion: An Anthropological View* (New York: Random House, 1966), p. 30.
42. Arthur C. Parker, *The Code of Handsome Lake, the Seneca Prophet*, New York State Museum Bulletins, no. 163 (Albany: University of the State of New York, 1913).
43. Bryan R. Wilson, *Magic and the Millenium* (New York: Harper & Row, 1973), pp. 385ff.
44. Annemarie A. Shimony, *Conservatism among the Iroquois at Six Nations Reserve*, Yale University Publications in Anthropology, no. 65 (New Haven: Department of Anthropology, Yale University, 1961).

Chapter Seventeen

Spirits Defend the Rights of Women: Spiritualism and Changing Sex Roles in Nineteenth-century America

Ann D. Braude

In March 1848, the people of Hydesville, New York, discovered that the spirit of a dead peddler would answer questions put to it by two adolescent girls, Kate and Margaret Fox.[1] They heard the spirit rap on the walls and furniture when the correct letter was reached as the girls recited the alphabet. Four months later, and forty miles down the Erie Canal, the first Woman's Rights Convention gathered at Seneca Falls to discuss the "social, civil and religious rights of women."[2] These apparently unprecedented events marked the beginnings of two mass movements: Spiritualism and Women's Rights. From the geographic proximity of their origins the two movements intertwined repeatedly as they challenged the existing norms of American life. Both faced ridicule for departing from the status quo, and both became enduring elements of American culture.

This essay presents a preliminary survey of the relationship between the religious content of Spiritualism and the changes in sex roles proposed by both Spiritualists and those in the Women's Rights movement. It will explore why the new religious doctrines of Spiritualism were meaningful to men and women who were ready to dispense with existing sex roles and create a new and expanded role for women in religion and society.

Many historians have noted a relationship between Spiritualism and women's rights in nineteenth-century America, but none have described the content of that relationship.[3] Both advocates and detractors of the time linked the two movements. Elizabeth Cady Stanton wrote with admiration that "the only religious sect in the world, unless we except the Quakers, that has recognized the equality of woman, is the Spiritualists."[4] A less sympathetic voice referred to "Women's Rights and Spiritualism, [as] illustrating the follies and delusions of the nineteenth century."[5] The two movements shared many leaders, participants and ideas. Not all feminists were spiritualists, but all spiritualists advocated women's rights, and women were in fact equal with men in spiritualist practice, polity, and ideology. At a time when no churches ordained women and many forbade them to speak in church, spiritualist women had equal authority, equal opportunities, and equal numbers in religious leadership.[6] Certainly, as Elizabeth Cady Stanton observed, spiritualists were the only religious group of which this could be said. Spiritualists put into action the unprecedented departures from existing sex roles advocated by the women's rights movement.

Spiritualism was based on the idea that contact with the spirits of the dead provided empirical proof of the immortality of the soul. Within a decade of the Hydesville rappings, thousands of Americans were gathering in "spirit circles" to make contact with their dead relatives. Individuals with "mediumistic powers" were discovered in households across the country. From the beginning, spirit communication occurred most frequently through the mediumship of the younger female members of families. Participation in Spiritualism was one of many ways in which American women expressed their dissent from Calvinism and their dissatisfaction with the roles available to them in the mainstream churches.

Women did not consciously choose to be mediums. Rather, they and their co-religionists believed that the spirits chose them and that they passively allowed spirits to communicate through them. Thus, the advent of mediumship did not require a decision to rebel against accepted female roles. Once spirits were in evidence, they could provide women with support and motivation to assume leadership despite public criticism. Emma Hardinge, a leading spiritualist who would enter a trance while on stage and then deliver lectures under spirit guidance, described her entrance onto the lecture circuit:

> that I, a woman, and moreover, *"a lady by birth,"* and *English*, above all, that I would go out, like "strong minded women," and hector the world, on public platforms! oh, shocking! I vowed rebellion—to give up Spirits, Spiritualism, and America; to return to England and live "a feminine existence" once again. With these magnanimous resolves upon me *one week, the next* saw me on a public platform, fairly before the world as a trance speaker.[7]

Another trance lecturer, Ascha Sprague, left her small town in Vermont and spent the rest of her life lecturing on behalf of spiritualism after she was healed through spirit intervention following seven years of invalidism.[8] Spirits, it seemed, encouraged women to do things which other forces militated against.

Spiritualism was conspicuous for the number and celebrity of its female leaders. Spiritualists were vocal advocates of the equality of the sexes and used every available opportunity to affirm this position. The following resolution, adopted at an Illinois Spiritualist Conference in 1860, is typical:

> Resolved, that in all things the rights of females are as sacred as those of males, that their opinions, when founded in like wisdom, are as worthy of being respected, and their privilege of a full, perfect, and free expression of opinions, is an inalienable right; consequently, any attempt, by whatsoever means, to restrict such privilege, is an unwarrantable assumption of power unbecoming of an enlightened people.[9]

Although some suffragists complained of individuals who put spiritualism before the struggle for the vote, Isabella Beecher Hooker's decision that spiritualism came first did not prevent her from corresponding with both Elizabeth Cady Stanton and Susan B. Anthony and playing a central role in the national suffrage campaign. Frances Ellen Burr, the president of the Hartford Woman Suffrage League, relied on spirit messages when planning the development of the national suffrage movement.[10]

What attracted followers to a movement which combined radical positions on social issues with unconventional religious practice? Religious women in nineteenth-century America had to overcome significant social contradictions in order to practice their faiths. The increasing identification of the qualities of piety with the qualities of femininity assured women of their spiritual superiority, yet they were asked to defer to men in all religious matters. Every Sunday they saw more of their sisters than their brothers in the churches they attended, yet they, the majority of members, were excluded from all decisions regarding the churches' operations. The religious instruction of the young was entrusted to them in Sunday schools, but they were forbidden to speak out loud during regular services. Told to serve God through their influence in the home, they saw men rule an ungodly and immoral society outside the home. Warned that their influence as mothers made them responsible for the spiritual fate of their children, they were asked to accept the Calvinist view that children who died without having a Christian conversion experience were damned to eternal punishment. The increased leadership of women during the Second Great Awakening in the early decades of the nineteenth-century deepened the existing contradictions. Their spiritual prowess was affirmed, but they were still denied ordination or positions of authority within church organizations.

Participation in Spiritualism was one way that American women resolved these contradictions. Instead of concluding that the qualities which made women especially suited to religion made them unsuited to public life, Spiritualism made the delicate constitution and nervous excitability commonly attributed to femininity a qualification for religious leadership. If women had special spiritual sensitivities, then it followed that they could sense spirits, which is precisely what mediums did. Spiritualism allowed women to discard Victorian limitations on women's role without questioning Victorian ideas about woman's nature.

The Bible was another source of contradictions between woman's spiritual competency and her subservient religious role. One woman troubled by this issue wrote to the spiritualist newspaper, *The Herald of Progress*:

> My eldest brother contests all my legal and moral rights upon Bible grounds. But sir, I may be a very wicked creature to argue my "rights" against such authority, but I cannot submit to be a Christian if such submission and resignation are demanded as incidental virtues in a woman. Will you state the Bible texts wherein the personal and intellectual rights of woman are made subservient to those of her brother.[11]

If the correspondent had addressed this problem to Lucretia Mott, Sarah or Angelina Grimké, Frances Willard, or any of a number of women of the period committed to reconciling Christianity and women's rights, she would have been assured that although Paul commanded women to remain silent and accept male headship, the Gospel also proclaimed that in Christ there was neither male nor female and that the Bible contained as many promises for her as it did for her brother. Far from trying to facilitate such a reconciliation between women and the Bible, the Spiritualist newspaper complied with the correspondent's request in full, and printed every damning verse from Paul's letters on its front page. Instead of suggesting what can be learned from other sections of the Christian Scripture, the newspaper explained what Christians could learn from Spiritualists. According to the editor,

> The Christian world . . . must learn that God's authority lies in the tranquil realms of eternal principles, written unmistakably in the constitution of mankind. It must learn that each is an eternal *fact with identical rights and parallel privileges which no other fact or personality has a right to curtail or embarrass.*[12]

Spiritualists found that when Christianity and women's rights conflicted, the principle of equality took precedence.

In his classic study of enthusiastic religion, Whitney Cross observed that Spiritualists, "probably more than other women's rights champions, frankly recognized aspects of equality beyond property or political safeguards."[13] Far from focusing narrowly on suffrage or property rights, Spiritualists advocated a broad range of reforms affecting women. They never disagreed about whether women deserved equal rights with men but only about the best means of achieving equality. The minutes of a Spiritualist convention held in Chicago in 1865 reflect the breadth of their concerns. After the officers had addressed the assembly, the first speaker from the the floor, Mrs. Parker,

> spoke in favor of the elective franchise for woman, as the foundation of all future guarantees of rights, and alluded to the fact that the tyrannical government of Austria had been before republican America in the granting of rights to women.

Next, Mrs. Dr. Stillman of Whitewater, Wisconsin rose to speak. According to the report, she

> ridiculed the idea of women going to the polls in a fashionable dress; while she was in favor of women's voting, she claimed that the reform dress must be adopted as a precedent movement; that the great demand of the day was *health*.

The report then quotes Stillman as saying "If women compress the chest so as to press out the very life, would they not vote, if fashion said so, for a very bad measure?" At the conclusion of Stillman's lengthy indictment of tight-lacing, petticoats, and insufficient exercise, the Assistant Secretary of the Society, Lois Waisbrooker, presented an opposing view.

> I believe every individual should wear that dress they feel most at home in. I have all the opposition which my spirit feels strong enough to bear.[14]

Waisbrooker, a Free Love advocate, had been subject to much derision for her Spiritualism and her radical social views. She felt unable to withstand the additional ridicule inevitably heaped on those who adopted the radical "American Dress," composed, like the bloomer costume, of a shortened skirt over loose trousers.[15]

Spiritualists believed that the advent of spirit communication heralded the arrival of a new era, in which humanity, with spirit guidance, would achieve hitherto impossible levels of development. The new era would be characterized by the accomplishment of a broad program of progressive social reforms, and a complete reformation of personal life. Women's rights would be at the center of the new order, which would also include abolition, temperance, vegetarianism, and a variety of other progressive reforms. The Spiritualist *Progressive Annual*, for example, listed not only spiritualist lecturers, but practicing women physicians, women instructors in light gymnastics, "practical dress reformers" who wear the "American costume," and speakers on the freedom and equality of the sexes.[16]

Spiritualists recognized that a new order in which women enjoyed complete equality would have to include a revision of men's roles in relation to women, and especially a reformation of the relationship between women and men in marriage. When the Chicago Spiritualist Convention of 1865 described above resumed after its noon recess, the minutes report that "a young couple present wished to be married." Mrs. H.F.M. Brown officiated. According to the minutes:

> She took the standard and dealt some severe blows against the marriage laws. She plead for the equality of wife and husband before the law as they are before God. She said the laws robbed the wife of her child, her property, of her name, and of her individuality. . . . She censured parents who suffered their children to rush blindly to the marriage altar. Mothers and fathers sell their beautiful innocent daughters for homes, a maintenance, and positions. . . . To these immolations may be traced the heart-aches, the suicides, the jealousies, elopements, insanity, drunkenness, and in fact all the ills and curses that call for prisons, asylums, doctors and preachers.

After further remarks, Brown performed the marriage, in a ceremony similar to the Quaker rite.

> By the linking of your hands we infer your hearts are already united, and that you only ask public recognition of the marriage already registered in heaven. Therefore by the authority invested in me by the state of Illinois, I pronounce you husband and wife.[17]

In contrast to the regular ceremony in which the wife's vow of obedience to her husband secured the established order, the Spiritualist wedding claimed that if women were legally and religiously recognized as men's equals, all society's ills would be cured. Spiritualists made it routine for a wedding to be the occasion of a declaration that men had no right to possess women and that the state had no right to interfere in individual relations. Previously, only the weddings of a few radicals like Lucy Stone and Robert Dale Owen had protested the injustice toward women written into the marriage laws, but the Spiritualist *Religio-Philosophical Journal* reported each month the names of couples joined in this unusual way.[18]

Spiritualism offered women a great deal from a political perspective, but what did it offer them religiously? Spiritualists viewed their movement as a corrective to the harsh doctrines of Calvinism, which they considered to be destructive to human hope and accountability. The points at which Spiritualism objected to Christianity were precisely the points at which a "True Woman" of the Victorian era would be appalled by Calvinism. Although gentler doctrines were preached from a number of pulpits by mid-century, Spiritualists found unacceptable vestiges of Calvinism in every denomination. As late as 1890, Abby Ann Judson, member of a famous family of Baptist missionaries, attributed her conversion to Spiritualism to her conscientious objection to Calvinist doctrines.[19] Ignoring the watered-down forms of Calvinism which characterized many popular denominations, Spiritualists recalled with horror the religious education of their youth. The clairvoyant Semantha Mettler described her feelings after being "cut off without hope" at the age of eleven by a debate with her Sunday school teacher.

> Why has God made the birds so happy, and me, a little child that has a living soul, with this terrible fear, like a phantom coming between me and the beautiful earth, stealing into my dreams with its terrible grimaces and casting its black shadows athwart the cheering sunlight?[20]

With the emergence of an evangelical domestic ideal during the Victorian period, women were encouraged to seek the fulfillment of their religious obligations in the exercise of their influence within the family circle, rather than in the pursuit of their own salvation. As their roles as mothers increasingly determined their primary social and religious identities, women were less and less willing to accept that those who died without having a Christian conversion experience were damned in spite of their mother's love. Nineteenth-century women refused to believe that a benevolent deity would cause their sons and daughters to be born if He knew all along that He would condemn some of them to eternal punishment in hell. The daughters of New England divines expressed their rejection of their fathers' harsh theology in sentimental novels which became the best-selling books of the nineteenth century. Antoinette Brown Blackwell, America's first woman minister, resigned her pulpit in 1854 when she recoiled from her congregation's expectation that she would hold up frightening images of punishment at the deathbed of an unconverted youth and at the burial of an illegitimate baby.[21]

Spiritualism was an extreme case of the rejection of Calvinism which pervaded women's culture. Spiritualists attributed dire tragedies to Calvinist beliefs and to the Roman Catholic view that those who died unbaptized would spend eternity in limbo. A Spiritualist newspaper reported that

> A poor victim of superstition, an Irish woman, gave birth to a child that did not survive its birth. She was so afflicted by her conception of its probable destiny because unbaptized, that she committed suicide by drowning. We have looked in Protestant journals in vain to discover a recommendation for penal enactments, to restrain teachings so obviously tending to insanity.[22]

According to this editor, Protestant Christians had not gone far enough in refuting Catholic doctrine.

Spiritualism provided a religious alternative that harmonized with the Victorian concept that "True Womanhood" was characterized by purity, piety, submissiveness, and domesticity.[23] It allowed believers to reject Calvinism without giving up a strong religious world-view that gave them hope of being reunited with their loved ones after death. As the century progressed, more and more Christians arrived at a similar compromise, but Spiritualism's wholesale dismissal of Calvinism as immoral had an appealing consistency. Spiritualists did not do away with punishment, but transformed it into a sort of probationary educational program through which individuals continued to grow in grace after death. All souls, no matter how debased at the time of their death, would eventually reach Summerland, the Spiritualist heaven.

The more a woman's identity derived from her family relations, the more she must have been devastated by the irreversible separation from family members at death. Although many nineteenth-century Christians leaned towards the Spiritualist position that individuals retained their personal identity after death, Spiritualism went farther than any other religion in promising to prevent the severance of family relations. Spirit messengers painted rosy pictures of life after death, in which reunited families picnicked by babbling brooks. Departed children and loved ones did not go to an unknown realm, but to a benign and familiar environment where the bereaved could imagine heavenly activities similar to family life on earth. Spiritualist families could be reunited before death by communication at a seance. The possibility of communicating with lost children was a great appeal of Spiritualism to bereaved mothers. The abolitionist Elizabeth Buffum Chace housed a medium in her home for two years after the last of her first five children died in infancy. Many years later, when Spiritualism had ceased to interest her, she remarked that "It used to seem true when we were receiving those communications from the children."[24]

A letter to a spiritualist newspaper from a woman in Wilmington, Delaware shows how desperately some women sought an alternative to orthodox theology. After losing the oldest of her three children she wrote that her spirit was "trembling on the verge of despair." According to the editor,

> She says "If the extreme passionate love of my darlings sway me too much, and is too selfish, I trust the excuse of sincere affection will obtain the Redeemer's mercy and pardon." The correspondent is a religious woman, belongs to a popular church, believes the Arminian creed, and very naturally doubts the eternal happiness of a baby boy whose spirit passed sky-ward three years ago. "The world," she writes, "is all a blank when thinking of the loved one lost, and I suspect the soundness of my judgement.[25]

Spiritualists and Women's Rights advocates shared the belief that women's experience as mothers gave them a heightened sense of values which justified departures from tradition. As mothers, they objected to the fate of their children in the theology preached by men and in the society controlled by men. Just as their legal and economic disabilities made them dependent on men for the physical welfare of their children, so their religious disabilities made them dependent on men for their children's spiritual welfare. Spiritualists concurred with women's rights advocates that women needed equal rights in order to control the conditions under which they raised their children. Spiritualism appealed both to women's desire for equality and to their concerns as mothers.[26]

In many ways, Spiritualists were simply extending the social and religious values of Victorian culture to their logical conclusions.[27] Spiritualism was an expression of authentic concerns which were central to the religious lives of many mid-century Americans, although most were satisfied with more conventional solutions. As liberal Protestantism and sentimental fiction brought heaven closer and closer to earth, it is not surprising that some people found the distance short enough to bridge. While Spiritualists were criticized for their materialistic portrayal of life after death, church-goers across the country enthusiastically peered through *The Gates Ajar* to see the apple trees and meadows of a heaven which looked very much like the New England village of novelist Elizabeth Stuart Phelps's girlhood.[28] Spiritualism epitomized the Victorian fascination with the dead and the hereafter.[29] Spiritualists merely articulated and acted on unorthodox thoughts which they shared with many other Americans.

Spiritualism also took seriously the Victorian view that the home was the true locus of religiosity. In the words of one Spiritualist, "Not in the church, not in the capitol, but in the family, came the first demonstrable recognition of immortal life and immortal love—the holiest truth to the holiest place."[30] Spiritualists secured the place of religion well within woman's sphere by relocating religious practice from the church to the home. Spirit circles gathered around dining room tables, an appropriate place for women to preside. Charles Beecher claimed that "It is not in its published literature, its periodicals, its lectures and its public mediums that the strength of the movement lies. It is in its family or home circles."[31]

If Spiritualists were only playing out Victorian ideals to their limits, why were they the target of harsh and incessant derision? Victorian culture was full of carefully balanced contradictions. As Barbara Welter has observed, the Cult of True Womanhood contained the seeds of its own destruction. Woman's piety often conflicted with passivity, while the maintenance of purity often conflicted with obedience.[32] When Spiritualists took seriously Victorian ideas about woman's nature, they found that these dictated radical departures from Victorian norms for woman's role. In woman's spiritual experience, they found a warrant for participation in public life. Spiritualism bolstered the claims of the women's rights movement by integrating them into a religious system that had a strong appeal to mid-century Americans. By blending the Victorian exaltation of female virtue with the extreme individualism of ante-bellum reform, Spiritualists created a model of female power which made sense to many women's rights activists.

Notes

1. This essay, in various forms, benefitted greatly from the careful reading and thoughtful comments of Molly Ladd-Taylor, Nancy F. Cott, and Sally Ann Stein. It is part of a larger study of the interaction between the movements of Spiritualism and Women's Rights which will appear in my dissertation. "American Spiritualism: Sex Roles and Religious Thought and Practice in a New Religious Movement." (Yale University).

2. Elizabeth Cady Stanton, Susan B. Anthony, and Mathilda Joslyn Gage, *The History of Woman Suffrage*, vol. 1 (New York: Fowler & Wells, 1881), p. 67.

3. There is no critical history of Spiritualism. The most helpful modern account is R. Lawrence Moore, *In Search of White Crows: Spiritualism, Parapsychology, and American Culture* (New York: Oxford University Press, 1977). Important contemporary accounts include Emma Hardinge, *Modern American Spiritualism: A Twenty Years' Record of Communion Between Earth and the World of the Spirits* (New York: published by the author, 1870), and Frank Podmore, *Modern Spiritualism: A History and a Criticism*, 2 vols. (London: Methuen and Company, 1902). Also helpful are Howard Kerr, *Mediums, Spirit Rappers, and Roaring Radicals: Spiritualism in American Literature, 1850–1900* (Urbana: University of Illinois Press, 1972), Marie Caskey, *Chariot of Fire: Religion and the Beecher Family* (New Haven: Yale University Press, 1978), Whitney Cross, *The Burned-Over District: The Social and Intellectual History of Enthusiatic Religion in New York, 1800–1850* (New York: Harper & Row, 1965), and E. Douglas Branch, *The Sentimental Years: 1836–1860* (New York: D. Appleton-Century Company, 1934). On feminism and Spiritualism, see Moore, *In Search of White Crows*, chaps. 3–4, Robert W. Delp, "American Spiritualism and Social Reform, 1847–1900," *Northwest Ohio Quarterly* 44 (1972):85–99, William Leach, *True Love and Perfect Union: The Feminist Reform of Sex and Marriage* (New York: Basic Books, 1980), and Mary Farrell Bednarowski, "Outside the Mainstream: Women's Religion and Women's Religious Leadership in Nineteenth-Century America," *Journal of the American Academy of Religion* 48 (1980):207–31.

4. Stanton, Anthony, and Gage, *History of Woman Suffrage*, vol. 3 (Rochester, New York: Susan B. Anthony, 1886), p. 530.

5. Fred Folio [pseud], *Lucy Boston: or, Women's Rights and Spiritualism, Illustrating the Follies and Delusions of the Nineteenth Century* (Auburn, N.Y.: Alden and Beardsley, 1855), is a satire which portrays the women's rights campaign as being accompanied by the appearance of the spirit of a mermaid. See also Henry James, *The Bostonians* (New York: Modern Library, 1886).

6. For the dates when the various Protestant churches opened leadership

positions to women, see Virginia Lieson Brereton and Christa Ressmeyer Klein, "American Women in Ministry: A History of Protestant Beginning Points," in *Women of Spirit: Female Leadership in the Jewish and Christian Traditions*, Rosemary Ruether and Eleanor McLaughlin, eds. (New York: Simon & Schuster, 1978).

7. Emma Hardinge Britten, *Six Lectures On Theology and Nature* ([Chicago?], 1860), p. 10.

8. Leonard Twynham, "Achsa W. Sprague (1827–1862)," *Proceedings of the Vermont Historical Society* 9 (1941):271–79.

9. As quoted in Britten, *Six Lectures*, p. 154.

10. Hannah Comstock to Isabella Beecher Hooker, 10 December 1874, Isabella Beecher Hooker Papers, Stowe-Day Memorial Library, Hartford, Connecticut; Milton Rugoff, *The Beechers, An American Family in the Nineteenth Century* (New York: Harper & Row, 1981), chaps. 22, 30. Frances Ellen Burr to Isabella Beecher Hooker, 1 November 1874, Isabella Beecher Hooper Papers. On the involvement of Beecher and Burr in the suffrage campaign see Stanton, Anthony, and Gage, *History of Woman Suffrage*, vol. 2 (New York: Fowler & Wells, 1881).

11. *Herald of Progress*, 12 May 1860.

12. Ibid.

13. Cross, *Burned-Over District*, p. 351.

14. *Religio-Philosophical Journal* 1 (1865):1.

15. On Lois Waisbrooker see Hal D. Sears, *The Sex Radicals: Free Love in High Victorian America* (Lawrence: Regents Press of Kansas, 1977).

16. *The Progressive Annual for 1862, Comprising an Almanac, a Spiritualist Register, and a General Calendar of Reform* (New York: A.J. Davis, 1862), p. 50; *The Progressive Annual for 1863* (New York: A.J. Davis, 1863), p. 41.

17. *Religio-Philosophical Journal* 1 (1865):1.

18. On radical weddings see Eleanor Flexner, *A Century of Struggle: The Woman's Rights Movement in the United States* (Cambridge: Harvard University Press, 1975), p. 64.

19. Joan Jacob Brumberg, *Mission for Life* (New York: The Free Press, 1980), pp. 161–63.

20. Frances H. Green, *Biography of Mrs. Semantha Mettler, the Clairvoyant, Being a History of Spiritual Development and Containing an Account of the Wonderful Cures Performed Through her Agency* (Boston, 1853), p. 15.

21. Elizabeth Cazden, *Antoinette Brown Blackwell: A Biography* (Old Westbury, New York: The Feminist Press, 1983), pp. 88–90.

22. *The Herald of Progress*, 17 March 1860.

23. Barbara Welter, "The Cult of True Womanhood," in *Dimnity Convictions: The American Woman in the Nineteenth Century* (Athens, Ohio: Ohio University Press, 1976), p. 21.

24. Lillie Buffum Chace Wyman and Arthur Crawford Wyman, *Elizabeth Buffum Chace, 1806–1899: Her Life and Its Environs* (Boston: W.B. Clarke Company, 1914), p. 107.

25. *Herald of Progress*, 4 February 1860.

26. For an example of the intertwining of the themes of religious and political equality in spiritualist thought, see Lois Waisbrooker, *Alice Vale: A Tale for the Times* (Boston: William White and Company, 1869).

27. This interpretation is suggested by Caske's argument that the Beechers' Spiritualism resulted from the persistence into the nineteenth century of their Calvinist anxiety about the fate of the soul after death. *Chariot of Fire*, chap. 10. On the culture of Victorianism see Daniel Walker Howe, "American Victorianism as a Culture," *American Quarterly* 27 (1975):507–32.

28. Elizabeth Stuart Phelps, *The Gates Ajar* (Boston: Fields, Osgood and Company, 1869).

29. Ann Douglas, "Heaven Our Home," and Stanley French, "The Cemetary as a Cultural Institution," both in *Death in America*, David Stannard, ed. (Philadelphia: University of Pennsylvania Press, 1975).

30. *Herald of Progress*, 25 March 1860.

31. Charles Beecher, *Spiritual Manifestations* (Boston: Lee and Shepard, 1879), p. 13.

32. Welter, "The Cult of True Womanhood," p. 41.

CHAPTER EIGHTEEN

From Shackles to Liberation: Religion, the Grimké Sisters and Dissent

FRANK G. KIRKPATRICK

As America has become increasingly secularized, it has become a commonplace assumption among some historians that an evangelical orientation necessarily correlates with a conservative political stance. One thinks initially perhaps of the new religious right which seems to be seeking a past that never was, or of the evangelical preachers of early twentieth-century fundamentalism who linked the truth of their gospel to the repeal of both liberal thought and what Billy Sunday called the social service nonsense of the Social Gospel. Even the revivalistic preachers of the 1940s and 1950s tended to link their evangelical message to a staunch anti-communism and a deep suspicion of the liberal social agenda.

A deeper reading of American religious history shows that this correlation between evangelical theology and conservative politics is far too simple. A clear counter example is provided by two remarkable social reformers of the ante-bellum period, Sarah (1792–1873) and Angelina (1805–1879) Grimké, who combined a deeply pietistic, evangelical faith with a social vision far in advance of the nation as a whole and even too radical with respect to women's rights for large segments of the already controversial abolitionist movement.

Most histories of the abolitionist and women's rights movements have discussed the effective work of the Grimké sisters. Their religious foundation and their conversion from the Episcopal Church to the Quakers are well known. But what has not been sufficiently analyzed or understood is how much their deep sense of a personal commitment to the Lordship of Jesus radicalized their evaluation of most of the traditional institutions, authorities, and practices not only of the social order but of organized religion itself, including their own Quakerism. Their piety was, for its day, radical because it went to the roots of the Christian faith, affirming what they saw as a deep, intimate, personal struggle to attain a perfect relationship with their Lord, Jesus Christ, and their hope of manifesting that relationship in a life of unceasing moral responsibility in a discipleship that would recognize no master but Christ. Through this discipleship the Grimkés radicalized the social implications of evangelicalism for an age which had been trying to domesticate the evangelical potential and to contain it within the structures of a male-dominated, slaveholding society.

EMERGING CONVICTIONS

The pre-abolitionist history of the sisters can be quickly sketched. They were born, fourteen years apart, to a distinguished, slave-owning Charleston, South Carolina family. "Something," Anne Firor Scott notes, "in the Grimkés' early experience had given them an independence of mind uncommon among nineteenth-century women."[1] Part of that something was an early revulsion, if not to slavery itself, then at least to its cruelty. Scott observes that slavery was particularly burdensome to the white women of the South because it was they who had the daily responsibility of oversight, especially of the house servants. Many white mistresses came to regard slaves as a trial, because of the difficult task of administration and care entrusted to them. Many also came to see that as women they were in many ways as much in thrall to their husbands and brothers as the slaves were. Mary Chestnut said she never saw a true woman who was not an abolitionist,[2] even though it was rare for southern women to act on this conviction.

The exact link between feminist and abolitionist concerns in the development of the Grimkés is not easy to discover. It does not seem to be the case that one obviously preceded and caused the other. Perhaps their awareness of the enslavement of women to men and of blacks to whites developed along similar lines and for many of the same reasons. The historical evidence is simply not complete enough to permit us to do more than guess which came first in the development of their consciousness of discrimination. The correlation in their own minds between slavery and the oppression of women certainly grew, and they became more articulate about it as they entered the ranks of the abolitionists in 1836 as the first female speakers on the issue of slavery and encountered hostility and suspicion even from within the leadership of the anti-slavery societies themselves. They were discouraged from speaking publicly to "promiscuous assemblies" (men and women together) and from linking the issues of women's rights and anti-slavery in their public addresses.

Religion was one outlet through which southern women could express some of the deeper feelings forbidden expression in the domestic circles of the South. Sarah and Angelina's first experience with formal religion was in the Episcopal Church to which the family belonged. One of the opportunities church participation gave to women was instructing the slaves, in a rudimentary way, in the Gospel. But the slaves were not permitted to read the Gospel themselves. The slaveowners, with the complicity of the churches, rightly sensed that if the slaves could read Scripture uninstructed by whites they might read into it insurrectionary or revolutionary possibilities. The uprising of Nat Turner in Virginia in 1831 and the Denmark Vesey conspiracy in Charleston in 1822 seemed to confirm this suspicion. But the contradiction involved in assuming that the slaves had sufficiently human souls to qualify for salvation but not enough humanity to learn salvation's journey for themselves may well have kindled in the sisters a sense of kinship with the slaves. Sarah, in particular, felt strongly called to the "masculine" profession of the law but was discouraged by her father and brother from pursuing it because of her sex. She was to say later, "with me learning was a passion. My nature [was] denied her appropriate nutriment, her course counteracted, her aspirations crushed."[3]

Both women were caught up early on in the revivalistic evangelism that swept the South during the Second Great Awakening in the first decades of the new century. Both sisters claimed conversion experiences. Sarah's was more private, but Angelina's, in 1826, led her for a while into the Presbyterian Church. The effects of her conversion, according to Katherine Lumpkin, were significant: "to do God's will on earth became her principal motivation" and led her to sense "a deep, compelling need to strip away those crippling bonds laid on her sex so that she could fully realize the powers that lay within her."[4]

Her days were "saturated with high purpose." Her diary records that she "had enlisted under the banner of the Cross . . . we must be about our Master's business."[5] It seems clear in retrospect that she was in the process of substituting one transcendent Master for all the corrupt and fallible masters of the human realm. By attaching herself so firmly and single-mindedly to one divine Lord, Angelina had discovered a means by which to move or reject all those human institutions and authorities which frustrated her vision of God's moral imperatives for her and the rest of humankind.

Sarah, meanwhile, had moved more and more toward the Quakers. She was attracted by their simplicity and intense spirituality. She, too, was looking for a way in which to live out her spiritual and moral commitment to a Master uncontaminated by human corruption. She was highly moved by reading in 1819 the famous Quaker spiritual exemplar and social reformer, John Woolman. When he referred to slavery as a burden which would grow heavier and heavier on the owners, he spoke to Sarah's own sense of its toll upon her soul. And when he concluded that, given the slaves' right as human beings to liberty, God would plead their cause and "happy will it be for such as walk in uprightness before him,"[6] Sarah could see that here was a moral imperative by which she could assure herself of living favorably in the sight of God.

Sarah eventually converted Angelina to Quakerism, by convincing her that the Quakers were "the most spiritual of any sect, the most obedient, the 'most crucified to the world.'"[7] Her conversion came when she "was finally convinced that true religion was at issue and that she could not escape what was at stake: to make her life consistent with the truth as she saw it."[8]

In spite of the fact that conversion to the Quakers solidified and justified Angelina's highest goal—to follow God alone—the price she had to pay was quite high. She was cut off, not only from her beloved Presbyterian community and its leader (who had become more than just a pastor to Angelina), but also from her Charleston friends, from the beliefs and customs of her own family, and even from the folkways of the region as a whole. Nevertheless, having made that break, Angelina, and Sarah before her, now were freed from the authority and coercion of their previous masters (including their father and brothers who had controlled both their lives and the lives of their slaves). "True believers," Angelina said in an angry exchange with her mother, "had but one Leader who would, if they followed Him, guide them into all truth."[9] It was "none but the power of God could ever have made me change," she declared, from her previous beliefs and behavior.[10]

When pressed about her growing opposition to slavery Angelina would always repeat Christ's words, "Do unto others as thou would'st have them do unto you . . . Would'st thou be willing to be a slave thyself?"[11] The alleged depravity of the slave, his unfitness for freedom, was countered by her argument that coercion and violence can never fit people for civilization: only moral instruction would suffice and this was denied the slave.

> But the root of the evil in Slavery is in the fact that the owners seldom thought of giving moral instruction . . . it [is] an institution so contrary to the spirit of the Gospel . . . a system which nourished the worst passions of the human heart.[12]

While she would later develop more detailed arguments about the economic dimensions of slavery, Angelina's fundamental objection continued to be that slavery was inconsistent with the *moral* responsibilities of the slaveowners and the moral potential of those who had been kept in bondage. Her own stand against slavery derived from a moral obligation she felt laid upon her by God's demand for spiritual and moral perfection in obedience to Him. Her belief that there were equal moral obligations placed upon all of God's creatures would later prove to be a crucial link between her demand for an end to slavery and for the legal establishment of rights for women.

> My idea is that whatever is morally right for a man to do is morally right for a woman to do. I recognize no rights but human rights. I know nothing of men's rights and women's rights. For in Christ Jesus there is neither male nor female . . . .
>
> This is part of the great doctrine of Human Rights and can no more be separated from Emancipation than the light from the heat of the sun; the rights of the slave and woman blend like the colors of the rainbow.[13]

She could even use this argument from moral responsibility to encourage two black women to attend a meeting at which they would undoubtedly encounter racial hostility and prejudice:

> I earnestly desire that you may be willing to bear these mortifications . . . They will tend to your growth in grace, and help your paler sisters *more* than anything else to overcome their own sinful feelings.[14]

Slavery, for Angelina, was evil not only for its oppression of the slave but also because of its corruption of white morality. It caused dissension in the white community, led owners to rely upon violence and the naked wielding of power, and prevented whites in slave-holding families from learning to do for themselves, causing them to grow up "unamiable, proud, and selfish"[15]—all moral failings which could only frustrate their moral relationship with God. Many years later, as the Civil War raged, Angelina could argue that the spiritual purity of the black man fighting for his freedom would have a morally salvific effect on whites:

> His heroism and self devotion and spirit of forgiveness will save us from curse of Slavery and the twin curse of Prejudice which like heels of iron have trodden him in the dust beneath our feet.[16]

Men of color, Sarah believed, would be "a remnant whose sufferings were preparing them to do a great work . . . ."[17]

THORNWELL'S COUNTER-ARGUMENT

In appealing to the notion of moral responsibility as the basis on which slavery should be overthrown, Angelina was utilizing an argument that could also be used, albeit in a transformed and distorted way, by the religious defenders of slavery. The most sophisticated and subtle argument on religious grounds ever developed in support of slavery drew precisely upon the notion of moral responsibility in order to claim that the slave's moral obligations were in no way infringed, and may in fact have been enhanced, by his servitude. It is ironic, perhaps, that the man who developed this argument most concisely and persuasively was a Presbyterian minister from the sisters' own Charleston, South Carolina, a man by the name of James Henley Thornwell. Though there is no evidence that the Grimkés responded specifically to Thornwell—they had left the state long before his views were published in 1850—the way in which they countered the general line of argument which he typified is highly revealing of the sophistication and radicality of their position. In his sermon, later published as a tract entitled "The Rights and the Duties of Masters," Thornwell acknowledged that "the same temper of universal rectitude is equally incumbent upon all,"[18] including those in servitude. This rectitude was equivalent to "the habitudes of holiness . . . the spirit of philanthropy . . . the spirit of piety . . . obedience to the law."[19] To be able to achieve this kind of rectitude required only a moral freedom, or the freedom of the inward man.

The fundamental question for Thornwell was whether the essential right of the slave, that is, his right to "the exercise of his moral nature," was incompatible with his being enslaved. Without this basic right "the fundamental law of his being" would be destroyed. But slavery did not deny or abridge this right. Slavery did not deny the slave the right to obey his master, nor did it curtail his freedom to be pious or charitable.

> The slave may come from the probation of *his* circumstances as fully stamped with the image of God, as those who have enjoyed an easier lot—he may be as completely in unison with the spirit of universal rectitude, as if he had been trained on flowery beds of ease.[20]

> If in the school of bondage he may be trained for the glorification and enjoyment of God, he is not divested of any of the rights which belong to him essentially *as a man*. He may develop his moral and religious nature—the source and measure of all his rights—and must, consequently, retain every characteristik [*sic*] of essential humanity.[21]

"The moral discipline of man is consistent with the greatest variety of external condition," one of which is slavery. As long as the slave shows his reverence to God by a "cheerful obedience to the lawful commands of his master,"[22] his moral character will be blessed in the sight of God. Having his *essential* moral rights fully intact even in slavery, therefore, the only things the slave lacks are *contingent* rights, such as the rights of the citizen and the free member of the commonwealth. But these contingent rights "do not spring from humanity simply considered" and thus are not relevant to his moral character.

Thornwell did not simply leave his argument at this abstract level, however. His ulterior motivation in developing, and certainly in applying the argument, was revealed when he added to the claim that contingent rights had no relation to essential rights the obviously unacceptable consequence, "for then they would belong to women and children!"[23] The refusal to distinguish between these two kinds of rights—a distinction which, Thornwell must have known, was denied by abolitionists and in particular by the two wayward daughters of Charleston—would, if "fully and legitimately carried out, . . . condemn every arrangement of society, which did not secure to all its members an absolute equality of position; it is the very spirit of socialism and communism."[24]

Not only was Thornwell not opposed to religious instruction for the slave, but he believed its effect would be to create in the slave "a sense of moral responsibility . . . which would be, at once, a security to the master and an immense blessing to the slave."[25] Thornwell even called upon the very Jesus to whom the Grimkés were always turning in order to support his position. He said of Jesus,

> He was no stirrer up of strife, nor mover of sedition. His "religion . . . is the pillar of society . . . the parent of social order, which alone has power to curb the fury of the passions, and secure to every one his rights; to the laborious, the reward of their industry; to the rich, the enjoyment of their wealth; to nobles, the preservation of their honors; and to princes, the stability of their thrones."[26]

By drawing a clear line between moral accountability and the social conditions within which that accountability could be exercised, Thornwell's argument destroyed the foundation on which social reform rests. As long as it could be maintained that external social conditions were irrelevant to the development of moral character, Thornwell's argument was the perfect defense of the status quo. He did not need to play down the importance of religion: in fact, he could extoll its significance as the only vehicle by which a division could be created between spiritual and social conditions. The irony is that the sermon was originally preached at the dedication of a church "erected . . . for the Benefit and Instruction of the Coloured Population."[27]

The force of the Grimkés' religious and moral position depended upon their ability to meet the fundamental assumptions on which Thornwell's argument rested. To this author's knowledge they never addressed the argument in the terms in which Thornwell cast it. However, their response is contained in their repeated and insistent claim that human moral responsibility knows no distinction of sex or race and that it therefore *presupposes* equal moral rights for all persons. In a dispute in the 1830s over whether they should speak publicly on behalf of women's rights while at the same time working for abolition, Angelina was to say that they did not need to speak *explicitly* of women's rights. "We speak of their *responsibilities* and leave *them* to *infer* their *rights*."[28] Moral reform meant " 'uplifting a great self-evident central principle [the equality of moral duties] before all eyes.' "[29]

It was clear to the Grimkés that Jesus made no distinction between persons when it came to moral responsibilities.

> Who has ever attempted to draw a line of separation between the duties of men and women, as *moral* beings, without committing the grossest inconsistencies on the one hand, or running into the most arrant absurdities on the other?[30]

Nevertheless, they chose for the most part not to mix public speeches against slavery with ones for the equal rights of women, as a concession to the entreaties of Theodore Dwight Weld and others who had feared that to do so would diminish the effectiveness of the sisters' abolitionist message.

The Centrality of the Lordship of Jesus

The strength and certitude of the Grimkés' position on the social issues before them arose out of their deep commitment to the Lordship of Jesus. Angelina continually complained about others in the abolitionist movement who, unlike herself, did not have "their hearts fixed trusting in the Lord alone . . . in simple faith on Jesus."[31] Sarah claimed that she was willing

> to spend and be spent in the cause of the enslaved, and . . . one of the best means of serving this cause is by the holiness of our lives that the mouths of gainsayers may be stopt, and that by near communion with the Lord Jesus we may be thoro'ly instructed in his will in all things.[32]

She reaffirmed her commitment to the principle that one must always come back to "the one simple point 'Follow after holiness without which no man shall see the Lord,' " and in this context mentioned the importance of her having been "born again."[33] Similar references to a "primitive simplicity to trust in the Lord," her desire to "follow her sure Leader in child-like confidence of undoubting faith," the need for a "simple obedience to the divine will," and the confidence that "if we trust in him we shall be preserved"[34] indicate how sincerely Sarah could say (in effect speaking for both of them) that her life had been "the panting of a soul after eternity."[35] Angelina could say of the anti-slavery cause that it strengthened her to "break the prison of my soul and come forth to the high and holy contemplation of Jehovah and of my fellow men as the image of my God."[36] Sarah also talked of how in reading the Scriptures her "spirit becomes one with Christ Jesus."[37]

Underlying these repeated affirmations of their relationship to Jesus and to the simple truths of God was a sense that both were on moral probation. Angelina confessed to Lewis Tappan in 1841 that:

> We shall be judged individually and not in the aggregate. We must give an account of the effects produced by our example, influence, etc. as individuals—*not* as communities,[38]

even though she disclaimed any ultimate responsibility for the consequences of her acts of discipleship ("I do not believe we are responsible for the consequences of doing the will of God").[39] Their confidence in the power of moral suasion alone was quite strong. They were convinced that, as Angelina put it, "moral suasion" will "bend" men's hearts to do the right. "The mighty engine of moral power" would drag in its rear all the reforms of the day.[40]

In her letters to Theodore Weld (the great evangelical anti-slavery leader whom she later married) after their engagement, Angelina disclosed a litany of spiritual exercises through which she was putting herself in preparation for the continuing task of moral suasion. As a form of spiritual growth and discipline they urged each other to tell the most egregious faults the one can find in the other. Angelina said to Weld at one point:

> I expect you to help me crucify the old man of sin and to crush down the first things of *pride* and self gratulation. O! Lord Jesus . . . purge out the old leaven and turn thy hand upon me until I am purified from dross. . . .[41]

It is not surprising in this regard that Sarah was attracted to the teachings of the spiritual perfectionist John Humphrey Noyes, later founder of the Oneida community. Weld himself had been influenced by Charles Grandison Finney who had developed his own brand of perfectionism, known as the Oberlin theology, which stressed the possibility of completely overcoming sin, at least inwardly or spiritually. It is likely that when Sarah wrote to Weld in 1837 that she had read with excitement some copies of the *Perfectionist*, edited by Noyes, she spoke for Angelina as well.[42]

SCRIPTURAL EXEGESIS

Although this highly personal, deeply intimate spiritual relationship to Jesus remained the core of the sisters' belief, included within it was a strong reliance upon Scripture as the revelation of God's will. They constantly made reference to the Bible as the only ground on which they will argue the morality of social issues. In her *An Appeal to the Christian Women of the South,* Angelina stated unequivocally that "The Bible is my ultimate appeal in all matters of faith and practice."[43] But the appeal is not a simple one. Both the *An Appeal to the Christian Women of the South* and Sarah's *An Epistle to the Clergy of the Southern States*[44] rest on an exegesis of Biblical texts which is informed, thorough, and detailed. The dominion of Adam over the animals was exegeted to show that it does not extend to other men. Paul's return of the slave Onesimus was put in context and dismissed as a support for slavery. Both sisters developed a Biblical exegesis of servitude in the Old Testament and used a rudimentary knowledge of Hebrew to do so. Such servitude, they claimed, with its Jubilee year of freedom, "was as different from American slavery, as Christianity is from heathenism," Hebrew having, in fact, no word at all for slave. And the gospel of Jesus Sarah nearly reduced to the proclamation: Liberty to the captive![45]

In partial answer to Thornwell's assumption that God supports the status quo, Sarah even developed a theme dear to liberation theologians today: that the prophetic dimension of the Bible is an authentic and accurate revelation of God's redemptive intent and that in that regard God "is in a peculiar manner the God of the poor and the needy, the despised and the oppressed."[46] And then she linked her strong sense of moral probation and individual responsibility with the Biblical message of liberation: "God has in infinite mercy raised up those [she recalls, in particular, the women of the Bible] who have moral courage and religion enough to obey the divine command, 'Cry aloud and spare not, lift up thy voice like a trumpet, and show my people their transgressions!' "[47] So that the point not be missed, she added immediately that the principles she was trumpeting in her speeches and writing "are the principles of the holy Scriptures."[48]

Later in their writings on women's rights, the sisters continued to use their exegetical skills. In a letter to Henry C. Wright they requested answers to some very specific exegetical questions, e.g., is "man" a generic term in the Bible, how does the word for man relate to the word for woman, what is the difference between the Greek and Hebrew in this regard, are minister, preacher and deacon synonomous in Ephesians 6:21, etc. They were even aware of possible corruptions in the text, and of earlier and later, interpolated passages.[49] Throughout they were convinced that only a thorough knowledge of the Bible would remove those distinctions and practices of men which perpetuate unjustified discrimination and the denial of human rights. As Sarah said to Jane Douglass, her black friend, in urging renewed study of the Bible, "Be not afraid to see the truth, . . . Disencumber your minds of the traditions of men and learn of Jesus."[50]

They were also astute enough to know that the traditions of men had often meant a male-biased interpretation of Scripture. While Sarah proclaimed that she was "willing to abide by its [the New Testament's] decision," she entered her protest

> Against the false translations of some passages by the MEN who did that work and against the perverted interpretations by the MEN who undertook to write commentaries thereon. I am inclined to think, when we [women] are admitted to the honor of

studying Greek and Hebrew, we shall produce some various readings of the Bible, a little different from those we now have.[51]

Part of their answer to Thornwell's argument, then, was to dig into the context of the Biblical writings to uncover those principles which supported their belief that God is for equality and liberty. To what extent they ignored those passages which would have confused or undermined their interpretation is not clear. Nevertheless, their interpretation of the Bible is not so idiosyncratic by modern standards as to render it obviously false or inaccurate.

THE GRIMKÉS' 'ULTRAISM' AND DISTRUST OF POWER

Building on the basis of their moral and spiritual relationship with Jesus and their interpretation of his will in Scripture, the sisters developed a host of ideas, which Angelina once summarized as their "ultraism,"[52] regarding power, authority, and institutions. This "ultraism" pushed the sisters into the category of radicals, in thought if not always in action. If Jesus was alone the Lord, then all forms of human dominion were automatically suspect. Human dominion, the desire to dominate and subordinate others, arose from a sinful lust for power. Slavery and the suppression of women were manifestations of that lust.

The lust of dominion inevitably produces hardness of heart, because the state of mind which craves unlimited power, such as slavery confers, involves a desire to use that power . . . .[53]

Consequently, the sisters came to distrust power in general and "the despotic control of man"[54] in particular. "Nothing but a narrow-minded view . . . can induce any one to believe in this *subordination* to a fallible being."[55]

Oppressive power was power exercised arbitrarily by persons over other persons. It violated what, to the Grimkés, was the injunction of Jesus to follow him alone, to be humble and to recognize the equal worth of others. The imposition of power on others inevitably worked to the detriment of both dominator and dominated. As Angelina said of slavery

Even were slavery not a curse to its victims, the exercise of arbitrary power works such fearful ruin upon the hearts of slaveholders that I would feel impelled to labor and pray for its overthrow with my last energies and my last breath.[56]

This kind of dominion of person over person is in reality, according to Angelina, the ascendency of the strong over the weak and the cause of war in all its forms. It arises when man places his trust in his own power as the illusory means to security. But it is an idolatrous trust that can be overcome only by placing oneself solely and completely in the hands of Jesus.

The question of power was also central to their discussion of women's rights. In 1838 Angelina had been challenged by the claims of Catherine Beecher that women are naturally inclined toward defenselessness and consequently a dependence upon the power of men, without which men would grant them nothing. Men, on the other hand, Beecher asserted, are combatants who are inclined to force and coercion, traits which make them reliable for the women who must depend upon them. While denouncing Beecher's appeal to "the generous promptings of chivalry" and the "romantic gallantry" which justify this dependence of women on men (which Angelina called "such littleness, . . . silly insipidities, such paltry, sickening adulation, sinful foolery"[57]), she stood Beecher's argument on its head by claiming that:

> If, by a *combatant*, thou meanest one who "drives by *physical force*," then I say, *man* has no more right to appear as *such* a combatant than woman; for all the pacific precepts of the gospel were given to *him*, as well as to her.

The "struggle for power," "coercive influences" "the use of force or of fear," are no more rightly exercised by men than by women. "All such influences are repudiated by the precepts and examples of Christ, and his apostles. . . . These 'general principles are correct,' if thou wilt only permit them to be of *general application*. . . ."[58]

Having evinced a deep suspicion of power arbitrarily exercised by human beings over their peers, it was a natural next step for the Grimkés to embrace the doctrine of non-resistance to evil, except through moral suasion. "The Christian," Sarah proclaimed, who "truly feels that he can say, 'The Lord is the strength of my life, of whom shall I be afraid,' asks not the aid of man in the day of peril; he feels that the arm of omnipotence is pledged for his preservation . . . he will not violate the command of his God 'resist not evil.' "[59] Later in the same letter she said: "I cannot describe to thee the blessed influence which my ultra Peace Principles have had upon my mind."[60] The following year Sarah wrote that her "whole being revolted so intuitively at the law of violence," that she was turning more and more to the"soul-elevating sentiments of the Sermon on the Mount," adding that "as I practice them my spirit becomes one with Christ Jesus."[61]

Responding to the tendency on the part of some abolitionists to take up arms in the struggle against slavery, Sarah asked "how can we expect His blessing upon our efforts, if we take carnal weapons to fight his battles? Are we walking in his steps? Is that mind in us which was also in Christ Jesus?"[62] The road to perfection, as Noyes and many others were arguing, could not include recourse to violence. If one trusted in the Lord then surely His truth, through the faithful moral discipleship of His followers, would ultimately prevail even if in the meantime suffering and persecution for the faithful were the price that must be paid.

Nothing, in fact, could more truly demonstrate one's moral purity than a willingness to die rather than compromise moral truth. As Angelina boldly proclaimed in her famous letter to William Lloyd Garrison of August 30, 1835:

> If persecution is the means which God has ordained for the accomplishment of this great end, EMANCIPATION: then . . . I feel as if I could say, LET IT COME; for it is my deep, solemn, deliberate conviction, that *this is a cause worth dying for*.[63]

Persecution might well be their lot should they embrace not only the cause of emancipation but also that of supporting it in a non-resistant, peaceful way. This, they acknowledged, would be "the greatest test of our faith."[64]

Rejection of Civil and Ecclesiastical Institutions

Aware that most human institutions and other forms by which human authority is maintained rest on the willingness to use violence or force, the Grimkés, like Garrison, were led ineluctably by the logic of moral purity to their distrust of *all* human institutions and structures of authority, of which slavery and the domination of women were only the most blatant examples. Angelina exclaimed to Weld:

> Civil Government is based on physical force, a physical force is forbidden by the Law of Love. If I have no right to *resist evil myself*, I have no right to call upon another to resist it for me, and if *I must not* call upon the Magistrate to redress my grievances, if *I* have no *right* to do so, then he can have no right to render me any such aid.[65]

It is God's government alone which is entitled to our obedience.

Consequently, as Sarah put it,

> The more I contemplate this sublime doctrine of acknowledgeing *[sic]* no government but Gods *[sic]*, of losing myself from all dominion of man both civil and ecclesiastical, the more I am persuaded it is the only doctrine that can bring us into that liberty wherewith Christ hath made us free.[66]

And to underscore the essential link she made between these radical conclusions for practice and her desire to be united in spiritual purity with Jesus, she added, "until we receive and believe this doctrine we have not that faith which over cometh the world, and without faith it is impossible to please God."[67] Their rejection of civil government clearly rests on their belief in the radically different kind of government God presides over. In a joint letter to Weld, they stated:

> All government, whether civil or ecclesiastical, conflicts with the govt. of Jehovah and that by the Christian, no other govt. can be acknowledged without leaning more or less on an arm of flesh.[68]

In these comments, Sarah and Angelina do not distinguish in any significant way between the authority of civil and ecclesiastical governments. Given their highly personal relationship with God, it is not surprising that they would feel little attachment even to human institutions which claimed to speak for Him. As we have seen, they both moved from a relatively superficial involvement in the Episcopal Church to the more spiritual and individualistic Quakers (Angelina having passed briefly through participation in the evangelical Presbyterians). But even the Quakers ultimately failed to hold their allegiance. The sisters' antisalvery work was more radical in practice than that which many Quakers, especially those still engaged in opposing the more liberal Hicksites, were willing to encourage or condone. And when Angelina married a non-Quaker, and Sarah participated in the wedding, they were disowned by the Meeting.

Gerda Lerner has said that following this disownment,

> All that remained was to live their humanitarian convictions according to their own, very personal interpretation of the Bible. The religious reformer ended up in making a religion of reform.[69]

I believe Lerner is wrong in this last claim because she overlooks the crucial fact that reform was to the Grimkés the outer manifestation of an even deeper inward commitment to achieving a singleness of mind, heart, and will with the only master they ever recognized, Jesus Christ. From what Sarah had called "the one simple point 'Follow after holiness without which no man shall see the Lord' "[70] it followed that "Civil government, Public worship, the Ministry, the sabbath, and other points connected with religion" should, along with "all *present* systems," be thrown into obscurity. She claimed that she could "almost rejoice in the prospect of a release from the duty. . . . of attending public worship."[71] And if that duty "is laid in the dust," then "the necessity of a regular ministry paid or unpaid delegated by human authority will cease."[72] And when that happens "the wicked and injurious distinctions which now prevail will vanish away and Christians feel in spirit and in truth that there is neither male nor female, but all are one in Christ."[73]

Sarah accused the churches, or sects, of substituting their own doctrines and practices for the simple truths of God, and argued that to submit to these would be analogous to the slavery under which the black men and women of the South were suffering so cruelly:

> Our slavery to ecclesiastical domination is tottering to its fall . . . the present system of Ch. discipline and the ministry can no more stand the light of the 19th century than the slavery of the Southern States.[74]

How great a loss it is when people

> permit their minds to be diverted by trying to discover what sect they shall join, thus seeking the living among the dead and substituting the creeds and the ordinances of man for that pure and holy communion which God designs shall exist between Christ and his disciples.[75]

By the end of 1837, Sarah and Angelina, in the course of an attack upon the growing "aristocracy that prevails among our colored brethren," confessed that they had given up going to any place of worship for "they are alike . . . places of spiritual famine."[76] Many years later, moved by William Miller's millenial prophecies, Angelina lashed out again at the churches, this time on the strength of her belief that the end of history was at hand:

> I fully believe in the downfall of every earthly throne, the overthrow of every political government, the annihilation of every Ecclesiastical Establishment and the dissolution of every sect and party under the sun. I feel the rocking of that great earthquake which is to shake down and whelm forever all organization, institutions, and every social framework of human device; but I am calm, hopeful, happy, for I see arising out of their ruins the Everlasting Kingdom of God.[77]

It is this radical distrust of everything institutional which stands between the soul and God that sets the Grimkés so decisively apart from James Thornwell, whose whole argument rests on the assumption that God has ordained institutions in order to guarantee order and security. The Grimkés' "ultraism" challenged the entire history of the Christian understanding of the state and the structures of social order developed originally by Augustine and given its decisive expression in the two-kingdoms doctrine of Luther. Only on the basis of such a radical challenge to the institutions and structures of men could the Grimkés provide an effective counter-argument to the subtle, nuanced, and powerful arguments of Thornwell, as well as to the charges made even by their closest allies that they were advocating too many causes at once, thus reducing the effectiveness of their work against slavery. Only people convinced, as they were, of the absolute truth, simplicity, and unity in one Lord of the morality to which their lives were witness could adopt the stance of sweeping ultraism.

When the sisters were challenged, for example, even by Weld, not to mix the cause of women's rights (which he supported in principle) with the cause of abolition lest they weaken the latter movement, Angelina, in reply to both Weld and John Greenleaf Whittier, declared without equivocation

> *The time* to assert a right is *the* time when *that* right is denied. *We must establish this right* for if we do not, it will be impossible for *us* to go on with the work of Emancipation . . . our *right* to labor in it *must* be firmly established; *not* on the ground of Quakerism, but on the only firm basis of human rights, the Bible.[78]

She went on to assert that moral reforms "are bound together in a circle like the sciences; they blend with each other like the colors of the rainbow, they are the parts only of our glorious whole and that whole is Christianity, pure *practical* Christianity."[79]

She attacked in particular appeals to expediency or concessions to political "realities." Those who would compartmentalize moral reforms on the grounds of "expediency" overlook the fundamental truth that Christianity is "a beautiful and harmonious system which would not be divided."[80] "O how lamentably superficial we are, to suppose that one truth can hurt another . . ."[81] "Abandon the law of expediency NOW and trust in Him who can pilot us thro' every storm."[82] In the course of this defense of uniting moral reforms, Angelina claimed that the work of the reformer is more akin to that of the politically outrageous prophets than to institutionally constrained priests. Prophets were unpaid (another attack on the paid ministry), and "as there were *prophetesses* as well as prophets, so there *ought* to be now *female* as well as male ministers."[83]

In abandoning the law of expediency, the Grimkés advocated an end not only to slavery but to racial prejudice in the North as well, the latter shocking even some of their antislavery supporters. Prejudice was a clear violation of Christ's command, "whatsoever ye would that men should do to you, do ye even so to them."[84] An "unholy and unreasonable prejudice" by Northerners is "doing the work of oppression on the free people of color in our midst. Let them learn to measure men, *not* by their complexions, but by their intellectual and moral worth,"[85] just as should be done with respect to women.

Because "woman in EVERY particular shares equally with man rights and responsibilities,"[86] the Grimkés, in an affirmation uniting all of their basic themes, drew the logical conclusion that,

> It is woman's right to have a voice in all the laws and regulations by which she is to be *governed* . . . and that the present arrangements of society, on these points, are a *violation of human rights, a rank usurpation of power,* a violent seizure and confiscation of what is sacredly and inalienably hers— . . .[87]

In fact, they argued, woman has every right to sit "in the Presidential chair of the United States."[88] They even linked racial prejudice to a denial of the sisterhood of all women. Angelina had appealed to women to oppose slavery because slave women "are our sisters; and to us as women, they have a right to look for sympathy with their sorrows, and effort and prayer for their rescue. . . ."[89]

THE WEDDING OF THEIR CONCERNS

An event which symbolically represented the linkage between most of the Grimkés' moral concerns and demonstrated how far they had moved in advance of the customs of their time was the wedding of the two spiritually driven abolitionists, Angelina and Theodore Weld in 1838.

The ceremony was written by the participants themselves, neither Angelina nor Weld feeling they could be bound by a prescribed set of words. They recognized the legitimacy of the state only to the extent of determining what was minimally necessary to have the marriage regarded as legal. They wished no official church recognition of the service. It will be remembered that by Angelina marrying a non-Quaker, and Sarah, simply by attending the service, had violated a Quaker tenet and were subsequently expelled from their Meeting. Many of the radical and conservative members of the abolitionist movement were present. Several black persons, including two former slaves who had once been owned by the Grimké family in South Carolina, were invited. A black minister offered up a prayer. Weld "alluded to the unrighteous power vested in a husband by the laws [of the country], over the person and property of his wife and he renounced 'all authority' thus accorded to him, except 'the influence which love would give to them over each other as moral and immortal beings.'" Weld also prayed that their union "be productive of enlarged usefulness, and increased sympathy for the slave."[90]

At the heart of the relationship between Weld and Angelina was an extended view of their understanding that men and women have equal moral rights and responsibilities. Their relationship consequently would be one of spiritual companions. As Sarah would put it in her letter on "Social Intercourse of the Sexes," the woman in the marriage would be "an intelligent and heaven-born creature, whose society will cheer, refine and elevate her companion, and . . . she will receive the same blessings she confers.[91] Using her exegetical skills she interpreted the word "help-meet" in the Septuagint as "manifestly" signifying a companion. "Now I believe," she concluded, "it will be impossible for woman to fill the station assigned her by God, until her brethren mingle with her as an equal, as a moral being . . ."[92] Certainly this is how Angelina and Weld regarded each other; as companions equally engaged in a spiritual discipleship to one Lord and Master, Jesus Christ. In joining themselves together they were not abandoning that discipleship but entering upon a life of companionship in which each would regard the other as an equal partner with the same moral rights and responsibilities. Nevertheless, Angelina once allowed herself to express puzzlement as to "why those of our own sex *cannot* fill the void in human hearts."[93]

After the wedding Angelina's active involvement in the abolitionist movement diminished steadily, and she underwent a lengthy struggle with despondency which has never been fully explained. Whatever the explanation, it seems evident that she never abandoned her beliefs and convictions. It is fitting to note that one of her and Sarah's last public acts came late in their lives, in the winter of 1870, when with forty women of Hyde Park, Massachusetts, they "walked through the driving snow to deposit their ballots in a separate box" in a demonstration in support of women's suffrage.[94]

What sustained and explained their lives of social reform, radical for its times, was nothing less than a commitment to a single-minded discipleship to Jesus Christ, as they interpreted his moral requirements in the context of their life-long search for moral and spiritual purity. This commitment transcended all human authorities and institutions. It resulted in a rejection of government, slavery, violence, arbitrary power, churches and sects, the ministry, and all the forms of discrimination by which women were treated as inferior in rights and responsibilities to men. It was a radical discipleship; but nothing less would have been able to move these remarkable women, Sarah and Angelina Grimké, from shackles to liberation in an age in which the former were a daily reality and the latter a hope too subversive to be more than a dream for most.

Notes

1. Anne Firor Scott, *The Southern Lady: From Pedestal to Politics 1830–1930* (Chicago: University of Chicago Press, 1970), p. 62.
2. Ibid., p. 48.
3. Sarah Grimké, "Education of Women" (essay), Box 21, Weld, MSS, quoted in Gerda Lerner, *The Grimké Sisters from South Carolina* (New York: Schocken Books, 1971), p. 29.
4. Katherine Du Pre Lumpkin, *The Emancipation of Angelina Grimké* (Chapel Hill: University of North Carolina Press, © 1974), p. 24.
5. Ibid., p. 25. While individual letters and tracts of Sarah and Angelina have been preserved, it is not always possible to separate the religious sentiments of one sister from those of the other. They tended to think and feel as one. Unless specifically noted in the text, the convictions and beliefs of one can reasonably be assumed to be those of the other as well.
6. *The Journal of John Woolman*, with an Introduction by John G. Whittier (Boston: Houghton Mifflin Company, 1871), pp. 104, 106.
7. Lumpkin, *Emancipation*, p. 32.
8. Ibid., p. 38.
9. Ibid., p. 47.
10. Ibid., p. 48.
11. Ibid.
12. Ibid., p. 49.
13. Angelina to Jane Smith, 10 August 1837, Ibid., p. 120.
14. Angelina to Jane Smith, 17 April, 20 January 1837, Ibid., p. 105.
15. Ibid., p. 46.
16. Angelina to E.J. Cutler, [n.d.] June 1863, Ibid., p. 217.
17. Sarah to Sarah Douglass, 23 November 1837, in *Letters of Theodore Dwight Weld, Angelina Grimké Weld and Sarah Grimké, 1822–1844*, 2 vols., ed. Gilbert H. Barnes and Dwight L. Dumond (New York: D. Appleton-Century Company, 1934), vol. 1.
18. James Henley Thornwell, "The Rights and the Duties of Masters, A Sermon Preached at the Dedication of A Church" (1850), in *Issues in American Protestantism*, ed. Robert L. Ferm (Garden City, N.Y.: Doubleday & Co., 1969), p. 191.
19. Ibid., p. 190.
20. Ibid.

21. Ibid., p. 191.
22. Ibid.
23. Ibid., p. 192.
24. Ibid., p. 189.
25. Ibid., p. 197.
26. Ibid.
27. Ibid., p. 189.
28. Angelina to T. Weld and John Greenleaf Whittier, 20 August 1837, Barnes and Dumond, *Letters*, vol. 1.
29. Sarah and Angelina to T. Weld, 20 September 1837, Barnes and Dumond, *Letters*, vol. 1.
30. Angelina Grimké, from *Letters to Catherine E. Beecher, in Reply to an Essay on Slavery and Abolitionism, Addressed to A.E. Grimké* (Boston, 1838), Letter XI, as found in *Up From the Pedestal: Selected Writings in the History of American Feminism*, Aileen S. Kraditor, ed. (Chicago: Quadrangle Books, © 1968), p. 61.
31. Sarah and Angelina to Gerrit Smith, 9 April 1837, Barnes and Dumond, *Letters*, vol. 1.
32. Sarah to T. Weld, 11 June 1837, Barnes and Dumond, *Letters*, vol. 1.
33. Ibid.
34. Sarah to Gerrit Smith, 28 June 1837, Barnes and Dumond, *Letters*, vol. 1.
35. Sarah to T. Weld, 2 February 1838, Barnes and Dumond, *Letters*, vol. 2.
36. Ibid.
37. Sarah to Gerrit Smith, 16 February 1838, Barnes and Dumond, *Letters*, vol. 2.
38. Angelina to Lewis Tappan, [n.d.] August 1841, Barnes and Dumond, *Letters*, vol. 2.
39. Sarah and Angelina to Henry C. Wright, 27 August 1837, Barnes and Dumond, *Letters*, vol. 1.
40. Angelina Grimké, *An Appeal to the Christian Women of the South* (Shrewsbury, New Jersey, 1836), pp. 26–27.
41. Angelina to Weld, 22 February 1838, Barnes and Dumond, *Letters*, vol. 2.
42. Sarah to Weld, 11 June 1837, Barnes and Dumond, *Letters*, vol. 1.
43. Angelina Grimké, *Christian Women*, p. 3.
44. Sarah M. Grimké, *An Epistle to the Clergy of the Southern States* (New York, 1836).
45. Ibid., p. 11.
46. Ibid., p. 12.
47. Ibid., p. 15.
48. Ibid.
49. Sarah and Angelina to Henry C. Wright, 27 August 1837, Barnes and Dumond, *Letters*, vol. 1.
50. Sarah to Jane Douglass, 23 November 1837, Barnes and Dumond, *Letters*, vol. 1.
51. Sarah Grimké, from "Province of Woman. The Pastoral Letter," *New*

England Spectator, reprinted in *The Liberator*, 6 October 1837, found in Kraditor, *Up From the Pedestal*, p. 54.

52. Angelina to Weld and Whittier, 20 August 1837, Barnes and Dumond, *Letters*, vol. 1.

53. Sarah M. Grimké, *Epistle to the Clergy*, p. 18.

54. Angelina Grimké, *Letters to Catherine E. Beecher*, Letter XII, in Kraditor, *Up From the Pedestal*, p. 64.

55. Ibid., p. 66.

56. Lumpkin, *Emancipation*, p. 172.

57. Angelina Grimké, *Letters to Catherine E. Beecher*, Letter XI, in Kraditor, *Up From the Pedestal*, p. 57.

58. Ibid., pp. 61–62.

59. Sarah to Gerrit Smith, 28 June 1837, Barnes and Dumond, *Letters*, vol. 1.

60. Ibid.

61. Sarah to Gerrit Smith, 16 February 1838, Barnes and Dumond, *Letters*, vol. 2.

62. Sarah to Sarah Douglass, 23 November 1837, Barnes and Dumond, *Letters*, vol. 1.

63. Lumpkin, *Emancipation*, p. 78.

64. Sarah and Angelina to Gerrit Smith, 9 April 1837, Barnes and Dumond, *Letters*, vol. 1.

65. Angelina to Weld, 21 January 1838, Barnes and Dumond, *Letters*, vol. 2.

66. Sarah to Gerrit Smith, 28 June 1837, Barnes and Dumond, *Letters*, vol. 1.

67. Ibid.

68. Sarah and Angelina to Weld, 20 September 1837, Barnes and Dumond, *Letters*, vol. 1.

69. Lerner, *The Grimké Sisters from South Carolina*, p. 357.

70. Sarah to Weld, 11 June 1837, Barnes and Dumond, *Letters*, vol. 1.

71. Ibid.

72. Ibid.

73. Ibid.

74. Sarah to Gerrit Smith, 28 June 1837, Barnes and Dumond, *Letters*, vol. 1.

75. Ibid.

76. Sarah and Angelina to Weld, 17 December 1837, Barnes and Dumond, *Letters*, vol. 1.

77. Quoted in Lerner, *The Grimké Sisters from South Carolina*, p. 308.

78. Angelina to Weld and Whittier, 20 August 1837, Barnes and Dumond, *Letters*, vol. 1.

79. Ibid.

80. Sarah and Angelina to Henry C. Wright, 27 August 1837, Barnes and Dumond, *Letters*, vol. 1.

81. Ibid.

82. Angelina to Weld, 27 August 1837, Barnes and Dumond, *Letters*, vol. 1.

83. Angelina to Weld and Whittier, 20 August 1837, Barnes and Dumond, *Letters*, vol. 1.

84. Sarah and Angelina on "The definite, practical means by which the

North can put an end to Slavery in the South," 1 March 1837, Barnes and Dumond, *Letters*, vol. 1.

85. Ibid.

86. Weld to Sarah and Angelina, 15 August 1837, Barnes and Dumond, *Letters*, vol. 1.

87. Angelina Grimké, *Letters to Catherine E. Beecher*, Letter XII in Kraditor, *Up From the Pedestal*, p. 65.

88. Ibid.

89. Quoted in Lerner, *The Grimké Sisters from South Carolina*, p. 161.

90. Sarah to Elizabeth Pease describing the wedding, 20 (?) May 1838, Barnes and Dumond, *Letters*, vol. 2.

91. Sarah Grimké, *Letters on the Condition of Woman and the Equality of the Sexes* (1838), in Kraditor, *Up From the Pedestal*, p. 57.

92. Ibid.

93. Angelina to Weld, 22 February 1838, Barnes and Dumond, *Letters*, vol. 2.

94. Eleanor Flexner, *Century of Struggle: The Women's Rights Movement in the United States* (New York: Atheneum, 1971), p. 165.

Chapter Nineteen

The American Catholic Bishops and Woman: From the Nineteenth Amendment to ERA

Antoinette Iadarola

According to historian Barbara Welter, nineteenth-century Americans enshrined women on a pedestal as encompassing the four feminine virtues of piety, purity, submissiveness, and domesticity. These attributes formed an ideology of true womanhood, of which Betty Friedan's "feminine mystique" is a linear descendant. Although building upon earlier Mariology and the cult of courtly love, this ideology arose in its nineteenth-century form as a part of the Romantic reaction against revolution and industrialization and their attendant threats to traditional values, especially the home. After marriage, man and woman became one and that one was man. Woman was to subordinate her entire being to her husband and continue to be submissive and passive. However, in matters of domesticity woman was to reign supreme, to be high priestess, for she was uniquely qualified to preside over her own domain, the home, which was viewed as a bulwark against the evils of an industrial society.[1]

Roman Catholics readily accepted this fixed model of woman, for it was rooted in a Christian theology and culture which held that such a model was ordained by God, embodied in the Virgin Mary, and revealed by a Pauline interpretation of scripture and/or the natural law. In addition, this view of womanhood was reinforced by biological differences and supported by a historical tradition which proclaimed the supremacy of patriarchal structures. In reply to the question, "What does it mean to say that nature intends women to do certain things?," Catholics posited a distinct role for each sex. A woman's specific role and function, a "woman's place," were clearly in the home as rearer of children and the nucleus of the family. Her power could best be exerted through her quiet influence on her husband and children. Any deviation from this role, critics charged, would upset the order of the universe and threaten the physical end of the human race.[2] This is an interesting point, for the characteristics of women were seen simultaneously as unchangeably rooted in woman's biological "nature" and yet something that would be "lost" instantly if she simply stepped out of her designated "place."

Catholic education for women reinforced these attitudes. As Rosemary Ruether convincingly argues, Catholic and non-Catholic women's colleges came into existence for very different reasons. Institutions such as Wellesley, Smith, and Radcliffe were established to "combat the myth of women's incapacity for the kind of college studies available to men," and they developed curricula and standards to rival male education. Separation was forced upon these institutions by male exclusion, not by the presence of any special feminine educational philosophy. On the other hand, Catholic women's colleges were founded with the rationale that women possessed a distinct nature and thus needed a specifically feminine education. According to Ruether, these institutions have been "handicapped by that Catholic feminism which decrees subservience as woman's nature and motherhood as her destiny. . . . Catholic women's colleges have suffered from the double handicap of the religious and the feminine ghetto."[3] In 1961, a survey of 109 presidents of Catholic colleges and universities which admitted women revealed that these administrators advocated a special curriculum in keeping with women's distinct nature, and over two-thirds of these presidents contended that the "essential role" of women is motherhood. The conclusion of one female educator summed it up: "Surely we do not want education to be the great leveler of the sexes. If this comes to pass, neither would excel in the particular gifts with which nature has endowed it."[4]

Supported by a distinct Catholic feminism in higher education, this "pedestal-Mary" concept of women gained momentum in the twentieth century, when, in 1930, Pope Pius XI described women's efforts for equality as debasing and unnatural. In his encyclical on marriage he solemnly echoed the traditional notion that the wife was the "heart of the home," the husband, "the head." In such an atmosphere, his successor, Pius XII, later asserted that: "The heroism of motherhood is the pride and glory of the Christian wife" and that "every woman is called to be a mother, mother in the physical sense; or mother in a sense more spiritual and more exalted, yet real, nonetheless." In the Pauline tradition, the pontiff exhorted wives to continue to be submissive to their husbands' authority and he warned: "Many voices will suggest rather a proud autonomy; they will repeat that you are in every respect the equal of your husband, and in many respects his superior. Do not react like Eve to these lying, tempting, deceitful voices."[5] It is interesting to point out that while many American Catholics viewed women as other "Marys," this stereotype contrasted with the view of woman as "Eve" which Pius XII alluded to in his remarks. James J. Kenneally persuasively argues that these stereotypes contributed in no small way to anti-feminism and influenced historians of Catholicism who have ignored the lives of Catholic women.[6]

These views persisted even in the reform-minded era ushered in by Pope John XXIII and the Second Vatican Council. The pope's 1963 encyclical *Pacem in Terris*, published in the same year as Betty Friedan's landmark book, *The Feminine Mystique*, stressed that woman's right to work was accepted only insofar as it did not conflict with her responsibilities as wife and mother, while the Second Vatican Council reaffirmed the preservation of the domestic role of women. The "Fathers" of the Council continued to view work for women as a stopping place between school and marriage.[7] In 1974 Paul VI declared:

> As we see her, woman is a vision of virginal purity . . . she is for man in his loneliness the companion whose life is one of unreserved loving dedication, resourceful collaboration and help, courageous fidelity and toil, and habitual heroic sacrifice . . . she is the Mother—Let us bow in reverence before her.[8]

Such an outlook leaves little room for sexual equality!

As a result of these perspectives, many American Catholics, male and female, have opposed the woman's movement in our history for they believe it to be a threat to an orderly society and women's natural position in the home. One of the greatest threats to these traditional concepts came from the suffragists who would dare to take woman "down from the pedestal" and throw her into the sordid world of politics. Early in the twentieth century the Catholic bishops of the United States put themselves solidly on record against woman's suffrage. During these years James Cardinal Gibbons (Baltimore) dominated the American scene as no other prelate has before or since. In an interview with the *New York Globe* in 1911 Gibbons outlined his argument:

> "Woman suffrage?" questioned the Cardinal. . . . "I am surprised that any one should ask the question. I have but one answer to such a question, and that is that I am unalterably opposed to woman's suffrage, always have been, and always will be. . . . Why should a woman lower herself to sordid politics? Why should a woman leave her home and go into the street to play the game of politics? Why should she long to come into contact with men who are her inferiors intellectually and morally? Why should a woman long to go into the streets and leave behind her happy home, her children, a husband and everything that goes to make up ideal domestic life? . . . When a women enters the political arena she goes outside the sphere for which she was intended. She gains nothing by that journey. On the other hand, she loses the exclusiveness, respect, and dignity to which she is entitled in her home."
>
> "Who wants to see a woman standing around the polling places; speaking to a crowd on the street corner; pleading with those in attendance at a political meeting? Certainly such a sight would not be relished by her husband or by her children. Must the child, returning from school, go to the polls to find his mother? Must the husband, returning from work, go to the polls to find his wife, soliciting votes from this man or that . . . ? Woman is queen," said the Cardinal in bringing the interview to a close, "but her kingdom is the domestic kingdom."[9]

Cardinal Gibbons repeated his argument two years later in a letter to the Maryland Association Opposed to Woman Suffrage: "Equal rights do not imply that both sexes should engage promiscuously in the same pursuits, but that each should discharge those duties which are adapted to its physical constitution." The cardinal charged that advocates of woman suffrage were preaching

> about women's rights and prerogatives and have not a word to say about her duties and responsibilities. They withdraw her from those obligations which properly belong to her sex and fill her with ambition to usurp positions for which neither God nor nature ever intended her.[10]

Through innuendo the cardinal suggested that voting was a full-time occupation and that casting the ballot in the American democracy was a form of prostitution! For Gibbons, the "pedestal-Mary" woman could not function outside the home without becoming Eve; if woman left her "domestic empire," this could only lead to disputes in the home and eventually to divorce, another Catholic concern related to the suffrage issue.

The Catholic fear for the preservation of the home and motherhood was further compounded by the juxtaposition of the birth control movement with the suffrage movement. In October 1915, Margaret Sanger, founder of modern "Planned Parenthood," returned from abroad and launched a crusade to legalize the dissemination of birth control information. She believed that married women could enter the political arena only if they limited their families and she concluded that female suffrage would inevitably lead to legal changes in states which prohibited birth control. Therefore, she publicly endorsed the suffrage movement while some suffrage leaders reciprocated by supporting her campaign. While contending that opposition to suffrage by Catholic leaders arose from concepts basic to traditional Catholic teaching, Eleanor Flexner, in her superb study *Century of Struggle*, conjectures that opposition became all the more heated because of the increasing attention given to the birth-control issue.[11]

Cardinal Gibbons's opposition continued. To the first National Anti-Suffrage Convention held in Washington on December 7, 1916, Gibbons sent a message which was delivered by Bishop William T. Russell (Charleston). The cardinal again argued the influence of woman as "queen of the domestic kingdom" and noted:

> As far as I have observed, it appears that woman suffrage, to the extent that it has been granted in this country, has not changed the result of the election. There has been a larger vote, but the results have been the same as they would have been if women had not voted. Thus it seems that our political life has not been benefitted or purified by the entrance of woman into the political arena, though the domestic life of those who have engaged in this political work must have been neglected, or at least impaired.[12]

This statement was widely disseminated by the National Anti-Suffrage group, as were similar statements by John Cardinal Farley (Los Angeles), Bishop John S. Foley (Detroit), Archbishop Sebastian Gebhard Messmer (Milwaukee), and Archbishop Henry Moeller (Cincinnati). Moeller went one step further. He asked that his clergy take the issue to the pulpit and "requested women not to fail to sign the anti-suffrage list if they do not wish to, or do not believe that they should enroll themselves under the banner of the suffragists. Pastors might urge the women . . . to declare themselves in regard to this matter when the opportunity presents itself."[13]

The issue was a heated one for Catholics. In 1913 Notre Dame debated the topic: "Should Woman Be Granted Equal Suffrage in the United States?" Notre Dame took the negative position and was defeated. News of the defeat made the front page of the Cincinnati *Catholic Telegraph* for it was the first loss of the debating team in twenty years![14]

When the Nineteenth Amendment was finally ratified in 1920, Catholic leaders opposed to suffrage implored Catholic women to vote in order to check those females who would use the ballot as a tool to legislate reforms threatening to the home and family. The National Council of Catholic Women was organized in 1920 to "stand as an invincible rampart against the onslaughts which are threatening the sanctity of the home, the indissolubility of the marriage bond, and the rights of parents in safeguarding the spiritual interests of their children."[15] Even the bishops' "Pastoral Letter of 1919" proclaimed that the franchise might prove an advantage; gentlewomen could purify and elevate political life as they can "reach the hearts of men and take away their bitterness . . . this is woman's vocation in respect to public affairs. . . ."[16] The Catholic hierarchy, and Gibbons in particular, in his attempt to Americanize the Catholic Church, went along with the Nineteenth Amendment, but voting was not to be viewed as a woman citizen's right. The vote of Catholic women must balance and, if possible, outweigh that of non-religious women.

Another pastoral issued in 1919 capsulized the American Catholic Church's future direction in regard to women. In February the National Catholic War Council, formed in 1917 by the hierarchy to mobilize Catholic support for the war effort, issued the "Bishops' Program of Social Reconstruction," a document advanced for its day in its social justice thrust, particularly in the area of labor reform.[17] The Program, signed by the Administrative Committee of the War Council, was drafted by Father John A. Ryan, who one year later would become the first head of the Social Welfare Department of the National Catholic Welfare Council, the postwar successor of the War Council. Ryan held this important position until 1945, and within the patriarchal family structure, he advocated a Family Living Wage, one of the most influential economic concepts to emerge from American Catholicism. Ryan published profusely and fought politically for his goals, one of which was defeat of the Equal Rights Amendment (ERA), first introduced in 1923.[18]

In this 1919 "Bishops' Program of Social Reconstruction," the bishops devoted one section, "Women War Workers," to the problem of readjustment created by the large number of women who had replaced men in the work force during the war years. The first "general principle" was that "No female worker should remain in any occupation that is harmful to health or morals." Among these occupations were streetcar conductor, streetcar guard and locomotive cleaner. Another "general principle" was the admonition "that the proportion of women in industry ought to be kept within the smallest practical limits."[19] Displaced female laborers should find suitable work in other areas or in domestic occupations. The message was clear: it was time to return to normalcy and that meant only one thing—women were to return to the home.

But the newly introduced ERA was seen by Catholic women as a threat to that "return to the home." In 1924 the National Council of Catholic Women, "a united Catholic womanhood," took an official stand against the Equal Rights Amendment at the annual convention held in St. Louis; the membership passed a resolution "protesting against the passage of the so-called Equal Rights Blanket Amendment because of the jeopardy in which it places the interests of women, and directing that representatives in Congress be informed of this protest."[20] Of course, Catholics were not the only ones to oppose ERA at this time. The Women's Bureau of the U.S. Department of Labor, the League of Women Voters, the National Federation of Business and Professional Women's Clubs, and the General Federation of Women's Clubs all came to support the ERA only as the years went by.

Discrimination against women is deeply rooted in the patriarchal structure of society. Whatever else it accomplished, the Nineteenth Amendment did not alter that structure. In predicting that women would act together to spearhead a drive for social change, the suffragists failed to realize that women were distributed throughout the social structure and had little opportunity to develop a sense of solidarity. The shift in formal legal and political status did not bring about a change in the definition of woman's or man's place, leaving the basic options available to the sexes unchanged.

In the 1920s and the 1930s the woman's groups sharply polarized over questions of ideology. One side, the feminists, believed that suffrage was only the first step in the campaign for freedom; the other side, the reformers, believed that the Nineteenth Amendment had completed the task of making women equal to men. Protective legislation became the crux of the differences between the two groups and these differences centered on opposing conceptions of female equality. The feminists were convinced that protective legislation discriminated against women and that women could only be free when they had achieved identity and equality with men in all areas of life regulated by the law. The reformers, on the other hand, believed that there were physical and psychological differences between men and women and that since these differences would never allow women to compete equally with men, special labor laws were needed to protect females. The feminists were committed to the philosophy that men and women were alike in principal attributes; the reformers held that women were the weaker sex in need of special legislation to preserve their rights.[21]

Many Catholics favored protective legislation. With Ryan, they believed first that women and society would be much improved if women did not engage in "extra-active" occupations.[22] These Catholic anti-ERA forces argued that women, forced into the job market against their will and nature, viewed their occupations as only temporary and, therefore, had no desire to organize themselves in labor unions. If women, then, were transient members of the working force not interested in organizing themselves, they would need protective legislation. This is the chief reason why Ryan and his colleagues in the National Catholic Welfare Conference believed in the necessity of protective legislation and thus opposed the Equal Rights Amendment.

But the perceived need for protective legislation waned during World War II when a labor shortage summoned women into the workforce in unprecedented numbers. In 1940, 48% of the country's single women were working; by 1944 that number had increased to 59%. Furthermore, in the interest of war production, married women were invited out of their sequestered homes and into the offices and factories of the country to perform "men's" jobs. The proportion of all married women who were employed jumped from 15.2% in 1940 to more than 24% by the end of 1945, and, as the fighting drew to a close, married women for the first time constituted close to a majority of women workers.[23] Most of the "protective" labor laws were waived during this period, without any apparent detriment to women. This enhanced the position of the Equal Rights Amendment advocates who had long contended that such laws not only were unnecessary but were in fact discriminatory rather than protective. "Rosie the Riveter" assumed folk-heroine status, and under the Lanham Act day-care centers were established for children of working mothers.

During the war, Catholic spokesmen continued to caution that working mothers imperilled the future of society and that "we shall have lost the war, if we lose the home."[24] Alarmed by the increasing number of women in industry, in 1942 the American bishops issued a statement: "we . . . express our grave concern about the Christian home in our beloved country in these crucial days. When mothers are engaged in industry a serious child care problem necessarily arises. Every effort must be to limit . . . the employment of mothers in industry. . . ."[25] Two years later they warned against turning the "mind and heart [of woman] away from the home, thereby depriving the family, State and Church of her proper contributions to the common welfare."[26] It is important to keep in mind that Ryan's influence was still strong at this time, and his view that men "would never be paid an adequate living wage while women were available to replace them" prevailed.[27]

Admonishments continued in the postwar period and well into the 1950s. In order to fulfill her proper role in society, "Rosie the Riveter" must take off her overalls and leave the grimy, immoral world of the ammunition factory to go home and have children, use the new superhighway to drive to the new supermarket, and live happily ever after in her new suburban ranch home—only to become, a decade later, the subject matter for Betty Friedan's research on "the problem with no name."[28] In 1958 a leading Catholic marriage manual asserted that outside employment might foster undesirable traits in a married woman by making her less willing to be dependent and passive, thus crippling her ability to make her husband happy. Contentment lay in the endless self-sacrifice of herself to her husband and would be endangered by a new-found aggressiveness.[29]

Psychiatrists, sociologists and anti-feminists debated the definition of woman's place.[30] The concept of "momism," the fetish of mother-worship, served as a springboard for the controversy over woman's proper role.[31] And while all this debate was going on, women quietly continued to enter the workforce, adding the second role of outside employment to the existing role of homemaker. What emerged in all this discussion as the nation entered the decade of the 1960s was the realization that any definition of woman's place must entail the creation of new roles for both women and men. Yes, the home remained a central focus for women, but it was no longer the only focus. Women were already in the process of defining for themselves their new sphere.

This was the situation of women when, at the end of the 1950s, Pope John XXIII summoned a Vatican Council to open "the windows of the Church and let in the fresh air."[32] In a truly Christian gesture, Pope John invited non-Roman Christian communicants to attend sessions of Vatican Council II as honored guests. This unprecedented gesture had an ironic twist, for the wives of Protestant observers arrived in Rome as hostesses to bishops, and some attended the debate on the floor of St. Peter's, while Roman Catholic women were absent. Even the great number of women in religious communities (four times as many as men), whose customs and rules were on the Council agenda for examination, had no representation on any of the conciliar commissions. The windows were opened, but gingerly.

Not until the second session of the Council did an advocate speak out on behalf of the presence of women at the Council as lay auditors. "Unless I am mistaken," observed the influential cardinal from Malines-Brussels, Leo Joseph Suenens, "women make up one-half of the world's population."[33] On September 8, 1964, Pope Paul VI issued the historic invitation: "women would be permitted to attend some sessions of the Ecumenical Council. . . . Certain nuns and leaders of Catholic women's organizations would be admitted as 'auditors' of debates of the third session of the Council. . . . on matters of interest to them."[34] Women could come in token numbers to the last two sessions to listen, but they were not permitted to speak from the floor of St. Peter's Basilica.

Ironically, it was the ensuing debate over women on the Council floor which focused public attention on certain rules in effect under Canon Law. For example, Canon 831 denies women the right to serve mass; Canon 1327 excludes women from preaching in the absence of clergy, whereas men are not excluded. In an attempt to change those Canon Laws which treated women as minors, a branch of a Catholic feminist organization was formed in the United States in 1965. The St. Joan's Social and Political Alliance was founded in London in 1911 by two English women primarily to work for woman's suffrage. This group, which until 1923 called itself the Catholic Women's Suffrage Society, believed that there was a strong effort on the part of the Church to make women communicants feel that feminism was out of bounds for Catholics. In order to educate themselves and the Church on the possibility of solidarity with feminist goals, Catholic women needed their own visible international organization. As the movement spread to other countries the word "international" was adopted. With members paying their own way to Rome, the Alliance "covered" the Council and submitted resolutions on the desirability of full participation of women in the Church, including ordination, and a revision of Canon Law.[35]

In the late 1960s the renewed feminist movement began to gain power and visibility in the United States, and in the years following Vatican II more attention was given to the theme "Women in the

Church." The Second Vatican Council included the following statement in its pastoral *Constitution on the Church in the Modern World*:

> With respect to the fundamental rights of the person, every type of discrimination, whether social or cultural, whether based on sex, race, color, social condition, language, or religion, is to be overcome and eradicated as contrary to God's intent. For in truth it must still be regretted that fundamental personal rights are not yet being universally honored.[36]

In 1976, in their pastoral on moral values, *To Live in Christ Jesus*, the U.S. bishops declared:

> As society has grown more sensitive to some new or newly recognized issues and needs (while at the same time growing tragically less sensitive to others), the movement to claim equal rights for women makes it clear that they must now assume their rightful place as partners in family, institutional, and public life. The development of these roles can and should be enriching for both women and men.[37]

The issue of sex discrimination was more specifically addressed in the bishops' call to action statement, *To Do the Work of Justice*, which was approved in 1978. It stated:

> Discrimination based on sex, because it radically undermines the personal identity of both women and men, constitutes a grave injustice in our society. . . . We will . . . study and dialogue regarding issues of concern to women and the eradication of sexist discrimination in current practices and policies.[38]

One portion of that study and dialogue has been several pastoral letters by American bishops.[39] These bishops have been sympathetic to women's rights, recognizing that "women have been and are still being denied their rightful place in society and in the Church."[40] In accordance with this recognition, many bishops have challenged their followers to raise "to a new level of awareness the issue of Christian feminism and the sin of sexism."[41] Some have come out in strong support of the Equal Rights Amendment.[42]

In 1972, the Leadership Conference of Women Religious (LCWR), the most powerful coordinating body representing 90% of all women's religious communities in the United States, decided to support the solidarity of women religious in the women's movement. This was understood in the sense that women religious would organize to campaign against the inequities of women in society, and the women's movement, in turn, would help sisters to understand their own identity as women and as religious women. In 1974 the assembly of the LCWR adopted the following resolutions:

> 1. That the LCWR supports the principle that all ministries in the Church be open to women and men as the Spirit calls them; and
> 2. That the LCWR affirms the principle that women have active participation in all decision making bodies in the Church.[43]

Spurred by this kind of leadership and activity, a major organization emerged within the American Catholic Church which is committed solely to promoting the ordination of women, the Women's Ordination Conference (WOC). The idea for a conference on this theme originated with a meeting of thirty-one women theological students and faculty at the Catholic Theological Union in Chicago in mid-December 1974. The meeting was called by a laywoman, Mary Lynch, and took place in Detroit in November 1975. In selecting staff and speakers, the conference planners were careful to balance religious women with laywomen leaders and scholars, both married and single. Registration was originally expected to be about 600, but the organizers underestimated the hunger for such a forum. The final registration was well over 1200 and included a few bishops.

The conference was a success for many reasons. First, it amassed a body of scriptural and theological material which already supported the priestly ordination of women.[44] This body of knowledge was largely unknown to the male hierarchy of the American Catholic Church. Second, it created an overwhelming experience of solidarity among the participants who had previously felt on the fringe and unsupported in their pursuit of the ordination of women. Third, the conference participants mandated that organizing staff continue as a network center to promote local conferences and support groups in as many states and as many communities as possible.

On January 27, 1977, the Vatican released the hastily assembled "Declaration on the Question of the Admission of Women to the Ministerial Priesthood." Acting on a mandate from Pope Paul VI, the Vatican Congregation for the Doctrine of the Faith explained the reasons for opposing female ordination. The declaration stated that the exclusion of women from the priesthood was founded on Christ's intent and is basic to the Church's understanding of ordination; therefore, the "church, in fidelity to the example of the Lord, does not consider herself authorized to admit women to priestly ordination." Exclusion, according to the congregation, was based not on concepts of women's natural inferiority and status of subjection, but rather on a sacramental bond between Christ, maleness and priesthood.[45]

Many were dismayed by the congregation's attempt to substitute for the traditional basis of exclusion—that is, the inferior position of women in a two-thousand year history of the church—a theological framework connecting maleness, Christ and priesthood. Carefully worded statements were issued by the WOC and the LCWR which unequivocally rejected the authority of the declaration and questioned its theological framework.[46] Opposition also came from quarters previously not interested in the issue. Twenty-three theologians, almost the entire faculty of the Jesuit School of Theology in Berkeley, sent an open letter to the pope through the then apostolic delegate in the United States, Archbishop Jean Jadot, pointing out the historical, scriptural, and theological untenability of the declaration.[47] Rosemary Ruether has concluded:

> One might say that if the Vatican lost its credibility for "infallibility" in matters of morals with the birth-control controversy, it lost its credibility for "infallibility" in matters of faith with the declaration on the admission of women to the priesthood. . . . Never has an official Vatican declaration been so roundly rejected and even ridiculed by both theological authorities and the general populace.[48]

In November 1978 the Second Conference on the Ordination of Women met in Baltimore to deal with "growing pains" and to clarify future goals and direction in regard to the push for the ordination of women. After that meeting, thirty women met with the Bishops' Liaison Committee with Religious and Laity at the annual meeting of the National Conference of Catholic Bishops (NCCB). At the General Assembly of the NCCB, Bishop Maurice Dingman (Des Moines) asked that a dialogue be conducted between the bishops and women on the issue of the participation of women in the life and ministry of the church. Other bishops supported the need for the dialogue, and under the direction of Archbishop John R. Quinn, President of the NCCB, a Bishops' Committee on Women in Society and in the Church was established to meet with representatives of the Women's Ordination Conference. In August 1979 the two groups agreed on the following goal of the dialogue: "To discover, understand and promote the full potential of woman as person in the life of the church."[49] The official dialogue participants consisted of six representatives of the WOC and six of the bishops' committee.

The two groups met in six sessions held between December 1979 and August 1981. The first three sessions focused on personhood as it is reflected in church teachings regarding men and women, the nature of patriarchy as a social system and its impact on church structures, and the question of the scriptural, theological, and institutional bases for change in accepted church teachings and practices. In the last three sessions of the dialogue the participants attempted a critical examination of theology, anthropology, scripture, and church and ministry as these topics relate to women. An interim report was issued by the NCCB on May 28, 1981, and a final report on April 27, 1982. The final report stated that "The challenge women offer the institutional church is to recognize that sexism is a sin." It recommended that "Christians at all levels engage in an ongoing dialogue and reflection on the issue of justice and equality for women," and stressed the need to review the Vatican Declaration on the Ordination of Women "in light of the insights of modern anthropology, sacramental theology and the practice and experience of women ministering in our American culture."[50]

While the Bishops' Committee on Women in Society and in the Church dealt with the ordination issue, it also had before it the issue of the Equal Rights Amendment. The evidence suggests that the Committee wished to issue a statement in support of the Amendment, but was prevented from doing so by the Catholic hierarchy on grounds that the passage of the Amendment would somehow have further legalized abortion, an issue of preeminent concern to the American bishops.[51] Those on the six-member committee took pains to separate support of ERA from any connotation of accepting abortion. In addition, they wanted to release the statement on their own behalf and had consulted with the family-life section of the Bishops' Department of Education, which apparently approved their conclusion that ERA would not threaten the stability of marriage and family life. Persons who are strongly anti-abortion could be just as strongly pro-ERA. An article in *America* magazine documented the evidence for this conclusion.[52]

Advance disclosure that the American bishops were considering a pro-ERA statement generated heavy mail from the anti-abortion "right to life" groups opposing the ERA. The NCCB's forty-eight member administrative board, which sets policy for the 345 U.S. Roman Catholic bishops, rejected the pro-ERA statement during an early May 1978 meeting in Chicago fearing that it would hurt anti-abortion efforts, particularly the bishops' support of the Human Life Amendment. Just as the birth control issue contributed to the bishops' decision to oppose women's suffrage, so the bishops were influenced by the abortion issue to remain silent on the Equal Rights Amendment.

The bishops were divided on the ERA issue. On June 2, 1982, twenty-three bishops issued a brief statement calling upon legislators in non-ratifying states to ratify the Equal Rights Amendment before the June 30 deadline. In the statement the bishops affirmed: "Equality under the law for all persons is a fundamental issue of justice."[53] Although, as already indicated, individual Catholic bishops had endorsed the ERA in their own dioceses, this was the first time a group of bishops joined in a common statement urging that the amendment be adopted. Bishop D'Antonio (New Orleans), explaining his endorsement, said: "The ERA spells simple common sense, like two and two make four. Justice demands it. I'd sin if I did not support it."[54]

It is difficult to assess at present where the women's movement in the Church will go in the immediate and long-range future. On November 12–13, 1983, preceding the annual meeting of the NCCB, the Bishops' Committee on Women in Church and Society sponsored a meeting attended by one hundred bishops and fifty women from a dozen national women's groups. The press was allowed to cover the three main talks—"Women in Scripture" by Sister Diane Bergant, "Origins of Ministry" by Francine Cardman and "Patriarchy in Society and the Church" by Elisabeth Schussler Fiorenza—but it was barred from the subsequent discussions. The scholarly presentations were well received and one bishop reported: "I think some bishops were shocked at how convincing they found the theological and scriptural presentations," including those challenging the Church's stance on the priestly ordination of women.[55]

At the ensuing meeting of the NCCB, the bishops agreed to write a pastoral letter on women in church and society. There are "important moral, social and ecclesial problems here," said Bishop Michael Kenny (Juneau), and he concluded: "Some of the injustices are in our own house."[56] Bishop Joseph Imesch (Joliet), who chaired the Committee on Women in Church and Society, asserted that the pastoral "would affirm those devoted women already serving the church and would offer new hope to those women who have experienced rejection or alienation." The bishops commissioned the letter only after Bishop Imesch gave assurances that, "The teaching of the church will be stated and respected in this document."[57] Commenting on the proposed pastoral, Sister Helen Flaherty, President of the Leadership Conference of Women Religious, expressed her concern because Bishop Imesch estimated that the letter would take two or three years to complete. Flaherty remarked: "My worry is that in two or three years it will be obsolete. I would rather they take some action . . . rather than putting down more words."[58]

In regard to the Equal Rights Amendment, the American bishops evaded taking a positive public stand on an important social justice issue. Their silence left them out of the mainstream of religious thought on the ERA. Among groups that endorsed ERA were the National Council of Churches, the United Church of Christ, and the nation's major organizations of Jews, Baptists, Methodists, Lutherans, Presbyterians, and Quakers. In 1977 the National Conference of Catholic Charities passed a resolution endorsing ERA, as did the Canon Law Society in 1979 and the Conference of Major Superiors of Men. Could an official Catholic position favoring ERA have made a difference in such states as Illinois, Missouri, and Louisiana—all three of which rejected the ERA?

But this is not the first time that the bishops have remained silent on an important social justice issue. One is reminded here of their silence at the 1852 Plenary Council in Baltimore when the issue of slavery was deliberately omitted from the agenda, an issue under much discussion by church leaders, and women's groups. The Catholic bishops of the ante-bellum period viewed slavery as a political, not a moral issue. It took them another 100 years to issue a statement on racism.

In any case women who are committed to change in Roman Catholicism know that they are committed for the long haul. George H. Tavard has written:

> the Church progressively abandoned the principle of Christian freedom in its application to the life of women within its own ranks and concerns, and in areas that could conceivably have escaped secular prejudice and social pressure. Instead, it adopted the principle of harmony with secular society . . . can the adoption of secular standards ever be justified when it results in restricting the freedom of the Gospel?[59]

We will never develop our religious traditions in meaningful ways without understanding the reasons for "secular prejudice and social pressure," the conscious and unconscious patterns that set our identities as men and women, the reasons for "restricting the freedom of the Gospel." For change means a rethinking and a "re-feeling" of our human formation as masculine and feminine. Change calls for the reevaluation for today and tomorrow of the models of womanhood that have been proposed by the Church. In regard to the ordination issue, it is impossible to imagine women being admitted to the Catholic priesthood without, at the same time, fundamental notions about hierarchy, theology, Church, and authority being questioned and modified. And perhaps this, more than women, is what the Catholic hierarchy really fears.

The U.S. bishops have boldly and aggressively articulated their view on Central America, abortion, nuclear armaments, tax credits for parents with children in private schools, cutbacks in federal funds for the poor. Is it too much to hope that in the near future a newly-energized Catholic hierarchy will take the forefront of the campaign for the rights of women in church and society?

Notes

1. Barbara Welter, "The Cult of True Womanhood: 1820–1860," *American Quarterly* 18 (Summer 1966):151–74; in the years following World War II, Betty Friedan charged that American women had been victimized by a set of ideas, a "feminine mystique," which was prevalent in society and defined female happiness as complete involvement in the roles of wife and mother; see Betty Friedan, *The Feminine Mystique* (New York: W. W. Norton Company, 1963).
2. James J. Kenneally, "Catholicism and Woman Suffrage in Massachusetts," *Catholic Historical Review* 53 (April 1967):43–44. See also, George H. Tavard, *Woman in Christian Tradition* (Notre Dame, Indiana: University of Notre Dame Press, 1973), chap. 6.
3. Rosemary Ruether, "Are Women's Colleges Obsolete," *Critic* 27 (October–November 1968):61–63.
4. M. Leonita Smith, "Catholic Viewpoints About the Psychology, Social Role and Higher Education of Women" (Ph.D. diss., Ohio State University, 1961), p. 118.
5. Pius XI, "Casti Connubi," 1930, as in *The Woman in the Modern World: Papal Teachings*, Benedictine Monks of Solesmes, eds. (Boston: St. Paul Editions, 1959), pp. 37–38; and in the same collection Pius XII, "To All Italian Women," October 1945, p. 131, and "To All Newly Weds," September 1941, pp. 68–69.
6. James J. Kenneally, "Eve, Mary and the Historians: American Catholicism and Women," *Horizons* 3 (1976):187–202.
7. John XXIII, *Peace on Earth* (Boston: St. Paul Editions, n.d.), pp. 10–11; "Pastoral Constitution of the Church in the Modern World," in *The Documents of Vatican II*, Walter M. Abbott, ed. (New York: Guild Press, 1966), pp. 257, 227, and 228 respectively.
8. "The Rise of Women in Contemporary Society: Address of Pope Paul VI to the Convention of the Union of Italian Catholic Jurists," 8 December 1974, *Pope Speaks* 19 (Spring 1975):316.

9. *New York Globe,* 22 June 1911; see Anti-Suffrage Documents, Sophia Smith Collection, Smith College (hereafter referred to as SSC), B7.

10. Extract from a letter of Cardinal Gibbons to the Maryland Association Opposed to Woman Suffrage, 22 April 1913, SSC.

11. Eleanor Flexner, *Century of Struggle,* 4th ed. (Cambridge: The Belknap Press of Harvard University Press, 1970), pp. 299, 369.

12. "A Message from His Eminence James Cardinal Gibbons to the National Association Opposed to Woman Suffrage," Washington, D.C., 7 December 1916, SSC, 67S.

13. "Some *Catholic Views* on *Woman Suffrage,*" pamphlet issued by the National Association Opposed to Woman Suffrage, n.d., SSC, 37S.

14. *The Catholic Telegraph* (Cincinnati), 5 June 1913.

15. "National Council of Catholic Women," pamphlet published by the National Catholic Welfare Council, Washington, D.C., n.d., SSC.

16. "Pastoral Letter of 1919," in *Our Bishops Speak, 1919–1951,* Raphael Huber, ed. (Milwaukee: Bruce Publishing Company, 1952), p. 46.

17. "Bishops' Program of Social Reconstruction," in Huber, *Our Bishops Speak,* pp. 243–60.

18. For a good biography on Father Ryan, see Francis L. Broderick, *Right Reverend New Dealer: John A. Ryan* (New York: The Macmillan Company, 1963).

19. "Bishops' Program of Social Reconstruction," in Huber, *Our Bishops Speak,* p. 250.

20. "Report of the President, National Council of Catholic Women, Fourth Annual Convention, St. Louis, Missouri, November 9–12, 1924," SSC.

21. For a full discussion of these events and issues, see J. Stanley Lemons, *The Woman Citizen: Social Feminism in the 1920s* (Chicago: University of Illinois Press, 1973), especially chap. 7, "Feminists Against Feminists"; see also William H. Chafe, *The American Woman: Her Changing Social, Economic, and Political Role, 1920–1970* (New York: Oxford University Press, 1972), chap. 5.

22. Broderick, *John A. Ryan,* p. 59.

23. "Changes in Women's Employment During the War," *Women's Bureau Bulletin,* no. 20 (Washington, D.C., 1944), p. 17.

24. "Bishop Duffy Deplores Mothers' Wartime Jobs," *Catholic Action* 24 (July 1942):6.

25. "Statements Issued by the Archbishops and Bishops of the United States on Victory and Peace, November 14, 1942," in Huber, *Our Bishops Speak,* p. 112.

26. "Statement on International Order of the Hierarchy of the United States, November 16, 1944," Ibid., p. 119.

27. Broderick, *John A. Ryan,* p. 59.

28. Friedan, *The Feminine Mystique,* pp. 15–16.

29. George A. Kelly, *The Catholic Marriage Manual* (New York: Random House, 1958), pp. 116–18.

30. See, for example, Ferdinand Lundberg and Marynia Farnham, *Modern Woman: The Lost Sex* (New York: Harper, 1947), Lundberg was a journalist,

Farnham a psychiatrist; Mirra Komarovsky, *Women in the Modern World* (Boston: Little, Brown, 1953); Elizabeth K. Nottingham, "Toward an Analysis of the Effects of Two World Wars on the Role and Status of Middle Class Women in the English Speaking World," *American Sociological Review* 12 (December 1947): 666–75; and Florence Kluckhohn, "Cultural Factors in Social Work Practice and Education," *Social Service Review* 25 (March 1951):38–48.

31. Philip Wylie, *Generation of Vipers* (New York: Farrar, Straus & Company, 1942).

32. Xavier Rynne, *The Second Session* (New York: Farrar, Straus & Company, 1964), p. 1.

33. Ibid., p. 117.

34. *The New York Times*, 8 September 1964.

35. *Bulletin of the St. Joan's International Alliance*, no. 1, August 1966, New York, SSC.

36. "Pastoral Constitution of the Church in the Modern World" in *The Documents of Vatican II*, Walter M. Abbott, ed. (New York: American Press, 1966), pp. 227–28.

37. National Conference of Catholic Bishops, *To Live in Christ Jesus* (Washington, D.C.: United States Catholic Conference, 1976), p. 24.

38. National Conference of Catholic Bishops, *To Do the Work of Justice* (Washington, D.C.: United States Catholic Conference, 1978), p. 17.

39. See for example, Bishop Carroll T. Dozier (Memphis, 1975), "Women: Intrepid and Loving," *Origins* 4 (Jan. 23, 1975):481; Bishop Victor H. Balke and Bishop Raymond A. Lucker (Crookston, MN and New Ulm, MN, 1981), "Male and Female—God Created Them," *Origins* 11 (May 5, 1981):333; Bishop John S. Cummins (Oakland, 1981), "Statement on Women in Ministry," *Origins* 11 (May 5, 1981):331; Archbishop Peter L. Gerety (Newark, 1981), "Women in the Church," *Origins* 10 (Feb. 26, 1981):582; and Bishop Matthew Clark (Rochester, 1982), "American Catholic Women: Persistent Questions, Faithful Witness," *Origins* 12 (Oct. 14, 1982):275.

40. Archbishop Peter Gerety, "Women in the Church," *Origins* 10 (Feb. 26, 1981):582.

41. Bishop Victor Balke and Bishop Raymond Lucker, "Male and Female—God Created Them," *Origins* 11 (May 5, 1981):333.

42. Bishops Michael McAuliffe (Jefferson City), Walter Sullivan (Richmond), Maurice J. Dingman (Des Moines), Raymond Lucker (New Ulm, MN), George Evans (Denver), and now-retired Charles Buswell (Pueblo), all supported ERA.

43. Quoted in Rosemary Ruether and Eleanor McLaughlin, *Women of Spirit* (New York: Simon and Schuster, 1979), p. 375.

44. Ann Marie Gardiner, ed., *Women and the Catholic Priesthood: An Expanded Vision. Proceedings of the Detroit Ordination Conference* (New York: Paulist Press, 1976).

45. "Declaration on the Question of the Admission of Women to the Ministerial Priesthood," *Origins* 6 (Feb. 3, 1977):524.

46. "Statements by the Women's Ordination Conference and the Leader-

ship Conference of Women Religious," *Origins* 6 (Feb. 10, 1977):545–48.

47. "Open Letter to Archbishop Jean Jadot," *Origins* 6 (Apr. 7, 1977):661–65.

48. Ruether and McLaughlin, *Women of Spirit*, pp. 380–81.

49. "Dialogue on Women in the Church: Interim Report," *Origins* 11 (June 25, 1981):83.

50. "Report on a Dialogue: The Future of Women in the Church," *Origins* 11 (May 21, 1981):8.

51. See Arlene Swidler, "Catholics and the E.R.A.," *Commonweal* 103 (Sept. 10, 1976):585–89; Elizabeth Alexander and Maureen Fiedler, "The Equal Rights Amendment and Abortion: Separate and Distinct," *America* 142 (April 12, 1980):314–18; "The ERA Movement," *The Humanist* 43 (July/August 1983).

52. Alexander and Fiedler, "Separate and Distinct," *America* 142 (April 12, 1980):314–18.

53. *National Catholic Reporter*, 11 June 1982.

54. Ibid.

55. Ibid., 25 November 1983.

56. Sisters of Charity, *Intercom*, December 1983, p. 8.

57. *National Catholic Reporter*, 25 November 1983.

58. Sisters of Charity, *Intercom*, December 1983, p. 8.

59. Tavard, *Women in Christian Tradition*, pp. 211–12.

Chapter Twenty

*Feminism and the Reevaluation of Women's Roles Within American Jewish Life**

Ellen M. Umansky

The impact of the feminist movement on the lives of American women has been much discussed and debated. In the last fifteen years, there clearly has been tremendous change in the ways in which women have been viewed by others and perhaps even more significantly, in the ways in which women have begun to view themselves. Traditional roles have been challenged and women increasingly have demanded greater participation in the political, social, educational and economic arenas of American life. These demands have, in turn, created new expectations. As women have begun to succeed at tasks outside of their so-called "natural domain," they have begun to explore new ways of developing their skills and talents. Subsequently, many have come to expect American society to sanction, if not facilitate, this exploration.

*I am grateful to the Blaustein Library of the American Jewish Committee, New York City, for making much of this research possible.

The American Jewish community has not been immune to the forces of feminism. Indeed, throughout the 1960s, a number of Jewish women—perhaps the most prominent of whom was Betty Friedan—began to take an active part in the burgeoning feminist movement. By 1974, *Ms.* magazine featured a series of essays that asked: "Is It Kosher To Be A Feminist?"[1] Implicit in the essays by Paula Hyman, Audrey Gellis and Bracha Sachs was a critique not only of women's roles in American society but also of the religious roles traditionally assigned to Jewish women.

One might argue, with justification, that the identification of many Jewish women as feminists during the 1960s and 1970s did not stem from an intrinsically *Jewish* commitment to women's equality. Indeed, I am not at all convinced that my forefathers (including the Biblical prophets and the rabbis of the Talmud) equated a just world with a non-sexist society. Perhaps for some women Judaism's general emphasis on seeking justice led to the conclusion that one has a responsibility—as a Jew—to fight injustice in accordance with one's own definition of what injustice is. Yet of equal if not greater significance is the fact that a high percentage of American Jewish women, like the majority of those involved in the feminist movement of the 1960s and 1970s, are white, middle class and college educated. Thus, the early commitment of many Jewish women to feminism tells us at least as much about the impact of acculturation and secularization on American Jewish life as it does about the Jewish commitment to justice.

Indeed, even today, there are many Jewish feminists who consider themselves to be only nominally Jewish. Others have left the Jewish community completely, viewing it—again with justification—as patriarchal and homophobic. By the late 1970s, however, the appearance of anti-Semitism in the women's movement[2] led a number of previously uncommitted and/or alienated Jewish women to reaffirm their identity as Jews while those already committed both as feminists and as Jews continued efforts, begun in the early '70s, to subject the Jewish community to feminist demands and expectations. Having achieved new opportunities for growth and self-expression outside of the Jewish world, they sought to attain within their Jewish lives what they could achieve or had achieved within American society.

Religiously-committed women began to seek greater participation within the synagogue as well as greater access to positions of religious and communal leadership. Some worked to develop prayers and rituals that would give expression to women's own sense of spirituality and some began to pursue advanced degrees in Jewish history and thought. All of these efforts revealed, and continue to reveal, the impact of feminism on American Jewish life. The feminist belief that "women have the same innate potential, capability, and needs as men, whether in the realm of the spirit, the word, or the deed" has irrevocably called into question Judaism's traditional understanding of women and has initiated a reformulation of women's religious and communal roles.[3] Although, as we shall see, women still have not achieved equality in any sphere of Jewish life, the changes that have occurred within the last ten years are encouraging, leading many to conclude that women's equality within Judaism is no longer a question of whether but of when.

This essay traces the development of Jewish feminism as both a movement and a more general commitment to the equality of women within Jewish life. Focusing on specific changes that have occurred in the last ten years, it seeks to show the ways in which women's religious and organizational participation within the American Jewish community has been altered as a result of feminist agitation. It begins with an exploration of women's religious lives, from a denominational and theological standpoint, and then examines women's access to positions of public leadership. Finally, it considers a number of questions which feminism poses regarding the future viability of the *halachic* Jewish legal system and the potential (or real) conflict between values derived from the Jewish tradition and those derived from feminism.

Exclusion and Participation within Religious Life

Jewish feminism—as a movement and as a perspective—has focused most clearly upon the traditional exclusion of women from much of Judaism's public religious life. The rabbis of the Talmud, those responsible for the formulation of Jewish law, argued that men and women, while possessing absolute dignity, equality and worth, were created as complements to one another. They claimed that God, employing a kind of Divine economy, intended men and women to occupy different societal roles so that together they might achieve wholeness. Thinking of women essentially as wives and mothers, they viewed the home as the natural domain of women, while maintaining that the public sphere of religious life, that of study and public worship, was the natural domain of men.[4]

The exemption of women from positive time-bound commandments (most within the realm of communal celebration or prayer), as well as their exclusion from the study of Torah, helped assure "that no legal obligation would interfere with the selection by Jewish women of a role which was centered almost exclusively in the home."[5] Jewish women weren't required to become wives and mothers—in fact the *mitzvah* (commandment) of procreation was incumbent only upon men—yet they were strongly urged to do so. The role of wife and mother was a "preferred" one and the only one in which women could participate fully.[6]

Within the synagogue, women were excluded from being counted in the *minyan* (the quorum of ten men necessary for public prayer), receiving an *aliyah* (being called to recite a blessing before the Torah reading), and leading the congregation in worship. The rabbis of the Talmud may have insisted that the religious roles of men and women were equal (women, after all, could claim the special *mitzvot* of kindling the Sabbath lights, preparing the dough for the Sabbath loaves, and observing the laws of family purity as their own), but as Paula Hyman has noted, despite these "necessary and noble" tasks, women's exemption from time-bound positive commandments, coupled with their lack of legal independence (for example, in matters of marriage, divorce, inheritance and in their inability to serve as legal witnesses in a Jewish court), "relegated women to a second-class status" with the "heart and soul of traditional Judaism"—communal study and prayer—remaining "the pursuits almost exclusively of men."[7]

While it might well be argued that up through the eighteenth century women were satisfied with their religious roles, Jewish emancipation in Europe led many women to rethink both their religious roles and their religious status. By the nineteenth century, greater participation in the economic, cultural and political life of Western and Central Europe, facilitated by the process of emancipation, had shattered the "medieval Jewish mind set" which embraced the notion that religion provided an all-encompassing framework for one's life.[8] As Judaism was reduced to just one of many aspects of existence and as new visions of enlightenment affirmed the validity of change, Jewish institutional and educational beliefs had to be adjusted in order to conform to the spirit of the modern age. While the extent to which these changes were made varied from country to country and community to community, both men and women, in an attempt to establish a modern Jewish identity, were forced to reevaluate both their understanding of Judaism and that which Judaism demanded.

Studies by Jacob Katz and others, focusing on emancipation in Western and Central Europe, have revealed the extent to which wealthy Jewish women were the first to take advantage of the opportunities which emancipation provided. Though for men enlightenment and secular education had to compete with the study of Torah,

> women, according to religious tradition, were exempted and excluded from studying the law, the main component of the Jewish traditional curriculum. . . . Thus the daughters of the well-to-do families in the ghetto were the first to benefit from the new opportunities. They were the first to learn the language of their neighbors, to acquire a familiarity with foreign languages and literature. They were also the ones to acquire the social graces that enabled them to move easily in a society not limited to Jews.[9]

The contrast between opportunities available to women in European society and those available to them within Judaism were striking. Emancipation enabled Jewish women to study, to move beyond the home and to seek new means of self-expression. It is thus not surprising that among eighteenth-century Jews who converted to Christianity, women were the first to do so.[10]

Henriette Herz and Rahel Varnhagen (whose salons were visited by some of the most celebrated intellectuals of the day) and Dorothea and Henriette Mendelssohn (daughters of the great Jewish philosopher, Moses Mendelssohn) are among the best known late eighteenth- and early nineteenth-century Jewish women who succumbed to the so-called "lure" of baptism. As I have argued elsewhere,[11] the attraction of Christianity for these women was not only social, as it was for most of their male counterparts, but religious—an opportunity, as they perceived it, to express their own religious natures more fully. This isn't to say that social considerations played no role whatsoever. Yet given the problems of remaining Jewish in a non-Jewish world, these women and hundreds if not thousands like them undoubtedly realized that they had less of a stake than did their male counterparts in retaining their Jewish identity. From their "enlightened" perspective, the roles to which Judaism had assigned them appeared limiting and their status subordinate if not inferior to that of Jewish men.

Emancipation helped create for Jewish women a new set of expectations. While in the eighteenth and early nineteenth centuries Jewish women could either remain Jewish and accept a religious role that seemed confining or reject this role and Judaism along with it, by the end of the nineteenth century, with the development of Reform Judaism in Germany and America, another option presented itself: namely, to redefine both Judaism *and* the religious roles of men and women.[12]

Reform Judaism set out to harmonize Judaism with what its leaders perceived to be the "spirit of the [modern] age." Part of its agenda, then, at least in theory was to modernize the role of Jewish women, making it more commensurate with that of women in the non-Jewish world. As early as 1846, at the Breslau Reform Rabbinical Conference, a committee organized to study the legal position of Jewish women declared that "the equality of religious privileges and obligations of women insofar as this is possible" was in accordance with their "religious consciousness, which grants all humans an equal degree of natural holiness."[13] To insure this equality, women were to be counted in the *minyan*, the benediction recited by Jewish males thanking God that they had not been created a woman was abolished, formal religious instruction for girls was introduced, and in the Reform Temple in Berlin women and men were seated on the same floor during the worship service.[14] By the end of the century, as the major focus of Reform shifted from Germany to the United States, Isaac Mayer Wise, one of the first rabbis in America to champion the cause of women's rights, had admitted girls into his synagogue choir in Albany, introduced family pews, and as President of Hebrew Union College, the Reform rabbinical seminary in Cincinnati, encouraged women to attend, though apparently none of his female students ever sought ordination.

Yet despite these advances, the commitment of nineteenth- and early twentieth-century Reform Judaism to women's equality was more theoretical than real. The movement as a whole did little to create new roles for women either in the synagogue or within its own organizational structure. In the early 1920s, the issue of ordaining women was first formally raised. While the Central Conference of American (Reform) Rabbis passed, by a vote of 56–11, a resolution affirming that the privilege of ordination could not justly be denied to women, Hebrew Union College's Board of Governors, empowered with reaching a final decision, voted not to change "the present practice of limiting to males the right to matriculate for the purpose of entering the rabbinate."[15] Twenty-three years later, in 1956, the Central Conference reaffirmed its earlier resolution, and Nelson Glueck, President of what had become Hebrew Union College-Jewish Institute of Religion, maintained that the College would ordain any woman who passed the required courses.

More than fifteen years were to pass, however, before Hebrew Union College admitted its first woman to the Reform rabbinate. Perhaps there would not have been such a delay had the institution either made its willingness to ordain women more widely known or actively recruited eligible female candidates. Instead, it wasn't until the late 1960s, as the burgeoning feminist movement began to create new expectations among women themselves, that women began to seek entrance into the rabbinate. Though not all of the sixty-one women ordained as Reform rabbis since 1972 think of themselves as feminists, most would readily admit that the feminist movement has helped break down sex-role barriers within the American Jewish community, paving the way for a greater acceptance of those women who, in becoming rabbis, have chosen to step out of their traditional female religious roles.

This isn't to say, however, that women ordained as Reform rabbis have gained universal acceptance even within the Reform movement. There are still congregations which consider interviewing a female candidate for a rabbinical position to be a mere formality and a few which refuse to interview women at all. Yet it is clear that the acceptance of women as Reform rabbis has steadily grown. The Central Conference has established a Task Force aimed at promoting greater acceptance of women rabbis within Reform congregations, its Placement Bureau stands—at least in theory—as "100% committed to placing women"[16] and HUC itself refuses to send a student rabbi to any congregation not willing to be served by a female rabbinical student.

While these efforts indicate that the acceptance of women rabbis still remains to some extent a problem, these and other efforts have succeeded in gaining women rabbis acceptance, at least in entry-level positions as assistant and associate rabbis and as Hillel and educational directors. What remains to be seen, as Rabbi Karen Fox recently noted, is how upwardly mobile women rabbis will become—whether they will succeed, for example, as rabbis of their own congregations and as senior rabbis with one or two assistants.[17] At present, because of their relatively recent ordination, few women are eligible for such positions. A number have gained solo pulpits though not without difficulty in some cases. As one female rabbi confided to me:

> There is a bottom line difference between male and female rabbis. Congregations believe that a female rabbi is going to want to have a baby, a decision that they believe will necessarily affect her more than the decision of her male colleagues to have a family will affect them.[18]

While this fear has prevented some women from gaining pulpits, the fact remains that some female rabbis, because they have wanted to have families, have not been overly aggressive in seeking congregational positions.

One senses here an ambivalence, reflecting a very real tension between feminism on the one hand and Judaism on the other. While the desire of women to become rabbis can be seen as an attempt to find fulfillment through a career outside of the home, the desire of these women (most of whom are now in their late twenties and early thirties) to have children reflects a more traditional—and more Jewish—understanding of women's social and religious role. At present, one-third of those seeking ordination as Reform rabbis are women. Those at Hebrew Union College and in the Central Conference believe that within the next ten years this figure will remain steady or, possibly, grow. As feminist values progressively take root within the American Jewish community, men and women may no longer identify rabbis who are women as "female rabbis." Yet before one can say the word "rabbi" without reference to gender, not only do more women have to be ordained but those who have been ordained need to earn greater acceptance.

Similar problems remain within the Reconstructionist movement which has been ordaining women since 1973. At present, fourteen women (almost 20% of all Reconstructionist rabbis since the movement's Reconstructionist Rabbinical College first opened in 1968) have received ordination. Of the forty-seven students enrolled in 1983, twenty-three (that is, almost half) are women.[19] From its inception in the 1930s, Reconstructionism has affirmed and worked towards achieving the equality of women in Jewish life. Yet as Rabbi Joy Levitt, ordained from the Reconstructionist Rabbinical College in 1981, quickly discovered, if a male "rabbi is good he will be well received" by his congregation, but "a woman has to be excellent."[20] In addition, with few role models to follow, women rabbis are often faced with a set of unique problems, including what to wear, what image to project, and the "more complex issue of the underlying sexual tensions which sometimes surface."[21] Finally, even if Reconstructionism's commitment to women's equality has been more evident than that of the other major Jewish religious movements in America, the small size of the Reconstructionst movement has forced many of its rabbis, male and female alike, to seek positions elsewhere—either in Reform or Conservative congregations or in Jewish organizations where, as we shall see, women have had greatest difficulty in achieving positions of influence and power.

While the relationship between feminism and the Reform and Reconstructionist acceptance of women as religious leaders may seem indirect, female agitation has directly forced the Conservative movement to reexamine its attitude towards women. In March of 1972, a group of women calling themselves "Ezrat Nashim" appeared at the Rabbinical Assembly convention to issue a "Call for Change." Among their demands were the full participation of women in religious observance, synagogue worship and decision-making bodies within synagogues and the general Jewish community; the recognition of women as witnesses in Jewish law; the right of women to initiate divorce; and the admission of women to rabbinical and cantorial schools.

Although the group's appearance at the convention was not sanctioned by the Rabbinical Assembly, the media attention which Ezrat Nashim received helped make its members "small scale celebrities within the Conservative movement."[22] As a result, the demands that they had made, all of which had been submitted to the Rabbinical Assembly's Law Committee, received a good deal of consideration. Early in 1973, the committee voted to count women in the worship quorum. In addition, its little-known 1955 decision allowing women to be called to the Torah was given new emphasis and the number of Conservative synagogues granting women *aliyot* significantly increased.[23]

The creation of the Jewish Feminist Organization in 1974 was, at least in part, due to the efforts of Ezrat Nashim. Recognizing the need for a larger, more activist organization, its members helped plan and lead a National Conference in 1973 on "The Role of Women in Jewish Life." A year later, at a second conference, the Jewish Feminist Organization was created; it sought "nothing else than the full, direct and equal participation of women at all levels of Jewish life." During the two years of its existence, the Jewish Feminist Organization served as an umbrella organization for numerous regional committees. Sponsoring seminars, consciousness-raising groups, bibliographical publications and other, specifically action-oriented proposals, it worked to become a force for "creative change in the Jewish community."[24] Though organizational problems led to its dissolution in 1976, subregional chapters continued to function, leading to the establishment of more informal groups that reevaluated and challenged women's traditional religious roles.

In 1973, the Rabbinical Assembly's Law Committee voted against the ordination of women as Conservative rabbis. More recently, however, the Conservative movement has reexamined this decision. In October of 1977, a "Commission for the Study of the Ordination of Women as Rabbis" was created. Composed of men and women, rabbis and laity, it attempted to determine whether Jewish law permitted the ordination of women and whether ethical, sociological, psychological, educational, symbolic and pragmatic considerations further supported (or opposed) women's ordination. The formation of this commission as well as its findings, which indicated that most of the Conservative laity were ready to accept women as congregational, spiritual leaders, clearly reflect new attitudes and expectations concerning the participation of women within Jewish religious life. The final recommendation of the commission that women be admitted into the Rabbinical School of the Jewish Theological Seminary of America "on a basis equal to that maintained heretofore for males"[25] was rejected by the Seminary itself, whose Senate of faculty and administrators, unable to reach a consensus, voted to table the issue indefinitely. Yet at the request of the Rabbinical Assembly (whose members narrowly defeated the application of a Reform rabbi, Beverly Magidson, to join the RA last spring), the Seminary has agreed to take another vote on October 24. Many, if not most Conservative rabbis, think that this time the recommendation to ordain women will pass. (The vote in fact passed by a wide margin. By a vote of 34–8, the Seminary faculty voted to accept women into the rabbinical program of the Jewish Theological Seminary beginning in the fall of 1984.)

Although the Orthodox movement in America shows little sign of even considering whether women should be ordained as Orthodox rabbis, changes that have occurred in the last ten years concerning women's religious roles clearly can be traced not simply to heightened feminist awareness within the Orthodox community but to feminist activity within the community itself. In 1972, a group of Orthodox women, identifying themselves as "Kol Isha," met to study *halachah* (Jewish law) as it pertained to women in an attempt to discover halachically acceptable avenues for change. While the group remained in existence for only a year, it met with a number of Orthodox rabbis, including Saul Berman of Stern College (Yeshiva University) and Steven Riskin of the Lincoln Square Synagogue in New York, both of whom have since addressed themselves to such issues as the religious education of women and the participation of women in public religious life.[26]

By the late 1970s, Orthodox women's "*minyanim*"—groups of ten or more women participating fully in a modified worship service—began to proliferate throughout the United States. According to Saul Berman in an interview published in *Response* in the spring of 1981, these groups "no longer excite the kind of opposition they did five or six years ago when . . . [they] . . . first began to gather." Their acceptance, Berman maintains, indicates that women's *minyanim* may well represent the first stage in a gradual process "which will ultimately involve a greater degree of participation and involvement by women in the synagogue service."[27] Although these women—and men—who have attempted to incorporate feminist values into Orthodox Jewish life represent only a minority of the Orthodox movement, they have become more visible and their demands are being heard. Maintaining that "the engagement of Judaism and feminism offers . . . new heights to scale, a deeper sense of maturity, and an enlarged scope of responsibility," Orthodox Jews like Blu Greenberg insist that

> if the hierarchy of the sexes serves no religious function, if Halakhah has the capacity for reinterpretation, if equality is a basic positive value in Judaism, then it behooves the [Orthodox] community and its leaders to take the initiative . . . [and] . . . search for new ways to upgrade religious expression and new means by which to generate equality for women in tradition.[28]

Creating New Rituals and Re-imaging the Divine

The increased participation of women within Jewish religious life has led to the creation of new rituals celebrating the life cycle of the Jewish woman. Naming ceremonies in honor of the birth of a daughter, blessings for menstruation and menopause, and the growing popularity of *Bat Mitzvah* attest to women's greater familiarity with Jewish liturgy and to new expectations concerning the celebration of their own membership in God's covenant with Israel. Traditionally, the first life-cycle ceremony in which women had a part was marriage, a ceremony in which a woman literally was "acquired" by her husband and in which her role primarily was passive. Within the last ten years, more egalitarian *ketubot* (marriage contracts) have been written,[29] and growing numbers of non-Orthodox couples, in direct and deliberate violation of Jewish law, have included women as witnesses in the signing of their *ketubah* as an expression of their belief in and commitment to the equality of women. Marriage ceremonies in which the bride and groom exchange rings and comparable vows have become relatively common (not in Orthodox circles, however, though even there attempts are being made to increase women's participation), and at the end of the ceremony one frequently sees the bride joining with her husband in breaking the traditional glass.

Rosh Hodesh—the celebration of the new moon—has become (again, within the last ten years) a holiday observed primarily if not exclusively by women. Prior to the eighteenth century and the age of emancipation, *Rosh Hodesh*, it seems, was recognized within the Jewish community as a "woman's holiday." This recognition may date back to the Biblical period, and certainly to the first centuries of the common era. By Talmudic times, it was held that God had given women *Rosh Hodesh* as a reward for the righteousness of their foremothers, those who wandered in the wilderness and went with Moses to Sinai but refused to give the men their jewelry to help make the Golden Calf. Through the seventeenth century rabbis maintained that women were to celebrate this holiday by abstaining from all work. While *Rosh Hodesh* has not been unknown in modern times, its rediscovery as a woman's holiday can be attributed to women's recent access to higher Jewish learning and their consequent familiarity with traditional Jewish texts. The celebration of *Rosh Hodesh* has led to the creation of rituals, some using traditional songs and prayers, others completely new. Groups regularly meeting to celebrate *Rosh Hodesh* have been in existence for several years. Most have neither appointed leaders nor fixed liturgies to which they must adhere. Instead, leadership responsibilities are either alternated or shared and the content of the celebration varies, with less traditional groups remarkably open to many kinds of spiritual exploration and expression.

Among the more startling innovations, perhaps because it is among the least familiar to many who have been initiated in the celebration of *Rosh Hodesh,* is the invocation of the Divine as *Shechinah,* She-Who-Dwells-Within. *Shechinah* is the feminine element of God, described in Jewish mystical literature but absent from daily Jewish prayer. Infused with a feminist awareness of their equality and the Jewish conviction that men and women were made in the image of God, Jewish women have begun to call on the Divine as *Shechinah,* She in whose image they—as women—have been created.

Prayers to *Shechinah* extend beyond *Rosh Hodesh* celebrations. One of the most beautiful is a blessing written by Rabbi Lynn Gottlieb to be said in place of the traditional prayer thanking God for not having been created a heathen or a slave and for having been created according to His will (women's traditional counterpart to the male blessing thanking God for not having created him a woman). Gottlieb's blessing begins: *"Bruchu Yah Shechinah"* (Blessed are you *Shechinah*) and goes on to thank the Divine for that which the worshiper is rather than for that which she is not. She thanks *Shechinah* for having created her a "journeying woman" (Gottlieb's translation of "ēvriyah," the feminine form of "ēvri" or Hebrew, whose root means "to pass") and a free woman *(bat horin)* and concludes *"Bruchu Yah Shechinah sheh astah ohtee eesha"* (Blessed are you *Shechinah* who made me a woman in your image).[30]

Jewish feminist theologians recently have begun to explore other means of re-imaging the Divine. In part, these efforts reflect an awareness of Mary Daly's critique of patriarchal God language, the realization, in other words, that as long as "God is in 'His' Heaven, ruling

'His' people," the position of women within Judaism will continue to be subordinate to that of men. Some have suggested retaining the word "God" but using feminine and masculine pronouns and adjectives in describing such a deity and in invoking His/Her name. Others have reclaimed the word "Goddess" to be used alongside of or in place of "God." Though the identification in Hebrew of the words for "Goddess" and "idol" make the name "Goddess" a problematic one,[31] the religious experiences of many Jewish feminist theologians have convinced them that such re-imaging is not just politically important but spiritually essential. As Judith Plaskow has argued, "The Goddess must be recognized as a part of God. For the God who does not include her is an idol made in man's image." Thus, she concludes:

> Acknowledging the many aspects of the Goddess among the names of God becomes a measure of our ability to incorporate the feminine and women into a monotheistic religious framework. At the same time, naming women's experience as part of the nature of the deity brings the suppressed experience of women into the Jewish fold.[32]

It remains to be seen whether these theological innovations will be accepted by the American Jewish community as a whole. Yet recent attempts by the Reform movement's liturgy committee to create more inclusive God language (for example, God as Ruler or Sovereign of Existence rather than King; Parent rather than Father), as well as the creation of non-sexist prayerbooks by a few local congregations, indicate that significant changes are already being made. Directly or indirectly, they can be attributed to a growing feminist awareness of women's equality and to a recognition of the importance of language in conveying the Jewish conviction that men *and* women are made in the image of God.

Leadership in the Jewish Community

During the last ten years, women have assumed roles of leadership within the American Jewish community, not only as rabbis and cantors but also as presidents of congregations and directors of various Jewish organizations. Women have pressed and continued to press for greater inclusion and participation in communal decision-making bodies. Despite the few inroads that have been made, however, leadership remains overwhelmingly in the hands of men.

Chaim Waxman, in a study of feminism's impact on American Jewish communal institutions published in 1980, discovered that throughout the 1970s there was little increase in the number of women serving as chief executive officers of Jewish organizations. In fact, the only "category" of organizations in which significantly more women served as chief executive officers in 1979 than in 1969 was that of community relations, where in 1979 29.1% (seven out of twenty-four) were women as opposed to almost none in 1969. Nevertheless, Waxman notes, "Even within this category, we find that there was a greater increase in the percentage of women chief executive officers between 1969 and 1973, before the feminist movement could have had any great impact, than 1973 and 1979." Thus, he concludes, "When viewed from the power perspective, it appears that the impact of feminism upon Jewish communal organizations has been negligible to virtually nil."[33]

A 1981 survey on the status of women in Jewish communal services seems to confirm Waxman's assessment. While indicating that a significant number of women are involved in Jewish communal organizations, it reveals that the vast majority remain in low professional levels, appearing to have "very limited access to top executive and administrative positions."[34] Reasons often given for excluding women from these positions include the supposed reluctance of women to travel and to work in the evenings, their lack of training in management and business skills, and their reluctance to take managerial jobs. Yet as Naomi Levine, formerly the Executive Director of the American Jewish Congress (and as such, the first woman to become head of a major Jewish organization that was not a separate women's group), has noted, "these arguments are excuses to cover up a deep attitudinal reluctance to see women in new roles."[35]

While in the last five years a number of major Jewish organizations have expressed a desire to develop new strategies for improving the position of women, it may take another decade before significant numbers of women attain positions of communal leadership on the professional level. On the lay level, attaining positions of power may take even longer: first, because access to these positions seems to be directly related to personal wealth (the argument is that an individual will be a more efficient fundraiser if he/she is also a large contributor); and second, because for the most part, those few women who have attained such positions do not seem to be feminists and have shown little if any interest in pressing for greater high-level involvement of women within their organizations. The Jewish Federation Council of Greater Los Angeles recently completed a study of women in Federation and Agency leadership roles. Concluding that woman's opportunity to move into top leadership positions within the Federation was limited, the study recommended

> that the Federation, applying the same standards to women and men, make a serious and sustained effort to involve greater numbers of women in leadership roles and committee chair positions.[36]

While important changes may occur in Los Angeles as a result of this study, other Jewish communities have barely begun to acknowledge women's exclusion and have done little, if anything, to include women in lay positions of influence and power.

Yet as Naomi Levine has argued, the Jewish community cannot undo the effect of women's liberation. "Women, particularly Jewish women," she writes, "are not going to lessen their interest in professional careers and they are not going to be satisfied any more solely with the role of the home maker."[37] Neither, one might add, will they remain content in assistant and entry-level positions and in lay positions that make little use of their own leadership potential.

Judaism vs. Feminism: A Conflict of Interest?

There are two final questions that need to be raised concerning the relationship between feminism and the American Jewish community. First, has the feminist critique of Judaism so threatened the *halachic* system that the integrity of *halachah* can no longer be maintained? Can one, in other words, adhere to *halachah* and work for change from within, or can women's equality be realized only by rejecting *halachah* all together? While Blu Greenberg views *halachah* as a primary commitment that cannot be sacrificed even for the achievement of feminist goals, Judith Plaskow has argued that women's subordination, rooted in the notion of woman as "Other," is so integral a part of *halachah* that piecemeal change will never eradicate women's inequality. She thus calls for a reaching beyond the tradition, to a new "understanding of Torah that begins with acknowledgement of the profound injustice of the Torah itself . . . [and its] . . . assumption of the lesser humanity of women."[38]

Yet no matter which stance towards *halachah* one adopts, the feminist who continues to identify as a Jew needs to raise a second question: is there a conflict between Jewish and feminist values and if so, to which should one adhere? In confronting this issue, Blu Greenberg has maintained that there are certain conflicts between feminism and Judaism, that feminism, for example, encourages a different kind of sexual morality, places greater emphasis on material success, and seems to reject the notion of sex-differentiated roles in favor of androgyny. In addition, feminism views the decision of whether to have children as one of individual choice while, at a time when the world Jewish population is actually decreasing, Judaism and the concern for Jewish survival dictate a commitment to the perpetuation of family life.

What is important here is not whether Greenberg's assessment of either Jewish or feminist values is correct. Rather, what emerges is a dichotomized view of existence, a potential—or real—conflict of interests that needs to be resolved in favor of one or the other. What is missing here is any concept of *Jewish feminist* values, values that emerge out of the experience of the Jewish feminist as she encounters the world, other people, and for many, God. To be fair, Greenberg's commitment to *halachah* discourages, if it does not prohibit, the evolution of such values. *Halachah*, even at its most flexible, allows no room for compromise or, it seems, for growth. Perhaps the work of creating values that reflect a commitment to both Judaism and feminism thus needs to be left to those who are not bound by the authority of Jewish law. Only once such work begins, however, will feminism emerge as a real force within American Jewish life, leading not only to greater involvement and participation by women but also to a new vision of what the American Jewish community should be.

During the last ten years, some have argued that feminism is a fad, and that feminist demands, if ignored, eventually will go away. This kind of argument has been used by opponents of women's ordination as well as by those who have opposed women's demands for greater participation in the worship service and greater access to positions of communal power. Yet those who hold this view fail to take feminism and women seriously. Despite conservative political trends in the United States and despite what some feel is a backlash against the feminist movement, the inroads that Jewish feminism has made, however few, are already too deep to be eradicated. Having tasted the fruit of the tree of knowledge, Jewish women are discovering that there is no road back to Eden.

NOTES

1. Paula Hyman, Audrey Gellis, Bracha Sachs, essays under heading "Is It Kosher To Be a Feminist?" *Ms.*, July 1974, pp. 76–83, 108–10.

2. See, for example, Letty Cottin Pogrebin, "Anti-Semitism in the Women's Movement," *Ms.*, June 1982, pp. 1–11, and Evelyn Torton Beck, ed., *Nice Jewish Girls: A Lesbian Anthology* (Watertown, Mass.: Persephone Press, 1982), especially pp. xiii–xxxvi and 250–61.

3. Blu Greenberg, *On Women and Judaism: A View from Tradition* (Philadelphia: Jewish Publication Society of America, 1981), p. 39.

4. For a fuller treatment of the rabbinic view of women, see Judith Baskin, "The Separation of Women in Rabbinic Judaism" included in this volume.

5. Saul Berman, "The Status of Women in Halakhic Judaism," in *The Jewish Woman: New Perspectives*, ed. Elizabeth Koltun (New York: Schocken Books, 1976), p. 122.

6. See Baskin (pp. 3ff.) for examples of women who did step out of their traditional roles and for rabbinic views of them.

7. Paula Hyman, "The Other Half: Women in the Jewish Tradition," in Koltun, *Perspectives*, p. 107.

8. Jacob Katz, *Tradition and Crisis: Jewish Society at the End of the Middle Ages* (New York: Schocken Books, 1971), pp. 270ff.

9. Jacob Katz, *Out of the Ghetto: The Social Background of Jewish Emancipation, 1770–1870* (New York: Schocken Books, 1978), p. 84.

10. Katz, *Out of the Ghetto*, p. 111.

11. See Ellen M. Umansky, *Lily Montagu and the Advancement of Liberal Judaism: From Vision to Vocation* (Lewiston, New York: Edwin Mellen Press, 1983), pp. 4–10, 210ff.

12. By the beginning of the twentieth century, other religious options within Judaism also appeared. What's more, as the Jews entered modernity, it became possible for women and men to remain within the Jewish community while identifying themselves as "secular Jews."

13. Report to the Breslau Conference, 1846, quoted in W. Gunther Plaut, *The Rise of Reform Judaism* (New York: World Union for Progressive Judaism, 1963), p. 254.

14. David Philipson, *The Reform Movement in Judaism* (New York: Ktav, 1967), p. 219. It should be noted that nearly thirty years after the Breslau Conference, confirmation was introduced within progressive European congregations as a ceremony which formally recognized the entrance of both boys and girls into Jewish communal life.

15. Michael A. Meyer, "A Centennial History," in *Hebrew Union College-Jewish Institute of Religion: At One Hundred Years* (Cincinnati: Hebrew Union College, 1976), p. 99.

16. Interview with Lynne F. Landsberg, Assistant Rabbi, Central Synagogue, New York City, 26 August 1983.

17. Karen L. Fox, "Whither Women Rabbis," *Religious Education* 76 (July–August 1981):363.

18. Interview with Judy Lewis, Rabbi, Temple Isaiah of Great Neck, Great Neck, New York, 25 August 1983.

19. Figures supplied by Rebecca T. Alpert, Dean of Students, Reconstructionist Rabbinical College, Wyncote, Pennsylvania (August 25, 1983).

20. *Consultation on The Role of Women in Jewish Religious Life: A Decade of Change 1972–1982: Papers and Summary of Proceedings* (New York: The American Jewish Committee, 1982), p. 12.

21. *Consultation on the Role of Women*, p. 13.

22. Alan Silverstein, "The Evolution of Ezrat Nashim," *Conservative Judaism* 30 (Fall 1975):45.

23. Anne Lapidus Lerner, "'Who Has Not Made Me a Man': The Movement for Equal Rights for Women in American Jewry," *American Jewish Year Book, 1977* (New York: American Jewish Committee, 1976), p. 22.

24. From preamble to interim constitution of the Jewish Feminist Organization, quoted in Lerner, "'Who Hast Not Made Me a Man,'" p. 7.

25. "On the Ordination of Women," *Conservative Judaism* 32 (Summer 1979): 78.

26. Roslyn Lacks, *Women and Judaism: Myth, History and Struggle* (Garden City, New York: Doubleday and Co., 1980), p. 169.

27. Saul Berman and Shulamith Magnus, "Orthodoxy Responds to Feminist Ferment," *Response* 40 (Spring 1981):6.

28. Greenberg, *On Women and Judaism*, pp. 37, 46.

29. And the Conservative movement has added a pre-nuptial agreement into its *ketubah* which empowers its *Bet Din* (Jewish court), in case of divorce, to act for the husband in giving the wife a *get* (bill of divorcement) should he refuse to do so.

30. Lynn Gottlieb, "Speaking Into the Silence," *Response* 41–42 (Fall–Winter 1982): 27.

31. For a fuller treatment of this issue see Ellen M. Umansky, "Re-Imaging the Divine," *Response* 41–42 (Fall–Winter, 1982):110–19 and also her "Possibilities and Problems of Creating a Jewish Feminist Theology," *Anima* (forthcoming).

32. Judith Plaskow, "The Right Question Is Theological," *On Being a Jewish Feminist: A Reader*, ed. with introductions by Susannah Heschel (New York: Schocken Books, 1983), p. 230.

33. Chaim I. Waxman, "The Impact of Feminism on American Jewish Communal Institutions," *Journal of Jewish Communal Services* 57 (Fall 1980):74–75.

34. Quoted in *Lilith*, issue no. 8 (1981):9.

35. Naomi Levine, "Keynote Address," *Consultation on the Response of Women's Organizations to the Changing Role of Women: Summary Proceedings* (New York: American Jewish Committee, 1979), p. 25.

36. "Jewish Federation Council of Greater Los Angeles Report of the Study Committee on Women in Federation and Agency Leadership," February, 1983 ("Women, Jewish—Organizational Participation," File, Blaustein Library, American Jewish Committee, NYC), p. 18.

37. Levine, "Keynote Address," in *Consultation*, pp. 28–29.

38. Plaskow, "The Right Question is Theological," in Heschel, *A Reader*, p. 231.

Contributors

Judith Baskin is Associate Professor of Judaic Studies, University of Massachusetts, Amherst, Massachusetts.

Ann D. Braude is Acting Instructor of Religious Studies, Yale University, New Haven, Connecticut.

William R. Darrow is Assistant Professor of Islamics and Middle Eastern Studies, Williams College, Williamstown, Massachusetts.

Walter B. Denny is Professor of Art History, University of Massachusetts, Amherst, Massachusetts.

Jane Dillenberger is Adjunct Professor of Theology and the Visual Arts, Pacific School of Religion, Berkeley, California.

Nancy Falk is Professor of Religion, Western Michigan University, Kalamazoo, Michigan.

Ellison Banks Findly is Assistant Professor of Religion and Intercultural Studies, Trinity College, Hartford, Connecticut.

Rosalind I. J. Hackett is Research Fellow in Religious Studies, University of Aberdeen, Scotland.

Yvonne Yazbeck Haddad is Associate Professor of Islamic Studies, Hartford Seminary, Hartford, Connecticut.

Antoinette Iadarola is Provost and Professor of History, College of Mount St. Joseph, Cincinnati, Ohio.

Frank G. Kirkpatrick is Associate Professor of Religion, Trinity College, Hartford, Connecticut.

Michael E. Lestz is Assistant Professor of History, Trinity College, Hartford, Connecticut.

Lou Ratté is an Independent Historian with the Connecticut Center for Independent Historians.

Sandra P. Robinson is Assistant Professor, Department of Religion, Duke University, Durham, North Carolina.

Annemarie A. Shimony is Professor of Anthropology, Wellesley College, Wellesley, Massachusetts

Nancy Schuster is a former faculty member, Wesleyan University, Middletown, Connecticut.

Jane I. Smith is Associate Dean for Academic Affairs and Lecturer in Islamics, Harvard Divinity School, Cambridge, Massachusetts.

Pauline Turner is Adjunct Professor, Anna Maria College, Paxton, Massachusetts.

Ellen M. Umansky is Assistant Professor of Religion, Emory University, Atlanta, Georgia.

Janice D. Willis is Associate Professor of Religion, Wesleyan University, Middletown, Connecticut.

Donna Marie Wulff is Assistant Professor of Religious Studies, Brown University, Providence, Rhode Island.

Index